COGNITIVE PSYCHOLOGY
AND INSTRUCTION

NATO CONFERENCE SERIES

I   Ecology
II   Systems Science
III Human Factors
IV Marine Sciences
V   Air—Sea Interactions

III HUMAN FACTORS

COGNITIVE PSYCHOLOGY AND INSTRUCTION

Edited by
Alan M. Lesgold
and James W. Pellegrino
Learning Research and Development Center
University of Pittsburgh
Pittsburgh, Pennsylvania

Sipke D. Fokkema
Free University
Amsterdam, The Netherlands

and

Robert Glaser
Learning Research and Development Center
University of Pittsburgh
Pittsburgh, Pennsylvania

Published in coordination with NATO Scientific Affairs Division

PLENUM PRESS · NEW YORK AND LONDON

Library of Congress Cataloging in Publication Data

NATO International Conference on Cognitive Psychology and Instruction, Free University of Amsterdam, 1977.
  Cognitive psychology and instruction.

  (NATO conference series: III, Human factors; 5)
  "Proceedings of the NATO International Conference on Cognitive Psychology and Instruction held at the Free University of Amsterdam, June 13-17, 1977, sponsored by the NATO Special Program Panel on Human Factors."
  Includes index.
  1. Educational psychology—Congresses. 2. Cognition (child psychology)—Congresses. I. Lesgold, Alan M. II. Nato Special Program Panel on Human Factors. III. Title. IV. Series. [DNLM: 1. Cognition—Congresses. 2. Psychology—Congresses. 3. Learning—Congresses. 4. Teaching—Congresses. W3 N138 v. 5 1977/BF311 N132c 1977]
  LB1051.N333 1977   370.15   77-27133
  ISBN 0-306-32886-0

Proceedings of the NATO International Conference on Cognitive Psychology and Instruction held at the Free University of Amsterdam, June 13–17, 1977, sponsored by the NATO Special Program Panel on Human Factors

© 1978 Plenum Press, New York
A Division of Plenum Publishing Corporation
227 West 17th Street, New York, N.Y. 10011

Printed in the United States of America

INTRODUCTION

Sipke D. Fokkema
Amsterdam, Free University

From June 13th - 17th, 1977 the NATO International Conference on Cognitive Psychology and Instruction, organized by the editors of this volume, took place at the Free University of Amsterdam. During this period approximately 150 psychologists representing 15 countries assembled for an exchange of scientific experiences and ideas. The broad aim of the conference, as indicated by its title, was to explore the extent to which theoretical and methodological developments in cognitive psychology might provide useful knowledge with regard to the design and management of instruction.

From a great variety of submitted papers the organizers attempted to select those that represented major problem areas being scientifically studied in several countries. For the organization of this book we chose to categorize the contributions according to the following general areas:

   I.   Learning

  II.   Comprehension and Information Structure

 III.   Perceptual and Memory Processes in Reading

  IV.   Problem Solving and Components of Intelligence

   V.   Cognitive Development

  VI.   Approaches to Instruction

The final paper in the volume is an extensive review and summary by Glaser, Pellegrino, and Lesgold, that examines the state of cognitive psychology (mainly as reflected in the contributions in this volume) with regard to instructional purposes. Each of the sections of the book also begins with a brief overview of the specific topics considered by the individual contributors within that section. Unfortunately, the planned size of this publication did not allow us to include all the papers that were presented at the conference. A list of authors and the titles of contributions that have not been included is placed after the Table of Contents.

The papers included in this volume differ in many respects other than problem area. On the one hand, the reader will find studies that originate within practical instructional settings, as well as studies that adhere to more classical laboratory conditions. On the other hand, and independent of this first dimension of variation, some of the studies are directed toward the opening of new theoretical avenues, while others present empirical data acquired by new types of designs and procedures. This diversity is to be expected and may be desirable at this point in time. However, this situation makes it difficult to arrive at a simple statement representing the main theme emerging from the conference. It appears that careful development of theory and critical design of experiments, representing either an applied or a basic research focus, is the prior requirement given the present state of affairs.

In surveying these reports of current research and theory, one should not forget that cognitive psychology is itself a recent development, and that relatively late in its short history, researchers became attracted by the practical problems within the vast field of formal education. Cognitive psychology in the United States had to establish itself in the face of a strong behavioristic and neo-behavioristic tradition. Thus, it first had to demonstrate its scientific value with respect to addressing some of the questions that behaviorism either failed to address or for which it offered inadequate explanations. There is little doubt that the ascendence of cognitive psychology was favored by the circumstance that several areas of psychological interest were being investigated that did not fit within the scope of interest of behaviorism. Some particular examples are the computer-simulation of human behavior and the information-processing approach to human performance. The concurrent developments within psycholinguistics assume a singularly important position among the historic factors that assisted in the breakthrough of cognitive psychology.

In the United States, the pioneering work of Bruner, Goodnow, and Austin (1956), and Miller, Galanter, and Pribram (1960) can be considered as initiating and furthering a principal change in approach, that only several years later would show its full impact on psychological research and theory. On the continent and in Great Britain, the cognitive point of view has a longer and smoother history. Since 1913, there have been several very influential contributions, and many supporting studies. The work of Selz (1913, 1935), Piaget (1947), and Bartlett (1932) immediately comes to mind. Of particular significance are Piaget's concepts of the operations of thought and Bartlett's concepts of "schema" (borrowed from Head). These concepts figure quite strongly in current cognitive theory. It is interesting to note, that with the sole exception of Selz, none of these European authors were interested in the problems of instruction.

It is typically the case that investigators using the term "cognitive psychology" give no further qualification. Nevertheless, for much of the work currently done under this broad label, the particular origin is often recognizable; be it simulation studies, verbal learning and memory studies, human performance, Piagetian theory, or otherwise. This situation contributes to the variation in the papers within this volume.

The area of individual differences, one of the most successful with regard to applied problems, is engaged in a fascinating process of becoming more integrated with the rest of psychology. This important change in the field is a consequence of linking concepts about personal characteristics with the properties of information-processing. There is also an enrichment in understanding individual differences because in information-processing studies of individual performance, the processes themselves appear to vary as a function of newly conceived organismic variables. The work of H. Simon (1976), L. Resnick and R. Glaser (1976), and R. Sternberg (this volume) are examples of this important trend.

We are aware of the fact that this collection of papers has some of the properties of the inn that one visits along the road to one's destiny. It is there, in an admittedly more or less noisy atmosphere, that past progress is evaluated, that one meets with some surprising characters, and that the prospects for further travel have to be estimated.

In the planning and execution of this conference and in the preparation of this volume we have benefited from the assistance, cooperation, and support of many people. We must first express our appreciation to the individual contributors who willingly adhered to our directives and provided the content for this volume. We were also greatly assisted by many who are not represented in this volume, but who invested great energy in this enterprise. They include: Dr. J. H. de Swart, Dr. S. Dijkstra, Ms. E. Kok, and Mr. H. Welmers, of the staff of the Laboratory of Experimental Psychology; and Ms. J. Sigfried and Ms. I. Hermanns-Vervaart, secretaries; all of the Free University. At the University of Pittsburgh we were assisted by Ms. J. Jewell and Ms. C. Faddis (technical editing); Ms. P. Stanton, Ms. P. Graw, and Ms. C. Hardaway (manuscript typing); Ms. C. Peel (graphics); Ms. G. Yaksic (composition); and Mr. D. Hanko (photography).

We are indebted to the NATO Scientific Affairs Division for its financial support of the conference and to the Free University at Amsterdam for its hospitality and for the services of its Congress Bureau.

The editors hope that this volume will be a valuable reference showing the scientific progress in those areas of cognitive psychology that are associated with the processes of learning and teaching.

References

Bartlett, F. C. Remembering. Cambridge: Cambridge University Press, 1932.

Bruner, J. S., Goodnow, J. J.& Austin, G. A. A study of thinking. New York: John Wiley, 1956.

Miller, G. A., Galanter, E. & Pribram, K. H. Plans and the structure of behavior. New York: Holt, Rinehart and Winston, 1960.

Piaget, J. La psychologie de l'intelligence. Paris: Colin, 1947.

Resnick, L. B., & Glaser, R. Problem solving and intelligence. In L. Resnick (Ed.), The nature of intelligence. Hillsdale, NJ: Lawrence Erlbaum, 1976.

Selz, O. Über die Gesetze des geordneten Denkverlaufs. Stuttgart: W. Spemann, 1913.

Selz, O. Versuche zur Hebung des Intelligenzniveaus. Eine Beiträge zur Theorie des Intelligenz und ihrer erziehlichen Beeinflüssung. Zeitschrift für Psychologie, 1935, 134, 236-301.

Simon, H. A. Identifying basis abilities underlying intelligent performance. In L. B. Resnick (Ed.), The nature of intelligence. Hillsdale, NJ: Lawrence Erlbaum, 1976.

Sternberg, R.J. Componential investigations of intelligence. This volume.

CONTENTS

I. LEARNING

II. COMPREHENSION AND INFORMATION STRUCTURE

Contents

VI. APPROACHES TO INSTRUCTION

ADDITIONAL CONFERENCE PRESENTATIONS

Joost Breuker, COWO, University of Amsterdam
   How Does One Know the Answer is Incorrect?

M. J. Coombs, University of Liverpool
   Representation and Memory for Medical Procedures

M. Corcia, C. Duchesne, J. Jacques, and M. Y. Caillebout, Université
Réné Descartes, Institut National de Recherche Pédagogique, Paris
   The More They Play the More They Think

Richard Cowan, University of Lancaster
   The Development of Conservation of Number: The Effect of Small
   Numbers

William Crano and Charles Johnson, Michigan State University
   Applying Cognitive Principles in Remedial Instruction

G. Erdos, University of Newcastle upon Tyne
   Role of Improvement on Tasks Measuring Field Dependence

Barry Gholson, Memphis State University
   Developmental Stages, Hypothesis Theory, and Individual Differences

J. A. M. Howe, University of Edinburgh
   Learning Through Building Computational Descriptions

Hans Marmolin, Lars-Göran Nilsson, and Hans Smedshammar, University of
Uppsala
   The Mediated Reading Process of the Partially Sighted

George Marsh, Morton Friedman, University of California at Los Angeles;
Veronica Welch and Peter Desberg, California State College at Dominguez
Hills
   Strategies in Reading and Spelling

James McCall, Jordanhill College of Education, Glasgow
   Judgments and Explanations: A Reexamination

John A. Self, University of Melbourne
   Computer-Based Socratic Teaching Via Hypothesis Theory

Lennart Svensson, University of Göteborg
    Cognitive Approaches in Learning

P. Vermersch and A. Weill-Fassina, Laboratoire de Psychologie du
Travail, Paris
    Functioning Registers and Answers' Analysis

Section I

LEARNING

Work in modern cognitive psychology has focused primarily on the processes that underlie perceptual, memorial, and problem-solving performance and has only indirectly investigated how these process skills are learned and how broader competences and knowledge are acquired. The papers in this section attempt to redress this balance by showing a direct concern with how knowledge structures and complex skills are acquired.

Van Parreren's invited address presents the general principles of a componential theory of cognitive learning, consisting of two forms of integration. One must learn to combine operations into higher-level sequences, but one must also learn how to decide which sequence of more elementary operations will be suitable for performing a novel task. Van Parreren devotes the bulk of his paper to a discussion of research in the U.S.S.R. on the abbreviations of cognitive and motoric operations that occur as simpler skills are assembled into more complex procedures.

The papers by Voss and Frederick Hayes-Roth consider old established topics in the psychology of learning - transfer and concept learning, and discuss them in terms of modern cognitive theory. Voss points out that classical transfer paradigms are much too restricted to address significant problems in the acquisition of complex knowledge and skills. He broadens the notion of transfer by studying individuals that have greater or less knowledge in a specific subject area and how they use their knowledge to acquire new information. Voss suggests that transfer is a function of the degree to which the structure of input information is related to the memory structure of an individual.

Frederick Hayes-Roth considers the problem of rule learning in terms of the question: What does it mean to learn from examples? Hayes-Roth studies the processes that people exhibit when they infer rules from examples that are presented to them. He proposes a theory for the classical task of conjunctive concept learning that combines two notions of knowledge representation: the structural represenation of a pattern, and production-rule operations that relate pattern descriptions. The theory describes a formal methodology that identifies criterial properties that establish commonalities among different examples as instances of the same rule. According to the theory, human

1

classification performance can be predicted on the basis of memory
strengths and cue validities of the combinations of properties that
occur in the course of a series of examples.

Norman's paper transmits an urgent message for change in
traditional methods of research on learning. He argues that if we are
seriously concerned with the acquisition of knowledge and the
development of expertise, then we must consider the learning of complex
topics with rich conceptual structures that takes years to accomplish
and may continually be updated and perfected. Norman speculates about
three ways in which complex knowledge and expertise might be acquired
over the course of time: "accretion," "restructuring," and "tuning."
Norman discusses characteristics of these three modes of learning in
terms of interference and transfer. A form of instruction is suggested
that compares the knowledge structure of the student and the knowledge
structure of the topic to be learned; discrepancies and confusions
between these two aspects are resolved through focused problems and
questions that the student must solve.

A BUILDING BLOCK MODEL OF COGNITIVE LEARNING

Carel van Parreren
Utrecht University
Utrecht, Netherlands

The view that cognitive development involves the successive formation of cognitive skills or operations has a long history in psychology. A prime example is Piaget's theory, in which it is postulated that concrete operations are formed after sensory motor schemas develop, and formal operations come into existence after concrete operations have been established. Furthermore, between the First and Second World Wars, Otto Selz, a German psychologist, constructed a theory that was based on a number of experimental investigations. Selz claimed that intelligence consists of a structured system of problem solving methods that must be acquired during development and that may be improved through teaching. Currently, the idea that teaching may be optimized if viewed as erecting a hierarchical structure in the learner, is well known from the publications of Robert Gagne (1970).

The building block model presented here differs from most others in several respects. First, although cognitive learning is considered to be comprised of placing "building blocks" on top of each other, resulting structure is not seen as one rigid whole, but rather as changing and flexible, since it has to be adapted to the actual task at a specific moment. This means that the same building blocks may be used and recombined whenever they are required for a new task. Thus, in our theory, cognitive learning is compared to the construction of a toy house from a child's box of bricks, rather than the building of a house in an adult manner. Every cognitive skill, once it is acquired, remains at the disposal of the subject even if it has been used before as a building block for the learning of a more complicated, higher skill.

The general argument can be seen in the following example. A person who wishes to enter the trade of cabinet making must first learn a number of elementary skills of carpentry. He must, for instance, master the skill of sawing. At a later stage of training, he will learn more complicated skills, e.g., say he will have to learn to make a dovetail joint in order to join two pieces of wood together. Of course, teaching him how to dovetail will only make sense if sawing has already been mastered. At a still later stage of training, the teacher may give the apprentice the task of constructing a chest for which he needs the

3

skill of dovetail joining. This example shows how the higher skills can
only be attained after mastery of more elementary skills, but it will
also be clear that the lower skills may be used to new purpose: The
pupil has not lost his competence at sawing as a result of learning the
higher skill of dovetail joining; furthermore he can use dovetail
joints for the construction of pieces of furniture other than chests.

Now we should discuss a second and more important difference
between our building block theory and other hierarchical models of
cognitive learning. The foregoing example can be used again. Having
completed technical school, the pupil has not only learned lower and
higher order skills, but he literally has these skills at his command.
As we mentioned earlier, the teacher could give him the task of making a
chest. It is important to remember that once the pupil has reached the
final stages of his schooling, it is no longer necessary for the teacher
to spell out the separate activities necessary for the job. Indeed, the
essence of skilled workmanship is that the craftsman who is asked to
produce an article will not only choose the correct construction for it,
but will be able to perform the whole sequence of required acts. The
higher skill is not only a combination of lower skills, but includes a
process of integration whereby the whole complicated sequence of acts
can be dealt with as a whole. Whereas, several successive commands were
necessary in the earlier stages of learning, at a later stage a single
instruction will be sufficient.

It is our contention that, where many cognitive skills are
concerned, learning consists of a process of integration. We further
contend that this integration takes place at two levels: on the level
of performance and at the level of command or control. Our third
assumption is that during the course of development, the primary form of
integration takes place at the level of performance, i.e., that as a
consequence of integration at this level, an integrated form of control
becomes possible. The reverse may also occur; that is, integration at
the level of control results in an integrated performance, but this
comes at a later stage of development and requires another kind of
process.

We will now discuss some experimental evidence for these
hypotheses. In an experiment by Denney and Acito (1974), children aged
two and three years were trained in a classification task. They were
asked to group geometric figures according to their similarity and in a
consistent manner. Starting from a random arrangement of the stimulus
objects, they had to sort them into sets in which all the objects were
alike on one or more of their dimensions, either shape, color, or size.
For adults or for children in a higher age group, a classification task
such as this would require only one initial instruction for smooth
performance of the task. For these older subjects, performance of the
task consists of one integrated activity; once they see the sorting
criterion, the motor part of the performance follows from the perceived
similarities. The young children who were employed as experimental
subjects in the experiment had no such integrated perceptual

classification activity at their command, so the simple unitary instruction to classify did not work. It is most interesting to note that of the two training procedures used by the experimenters, the successful one consisted of a modeling with verbalization procedure, which turned out to be a way of <u>dissecting</u> the higher, perceptual skill that the subjects had not yet mastered, into separate successive part-skills of a lower order. Such part-skills were "scanning," "comparing," and "rejecting." Each was, in its turn, elicited by an instruction in the form of modeling with verbal comment:

> In modeling scanning, the experimenter moved his head around in a very obvious way to indicate that he was looking at the entire stimulus array, often making statements such as, "Let's see, I have to look at all the pieces so I'll get all the ones that look alike," or "Let's see, are there any more that look like those?" In modeling, comparing, and rejecting, the experimenter occasionally picked out an incorrect piece, placed it in the group he was formulating, looked at it, and then returning it to its original position, said something like, "No, that one doesn't belong. It's not the same as the others." (Denney & Acito, 1974, p. 40)

The results of the training were most impressive; on a posttest, which used a different stimulus array consisting exclusively of triangular shapes, but which varied in color, size, and pattern, 11 of the 17 subjects showed a consistent system of sorting, whereas in the control group only two of the children were successful in completing a true classification. The authors do not provide information about the nature of the activity used by the successful children, i.e., whether any form of integration of the instructed lower skills into a unitary form had taken place. Certainly some integration must have taken place, for otherwise it is difficult to understand how it was possible for the children to transfer the sequence of separate acts to an essentially different stimulus array. However, we need not speculate on this, because it is quite certain that these same children will ultimately acquire the activity of classification along perceptually given dimensions in a unified way, as one integrated perceptual skill, just as each of us has at his disposal. This means that in the course of development, a form of learning is taking place in which a sequence of separate acts undergoes a kind of fusion whereby they are molded into one integrated whole. It is this formation of a unified activity that is so very well suited to intentional control, either through one initial instruction, or self-instruction. This again paves the way for using the skill of classifying in more complicated forms of behavior, as in a problem solving task.

Formation of Perceptual Acts

For a theory regarding the learning of cognitive skills, it is of course necessary to analyze how an integrated unitary activity is formed from a sequence of lower, more elementary activities. Soviet psychologists have discovered a crucial kind of process in this respect. It is called sokraščenie dejstvija, abbreviation of the action. By this they mean that in the process of learning skills, including cognitive skills, a short contracted form of action results from an originally elaborate action that often consists of a number of separate steps or part-actions. From a close study of several experimental papers in which Soviet psychologists refer to the concept of abbreviation in learning processes, it appears that at least three different forms of such abbreviation must be distinguished.

One of these forms seems to take place in the learning of perceptual classification, as in the study by Denney and Acito. The adult act of seeing immediately what belongs to what, evolves out of a more elaborate process that comprises the manual bringing together of two objects in order to see whether they are similar in some respect, and subsequently placing them into one group, or rejecting one object and returning it to the original array. The greater part of this motor activity is discontinued at a later stage, and the comparison is made "from a distance." It is quite interesting to note that every form of comparison seems to have its own original motor behavior. For instance, comparing two blocks according to size originates from the act of placing one on top of the other in such a way that one can be seen whether or not the edges are flush.

Leonid Venger, a psychologist from the Moscow Institute for Research of Preschool Education, who wrote a very interesting book on Perception and Instruction (1969), analyzed this form of abbreviation - which he described as the formation of perceptual acts. I shall mention only one of his discoveries, which may be illustrated by a learning process that many of us will have observed for ourselves. A very common toy for babies consists of a number of similarly formed hollow objects, for example, cubes with one side missing and that differ in size. One kind of action these cubes invariably evoke from the learner is to try to insert one cube into another. Initially, this action is attempted in a haphazard, trial and error way. But, there comes a stage (which characteristically does not occur spontaneously with feeble-minded children, as Venger observed) when the child reduces the gross motor activity and moves the cubes in a more subtle way as he or she scrutinizes the relative position of the cubes. The child's movements have, as Venger remarked, acquired a new goal: The child is no longer aiming at the result directly, but is performing orienting movements, which have the function of inspecting the arising possibilities, getting acquainted with the situation, and so on. Of course, this kind of behavior will more often be successful than blind trial and error. Now, this stage of orienting action gives way to a later one that is still more abbreviated: The child looks at the cubes, selects one that will fit into another, and handles it in the correct way so that one will slip into the other. The motor part of the action has then been reduced, smoothed out to just those movements that are essential for reaching the sought-after result. All the other movements have been omitted and have been replaced by purely perceptual activity.

Automatization

We cannot dwell upon the subject of abbreviation through the formation of perceptual acts. Fortunately, some of the relevant Soviet publications have been translated into English, for example, part of Venger's aforementioned book (1969) and some very important papers by Zaporožec (1969, 1970). There are other kinds of abbreviation that should also be discussed. I shall deal with one of them succinctly because it is far more important for the learning of motor skills than of cognitive skills. It is the process through which automatic ways of responding are learned, and more information concerning it can be found in Western than in the Soviet sources. Such automatic responses can be observed during the course of learning to drive a car and in several other kinds of motor activity, such as sports, gymnastics, or in the playing of musical instruments. A very penetrating study of this process of forming automatisms was conducted by the Belgian psychologist, Van der Velt (1928). The abbreviation of action that occurs in these cases does not result from the dropping out of motor actions, but the elimination of parts of the activity that take place on the mental plans, "in the head." At the beginning of the learning process, the motor action has to be controlled step by step through external instruction, or self-instruction (consider the way in which we learn to swim during swimming instruction). Later, the motor activity can more easily be left to itself, though in all cases some form of control remains necessary. Integration on the level of control manifests itself here in the decrease of the number of control-points. But reducing control is only feasible for the subject because on the level of performance, the action has fused into a fluent motor pattern (what Wolfgang Kohler has called a motor Gestalt). The motor integration is clearly the primary process here, though the possibilities for using the acquired motor skill as a building block for higher units depend on the residual number of control points.

Selecting the Shortest Route to the Goal

Let us now consider the third form of abbreviation. I shall introduce it by illustration in an experiment by Veklerova, (1974; see also Těplen'kaja, 1972), a pupil of one of the most influential Soviet instructional psychologists, Gal'perin. Veklerova tested a training procedure for the formation of concepts with children of kindergarten age. She used a training procedure that was introduced by Gal'perin, (1957, 1969), and which is quite remarkable because it permits the training of young children in cognitive tasks with a high degree of generality, i.e., through which the subjects can cope with a very wide range of transfer tasks. In Veklerova's experiment, she trained her subjects in the well-known Vygotskij classification task, in which the subject has to form groupings of a set of blocks that vary in width, color, shape, and height. Veklerova's training aimed at the level of real concepts, which according to Vygotskij (1962), is only accessible to pupils over twelve years of age. Furthermore, she was interested to see if the mastering of the conceptual classification of the Vygotskij blocks would have any influence on other classification tasks, i.e., whether the subjects had learned a more general form of conceptual behavior.

It is impossible to describe here the elaborate training procedure that Veklerova used. For our purpose it is important to note that the Gal'perin training procedure starts from an elaborate form of action, instigated and controlled by detailed verbal instructions from the experimenter, and performed on an overt, motor level, with as many concrete props as may be devised for separate parts of the total action. For instance, the children are taught to observe one attribute of the stimulus objects at a time by performing "measurements" with concrete measuring instruments. Thus, they learn to pay attention to the size of the blocks by placing them on a coin that is equal in size to the large blocks, but larger than the small blocks. This kind of identification of separate features by way of manual activity is thereupon gradually replaced by perceptual actions. Of course, it is the first form of abbreviation that takes place here, and it is one of the characteristics of Gal'perin's theory of instruction that it deliberately guides the abbreviation process.

In Veklerova's experiment, however, we find another form of abbreviation that is equally directed by training instructions. To illustrate this we must consider another part of her training procedure. The children who participated in the experiment had to learn to attend to separate features of the blocks, as well as to the critical features for a given concept. They also had to know the type of rule that applies for a conjunctive concept. In the special case of the Vygotskij concepts, this means that it is only permissible to conclude that a block belongs to a certain conceptual class when it has been ascertained beforehand that both critical feaaures are present. If one or both of the features are lacking, or if the child could not know whether the object has both critical features (which might happen in those cases where the experimenter did not show a block, but gave a verbal description), other conclusions have to be drawn, either that the concept does not apply, or that it is not known whether it applies. These methods of reasoning were taught to the children with the help of a logical scheme that the children could read off from a card placed in front of them, which resembled the following:

```
            1        +  +  -  -  -  ?  +  ?  ?
            2        +  -  +  -  ?  -  ?  +  ?
                    ---------------------------
Conclusion           +  -  -  -  -  -  ?  ?  ?
```

The children were taught to determine whether the first and then the second feature of the concept would apply, and then to look for the column of the logical scheme where this particular combination could be found. Underneath the symbols for the first and the second feature, they then found the conclusion that followed from the combination. During the course of the teaching-learning process, the children were able to reason without further help from the logical scheme. Since they also reached the correct conclusions in cases in which incomplete descriptions were given, it must be concluded that they had discovered short-cuts such as "If both critical features are present, the concept applies," "If one of them is missing, it does not apply," or even, "If one feature is present but you do not know about the other, or if you do not know about either, then you cannot say if the concept applies." (The other possible interpretation of the results would be that the subjects memorized the whole logical scheme, but since the children gave their replies rapidly, this possibility is highly improbable.)

Veklerova sums up this part of the learning process as an abbreviation of the action, and an abbreviation it indeed is. But, it is a new, third kind of abbreviation. It does not belong to the first kind, because no motor act is transformed into a perceptual one. Nor can we classify it as an abbreviation of the second kind, because although a mental process is reduced, it is not because a motor action (which was guided by it) may now be left to itself. With the type of abbreviation we are now considering, a mental act is dropped because the subject realizes that it is superfluous and that the same result can be reached without performing it. It would appear that the subject stops performing the part-action because he or she has attained the insight that with or without it, the total action will give the same outcome and it is easier to choose the shortest way of performing the action.

Thus, this third kind of abbreviation, which is an outstanding feature of the learning of cognitive skills, really rests on the subject's discovery of identity between two different paths to a goal and the selection of the shortest route to the goal. It is possible to find instances of this insightful abbreviation in several different cognitive learning situations. To cite one example, let us consider how we learned to add. At the very first stage, in adding three and two, we counted three blocks on one part of our desk, and counted two at another. We then placed all the blocks together and counted the newly formed group. This elaborate method of addition sooner or later underwent a series of abbreviations. One of these is no longer counting from one to five to find the total, but starting immediately from the total number of blocks in the first group, i.e., only counting from three onwards: 3, 4, 5. This was only possible because we discovered that with the original method, we counted the first group twice, and that the results were, of course, the same on both occasions. We then further dropped the second counting. One can also see that, in this case, abbreviation of the total action results from the discovery of identity between two paths to the goal.

The type of abbreviation that is based on the discovery of identity relations seems to be a higher and more difficult achievement than the two others. Most of the examples that I have been able to find thus far seem to occur with children who have reached at least kindergarten age. Every time one finds such a case, it is experienced as a specimen of genuinely intelligent behavior. It is significant that the Soviet psychologist Kruteckij (1976), who examined the ways in which pupils of 14 years and over solved mathematical problems, found that with children who were mathematically gifted, the abbreviations occurred at a far higher rate than with normal pupils during the solving of a series of comparable problems. That this form of abbreviation is a higher and more intellectual achievement is also connected with the fact that it represents the reverse relationship between the level of control and the level of performance. In these cases, the abbreviation is discovered on the cognitive plane, and only after this has happened is the performance altered in a corresponding way. Here we have, for the first time, a case of a deliberate alteration of a <u>plan</u> of action.

It remains now to discuss the implications of the building block model for teaching. Can we deliberately influence abbreviation processes in order to advance cognitive development? The peculiar thing is that the three different forms of abbreviation processes cannot be influenced in themselves, but we can still take advantage of them for instructional purposes. We cannot influence abbreviation directly because all three forms occur spontaneously, or, as I prefer to call it, <u>autonomously</u>. It is not only the first two but also the third form that is an autonomous process, because the discovery of identity occurs suddenly with every child even when we try to explain the identity to the child. The difference between the first and second types of abbreviation and the third type is that the latter type represents a non-continuous process, whereas the other two types represent a continuous process.

Nevertheless, it is possible to influence the process in an indirect way. We may induce the child to perform specific kinds of actions in which we anticipate that (on the grounds of experience or intuitive knowledge) the desired forms of abbreviations will probably occur sooner or later. It is here that fruitful research problems for instructional psychology arise. If we knew more about the conditions of the different forms of abbreviation, we could benefit more than we have thus far, because we could choose forms of action that are optimal for abbreviational possibilities, with the result that we could provide the child with a rich and varied array of integrated building blocks in a more efficient and pleasurable way than we do now. But - apart from our insufficient knowledge of abbreviation processes--we should guide the <u>actions</u> of the child through our instruction, and not only inform the child about, or reward him or her for, the <u>achievements</u> we wish the child to reach. Traditional reinforcement procedures only inform the subject that his or her achievement was all right, or reached a quantitative criterion. Of course, feedback could be used in such a way that it informs the learner about qualitative aspects of the activity, but it is only in the rarest of cases that this is done in psychological laboratories and in schools. Modeling certainly is more promising, because the activity is demonstrated to the learner, but its effects are better still when it used in conjunction with verbal instructions that assist the learner to analyze what is being seen. Verbal instruction in this case is action-centered. Goal-centered verbal instructions have been shown to have less impact on learning (Pijning, 1975).

I would like to end with a word of warning. Teaching pupils to perform specified actions suppposes a language in which actions may be described. Now, most of the language systems currently being used by cognitive psychologists are of a purely logical nature. Man's cognitive activity in these descriptions is reduced to a number of rational procedures. However, human activity is not totally rational. There are rational components in it, which flow directly from the action's goal, but there are others that are evoked by the situation or field with which the subject is confronted. What we need in psychology in general, and in instructional psychology in particular, is an action language, a language through which the complicated interaction between intentional factors and field factors in human activity may be adequately expressed.

Footnotes

Reference to Soviet sources is only made to translations, so far as they exist. The year of original publication is mentioned, however. The international transliteration system for Russian has been used. Where translated texts use another spelling, this is given between parentheses.

References

Denney, N. W., & Acito, M. A. Classification training in two- and three-year-old children. Journal of Experimental Child Psychology, 1974, 17, 37-48.

Gagne, R. M. The conditions of learning. New York: Holt, Rinehart, and Winston, 1970.

Gal'perin, P. J. An experimental study in the function of mental actions. In B. Simon (Ed.), Psychology in the Soviet Union. London: Routledge and Kegan Paul, 1954, 1957.

Gal'perin, P. J. Stages in the development of mental acts. In M. Cole & I. Maltzman (Eds.), A handbook of contemporary Soviet psychology. New York: Basic Books, 1969.

Kruteckij, V. A. (Krutetskii) The psychology of mathematical abilities in school children. Chicago: University of Chicago Press, 1968, 1976.

Pijning, H. Leren van een groot-motorische vaardigheid. Dissertation, Utrecht University, 1975.

Tëplen'kaja, Ch. M. (Tjoplenkaja) Zum Problem der Begriffsbildung bei Kindern. In J. Lompscher (Ed.), Probleme der Ausbildung geistiger Handlungen. Berlin (DDR): Volk und Wissen, 1968, 1972.

Veklerova, Ch. M. Formirovanie logičeskich struktur u staršich doškol'nikov. Avtoreferat dissertacii, Moskva, 1974.

Velt, J. van der L'apprentissage du mouvement et l'automatisme. Dissertation, Louvain University, 1928.

Venger, L. A. Vosprijatie i obučenie. Moskva: Prosveščenie, 1969.

Venger, L. A. Selections from L. A. Venger's monograph: "Perception and learning." Soviet Psychology, 1971-72, 10, 1-108.

Vygotskij, L. S. (Vygotsky) Thought and language. New York: Wiley, 1934, 1962.

Zaporožec, A. V. (Zaporozhets) Some of the psychological problems of sensory training in early childhood and the preschool period. In M. Cole & I. Maltzman (Eds.), A handbook of contemporary Soviet psychology. New York: Basic Books, 1969.

Zaporožec, A. V. (Zaporozhets) The development of perception in the preschool child. In Cognitive development in children. Five monographs of the Society for Research in Child Development. Chicago: University of Chicago Press, 1970.

COGNITION AND INSTRUCTION: TOWARD A COGNITIVE THEORY OF LEARNING

James F. Voss
University of Pittsburgh
Pittsburgh, Pennsylvania, U.S.A.

Contemporary cognitive psychology has focused upon problems of perception and memory, an emphasis that has led to an apparent decrease of research in the area of learning.[1] A reasonable question to ask, therefore, is whether the cognitive movement has neglected the study of learning, or whether cognitive psychology has incorporated the concept of learning, but has done so under a different terminology.

I would like to offer a two-part answer to this question. The first part of the answer is that the study of learning indeed exists within cognitive psychology. Bower (1975),for example, has argued that learning involves the addition of nodes and relational links among nodes; John Anderson (1976) has implied that learning also involves an inductive system and the addition of new productions to the existing repertoire; and Rumelhart and Norman (1975) have described learning in terms of the accretion, tuning, and restructuring of schema. The second part of the answer, however, is that although the concept of learning may be found in cognitive psychology, it also must be conceded that the cognitive view of learning is vague, is abstract, and, most important, is lacking a substantive data base. I would, therefore, like to argue that there is a distinct need to develop a more explicit statement of the concept of learning within the cognitive framework, and I would add that such a statement is necessary if cognitive theory is to provide a basis for instructional research, theory, and practice. It is the purpose of this paper to consider some issues that pertain to this assertion. In the next section of the paper, three principles involving the concept of learning within cognitive psychology will be considered.

Learning and Cognition: Three Principles

Principle 1

What generally has been termed learning, whether occurring inside or outside of the laboratory, almost always is transfer.[2] In one sense, this point is obvious and trivial; in another sense, the implications of this principle have, almost without exception (e.g., Ferguson, 1954,

13

1956), not been fully explored, probably because we know so little about transfer.

The classic transfer paradigm is (a) Learn A then Learn B versus (b) learn a control task then Learn B; transfer is measured by comparing B acquisition in the two conditions. With the use of such a paradigm, negative transfer has been found in highly specific paradigm situations, although this assertion may sometimes be questioned because of control group issues.[3] Also, positive transfer has been obtained under a number of conditions, including (a) highly specific mediational paradigms (e.g., Postman, 1962); (b) as a learning-to-learn effect (e.g., Duncan, 1960); (c) under conditions in which strategy training transfers to a new situation (e.g., Olson, 1977); (d) under conditions involving use of so-called "advance organizers," although these data are somewhat inconsistent (see, however, Royer & Cable, 1976); and (e) under conditions in which principles are applied to specific situations (e.g., Judd, 1908). With respect to theory, transfer is not well understood; we, in essence, have not gone very far past the "identical elements" theory. In some ways, our relatively poor understanding of transfer is amazing, since our educational systems are based fundamentally upon assumptions of transfer.

The conception of transfer that is based upon the classical transfer paradigm is, however, too narrow. The transfer to which I am referring involves learning (Task B) in relation to the previous learning of the individual (A learning). Moreover, by A learning, I mean not the acquisition of a specific list or set of materials (although such acquisition may be part of A learning), but rather the knowledge and skills that the individual brings into the Task B situation. Moreover, a corollary of this view is that there cannot be a baseline control that involves no A learning, since every individual has developed knowledge and skills in some way. Thus, learning in this view consists of an interaction of the knowledge and skills the individual brings into and uses in a given situation with the information and demands of the situation.

We shall now consider some research we have conducted that bears on these issues. We employed the contrastive method (Chase & Simon, 1973; Hunt, Front, & Lunneborg, 1973) and isolated two groups, with each individual of one group having a highly developed knowledge of a particular subject-matter domain, while the second group knew much less about the area. The knowledge domain we used was baseball, and the groups were equated on a reading comprehension test. We conducted a series of eight experiments that were designed to isolate structure and process differences that could account for performance differences in the two groups, assuming such performance differences would occur. Our experiments included a number of memory and processing tasks, as well as a multidimensional scaling study on the knowledge of a particular set of relationships within the particular knowledge domain. Two conclusions of the work are considered.

The first is that domain-related concepts of the high knowledge individual are more differentiated than the concepts of the low knowledge individual. Moreover, if one assumes that the meaning of a concept consists of the relationships of that concept with other concepts (dc Saussure, 1959; Lyons, 1969), then the conceptual structure of the high knowledge individual may be assumed to have more concepts and more interrelationships among these concepts.

This hypothesized difference in conceptual differentiation has three important implications. First, the high knowledge person is able to identify knowledge-related material more precisely and more quickly than the low knowledge individual, and this difference produces a more precise encoding and storage of the information. Second, because of this superiority in storage precision, retrieval is made easier for the high knowledge person. Third, the differences of the high and low knowledge individuals suggest that depth or level of processing differences exist at a semantic level and that these differences are characterized by encoding uniqueness (Lockhart, Craik, & Jacoby, 1976).

The second conclusion of this work involves the role of context; the high knowledge individuals have a much greater knowledge of contingent relations and are more adept at using this knowledge. An experimental example illustrates this conclusion.

The experiment involved presentation of 24 target sentences, with eight sentences occurring under each of three conditions. In one condition, there were, at input, two context sentences that preceded any particular target sentence. In the second condition, there was one context sentence preceding each target sentence at input, and in the third condition, no context sentences preceded the target sentence at input. The target sentences were presented in capital letters, with the context sentences presented in regular typing format. The context sentences and the target sentences formed a sequentially meaningful unit in terms of the subject matter.[4]

After presentation of the sentences, recall involved two stages. In the first, no context sentences were presented and the individual was asked to recall the target sentences; in the second, recall was tested by presenting the context sentences and asking the individual to recall the related target sentences. Figure 1 represents the results of the first recall test. The results indicate that at uncued recall, the high knowledge individuals show an increase in recall with the number of context sentences at input, whereas recall decreased for the low knowledge individuals.

Our explanation of these findings is that because the high knowledge individuals had perceived the sentences as a unit at input, they were able to generate the respective target sentence if they recalled a related context sentence. However, at input, the low knowledge subjects probably did not understand the relationships between the context sentences and target sentences, and this led to interference

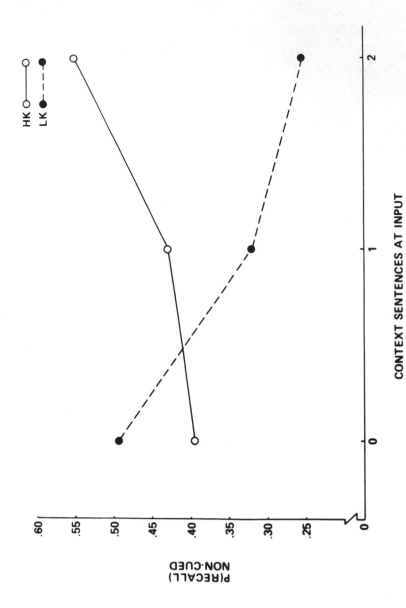

Figure 1.   Probability of recall in non-cued condition for High-knowledge (HK) and Low-knowledge (LK) groups as a function of number of context sentences at input.

in the processing of the material when it was presented. With respect
to the subsequent cued recall, the high knowledge group was able to
recall more new target information (not recalled in uncued recall) than
the low knowledge group.

These results clearly illustrate the strong effect of context in
the high knowledge group when the context maps onto their existing
knowledge. Moreover, for the low knowledge individuals, context
produced difficulty in acquiring new information. This latter finding
at least suggests that information presented successively in a classroom
about a particular subject matter could become increasingly difficult
for individuals with relatively poor understanding of the information.

Other results we have obtained also support the conclusion that the
high knowledge individual's store of contingent relations is critical;
e.g., the high knowledge individuals recalled domain-related information
more readily than low knowledge individuals in a memory span type of
study, and they also were able to make more appropriate predictions
regarding events that could occur under a given set of circumstances.

Our results thus suggest that knowledge of a given domain builds up
an internal context that the individual is able to utilize when new
inputs of domain-related information occur. However, low knowledge
individuals lack the appropriate internal context; for them,
understanding the external events is quite difficult because they are
unable to interpret the events in terms of their knowledge structure.

Our work also indicated that knowledge of contingent relationships
is of considerable importance to the operation of working memory.
DeGroot (1966) and Chase and Simon (1973) emphasized the importance of
perceptual chunking in chess experts. Our work led to a somewhat
modified view of chunking for high knowledge individuals. The top panel
of Figure 2 presents the traditional view of the chunk, and we think
this description holds for our low knowledge individuals; they
understand discrete pieces of information reasonably well, but often
fail when they try to relate information that was not presented
contiguously. However, the lower panel, which describes what we term a
flowing chunk, depicts our view of chunking in the high knowledge
individuals. What the diagram is meant to depict is that the knowledge
of contingent relations is extremely substantial in the high knowledge
individuals. Moreover, the transitions are accomplished in such a
manner as to make chunk boundaries almost indistinguishable. This
notion, if correct, suggests that either working memory capacity is
extremely large for the high knowledge person, or long-term memory is
extremely accessible and information flows into working memory with such
ease that it provides a relatively large functional working memory
capacity. To carry this point one step farther, if we assume that
learning involves the integration of relevant working memory components
with new input, it is clear that the high knowledge individual has an
overwhelming advantage compared to the low knowledge person, because so

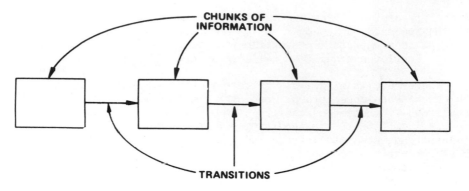

TRADITIONAL VIEW OF CHUNKS

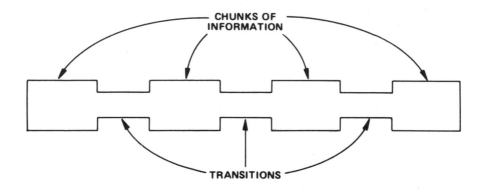

THE CONCEPT OF FLOWING CHUNKS

Figure 2.   Traditional view of chunks (low knowledge) and concept of flowing chunk
(high knowledge).

much   information is available in the high knowledge individual.
Incidentally, one cannot help but note how our findings tend to resemble
differences obtained as a function of age. Indeed, the question of the
extent to which particular age differences may essentially be knowledge
differences is an important, unresolved problem.

It is tempting to state our findings using terms such as schema (Bartlett, 1932; Spiro, 1977), scripts (Schank, 1975), frames (Minsky, 1975), or macrostructures (Kintsch & van Dijk, 1975). However, while it is clear that our high knowledge individuals do have generalized knowledge structures of domain-related information, it also is true that, at least for baseball knowledge, the information that could go into a schema is often probabilistic; i.e., in any given situation, there is not one event that is related but any number of events that are potentially related. The subsequent input, then, is specific; and in order to place that input into a schema or script, it is necessary that the specific input be differentiated conceptually from other possible inputs. In other words, the schema consists of not only generalized contingent relations, but also of differentiated concepts. Indeed, we are reminded of Locke's (1956) notion that the concept of triangularity is general, and does not refer to specific triangles; i.e., it is not equilateral or isoceles, etc.; and we then are reminded of Berkeley's (1971) counter-argument, that whenever he thinks of triangularity, he thinks of a specific triangle. We, in other words, do not question the existence of generalized knowledge structures, but we question whether they exist apart from specific experiences and whether people really place information in vacant slots. It is more likely t..at people identify input information in terms of what they already know. The results considered to this point lead to our general second principle.

Principle 2

When learning is viewed as transfer, the primary factor influencing learning is the knowledge the individual brings into and uses in the particular learning situation. Moreover, the knowledge the individual has of the particular subject matter is of great importance. The extent to which knowledge of one domain may be useful in learning new information of another domain is, of course, an open question; we do not know how specific or how general transfer effects really are.

To introduce the third principle, I shall briefly present a few results from another line of research we have been pursuing. This work has consisted of studying how understanding of a prose passage is related to the memory structure of the individual. We have employed multidimensional scaling procedures in order to assess the conceptual relations existing in the memory structure of the individual, and we then used the same procedures to assess the conceptual relations that the individual develops when a prose passage is read. Our passages were about various animals. Previous work (Henley, 1969; Rips, Shoben, & Smith, 1973) indicated that when people rate animals for similarity, size is the strongest determinant of the ratings. A story was constructed in which there were two classes of animals, animals that were helpful and those that were not helpful. Two versions of the story were constructed that were identical except for the roles of the

specific animals. In one case, the story structure was consistent with
the memory structure;   i.e., small animals were helpful and large
animals were not helpful. In the second version, the helpful group
included both large and small animals, as did the nonhelpful group.
After reading one or the other version of the story, subjects rated the
animal terms for similarity as the terms had occurred in the story
context.

        The important finding was that second-grade children apparently
understood the story better when the concepts were consistent with the
memory structure.   When the story was not congruent, it was not
understood as well.   This difference of story version diminished by
fourth grade, and college students had little difficulty with the
inconsistent version.   Moreover, the results of another study provided
evidence suggesting that when a prose passage structure was similar to
the memory structure, recall was better for the individuals whose memory
structures were most closely related to the passage structure, as
measured by distances in subject space using the INDSCAL procedure
(Carroll & Chang, 1970); however, when the passage was different than
the memory structure,   the passage was better recalled by individuals
with a larger distance (change) between their memory structure and
passage structure. These results suggested the third principle.

Principle 3

        When learning is viewed as transfer and when the most important
factor in learning is taken to be the knowledge of the individual,
learning is a function of the degree to which the structure of the input
information is related to the memory structure of the individual.
Furthermore, our results suggested a possible fourth principle, namely,
that flexibility in the use of one's knowledge may be related to
learning new information when the new information differs substantially
from the memory structure.   This general view is, of course, in line
with many similar statements (e.g., Anderson, 1977; Anderson & Ortony,
1975;   Moore & Newell, 1974;   Rumelhart & Ortony, 1977).   In the
concluding section, implications of the present view for instruction
will be considered.

Implications for Instruction

        First, the present view indicates that more must be learned about
knowledge and how to conceptualize knowledge. Work on this problem has,
of course, been quite substantial in recent years.   For example,
Anderson (1976) has examined the ways to handle the differences of
declarative and procedural knowledge (Ryle, 1949), Polanyi's (1966)
distinction of tacit and explicit knowledge has been frequently cited,
and a number of papers in the Anderson, Spiro, and Montague (1977)
volume, especially Broudy's (1977) chapter, are concerned with issues of
knowledge representation. This work, in all probability, is only the

beginning of such study.

A second instructional implication is that there is a need to develop measuring instruments that give us a better idea of what an individual knows. Furthermore, such instruments will be needed not only to assess traditional knowledge, i.e., subject-matter content, but also to develop means of measuring processing skills. The problems of assessing knowledge in this way are, in fact, quite substantial. Knowledge representations as described by a number of current investigators may be quite fruitful; but, it may be another matter when one assesses what the individual knows specifically, and then tries to relate that information to the hypothetical knowledge structure.

A third implication is the need to determine the nature and importance of knowing, i.e., the person's awareness of what he or she knows. Currently, questions of knowing are being studied most extensively in the developmental area (e.g., Brown, 1975; Kreutzer, Leonard, & Flavell, 1975), although there is some activity in the adult area (e.g., Gardiner & Klee, 1976; Vesonder & Voss, Note 1).

A fourth implication is that if we assume that when a person learns about a given topic, his or her knowledge structure becomes more like the knowledge of the field as it is described by the experts of the area (Shavelson, 1972), then it would seem important that appropriate descriptions be developed that portray the knowledge of particular subject-matter areas. Such descriptions could serve as reference points that then could be compared to the knowledge structure of a particular individual. Moreover, how that structure may change with training and approach the reference point could also be determined.

The fifth and last implication is that we need to determine how important the specific, domain-related knowledge of the individual is for learning, as opposed to general knowledge. Furthermore, we need to determine how specific and more general content in an instructional event may interact with the specific and the general knowledge of the individual (cf. Mayer, Stiehl, & Greeno, 1975).

The viewpoint advocated in this paper calls for a reorientation with respect to instructional process. The view specifically indicates that instructional improvement may take place when we learn more about the relation of experience and knowledge to learning. In order to accomplish this goal, it will be necessary to develop better and more sensitive instruments than are currently in existence, instruments that will provide an estimate of knowledge and processing skills.

This paper has argued that learning should be viewed as transfer because such a perspective will help to develop a reasonable concept of learning within the cognitive framework and will help to develop a cognitive theory of learning. It is uncertain, however, whether cognitive theory, as it exists today, is capable of answering this challenge. In cognitive psychology today, there is a wave of

rationalism, which is leading to a proliferation of models that are
sometimes not testable, not tested, or not compared. It is difficult to
see where this movement will lead. Perhaps the real message of this
movement is that it portrays a need for new and creative ways to frame
problems and ask experimental questions. Perhaps cognitive psychology
is starting to identify the really important issues, but does not know
how to address them. In addition, there seems to be a tendency today to
use hypothetical concepts and labels as though they were explanations.
What is a script but a name for an organized, recurring class of events?
The use of such labels may be helpful in a heuristic way, but such use
may also be deceptive, in the sense that providing a label does not
necessarily help us to understand the problem at hand. Concepts such as
scripts, frames, macrostructures, active memory structures, etc., should
lead to a theory that will explain phenomena, and should generate new,
significant lines of inquiry. There appears to be a question of whether
such developments are taking place to a significant degree. The
significant issues are at hand, but the means to define, understand, and
explain them are not clear. Possibly, such skepticism is too
pessimistic. Hopefully, transfer will occur in the psychological
community, and today's knowledge will interact with tomorrow's input in
order to provide a meaningful concept and theory of learning within the
cognitive framework.

Footnotes

This paper is supported by the Learning Research and Development
Center of the University of Pittsburgh and funds from the University of
Pittsburgh. The author wishes to thank Gay Bisanz, Harry Chiesi, Ron
LaPorte, George Spilich, Kathy Studeny, and Gregg Vesonder for their
contributions to the paper, as well as Drs. Alan Lesgold and James
Pellegrino for their comments on a preliminary draft of the paper.

1. In as strongly a learning-oriented publication as the Journal
of Experimental Psychology, we find that in 1956, 25% of the articles
had the word "learning" in the title, whereas this percentage decreased
to 19% in 1966, and to 9% in 1976 (Human Learning and Memory section).

2. This statement refers primarily to the traditional study of
human learning and memory in the verbal context, and not to questions of
classical and operant conditioning. Also, in a general sense, any
multiple trial experiment could be regarded as transfer, with trial $n +
1$ performance being a function of trial n, $n - 1$, etc., performance.

3. When A-B, A-C acquisition is compared to D-B, A-C acquisition,
we say negative transfer occurred when second list acquisition in the
latter condition is superior to acquisition in the former. However, if
first-list learning is taken as the baseline control, we find that both
groups often show positive transfer, with the A-B, A-C condition showing
less positive transfer.

4. Each sentence was presented for 8 sec. When one context sentence was presented with the target sentence, both sentences were presented for 16 sec, and similarly, with two context sentences and the target sentence, the total presentation time was 24 sec. The participants were instructed that they would be tested on the target sentences and that the other sentences were present to help them learn the target sentences.

Reference Note

1. Vesonder, G. T., & Voss, J. F. On the prediction of one's own correct responding. Unpublished manuscript. University of Pittsburgh, 1977.

References

Anderson, J. R. Language, memory, and thought. Hillsdale, N. J.: Lawrence Erlbaum Associates, 1976.

Anderson, R. C. The notion of schemata and the educational enterprise: General discussion of the conference. In R. C. Anderson, R. J. Spiro, & W. E. Montague (Eds.), Schooling and the acquisition of knowledge. Hillsdale, N. J.: Lawrence Erlbaum Associates, 1977.

Anderson, R. C., & Ortony, A. On putting apples into bottles - A problem of polysemy. Cognitive Psychology, 1975, 7, 167-180.

Anderson, R. C., Spiro, R. J., & Montague, W. E. Schooling and the acquisition of knowledge. Hillsdale, N. J.: Lawrence Erlbaum Associates, 1977.

Bartlett, F. C. Remembering. London: Cambridge University Press, 1932.

Battig, W. F. Sequential learning and thought: An overlooked communality. In J. F. Voss (Ed.), Approaches to thought. Columbus, Oh.: Merrill Publishing Co., 1969.

Berkeley, G. A treatise concerning the principles of human understanding. Menston, England: Scholar Press, 1971.

Bower, G. H. Cognitive psychology: An introduction. In W. K. Estes (Ed.), Handbook of learning and cognitive processes (Vol. 1). Hillsdale, N. J.: Lawrence Erlbaum Associates, 1975.

Broudy, H. S.   Types of knowledge and purposes of education.   In
    R. C. Anderson, R. J. Spiro, & W. E. Montague (Eds), Schooling and
    the acquisition of knowledge. Hillsdale, N. J.: Lawrence Erlbaum
    Associates, 1977.

Brown, A. L.   The development of memory: Knowing, knowing about
    knowing, and knowing how to know. In H. W. Reese (Ed.), Advances
    in child development and behavior (Vol. 10). New York: Academic
    Press, 1975.

Carroll, J. D., & Chang, J. J. Analysis of individual differences in
    multidimensional   scaling   via   an   N-way   generalization   of
    Eckart-Young decomposition. Psychometrika, 1970, 35, 283-319.

Chase, W. G., &   Simon, H. A.   Perception   in   chess.   Cognitive
    Psychology, 1973, 4, 55-81.

Collins, A., & Loftus, E. A spreading-activation theory of semantic
    processing. Psychological Review, 1975, 82, 407-428.

de Groot, A. D. Perception and memory versus thought: Some old ideas
    and recent findings.   In B. Kleinmuntz (Ed.), Problem solving:
    Research method and theory. New York: Wiley, 1966.

de Saussure, F. Course in general linguistics. New York: McGraw-Hill,
    1959.

Duncan, C. P. Description of learning to learn in human subjects.
    American Journal of Psychology, 1960, 73, 108-114.

Ferguson, G. A. On learning and human ability.   Canadian Journal of
    Psychology, 1954, 8, 95-112.

Ferguson, G. A. On transfer and the abilities of man. Canadian Journal
    of Psychology, 1956, 10, 121-131.

Gardiner, J. M., & Klee, H.   Memory for   remembered   events: An
    assessment of output monitoring in free recall. Journal of Verbal
    Learning and Verbal Behavior. 1976, 15, 227-233.

Henley, N. M. A psychological study of the semantics of animal terms.
    Journal of Verbal Learning and Verbal Behavior, 1969, 8, 176-184.

Hunt, E., Frost, N., & Lunneborg, C.   Individual   differences   in
    cognition: A new approach to intelligence. In G. H. Bower (Ed.),
    The psychology of learning and motivation (Vol. 7).   New York:
    Academic Press, 1973.

Judd, C. H. The relation of special training to general intelligence. Educational Review, 1908, 36, 28-42.

Kintsch, W., & van Dijk, T. A. Comment on se rapelle et on resume des histoires. Langages, 1975, 40, 98-116.

Kreutzer, M. A., Leonard, C., &Flavell, J. H. An interview study of children's knowledge about memory. Monographs of the Society for Research in Child Development, 1975, 40(1).

Locke, J. An essay concerning human understanding. New York: Gateway Editions, Inc., 1956.

Lockhart, R. S., Craik, F. I. M. & Jacoby, L. Depth of processing, recognition and recall. In J. Brown (Ed.), Recognition and recall. New York: Wiley, 1976.

Lyons, J. Introduction to theoretical linguistics. Cambridge, Mass.: Cambridge University Press, 1969.

Mayer, R. C., Stiehl, C., &Greeno, J. G. Acquisition of understanding and skill in relation to subjects' preparation and meaningfulness of instruction. Journal of Educational Psychology , 1975, 67, 331-350.

Minsky, M. A framework for representing knowledge. In P. H. Winston (Ed.), The psychology of computer vision. New York: McGraw-Hill, 1975.

Moore, J., & Newell, A. How can Merlin understand? In L. W. Gregg (Ed.), Knowledge and cognition. Potomac, Md.: Lawrence Erlbaum Associates, 1974.

Olson, D. R. The languages of instruction: The literate bias of schooling and the acquisition of knowledge. Hillsdale, N. J.: Lawrence Erlbaum Associates, 1977.

Polanyi, M. The tacit dimension. Garden City: Doubleday, 1966.

Postman, L. Transfer of training as a function of experimental paradigm and degree of first-list learning. Journal of Verbal Learning and Verbal Behavior. 1962, 1, 109-118.

Rips, L. J., Shoben, E. J., & Smith, E. E. Semantic distance and the verification of semantic relations. Journal of Verbal Learning and Verbal Behavior, 1973, 12, 1-20.

Royer, J. M., & Cable, G. W. Illustrations, analogies, and facilitative transfer in prose learning. Journal of Educational Psychology, 1976, 68(2), 205-209.

Rumelhart, D. E., & Norman, D. A.   The active   structural   network.   In
     D. A. Norman   &   D. E. Rumelhart (Eds.), Explorations in cognition.
     San Francisco: W. H. Freeman, 1975.

Rumelhart, D. E., & Urtony, A.   The   representation   of   knowledge   in
     memory.   In   R. C. Anderson, R. J. Spiro, & W. E. Montague (Eds.),
     Schooling and the   acquisition   of   knowledge.   Hillsdale,   N. J.:
     Lawrence Erlbaum Associates, 1977.

Ryle, G.   The concept of mind.   London: Hutchinson, 1949.

Schank, R. C.   The role of memory in language processing.   In   C. Cofer
     (Ed.),   The   structure   of   human   memory.   San   Francisco:
     W. H. Freeman, 1975.

Shavelson, R. J.   Some   aspects   of   correspondence   between   content
     structure   and cognitive structure in physics instruction.   Journal
     of Educational Psychology, 1972, 63, 259-263.

Spiro, R. J.   Remembering information from text: The "state of   schema"
     approach.   In R. C. Anderson, R. J. Spiro, & W. E. Montague (Eds.),
     Schooling and the   acquisition   of   knowledge.   Hillsdale,   N. J.:
     Lawrence Erlbaum Associates, 1977.

LEARNING BY EXAMPLE

Frederick Hayes-Roth
The Rand Corporation
Santa Monica, California 90406

What is Learning By Example?

Everyone has many personal experiences of learning by example. While much psychological research has investigated "concept learning" (cf. Bruner, Goodnow, & Austin, 1956; Hayes-Roth & Hayes-Roth, in press; Hunt, 1952), that rubric is too narrow to embrace the variety of situations in which learning by example occurs. A brief list of such situations includes:

1. Traditional concept learning, such as inducing the class characteristics of "triangle": "Three distinct line segments such that each line segment is coterminous, with a different line segment at each of its endpoints." Such a rule can be induced from various examples of triangles; all examples necessarily manifest the rule, although they may differ from one another in irrelevant ways (e.g., in absolute and relative size, shape, orientation, color, texture). Note that although most traditional concept learning tasks employ only attribute-value descriptions, this learning task requires higher order, relational logic to characterize the structural constraints among the lines of a triangle.

2. Serial pattern learning, such as predicting the next item in a conceptually organized sequence. Traditional research on this problem has centered on mathematical sequences of symbols and various algorithmic models of memory processes for simulating the sequence generator. Other examples of this type of behavior include anticipation of expectable events (e.g., words or topics in a text that are predictable from preceding context) and prediction of cyclic phenomena. In these situation, subsequences of the preceding sequence of items serve as examples from which the sequence generation rule is induced.

3. Transformation learning, such as inducing the rule for converting active sentences to semantically equivalent passive sentences. Presumably, this type of general syntactic procedure is abstracted from examples of semantically equivalent pairs of sentences

----

27

illustrating such a transformation. The use of transformations, however, extends far beyond the domain of syntax. Newell and Simon (1972) have shown that similar types of rules (called productions) provide an excellent model of human problem solving activity. Their theory postulates that the problem solver applies these productions (described below) to internal representations of the problem whenever the properties of the problem state satisfy the rules' conditions. These rules, too, are presumably inferred by generalizing previous experiences, including both trial-and-error successes and instructive examples.

4. Category learning, such as including the sets of words that are adjectives and those that are nouns, and the associated rule of English grammar that adjectives may precede nouns but not vice versa. While such formal categories and grammatical principles may not be consciously understood, behavioral evidence of this sort of learning is ubiquitous. It is hypothesized in this case, too, that learning results from experience of examples.

Learning by example, as a theory of the way concepts and general rules are induced, could be compared with other learning theories in a variety of ways. Only in the case of learning by example, however, has research progressed sufficiently to enable the theory to account for what is learned as well as specifying conditions under which learning occurs. For this reason, this learning theory is especially practical. In the subsequent sections, the theory is outlined and its most important implications are considered.

How Can Learning from Examples Occur?

Early work by cognitive psychologists on concept learning identified a variety of types of concepts that could be learned according to the logical structure of the corresponding propositional formulae (cf. Bruner, Goodnow, & Austin, 1956; Hunt, 1952). Thus, conjunctive concepts are those for which class membership rules are expressible in terms of conjunctions of two or more criterial attributes. Similarly, relational concepts are those requiring specific relations to hold among objects or features in all examples of the concept. This taxonomy stimulated a vast amount of research. In particular, the type (logical structure) of concepts, strategies for hypothesis testing, effects of positive or negative examples, and amount and delay of feedback, were heavily investigated.

Recently, a new approach to the learning problem has been taken, stemming from combined interests in computer-based learning and cognitive models of human learning. The thrust of this research is to develop mechanisms that can model the kind of learning that people exhibit when provided with examples of general rules. This change in emphasis has produced a new orientation to the basic issues. The chief variables of interest in the current research are what kinds of logical descriptions actually underlie cognitive processes, and how these can be inferred directly from examples (cf. Hayes-Roth, 1976, 1977a; Hayes-Roth & Hayes-Roth, in press; Hayes-Roth & McDermott, 1976a,b; Michalski, 1973; Vere, 1975, in press; Waterman, 1975a,b; Williams, 1972; Winston, 1975).

Several researchers have come to the conclusion that a significant amount of human knowledge is representable in two basic conceptual forms. One is a structural representation of a pattern, such as a propositional formula describing the prototypic triangle (see Example 1 above), or a predicate calculus expression representing a prototypic active sentence that can be transformed into passive voice. The second type of knowledge structure is a production rule that relates two pattern descriptions by a transformational rule: Whenever the pattern called the "condition" is matched by events in memory, the pattern called the "action" component is executed. Such condition-action rules have now been successfully employed to model a wide range of intellectual functions, including syntactic and semantic processing in connected-speech understanding (Hayes-Roth & Mostow, 1976; Hayes-Roth, Mostow, & Fox, 1977), human problem solving (Newell, 1973; Newell & Simon, 1972), and medical diagnosis (Shortliffe, 1976).

The benefit of such an approach to knowledge representation is multiplied considerably by the fact that both of the proposed types of knowledge structures can be induced from examples. Extending and generalizing the early work on conjunctive concept learning, an operational theory has been developed for learning structural representations of patterns and production rules from examples. The essence of the theory is the same as suggested by Galton (1907) in the form of a "composite photograph" theory of concept formation. Galton converted the contemporary technology of photography into a theory for explaining how it was possible to combine various images of the same object into a generalized form that could serve as a template for recognizing all variants of the basic image. His theory was, simply, that the memory representation of an object's image was like a photographic transparency. Thus, by overlaying multiple representations derived from different views of the same object, a composite photograph would emerge in which the invariant properties would be accentuated and properties that differed among alternative views would be attentuated. The collection of emergent common properties would constitute a template defining the concept. Subsequent images of the same object would necessarily match this template, because they too would exhibit properties criterial to the general concept.

Of course, Galton's theory was little more than a metaphor. Combining Galton's key insight with contemporary technology, however, yields a powerful model of the learning process (Hayes-Roth, 1976, 1977a; Hayes-Roth & McDermott, 1976b). In brief, the learning process is modeled in the following way. At any moment, the learner is viewed as possessing a current stock of predicates that he/she uses to delimit, label, describe, and relate objects, actions, and events. This knowledge is conceived of as a set of properties and case frames applied in forming descriptions of instructional examples. A formal methodology has been developed to convert such case relational descriptions of events into equivalent graph structures. Then, by comparing the graph representations of several illustrations of the same concept or rule, and extracting the subgraph that is common to all (or many) of them, an hypothesis about the criterial properties and relations of the general class is generated. As Galton proposed, different examples of the same class concept will all exhibit the criterial properties constituting the general rule. These are directly identified by finding the structural sub-representation that is common to the various descriptions. Thereafter, the learner can recognize novel instances of the general rule by detecting that the stimulus manifests those properties inferred to be criterial. Furthermore, newly learned patterns (like "triangle") increase the learner's stock of descriptive predicates.

At the same time as this process of learning by comparison identifies the commonalities among different examples of the same rule, one of its by-products is a discovery that particular sets of different properties reliably occur as alternatives in similar descriptive contexts. In fact, categories (such as "noun" and "adjective") are immediately identifiable by noting that specific sets of values occur in comparable contexts in different examples (e.g., "red" or "white" or "blue" all can precede "house" or "flag" or "paint"). Once such categories are identified, the learner can describe subsequent events using these novel properties. Thus, both concept and category learning produce an expansion of predicates available to the learner.

Finally, transformations or problem solving production rules can be induced from before-and-after pairs illustrating their application. In this case, antecedent and consequent components are compared to their respective counterparts in several examples. In this way, general condition-action patterns common to all examples are inferred. These learned rules explain how variables are bound and substitutions should be made from constants in a problem context (the condition) to the associated action.

As an illustration, consider the problem of inducing an unknown rule of transformational grammar from the following three antecedent-consequent example pairs:

1. "The little man sang a lovely song."
    "A lovely song was sung by the little man."

2. "A girl hugged the motorcycles."
    "The motorcycles were hugged by a girl."

3. "People are stopping friendly policemen."
    "Friendly policemen are being stopped by people."

The relational descriptions of these sentence pairs consist of three types of components: (a) syntactic phrase structures and markers (e.g., NUMBER:SINGULAR, TENSE:PRESENT); (b) a property that distinguishes elements of the antecedent sentence from elements of the consequent sentence (EVENT:e1 and ANTECEDENT:e1, as opposed to EVENT:e2 and CONSEQUENT:e2); and (c) same-type relations joining any pair of antecedent and consequent syntactic components that are identical types (i.e., are distinct tokens of the same type or, equivalently, are the roots of identical directed phrase structure graphs). The case frame description of the first sentence pair is shown below.

```
{{ANTECEDENT:e1, CONSEQUENT:e2},
{S:s1, NP:np11, VP:vp1, EVENT:e1},
{S:s2, NP:np21, VP:vp2, EVENT:e2},
{NP:np11, DET:the1, ADJ:little1, NOUN:noun11, EVENT:e1},
{NP:np21, DET:a1, ADJ:lovely1, NOUNnoun21, EVENT:e2},
{NOUN:noun11, NST:man1, NUMBER:n11, EVENT:e1},
{NOUN:noun21, NST:song1, NUMBER:n12, EVENT:e2},
{SINGULAR:n11, EVENT:e1},
{SINGULAR:n12, EVENT:e2},
{VP:vp1, AUX:aux11, VERB:verb11, NP:np22, EVENT:e1},
{SAME!NP:np21, SAME!NP:np22},
{NP:np22, DET:a2, ADJ:lovely2, NUUN:nuun22, EVFNT:e1},
{SAME!NOUN:noun21, SAME!NOUN:noun22},
{NOUN:noun22, NST:song2, NUMBER:n13, EVENT:e1},
{SINGULAR:n13, EVENT:e1},
{VP:vp2, AUX:aux12, PB:pb1, VERB:verb12, PP:pp1, EVENT:e2},
{AUX:aux11, AUXST:have1, TENSE:t11, NUMBER:n15, EVENT:e1},
{AUX:aux12, AUXST:have2, TENSE:t12, NUMBER:n16, EVENT:e2},
{SAME!AUX:aux11, SAME!AUX:aux12},
{VERB:verb11, VST:sing1, TENSE:t21, NUMBER:n15, EVENTe1},
{VERB:verb12, VST:sing2, TENSE:t22, NUMBER:n16, EVENT:e2},
{SAME!VERB:verb11, SAME!verb:verb12},
{PB:pb1, PBST:be1, TENSE:t23, NUMBER:n16, EVENT:e2},
{SAME!TENSE:t11, SAME!TENSE:t12},
{SAME!TENSE:t21, SAME!TENSE:t22, SAME!TENSE:t23},
{SINGULAR:n15, EVENT:e1},
{SINGULAR:n16, EVENT:e2},
{PRESENT:t11, EVENT:e1},
{PRESENT:t12, EVENT:e2},
{PAST-PART:t21, EVENT:e1},
{PAST-PART:t22, PAST-PART:t23, EVENT:e2},
{PP:pp1, PREP:by1, NP:np12, EVENT:e2},
{SAME!NP:np11, SAME!NP:np12},
{NP:np12, DET:the2, ADJ:little2, NOUN:noun12, EVENT:e2},
{SAME!NOUN:noun11, SAME!NOUN:noun12},
{NOUN:noun12, NST:man2, NUMBER:n14, EVENT:e2},
{SAME!NUMBER:n11, SAME!NUMBER:n12, SAME!NUMBER:n13},
{SAME!NUMBER:n14, SAME!NUMBER:n15, SAME!NUMBER:n16},
{SINGULAR:n14, EVENT:e2},
```

```
{THE:the1, EVENT:e1},
{THE:the2, EVENT:e2},
{SAME!WORD:the1, SAME!WORD:the2},
{LITTLE:little1, EVENT:e1},
{LITTLE:little2, EVEN1:e2},
{SAME!WORD:little1, SAME!WORD:little2},
{MAN:man1, EVENT:e1},
{MAN:man2, EVENT:e2},
{SAME!WORD:man1, SAME!WORD:man2},
{HAVE:have1, EVENT:e1},
{HAVE:have2, EVENT:e2},
{SAME!WORD:have1, SAMF!WORD:have2},
{SING:sing1, EVENT:e1},
{SING:sing2, EVENT:e2},
{SAME!WORD:sing1, SAME!WORD:sing2},
{A:a1, EVENT:e1},
{A:a2, EVENT:e2},
{SAME!WORD:a1, SAME!WORD:a2},
{LOVELY:lovely1, EVENT:e1},
{LOVELY:lovely2, EVENT:e2},
{SAME!WORD:lovely1, SAME!WORD:lovely2},
{SONG:song1, EVENT:e1},
{SONG:song2, EVENT:e2},
{SAME!WORD:song1, SAME!WORD:song1},
{BE:be1, EVENT:e2},
{BY:by1, EVENT:e2}}
```

This corresponds to Figure 1. When the descriptions of all three sentence pairs are compared, the learning algorithm induces the rule illustrated in Figure 2. Here, same-type relations that were common to all examples have been retained and are represented by arrows linking subgraphs in the antecedent sentence structure with corresponding subgraphs in the consequent sentence structure. These correspondences represent identical quantified variables in the left- and right-hand sides of the inferred production. When the rule is applied, the actual parameter in a stimulus event that matches the antecedent will be bound to the corresponding locus of the consequent structure. If this is done, the inferred production will effect the active-to-passive transformation rule.

This theory has led to development of several successful computer learning algorithms. These have been used to infer concepts in a variety of language processing tasks, including: learning to discriminate among vowels occurring in natural, connected speech (Burge & Hayes-Roth, 1976); learning to recognize words by discovering finite-state network representations comprising sequences of sets of alternative, acoustically labeled phones evident in examples (Fox & Hayes-Roth, 1976; Hayes-Roth & Burge, 1976); induction of general syntactic rules for active-to-passive, equi-noun deletion, and other transformations (Hayes-Roth, 1977a; Hayes-Roth & McDermott, 1976b); and induction of grammatical and semantic categories of words and phrases from a corpus of language (Hayes-Roth, 1976).

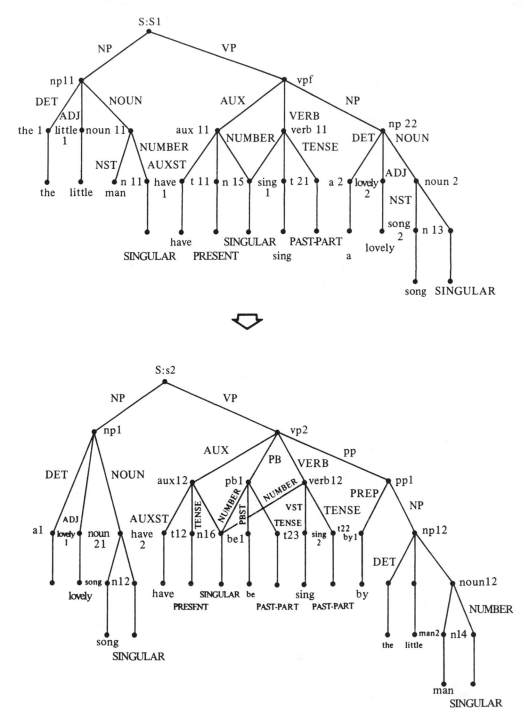

Figure 1. Graphical representation of the first example of the active-to-passive transformational rule.

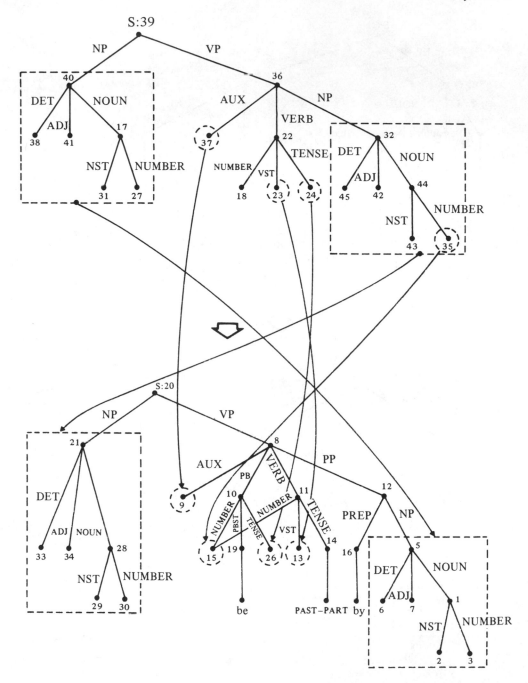

Figure 2. Graphical representation of the induced active-to-passive transformational rule.

Application of the theory to human learning tasks has shown that concept learning occurs when criterial combinations of properties common to examples of the same class are encoded and strengthened in memory (Hayes-Roth & Hayes-Roth, 1976, in press). Human recognition and classification performance is most accurately predicted by postulating that decisions are based on the memory strengths and cue validities of combinations of properties occurring in earlier examples. The significance of property combinations abstracted from instructional examples is a persistent and powerful phenomenon. Even when subjects are taught to apply a general rule and are subsequently trained by practicing with specific examples, their recollection of training instances and classification of subsequent items are more accurately predicted by the proposed learning theory than by theories postulating storage of an abstract or symbolic prototype plus transformational rules that accommodate variations from prototypes (Hayes-Roth & Hayes-Roth, in press).

When Does Learning by Example Occur?

The results of the research mentioned above suggest that we learn general rules, in the form of criterial combinations of properties and relations among objects, whenever we practice applying a rule or try to learn an unknown rule with instructive examples. This learning apparently occurs even when ostensibly unnecessary; i.e., if a general rule for a new concept is presented first, subsequent practice with specific examples of the rule results in learning of generalized representations that are abstracted directly from observed properties and relations of the specific examples. In short, if examples are used, they have a significant effect on what is learned (Hayes-Roth & Hayes-Roth, 1976, in press).

How Can Positive Effects of Learning Be Promoted?

This theory of learning predicts that each instructional example causes learning of relevant and irrelevant criteria that are consistent with it. Thus, undesirable learning must be controlled. Two methods for limiting learning of irrelevant generalities are: (a) present examples with the fewest irrelevant characteristics, and (b) insure that multiple examples of the same general rule vary maximally on irrelevant dimensions.

The theory also predicts that examples are the most powerful mechanism for instilling effective rule-directed behavior. They apparently influence behavior more than presentation of formal statements of general rules. Thus, learning can be most facilitated by first identifying the criterial properties and relationships of the knowledge to be acquired, and then insuring that each example manifests all criterial characteristics.

Other conditions that might promote learning by example are discussed in the next section.

Research Directions and Potential Applications

First, consider the important questions that are raised by these results. Among them are the following:

Is teaching with counterexamples effective? Results of earlier concept learning studies suggest that subjects have difficulty learning from negative information. This would also be predicted by the current theory.

What presentation sequence of rules and examples best promotes rapid learning?

How can examples be constructed to facilitate abstraction of more than one principle at a time?

Are informationally rich, embellished examples more effective or less effective than impoverished, bare-bones examples constructed to minimize irrelevant information?

Are variants of the teaching by example paradigm, such as teaching by analogy or anecdote, effective? How can the positive or negative effects associated with these alternatives be predicted?

Finally, consider the implications of this work for instructional applications. The following instructional paradigm appears to be warranted: The pattern characteristic or condition-action rule to be learned should be analyzed to identify its criterial properties and relations; competence in detecting and coding these attributes should be presented that manifest, in a salient way, the criterial properties and relations; and, finally, the multiple examples should be explicitly compared to highlight their commonalities. On the basis of evidence accumulated to date, this paradigm can be expected to promote rapid and effective learning.

References

Bruner, J. S., Goodnow, J. J., & Austin, G. A. A study of thinking. New York: Wiley, 1956.

Burge, J., & Hayes-Roth, F. A novel pattern learning and classification procedure applied to the learning of vowels. Proceedings of the 1976 I.E.E.E. International Conference on Acoustics, Speech and Signal Processing, Philadelphia, 1976, 154-157.

Fox, M. S., & Hayes-Roth, F. Approximation techniques for the learning of sequential symbolic patterns. Proceedings of the Third International Joint Conference on Pattern Recognition, Coronado, California, 1976, 616-620.

Galton, F. Inquiries into human faculty and its development. London: Dent, 1907.

Hayes-Roth, B., & Hayes-Roth, F. A comparative psychological investigation of pattern classification theories. Proceedings of the Third International Joint Conference on Pattern Recognition, Coronado, California, 1976, 224-227.

Hayes-Roth, B., & Hayes-Roth, F. Concept learning and the classification and recognition of exemplars. Journal of Verbal Learning and Verbal Behavior, (in press).

Hayes-Roth, F. Patterns of induction and related knowledge acquisition algorithms. In C. Chen (Ed.), Pattern recognition and artificial intelligence. New York: Academic Press, 1976.

Hayes-Roth, F. Uniform representations of structured patterns and an algorithm for the induction of contingency-response rules. Information and Control, 1977, 33, 87-116.

Hayes-Roth, F. The role of partial and best matches in knowledge systems. In D. A. Waterman & F. Hayes-Roth (Eds.), Pattern-directed inference systems. New York: Academic Press, in press.

Hayes-Roth, F., & Burge, J. Characterizing syllables as sequences of machine-generated labelled segments of connected speech: A study in symbolic pattern learning using a conjunctive feature learning and classification system. Proceedings of the Third International Joint Conference on Pattern Recognition, Coronado, California, 1976, 431-435.

Hayes-Roth, F., & McDermott, J. Learning structured patterns from examples. Proceedings of the Third International Joint Conference on Pattern Recognition, Coronado, California, 1976, 419-423. (a)

Hayes-Roth, F., & McDermott, J. Knowledge acquisition from structural descriptions. Pittsburgh: Working paper, Department of Computer Science, Carnegie-Mellon University, 1976. (b)

Hayes-Roth, F., & Mostow, D. J. Syntax and semantics in a distributed logic speech understanding system. Proceedings of the 1976 I.E.E.E. International Conference on Acoustics, Speech and Signal Processing, Philadelphia, 1976, 421-424.

Hayes-Roth, F., Mostow, D. J., & Fox, M. Understanding speech in the Hearsay-II system. In L. Bole (Ed.), Natural language communication with computers. Berlin: Springer-Verlag, 1977.

Hunt, E. B. Concept learning: An information processing approach. New York: Wiley, 1952.

Michalski, R. S. AQVAL/1--Computer implementation of a variable valued logic system VL1 and examples of its application to pattern recognition. Proceedings of the First International Joint Conference on Pattern Recognition, Washington, D.C., 1973, 3-17.

Newell, A. Production systems: Models of control structures. In W. Chase (Ed.), Visual information processing. New York: Academic Press, 1973.

Newell, A., & Simon, H. Human problem solving. Englewood Cliffs, N.J.: Prentice-Hall, 1972.

Shortliffe, T. MYCIN: A program for computer-based medical consultations. New York: Elsevier North-Holland, 1976.

Vere, S. A. Induction of concepts in the predicate calculus. Proceedings of the Fourth International Joint Conference on Artificial Intelligence, Tbilisi, U.S.S.R., 1975, 281-287.

Vere, A. A. Induction of relational productions. In D. A. Waterman & F. Hayes-Roth (Eds.), Pattern-directed inference systems. New York: Academic Press, in press.

Waterman, D. A. Adaptive production systems. Proceedings of the Fourth International Joint Conference on Artificial Intelligence, Tbilisi, U.S.S.R., 1975, 296-303. (a)

Waterman, D. A. Serial pattern acquisition: A production system approach. Pittsburgh: CIP Working Paper, Department of Psychology, Carnegie-Mellon University, 1975. (b)

Williams, D. S. Computer program organization induced from problem examples. In H. A. Simon & L. Siklossy (Eds.), Representation and meaning. Englewood Cliffs, N.J.: Prentice-Hall, 1972.

Winston, P. H. Learning structural descriptions from examples. In P. H. Winston (Ed.), Psychology of computer vision. New York: McGraw-Hill, 1975.

NOTES TOWARD A THEORY OF COMPLEX LEARNING

Donald A. Norman
Department of Psychology
University of California, San Diego
LaJolla, California, U.S.A.

I do not care about simple learning. I am not interested in the kind of learning that only takes 30 minutes. I want to understand real learning, the kind we all do during the course of our lives, the kind of learning that takes years to accomplish and that may, indeed, never be completed. I want to understand the learning of complex topics. A complex topic is one with such a rich set of conceptual structures that it requires learning periods measured in weeks or even years. The learning of complex topics differs from the learning that can be completed in minutes. I have estimated that to become an expert in a complex topic requires at least 5000 hours of study. Where does this estimate come from? I made it up. But it is remarkably robust, having been defended for a wide variety of topics.

Let me offer an operational definition of complexity in a topic: There must exist experts. The existence of experts requires a topic to have sufficient complexity that considerable study is involved. Topics that qualify under this definition include mathematics, languages, table-tennis, piano playing, poker, psychology, history, cooking, and computer programming. Thus, the topics include motor skills, intellectual topics, procedurally-based topics, fact-based topics, and all sorts of mixtures.

Consider what it takes to become an expert: several years of hard work studying and practicing the topics, thinking of them much of the day, for most of the year. A year contains about 2000 hours (of 40-hour weeks). Two-and-a-half years of full-time study does not seem an outrageous amount of time to transform a university student into a professional psychologist, or a beginning tennis player into a professional, and so on. In fact, viewed this way, the time seems low.

The Acquisition of Knowledge

When we come to the study of learning - especially the learning of complex material - the problems of memory representation seem central. Most workers agree that information within memory is stored in organized units. What form these units take is not clear. Several different

39

proposals are viable, and the current literature on memory speaks in such terms as schemas, schemata, frames, scripts, plans, images, and so on. Moreover, one can debate the details of the representation, whether it should be continuous, discrete, declarative, procedural, active network structures, feature lists, or what not.

For our current purposes, however, it turns out that we can ignore the details of the representation as long as we accept the fact that some organized form of representation must be present. It is important that the knowledge structures provide a framework for whatever new knowledge is to be acquired. I will use the term knowledge module (KM) as a neutral name for the units of memory structure. One KM can contain within it other KMs, thus providing higher-level organization to conceptual knowledge and to the KM structures themselves.

How can new knowledge be acquired? Rumelhart and I have suggested that there are three ways to acquire new knowledge. First, new knowledge can be added to the framework provided by existing KMs; call this mode of acquisition accretion. Second, new KMs can be formed, reconceptualizing knowledge about a topic; call this mode restructuring. Third, existing KMs can be made more efficient by specializing the information contained within them for the particular task required of them; call this mode tuning. These three modes of learning were first proposed in Rumelhart and Norman (in press).

Accretion

Whenever an existing KM acts as a guiding structure for the acquisition of new knowledge, we call this process learning by accretion. Essentially, the mode of accretion is simply the addition of new information either within or guided by existing structures. There are two ways accretion might occur. First, an existing KM may have incomplete structures (amounting to unfilled arguments or unspecified arguments or unfilled slots). Accretion in this case is simply acquiring the appropriate information to fill out the existing KM structure. Second, new knowledge may be guided by an existing KM. Thus, an existing KM acts as a prototype module for the construction of a new KM.

Accretion is necessary to provide a data base upon which appropriate knowledge modules can later form (through restructuring). Late in the process of learning, when most of the appropriate KMs exist, accretion seems to be needed to fill out the knowledge.

In general, because accretion is a straightforward addition of knowledge to existing KMs, it is the type of learning studied most frequently in the psychological literature, especially in the field of paired-associate learning. Accretion learning requires study, probably with the use of mnemonic aids (and deep levels of processing). It can be tested by conventional recall and recognition techniques.

Restructuring

This mode is often characterized by new insight into the structure of the topic. It is at this phase that we expect the learner to say, "Oh, now I understand," or to show evidence of jumps in understanding. If accretion is knowledge acquisition, restructuring is knowledge understanding. Although restructuring is probably the most dramatic of the learning phases, we also expect it to be the most infrequent of the phases and the most difficult to produce. Of course, minor restructuring need not be dramatic, but it is still a characteristically different mode of learning than accretion.

Notice that there need be no formal addition of knowledge by the student during restructuring. Thus, one can imagine a "pure Socratic tutorial" in which the instructor only asks questions of the student, carefully avoiding the presentation of knowledge not already known by the student. But by skillful questions, the student can be led to recognize deficiencies within existing KMs, and then to recognize analogies among the KMs needed for the topic being learned and the structures of other topics. Thus, by analogy, metaphor, and inference based on different existing KMs, the student comes to restructure the knowledge base for the topic being studied. Whether it is actually possible for "pure" restructuring to take place in the complete absence of new information is not known, but consideration of the pure situation helps provide an understanding of the mode.

Restructuring requires good teaching. Examples and appropriately selected analogies and metaphors seem appropriate, as do such tutorial techniques as the Socratic Dialogue. Tests of the knowledge should cover conceptual understanding.

Tuning

Even after all the basic structures and concepts are present, that is, after the phases of restructuring and accretion are completed, there is still another aspect of learning. With continued use of the material about a topic, performance becomes smoother, more efficient, less hesitant. Eventually, performance of the task reaches a stage of automation, in which less processing resources appear to be needed to perform. This is the mode of learning called tuning. During tuning, the proper KMs and concepts are assumed to be present, but the structures need to be refined. Unnecessary computation needs to be eliminated, unnecessary variables need to be replaced with particular values. Some information that was previously computed or inferred is stored directly. Thus, during tuning, many (thousands) of special cases are acquired as specialized KMs.

Repeated use of knowledge seems to be required for tuning to take place, that is, practice and problem solving. And, if the evidence on motor skills can be thought to be relevant to the learning of complex conceptual skills (and one suspects that there is more in common among these areas than might initially be suspected), tuning can continue over the lifetime of the individual. Tuning seems best accomplished by practice at the task or in using the concepts of the topic matter. Tests of tuning should be measures of speed and smoothness. Performance under stress or pressure may be a good measure.

The Sequence of the Modes of Acquisition

The different modes of learning do not necessarily occur in sequence. Presumably they co-occur, with the student accreting knowledge about one aspect of a topic while simultaneously restructuring knowledge about other aspects, and conceivably tuning the use of the knowledge about still a third aspect. Still, one expects that over the course of learning about a particular topic, there will be phases in which the mode of learning is primarily of one form.

Consider a hypothetical learning situation in which a student starts to study some particular topic. At the very start of learning, accretion should be the primary mode, with restructuring starting only after the initial knowledge builds up. With time, restructuring becomes the dominant mode of learning. Following that, one might very well expect accretion to become dominant again, but this time the new knowledge is added to the appropriate knowledge structures. During all this, tuning is steadily gaining in importance, as the basic structures and concepts of the topic are becoming more completely acquired. Finally, in the last stages of learning, tuning is dominant.

All three modes of learning are probably always present, however, because learning a complex topic has neither a definite starting point nor a definite ending point. The start always builds upon previously acquired material (thereby making unclear where the start really occurs). There is no limit to the knowledge that can be acquired about some topics. Figure 1 shows a hypothetical example of the division of effort among the three modes of learning during the time course of study of a complex topic.

Some behavioral predictions can be made about differences to be expected during the different modes of learning. Inasmuch as Figure 1 provides a reasonable description of the relative importance of the different modes, one could expect to get reasonable behavioral observations by tests at different times in the learning of new materials. In particular, the modes of learning differ in the kind of instructional procedures that are most relevant; the test of knowledge that seems most appropriate; the ability to transfer the newly acquired knowledge to other,related topics; and the susceptibility to interference from the simultaneous learning of related topics. Table 1 summarizes these properties.

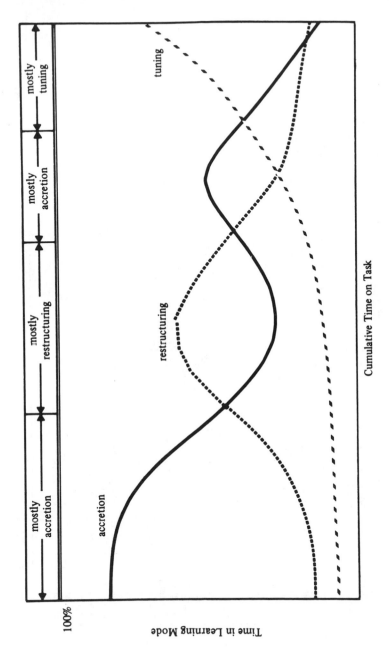

Figure 1. Hypothetical time division of effort in the three learning modes during the study of a complex topic.

Table 1. Characteristics of the Three Modes of Learning

Mode	General characteristic	Attributes of the student's knowledge structures	Learning strategy	Testing	Interference from related topics	Transfer to related topics
Accretion	Adding to the amount of knowledge: traditional verbal learning.	Accumulation of knowledge according to existing KMs.	Study, probably using mnemonic systems and good depth of processing.	Factual tests: short answers; multiple choice. Basic recall and recognition tests.	High	Low
Restructuring	Insight. Feeling of understanding material that was previously disorganized. Often accompanied by "oh," or "aha."	New structures for KMs are formed.	Thought, teaching by example, analogy, metaphor. Socratic dialogue.	Conceptual tests. Questions that require inference or problem solving.	Medium	High
Tuning	Making existing KMs more efficient. No new knowledge or structures, but refinement of current skills.	The parameters of KMs are adjusted for maximum efficiency. Special cases are directly encoded.	Practice	Speed, smoothness. Performance under stress or pressure.	Low	Of general knowledge: high. Of specific (tuned) knowledge: very low.

Note especially the different predictions for transfer and interference. In the early stages of accretion, before appropriate KMs are acquired, one expects transfer of knowledge to new (related) tasks to be low, and interference from simultaneous learning of similar materials to be high. After restructuring has taken place, one expects that there will be good transfer to new, related topic matters. Simultaneous learning of similar topics can cause interference, however, especially where the conceptual structures for one topic might erroneously be applied to the other.

After considerable tuning has occurred, one expects the KMs for the topic matter to be rather specialized, thereby minimizing the susceptibility to interference from the simultaneous learning of similar topics. Transfer of general knowledge should remain high, but transfer of KMs developed through specialized tuning should be very low. The general conceptualizations acquired in restructuring and accretion are still present and are still transferable, possibly with less chance for incorrect application because of the tuning phase.

Comments on Instruction

Knowledge in a complex topic is organized into conceptual structures. The student and the instructor share complementary aspects of a common effort. The goal is to establish appropriate knowledge structures within the memory structures of the student. In some sense, the task is to compare the knowledge structures of the student and that of the topic, and then to present the student with the discrepancies. This picture is useful, but note that because it is so oversimplified, it suffers from several problems. Often the student has erroneous information that must be corrected before the new information can be acquired. There are different levels of understanding of knowledge, and unless the student does the proper processing activities at the time of acquisition of the new knowledge, there will be deficiencies in the knowledge structure. Simple acquisition of the statements of the knowledge do not necessarily suffice. The last problem is that the statement assumes that one can always do a direct comparison of knowledge structures. But the structures of the student may be in a different format from the structures assumed to be present in the topic that is to be learned.

Teaching Learning Strategies

If the organization of the material to be learned is important, but if it is likely to differ for each student, then a likely and obvious ploy is to have the student control the course of learning. Unfortunately, numerous experiments exploring the possibility of giving students control of the teaching environment fail to reveal any benefits. One possible reason for the discrepancy between intuition and data is that the average student has very little knowledge about the principles of learning. Students have a "naive learning theory," together with a "naive psychology" that is quaint, but erroneous. For example, college students, to a surprisingly large extent, believe that rehearsal is an effective procedure for learning; whereas, it is in fact one of the poorest methods. Some training in mnemonic skills, some understanding of depth of processing and availability notions, perhaps an understanding of the models of accretion, restructuring, and tuning (and the differences in learning skills required for each phase) could conceivably make a difference. Students should also understand their own learning styles so that they can tailor their learning strategies to their own strengths (Pask, 1975; Snow, 1977).

Papert and collaborators (Papert, 1977) have emphasized the development of "debugging" skills in the student, a term used to describe the development of self-assessment and correction of basic knowledge structures - a skill I would claim to be important in restructuring. Some recent work has examined the possibility that a student can be trained to be a good learner, but, as yet, there are no conclusive results.

Critical Confusion

Learning is best done for a purpose. To this end, it is important that a student be able to have a focus when acquiring complex material. Consider, for example, what happens when we, ourselves, learn something new. For example, I recently learned how to use a new computer system. To do this, I found myself first reading the tutorial manuals associated with the documentation, then trying to do this on the computer. I had to make up problems for myself, then puzzle out how to accomplish the goal while working at the computer terminal. I had to read the manual about five times, each time picking up new conceptualizations and new specific information. I discovered that information was continually being confused and clarified.

I wish to propose that critical confusion is an important aspect of learning. Learning is not a passive activity; the learner must actively construct the relevant knowledge structures. The topic matter of a complex subject contains far too much information to be assimilated at one pass. Therefore, either the instructor must tailor the information just right, or the learner must go at the complex body of information seeking information with a restricted point of view. Many different points of view will be necessary to claim mastery of the material, but by being focused, learning seems to be optimized. Without focus, the proper data structures are not clear; there are too many alternatives, and the student is left without clear guidance.

Focus can appear to be provided in several ways. One technique is to provide specific problems that the student must solve, thus the attempt to learn to solve them guides the acquisition of knowledge. A second technique is deliberately to confuse the student by presenting issues and problems that exceed the student's capabilities. If this is done properly, it should create a guided confusion, confusion in just those critical areas that one then wishes to teach. Finally, one can present the student with questions during the study of the material, the questions thereby providing guidance to the interpretation of the information, specifying the important dimensions that should be learned. This is the mathemagenic questions technique studied by Rothkopf (1970).

It is amusing to note that should the notion of "critical confusion" be verified experimentally, then the effective instructor will be one who leaves the student confused. Clarity of instruction may not be virtuous, for it can lead to superficial levels of understanding. This interpretation is consistent with recent views of depth of processing in memory research: Better memory storage and retrieval results from active processing of the material that is to be acquired. Passive listening or reading, with apparent understanding, probably minimizes the processing and, hence, the efficacy of memory encoding.

Summary

In this paper, I have put together a number of related issues. For one, the analysis of the problem of learning a complex topic shows that a number of different issues are involved. Second, learning is not a unitary process. There are different modes of learning, each with different behavioral and instructional assumptions. Finally, there are issues of instructional strategy that result from both the general properties of learning and memory and the differences among the modes of learning. In addition, subjects need to acquire appropriate knowledge of their own learning capabilities in order to perform the necessary active processing on the material presented to them, and to incorporate it properly into their knowledge structures.

At the moment, the basic principles discussed in this paper are hypothetical, verified primarily by observations of the learning process and by analysis of the known properties of memory and learning. More empirical work is required. Hopefully, the principles in this paper can provide a guide, not only to our better understanding of the theoretical concepts of learning, but also to better instructional procedures.

Acknowledgments

The work reported in this paper was supported by the Advanced Research Projects Agency and the Office of Naval Research of the Department of Defense and was monitored by ONR under Contract No. N00014-76-C-0628.

References

Papert, S.   Teaching children thinking.   Programmed   Learning   and
    Instructional Technology, 1972, 9.

Pask, G. Conversation, cognition and learning.   Amsterdam: Elsevier,
    1975.

Rothkopf, E. Z. The concept of mathemagenic activities.   Review of
    Educational Research, 1970, 40, 325-336.

Rumclhart, D. E., & Norman, D. A. Accretion, tuning and restructuring:
    Three modes of learning.   In R. Klatsky & J. W.Cotton (Eds.),
    Semantic factors in cognition. Hillsdale, NJ: Lawrence Erlbaum
    Associates, in press.

Snow, R. Research on aptitudes: A progress report (Technical Report
    No.   1, Aptitude Research Project).   Stanford, CA: Stanford
    University, School of Education, 1977.

Section II

COMPREHENSION AND INFORMATION STRUCTURE

This section begins with two invited papers that connect the area of discourse comprehension with other concerns of this book. Frijda emphasizes that learning from a discourse is an intelligent act, heavily dependent on intellectual skills and prior experience. Like Clark and Haviland (1977), he suggests that deep, rich memory representations are formed in the comprehender only when he or she treats the task of comprehension as a problem-solving task. He goes on to develop a characterization of comprehension in which the internal (mental) structure is the goal and schemata are the criteria which judge the match between incoming text and the memory structure that is being constructed.

Anderson investigates one part of his claim. Specifically, he shows how a person's particular experiential background, in terms of known schemata and also in terms of varying dispositions to invoke different schemata, influences what he knows after reading a passage. Often, the differences are only qualitative, i.e., the number of facts learned is constant - which facts are learned varies.

In contrast to the first two papers, which emphasize variability in comprehension due to variability in the comprehender, the papers by Barbara Hayes-Roth and by Thorndyke emphasize the role played by the structure and specific wording of text. Hayes-Roth presents reasonable evidence that whether words and lower-level discourse forms are repeated or varied from one text segment to the next (e.g., with synonyms) or not exerts great influence on the extent to which internal representations for the two segments are integrated. Thorndyke illustrates the role of slightly more global discourse structure in learning from text. Independent, for the most part, of the comprehender, transfer between consecutive passages is a function of the relationship between passage structures.

The final two papers explore issues in the role of nonverbal information in comprehension. Stenning asks whether verbal messages concerning how to get someplace are represented more concretely than is appropriate to the wording. Cornoldi presents evidence suggesting the need for a cognitive theory to explain the effects of imagery mediation on learning and memory.

49

MEMORY PROCESSES AND INSTRUCTION

Nico H. Frijda
Universiteit van Amsterdam
Amsterdam

Transformational Aspects of Information Processing

The past decade has seen considerable theoretical advances with respect to the representation of knowledge in memory. These advances have yielded a much clearer picture of the knowledge structure that is to be established in the instructed subject (Rumelhart, Lindsay, & Norman, 1972; Schank, 1975a). There have also been advances in understanding the importance of inference procedures, as well as the influence of previous knowledge upon the processing of new information (Abelson, 1975; Minsky, 1968, 1975; Schank, 1975b). However, these insights and advances are fragmentary in several important respects, particularly with regard to advancing instructional theory. Although a reasonably clear understanding of knowledge representation has emerged, there have been few theoretical and experimental advances in the understanding of knowledge acquisition and utilization. There is little that offers promise towards a theory of cognitive learning.

Existing models of memory obviously deal with acquisition processes. An example is the work on natural language understanding and pattern learning (e.g., Winston, 1973). However, the usual approach of studying the processing of single sentences, or a few sentences strung together, does not lead to full confrontation with one of the predominant features of human knowledge acquisition, namely, the considerable transformation that the information must undergo on its way to storage. Transformation of incoming information appears to be an essential aspect of the processing of complex information. This is not due to some peculiarity of the human information processing system, but instead seems intrinsic to efficient information storage and utilization. It also is necessary in order to make accessible the information contained in the messages presented or intended by the sender of the message concerned, since the information may not be expressed, or even expressible, explicitly in any of the message elements as such, but resides in their succession or their relationships.

The transformation I have in mind can probably best be characterized as the transformation of sequential inputs into hierarchical structures, or, more generally, into structures that are ot primarily sequential in nature. Such transformation occurs, and is needed, in information processing in many different domains. Perhaps the clearest example is offered by text comprehension, or the comprehension of discourse. When reading a story or novel, a plot is discerned, a topic identified, a general line of events recognized; characters obtain contours, and a moral or general view is possibly extracted. These are the types of information that find their way into summaries, and this should be the case, since the plot or topic, major line of events, characters, and moral may be what the text is primarily intended to convey. Similar types of information may well constitute the intended goal of an instructional or scientific text. However, none of the above may be explicit in any single sentence of the text. They may constitute the meaning or substance of entire passages or of the story as a whole. The information in the separate sentences somehow gives rise to these more global representations, which van Dijk (1975) refers to as "macrostructures."

The information in the individual sentences is transformed into the macrostructure, a representation of the major events linked together by causal relationships, and a representation of the major reasons or arguments for the occurrence of these events. Such information may even become a single macroproposition, as in "Crime leads to punishment." However, this does not mean that the full descriptions are discarded. At least some of the fine grain is usually retained, and generally must be retained to accomplish the learning purpose or to enrich the reader's mind. In fact, the macrostructure often seems to serve as a retrieval cue or plan for finer grain details (van Dijk & Kintsch, 1976; Kintsch, 1974). This means that the detailed information must be appropriately placed within the macrostructure, and the appropriate function (as setting, condition, etc.) must be designated. Bundles of details are grouped under their respective macro-elements, and may only be connected to the details following them by this subordinate path. The information from separate sentences may well be organized at several levels, and thus subsequently can be summarized at more than one level. As an example, "Hamlet" begins with Hamlet's father's ghost communicating his murder to his son; or it may be said to begin with the ghost's first appearance to the three men and Horatio; or it may be said to begin with the change of watch in the cold; or, again, it may be said to begin with Bernardo hailing Francesco. Of course, it begins with Bernardo saying "Who's there?." The situation, with respect to this type of transformation, is not very different when the elements in the macrostructure are mentioned explicitly as subtitles, outlines, or direct statements in the text. Even then, the detail must be perceived as belonging to a particular macro-element in a particular way, and some amount of rearrangement must occur.

Transformations of an input sequence occur not only in creating a macrostructure. They may also occur because the sequence of the story does not correspond to the sequence of events (Hamlet relating to Horatio, after his return, his voyage to England); or because different lines of events cross in the story. They occur, most importantly, in the gradual development of compound representations of entities, such as the personality of a character in a novel or of the state of affairs at a given moment in time. A character, for instance, may be conceived as a mode in the representational structure. This mode is gradually enriched by information coming in as the story continues, until the total picture is obtained. There also must be aspects of the representation that contain the development of affairs at a given moment, just as the board with a chess position represents the history of all moves made in that game.

The need for transformation is not peculiar to literary prose, in which much is implicit. It is similarly present in processing scientific prose. If a problem statement is declared as such, the text proper must be ordered as the value of that statement; the experimental manipulation must be linked to some aspect of the problem statement and the experimental result must be seen as congruent in some way to the prediction, and this to the hypothesis, and so on. All this, which must be "understood," can be explicitly mentioned in captions or text elements that give reasons, ground-consequence-relations, and so forth. But the more extensive the structural indications given in the text, the larger the discrepancy tends to be between text order and internal structure of the representation. Explanations of how and why an experimental manipulation follows from an hypothesis interrupt the flow of major reasoning, cause the elements belonging together (hypothesis or manipulation) to be remote in written space, and, therefore, in moment of reading. They increase the need for distinguishing structure indications from content indications; they increase the need for cross-referencing indications, in particular when the elements of one set of statements - say of the theory - each are related to different aspects of another set of statements - say the experimental set-up. Complete structural indications spread out in reading time what has to become a non-temporal whole in the internal representation.

The need for transformation is inherent, it would seem, in the verbal mode of information transmission. However, it is not restricted to that mode. In personally experienced events, much of the same occurs. Meanings, topics, and plots are not seen but understood, and macrostructures emerge much as on the basis of written events, with only helpful chapter headings missing.

Aspects of Cognitive Skills

Let us now consider the situation involved in the learning of skills and principles, cognitive skills, in particular. Descriptions of principles or methods, in such a manner that they can be applied, invariably involve a considerable gap between the literal content of these descriptions and the internal structure they are meant to establish. This obviously holds where skills involve the integration and mutual adjustment of part-skills, and the utilization of continuous feedback information, as is the case with sensory-motor skills or with reading. This also is the case for all those cognitive skills that must be capable of dealing with a large, and often quite unpredictable, set of conditions - the majority of skills of interest. Take, for instance, theorem-proving in elementary geometry. It is possible to formulate useful and reasonable efficient procedures, as demonstrated by Gelernter's computer program (1963). It does not seem possible, however, to teach these same procedures to human subjects in the same relatively determinate fashion. The reason is a human's incapacity for systematic memory search (of theorems to be used, or of features to be checked), and the fact that it is unfeasible to teach a human subject to construct complete subproblem-trees during problem solving. Consequently, instruction has to take one of two forms: It either consists of an algorithm that does not correspond to what the subject is finally supposed to do; or it consists of hints, general and open recommendations, and the like. Resnick and Glaser (1976), for instance, point out that instructions for teaching children a flexible procedure for subtraction would be far too complex for them to handle; furthermore, they spontaneously develop, on the basis of a simple algorithmic method, a more flexible approach. Resnick and Glaser state that the children must "invent" the method, and that many of them actually do so.

The other kind of instruction is illustrated in the work of Landa (1975). His instructional program for learning to prove geometry theorems is composed of instructions such as "Look at what is given and analyze its properties" or "Reconsider your line of effort." Because of its indeterminacy, he calls his teaching program "heuristic." He points out that to achieve results with such a program, one has to "resuppose in a problem solver certain specific abilities such as, for instance, the ability to estimate probabilistically . . . to imagine into which figure some geometric element may go" (p. 243), and "to shift from one mode of action to another, to change the order of actions" (p. 250).

The "insufficiency" of instruction is illustrated by instructional practice in the domains indicated. Proficiency ensues by giving verbal instruction of the kind mentioned, and guided exercises that, in some mysterious fashion, let the proper inner representations emerge, if they do so at all.

The discrepancy between instruction presented and inner representation derives in part from the essential problem solving aspect of many intellectual skills. A flexible cognitive method does not consist of a linear program with a larger or smaller number of branching points. It consists, rather, of a collection of goals and subgoals, each provided with a set of criteria for judging the appropriateness of possible solutions, given the circumstances of the moment. The criteria serve to test whether the outcome of a solution corresponds to what is needed. Vital in this structure is the provision for matching information with requirements, rather than having fixed couplings between requirements and solution means, or having only such couplings. To clarify this, take the solution process in a weight seriation task.

A subject may be looking for the next heaviest object. He stumbles upon a rather heavy one and puts it at a provisional position in the series, having recognized solution value and changing his tactics accordingly.

It may be pointed out that this problem solving structure is proper not only to developed skills, but to developed action concepts - word-meanings also - insofar as these reflect understanding of the action involved. "To roast," for instance, refers to a frame describing not only the action sequence of roasting, or several of these (roasting beef in the oven is different from roasting a duck on a spit), but the end result to be obtained, the exigencies for achieving that (heat and fat), the exigencies for their application (a heat source, something to hold the meat away from but close to the fire, a means to retain the fat), and so forth. It may also be pointed out that the emergence of a problem solving structure implies a reversal of sequence in the internal representation when compared with the sequence of an action description or algorithm. To the extent that a program is a deductive plan, the goal comes first, then its condition, then the conditions for that, and so forth. At execution time, the corresponding events follow in reverse order.

Quite generally, then, knowledge acquisition involves a gap, a discrepancy between what is presented and what is to be acquired. This holds for knowledge acquisition both inside and outside explicit instructional situations. The gap can only be bridged, or the discrepancy overcome, by some "autonomous" transformational activity, since, if the foregoing analysis is correct, the transformational activity usually is not (and often cannot) be fully determined by the instructional material and procedures. I call it autonomous also, since people often do manage to construct the desired representations. They do obtain macrostructures (cf. Gentner, 1976) and they achieve flexible problem solving skills (Resnick & Glaser, 1976) without being told to do so, or how to do so.

The foregoing leads to some preliminary conclusions regarding the instructional process. The first is that learning in a strict sense is not possible. That is, it is usually impossible to present the learner with precisely what he wants, or should want, to acquire. It can be approximated to a greater or lesser degree, but instructional materials and resultant internal cognitive structures typically cannot be the same.

Also, it is not possible for the learner simply to sit and absorb the materials presented if meaningful learning is to occur. It is also impossible for the teacher to govern the necessary processing activities of the learner directly. Thus, the second conclusion is that control by the instructional process or by the teacher over an individual's learning process can never be complete. At best, control can be partial and can only trigger and direct the learner's autonomous transformational activities.

Transformational Processes

For a fuller understanding of the cognitive learning process, it may be useful to inquire into the nature of transformational activities. It is obvious that we will be unable to do so with respect to the entire domain that concerns us, since: (a) There exists no theory of cognitive learning; (b) there is little theorizing on the subject of why intelligence and learning are related, other than sometimes defining intelligence as the ability to learn; and (c) there is hardly any research on the constructive processes involved in learning, as in learning generalities that lead to new concepts such as "mass" in physics, or "insight" in psychology. Nevertheless, we may try to probe into some aspects of knowledge acquisition, namely, text processing and the establishment of macrostructures. We take our hypotheses in part from the existing literature, notably van Dijk (1977) and van Dijk and Kintsch (1976), and in part from our own preliminary work towards a model of text processing.

What then, may be the transformational activities involved in bridging the mentioned gap? In other words, what are the processes that are needed for the emergence of a rearranged structure, i.e., the macrostructure plus finer grain detail in its appropriate place?

The overall process may be described as involving ordering, integration, and reconceptualization.

Ordering means several things. As an incoming sentence is understood, i.e., an internal representation is formed, its information should be ordered with respect to the information structure already constructed. This amounts to finding role relations to that structure, or to elements of the structure, and to finding connections with those other elements. Sometimes this is easy, as in the sentence-pair, "The boy saw something. It was a girl he saw." Sometimes it may be difficult, because: (a) referential terms are obscure, (b) the conceptualizatin of the role-slot that the new sentences is to fill is remote because so many elements have to be ordered at the same time, (c) a number of "slots" may be waiting to be filled and it has to be determined whether the new information belongs in one of these, or (d) because a considerable amount of work has to be performed before the element can be definitely placed at all.

This considerable amount of work derives from a second aspect of ordering: unit formation. When a sentence is read, it must be decided whether its information contributes to the completion of a macro-element under construction, or whether it begins a new element. This implies processes of segmentation and unit formation. Concurrently with ordering the information of a sentence in its macro-element, these macro-elements themselves are formed, and ordered with respect to each other; this may occur at various levels. This also means that each time a new sentence is read, the element to which information is added must be determined, that is to say, a decision must be made about the level or levels at which ordering should take place.   It may, at any given moment, be unclear which slot in which macro-element is going to be filled during the formation of a subordinate element.

The process of unit formation - formation of macro-elements - may again be easy or difficult.   It entails the processes that van Dijk discussed in his "macrostructuring rules": generalization, deletion, integration (in his sense), and construction.   Generalization, for instance, is the replacement of a set of information elements by their common denominator, such as when a lengthy landscape description is grasped as the description of a gloomy landscape.   This conceptualization as a whole, as indicated before, is linked to the preceding or ensuing structure. Generalization in this sense is easy when the elements going into the new unit are rather similar; it is difficult when the common role, which may be required by the structure into which it must go, has to be discovered or constructed.

The segmentation involves some kind of "reconceptualization." At least, the content of a segment becomes reconceptualized when the resulting macrostructure is described in a summary.   The node of the network, under which the details are subsumed, is given a new global description ("landscape").   It may be assumed that the internal representation of this node may be provided with a corresponding inner description, being the subject's "realization" of the meaning of the entire corresponding passage. For our purpose, it does not matter much whether reconceptualization is executed at storage time, or at retrieval time, when "reading" the nodes constituting the macrostructure.   The required cognitive process, consisting of abstractive and, certainly in part, inferential activity, remains the same. Evidence for its occurrence at storage time was presented by Frederiksen (1975).

The ordering of information elements, the construction of units, and this reconceptualization may be easy and natural, because role and connectivity indications and "macropropositions" are given in the text: "A man planned a killing, and as preparation, he took several measures: he . . .," or because previous knowledge provides a solid foundation for ordering - the much discussed "frames" or "scripts" in memory providing the relationship or connectivity between elements that are not mentioned explicitly in the text, as in "The man swung his knife and the old shopkeeper fell to the ground" (Minsky, 1975, Schank, 1975b).   It also may be difficult, demanding inference of various degrees of complexity, determinacy, and explicitness. The construction of units often requires abstraction of various sorts: Perceiving other than superficial similarities or functional dependencies (Hamlet's protracted introspective indecision) and, most of all, discerning what is essential, what are the major events and their major conditions.

The work involved in the processes described may be considerable, in particular because of the load placed upon working memory. This is the case even in reading, when unfinished structures at different levels may have to be kept in abeyance, where one or more of these has to be

held while processing other parts of the story, and where separate words
and sentences are held while their meanings are being retrieved or
constructed.   This load on working memory is heavier still when
listening to discourse, when all this has to be performed in "real time"
and any backtracking interferes with intake of new information.

It has been stressed that the processes involved may be easy or
difficult.   At any rate, they are not automatic, at least not beyond a
certain degree of text complexity.   This appears from the fact, often
neglected in current literature on story recall, that people differ
greatly in their amount of text understanding or text recall,
particularly from the point of view of integration and ordering.
Kintsch and van Dijk (1975) report that story recall, to a large extent,
misses essential points or coherent macrostructure; it often consists
of a sequence of unconnected and not always unimportant facts.   Delayed
recall protocols of scientific prose passages in an experiment by
Oostendorp (1977) manifest the same deficiencies.

The description of possible necessary processes does not yet
provide a satisfactory explanation of the rise of macrostructures, or,
rather, the rise of that internal representation that consists of some
of the base information organized along with macrostructures of
different scope and levels.   Assuming that there is a mechanism endowed
with the processing capabilities described above, we still must ask why
and when it uses those capabilities, and to what extent.   Why does
"understanding" arise at all?   In other words, one may pose the question
about what mechanism governs text organization and text understanding.

Under some conditions, the situation is rather transparent: People
sometimes read or listen with the intention of grasping gist, the
general outline of events or major propositions.   The task motivating
the reading may prompt this, for instance, when it consists of searching
for the answer to a specific question to judge whether the story is
suitable for a juvenile audience.   The reading or listening goal sets
the level of categorization and it should correspond to that of the
goal.   The goal may exert its ordering effect in a similar way for
different reasons: for information reduction in retention or
reproduction, discarding much of the lower-level information after the
macrostructure has been abstracted; or in order to construct a
retrieval plan for more than just the macrostructure.   The goal may be
able to do this by focusing the processing upon "major events," either
in general, or those corresponding to that goal.

Under conditions such as reading a novel, the formation of
macrostructure seems to be entirely determined from within.   At least to
some extent, it is governed by the identification of "major events,"
major events being defined as those events that permit the construction
of a macrostructure.   The major events may be recognized as such, and
used to form that macrostructure, because their connections (and not
those of the specific actions and situations) constitute the
connectivity of the story; or, because it is these events that are

informative, or arouse interest and emotion.

The principal point here is tht some focusing upon "major events," with the readiness as well as the ability to note them, is a necessary supposition for explaining the structure I am discussing.

In the process of structuring, major events engender major events: The upshot of the first chapters of the book I am reading is a murder, and I wait for ensuing delight or punishment, or both. Major events obviously can do so only because of the presence, in the reader's mental store, of event schemas, scripts, frames, or whatever the name given those memory dispositions upon which expectations are based. Event schemas, as I prefer to call them here, provide the slots in which information elements are placed as they come in, guiding their ordering in advance. If the information in a new sentence does not refer to delight or punishment, or any other reasonable consequence of murder, it may constitute the first element of an entire segment that as a whole, is such a consequence. Two important issues must be noted. First, organization and level of reconceptualization ensue only if the appropriate schema is in fact evoked in the form of an expectation, a curiosity with specific direction, and if future events are in fact recognized as fulfillments. None of these is necessary or automatic; the respective cognitive processes depend upon ability and willingness of the subject. Second, the operation of schemas has, or may have, a problem solving character. That is, the "schema" consists of a set of criteria for judging the appropriateness of incoming events. Current theoretical considerations of natural language processing, in my view, too often treat expectations, frames, and scripts as sequences of probable facts. Instead, I would suggest that an intelligent understanding system is provided with tests for fit, and with means for noticing fit between matched events with variable degrees of risk or effort. Moreover, the event schemas that operate in text processing are, to a large extent, quite general; they are notions such as "intentions tend to lead to this fulfillment, or else," or "chains of change continue unless they are stopped or come to a natural state of rest."

By governing ordering and level of reconceptualization, event schemas that are evoked by some major event (or prior macrostatement) motivate the operations of "deletion," "generalization," "integration," and "construction" mentioned by van Dijk.

Subsumption of detail under a macrostructure mode, or nonretention of such detail, can occur because the event schema dictates that the detail be so organized and conceptualized. It is comparable or sometimes even identical to skipping pages in a novel that describe the lovely countryside where a love encounter is to take place, because we already know that it is going to happen in the open in the Cotswolds, and we are curious about the consummation that is sure to be depicted next. Similarly, for "generalization" - the replacement of "John buys apples, oranges, and bananas" by "John buys fruit" - is motivated by the tendency to complete an event schema of a succession of actions.

Let me summarize the main argument in the preceding considerations. Text processing consists of building an integrated, hierarchical structure out of a sequence of information elements, sentences, and paragraphs. The construction of this hierarchical structure involves activities of ordering, integration, and reconceptualization, or at least of recognition of the meaning and function of larger bodies of information as a whole in the total structure. These activities, in turn, demand operations of structuring, recognition of functions, of abstraction of various kinds, of the discrimination of essentials and elaborations, and of inferencing of varying degree of complexity. Ordering, integration, and their executing operations are supported by cognitive dispositions, here called "event schemas"; these event schemas, at their best, are utilized in a problem solving fashion, that is, as goals for integrative or "understanding" effort. Ordering, integration, and reconceptualization are motivated by the knowledge-acquisition goals on the one hand, and by the focusing upon "major events" and their detection on the other. They involve an "effort after meaning," a search for gist.

In the above tentative analysis of text processing, one is struck by the fact that the difficulties of the task appear to be precisely those that are characteristic for tasks used as tests of intelligence. More precisely, they are the same as the "characteristic difficulties," as Elshout (1976) has called them, of tests for "general reasoning" or CMS in Guilford's system (Guilford, 1967). In fact, the problems encountered in text understanding are quite similar to those that are found in, for instance, arithmetical reasoning problems, such as "A is 10 years older than C, and B is 15 years older than A was 10 years ago. The sum of their ages is 55. How old is B?" There, too, the problem is mainly to identify the relevant elements, to identify identical elements in different sentences or different guises, to perceive their relations, and to construct, in short, an adequate representation of the problem situation. There are, indeed, indications that text comprehension correlates substantially with intelligence (Carroll, 1974), and that it loads, in particular, upon this general reasoning factor as well as upon an inferential reasoning factor (Evaluation of Semantic Implications, Kunst, 1974). At any rate the present analysis, if correct and more generally valid, explains the relation between learning and intelligence: Learning requires much the same cognitive operations as many problem-solving tasks or intelligence test items. Knowledge acquisition is intellectual work, involving a high measure of structuring, transformational activity.

Transformational Processes in Cognitive Skill Acquisition

The importance of transformational processes in learning may be further illustrated by some brief remarks on the establishment of problem solving methods. They must be brief because the matter is obscure. It is obscure how, by what mental process, the subject escapes from a rigid algorithm into a flexible approach. That the transformation does occur is evident. It can be observed that subjects, when faced with a new task, adopt a way of handling the task and rapidly develop this into something that adapts itself to minor and unforeseen situational variables. Also, when taught some problem solving method, subjects have to "appropriate" this method, i.e., make it "their own"; when they cannot do this, they offer resistance to the solution principles taught (Elshout-Mohr, 1976). Probably one of the major aspects of the change-over from rigid algorithm to flexible approach is the fragmentation of the rigid method into a production-system, governed by constant feedback from the main goal. It is perhaps useful to view this as the subject's perception of the function or purpose of the segments of the solution method, and the replacement of these segments by their respective functions as the subgoals: or, alternatively, as the transformation of the main goal in a collection of mutually dependent subgoals, each of which may or may not call up one of the original method segments.

        To the extent that this analysis is also valid for other forms of learning - for the acquisition of cognitive skills in particular - it may contribute to the emergence of a theory of cognitive learning. Cognitive learning would appear as an active process, involving the application of cognitive skills representing various kinds of integrative and transformational activity. The analysis suggests a much closer relation between cognitive learning and problem solving than is generally brought forward, since the activities involved are quite similar to those involved in intellectual tasks.

        The preceding leads to the consideration of instructional consequences. How can cognitive learning be improved, or can it? Obviously, the need for transformational activity, or its degree of difficulty, differs greatly among learning materials. Texts may or may not possess a clear structure with distinct indication of concepts and functions at a macrolevel.

        Instructional material can often be more closely matched with: (a) the internal representation that the subject is to acquire, and (b) the processing activities necessary to acquire that internal representation. A clear example of how and why this can be done may be found in modern mathematics, where, for instance, function notations mirror the operations the subject has to perform. However, lessening the need for transformational activity cannot do away with it entirely; the structure of the information presented and its internal representation (or, rather, the inner structure of the information) are different.

        Even where the latter structure can be approximated, or at least its ingredients can be made explicit, there are limits to the extent that this should be done. We have already pointed out that making all structural relations explicit in a text will tend to make it either too boring, or too complex, or both (explications have to be processed,

too).   Descriptions of cognitive procedures are either abstract and
useless, or demand precisely the activities indicated, or they are
hopelessly complicated; only a large-scale computer can profitably read
a true problem solving program.

From a somewhat different perspective, the question may be raised
about the utility of aids that lessen the need for transformational
activity in instructional materials, and the conditions when such aids
are useful. Material that offers little intellectual challenge may lure
the subject into rote learning and away from transformational and
integrative work that still must be performed. Moreover, text
difficulty of the kind under consideration here may affect only learning
time without affecting retention or understanding; evidence for such a
possibility was provided by Kintsch and van Dijk (1975).   Also,
transformational activity may yield fruitful side-effects, such as
reconceptualization at a higher level than required, or the discovery of
critical deficiencies in the arguments presented. All of this is to
assert that improvements in learning materials and instructional
procedures can at best lead to marginal gains, or only yield gains in
time. They can be marginal at best, since the major obstacles to
efficient learning seem to reside in the weakness of the cognitive
activities involved.

Thus, one might want to improve these activitives, and, in view of
what has been said before, this amounts to improving problem solving
ability or its components. Again, in view of what has been said before,
it is doubtful that this can be achieved, since training in problem
solving presupposes precisely what it wants to produce: transformation
of complex instructions into a different coherent internal structure.
What is required is training not in some task-specific problem solving
algorithm, but in general structuring ability.

The pessimistic view on the trainability of problem solving skills,
or of learning effectiveness, is not only based upon the above
theoretical considerations. It is an outcome of varied problem solving
training experiments.

I think that a survey of existing research - including unpublished
studies - will yield the following conclusions. Training in problem
solving frequently yields positive, often considerable effects (e.g.,
Elshout-Mohr, 1976; Covington & Crutchfield, 1965; Landa, 1976).
These effects are more pronounced in capable subjects than in poor
subjects (Inhelder, Sinclair & Bovet, 1974). The training effects,
where they exist, are of short duration (e.g., Kohnstamm, 1976). Seldom
if ever do training effects generalize to tasks other than the training
task (e.g., Elshout-Mohr, 1976; Kilpatrick, 1969; Kunst, 1977).

These discouraging results may be due to deficient training
procedures.   Theoretical analysis suggests that it is not a training
deficiency. It is more likely that problem solving proficiency cannot
be greatly improved by training. If this is true, the transformational

activities so basic in knowledge and skill acquisition may well depend primarily upon intelligence. This is hardly a surprising statement, but it emphasizes that learning ability rests upon generalized cognitive skills. Even if learning ability depends upon intelligence, this does not preclude the possibility that it may be improved, although not by training. There are several reasons to envisage this possibility. The first reason is that the skills involved are of a general nature. Their manifestation in explicit instructional situations may not be the most appropriate and unrestricted area in which to reinforce them. Moreover, because of their general nature, if they have not been optimally developed during the subject's lifetime, it is illusionary to suppose that they can be drastically improved during training sessions of restricted duration and variety. Second, skills in general are not taught but are given occasion to develop. They are not acquired by instruction, but by experience, when occasion for this experience is presented. The extent to which instructional guidance of this experience is useful depends upon the nature of the skill.

If the above is true, what would be needed for the improvement of learning ability would be that ample occasion is created for problem solving activities to manifest themselves over long periods of time and over a wide range of situations. This amounts to saying that instruction would profit not so much from improvement in instruction, but from improvement in the intelllectual environment both inside and mostly outside the instructional situation. There is, it would seem, no other way.

It is not so clear what kind of environment or situation will give occasion for problem solving activities to manifest themselves, or to be forced to manifest themselves. There may be only one real condition for this: That is, the carrying of responsibility for understanding and for coping with problem solving situations. The carrying of responsibility would seem the main force for a problem solving goal to arise in some manner with which the subject identifies. Having such goals may well be the major source from which corresponding problem solving skills develop.

References

Abelson, R. P. Concepts for representing mundane reality in plans. In D. G. Bobrow & A. M. Collins, (Eds.), Representation and understanding. New York: Academic Press, 1975.

Carroll, J. B. Defining language comprehension: Some speculations. In J. B. Carroll & R. O. Freedle, (Eds.), Language comprehension and the acquisition of knowledge. Washington: Winston, 1972.

Covington, M. V. & Crutchfield, R. S. Facilitation of creative problem
    solving. Programmed Instruction, 1965, 4, 3-5.

Elshout, J. J. Karakteristieke Moeilijkheden in het Denken.   Ph.D.
    dissertation, University of Amsterdam, 1976.

Elshout-Mohr, M. Training in Denkstrategieën.   Ph.D.   dissertation,
    University of Amsterdam, 1976.

Frederiksen, C. H. Acquisition of semantic information from discourse:
    Effects of repeated exposure. Journal of Verbal Learning and
    Verbal Behavior, 1975, 14, 158-169.

Genter, D. R. The structure and recall of narrative prose. Journal of
    Verbal Learning and Verbal Behavior, 1976, 15, 411-418.

Guilford, J. P.   The nature of   human   intelligence.   New   York:
    McGraw-Hill, 1967.

Inhelder, B., Sinclair, H., & Bovet, M. Learning and the development of
    cognition. Cambridge: Harvard University Press, 1974.

Kilpatrick, J. Problem-solving in mathematics. Review of Educational
    Research, 1969, 39, 523-534.

Kintsch, W. The representation of meaning in memory.   Hillsdale, NJ:
    Lawrence Erlbaum Associates, 1974.

Kintsch, W., & van Dijk, T. A. Comment on se rappelle et resume des
    histoires. Languages, 1975, 40, 98-116.

Kohnstamm, G. A. Het proefkrèche-projekt. Amsterdam, 1976.

Kunst, H. Algemeen redeneren: Onderzoek naar psychologische inhoud.
    Ph.D. dissertation, University of Amsterdam, 1977.

Landa, L. Instructional regulation and control. Englewood Cliffs, NJ:
    Education Technology Publications, 1976.

Minsky, M. Semantic information processing.   Cambridge: MIT   Press,
    1968.

Minsky, M. A framework for representing knowledge.   In P.   Winston,
    (Ed.), The psychology of computer vision. New York: McGraw-Hill,
    1975.

Resnick, L. B., & Glaser, R. Problem solving and intelligence.   In L.
    B.   Resnick (Ed.), The nature of intelligence. Hillsdale, NJ:
    Lawrence Erlbaum Associates, 1976.

Rumelhart, D., Lindsay, P., & Norman, D. A.   A   process   model   for
    long-term   memory.   In E.   Tulving & W.   Donaldson (Eds.),
    Organization of memory. New York: Academic Press, 1972.

Schank, R. C. Conceptual information processing.   Amsterdam: North
    Holland, 1975. (a)

Schank, R. C. The structure of episodes in memory. In D. G. Bobrow &
    A. M. Collins (Eds.), Representation and understanding.   New
    York: Academic Press, 1975. (b)

van Dijk, T. A. Text and context. London: Longmans, 1977.

van Dijk, T. A., & Kintsch, W.   Cognitive psychology and discourse:
    Recalling and summarizing stories.   In W. V. Dressler (Ed.),
    Trends in text linguistics. Berkin: de Gruyter, 1976.

van Oostendorp, H.   Het Effect van Structuur-explicitering van een
    Studietekst op de Retentie. Masters thesis, University of
    Amsterdam, 1977.

Winston, P. Learning to identify block structures. In R. L. Solso
    (Ed.), Contemporary issues in cognitive psychology: The Loyola
    Symposium. Washington, DC: Winston, 1973.

SCHEMA-DIRECTED PROCESSES IN LANGUAGE COMPREHENSION

Richard C. Anderson
University of Illinois at Urbana-Champaign
Urbana, Illinois, U.S.A.

This paper will attempt to develop the thesis that the knowledge a person already possesses has a potent influence on what he or she will learn and remember from exposure to discourse. It begins by outlining some assumptions about the characteristics of the structures in which existing knowledge is packaged. Next, based on these assumptions, it presents a speculative theoretical treatment of the processes involved in assimilating the information and ideas in discourse. This is the topic that will be given most attention in this paper. Data consistent with the theory will be summarized. It should be emphasized in advance, however, that the experiments to date show at most that the theoretical notions are interesting and plausible. The research has not advanced to the point where there is a firm basis for choosing between competing accounts. Finally, some observations will be made about the implications of this research for education.

Schematic Knowledge Structures

Like many others (Ausubel, 1963; Minsky, 1975; Schank & Abelson, 1975; Bower, 1976; Rumelhart & Ortony, 1977), I find it useful to postulate that knowledge is incorporated in abstract structures that have certain properties. These structures will be called schemata, in deference to Piaget (1926) and Bartlett (1932), who introduced the term to psychology. What follows is an amalgam of my own thinking and that of other theorists.

A schema represents generic knowledge; that is, it represents what is believed to be generally true of a class of things, events, or situations. A schema is conceived to contain a slot, or placeholder, for each component. For instance, a Face schema (Palmer, 1975) includes slots for a mouth, nose, eyes, and ears. Encoding a particular object is conceived to be a matter of filling the slots in the schema with the features of the object. Part of schematic knowledge is the specification of the constraints on what normally can fill the slots. An object will be recognized as a face only if it has features that qualify as eyes, a mouth, a nose, and so on. To be sure, the constraints on the slots in a Face schema are flexible enough that we

67

can tolerate considerable variation, as in a sketchy drawing in a comic strip, the stylized and transformed representation in a cubist painting, or the exaggerated portrayal in a political cartoon (Gombrich, 1972). Nonetheless, there are limits beyond which an object is no longer a face.

The encoded representation of a particular thing or event consists of a copy of the schemata that were brought to bear in interpretation, plus the information inserted in the schemata's slots. Such particularized representations are called <u>instantiated</u> schemata (cf. Anderson, Pichert, Goetz, Schallert, Stevens, & Trollip, 1976). The slots in a schema may be instantiated with information that could be said to be "given" in the situation, or message, but often slots are filled by inference.

A schema is a knowledge "structure" because it indicates the typical relations among its components. A Face schema will represent the relative spatial positioning of the eyes and nose, for instance. Another attribute of schemata with structural significance is that they exist at various levels of abstraction and embed one within another (Rumelhart & Ortony, 1977). Contrast the knowledge that (a) a face has eyes, (b) an eye has a pupil, (c) a pupil dilates in the dark. It is apparent that these propositions are arranged in decreasing order of importance to faces. This variation in importance can be captured by assuming that Eye is a subschema embedded in the Face schema; and that Pupil, in turn, is a subschema of Eye. It is assumed that a person can employ a dominant schema without necessarily accessing the knowledge available in embedded subschemata. On the other hand, should the occasion demand it, the full meaning of a subschema can be unpacked and a deeper interpretation given.

To comprehend a message is to place a construction upon it that gives a coherent formulation of its contents. In schema terms, a "coherent formulation" means a one-to-one correspondence between the slots in a schema and the "givens" in the message. It is instructive to examine the comprehension of a sentence devised by Bransford and McCarrell (1974), for which a subsuming schema is not readily appparent: <u>The notes were sour because the seams split</u>. The syntax is simple and the individual words are easy, yet the sentence as a whole does not immediately make sense to most people. However, the sentence becomes meaningful as soon as one hears the clue <u>bagpipe</u>. Why is this clue effective? An answer is that it enables the conception of a framework that maps onto a possible world. Within the framework, each word in the sentence can be construed to have a referent with a sensible role to play in the possible world. That is to say, the clue allows one to invoke a schema containing slots for the objects, actions, and qualities mentioned in the sentence. The schema gives a good account of the sentence and, therefore, there is the subjective sense that it has been comprehended.

Conceptions of the Reading Process

According to one view, reading is a "bottom-up" or "data-driven" process (Bobrow & Norman, 1975). There is a series of discrete processing stages, each corresponding to a level of linguistic analysis. Analysis proceeds from the most primitive low-order level to the most complex high-order level. As a first step, feature analyzers are brought to bear on discriminate horizontal, vertical, and oblique line segments; open and closed loops; intersection with a horizontal plane; and so on. From these, letters are identified. Strings of letters are analyzed into clusters with morphophonemic significance. Words are recognized. Strings of words are parsed into phrase constituents. Word meanings are retrieved from the subjective lexicon. Eventually, a semantic interpretation of a sentence is produced. Sentence meaning is conceived to be the deterministic product of the lower-order levels of analysis and, presumably, the meaning of a text is a concantenation of the meanings of its component sentences.

Another view holds that reading is essentially a "top-down" or "conceptually driven" process. Rather than analyzing a text squiggle by squiggle, the reader samples it to confirm or reject hypotheses about its content. In other words, reading is conceived to be a psycholinguistic guessing game (Goodman, 1976). The reader's expectations represent a form of preprocessing that should expedite and speed up subsequent analysis. Occasionally, expectation would be predicted to override the print, as appears to happen when children make miscues in oral reading, substituting semantically related words in place of those given.

There is an interesting difference between the bottom-up and top-down theories about reading in their treatment of ambiguity. According to the former view, a high-order process does not affect low-order processes. Each stage takes as its input the output from the preceding stage. If an ambiguity arises at any stage, the alternative interpretations are sent forward for resolution at a later point. For instance, it would be supposed that all of the meanings of a homonym are accessed. Eventually, if the message as a whole is not ambiguous, a process operating on syntax, semantics, or pragmatics at the phrase, sentence, or text level, will permit a choice among the homonym's senses.

From the perspective of a bottom-up model, reading is a matter of growing a tree of possible interpretations. Any stage may add new branches, or prune some of those already there. From the perspective of a model that admits of possible top-down influences, on the other hand, not all of the branches need be grafted on to the tree in the first place. Emerging high-order expectations may forestall some interpretations before they occur. With respect to the meaning of a homonym, it might be expected that normally only the contextually most appropriate meaning would be accessed. This is the implication of research by Schvaneveldt, Meyer, and Becker (Note 1), using a lexical decision task. For instance, money was identified as a word faster in the sequence save, bank, money than in either river, bank, money, or the control sequences save, date, money or fig, date, money. If all senses of a word were activated, bank should have primed money to some extent, even when preceded by river, but this did not happen. Converging evidence has been obtained by Swinney and Hakes (1976), who found, using a phoneme monitoring task, that a disambiguating context of a sentence or two can constrain the interpretation of a subsequently encountered homonym.

Of course, it is surely simplistic to imagine that reading is either a bottom-up or top-down process. Rumelhart (1976) has presented a persuasive case that reading must involve continuous interactions among many levels of analysis. This paper deals with how concepts brought to a text influence comprehension, learning, and recall; but, to assert the obvious, the processes involved in analyzing the print itself are also crucial.

Schemata and Text Interpretation

We have used various devices to get people to bring different schemata into play when reading text. Several studies have employed whole passages that were ambiguous. For instance, Schallert (1976) constructed passages that could be given two distinct interpretations. One of the passages told of a character who was afraid that his best pitchers would crack in the heat. The passage was entitled "Worries of a baseball manager" or "Worries of a glassware factory manager." Scores on a multiple-choice test--constructed so that the interpretation of pitcher and other similarly ambiguous elements could be distinguished--indicated that the interpretation of this and other passages was strongly related to the title.

In the absence of strong contextual cues, such as titles and introductions, the schemata by which people assimilate ambiguous passages can be expected to depend upon their background and life situation. Anderson, Reynolds, Schallert, and Goetz (1977) wrote the following passage:

> Every Saturday night four good friends get together. When Jerry, Mike, and Pat arrived, Karen was sitting in her living room writing some notes. She quickly gathered the cards and stood up to greet her friend at the door. They followed her into the living room but as usual they couldn't agree on exactly what to play. Jerry eventually took a stand and set things up. Finally, they began to play. Karen's recorder filled the room with soft and pleasant music. Early in the evening, Mike noticed Pat's hand and the many diamonds. As the night progressed the tempo of play increased. Finally, a lull in the activities occurred. Taking advantage of this, Jerry pondered the

arrangement in front of him. Mike interrupted Jerry's reverie and said, "Let's hear the score." They listened carefully and commented on their performance. When the comments were all heard, exhausted but happy, Karen's friends went home.

Most people interpret this passage in terms of an evening of cards but it can be interpreted as being about a rehearsal of a woodwind ensemble. Another passage is usually perceived to be about a convict planning his escape from prison; however, it is possible to see it in terms of a wrestler hoping to break the hold of an opponent. These passages were read by a group of physical education students and by a group of music students. Scores on a multiple-choice test and theme-revealing disambiguations and intrusions in free recall indicated that the interpretations given to passages bore the expected strong relationships to the subject's background. An example of an intrusion showing a card theme was, "Mike sees that Pat's hand has a lot of hearts." One showing a music theme was, "As usual they couldn't decide on the piece of music to play."

Of special significance to the discussion in this section are responses on a debriefing questionnaire. Subjects were asked whether they became aware of another possible interpretation of either passage. The interesting fact is that 62% reported that another interpretation never occurred to them, while an additional 20% said they became aware of an alternative interpretation during the multiple-choice test or when responding to the debriefing questionnaire. Less than 20% said they were aware of a second interpretation while reading a passage. Many people would not wish to place too much stock in retrospective reports. Still, these are the results that would be expected on the basis of top-down, schema-based processing.

Gordon Bower (cf. Note 2) and his coworkers at Stanford have completed several studies that parallel those done in my laboratory. One study involved stories about characters who visit the doctor. An examination is completed and the doctor smiles and says, "Well, it seems my expectations have been confirmed." The base story was, in Bower's words, "a sort of neutral Rorschach card onto which subjects would project their own meanings" (Note 2, p. 8). The introduction to one version of the story describes the character as worried about whether she is pregnant. Here subjects tended to recall the doctor's remark as, "Your fears have been confirmed" or simply, "You're pregnant." An alternate introduction described the main character as a wrestler worried about being underweight. Subjects who read this version remembered that the doctor told the character he was gaining weight.

In another study, Bower and his assocites used a story about a series of mishaps that happen when a TV commercial involving water skiing is filmed. Alternate introductions were written to cause the reader to identify with either Harry, the boatdriver, or Rich, the water skier. On a recognition test, subjects tended to rate, as explicitly

part of the text, statements formulated from the perspective of the
character with whom they were led to identify. For instance, more
subjects given the water skier than the boatdriver introduction
identified, "The handle was torn from Rich's grasp as the boat
unexpectedly jumped ahead," as a proposition from the text. The reverse
was true of the parallel formulation of the same episode written from
the boatdriver's perspective: "Rich slipped and lost control and the
handle went skipping across the water."

The general point illustrated by these experiments is that the
meaning of a text arises in an interaction between the characteristics
of the message and the reader's existing knowledge and analysis of
context. Ambiguous passages are useful for making transparent the role
of world knowledge and context. However, there is every reason to
suppose that they are equally important when comprehending material that
would be said to be "unambiguous." A message has an unambiguous meaning
just in case there is consensus in a linguistic community about the
schemata that normally will subsume it. The role of knowledge of the
world is merely less obvious to the psychologist doing prose memory
research in these cases, for the author, reader, and the judges who
score the protocols employ complementary schemata, and thus give
essentially the same interpretation to the material.

Schemata and the Significance of Text Elements

Since Binet and Henri (1894; also, Thieman & Brewer, in press)
worked with French school children at the end of the nineteenth century,
it has been known that people are more likely to learn and remember the
important than the unimportant elements of a prose passage. No doubt,
authors provide linguistic cues to the important points in a text;
however, I shall argue that importance is largely a derivative of the
schemata the reader imposes on the text.

The schema brought to bear on a text will contain embedded
subschemata that generally can be conceived to form a hierarchy. The
position of a subschema in the hierarchy is one index of its importance.
Significant text information instantiates higher-order slots in the
structure. The schema could be said to "give" such information its
importance. It follows that the importance of a text element would vary
if readers were caused to invoke schemata in which the text element
played a greater or lesser role. This hypothesis has been investigated
in two lines of research in my laboratory.

Anderson, Spiro, and Anderson (1977) wrote two passages--one about
dining at a fancy restaurant, the other a closely comparable story about
shopping at a supermarket. The same eighteen items of food, attributed
to the same characters, were mentioned in the same order in the two
stories. Subjects read one of the stories and then, after an interval,
attempted recall.

The first prediction was that the food items would be better learned and recalled when presented in the restaurant narrative. The reasoning was that a dining-at-a-fancy-restaurant schema contains a more finely articulated structure; that is, certain categories of food will be ordered and served. Also, there are constraints on the items that can fit into these categories: Hot dogs will not be the main course, nor Koolaid the beverage. Just about any food or beverage fits a supermarket schema. This prediction was confirmed in two experiments.

The second experiment involved food categories determined on the basis of a norming study to have a high or a low probability of being in an individual's restaurant schema. An entree and a drink during the meal are examples, respectively, of the high and low categories. An entree is an essential element. No fine meal would be complete without one. A drink during dinner is a less central, perhaps optional, element. Subjects who read the restaurant story recalled substantially more of the foods and beverages from three high probability categories than subjects who read the supermarket story. In contrast, there was no difference between the two passages on items from three low probability categories. This shows that the restaurant narrative did not indiscriminately facilitate performance, as would be expected if it were more interesting, coherent, or memorable overall. Instead, as predicted, there was selective enhancement of items from just those categories that have special importance in a restaurant schema.

The next prediction was that subjects would more accurately ascribe foods to characters when given the restaurant story. Who gets what food has significance within a restaurant schema, whereas it does not matter in a supermarket who throws the brussel sprouts into the shopping cart. In both experiments, the conditional probability of attributing a food item to the correct character, given that the item had been recalled, was higher among subjects who received the restaurant story than the supermarket story.

Finally, it was predicted that order-of-recall of food items would correspond more closely to order-of-mention for subjects who read the restaurant passage. There is not, or need not be, a prescribed sequence for selecting foods in a grocery store, but at a fine restaurant it would be peculiar to have a strawberry parfait before the escargot. In the first experiment, the average correlation between recall order and order of mention was significantly higher for the group that received the restaurant narrative. The trend was in the same direction, but not significant in the second experiment, perhaps because recall was attempted shortly after reading. There had been an hour and a half interval before recall in the first study. Maybe surface order information is available shortly after reading, and this makes the generic order information, inherent in a schema, superfluous.

The experiments just described used the device of weaving the same information into two different narratives in order to get readers to assimilate that information to two different schemta. The device in a second, parallel line of research was to ask subjects to read a narrative from alternative points of view that, presumably, caused them to invoke different schemata. Pichert and Anderson (1977) asked subjects to read stories from one of two perspectives or from no directed perspective. One of the stories ostensibly was about what two boys do when skipping school. They go to one of the boys' homes, since his mother is never home on Thursdays. It is a well-to-do family with a luxuriously appointed home. It has a number of attractive features, such as spacious grounds, a tall hedge that hides the house from the road, and a new stone fireplace. However, it also has some defects, including a musty basement and a leaky roof. The family has many valuable possessions--silverware, a coin collection, a color TV set. Readers were asked to approach the story from the viewpoint of a burglar or a prospective homebuyer. Obviously, a coin collection is important to a burglar, but unimportant to a homebuyer. The opposite is true of a musty basement or a leaking roof. In a preliminary experiment, the average intercorrelation of rated idea unit importance across three perspectives on each of two stories was determined to be quite low, which is in itself evidence that schemata determine the significance of text elements.

The next experiment manipulated perspective to investigate the effects of schemata on text learning and recall. The previously obtained ratings of idea unit importance were strongly related to immediate recall and, independently, to delayed recall. This was true just of ratings obtained under the perspective the subject was directed to take, not other possible but nonoperative perspectives. Ratings of importance under the operative perspective was a significant predictor of recall in five of six stepwise multiple regression analyses (one for each of three perspectives on each of two stories). It was the only significant predictor in four of these analyses.

The past few years have seen increasing refinement of the notion of importance in terms of theories of text structure (cf. Kintsch, 1974; Meyer, 1975; Rumelhart, 1975; Mandler & Johnson, 1977). These are more properly regarded as theories of the structure of the schemata by which a linguistic community normally will subsume a message, as some theorists expressly acknowledge. But a text need not be read "normally." Depending on the reader's goal, task, or perspective, he or she may override the conventions a linguistic community ordinarily uses to structure a text. When the schema changes, then, so will the importance of text elements.

Possible Effects of Schemata on Encoding and Retrieving Text Information

This section gives a more detailed account of some of the mechanisms by which schemata may affect the processing of text information. The central phenomenon to be explained is the primacy of important text in recall, illustrated in the preceding section.

Significant text elements might be better recalled because they are better learned. In other words, the effect might be attributable to a process at work when a passage is read. An attractive possibility is that the schema provides the device by which a reader allocates attention. Extra attention might be devoted to important text elements, whereas insignificant elements might be skimmed or processed less deeply. A second possibility on the encoding side is that a schema provides "ideational scaffolding," to use Ausubel's (1963) apt term, for selected categories of text information. A schema will contain slots for important information, but may contain no slots, or only optional slots, for unimportant information. According to this view, information gets encoded precisely because there is a niche for it in the structure. This is an interesting idea, but as yet I have been unable to think of any implication of the ideational scaffolding hypothesis that might permit it to be distinguished from the regulation-of-attention notion.

The fact that people recall more important than unimportant text elements might be due to processes at work when information is retrieved and used, instead of, or in addition to, processes acting when the information was initially encoded. There are several possible retrieval mechanisms that fall out of a schema-theoretic orientation, which might account for the primacy of important text information in recall.

The first can be called the "retrieval plan" hypothesis. The idea is that the schema provides the structure for searching memory. Consider for illustration the burglar perspective on the story about two boys playing "hooky" from school. The rememberer will possess the generic knowledge that burglars need to have a way of entering a premise; that they are interested in finding valuable, portable objects that can be "fenced" easily; that they are concerned about avoiding detection; and that they aim to make clean "getaways." Memory search is presumed to start with the generic concerns of a burglar. Generic concerns implicate selected categories of text information. For instance, the fact that all burglars need to enter the place to be robbed is assumed to provide a mental pathway or implicit cue for the specific proposition that the side door was kept unlocked. On the other hand, information in a text that may have been encoded, but does not connect with the schema guiding memory search, should be relatively inaccessible. For example, the passage about the boys playing hooky from school asserts that the house has new stone siding. Presumably, there are no pointers in a burglary schema to information of this type and, thus, this information is unlikely to be retrieved even if it were stored.

We have named another possible retrieval explanation the "output editing" hypothesis. The assumption is that the schema contains within itself an index of importance. The rememberer establishes a response criterion based jointly on this index, motivation, and demand characteristics. There are several variants on how output editing might work. In crudest form, the subject simply might not write down information that occurred to him or her because it falls below the response criterion.

    I will consider, finally, the possibility that people may   remember
more   important   than   unimportant   information   because of a process of
"inferential reconstruction" (Spiro, 1977). There may be information
missing from memory, either because the information was not stored, or
because it was forgotten. The conceptual machinery of the schema and
the information that can be recalled may permit the rememberer to fill
gaps by inference. Anderson, Spiro, and Anderson (1977) have
illustrated how the process might work as follows. Suppose that a
person is trying to recall a story about a meal at a fine restaurant
(see the preceding section). The beverage served with the meal cannot
be recalled, but since there is a slot in a restaurant schema for such
an item, the rememberer is led to try to reconstruct one. If the
information that beef was served for the main course can be recalled,
then red wine may be generated as a candidate beverage. There are a
couple of possible scenarios at this point. Red wine might be produced
simply as a plausible guess.   A good guess and an element actually
remembered often will be indistinguishable to a judge, particularly one
applying lenient, gist-scoring criteria. Or, it might be that once a
candidate element, such as red wine, has been produced, it is checked
against an otherwise inaccessible memory trace. To say this another
way, the process might be one of generation, followed by recognition and
verification (Kintsch, 1974).   In any event, the foregoing gives an
account of the primacy of important text information, for the schema is
more likely to contain the concepts for reconstructing important than
unimportant elements.

Evidence for Encoding and Retrieval Benefits

    We have completed several experiments to determine whether schemata
have   independent   effects   on   the   encoding and retrieval of text
information and, if so, to begin to pin down the specific mechanisms
that are responsible.   My student, James Pichert, and I (Anderson &
Pichert, 1977) asked undergraduates to read the story about two boys
playing hooky from school, from the perspective of either a burglar or a
homebuyer. The story was recalled once from the same perspective from
which it had been read. Then everyone recalled the story for a second
time. Half of the subjects did so again from the same perspective. The
other half changed perspectives. Based on previously obtained ratings,
a cluster of information important to a burglar but unimportant to a
homebuyer (e.g., a collection of rare coins), and another cluster
important to a homebuyer but unimportant to a burglar (e.g., a
fireplace), were identified. As expected, subjects produced on the
second recall a significant amount of new information--that is,
information that had not been recalled the first time--that was
important in the light of the new perspective, but that was unimportnat
in terms of the perspective operative when the passage was read and
recalled the first time. There does not appear to be any way to explain
this finding solely in terms of encoding mechanisms. Thus, it seems to

be rather strong evidence for a retrieval mechanism independent of encoding.

In the preceding section, three explanations within schema theory for an influence on retrieval were discussed. To review briefly, the first is the retrieval plan hypothesis: A new schema will furnish implicit cues for different types of text information. The second is the output editing hypothesis: When the schema changes, different types of information are above a response criterion. The third is the inferential reconstruction hypothesis: A new schema will provide the concepts for infering different categories of important but unavailable information.

In a follow-up study, Pichert and I replicated the retrieval benefit identified in the experiment described above. We also collected subjects' introspective descriptions of the processes of learning and remembering. Most subjects discussed strategies and tactics for remembering in a manner consistent with the retrieval plan hypothesis. A number said, in so many words, that reviewing the concerns of a burglar or homebuyer caused them to think of previously unrecalled information related to these concerns. For example, one subject said, "I was thinking. . . was there anything wrong with the house? And then I remembered the basement was damp." Another said, "I remembered [the color TV] in the second one, but not the first one. I was thinking about things to steal, things to take and steal...."

The self-report protocols generally gave little support to the output editing hypothesis. Most subjects insisted that they wrote down everything they could remember. John Surber, another student of mine, manipulated the incentive for recall. He reasoned that if the increment in recall in the perspective-shift group were due to output editing, then the increment would disappear under conditions of high incentive. What he actually found was a difference in favor of subjects who shifted perspective, regardless of whether a 25 cent bonus was paid for each new idea. Thus, two strands of evidence weigh against an output editing interpretation of the results of this series of experiments. I do not wish to argue that people never suppress information available to them, only that this probably was not a major factor under the conditions that have prevailed in our research.

Spiro (1977) has obtained convincing evidence for reconstructive processes in memory for discourse. Subjects read a story about a couple engaged to be married. The man is strongly against having children. In one version of the story, the woman is elated to find this out because she doesn't want children either. In the other version, she is horrified because a large family is important to her. Several minutes after reading the story, subjects are told either that the couple did get married or that they broke up. Based on the assumption that people's common-sense psychology of interpersonal relations could be represented in terms of Heider's principle of structural balance, Spiro predicted the particular types of "reconciling errors" subjects would introduce into their recall protocols when the situation described to them was imbalanced. For instance, when the couple got married despite the serious disagreement about having children, it was argued that subjects would modify the story to reconcile the incongruity by claiming, for instance, that "the problem was resolved when they found out that Margie couldn't have children anyway." The expected types of reconciling inferences appeared with increasing frequency over a retention interval of six weeks. Subjects were more confident their inferences had been part of the story than they were that propositions that had an explicit basis in the text had been present.

The perspective shift studies described earlier in this section all showed a retrieval benefit, but, for a couple of reasons, none clearly established that schemata have an encoding influence as well. This was the purpose of another experiment completed by Jim Pichert and me. A story was recalled just once, from either the same perspective from which it was read, or from a different one. Both the perspective from which the story was read and the perspective from which it was recalled, which were orthogonal factors in the design employed, had a substantial effect on performance. Thus, both encoding and retrieval influences were demonstrated.

When asked how the assigned perspective affected the manner in which the story was read, most subjects described a process of directing attention to important elements. For example, one subject told to take the burglar perspective said, "I kept in mind all of the critical things a burglar would be looking for, such as getting in and out, the items that it would be easy to move and take from the house itself." One assigned the homebuyer perspective reported, "I spent most of the time looking for items to be interested in when buying a house." A straightforward way to get converging evidence on the regulation-of-attention hypothesis would be to time subjects on chunks of text material whose importance has been manipulated in some way. We have not done experiments of this type yet.

In summary, this section reviewed evidence that a schema operative when a passage is read affects encoding, possibly by directing attention to text elements that are significant in the light of the schema. Evidence was presented that shows that the schema affects remembering later, probably in part by providing the plan for searching memory. Schemata probably also provide the basis for inferential elaboration when a passage is read, and inferential reconstruction when there are gaps or inconsistencies in memory.

Implications of Schema Theory for Education

Text information is interpreted, organized, and retrieved in terms of high-level schemata. It follows that the student who does not possess relevant schemata is going to have trouble learning and remembering the information encountered in stories and textbooks.

Consider, for illustration, the description of an unfamiliar nation in a geography text (cf. Anderson, Spiro, & Anderson, 1977). The mature student will bring to bear an elaborate Nation schema that incorporates well-formed subschemata for assimilating information about the topography, climate, economy, culture, and political system. It is only a slight oversimplification to say that the task for the advanced student is simply to fill the slots in an already formed schema with the particular information in the text about the unfamiliar nation. The information will be readily acquired and, once acquired, easily retrieved when needed.

How about the young reader, who, for the sake of the argument, will be assumed not to possess a refined Nation schema? In the worst case, a description of an unfamiliar nation would be unintelligible to such a reader, like the Bransford and Johnson (1973) passages for mature readers, where a schema-evoking context was not provided. More likely, the young reader will have a partly formed Nation schema sufficient for some level of understanding of the material, but that will not enable a representation of great depth or breadth.

Whether people possess the schemata appropriate for assimilating a text should be an important source of individual differences in reading comprehension. Smiley, Oakley, Worthen, Campione and Brown (1977) have obtained some evidence suggesting that this may be the case. Good and poor readers drawn from seventh-grade classes read one folktale and listened to another. Following each story, they were tested for comprehension and recall. Under both reading and listening conditions, good readers recalled a greater proportion of the stories, and the likelihood of their recalling a particular element was an increasing function of the element's structural importance. Poor readers not only recalled less of the stories, but their recall was not as clearly related to variations in importance. Smiley et al. went on to show that it was necessary to test children as young as first grade before finding another group that showed as little sensitivity to gradations of importance as poor reading seventh graders (see also Brown & Smiley, 1977). On the other hand, Perfetti and Lesgold (in press) have summarized several studies that, by and large, have not revealed substantial differences between good and poor readers in sensitivity to sentence structure or text structure.

Thus, based on evidence already available, it is too early to say whether variations in high level schemata, or facility in using these schemata, will turn out to be a consistent difference between good and poor readers. I hope only to have shown that this is a very reasonable place to look for differences. If differences are consistently found, there will be implications for diagnosis, design of lesson materials, and approaches to teaching.

Reference Notes

1. Schvaneveldt, R. W., Meyer, D. E., & Becker, C. A.   Contextual constraints on ambiguous word recognition. Paper presented at the meeting of the Psychonomic Society, Boston, November 1974.

2. Bower, G. H. On injecting life into deadly prose: Studies in explanation seeking.   Invited   address   at   meeting   of   Western Psychological Association, Seattle, Washington, April 1977.

References

Anderson, R. C., & Pichert, J. W.   Recall of previously unrecallable information following a shift of perspective (Technical Report 41). Urbana, IL: University of Illinois, Center for the Study of Reading, April 1977.

Anderson, R. C., Pichert, J. W., Goetz, E. T., Schallert, D. L., Stevens, K. V. & Trollip, S. R. Instantiation of general terms. Journal of Verbal Learning and Verbal Behavior, 1976, 15, 667-679.

Anderson, R. C., Reynolds, R. E., Schallert, D. L., & Goetz, E. T. Frameworks for comprehending discourse. American Educational Research Journal, 1977, in press.

Anderson, R. C., Spiro, R. J., & Anderson, M. C.   Schemata   as scaffolding for the representation of information in connected discourse (Techical Report 24). Urbana, IL: University of Illinois, Center for the Study of Reading, March 1977.

Ausubel, D. P. The psychology of meaningful verbal learning. New York; Grune and Stratton, 1963.

Bartlett, F. C.   Remembering. Cambridge, England: The   Cambridge University Press, 1932.

Binet, A., & Henri, V. La memoire des phrases. L'annee Psychologique, 1894, 1, 24-59.

Bobrow, D. G., & Norman, D. A. Some principles of memory schemata.   In D. G. Bobrow & A. M. Collins (Eds.), Representation and understanding: Studies in cognitive science. New York: Academic Press, 1975.

Bower, G. H. Experiments in story understanding and recall.   Quarterly Journal of Experimental Psychology, 1976, 28, 511-534.

Bransford, J. D., & Johnson, M. K. Considerations of some problems of comprehension. In W. G. Chase (Ed.), Visual information processing. New York: Academic Press, 1973.

Bransford, J. D., & McCarrell, N. S. A sketch of a cognitive approach to comprehension. In W. Weimer & D. Palermo (Eds.), Cognition and the symbolic processes. Hillsdale, NJ: Erlbaum, 1974.

Brown, A. L., & Smiley, S. S. Rating the importance of structural units of prose passages: A problem of metacognitive development. Child Development, 1977, in press.

Gombrich, E. H. J., Hochberg, J., & Black, M. Art, perception, and reality. Baltimore: Johns Hopkins University Press, 1972.

Goodman, K. S. Reading: A psycholinguistic guessing game. Journal of the Reading Specialist, 1976, 4, 126-135.

Kintsch, W. The representation of meaning in memory. New York: John Wiley & Sons, 1974.

Mandler, J. M., & Johnson, N. S. Rememberance of things passed: Story structure and recall. Cognitive Psychology, 1977, 9, 111-151.

Meyer, B. J. F. The organization of prose and its effects on memory. Amsterdam: North-Holland Publishing Company, 1975.

Minsky, M. A framework for representing knowledge. In P. H. Winston (Ed.), The psychology of computer vision. New York: McGraw-Hill, 1975.

Palmer, S. E. Visual perception and world knowledge: Notes on a model of sensory-cognitive interaction. In D. A. Norman, D. E. Rumelhart, & the LNR Research Group, Explorations in cognition. San Francisco: Freeman, 1975.

Perfetti, C. A., & Lesgold, A. M. Discourse comprehension and sources of individual differences. In M. Just & P. Carpenter (Eds.), Cognitive processes in comprehension. Hillsdale, NJ: Erlbaum, in press.

Piaget, J. The language and thought of the child. New York: Harcourt, Brace, 1926.

Pichert, J. W., & Anderson, R. C. Taking different perspectives on a story. Journal of Educational Psychology, 1977, in press.

Rumelhart, D. E. Notes on a schema for stories. In D. G. Bobrow & A. M. Collins (Eds.), Representation and understanding: Studies in cognitive science. New York: Academic Press, 1975.

Rumelhart, D. E.   Toward an interactive model of reading.   In S.   Dornic
    (Ed.), Attention and performance VI.   London: Academic Press,
    1976.

Rumelhart, D. E., & Ortony, A.   The representation of knowledge   in
    memory.   In R.   C.   Anderson, R.   J.   Spiro, & W.   E.   Montague
    (Eds.), Schooling and the acquisition of knowledge.   Hillsdale, NJ:
    Erlbaum, 1977.

Schallert, D. L.   Improving memory for prose: The relationship between
    depth of processing and context.   Journal of Verbal Learning and
    Verbal Behavior, 1976, 15, 621-632.

Schank, R., & Abelson, R. P.   Scripts,   plans,   and   knowledge.
    Proceedings   of   the   Fourth   International   Joint   Conference   on
    Artificial Intelligence.   Tbilisi, Georgia: U.S.S.R., 1975.

Smiley, S. S.,   Oakley, D. D.,   Worthen, D.,   Campione, J. C., &   Brown,
    A. L.   Recall of thematically relevant material by adolescent good
    and poor readers as a function of written versus oral presentation
    (Technical Report 23).   Urbana, IL: University of Illinois, Center
    for the Study of Reading, March 1977.

Spiro, R. J.   Remembering information from text: Theoretical   and
    empirical issues concerning the 'State of Schema' reconstruction
    hypothesis. In R.   C.   Anderson, R.   J.   Spiro, & W.   E.   Montague
    (Eds.), Schooling and the acquisition of knowledge.   Hillsdale, NJ;
    Erlbaum, 1977, in press.

Swinney, D. A., & Hakes, D. T.   Effects of prior context upon lexical
    access during sentence comprehension.   Journal of Verbal Learning
    and Verbal Behavior, 1976, 15, 681-689.

Thieman, T. J., & Brewer, W. J.   Alfred Binet on memory for ideas.
    Genetic Psychology Monographs, in press.

STRUCTURALLY INTEGRATED VERSUS STRUCTURALLY SEGREGATED
MEMORY REPRESENTATIONS: IMPLICATIONS FOR THE
DESIGN OF INSTRUCTIONAL MATERIALS

Barbara Hayes-Roth
The Rand Corporation
Santa Monica, California 90406

Students regularly receive conceptually related information from several different sources. For example, a student might study several textbook chapters concerning U.S. involvement in World War II. All of the studied information would be related at a general topical level. In addition, some of the information would be related in more specific ways. For example, the student might learn that the U.S. took various actions during the war, including bombing Hiroshima and Nagasaki, liberating France, giving monetary aid to China, etc.

The student's task is not simply to memorize studied information, but to organize it in memory. A critical feature of this memory organization is the degree to which particular subsets of the information are structurally integrated or segregated. Structurally integrated memory representations share common sub-representations, while structurally segregated memory representations do not. Consider the memory organization of knowledge about U.S. involvement in World War II shown in Figure 1. In this organization, all propositions regarding actions taken by the U.S. are structurally integrated because they all share a common sub-representation of "U.S." Alternatively, consider the memory organization shown in Figure 2. In this organization, propositions regarding actions against ememies ("bombs", "captures") are structurally integrated and propositions regarding actions toward allies ("commands", "aids", "liberates") are structurally integrated, but the two sets of propositions are structurally segregated. In other words, separate sub-representations of "U.S." are involved in representations of the two sets of propositions.

Structurally integrated and structurally segregated memory representations have different properties. Structurally integrated representations emphasize the common features of related propositions

----

83

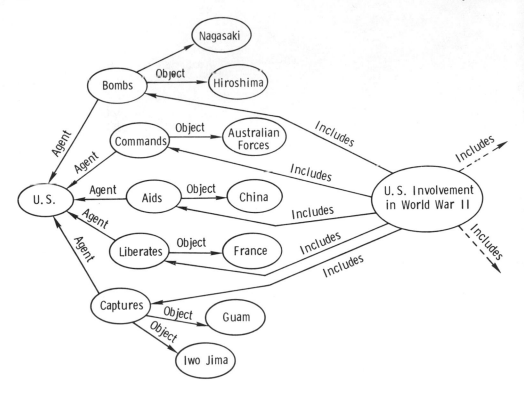

Figure 1.   Example of a structurally integrated memory representation.

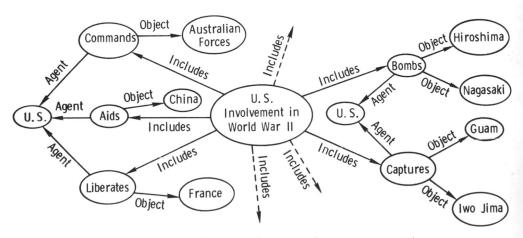

Figure 2.   Example of a structurally segregated memory representation.

and the configural effects produced by simultaneous consideration of all related propositions. They deemphasize individual propositions and, as a result, may exhibit interference during attempts to access isolated propositions. These effects derive from a tendency for any activation of the shared sub-representation to diffuse throughout all of the propositions, rather than being focused on any one proposition. Structurally segregated representations, on the other hand, obscure the common features of related propositions and any configural effects, while emphasizing individual propositions. These effects derive from a tendency for activation to be concentrated on particular propositions, with fewer structural linkages present to diffuse that activation among conceptually related memory representations.

Each kind of memory representation is adaptive under certain circumstances, depending upon the kinds of relations that occur in the studied text(s) and the nature of the performance required following study. Integrated memory representations are adaptive for higher-order cognitive processing, such as summarization, generalization, and inference. Segregated memory representations are adaptive for fast, accurate learning and remembering of specific propositions. For example, after learning about various actions taken by the U.S. during World War II, the student might be required to draw inferences about the general nature of U.S. activities toward allies. A structurally integrated memory representation of the relevant propositions, as illustrated in Figure 2, would facilitate inference in two ways. First, it would emphasize the common characteristics of the various actions toward allies (e.g., that the U.S. actively cooperated with allies). Second, it would facilitate simultaneous activation of all relevant propositions, enabling more elaborate cognitive analysis of the configural properties of actions toward allies (e.g., that the U.S. played a supportive leadership role toward allies). It might also be important for the student to remember specific action toward allies. Structurally segregating memory representations of these propositions from those regarding actions toward enemies would facilitate performance in two ways. First, it would maximize the probability that individual propositions would be retrieved, because processing capacity would be divided among a relatively small number of proposition representations. Second, it would restrict activation of related propositions that might be confused with target propositions.

Organizing studied information in memory in an appropriate way is a critical aspect of the learning process. It is difficult because the student must first detect conceptual relations in the studied material, and then determine which propositions should be organized in structurally integrated versus structurally segregated memory representations. Further, establishing integrated versus segregated memory representations may not always (or ever) result from conscious decisions, but may sometimes occur automatically during reading. Thus, it seems likely that even good students will frequently acquire suboptimal memory representations.

An obvious implication of the above analysis is that learning could be improved by assisting the student in detecting conceptual relations in studied material, determining which propositions should be organized in structurally integrated and segregated memory representations, and establishing the appropriate memory organization. If these processes occur automatically during reading, it may not be sufficient to provide some adjunct aid to the student during study. A better approach may be to present the studied material in a form that automatically promotes the desired memory organization.

One technique for doing this is suggested by a recently proposed theory of the representation of meaning in memory (Hayes-Roth & Hayes-Roth, 1977). The theory assumes that the meaning of a verbal input is represented in memory in a linguistic form that bears a close resemblance to the surface form of the input. In particular, the words used in the input are assumed to be the basic units of its memory representation. The theory contrasts with the more prevalent view that the meaning of a verbal input is represented in memory in a canonical form that is more abstract than the words used in the input.

One of the findings of Hayes-Roth and Hayes-Roth is particularly relevant here. Several previous studies had shown that when students learn propositions that involve common words (e.g., all of the propositions regarding U.S. activity during World War II), interference in memory occurs for each of them (Anderson, 1974; Hayes-Roth, 1977; Thorndyke & Bower, 1974). That is, students do not remember the propositions as well as they remember those that are unrelated to other learned propositions. This suggests that the students formed integrated memory representations of related learned propositions. Hayes-Roth and Hayes-Roth found tht this kind of interference could be eliminated by paraphrasing the common words in one of the sentences (e.g., by replacing "U.S." with "American" in propositions regarding U.S. activity toward enemies). This finding suggests that paraphrasing the common words induced segregated memory representations of related propositions. The implications are obvious: If memory for individual propositions is desired, conceptual relations in studied material should be worded as differently as possible to promote development of segregated memory representations. If higher-order processing, such as inference, is desired, conceptual relations should be worded as similarly as possible to promote development of integrated representations. We have been investigating these prescriptions in learning contexts closely approximating natural instructional contexts. Two examples are discussed below.

Consider the case in which the student must read several texts that are similar in the general outline of the information presented, but different in detail. The following excerpts are from two texts of this sort:

Text 1. The Spring Episode was the first revolution
in Morinthia. The outbreak occurred shortly before dawn on
April 17, 1843. The revolution was undoubtedly caused by
the tyranny imposed upon the Morinthian people by King
Egbert, the dictator. For months, Egbert had extracted
half of all the earning of the people. However, the
immediate cause of the outbreak appeared to be a minor
crime committed several days earlier. A peasant had
poached several chickens from the royal henhouse to serve
at his daughter's wedding. It seemed a minor offense to
the people, but in Morinthia, everyone who disobeyed the
law was punished severely . . .

Text 2. The November Episode was the first revolution
in Caledia. The outbreak occurred shortly after midnight
on November 1, 1737. The revolution was undoubtedly caused
by the tyranny imposed upon the Caledian people by King
Ferdinand, the dictator. For months, Ferdinand had refused
to allow the representatives of the people to participate
in the government. However, the immediate cause of the
outbreak appeared to be a minor crime committed several
days earlier. A stable boy had drunk a bit too freely at
the local tavern and disturbed the town with his singing
while making his way home. It seemed a minor offense to
the people, but in Caledia, everyone who disobeyed the law
was punished severely . . .

Texts 1 and 2 describe similar political events in two different
countries. In both cases, a first revolution is named, dated, and
attributed to the tyranny of a dictatorial king. The immediate cause of
each revolution is a minor crime committed by an ordinary person who is
punished severely. In both cases, it is commonplace to punish severely
those who disobey the law. The two texts also difffer in important
ways: the name and time of occurrence of the revolution, the name of
the king, the expression of the king's tyranny, and the particular crime
committed.

Because the conceptual relations in texts 1 and 2 are worded
identically, structural integration of the memory representations of the
two texts will be automatic. In other words, the memory representations
of the texts will share many common sub-representations. This
integration will result in interference in the student's ability to
remember which details are associated with which revolution. In order
to deter integration of the two memory representations, minimize the
interference, and thereby improve the student's retention of the
material, the conceptual relations should be paraphrased in one of the
texts, as in the following alternative to text 2:

Text 3. The first Caledian rebellion was called the
November Episode. The uprising happened on November 1,
1737, just after midnight. The oppression of the Caledians

by King Ferdinand, the autocrat, was clearly the cause of
the rebellion. For months, Ferdinand had refused to allow
the representatives of the people to participate in the
government. But an insignificant crime that had occurred a
few days before seemed to be the immediate cause of the
uprising. A stable boy had drunk too much at the local
tavern and disturbed the town while making his way home.
The Caledian citizens thought it was an insignificant
misdemeanor, but all those who violated the Caledian law
were punished harshly . . .

We have been working with pairs of related texts in which
conceptual relations are represented by either same (e.g., text 2) or
paraphrase (e.g., text 3) wordings. We find, over a variety of topics,
that students remember text-specific details better (20% improvement)
when the conceptual relations are paraphrased. Thus, a simple technique
for improving the effectiveness of instructional materials is to word
texts that are similar in outline, but different in detail, as
differently as possible to promote segregated memory representations.

On the other hand, some learning tasks can be facilitated by
establishing integrated memory representations. One such task is
inference from several texts that present complementary information.
Consider, for example, the following excerpt:

Text 4. The second Morinthian rebellion was called
the Curfew Episode. It provided the setting for several
important events in the life of Albert Profiro, a young
Morinthian tradesman. The uprising happened on March 22,
1844, the day after a group of youths were discovered to
have violated the curfew law. The law had been a source of
friction between the townspeople and the government for
some time. The people welcomed the opportunity to flood
the streets, throwing stones and damaging property. Albert
took it upon himself to try to calm the people. Although
Albert hated all autocrats and their governments, he hated
anarchy in the streets even more . . .

Text 4 describes political events that are complementary to those
described in text 1. Both texts are about Morinthian revolutions and
some of the associated events. Text 1 describes the first revolution:
its causes, what happened during the revolution, and how it was
resolved. Text 4 focuses on how the second revolution affected the life
of a particular individual. Note that integration of the information in
both texts would enable one to draw certain inferences that could not be
drawn if given knowldge of the informtion in only one or the other of
the texts. For example, one could infer that Albert Profiro hated King
Egbert because (a) King Egbert was a dictator (Text 1), (b) Albert
Profiro hated all autocrats (Text 4), and (c) a dictator is an autocrat
(by definition).

The student's ability to draw appropriate inferences depends upon integrating the relevant premises from the two texts, that is, upon recognizing conceptual relations between the representations of the two texts (e.g., between "dictator" and "autocrat"). Because conceptual relations in the two texts are worded differently, distinctive memory representations will be established automatically, hampering integration of the relevant premises. In order to promote establishment of common sub-representations, facilitate integration of the relevant premises, and thereby improve the student's ability to draw appropriate inferences, the conceptual relations between the two texts should be worded as similarly as possible, as in the following alternative to text 4:

> Text 5. The Curfew Episode was the second revolution in Morinthia. It provided the setting for several important events in the life of Albert Profiro, a young Morinthian tradesman. The outbreak occurred on March 22, 1844, the day after a group of youths were discovered to have disobeyed the curfew law. The law had been a source of friction between the townspeople and the government for some time. The people welcomed the opportunity to flood the streets, throwing stones and damaging property. Albert took it upon himself to try to calm the people. Although Albert hated all dictators and their governments, he hated anarchy in the streets even more . . .

We have been working with pairs of related texts in which conceptual relations are represented by either same (e.g., text 5) or paraphrase (e.g., text 4) wordings. We find, over a variety of topics, that students draw more accurate inferences (50% improvement) when the conceptual relations have the same wordings. This is true even when students are permitted to look back at the text during inference. Thus, a simple technique for improving the effectivenss of instructional materials is to word texts that present complementary information as similarly as possible to promote integrated memory representations.

Conclusions

Simple wording manipulations on study materials can be used to influence the organization of the material in memory and students' ability to use the stored information. Differently worded texts promote structurally segregated memory representations, facilitating memory for specific propositions. Similarly worded texts promote structurally integrated memory representations, facilitating inferencing and other higher-order cognitive processing of the stored information.

References

Anderson. J. R.   Retrieval of propositional information from long-term
    memory.   Cognitive Psychology, 1974, 6, 451-474.

Hayes-Roth, B.   Evolution of cognitive structures   and   processes.
    Psychological Review, 1977, 84, 260-278.

Hayes-Roth, B., & Hayes-Roth, F.   The prominence of lexical information
    in memory representations of meaning.   Journal of Verbal Learning
    and Verbal Behavior, 1977, 16, 119-136.

Thorndyke, P. W., & Bower, B. H.   Storage and retrieval processes in
    sentence memory.   Cognitive Psychology, 1974, 6, 515-543.

KNOWLEDGE TRANSFER IN LEARNING FROM TEXTS

Perry W. Thorndyke
Rand Corporation
Santa Monica, California, U.S.A.

The acquisition of knowledge through reading text is a common source of learning in an instructional setting. In a typical learning environment, a student must study texts containing information on related topics and situations, and then integrate that information into a coherent knowledge representation. As any educator knows, the knowledge actually acquired by a student in this situation is only a small subset of all information to be learned. This paper investigates the influence of the structure of presented textual information on the learning of related information. In essence, the following question is addressed: When sets of topically related material containing shared knowledge are to be learned, how are they best presented to the learner? The motivation for this research has been to discover techniques for organizing information that will optimize learning.

Our approach to this instruction problem has been to manipulate experimentally what knowledge is available to a learner (the TRAINING material) and how well the knowledge is learned, and then observe how that knowledge influences the acquisition of new information (the TARGET material) related to the training material. This general method has a long history in experimental psychology, especially in paired-associate studies, and is referred to as the proaction paradigm. In the research reported here, we have tried to use meaningful texts as experimental stimuli in an attempt to approximate normal learning environments. This has necessitated the definition of more complex relationships between training and target materials, and a more complex characterization of what a subject has learned than is customary in traditional verbal learning experiments.

For example, I have previously distinguished two types of knowledge in texts containing event sequences: content and narrative structure (Thorndyke, 1977). Narrative structure can be thought of as a syntactic structure for describing well-formed stories. It expresses text-level knowledge about the organization of events in the passage: the setting of the passage, the goal of the main character in the passage, the

----

91

events comprising attempts of the main character to achieve the goal, and the resolution of the initial problem. The rules for the organization of events into a problem-solving sequence can be expressed independently of the particular selection of characters, goals, or particular actions. That is, the situation-event contingencies that characterize the organization of events into episodes, and episodes into plots, provide a grammatical description of stories, just as a linguistic deep-structure representation characterizes intra-sequential relationships. A story encoded according to this structural analysis is represented as a hierarchy with intermediate nodes corresponding to abstract structural elements of the plot organization, and terminal nodes corresponding to actual propositions from the story.

Text content, on the other hand, expresses knowledge at the level of individual sentences. The content of a sentence is represented by both a <u>syntactic structure</u> and a <u>semantic structure</u>. The semantic structure consists of a relation, or <u>predicate</u>, and its arguments, or <u>details</u>. This distinction between text structure and content has been noted elsewhere in discussions of text "macro-structure" and "micro-structure" (van Dijk & Kintsch, 1977). Research in cognitive psychology has recently investigated the memory representation of both text structure (Rumelhart, 1975; Thorndyke, 1977; Mandler & Johnson, 1977) and text content (Kintsch, 1974; Meyer, 1975; Frederiksen, 1975). These distinctions will be useful below in characterizing the kind of information a learner acquires from a text.

When a person reads a text, the knowledge that he extracts from it includes not only the individual facts, but the relationships among the facts. This latter knowledge permits him to integrate all of the information from the text into a representation in memory that is not merely a concatenation of sentences. Rather, the memory representation will reflect the organization of sets of sentences into higher-order functional elements that compose well-formed texts. Thus, learning from text is assumed to require the acquisition of individual facts <u>and</u> the combination and integration of these facts into higher-order text structures. If this is true, one ought to be able to improve learning of a text either by facilitating the learning of individual facts or by simplifying the integration process. Methods for accomplishing both goals are proposed and examined below. The latter technique is considered first.

Transfer of Structure

In one experiment (Thorndyke, 1977), subjects were presented with a narrative passage of approximately 200 words to study for 90 seconds and learn. The text was a narrative account of a hypothetical island, the inhabitants of which tried to win senate approval for the construction of a canal. Following this story, subjects were presented a second story of the same length to read and remember. After a short delay, subjects were asked to recall the entire second story. The second story bore one of three relationships to the first story. In the REPEATED STRUCTURE condition, the second story had a narrative structure identical to the first story, but had entirely different content. In this condition, the second story was about a farmer whose animals were trying to convince him to build a new barn. The role of the events of the story in the problem-solving framework were identical to those of the first story, but the topic, characters, and particular actions were completely unrelated in the two stories. Thus, a single representation of a narrative structure, formulated according to a grammar of plot organizations (Thorndyke, 1977), was used to produce two stories with unrelated details. In the REPEATED CONTENT condition, the second story repeated some of the semantic content of the first story in a new narrative framework. That is, the second story was about the farmers and senators of the island engaged in a new, unrelated series of episodes. In this condition, then, the representations of narrative structure were different for the two stories, but the characters in the stories were the same. In the UNRELATED condition, the second story shared neither content nor narrative structure with the first story. Hence, this story served as a control condition against which to measure the transfer effects of structure and content.

Across all subjects, the mean free recall for the facts of the UNRELATED second story was 51%. However, in the REPEATED STRUCTURE condition, subjects' recall was 62%, a 22% improvement over the control condition. On the other hand, recall of the REPEATED CONTENT story was 37%, a decrease of 28% relative to the control story. These results were interpreted as evidence for the use by subjects of organizing frameworks for integrating the facts of a text. In the REPEATED STRUCTURE condition, subjects learned during the Story 1 presentation a structure for encoding the story events into a well-formed narrative description. This structure consisted of a hierarchy of abstract conceptual relationships among characters, goals, and event sequences for attaining these goals. When the second story was presented, subjects could use the same framework encoded for Story 1 to encode the new characters and events of Story 2 at the terminal nodes of the hierarchy. Hence, the task of learning the new facts was simplified by the prior learning of the integrating structure.

Other experiments (Thorndyke, 1977; Experiments I and II) have confirmed that learning an organizing framework affects the ability to learn individual facts in a text. When the same text content was presented in a variety of meaningful structural forms, comprehensibility and subsequent recall of the text were found to be a monotonically increasing function of the structural similarity between the text and a well-formed, goal-directed narrative (as defined by the grammar). That is, the ease of learning a fact appears to be dependent on the context or structure in which that fact is presented, as well as how well that structure is previously learned.

However, in the REPEATED CONTENT condition, the transferred information comprised particular predicates of the setting, namely, location and character information. But in Story 2, the characters previously learned were assigned to different roles and relationships than in Story 1. So the benefits of transferring some detailed information (the character names and location of the events) for learning Story 2 were outweighed by the interfering effects of having integrated those facts in a way inappropriate for learning Story 2. Thus, net interference was observed for Story 2 learning in the REPEATED CONTENT condition relative to the UNRELATED condition.

Transfer of Content

It is often the case that a student must learn several facts with the same general form. In this case, it may be desirable to facilitate learning of the individual facts that share the common form. The constraints on the learning of several facts with similar content were examined in another series of experiments, in which transfer effects of structure were tested at the level of individual facts within a text. In this study, a subject was required to learn facts that shared common predicates and topics, but differed in detailed knowledge, a situation commonly faced by a learner. For example, one might want to teach the following information about Mount Rushmore:

Mount Rushmore has four figures represented on it. George Washington was the first President and lived at Mount Vernon. Thomas Jefferson was the third President and lived at Monticello. Abe Lincoln was the 16th President and lived in a log cabin. Theodore Roosevelt was the 26th President and lived at Sagamore Hill.

One way to conceptualize the knowledge contained in this description is to note that the construction, "Person i was the nth President and lived at location l," is a predicate repeated four times with different details each time. The repetition of predicate forms across the four sentences might be expected to facilitate learning of the presented information, since the knowledge of the predicates could be used to encode new details in already existing predicate structures. As predicate structures are repeated, their strength in memory should increase. Thus, as learning progresses, acquisition of new facts should be facilitated by increasing memory strength of the semantic predicate.

In addition, however, changing some details across occurrences of the predicates should produce competition for associations between the changed details and the predicates. As each new fact is learned, the number of details associated with a predicate increases, thus producing interference among the set of learned details. Such interfering effects should have a negative effect on learning. Therefore, as the number of repetitions of the shared structure is increased, there should be initial facilitation of learning (due to predicate repetition) followed by interference in learning (due to competition for associations) (Hayes-Roth, in this volume).

In an experiment designed to test these hypotheses (Thorndyke, Note 1), subjects were presented n passages in succession (n=1, 2, 3, 4, or 8) that were different examples of the same general concept (e.g., passages about n different constellations), followed by a target passage for study and recall. Each sentence in the target passages had a corresponding sentence at the same serial position in all n training passages that bore a particular relationship to it. For example, suppose sentence 5 of the target passage was "This constellation was originally charted at Palomar Observatory." Then sentence 5 of all preceding constellation passages was one of three types. In the REPEATED condition, the entire sentence (predicate and detail) was repeated intact (i.e., "This constellation was originally charted at Palomar Observatory"). In the CHANGED condition, the predicate was identical, but the detail was changed for each of the n passages (e.g., "This constellation was originally charted at Mount Wilson Observatory" might be one of the n such prior sentences). In the UNRELATED condition, there was no similarity between the target sentence and the corresponding training sentences (e.g., "This constellation is part of a gaseous nebula" might be one such sentence).

The relationship of interest was how recall of a fact, both predicate and detail, would be influenced by the type of information transferred among passages about that fact and the number of prior exposures to the information. The results are shown in Figure 1. The "0" point on the abscissa is the mean of all target sentences in the UNRELATED condition. Note that for the REPEATED sentences, recall of both predicates and details increased with number of presentations, demonstrating the well-known effect of repetitions on learning. Similarly, recall of the constant predicate in the CHANGED condition (i.e., "This constellation was originally charted somewhere") increased over number of presentations, even though the detail associated with the predicate varied across passages. Thus, the practice effect obtained for the REPEATED sentences was also obtained for the repeated portion of the CHANGED sentences. Such selective facilitation of predicate learning has also been demonstrated in a retroaction paradigm (Bower, 1974).

On the other hand, recall of the CHANGED detail, that part of the sentence that varied across texts, was initially facilitated, then interfered with, and finally reached asymptote. Thus, prior training on the CHANGED predicates strengthened their memory representation and facilitated learning of the associated details until the interfering effects of competing associations produced decrements in recall of the details. This inverted U-shaped function demonstrating the combined effects of facilitation and interference during learning has been demonstrated with other types of experimental materials as well (Hayes-Roth, 1977).

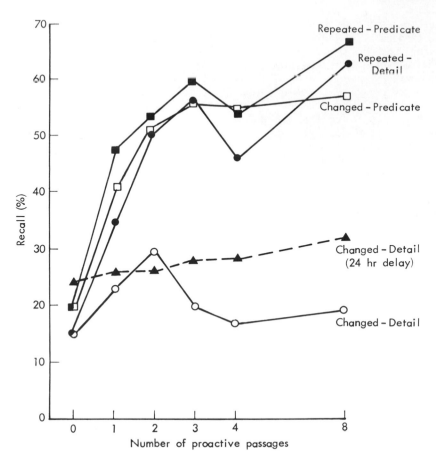

Figure 1. Free recall of facts from a text as a function of type and frequency of prior knowledge presented about the facts.

     In another experimental condition, it was found that delaying the presentation of the target passage for 24 hours after the training sequence produced no differences in recall of CHANGED details across number of prior proactive passages. That is, when training materials preceded the target materials by a long time interval, the degree of learning was independent of the number of prior presentations of the shared predicate. This result is shown by the dashed lines in Figure 1. Furthermore, for a given number of prior presentations of a predicate, less interference was produced by a 24-hour interval between training and target presentations than by immediately following the training material with the target material. The superiority of recall in the delay condition suggests that interference due to competing associations among related items can be eliminated completely by reducing the confusability between the training materials and the related target material to be recalled.

Conclusions

The results presented here of the influential nature of structural contexts on the learning of facts contained in the contexts may have important implications for the design of instructional texts and techniques. Some of these implications are described below, in the context of the experimental results reported here.

1. Knowledge of the structure of material can facilitate learning of the material. That is, advance knowledge of the context in which a fact will occur and the relevance of the fact will facilitate learning the fact. This suggests that effective teaching materials and procedures might emphasize the organizational and structural characteristics of the material to be learned. One might, for example, teach a subject domain in a top-down hierarchical fashion, by making explicit during initial exposures the general form or structural characteristics of the material to be presented, and by gradually increasing the degree of detail and specificity. Thus, initial learning would consist of acquisition of the appropriate general structure, while subsequent learning would require the acquisition of detailed facts to fill out the overall organizational framework. This presentation strategy has been termed "web teaching" (Norman, 1973). This instructional strategy might be implemented as both organizational and spatial phenomena: Material organized in a structure-sensitive manner might be presented with visual cues such as spatial organization and segmentation. Such a method would exploit the power of mental imagery as a storage and retrieval aid as well as utilizing optimal organizational characteristics. The use of structural information as an advanced organizer has been proposed elsewhere (Ausubel, 1963; Mayer & Greeno, 1972) and has been occasionally implemented with some success (Ward & Davis, 1939).

2. Making facts available that can be substituted for a to-be-learned fact interferes with learning. Such substitutions can consist of either new relationships among previously learned concepts, or details that share the same semantic predicate. Conversely, however, this interference can be minimized by instructional techniques that highlight the differences between the potentially confused facts. Such techniques might include (a) spacing the learning of the related facts over time, or (b) changing the surface features of the related information by embedding it in varying syntactic forms (Hayes-Roth, this volume). Both techniques appear to permit shared structures to be learned and transferred to new contexts advantageously while particular contexts remain differentiated.

Footnote

The research reported here was partially supported by Contract No. DAHC15-73-0181 from the Defense Advanced Projects Research Agency of the Department of Defense.

Reference Note

1. Thorndyke, P. Facilitating and interfering transfer effects in memory for narrative discourse. Paper presented at the meeting of the Psychonomic Society, St. Louis, 1976.

References

Ausubel, D. The psychology of meaningful verbal learning. New York: Grune & Stratton, 1963.

Bower, G. Selective facilitation and interference in retention of prose. Journal of Educational Psychology, 1974, 66, 1-8.

Frederiksen, C. Representing logical and semantic structure of knowledge acquired from discourse. Cognitive Psychology, 1975, 7, 371-458.

Hayes-Roth, B. The evolution of cognitive structures and processes. Psychological Review, 1977, 84, 260-278.

Hayes-Roth, B. Structurally integrated versus structurally segregated memory representations: Implications for the design of instructional materials. In this volume.

Kintsch, W. The representation of meaning in memory. Potomac, Md.: Erlbaum, 1974.

Mandler, J., & Johnson, N. Remembrance of things parsed: Story structure and recall. Cognitive Psychology, 1977, 9, 111-151.

Mayer, R., & Greeno, J. Structural differences between learning outcomes produced by different instructional methods. Journal of Educational Psychology, 1972, 63, 165-173.

Meyer, B. J. F. The organization of prose and its effects on memory. Amsterdam: North-Holland Publishing Co., 1975.

Norman, D. Memory, knowledge, and the answering of questions. In R. Solso (Ed.), Contemporary issues in cognitive psychology: The Loyola Symposium. Washington, D. C.: V. H. Winston, 1973.

Rumelhart, D. E. Notes on a schema for stories.   In D. G. Bobrow &
    A. M. Collins (Eds.), Representation and understanding. New York:
    Academic Press, 1975.

Thorndyke, P. Cognitive structures in comprehension and memory of
    narrative discourse. Cognitive Psychology, 1977, 9, 77-110.

van Dijk, T., & Kintsch, W.   Cognitive psychology   and   discourse:
    Recalling and summarizing stories. In W. Dressier (Ed.), Trends in
    text-linguistics. New York: deGruyter, 1977.

Ward, A., & Davis, R. Acquisition and retention of factual information
    in seventh-grade science during a semester of eighteen weeks.
    Journal of Educational Psychology, 1939, 30, 116-125.

ON REMEMBERING HOW TO GET THERE:
HOW WE MIGHT WANT SOMETHING LIKE A MAP

Keith Stenning
The University of Liverpool
Liverpool, England, U.K.

The hallmark of imagery, whether it is mental or externalized in some expressive medium, is that imagery is specific. It is the purpose of this paper to define a precise sense of specificity, to use this definition to redefine the issues between image and propositional theories of memory representations, and to present a report of an experiment which illustrates this approach to imagery.

I shall define specificity as a property of representation systems; for example, maps, rather than as a property of particular images; for example, the one-inch ordnance survey map of Liverpool. A representation system is specific with regard to some class of information if, for any state of affairs represented in the system, that class of information must be specified. Thus, maps are specific with regard to directional information such as right and left turnings, because for any junction represented on a map, that junction must be specified as a right or left turning relative to some major road. In this respect, maps contrast with descriptions couched in a language of the logical power of English. It is easy to describe a route in English without specifying whether turnings are to the right or to the left: "Go down the street to the library and turn over the bridge." English allows us to remain vague about spatial relations that maps insist that we specify. Note that specificity is not a property defined on particular representations: A particular English description of a route can specify spatial relations, but what makes maps specific is that certain relations must be specified in any map. In fact, a language of the logical power of English does not appear to be specific with regard to any class of information: We can always avoid specifying any piece of information about a state of affairs, even if at the expense of some periphrasis.

Spatial relations are not the only type of information whose specification image systems may force. Another example is provided by referential relations. If we diagram a world in which there are just three people, one short and two tall, one dark and two fair, we are forced to choose between two alternative distributions of these properties; or in a logician's terms, two models of the foregoing

101

description of the world. There can be one short dark person and two
tall fair ones, or there can be one short fair person, one tall fair
person, and one tall dark person. Again, English provides the logical
power to be vague about this choice, whereas diagrams do not.

This contrast is not merely one between symbolic and iconic systems
of representation;   there are artificial languages as well as sub-
languages of natural languages that are also specific with regard to
referential or spatial relations.   A language whose only referential
device is logical constants, paired in a one-to-one fashion with
referents, is also a representational system that is specific with
regard to referential information; any two facts about objects stated
in such a language determine whether they are facts about the same
objects or about different objects (see Stenning, in press).

With this much definition of specificity, let us turn to a
redefinition of some issues of representation. The debate between image
and propositional theories of human memory is an old one.   Recently,
Pylyshyn (1973)   and   others   have argued that the only viable
representations that we have for manipulating and   storing information
are classes of descriptions (e.g., sets of statements, data bases,
etc.), and that any subjective experience that we may have of
representations like our immediate sensory intake must be epiphenomenal
with regard to our ability to manipulate and store knowledge.   Other
recent work has attempted to establish that distinctively sensory
representations function as the basis for success at a variety of memory
tasks (e.g., Paivio, 1971). Kosslyn and Pomerantz (1977) have reviewed
evidence from several tasks that they argue is difficult to explain on
the basis of propositional representations. Both sides of this debate
focus on the question of how similar sensations are to memory
representations, and ask whether talk of images can be reduced to talk
of propositions or descriptions. Both make the assumption that to claim
that   knowledge   representations   are propositional is to make a
substantive claim about them. The sides differ as to whether they
believe the reduction can be performed, and whether the substantive
claim is correct. But descriptions couched in the propositions of
languages of the logical power countenanced by these authors have no
limitations in what they can represent or leave unrepresented.   The
propositionalist position should not be seen as a theory that might
reduce all talk of images to talk of descriptions, but rather as a
skeptical position.   The propositionalist is skeptical that anything
substantive can be said about the form of knowledge representations.

A propositionalist may place limitations on the language of
description that he countenances, but insofar as he argues for
descriptions and against images, he in no way limits the range of
possible representational systems.   As a skeptic, he places the onus
upon the imagist of demonstrating such limitations in the form of
demands that some mental representation makes for specific information.
Much of the enthusiasm for frames, scripts, plans, and schemata in the
literature can be seen as a response to the realization that

propositionalist claims are inherently skeptical about the possibility of saying anything interesting about the form of representation of human knowledge. These devices introduce specificity in the sense defined above; they contain variables that must be filled, if not by extrinsic information coming in from the world, then by "default" values supplied by the representer (Minsky, 1976).

The psychologist who takes an imagist position must find a type of image that is obligatorily specific with regard to certain information and must demonstrate that the representations people use in performing some task in fact illustrate just this specificity. For the most part, psychological work that has tried to argue for images has not made this attempt, but has, instead, correlated reports of the availability or vividness of people's experienced imagery with their success on a task (e.g., Paivio, 1971), or has varied instructions to "use imagery" and examined the effects of such instructions (e.g., Bower, 1970). Such an approach is necessarily open to the propositionalist criticism that it could be any feature common to things that people call imageable that leads to the observed correlations. Further, such an approach can tell us little about the nature or functioning of the representations used, except that they are accompanied by what people call mental images. A propositionalist who believes these images to be epiphenomenal will not be impressed.

The work reviewed by Kosslyn and Pomerantz (1977) provides stronger evidence for the functional involvement of representations that are specific in a variety of tasks. Kosslyn's own work on image size (Kosslyn, 1975) argues that the images his subjects employ are specific as to relative size, even though there is no reason why this should be particularly useful in the tasks studied. Shepard and his colleagues' work on "mental rotation" (see Shepard & Metzler, 1971) makes the point that there are no available models of rotation procedures that operate on propositional representations and still give the result that the time taken to rotate is linearly related to the angle through which it moved. This underlines the fact that the propositionalist position is skeptical rather than reductionist: It is not that there are available models of these tasks that operate on propositional representations, that is, models to which we could seek to "reduce" our talk about images. It is odd to talk of reduction before we have anything to reduce to, but it is perfectly sensible to maintain a skepticism about a scientific enterprise until it has produced some evidence for its direction.

In addition to the work arguing for images as representations in a wide variety of tasks, there is a considerable body of literature that specifically investigates people's knowledge of places (e.g., Lynch, 1960; Downs & Stea, 1973; Siegel & White, 1975). Some authors (e.g., Kaplan, 1973) have been careful to leave open whether people's knowledge of places take the form of cartographic maps, and they reserve the use of the term "cognitive maps" for this reason. Authors such as Hardwick, McIntyre, and Pick (1976) have argued for the map-like nature of children's and adults' knowledge of places.

All the studies mentioned so far either present physical images to
the subject, investigate knowledge acquired through acquaintance with
real places, or give explicit instructions to form mental images. The
present experiment sought to demonstrate the specificity of mental
representations by presenting only verbal information without
instructions as to image, and then looking for evidence of subjects'
preference for memory representations of spatial information that
exhibit a specificity in common with mapping systems. Remembering a set
of verbal directions in order to follow an unknown route is a common
enough task, and calls on a part of our fundamental ability to get
around in the world. It is also a task that elicits reports of imagery
from many people. It is possible to describe routes in ways that differ
only in that a junction is described as "to the left," "to the right,"
or in an unspecified direction: "Go along the street until you reach
the Post Office and then turn

```
               | right |
               |   φ   |
               | left  |
```

up the hill." I shall refer to these three forms of description as R
(for right), L (for left), and V (for vague).

The relations between the meanings of these three descriptions is
shown in the left half of Figure 1, both as a hierarchy of distinctions
and as a matrix of features. In order to be able to relate "turn right"
and "turn left" to the unmodified verb "turn," both must be seen as
containing specifiers of direction. Notice that in such a
representation, R and L descriptions share one more feature with each
other than either does with V descriptions. On the basis of such a
representation, we would expect R and L to be more confusable with each
other than either is with V.

The relations between V, R, and L, as represented in a mapping
system, are shown in the right half of Figure 1. Since in a map any
turn off a route must be specified as to the right or to the left with
respect to the through road, V, R, and L descriptions must all lead to
directional specifications. In the case of V descriptions, this
direction value will be a default value, whereas for R and L, it will be
extrinsic information. Such a representation does not allow a
prediction of the relative similarity, and therefore confusability, of
V, R, and L, since all share one feature and differ in another.
However, the directional dimension is primary to this medium or
representation, and it is reasonable to predict that it will be more
accurately preserved than the "default/extrinsic" dimension. If this is
the case, V should be more confusable with R and with L than either R or
L are with each other. This is precisely the opposite prediction than
that expected if these distinctions are structured as descriptions, and
so it is possible to investigate the nature of subjects' memory
representation of this information by examining patterns of confusions
between the three forms and the relative accuracies with which features
are preserved in memory.

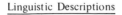

Linguistic Descriptions   Mapping Systems

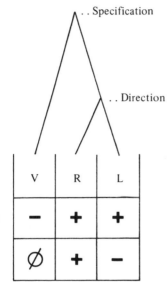

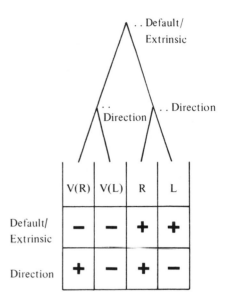

Specification:

    − = unspecified

    + = specified

Direction:

    − = left

    + = right

    φ = not classified on
        this feature

Default/Extrinsic:

    − = information is default
        value added by S to
        construct representation

    + = information is an extrin-
        sic value derived from
        route description

Direction:

    − = junction is to the left
        in representation

    + = junction is to the right
        in representation

Figure 1. Two feature representations for route choice points.

Method

Thirty subjects were given written sets of directions along hypothetical routes that contained twelve "choice points" that could be naturally described in the three ways illustrated above. They were instructed to study the directions just as though they were going to have to follow them, and were given as much time as they felt they needed to do this. They were told that they would have to perform a recall of the route, and would subsequently make some recognition judgments that would be presented as follows.

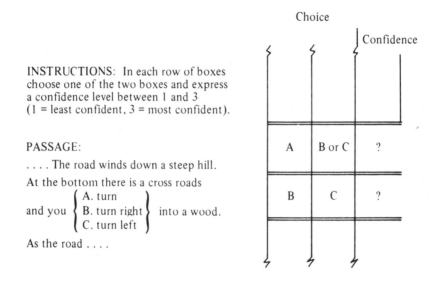

Figure 2. An example section from the recognition test.

The passage of directions was typed out with three forms of description marked as alternatives at each choice point. Two questions were presented for each of these choice points, which asked the subject to choose between different combinations of the three numbered alternatives and to express a confidence in the answer given. Figure 2 shows an example of one choice point and its associated questions as they were presented for recognition. Subjects were instructed that they must answer all such questions; if they thought both alternative answers to a question were incorrect, they were told to guess which was more likely.

FREQUENCIES OF FIRST CHOICE BETWEEN V, R & L.

Stimulus Presented

	V	R	L	
V	184	42	40	266
R	34	174	15	223
L	22	24	185	231
	240	240	240	720

First Choice At Recognition

Confusions:
$\underline{V}$ with $\underline{R}$ & $\underline{R}$ with $\underline{V}$ = 76
$\underline{V}$ with $\underline{L}$ & $\underline{L}$ with $\underline{V}$ = 62
$\underline{R}$ with $\underline{L}$ & $\underline{L}$ with $\underline{R}$ = 39

Accuracies:
$\underline{P}$ correct when presented $\underline{V}$ = .77
$\underline{P}$ correct when presented $\underline{R}$ = .73
$\underline{P}$ correct when presented $\underline{R}$ = .77

FREQUENCIES OF JUDGMENTS OF FEATURES

Answers to question "Was junction $\underline{V}$ ($\underline{Sp}^-$) or was it $\underline{R}$ or $\underline{L}$ ($\underline{Sp}^+$)?"

Stimulus Presented

	Sp^-	Sp^+	
Sp^-	184	82	
Sp^+	56	398	
	240	480	

Recognition Response

$\underline{P}$ correct = .80

Answers to question "Was junction $\underline{R}$ or $\underline{L}$?"

Stimulus Presented

	R	L	
R	203	27	230
L	37	213	250
	240	240	480

Recognition Response

$\underline{P}$ correct = .87

Figure 3. Recognition judgments analyzed by target preferred and by feature preferences.

Subjects were presented with two such passages, two recall tests, and two recognition tests. The order of presentation of the passages was counterbalanced. Each subject was presented with four choice points in form R, four in form L, and four in form V in each passage. All choice points were obtained by permuting the forms in a Latin Square.

Results and Discussion

In this brief report, I will concentrate on the results of the recognition tests that are tabulated in Figure 3. From the table of "first choices" (the form of description that the subject thought was most likely to have occurred in the passage that he read), we can compute the subjects' accuracy in each of the three presentation conditions averaged across all choice points, and the number of confusions between all possible pairs of stimuli and responses. Although the probabilities of correct recognition of V, R, and L are essentially identical (.74, .70, and .74), the numbers of confusions between V and R and V and L are greater than the number of confusions between R and L (76 and 62 are both greater than 30).[1] From the separate tables for confusions between features (the bottom half of Figure 3), we can see that the probability that the direction feature is maintained correctly in memory is greater than the probability that the specification feature is correct (.87 > .80).[2] This pattern of confusions and feature accuracy is exactly what distinguishes the structure of the map representation from the semantic structure of the English descriptions, and suggests that subjects freely choose to construct a map-like representation of a route when given a description of the route, and that they do this at least in part by supplying default specifications for spatial relations that are not supplied in the description.

It should be remembered that this result does not support the view that subjects' representation of this information is just a map. Subjects are quite good at maintaining the information represented by the feature "default/extrinsic." The question arises how this information is represented in memory. Here, the present analysis can say very little. It appears that "right" is more often chosen as a default than "left": When V is presented, R is more often responded than L (34 R:22 L), even though when R or L is presented, there is a bias among confusion responses toward L and against R (24 L:15 R). There are many other ways of analyzing these data, as well as the recall data, which cannot be included here. I would like to offer this brief report as an example of an approach to a very general question of the demands that a form of representation makes for the specification of information, and as providing some evidence (in a particular case) that subjects choose an image representation in a qualified but precise sense of that term.

Footnotes

1. Sign tests for the significance of these differences show the following results:

The number of VR confusions is significantly greater than the number of RL confusions. (By subjects $p < .001$, by items $p < .025$). The number of VL confusions is significantly greater than the number of RL confusions. (By subjects $p < .032$, by items $p < .008$).

2. Sign tests for the significance of this difference showed that Pcorrect R/L is greater than Pcorrect Sp-/Sp+. (By subjects $p < .001$, by items $p < .002$).

References

Bower, G. The analysis of a mnemonic device. American Scientist, 1970, 58, 496-510.

Downs, R. M., & Stea, D. (Eds.), Image and environment. Chicago: Aldine, 1973.

Hardwick, D. A., McIntyre, C. W., & Pick, H. L. The content and manipulation of cognitive maps in children and adults. Monographs of the Society for Research in Child Development, 1976, 41(3, Serial No. 166).

Kaplan, S. Cognitive maps in perception and thought. In R. M. Downs & D. Stea (Eds.), Image and environment. Chicago: Aldine, 1973.

Kosslyn, S. M. Information representation in visual images. Cognitive Psychology, 1975, 7, 341-370.

Kosslyn, S. M., & Pomerantz, J. R. Imagery, propositions and the form of internal representations. Cognitive Psychology, 1977, 9(1), 52-76.

Lynch, K. The image of the city. Cambridge, MA: MIT Press, 1960.

Minsky, M. A. A framework for representing knowledge. In P. H. Winston (Ed.), The psychology of computer vision. New York: McGraw-Hill, 1975.

Paivio, A. Imagery and verbal processes. New York: Holt, Rinehart & Winston, 1971.

Pylyshyn, Z. W. What the mind's eye tells the mind's brain: A critique
    of mental imagery. Psychological Bulletin, 1973, 80, 1-24.

Shepard, R. N., & Metzler, J. Mental rotation of three-dimensional
    objects. Science, 1971, 171, 701-703.

Siegel, A. W.,   &   White, S. H.   The   development   of   spatial
    representations of large-scale environments. In H. W. Reese (Ed.),
    Advances in child development (Vol.   10).   New York: Academic
    Press, 1975.

Stenning, K. Anaphora as an approach to pragmatics.   In M. Halle,
    G. A. Miller   &   J. Bresnan   (Eds.),   Linguistic   theory   and
    psychological reality. Cambridge, MA: MIT Press, in press.

SOME REFLECTIONS CONCERNING THE ROLE OF IMAGERY IN
MEMORY AND LEARNING PROCESSES

Cesare Cornoldi
University of Padova
Padova, Italy

The purpose of this report will be to consider some problems involved in research on the role of imagery in memory and to evaluate the implications of imagery research for the learning and teaching processes. In particular, some controversial points in this field will be considered with respect to some experimental results we have obtained at the Psychology Institute of Padova.

Research on imagery has been particularly concerned with the relationship between imagery processes and memory. Such research can be grossly differentiated according to whether the approach is neomentalistic in the Paivio (1975) sense, or the approach is strictly cognitive. The difference between these two approaches is especially apparent in the choice of the dependent variable, which is imagery itself within the cognitive approach versus memory performance within the neomentalistic approach. The cognitive approach is oriented toward a thorough analysis of the structure, properties and functions of images, and suggests the necessity of analyzing the nature of images with respect to their development and differentiation. The neomentalistic approach considers imagery an intervening, substantially unitary, variable that is operationally definable in three ways: (a) on the basis of the stimulus characteristics (visual and high imagery stimuli have a great probability to activate imagery processes); (b) on the basis of the instructions given to the subject to use imagery strategies; and (c) on the basis of individual differences in imagery, identified by either self-evaluation or objective tasks (Paivio, 1975). The neomentalistic approach has clearly shown that imagery facilitates the acquisition and retention of stimulus material, that such effects depend on the nature of the task (e.g., Begg & Paivio, 1969; Paivio, Smythe, & Yuille, 1968; Sheehan, 1972), and that imagery has clear instructional implications (Atkinson, 1975).

Although research in this field was initially focused on adult memory performance, similar results were sometimes observed with children (e.g., Levin, Hawkins, Kerst, & Guttmann, 1974; Smirnov, 1973). For example, we have selected 24 words representing three different levels of imagery value I: high (I > 5.63), medium (5.62 > I

> 4.39), and low (4.38 > I), from a sample of commonly used words rated
on a seven-point imagery scale by 40 fifth grade children (Girardi,
1973-74). The words were presented (in a random order that varied for
every two subjects) to 48 fifth grade children in a four-trial free
recall task. Results which are represented in Figure 1 showed
significant effects of trials and of imagery value, repeating the same
trends which were observed in an experiment that has been conducted with
adults following the same procedures (Cornoldi, 1976).

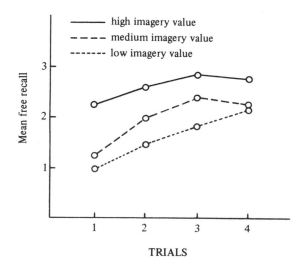

Figure 1. Mean free recall by fifth-grade children of nouns varying in imagery value.

Theoretically, it seems more consistent to assume that imagery
processes should be especially useful in the case of children's memory.
In fact, imagery codes should have prior and more complete development
than verbal code, as is asserted in many genetic theories, e.g., by
Blonski (Smirnov, 1973), Bruner (Bruner, Olver & Greenfield, 1966) and
Piaget (Piaget & Inhelder, 1966). Nevertheless, many experimental
results seem to indicate the opposite trend, with imagery negatively
affecting children's memory while simultaneously facilitating adults'
memory (e.g., Milgram, 1967; Rohwer, 1970). These results, however,
must be evaluated by considering several possible explanations: (a) the
typical verbal test modality that does not directly examine information
imaginally encoded; (b) the nature of the paired-associate paradigm,
which is essentially verbal and can be also very unnatural for children;
(c) the extrinsic relation that sometimes ties verbal and pictorial
materials; and (d) the difficulty that a child may experience in moving
from one code to the other one. A failure in paired-associate tasks

could be determined by translation difficulties rather than by a loss of the imaginally coded information or an inability to retrieve such information. For example, in situations where pictorial materials accompany verbal items, children sometimes appear to pay more attention to pictorial materials, but they are tested only with the verbal stimuli, thus putting them at a disadvantage. When the test is verbal, only specific, adequate pictorial accompaniment favors retention, as Lesgold, Levin, Shimron and Guttmann (1975) have shown for children's prose learning.

Another point that is puzzling and has clear instructional implications, involves the influence of imagery on long-term retention. Some researchers who have analyzed the retention of imaginally coded stimuli after long delays, have argued that there was no imagery advantage beyond that achieved in initial acquisition, and in some cases there was even a higher rate of loss (e.g., Baranov, quoted in Smirnov, 1973; Hasher, Riebman, & Wren, 1976; Postman & Burns, 1973). Some of these results may be explained by the above-mentioned considerations. Moreover, observing that high imagery items only maintain (either totally, or partially) an initial acquisition advantage does not deny the fact - which is practically most relevant - that, when time devoted to the learning of some material is held constant, imagery processes produce higher long-term retention.

It seems possible to isolate situations where there is a specific interaction between imagery processing and delay of the retention test, i.e., imagery effects may sometimes be more evident after long retention intervals than after short intervals. We observed such a significant interaction by visually or verbally presenting a narrative passage to fifth grade children and testing their retention after one or 90 days. Visual-pictorial presentation was in the form of a silent movie, while verbal presentation, involved oral presentation by a teacher. The passage told the story of a black child who steals a pineapple in a tropical garden. It was chosen because of its capacity to maintain the attention of the children. Verbal recall of children was quantified by dividing the story in 16 blocks and assigning a value of 0-3 for each story segment based upon the completeness of recall (this evaluation appeared highly reliable, since the judge's scores for each subject highly correlated, $r = .99$, with the scores assigned by a control judge). Mean recall scores for each group are represented in Figure 2. Variance analysis revealed a significant effect of time interval and a significant interaction; nevertheless, no effect of modality of presentation was observed.

These results suggest that different kinds of materials can have different effects on memory, and that it can sometimes be useful to provide both verbal and pictorial representations. With respect to Paivio's (1971) dual-encoding, and in our opinion, such a presentation should also promote the establishment of connections between the two types of representations and thus should aid the individual in the task of translating the information between representations (codes).

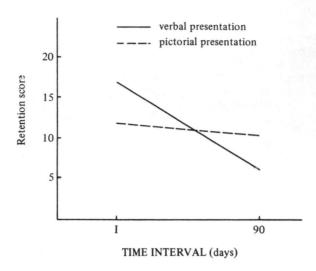

Figure 2. Mean recall score for fifth-grade children of a visually or verbally presented story after 1 or 90 days.

Furthermore, in a situation with verbal and pictorial presentation and the usual verbal test, it is useful to analyze whether the order of presentation (verbal-pictorial versus pictorial-verbal) affects performance. With children 9-10 years old, Davies, Milne, and Glennie (1973) observed that a double presentation of words did not always favour retention and that a pictorial-verbal presentation order yielded superior retention performance compared to a verbal-pictorial order. In a comparison between the effects of a talking didactic picture presenting concepts of temperature and the effects of a corresponding verbal lesson, Funari, Guarda, and Varin (1970) observed the opposite trend. Paivio and Csapo's (1973) research with adults and a repetition of Davies's experiment with adults, (Negrini, 1975-76) showed that presentation order does not affect performance. This difference between adults and children could be effectively due to a developmental trend, but it could also be due to the nature of the material. The Funari et. al. film was difficult to understand immediately, whereas the Davies et al. pictorial materials probably led to immediate verbal labeling. These two characteristics were not present in our narrative story. This story was presented to four other groups of fifth grade children, either in the pictorial-verbal order or in opposite order, maintaining the same procedure of the preceding experiment. Analysis of variance showed only a time effect, i.e., lower recall scores after 90 days; a slight advantage of verbal-visual presentation was not significant. Comparison between the performance with only one modality of presentation of the preceding experiment and the present performance (see Figure 3) revealed that a double presentation favours retention and prevents the considerable long-term forgetting that was observed in the single verbal presentation condition. In light of this result, we conclude that joint verbal and visual presentation creates conditions for a strong memory representation of school-related information. This kind of dual presentation could be inserted in a more general program that would attempt to utilize both verbal and imagery processes, and promote the development of skills for translation across memory codes or representations. With regard to the influence of presentation order on memory performance, it must be observed that the initial representation is not simply added to the second representation, but also offer a context for the processing of the subsequently presented material. Different results may be explained by evaluating the comprehension and degree of elaboration respectively required by the initial and subsequently presented material. For example, Royer and Cable (1975) have shown that concrete, easily understood material leads to positive transfer in the learning of more difficult, abstract material. If both verbally and pictorially presented materials are easily understandable, as in the case of our story, presentation order should not be particularly important.

The present discussion suggests that it is necessary to analyze carefully the nature of the materials and of the processes involved in different groups of subjects. For example, with respect to visual stimuli, Zinchenko (see Zaporozhets & Zinchenko, 1966) observed that 3-year-old children are not able to analyze adequately or recognize schematic visual stimuli, whereas they are successful with a meaningful picture. In some pilot research, we have observed that recognition memory of first grade children for random shapes (Attneave & Arnoult, 1956) is superior when the shapes are simple (six points) rather than complex (24 points), whereas for third grade children, there are no differences in performance, and fifth grade children are more accurate on the complex shapes.

Another problem in this area that we can discuss in light of our own data involves the identification of (possible) individual differences in imagery. It has been suggested that subjects with learning disabilities have visual abilities (e.g., Guyer & Friedman, 1975), so that it would be suitable to individuate such subjects and to plan particular learning programs for them. (A particular case of this perspective is represented by individuals suffering brain damage in only one hemisphere.) Nevertheless, it appears difficult to obtain valid (more than reliable) imagery measures, and attempts at measuring imagery, both by self-evaluation and performance tests, produce ambiguous results. For example, in the free recall experiment discussed earlier, the children were also given two imagery tests: an adaptation of the self-evaluation questionnaire VVIQ (Marks, 1973), where the items were presented only with open eyes, and the Gottschaldt test, Form A (Thurstone, 1944), which Di Vesta, Ingersoll, and Sunshine (1971) have shown to be a good imagery test. If tested imagery ability and imagery effects associated with high imagery words reflect the same mental

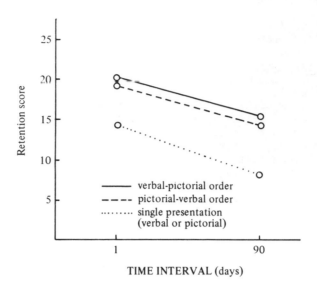

Figure 3. Mean story recall score for fifth-grade children as a function of modality of presentation and retention interval.

process, a positive correlation should be found between imagery test scores and high-low word imagery differences in recall. The results did not confirm this expectation, with all correlations slightly (but not significantly) negative.

In conclusion, the ncomentalistic approach, which has been followed in imagery research, has offered many important results. Nevertheless, it now appears necessary to have a more cognitively oriented analysis of imagery. The ambiguous results of research on certain problems is due to the unsatisfactory knowledge of what images and imagery are. Under the name of imagery, many entities are subsumed that are diverse and whose empirical issues are sometimes different. In fact, there are differences in the stimulus contexts that are used, in the imagery abilities that are involved, in the imagery strategies, and in the opinion that a subject has of his own images, as is shown by variations observed in the evaluation of image latencies (from about a half-second to some seconds), and in self-evaluation questionnaires. Therefore, it appears not only useful to consider imagery as an intervening variable, but also necessary to analyze in the most direct way imagery processes and representations, in order to elucidate their nature, developmental trends, components, specifications, relations, and peculiarities, with respect to verbal processes. As an example, consider the case of the processing and retention of a complex visual stimulus. In the analysis of this situation, I think we should take into account the genetic trend that progressively develops from elementary analysis abilities through more subtle discrimination-retention capacities, the development of repertory of visual patterns or schemata that help the subject in the analysis of visual stimuli, and the modality of the interactions between the iconic representations and either the representation of other kinds of sensory-motor informations, or the first forms of verbal language. Furthermore, we should study the components that constitute these visual schemata, and the rules of use and of hierarchical organization of the schemata, the capacity of analysis of the visual-imaginal system, and whether (and how) different processes (imaginal versus verbal) correspond to different formats of representation in semantic memory.

Footnotes

1. Assistants in this research included A. Bonetti, P. Girardi, and T. Pravadelli.

References

Atkinson, R. C. Mnemotechnics in second-language learning. American Psychologist, 1975, 30, 821-828.

Attneave, F. & Arnoult, M. The quantitative study of shape and pattern perception. Psychological Bulletin, 1956, 53, 452-471.

Begg, I., & Paivio, A. Concreteness and imagery in sentence meaning. Journal of Verbal Learning and Verbal Behavior, 1969, 8, 821-827.

Bruner, J. S., Olver, R. R., & Greenfield, P. M. Studies in cognitive growth. New York: Wiley, 1966.

Cornoldi, C. Memoria e immaginazione. Padova: Patron, 1976.

Davies, G. M., Milne, J. E., & Glennie, B. J. On the significance of "double encoding" for the superior recall of pictures to names. Quarterly Journal of Experimental Psychology, 1973, 25, 413-423.

DiVesta, F. J., Ingersoll, G., & Sunshine, P. A. A factor analysis of imagery tests. Journal of Verbal Learning and Verbal Behavior, 1971, 10, 471-479.

Funari, F., Guarda, G., & Varin, D. Studio comparato sull'apprendimento mediante film didattico e lezione. Ikon, 1970, 20(74), 59-79.

Girardi, A. P. Calcolo del valore d'immagine di 258 parole valutate da bambini di dieci anni. Tesi di Laurea, Facolta di Magistero, Anno Accademico 1973-74.

Guyer, B. L., & Friedman, M. P. Hemispheric processing and cognitive styles in learning-disabled and normal children. Child Development, 1975, 46, 658-668.

Hasher, L., Ricbman, B., & Wren, F. Imagery and the retention of free-recall learning. Journal of Experimental Psychology: Human Learning and Memory, 1976, 2, 172-181.

Lesgold, A. M., Levin, J. R., Shimron, J., & Guttmann, J. Pictures and young children's learning from oral prose. Journal of Educational Psychology, 1975, 67, 636-642.

Levin, J. R., Hawkins, P., Kerst,S. M., & Guttmann, J. Individual differences in learning from pictures and words: The development and application of an instrument. Journal of Educational Psychology, 1974, 66, 296-303.

Marks, D. F. Visual imagery differences in the recall of pictures. British Journal of Psychology, 1973, 64, 17-24.

Milgram, N. A. Verbal context versus visual compound in paired-associated learning by children. Journal of Experimental Child Psychology, 1967, 5, 597-603.

Negrini, R. Ipotesi della dopia codifica: Un controllo sperimentale del recupero, dei disegni e nomi compiuto con songetti adulti. Tesi de Laurea, Facolta di Magistero dell'universita di Padova, Anno Academico 1975-76.

Paivio, A. Imagery and verbal processes. New York: Holt, 1971.

Paivio, A. Neomentalism. Canadian Journal of Psychology, 1975, 29, 263-291.

Paivio, A., & Csapo, K. Picture superiority in free recall: Imagery or dual coding? Cognitive Psychology, 1973, 5, 1976-206.

Paivio, A., Smythe, P. C., & Yuille, J. C. Imagery versus meaningfulness of nouns in paired-associate learning. Canadian Journal of Psychology, 1968, 22, 427-441.

Piaget, J., & Inhelder, B. L'image mental chez l'enfant. Paris: Presses Universitaires de France, 1966.

Postman, L., & Burns, S. Experimental analysis of coding processes. Memory and Cognition, 1973, 1, 503-507.

Rohwer, W. D., Jr. Images and pictures in children learning: Research results and instructional implications. In H. W. Reese (Chm.), Imagery in children's learning: A symposium. Psychological Bulletin, 1970, 73, 393-403.

Royer, J. M., & Cable, G. W.   Facilitated   learning   in   connected discourse. Journal of Educational Psychology, 1975, 67, 116-123.

Sheehan, P. W. A functional analysis of the role of visual imagery in unexpected recall.   In P.   W. Sheehan (Ed.), The functions and nature of imagery. New York: Academic Press, 1972.

Smirnov, A. A. Problems of the psychology of memory., (English translation).   New   York: Plenum Press, 1973. (Originally published, Problemy Psikhologii Pamyati, Moscow, 1966)

Thurstone, L. L. A factorial study of perception. Chicago: University Press, 1944.

Zaporozhets, A. V., & Zinchenko, V. P.   Development   of   perceptual activity and formation of a sensory image in the child. In Psychological Research in U.S.S.R. Moscow: Progress Publishers, 1966, 393-421.

Section III

PERCEPTUAL AND MEMORY PROCESSES IN READING

     Levy's invited paper gives a good outline of earlier work on the
role of phonological coding processes in reading and then presents
evidence from phonological suppression experiments that phonological
codes need to be generated in the course of reading if anything other
than vague gist is to be remembered from the text.   The experiments,
combined with other recent work cited by Levy, provide a new level of
understanding of the role of visual vs. verbal codes in reading.   The
traditional question has been, "Does one need to access verbal codes to
apprehend the meaning of a word that is seen?" We can now attend to a
more useful question: "Which comprehension processes depend upon verbal
codes?"

     There are four papers on individual differences in word reading
skills that follow Levy's paper. All are, to some extent, complements
to her paper, in that they look at individual differences in simple word
encoding or recognition processes. The four papers can be located on a
continuum of differential support for the claim that phonological
encoding ability is what distinguishes the more-skilled reader.
Frederiksen's paper is closest to the positive end of that continuum,
while the remaining papers are a bit more neutral. He offers detailed
analyses of relatively complex experiments that tend to show that
less-skilled high-school readers are slower on tasks such as lexicality
judgments - but only in circumstances that seem to require phonological
evidence.

     In a paper that is very compatible with Frederiksen's,
Scheerer-Neumann shows that poor readers are less sensitive to subword
structure than are better readers.   If one accepts the Frederiksen
interpretation that phonological coding efficiency is the primary
distinguisher of the better reader, there is still work left to do in
explaining the Scheerer-Neumann finding. Similarly, there is work to be
done to try to tie in the findings of Rayner and Posnansky that word
recognition progresses with age (expertise?) from a letter-by-letter
process to a more wholistic one.

     The McClelland and Jackson paper offers an alternative to
Frederiksen's theoretical analysis.   They claim that existing data,
especially theirs, suggests that a very general memory access capability

121

is more efficient in better readers. They suggest that all (verbal) memory accesses are faster in better readers, not just phonological code access. Their paper is also unique among the four in comparing above-average to average adult readers; the others use children ranging from first grade (age 6) to high school (ages 14 to 18).

The remaining three papers do not tie as directly to the issues raised thus far. Jarvella, in the latest of a series of reports on this topic, explores the circumstances that cause direct memory for the wording of discourse to begin fading after a given clause is processed.

Farnham-Diggory's paper studies performance in two tasks that are thought to be good predictors of reading readiness. The paper brings to mind Frijda's suggestions that comprehension will require general problem solving skills as well as specific knowledge and specific perceptual skills. It also uses a methodology very similar to that used by Snow's paper in a later section. The hemispheric asymmetry study of Davidoff, Cone, and Scully, which concludes this section, seems to demonstrate that learning to read is associated with an extremely strong general change in the organization of the brain, presumably more of a software than a hardware nature.

SPEECH PROCESSING DURING READING

Betty Ann Levy
McMaster University
Hamilton, Ontario, Canada

Even for Huey (1908), whose insights into reading still guide modern research, confusion surrounded the role played by speech processing during reading. While he claimed, "There can be little doubt that the main meaning comes to consciousness only with the beginning of the sentence utterance, and the reader does not feel he has the complete sense until he has spoken it" (p. 147), he also admitted that "Purely visual reading is quite possible, theoretically" (p. 117). Why do we so frequently find ourselves subvocalizing while we read, if we can read in a purely visual manner? The focus of this paper will be on the function served by speech processing while reading, and on where in information processing models such speech recoding mechanisms should be located.

The paper is divided into four main sections. The first section summarizes evidence suggesting that speech recoding is necessary for lexical access. The second section offers support for the view that speech recoding is useful for memory during comprehension. The third section considers situations where comprehension may occur without speech recoding, and the final section includes a discussion of reading models, with some closing comments on instruction. Throughout the paper, both speech recoding and reading have been used as very general terms. Reading has been equated with the visual processing of language. Whether the evidence discussed will prove to be relevant to 'real' reading is unknown. Speech recoding includes all "transformations of printed words into any type of speech based code, whether it be articulatory, acoustic, auditory imagery, or a more abstract code" (Kleiman, 1975, p. 323). Since there is little evidence as to which of these is most appropriate for the research to be discussed, use of the general term avoids prejudging such issues.

Figure 1 is Copyright 1975 by Academic Press, Inc.; Figures 2, 3, and 7 are Copyright 1977 by Academic Press, Inc. All were reproduced by permission.

Speech Recoding During Lexical Access

Early evidence from studies of short-term memory and word recognition pointed to a need for speech recoding in accessing an item in the mental lexicon. It was often assumed that short-term memory was a phonemic store, which held language signals until they made contact with their long-term semantic representations. Thus, visually presented language was converted to a phonemic form, by overt or covert articulation, for further processing into memory. Five types of evidence supported this position. First, tachistoscopically presented arrays of letters were largely forgotten 250-500 msec following presentation, suggesting that visual representations fade very rapidly from memory (Sperling, 1960). Second, errors observed in short-term recall resembled those found in listening, even for visually presented lists, leading to the conclusion that visual events were phonemically encoded in short-term memory (Conrad, 1964). Third, the last few items were better retained if they were presented auditorily rather than visually (Murdock, 1967). One explanation was that auditory items were compatible with the short-term memory code, but visual items required additional processing to transform them to a phonemic form. A further piece of evidence was the strong correlation between recallability and loudness of the vocalization (silent to whispered to loud reading; Murray, 1965). It appeared that enhancing translation to a speech code improved the retention of visual speech. A final supporting result was that visual recall was markedly reduced when speech recoding was suppressed, by asking subjects to repeat an irrelevant syllable during the list presentation. Auditory recall was unaffected under these conditions (Levy, 1971; Peterson & Johnson, 1971). Together, these five phenomena suggested that visually presented language is rapidly forgotten unless it is converted to a speech code. The stronger claim made was that this phonemic conversion was a necessary step, since short-term memory precedes long-term semantic analysis.

Further supporting evidence came from studies of word identification, where the issue was whether reading consisted of an additional grapheme to phoneme conversion stage added to the mechanisms used in listening comprehension. Three types of evidence favored this view. First, in some visual identification tasks, response times increased with increasing number of syllables, even when the number of letters per word was constant (Ericksen, Pollack, & Montague, 1970; Klapp, 1971). This finding could indicate that the visual items were translated to a phonemic form which took longer the more syllables involved. However, since a syllable length effect was not observed in other visual tasks, a strategy rather than a necessary process may be involved (Klapp, Anderson, & Berrian, 1973; Johnson, 1975; Theios & Muise, 1976). Second, in a lexical decision task where subjects must decide whether an item is or is not a word, decision times are slower when the nonwords sound like real words, such as "brane" (Meyer & Ruddy, Note 1; Rubenstein, Lewis & Rubenstein, 1971). The idea here was that the phonemic similarity with a real word should have influenced rejection time for nonwords only if phonemic translation of the graphemic display had occurred. Third, CVC trigrams take longer to classify as nonwords than CCC trigrams, perhaps because they are pronounceable and are thus processed beyond the phonemic stage. While this accumulated evidence from word recognition and short-term memory may be taken to indicate that phonemic translation often occurs during visual processing, it cannot support the stronger claim that lexical access can only be achieved via speech recoding. Other evidence argues against this stronger claim.

In both the short-term memory and word recognition literature, evidence is available which suggests that phonemic translation can be bypassed, without failure in comprehension. Kroll, Parks, Parkinson, Beiber, and Johnson (1970) asked subjects to shadow auditorily presented letters, while an auditory or a visual memory letter was being presented. The auditory shadowing task was used to prevent speech recoding of the visual letters, and to prevent auditory rehearsal. Even 30 sec following presentation, visual memory letters were better retained than auditory letters. Since speech processing had been disrupted by shadowing, a speech-based, short-term memory was not needed for the long-term retention of visual items in this case. Further, Warrington and Shallice (1969) described a patient whose auditory digit span was reliably only a digit or two, while his long-term memory was quite normal. This patient could not have been using a phonemic short-term memory from which to access long-term memory locations. Finally, Conrad (1970, 1971) demonstrated that some deaf children do not phonemically recode visually presented language, yet their retention is unharmed for both lists and prose passages. The sequential stage model, with a phonemic short-term memory preceding semantic long-term memory, could not handle results such as those described above, thus opening the way for memory theorists to adopt more flexible processing systems (Craik & Lockhart, 1972; Baddeley & Hitch, 1974).

A case against the necessity of phonemic recoding for comprehension was also made in the literature on reading. First, since naming times appeared to be about 200 msec longer than lexical decision times, it seemed unreasonable to suppose that naming preceded lexical access (Theios & Muise, 1976). One possible problem with this comparison is that naming times also include time to program a verbal response, which may increase latency. Second, studies of misspellings indicate that both Greek and American subjects read more slowly, even when the misspellings do not alter the underlying phonemic translations (Bower, 1970; Theios & Muise, 1976). If grapheme-to-phoneme conversion had been used, these readers should not have been adversely affected, since this conversion was unambiguous and yielded a correct phonemic transcription of the passage. A third finding was that judgments about the semantic acceptability of a phrase were not slowed down when that phrase sounded sensible (e.g., tie the not; Baron, 1973). It appears then that a phonemic representation was not consulted in making this meaning decision. Fourth, Kleiman (1975) demonstrated that suppressing speech recoding slowed decision times for phonemic judgments more than for semantic judgments. If phonemic recoding preceded meaning access, the semantic and phonemic judgments should have been equally affected. Also, Green and Shallice (1976) demonstrated that misspellings affected semantic decisions more than phonological ones, suggesting an influence of the visual display beyond the phoneme stage. They further demonstrated that semantic judgments are unaffected by syllabic length, as would have been expected if graphemes were first converted to a phonemic code before being passed on to the semantic analyzers. A final source of evidence comes from work with phonemic dyslexic patients. These patients make visual and/or semantic errors when reading words, but phonemic confusions are rarely observed (Marshall & Newcombe, 1966; Shallice & Warrington, 1975). These dyslexics are also unable to read aloud orthographically acceptable nonwords and are not affected by the homophonic similarity of nonwords to real words in a lexical decision task (Patterson & Marcel, 1977). These latter findings suggest that the patients are unable to make grapheme to phoneme conversions, while the error data suggest that their reading represents visual to semantic processing, without an intervening phonemic stage. Together, these six sources of evidence argue against the view that visual signals must be converted to a speech format in order to gain access to meaning.

Speech Recoding for Memory and Comprehension

The previous section indicated that while speech recoding sometimes occurs during visual processing, it is not necessary for lexical access. However, other roles for speech recoding in the course of word processing need still to be considered. A common claim is that the speech code is a useful format in which to hold items until the entire string can be comprehended (Conrad, 1972; Norman, 1972). After a detailed review of the literature on speech recoding, Conrad (1972) concluded that speech may well be the best possible form for remembering words, and that "reading is most certainly possible with no phonology involved at all, but that with phonology it is great deal easier" (p. 237). The ease would arise from better retention of words until comprehension had occurred. Supporting evidence for this position has recently been provided with both fluent and beginning readers.

Unskilled Reading

Several investigators have suggested that beginning and poor readers may use speech recoding to aid their memory during comprehension. Hitch and Baddeley (in press) suggested that an articulatory loop (a speech recoding subsystem in their working memory model) may be used to aid phonemic blending when beginning readers sound out words. They further speculated that this articulatory loop may be useful in retaining order information and important items needed for comprehension. That children do have problems in phonemic processing has recently been demonstrated, though the problem is even more basic than blending. They appear to be unable to segment words into phonemes. This conclusion arises from a series of findings reported by

I. Liberman, Shankweiler, and their Haskins colleagues. They have shown that by first grade, children can identify the number of syllables in words, but are still unable to indicate the number of phonemes in words. This is important in that learning to read may well require breaking the visual display into its speech components (I. Liberman & Shankweiler, in press; I. Liberman, Shankweiler, A. Liberman, Fowler, & Fisher, 1976). Also, analyses of the errors made by beginning readers indicated that more errors occurred on final than on initial consonants. Unlike vowel errors, the consonant errors tended to share phonetic features with the correct response. These data were taken to indicate that children form phonetic representations of consonants during reading. Because of the problem of phoneme segmentation, consonants appearing later in the word are more prone to error than the first and most distinctive consonant (Fowler, I. Liberman, & Shankweiler, 1976). Finally, for both auditory and visual presentation, good readers are more susceptible to acoustic confusions in a short-term memory task than are poor readers, perhaps because good readers use phonemic processing, making them more susceptible to speech errors. The conclusion offered from this series of observations was that a phonemic representation is important in reading, largely because it acts as a good memory representation from which message comprehension can occur (Shankweiler & I. Liberman, 1976).

Working at a quite different level of analysis, Perfetti and Lesgold (in press) came to a very similar conclusion about the role of "verbal" processing during discourse comprehension for both reading and listening. They argued that while good and poor readers do not differ in the amount of "storage-space" available, they do differ in verbal processing speed. Poor readers appear to encode verbally more slowly than fast readers, which puts them at a disadvantage in retaining discourse wording. As Perfetti and Lesgold point out, "The poor reader is slower at getting to the point in the comprehension process beyond which exact wording is not needed, but he is also poorer at retaining exact wording. Thus, he is confronted with a double whammy - slower processing and lower tolerance (in terms of working memory) both of which combine to create more processing needs than might otherwise exist." While no attempt has been made here to review the available literature on developmental differences, the two examples cited provide clear indication that a short-term memory view of speech processing is proving useful in understanding problems of the unskilled reader.

Fluent Reading

Subvocal speech activity, as measured by EMG recordings indicates that adults also subvocalize while they read. Hardyck and Petrinovich (1970) attempted to suppress subvocal speech, using a feedback technique, in order to demonstrate that subvocal speech hindered reading. Berkeley undergraduate readers had no difficulty in suppressing their subvocal activity during easy reading and without loss of comprehension. When asked to read difficult passages, however, they were unable to prevent their subvocalizations, and attempts to do so led

to poorer comprehension. Since comprehension was measured by a memory
test administered after the passage had been read, the subvocal activity
may have been needed to aid memory.

     Further evidence for speech recoding in memory comes from studies
in which speech translation was prevented by asking subjects to engage
in a subsidiary verbal task. Kleiman (1975) asked subjects to shadow
auditorily presented digits while they made decisions about word pairs
or phrases. This shadowing activity had little effect on decision times
for graphemic and synonymity judgments, but phonemic and sentence
acceptability judgments were slowed down by the shadowing requirement.
Kleiman argued that meaning can be accessed without speech recoding (as
in synonymity judgments), but that speech recoding acts as a useful
holding code to maintain sentence wording until semantic integration
occurs, as is necessary for making sentence acceptability judgments.

     My own research on speech responding is logically quite akin to
Kleiman's, and follows from an earlier observation that suppressing
speech recoding, by asking subjects to say an irrelevant syllable,
adversely affected visual, but not auditory, short-term memory (Levy,
1971). To relate this observation to reading, the change detection
paradigm described by Sachs (1967) was used. In the first studies, sets
of three unrelated sentences were presented serially, followed
immediately by a test sentence. Subjects simply indicated whether the
test sentence was identical to or changed from its presentation version.
The sentences were all seven words in length, and of the form: article,
adjective, noun, verb, article, adjective, noun. Two types of changes
were tested: (a) lexical, in which a synonym had been substituted for
one of the sentence nouns, thus changing the wording without altering
the sentence meaning; and (b) semantic, which consisted of
interchanging the subject and object nouns, thus changing the sentence
meaning while leaving the wording and syntactic form intact. For
example, if the original sentence was The furry kittens approached the
purring mother, a lexical change might be The furry cats approached the
purring mother, and a semantic change would be The furry mother
approached the purring kittens. Subjects were never required to
indicate which type of change had occurred, and changed and identical
test sentences were equiprobable. Additional (and unanalyzed) control
items contained changes in an adjective or the verb, to ensure that
subjects read the entire sentence and not just the nouns.

     To examine the effects of modality on the retention of sentence
wording and meaning, the first studies compared listening with reading.
Subjects read aloud, read silently, or read while counting quickly and
continuously from one to ten while they read (to prevent vocalization).
The idea was to compare comprehension during reading, with different
degrees of vocalization of the material read. Figure 1 (from Levy,
1975) shows the main findings. The data were converted to a P(hit) –
P(false alarm) measure to correct for response biases (analyses using d'
scores yield the same results). Two points should be noted. An
auditory advantage, through auditory presentation or reading visual

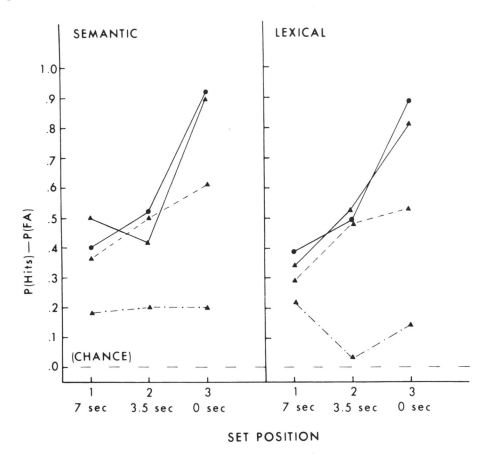

Figure 1.   Retention curves for four vocalization conditions, using lexical and semantic measures:
●——● auditory; ▲——▲ visual-vocalized; ▲---▲ visual-silent; ▲-·-▲ visual-suppressed
(from Levy, 1975).

sentences aloud, is localized in the final sentence only. Thus, additional auditory information is available following listening to briefly aid processing. Also, suppressing speech responding (by counting) causes a large retention decrement for both the wording and the meaning of visually presented sentences, and this effect covers all sentence positions.

In order to claim that the suppression decrement observed above represents a problem in fluent reading, a further test is required. According to Gleitman and Rozin (1976), a deficit in fluent reading can only be claimed if one first ensures that the deficit would not occur if the message had been heard and not seen. That is, the problem is in reading, and not in general comprehension under the task conditions used. To demonstrate that the suppression decrement represents a reading failure, a further study comparing silent and suppressed vocalization for both auditory and visual presentation was conducted. With unpracticed subjects, a small, inconsistent suppression decrement was observed in the auditory modality (Levy, 1975), but this disappeared when relatively practiced subjects, who completed several sessions with the task, were used. Figure 2 (from Levy, 1977) shows the main findings, and the modality specificity of the suppression decrement is quite clear here. From these findings, it can be claimed that a reading, rather than a general language comprehension, problem is involved here, since the suppression effect occurs in fluent reading, while not affecting listening.

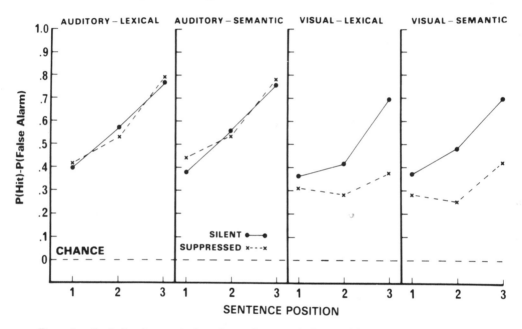

Figure 2.   Lexical and semantic detection performance in four modality-vocalization conditions (from Levy, 1977a).

A second possible interpretation of the suppression decrement is also taxed by the modality specificity of the effect. It could be claimed that counting affects reading simply because the subject must perform two tasks at once and has insufficient processing resources available. By this view, however, an auditory decrement should also be observed, since counting requires processing capacity during listening as well. However, no decrement in performance occurred for listening. One could further argue that the reading deficit was merely due to unfamiliarity with performing these particular tasks together, or that reading requires more attention than listening and therefore the additional task causes greater disruption in processing (Baron, 1976).

To examine the processing requirements during reading in more detail, three further studies were conducted. The first looked at the effect of practice on the visual suppression effect. The idea was that if the deficit was due to the subjects' unfamiliarity with counting while reading, then over days of practice, the suppression decrement should at least be attenuated (Levy, 1977). Subjects therefore returned for four sessions of practice, during which time they read 768 sentences, 384 of them while counting. This should have been sufficient practice to show some attenuation of the suppression decrement. As Figure 3 clearly shows, this was not the case. No change in the magnitude of the suppression decrement approached statistical reliability. The unfamiliarity argument seems unlikely in view of these data.

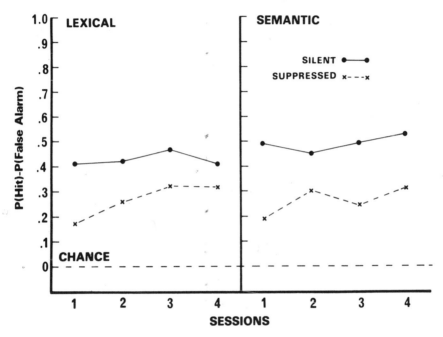

Figure 3.   Lexical and semantic detection performance across four sessions of practice (from Levy, 1977a).

However, it might be argued that the rate at which the sentences were presented (2.0 to 3.5 sec per sentence) allowed insufficient time for processing. That is, the time limit pressed processing capacity to the point where counting overtaxed the system. If more time was available, then sufficient capacity might be available to handle both the reading and counting requirements. Michael Withey therefore conducted two studies to examine the resource limitations imposed by presentation rate. In the first study, he used a self-paced procedure, with subjects being told to read each sentence until they understood it, as they would be given a memory test after each set of three sentences. They were given practice in detecting both lexical and semantic changes. Reading time was measured for each sentence and the experiment was carried out over three days of practice, with silent and suppressed reading measured on each day. The idea was that subjects should develop an optimal reading rate for each vocalization condition, and changes in strategy might be observed over days of practice. Figure 4 shows the mean reading time for each sentence, over the three days of practice. Surprisingly, at all sentence positions, subjects read faster when counting than when reading silently. Further, the strategy adopted over days was to read faster yet, and in the suppressed condition, a development that looks like "get to the end fast" was observed. Lest this appears to support the speed reading claim that reading is faster if subvocalization is suppressed, I hasten to point out that comprehension was poor, as indicated in Figure 5 by both lexical and semantic detection levels during suppression. Thus, left to their own devices, subjects did not appear to adopt a reading speed that led to better comprehension during suppression, despite their feeling that they were performing badly on the memory task.

While one plausible interpretation of these tasks is that subjects were frustrated and simply wanted to end the experiment as quickly as possible, a more constructive view is that they realized that reading more slowly would not help them, so they read as quickly as possible, hoping that some peripheral memory information might still be available to help them with the test. By this view, slower rates of presentation

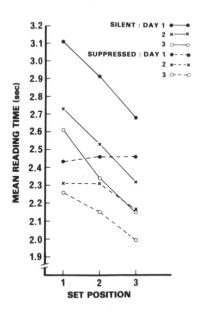

Figure 4. Reading times for silent and suppressed vocalization, across three days of practice.

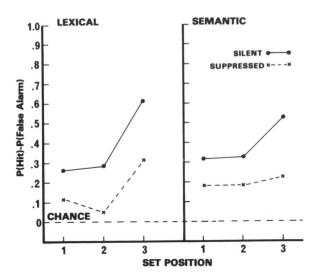

Figure 5.   Lexical and semantic detection performance following self-paced
presentation.

would not eliminate the suppression decrement.   In Withey's second
experiment, sentences were therefore presented at rates of 2, 4, or
6 sec per sentence. Since there were only five content words per
sentence, this provided a full second for reading each critical word at
the slowest rate of presentation.   Figure 6 presents the important
findings.   While detection improved with increasing presentation rate,
this effect did not interact with vocalization condition.   That is,
there was no attenuation of the suppression decrement as presentation
rate increased. Providing more time (and presumably, therefore, more
processing resources) did not eliminate the usefulness of speech
responding.

In summary, the suppression decrement does not occur during
listening, even though the processing requirements should be similar to
those of reading. Practice does not lead to an attenuation of the
decrement.   Further, given control over reading rate, subjects are
unable to adopt a reading rate that improves their comprehension.
Finally, even very long presentation rates do not lead to a lessening of
the suppression decrement. Given these findings, it seems unlikely that
any simple notion of processing capacity overload could offer a complete
explanation of the phenomenon described. A more acceptable view is that
counting interferes with a process important in reading.

Comprehension Without Speech Reading

From the studies reviewed in the last section, a fairly strong case
can be made that speech responding aids sentence memory. The further

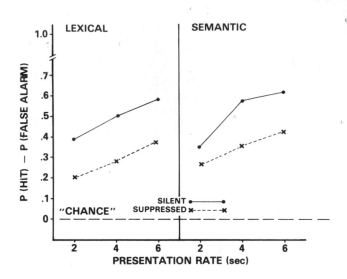

Figure 6.   Lexical and semantic detection performance at three rates of presentation.

claim that speech responding also aids comprehension depends on the
assumption that memory is involved in comprehension. By a sequential
stage view favored in many reading models, this assumption is
reasonable.   That is, one must process the words, which are then stored
until parsing and integration mechanisms "understand" the sentence
message (e.g., Gough, 1972; Kleiman, 1975). In the final section of
the paper, alternative views of the relationship between word and
meaning processing will be discussed. First, however, a summary of
evidence relating speech responding to comprehension or to meaning
analyses will prove enlightening.

      Several lines of evidence point to the necessity of an explicit
memory requirement before speech responding effects will be observed.
That is, only when a memory requirement is made explicit, or when it is
necessitated by the nature of the task, will the speech conflict effect
be evidenced.   Baron (1976) compared the latencies to make sound and
spelling judgments, when subjects were required to hold the items in
memory, as opposed to when the items were visually available. The idea
was that spelling judgments would be faster than sound judgments, since
they did not require speech recoding, but only when the items were
available and did not have to be held in memory. The data supported
this view, with spelling judgments being faster than sound judgments
when the stimuli were present but not when they were held in memory.
Baron also tested three-term series problems (e.g., John is taller than
Jack; Jim is taller than Jack; Jim is shorter than Jack), with
subjects responding true or false.   Here, it is necessary to keep the

three terms in memory to solve the problem. If subjects were required to say "oh" after reading the sentences, their decision times were slower. They reported that "oh" disrupted their memory, forcing them to read again. Baron argued from both of these demonstrations that when memory is involved in a comprehension task, speech recoding will be observed, since a phonemic code serves to hold words in memory.

Similarly, Smith (Note 2) gave subjects both single sentence existential affirmatives, such as "Some chairs are furniture," and three-term syllogisms, like those used by Baron, with subjects making true-false decisions. Two discrete and two continuous types of interference tasks were compared for listening and for reading. Discrete verbal interference consisted of subjects saying "oh" after reading (hearing), while discrete nonverbal interference was a tap following reading (hearing). The continuous tasks were carried out during reading (listening), with the verbal form being the subject repeating "hi-ya," and the nonverbal form tapping repeatedly. While there was no difference in error rates or decision times for the verbal versus nonverbal forms of interference during listening, the reading task was more affected by verbal, than by nonverbal interference. For both existential affirmatives and syllogisms, reaction times were greater for verbal than nonverbal discrete tasks. For syllogisms, the error rates were higher for both discrete and continuous verbal than nonverbal interference. Some qualification of the findings was needed, in that the interference was more pronounced and reliably found for female than for male subjects. Smith concluded from her data that continuous and perhaps automatic repetition (e.g., "hi-ya") may not sufficiently tax the central speech system to prevent speech recoding while reading. However, the more demanding operation of programming even a simple speech response, such as "oh," is sufficient to disrupt other speech encoding. As can be seen from the discrete interference task, the comprehension of both existential affirmatives and syllogisms appears to involve a speech recoding stage. Both of these tasks also involve a memory requirement in their solution.

In a rather different paradigm, Potter and Kroll (Note 3) presented sentences visually at a rate of twelve words per second. The sentences (eight, ten, twelve, or fourteen words in length) consisted of all words, or words plus one picture (representing the replaced word). The subjects either made judgments about the sentence's plausibility, or they recalled it verbatim, or they did both tasks. The reasoning behind this study was that since pictures take longer to name than words, the presence of a picture should disrupt the speech recoding of the sentence. If comprehension (plausibility judgments) and/or memory (verbatim recall) were dependent on speech recoding, then the rebus (picture) sentences should show slower plausibility judgments, with more errors and/or poorer verbatim recall than the all-word sentences. In fact, plausibility judgments were about 100 msec slower, and verbatim recall was lower (84% versus 88% correct) for rebus than for regular sentences. However, as Potter and Kroll point out, retention was very high and 100 msec is a very small disruption, suggesting that speech

recoding was not very critical to performance. Since retention was so
good, the memory load may have been insufficient to require speech
recoding. Nonetheless, the data do suggest that some meaning processing
occurred without a speech recoding stage.

    Finally, Baddeley (personal communication) has conducted studies in
which he varied the nature of the subsidiary task in which subjects
engaged while they made category judgments. The judgments were of the
form, Does a canary have wings? or, Is a canary a living creature? The
subsidiary tasks were counting repeatedly from one to six (suppression),
or repeating six random digits held in memory (memory load), and these
were compared with silent reading. He found that while memory load led
to consistent reaction time increases, suppression has no consistent
effect over trials. A tentative interpretation was that while simply
preventing articulation (suppression) may have interfered initially with
performance, because subjects adopted a speech recoding strategy, over
trials they dropped this strategy and the suppression effect
disappeared. Memory load, on the other hand, taxes central working
memory capacity. These data look quite similar to those of Smith, where
the simple continuous task was insufficient to reliably prevent speech
recoding, while the more demanding "oh" succeeded in disrupting speech
processing. Unfortunately, a nonverbal comparison is unavailable in
Baddeley's memory load condition, making it unclear whether speech
recoding or general processing capacity was the limiting factor.   While
these studies do not give a very clear picture of the relationship
between speech recoding and comprehension, they do suggest   that
comprehension can occur without speech recoding in some instances, and
that processing or memory load is a critical component in whether a
speech conflict effect is observed.   The problem is in defining the
relationship between processing load, speech responding, and
comprehension.

    The problem of comprehension and memory requirement surfaced in my
own work in considering the relationship of speech responding to the
measures used. In the studies described to date, no differences in the
suppression decrement existed for the lexical and semantic measures.
This may be because the processing of wording and meaning are equally
affected by suppression, since these represent sequential stages in
sentence processing. However, it may also be due to the use of
unrelated sentences, which may have encouraged a literal rather than
semantic processing strategy. Perhaps the subjects were not "reading
for meaning" as they would with thematic texts, thus our measures both
reflected memory for wording. To examine the relationship of
thematicity to speech suppression, thematic paragraphs were constructed,
with seven sentences per paragraph. The seven sentences consisted of
one sentence (which would be tested), surrounded by six context
sentences, all forming a little story.   The stories also had titles
reflecting their main idea, and subjects were instructed to relate the
seven sentences to the story theme to make them more memorable.   A
second group of subjects received the same tested sentences, but the six
context sentences were scrambled across sets to give unrelated passages.

No titles were used and subjects were told to remember all seven unrelated sentences. In fact, only the final three sentences in each set were tested (though foil tests of the earlier four were used to ensure they were read), because we also varied the point in the passage at which the subject began suppressing his speech responding (i.e., counting). The idea was that if suppression began immediately, thematic processing might be discouraged, whereas once comprehension had begun, it might be unsuppressable. However, no effect of this manipulation occurred. The final three sentences were tested with both lexical and semantic changes, as in earlier studies. Table 1 contains examples of the material used. In brief, then, the study consisted of two groups of subjects, one reading seven sentence paragraphs, one reading unrelated sets. Each group participated in three sessions. During each session, half of the passages were read silently and half while counting. Also lexical, semantic, and identical tests were given (plus unanalyzed verb and adjective foils as before).

Table 1.   Examples of Thematic Passages and Test Sentences

I   A Summer Ride

The lone rider reached the grassy knoll.
The young boy stroked his horse's neck.
The prancing steed tossed his tawny mane.
The adventurous boy viewed the wide plain.
A thick wood became his new interest.
His thirsty horse lapped some clear water.
The quiet lake bordered the peaceful forest.*

The quiet lake bordered the peaceful <u>woods</u>. (lexical)

The quiet <u>forest</u> bordered the peaceful <u>lake</u>. (semantic)

II   The New House

The young couple admired their new home.
An exquisite lamp lit the living room.
An antique clock graced the west corner.
Deep luxurious carpets covered the wooden floor.
The flowered sofa accented the colonial decor.
The greenish room matched the gold drapes.*
A quaint fireplace added the final touch.

The greenish room matched the gold <u>curtains</u>. (lexical)

The greenish <u>drapes</u> matched the gold <u>room</u>. (semantic)

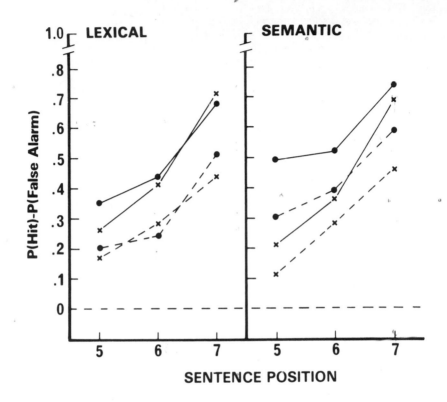

Figure 7.   Lexical and semantic detection performance for thematic and unrelated passages: Thematic-silent, ●——●; thematic-suppressed, ●---●; unrelated-silent, X——X; unrelated-suppressed, X---X (from Levy, 1977a).

Figure 7 (from Levy, 1977) contains the main findings. From the lexical measure, shown in the left-hand panel, it is clear that there is no effect of thematicity, but a large suppression decrement. That is, the relatedness of the sentences did not help discrimination between synonyms that did not alter meaning. Speech responding was still critical. The right-hand panel showing the semantic measure gives quite a different picture. Here, thematic passages were better remembered than unrelated ones, but suppression affected the processing of both types of material <u>equally</u>. Analyses indicate that these main effects are highly significant, with no trace of an interaction between them. Thus, we have independent meaning and speech responding effects occurring simultaneously. This study is important on two counts. Clearly, our lexical and semantic measures reflect different forms of processing. The semantic measure captures variations in meaningfulness not seen in lexical detection. Also, the suppression effect occurs in both measures, with no dependency on meaningfulness. A straightforward interpretation of these findings is that the analyzers that deal with meaning are not those that are affected by speech responding.

How can the independent thematicity and speech responding effects be explained? One possibility is that the measure reflects two aspects of comprehension. The particular testing sequence used involves identical, lexical, and semantic tests occurring at random. Thus, subjects were always prepared for changes in wording as well as meaning. If speech responding affected mechanisms used to maintain word memory, while thematicity affected independent meaning processors, both could ultimately contribute to semantic detection performance. That is, the semantic measure could reflect the contribution of the meaning analyzers to general gist recognition, while it also reflected the more detailed contribution of wording memory provided by the speech component. For example, the sentence <u>The passionate girl kissed the receptive fellow</u> may indeed be more memorable in the context of a story about a romantic walk beside a moonlit stream than in the context of unrelated sentences. However, memory for who took the initiative may still be enhanced by a strict word order record, i.e., <u>girl</u> came before <u>fellow</u>. Since all of our sentences were actives, such a strategy allows contributions of gist, as well as word order, to influence semantic detection.

To test the plausibility of this word versus gist memory interpretation, one further study (Levy, in press) was conducted. This time, we had two main testing groups--one group made identity versus change discriminations as before, but the second group made paraphrase judgments. In the paraphrase tests, wording changes occurred in both yes and no versions, thus identify was never tested, and subjects should not have been encouraged to maintain exact wording. Table 2 contains examples of paragraphs, plus tests. In paraphrase tests, two words per sentence were changed, with one version maintaining the sentence meaning, while the other altered it. Both versions could have occurred in the story, but the yes version "fit better." The paragraphs and unrelated sets were largely as in the previous experiment, but this time, sentence positions two to seven were tested (not just the final three positions). This allowed us to better observe the memory durations of the effects observed. The lexical-semantic and paraphrase detection groups were both divided into two subgroups, with one subgroup reading thematic passages for three sessions, while the other read unrelated passages. Again, within each session, half of the passages were read silently and half while counting.

Table 2. Examples of Thematic Paragraphs and Lexical, Semantic, and Paraphrase Tests

I An Emergency

The hospital staff paged the busy doctor.
The solemn physican distressed the anxious mother.
The sobbing woman held her unconscious son.
A speeding truck had crossed the mid-line.
Her oncoming car was hit and damaged.
Her child had plunged through the windshield.
The medical team strove to save him.

The solemn physician distressed the anxious woman. (lexical)

The solemn mother distressed the anxious physican. (semantic)

The solemn doctor upset the anxious mother. (paraphrase - yes)

The solemn officer helped the anxious mother. (paraphrase - no)

II A Lost Boy

The lost boy searched the crowded street.
His careless mother had forgotten about him.
The concerned policeman approached the worried child.
The kindly man dried the boy's tears.
The young lad gave his home address.
And the police cruiser escorted him home.
In future his mother was more careful.

The concerned policeman approached the worried youngster. (lexical)

The concerned child approached the worried policeman. (semantic)

The concerned officer approached the upset child. (paraphrase - yes)

The concerned woman approached the carefree child. (paraphrase -no)

Figure 8 gives the main findings for the lexical-semantic detection subjects. The picture is very similar to the earlier experiment, but with qualifications as to the memory range affected. For the lexical measure, there was no effect of thematicity, but a substantial suppression decrement. However, the suppression effect covers the final sentence positions only, as detection during silent reading reaches "floor levels" in the early sentence positions. Thus, the interpretation of the suppression effect disappearance is ambiguous, as it may simply be due to the low levels of silent recall. However, in view of earlier findings (Sachs, 1967; Begg, 1971), these floor performance levels may be due to the dissipation of word memory after about 7 sec. If the suppression effect is related to word retention, it would also dissipate after this interval. For the semantic measure, there was an effect of thematicity and an effect of suppression, but no interaction of the two. Thus, the two independent effects of the earlier study are also found here. While the thematicity effect extended over the range of sentence positions tested, the suppression decrement is unreliable over the early sentence positions. Thus, the thematicity and suppression effects seem to differ in their memory duration, with thematicity being a long-term effect, but suppression a short-term effect. For the thematic case, at least, the attenuation of the suppression effect does not seem to be attributable to floor performance levels.

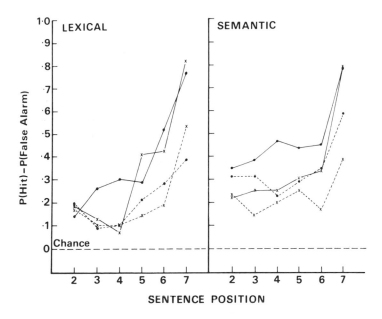

Figure 8.   Lexical and semantic detection performance for thematic and unrelated passages: Thematic-silent, ●———●; thematic-suppressed, ●---●; unrelated-silent, X———X; unrelated-suppressed, X---X (from Levy, 1977b).

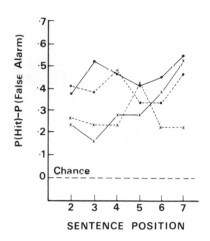

Figure 9.   Paraphrase detection from thematic and unrelated passages: Thematic
silent,●———●; thematic suppressed, ●---●; unrelated-silent, X——X;
unrelated suppressed, X---X (from Levy, 1977b).

        Figure 9 shows the findings for the paraphrase test.   While these
data   are more variable than the detection results, several findings are
quite clear.   Suppressing speech responding had no effect on paraphrase
detection, while thematicity aided such discriminations.   Further, there
are no effects of sentence position,   suggesting that more peripheral
forms of memory do not affect this test.   Taken together, the findings
for both lexical-semantic and paraphrase tests suggest that meaning
analyses   do   occur   independently   of speech responding during reading.
That is, comprehension of the basic gist of a sentence does not seem to
depend   on   speech   processing.   However, speech processes do aid memory
for wording, which may be critical when order of events must be
remembered.   A similar suggestion was made by Saffran and Marin (1975),
from studies of a patient with a deficiency in auditory short-term
memory.   This patient's auditory digit span was less than three items.
While the patient was unable to recall the exact wording of sentences,
he could usually supply a reasonable paraphrase of the sentence meaning.
This was not true, however, for reversible sentences (such as those used
in the lexical-semantic task here) where it is necessary to remember the
order of the nouns in order to comprehend the sentence message.   As with
the   suppression effect, then, this patient appeared to be able to
process general gist without a speech code, but when word order was
essential   to comprehension, poor speech encoding led to poor retention.
The argument, then, is not that speech responding is necessary for
comprehension, but that speech analyses provide additional detailed
information about the order of events.   This may or may not be useful in
reading, depending on the nature of the reading task set.

Models and Instruction

The original problems posed were: Is speech recoding useful during
fluent reading, and if so, where in the information processing stream
should such processes be located? The data discussed support the claim
that speech recoding is useful in providing specific information that
may not be required in all reading tasks. It does not appear to be
necessary for lexical access to single words, nor is it impossible to
understand the gist of short passages without speech recoding.   Rather,
speech recoding is useful when details of the presented message must be
held in memory to complete a comprehension task (e.g., syllogism
solution), or when memory for detail is required (e.g., our semantic
detection task). The memory component seems critical. If comprehension
is not too difficult, it can be carried out on-line and probably rarely
requires speech recoding.   Most of the data reviewed fit this
conclusion.

Where, then, should speech processes be located in the information
stream?   The simple answer is to say in short-term or working memory,
but this answer needs considerable elucidation.   Kleiman (1975)
described in some detail a working memory model for comprehending
sentences. In this model, single words can achieve lexical access
without speech recoding, but when several words (phrases or sentences)
must be kept accessible in memory for complete message comprehension,
then speech recoding occurs. It serves as a holding device for words so
they remain available for parsing and integration mechanisms.   Thus,
speech recoding precedes sentence comprehension, which in turn precedes
mechanisms dealing with thematic context. While capturing the need for
memory for wording and the role that speech recoding plays there, this
model maintains a sequential stage position. That is, speech recoding
occurs prior to and provides a data base for later meaning stages.

Such a stage view necessitates a dependency relationship, in that
disruption of speech stages should also disrupt or eliminate later
meaning processing, since the data being fed into the meaning stage
should be poor.   Such a system would then be unable to explain a
suppression decrement that was independent of the thematicity effect.
It would also have trouble describing a fascinating series of findings
by Marcel (Note 4) and by Allport (1977), which indicate considerable
comprehension of meaning when subjects are unaware of what item was
presented. Marcel (Note 4) used a masking procedure in tachistoscopic
recognition, but asked subjects to make three sorts of judgments: (1)
Was a word presented?   (2)Which of two words did it resemble
graphically?   (3)Which did it resemble semantically? Surprisingly,
Marcel found that chance performance was first reached on the
presence-absence judgments, then on the graphemic judgments, and lastly
on the meaning judgments. That is, subjects could make above-chance
choices on the basis of meaning when they could not identify the visual
characteristics of the word and claimed that in fact no word was
presented.   Because these findings are open to several interpretations,
Marcel provided a more clever version of his meaning effect. He used an

associative priming procedure, where lexical decision latency to a word is increased if a word immediately preceding it is related in meaning. Thus, "nurse" is responded to faster if it is preceded by "doctor," rather than "chair." Marcel, however, masked the first stimulus until subjects reported not seeing a word (doctor). Despite not "seeing" doctor, nurse was still responded to faster if preceded by doctor than by chair. This associative priming effect seems to suggest meaning processing, without word identification. In a similar vein, Allport (1977) demonstrated that under conditions where subjects could not report the word presented, their errors were frequently semantically related to the correct word. That is, normal subjects made errors which preserve meaning rather like the errors of some phonemic dyslexic patients. Both of these demonstrations of meaning, despite lack of item identification, present an explanatory problem for models that uses sequential stages with word identity preceding meaning.

A second working memory model, proposed by Baddeley and Hitch (1974, also Hitch and Baddeley, in press), is more flexible in that it does not postulate sequential stages. Here, the articulatory loop could deal with word order and be disrupted by suppression, while in parallel, the executive processor deals with meaning. This system can then produce independent speech suppression and thematicity effects. Several problems must be noted, however: (a) the articulatory loop is said to maintain about three words or one and a half seconds of speech, estimates far too small to cover the range of the suppression decrement; (b) there is no obvious reason why the executive processor should become speech based with heavy memory loads (e.g., Smith, Note 2), since this is not a speech processor; and (c) since the executive processor has been assigned no particular characteristics, it provides little guidance in understanding or predicting such important things as how thematicity affects processing. It may well be that the executive processor encompasses all types of processing other than speech responding, and comes to look rather like the message center of an interactive model (e.g., Rumelhart, 1976) or again, it may be similar to the logogens in Morton's (1969) recognition model, which sum incoming information irrespective of source. Without further elaboration of the function of the executive processor, such a view of working memory provides little guidance in understanding the many processes and their interactions likely to be observed in reading research. In summary, the sequential models (even the more flexible ones such as levels of processing, Craik & Lockhart,1972) have some difficulty in handling independent meaning analyses, since these are assumed to be preceded by word identification and to be provided with data from earlier stages. These models are considerably taxed by the available data on reading.

An alternative to these models is the top-down view, where the reader is seen as a problem solver. The direction of processing control is from the cognitive system downward. That is, the cognitive system forms hypotheses about what is being read and then samples the stimulus array to confirm its view. A full stimulus analysis is not necessary for comprehension to occur. While some theorists allow sampling from both visual and speech levels of analyses (e.g., Goodman, 1970), others specifically exclude speech analyses from the realm of fluent reading (e.g., Smith, 1973). Clearly, by this view, meaning analyses neither follow nor are dependent upon speech responding. Another alternative is an integration of these views, exemplified by Rumelhart's (1976) interactive model of reading.   By this view, analyses occur simultaneously and interactively at several levels of analyses.   That is, the direction of control is neither bottom-up nor top-down. Rather, each level of analysis (e.g., visual features, letters, syntax, meaning, etc.) forms hypotheses about what message has occurred in its domain of responsibility. Each level uses "hints" from the hypotheses of other levels, which are publicly displayed in the message center. Comprehension appears to be an understanding of the message by the accumulation of information from all levels, with no one analysis necessarily preceding any others.

The top-down model seems unlikely in view of the speech effects observed in reading. If speech translation is eliminated from the realm of fluent processing, then no suppression effects, nor speech conflicts of the type observed by Baron and by Smith, should be observed. Thus, while top-down views handle thematicity effects and on-line comprehension (e.g., Potter & Kroll, Note 3), they offer no guidance on the speech responding effects.   For the top-down views that allow sampling from speech as well as other levels, the mechanisms for relating information from various sources must be specified.   The simplest view would be to suppose that the stronger the semantic hypotheses, the less sampling of stimulus input would be needed.   Thus, in our studies, one might have expected an attenuation of the suppression decrement for more meaningful passages, where the semantic control should be greater and less sampling required. Clearly, this did not occur. If information is sampled irrespective of the "goodness" of the semantic input, then such models would not differ from interactive view, where all levels process within their realm of responsibility and all information is public. Such a view can clearly handle independent effects from different types of information and suggests interesting directions to pursue in future research.

It is clearly in the area of the interaction between the semantic and peripheral processing systems that much important information about reading lies. While much of recent memory and word recognition work has been guided by a sequential stage framework of thought (with notable exceptions, e.g., Morton, 1969; Neisser, 1967), other views now seem to open more fruitful lines of pursuit. The ideas that general meaning may be perceived in advance of identification of exact wording and that additional analyses (visual, speech, etc.) may be used to specify exactly what was presented, offer food for future research thought.   It may be the case that for some forms of fluent reading, detailed identification is unnecessary, and forcing the subject to know the words read actually hinders the fluency of his processing. On the other hand, it seems equally limited to decide that this is fluent processing and that other forms are irrelevant or inferior forms of reading. When one

reads unfamiliar or difficult passages or when one reads to acquire   new
information,   meaning   processing   may   well   need buttressing from more
detailed, peripheral identification systems, even for   the   most   fluent
reader.   Our models of reading will want to incorporate many processors,
with specification of their interactions under different   circumstances,
to   capture   the   variety   of   observations   in   reading   for   different
purposes.

        Such a confusing state of affairs does not lead to an   easy   recipe
for   instruction   in   fluent   reading.   Oral   reading   may enhance word
identification or grapheme-phoneme conversion processes, while hindering
general   meaning   analyses   when   only general concepts need be grasped.
When speed reading instructors point out to adult readers the   power   of
preview   and   of rapid visual scanning, they demonstrate very useful and
frequently unknown skills.   However, when reading difficult or technical
material,   or when searching for a particular piece of information, more
detailed analyses may be required.   In these cases, speech encoding   may
be   particularly   useful.   Knowledge of the flexibility of human visual
processing skills, as well as the losses and payoffs involved when using
different   reading   strategies,   may well lead to more optimal (fluent?)
reading by adults.

        For beginning readers,   the   picture   may   prove   quite   different.
While considerable interest has been shown in whole word versus phonetic
reading   instruction,   not   too   much   effort   has   been   expended   on
demonstrating   cognitive   control   skills   to   children.   This   may   be
sensible, since these skills must depend on acquired   knowledge   of   the
world and of language.   We must keep in mind, however, that our ultimate
aim is to show the child how to rapidly acquire knowledge,   not   how   to
pronounce words.   The real question is whether the developmental process
is such that semantic skills are optimally acquired once the buttressing
skills   are   there to fall back on.   Liberman and Shankweiler (in press)
report   some   success   in   aiding   beginning   readers   by   teaching   the
relationship between print and speech.   Maybe in reading also, the child
must also learn to walk before he can   run.   Learning   how   to   process
language signals slowly may be necessary before fluency can be attained.

                                                Footnotes

        This paper was prepared while the author was on   sabbatical   leave,
visiting   the   MRC Applied Psychology Unit, Cambridge, England.   I thank
my   Unit   colleagues   for   many   stimulating   discussions   that   heavily
influenced   views   presented   in this paper.   I also thank the technical
and secretarial staff for their assistance in preparing the   manuscript.
The   research   reported   was   supported by Grant A7657 from the National
Research Council of Canada.

        1.   Unpublished experiments   toward   a   Master's   thesis,   McMaster
University.

Reference Notes

1. Meyer, D. E., & Ruddy, M. G. Lexical-memory retrieval based on graphemic and phonemic representations of printed words. Paper read at the Psychonomic Society Meeting, St. Louis, November 1973.

2. Smith, M. C. Evidence for speech recoding when reading for comprehension. Paper read at the Psychonomic Society Meeting, St. Louis, November 1976.

3. Potter, M. C., & Kroll, J. F. Pictures in sentences: Comprehension and recall. Paper read at the Psychonomic Society Meeting, St. Louis, November 1976.

4. Marcel, T. Unconscious reading: Experiments on people who do not know that they are reading. Paper given to the British Association for the Advancement of Science, 1976.

References

Allport, D. A. On knowing the meaning of words we are unable to report: The effects of visual masking. In S. Dornic & P. M. A. Rabbitt (Eds.), Attention and performance VI. London: Academic Press, 1977.

Baddeley, A. D., & Hitch, G. Working memory. In G. H. Bower (Ed.), The psychology of learning and motivation (Vol. 8). New York: Academic Press, 1974.

Baron, J. Phonemic stage not necessary for reading. Quarterly Journal of Experimental Psychology, 1973, $\underline{25}$, 241-246.

Baron, J. Mechanisms for pronouncing printed words: Use and acquisition. In D. LaBerge & S. J. Samuels (Eds.), Basic processes in reading: Perception and comprehension. Potomac, Md.: L. E. Erlbaum, 1976.

Begg, I. Recognition memory for sentence meaning and wording. Journal of Verbal Learning and Verbal Behavior, 1971, $\underline{10}$, 176-181.

Bower, T. G. R. Reading by eye. In H. Levin & J. P. Williams (Eds.), Basic studies on reading. New York: Basic Books, 1970.

Conrad, R. Acoustic confusions in immediate memory. British Journal of Psychology, 1964, $\underline{55}$, 75-84.

Conrad, R. Short-term memory processes in the deaf. British Journal of
    Psychology, 1970, 61, 179-195.

Conrad, R. The effects of vocalization on comprehension in the
    profoundly deaf. British Journal of Psychology, 1971, 62, 147-150.

Conrad, R. Speech and reading. In J. F. Kavanagh & I. G. Mattingly
    (Eds.), Language by ear and by eye: The relationships between
    speech and reading. Cambridge: Massachusetts Institute of
    Technology Press, 1972.

Craik, F, I. M., & Lockhart, R. S. Levels of processing: A framework
    for memory research. Journal of Verbal Learning and Verbal
    Behavior, 1972, 11, 671-684.

Ericksen, C. W., Pollack, M. D., & Montague, W. E. Implicit speech:
    Mechanisms in perceptual coding. Journal of Experimental
    Psychology, 1970, 84, 502-507.

Fowler, C. A., Liberman, I. Y., & Shankweiler, D. On interpreting the
    error pattern in beginning reading. Status Report on Speech
    Research, SR-45/46. Haskins Laboratories, 1976.

Gleitman, L. R., & Rozin, P. The structure and acquisition of reading,
    I: Relations between orthographics and the structure of language.
    In A. Reber & D. Scarborough (Eds.), Marks to meaning. Potomac,
    Md.: L. E. Erlbaum, 1976.

Goodman, K. S. Psycholinguistic universals in the reading process.
    Journal of Typographic Research, 1970, 4, 103-110.

Gough, P. B. One second of reading. In J. F. Kavanagh &
    I. G. Mattingly (Eds.), Language by ear and by eye: The
    relationships between speech and reading. Cambridge:
    Massachusetts Institute of Technology Press, 1972.

Green, D. W., & Shallice, T. Direct visual access in reading for
    meaning. Memory & Cognition, 1976, 4, 753-758.

Hardyck, C. D., & Petrinovich, L. F. Subvocal speech and comprehension
    levels as a function of the difficulty level of reading materials.
    Journal of Verbal Learning and Verbal Behavior, 1970, 9, 647-652.

Hitch, G. J., & Baddeley, A. D. Working memory and information
    processing. In Memory Processes, Block 3, Part one, 0303 Cognitive
    Psychology. The Open University, in press.

Huey, E. D. The psychology and pedagogy of reading. Cambridge:
    Massachusetts Institute of Technology Press, 1968. (Originally
    published, 1908)

Johnson, N. F. On the function of letters in word identification: Some data and a preliminary model. Journal of Verbal Learning and Verbal Behavior, 1975, 14, 17-29.

Klapp, S. T. Implicit speech inferred from response latencies in same-different decisions. Journal of Experimental Psychology, 1971, 91, 262-267.

Klapp, S. T., Anderson, W. G., & Berrian, R. W. Implicit speech in reading, reconsidered. Journal of Experimental Psychology, 1973, 100, 368-374.

Kleiman, G. M. Speech recoding in reading. Journal of Verbal Learning and Verbal Behavior, 1975, 14, 323-339.

Kroll, N. E. A., Parks, T. E., Parkinson, S. R., Beiber, S. L., & Johnson, A. L. Short-term memory while shadowing: Recall of visually and aurally presented letters. Journal of Experimental Psychology, 1970, 85,220-224.

Levy, B. A. Role of articulation in auditory and visual short-term memory. Journal of Verbal Learning and Verbal Behavior, 1971, 10, 123-132.

Levy, B. A. Vocalization and suppression effects in sentence memory. Journal of Verbal Learning and Verbal Behavior, 1975, 14, 304-316.

Levy, B. A. Reading: Speech and meaning processes. Journal of Verbal Learning and Verbal Behavior, 1977, in press.

Levy, B. A. Speech analysis during sentence processing: Reading versus listening. Visible Language, in press.

Liberman, I. Y., & Shankweiler, D. Speech, the alphabet, and teaching to read. In L. Resnick & P. Weaver (Eds.), Theory and practice of early reading. Hillsdale, N. J.: Lawrence Erlbaum Associates, in press.

Liberman, I. Y., Shankweiler, D., Liberman, A. M., Fowler, C., & Fischer, F. W. Phonetic segmentation and recoding in the beginning reader. In A. S. Reber & D. Scarborough (Eds.), Marks to meaning. Potomac, Md.: L. E. Erlbaum, 1976.

Marshall, J. C., & Newcombe, F. Syntactic and semantic errors in paralexia. Neuropsychologia, 1966, 4, 169-176.

Morton, J. The interaction of information in word recognition. Psychological Review, 1969, 76, 165-178.

Murdock, B. B. Auditory and visual stores in short-term memory.   _Acta Psychologica_, 1967, _27_, 316-327.

Murray, D. J. Vocalization-at-presentation and immediate recall, with varying presentation rates.   _Quarterly Journal of Experimental Psychology_, 1965, _17_, 47-56.

Neisser, U. _Cognitive psychology_. New York: Appleton-Century-Crofts, 1967.

Norman, D. A. The role of memory in the understanding of language.   In J. F. Kavanagh & I. G. Mattingly (Eds.), _Language by ear and by eye: The relationships between speech and reading_.   Cambridge: Massachusetts Institute of Technology Press, 1972.

Patterson, K. E.,   &   Marcel, A. J.   Aphasia,   dyslexia   and   the phonological coding of written words.   _Quarterly Journal of Experimental Psychology_, 1977, in press.

Perfetti, C. A., & Lesgold, A. M. Discourse comprehension and sources of individual differences.   In M. Just & P. Carpenter (Eds.), _Cognitive processes in comprehension_. Hillsdale, N. J.:   Lawrence Erlbaum Associates, in press.

Peterson, L. R.,   &   Johnson, S. T.   Some   effects   of   minimizing articulation on short-term retention. _Journal of Verbal Learning and Verbal Behavior_, 1971, _10_, 346-357.

Rubenstein, H., Lewis, S. S., & Rubenstein, M. A. Evidence for phonemic recoding in visual word recognition. _Journal of Verbal Learning and Verbal Behavior_, 1971, _10_, 647-657.

Rumelhart, D. E. Toward an interactive model of reading. In S. Dornic & P. M. A. Rabbitt (Eds.), _Attention and performance_ VI. Hillsdale, N. J.: Lawrence Erlbaum Associates, 1977.

Sachs, J. S. Recognition memory for syntactic and semantic aspects of connected discourse. _Perception & Psychophysics_, 1967, _2_, 437-442.

Saffran, E. M., & Marin, O. S. M. Immediate memory for word lists and sentences in a patient with deficient short-term memory. _Brain and Language_, 1975, _2_, 420-433.

Shallice, T.,   &   Warrington, E. K.   Word recognition in a phonemic dyslexic patient.   _Quarterly Journal of Experimental Psychology_, 1975, _27_, 187-199.

Shankweiler, D., & Liberman, I. Y.   Exploring the relations between reading and speech.   In K. M. Knights & D. K. Bakker (Eds.), _Neuropsychology of learning disorders: Theoretical approaches_. Baltimore: University Park Press, 1976.

Smith, F. Psycholinguistics and reading. New York: Holt, Rinehart &
    Winston, 1973.

Sperling, G. The information available in brief visual presentation.
    Psychological Monographs, 1960, 74, (11; Whole No. 498).

Theios, J., & Muise, J. G. The word identification process in reading.
    In N. J. Castellan, Jr., & D. Pisoni (Eds.), Cognitive theory (Vol.
    2). Potomac, Md.: L. E. Erlbaum, 1976.

Warrington, E. K., & Shallice, T. The selective impairment of auditory
    verbal short-term memory. Brain, 1969, 92, 885-896.

ASSESSMENT OF PERCEPTUAL, DECODING, AND LEXICAL SKILLS
AND THEIR RELATION TO READING PROFICIENCY

John R. Frederiksen
Bolt Beranek and Newman Inc.
Cambridge, Massachusetts, U.S.A.

A central problem in evaluation research is the assessment of effects of instructional strategies on specific information processing skills. The goal of the research project on which I shall report is to develop and validate techniques for measuring perceptual and cognitive skills that are related to reading proficiency, and to investigate how deficiencies in particular skills may limit an individual's ability to read with speed and comprehension. The measures to be developed are chosen to represent five skill domains or levels of processing, as illustrated in Figure 1.

1. The Perceptual Level includes processes involved in the encoding of visual information, scanning a visual image, recognizing patterns, encoding of graphemic or supragraphemic units, and storing the order of encoded visual units.

2. The Decoding Level includes skills involved in the translation of English orthographic patterns into derived phonemic patterns.

3. The Lexical Level includes skills involved in utilizing available evidence for accessing the lexicon, in retrieving lexical information of either a semantic or articulatory nature, and in making semantic and lexical decisions on the basis of retrieved information.

4. The Phrasal Level includes skills involved in the use of propositional and syntactic structure to guide lexical search and retrieval, in the construction of a running model of text, and in the use of contextual information in making lexical identifications and semantic decisions.

5. Interactions among processes occurring at different levels constitute a fifth domain of interest. To take one example, the presence of phrase level constraints on a lexical item can influence the mode of lexical access and the use of decoding processes in lexical retrieval. Such interactions can be expected to contribute to a fluent, integrated approach to reading.

153

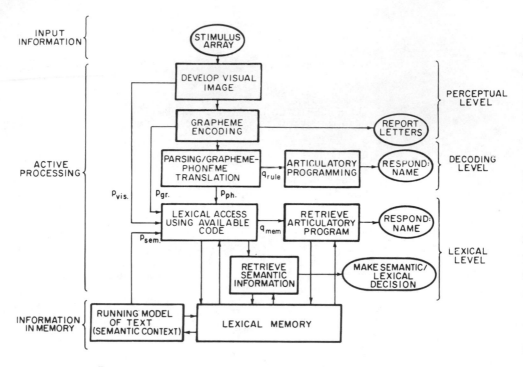

Figure 1.   The general conceptual model underlying the experiments.

I shall review a set of experiments we have carried out that are aimed at the measurement of processing strategies and levels of processing accuracy and efficiency in a number of these domains. The following general approach has been taken: On the basis of pertinent existing theory, experimental tasks are chosen for each domain, and variables are selected that allow us to manipulate the degree to which the relevant processing skill contributes to task performance. Validation of the experimental procedures is based upon the correspondence between theoretical predictions and experimental results, and on their relationship to an external measure of reading ability. Contrasts among the experimental conditions are then defined that (a) represent selected processing skills within the domain under investigation, and (b) are related to an individual's level of reading ability. The individual subject's scores on these contrasts serve as measures of processing skill.

The Perceptual Domain

In order to measure skills in the perceptual domain, a letter identification task was selected. Subjects were asked to report all of the letters they could identify in a masked, briefly-presented stimulus array,.   While a third of the stimulus items were four-letter English words, the remaining items were English-like four-letter arrays in which two letters were masked during the exposure so that only a single pair of adjacent letters was available for the subject to report.   The critical (unmasked) letters were either the first two letters (e.g., KN--), the middle two letters (e.g., -NC-), or the final two letters (e.g., --RD).   In addition to varying in their location, the critical bigrams were chosen to represent two sources of redundancy in English orthography: (a) redundancy due to sequential constraints that occur among letters, and (b) redundancy due to positional constraints on letter occurrence.   Accordingly, the critical bigrams varied in the overall frequency with which the letters occur together in English prose (e.g., TH (high), GA (middle), and LK (low), and in their likelihood of occurring in their presented position in a normal, four-letter English word (e.g., TH-- (high) vs. -TH- (low)).[1]

To make the task perceptually demanding, the stimulus array was preceded and followed by a 300 msec masking field, and the stimulus duration chosen was the shortest duration that would still allow 95% of the stimulus letters to be correctly reported (generally 90-100 msec). Finally, in order to relate performance to reading skill, the 20 subjects (high-school students) were divided into four levels (quartiles) on the basis of Nelson-Denny reading test scores.

We found that our subjects were sensitive to the manipulations of sequential and spatial redundancy. Bigrams having low, middle, and high probabilities of occurrence were reported correctly 88%, 92%, and 93% of the time, respectively; bigrams occurring in unlikely and likely locations were reported correctly 90% and 92% of the time.   These differences, while small in magnitude, were highly reliable (p<.001 and p<.005, respectively) and suggest that letters within an orthographically regular array are not processed independently, and that positional cues can facilitate encoding.

In addition to these general results, we found that subjects who vary in reading ability differ reliably both in their rate of scanning a perceptual array, and in their sensitivity to redundancy built into the stimulus.   In Figure 2, we have plotted mean identification latencies for bigrams occurring in each of three positions within a four-letter array for subjects at each ability level.   While overall letter identification latencies are longer only for the poorest group of readers, the slopes of the array-length functions decrease as reading ability increases.   The high rate of scanning obtained with high ability readers (250 letters/sec) is five times that obtained with the poorest readers (48 letters/sec), and suggests that the strongest readers may be processing letters in parallel.   The interaction between bigram frequency and reading ability is illustrated in Figure 3.   The magnitude of the bigram effect decreases as reading ability increases.   While high ability readers are capable of efficiently processing letters that occur together in English over a broad frequency band, low ability readers'

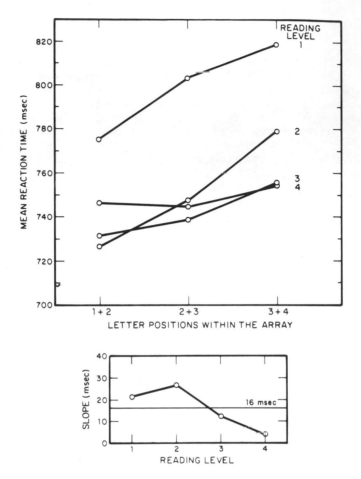

Figure 2.   Mean reaction times in letter identification plotted as a function of
bigram location and reading level. The slopes of fitted lines are plotted
at the bottom of the figure for each reading level.

efficiency in processing is limited to letter pairs that typically occur
together, with high frequency.

    For all subjects, the effect of bigram probability is most marked
when the critical pair of letters is presented in the first two
positions, and appears to decrease as the position of the letter pair is
moved from left to right within the array (see Figure 4). Finally,
positional redundancy was found to influence letter identifications only
when the bigrams are of low frequency and in the first position. In
that instance, bigrams having high positional likelihoods were
identified an average of 14 msec faster than were those having low
positional likelihoods.

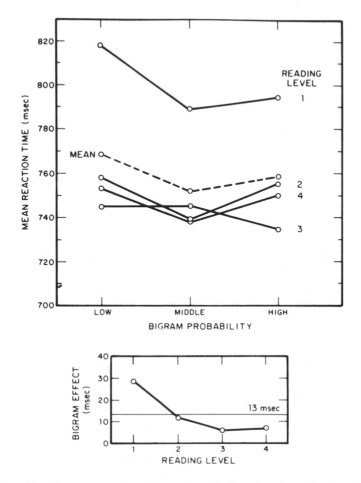

Figure 3.   Mean reaction times in letter identification, plotted as a function of
            bigram probability and reading level. The size of the bigram effect
            (mean for low frequency bigrams minus the mean for middle and high
            frequency bigrams) is plotted at the bottom of the figure for each
            reading level.

     To summarize, we found differences in processing efficiency at the
perceptual level between subjects who are high or low in overall reading
ability. Low ability readers scan a visual array more slowly than do
high ability readers, and they are slower in identifying letters when
they do not occur in a predictable sequence. The fact that readers, in
general, are able to exploit sequential and positional redundancies
characteristic of English orthography suggests that the processing of
individual letters does not proceed independently from the processing of
adjacent letters (cf. Landauer, Didner, & Fowlkes, Note 1).

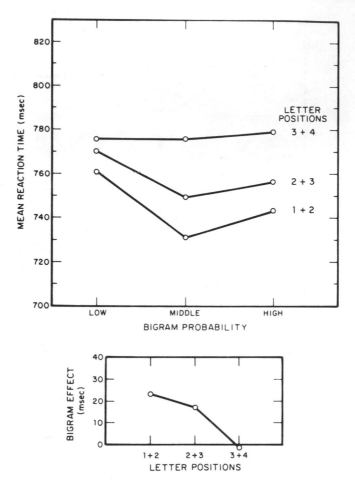

Figure 4.   Mean reaction times in letter identification, plotted as a function of
bigram location and bigram probability. The size of the bigram effect
is plotted at the bottom of the figure for each location.

The Decoding or Word-Analysis Domain

To study differences in decoding skills among readers, we selected
an oral reading (or pronunciation) task. Our strategy here was to vary
difficulty in decoding arrays of letters by manipulating the
orthographic structure of our stimulus materials. We can determine the
effect of orthographic variations on decoding latencies by studying
subjects' responses in pronouncing pseudoword items. If the pattern of
response times observed in the pronunciation of words is found to
resemble that obtained in this pure decoding situation, we will have
evidence for a decoding component in lexical retrieval. Absence of such
a pattern of response times will indicate that some other form of code
is utilized in gaining access to the lexicon.

The stimuli were words of high and low frequency, and pseudowords derived from the words by changing a single vowel. The words and pseudowords included 22 separate orthographic forms representing variations in length (four, five, and six letters), number of syllables (one and two), length of first syllable (two or three letters), type of vowel (primary or secondary; cf. Venezky, 1970), presence of a silent-e marker, and length of initial and terminal consonant clusters. These $\overline{22}$ forms were matched on initial letter (and phoneme). The stimulus array was exposed for 50 msec without any masking stimuli. The subjects were the same ones who participated in the previous experiment.

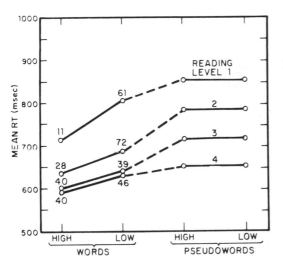

Figure 5. Mean onset latencies obtained in the pronunciation experiment for high and low frequency words and pseudowords, plotted separately for subjects at four reading levels.

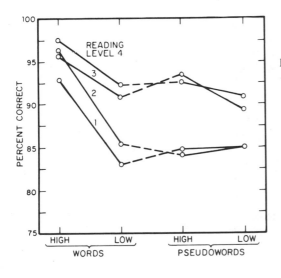

Figure 6. Percentage of correct responses obtained in the pronunciation experiment for high and low frequency words and pseudowords, plotted separately for subjects at four reading levels.

   In Figure 5, we see that there are significant differences in onset
latencies   for   subjects   having   different   reading   levels,   and   the
magnitude of these differences is greater for pseudowords than it is for
low   frequency   words,   which   is,   in   turn,   greater than that for high
frequency words.   Percentages of correct pronunciations   are   shown   in
Figure   6.   Skilled readers make fewer errors in pronouncing pseudowords
and low   frequency   words   than   do   less   skilled   readers,   but   these
differences   in   accuracy   of   pronunciation   are   not   present when the
stimuli are common words.   In summary, readers appear to differ in   both
the   accuracy   and   efficiency   with   which they decode English spelling
patterns, and the differences in performance for high   and   low   ability
readers   are   most   marked   when   the   letter patterns to be decoded are
unfamiliar.

   Turning to the effects of variations in orthographic structure,   22
separate   orthographic forms were represented within each of the classes
of   stimuli   (words   and   pseudowords   of   high   and   low   frequency).
Restructing our attention for the moment to pseudoword decoding, we find
that the differences in mean onset latencies across these 22   forms   are
reliable,   the   average   reliability   across   the four groups of readers
being .72 (for Levels 1 to 4, respectively: .69, .90,   .57,   and   .73).
Next, we can compare the effects of orthographic variables on mean onset
latencies   for   words   with   those   for   pseudowords   by computing   the
correlations (calculated over the 22 forms) between mean onset latencies
for pronouncing high and low frequency words with those for pseudowords.
These correlations, expressed as percentages of the reliable variance in
pseudoword decoding times,   are   also   given   in   Figure   5.   For   poor
readers,   latencies   for naming high frequency words are not predictable
from pseudoword decoding times (11% and 28%), while latencies for naming
low   frequency words are closely related (61% and 72%) to those obtained
for pseudowords having similar orthographic forms.   However, in the case
of   high   ability readers, latencies for naming words are predictable to
the same degree for both high and low frequency words.   For low   ability
readers,   the   identification   of   low   frequency   words   utilizes
word-analysis (decoding) skills similar to those that   are   required   in
pronouncing   pseudowords,   but   the   recognition of high frequency words
relies on more holistic properties of words -   presumably   their   visual
characteristics,   as   Perfetti and Hogaboam (1975) have suggested.   High
ability readers, on the other hand, are efficient decoders and   tend   to
employ   those highly developed skills in the recognition of high as well
as low frequency words.

   A detailed analysis   of   the   effects   of   particular   orthographic
variables   on word recognition latencies is shown in Figure 7.   Here are
shown the results of planned comparisons among orthographic forms, which
yielded   significant effects in the decoding of pseudoword items.   Onset
latencies are longer for items having longer initial consonant clusters.
They are longer for pseudowords and low frequency words having secondary
vowels (e.g., SAID) than for those having primary vowels   (e.g.,   SONG),
and these differences are larger for poor readers than for good readers.
Onset latencies for two-syllable items   exceed   those   for   one-syllable

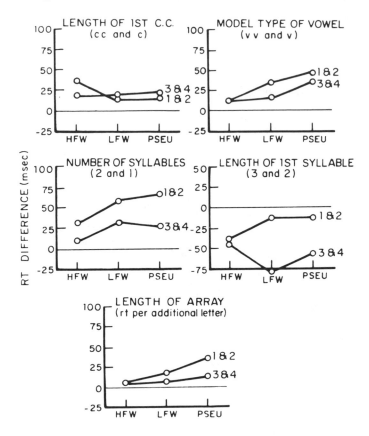

Figure 7.   Differences in onset latencies for the planned comparisons among orthographic forms as a
function of stimulus type (high frequency words, low frequency words, and pseudowords).
Separate plots are given for readers at the top two and bottom two levels.

items, and these effects are greater for poor readers than for good
readers. The syllable effects appear to be larger when the initial
syllable is two letters long, than when it has three letters. Finally,
the increase in response time for each added letter is greater for poor
readers than for good readers, and depends upon word frequency.
Together, these results show that readers of varying ability differ
substantially in their efficiency in decoding the more complex
orthographic forms.

The Lexical Domain

The purpose of the lexical decision experiment was to investigate
methods used for decoding and lexical access during silent reading by
subjects who vary in overall reading ability. In addition, we were

interested in evaluating the effects of manipulating the visual
familiarity of a letter array on subjects' performance in decoding and
lexical retrieval. This was accomplished by altering the letter cases
used in presenting stimulus words and pseudowords. Visually familiar
stimuli were presented in a consistent letter case (e.g., WORDS or
words), while visually unfamiliar stimuli were presented using a mixture
of letter cases (e.g., WoRd).

The effects of case mixing on times for lexical decisions can be
anticipated on the basis of an analysis of decoding presented in Figure
8. When stimuli are presented in a consistent case, multiletter units
can be directly identified, leading to a simplification in the decoding
process. Presenting items in mixed cases decreases the size of visually
encodable units, and increases decoding demands, since decoding must
begin with a larger number of initial units. Mixing letter cases
should, therefore, increase the magnitude of array-length effects, which
are attributable to letter encoding and processes of decoding; however,
mixing of letter cases should not lead to an increase in size of
syllable effects, since syllabication is thought to take place after
decoding of the letter array. We expect the effects of letter mixing to
be greater for poor readers than for good readers, since any increase in
the demands placed upon decoding skills will have a particularly strong
impact on readers who are poor decoders.

The effects of mixing letter cases on word frequency effects should
be minimal for high ability readers, since for these readers, the coded
phonemic representation accurately portrays the stimulus item that
furnishes the basis for lexical retrieval. For poor readers, however,
the picture is expected to be different. Poor readers are not only

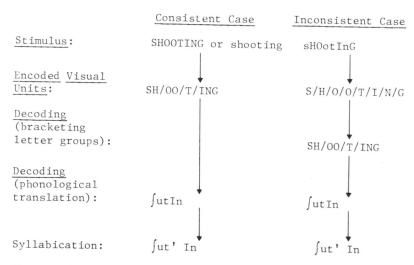

Figure 8.   Hypothetical processing stages in decoding under single case and mixed
             case conditions.

deficient in decoding skills; they tend to employ visual strategies for word recognition when a word is familiar to them. The effect of case mixing is simultaneously to eliminate the possibility of using a visual recognition strategy and to increase the difficulty of successful decoding, thus obtaining an accurate phonemic representation of the stimulus. Since poor readers must base their lexical decisions on an imperfect representation of the stimulus, they can be expected to require additional time for lexical retrieval.

    The stimulus items included in the experiment were words and pseudowords varying in length (four, five, and six letters), syllabic structure (one and two syllables), and frequency class (four equal logarithmic frequency intervals). The subject's task was to judge whether an item was a word or pseudoword, and to respond by depressing an appropriate response key. One group of subjects was presented with items in a consistent letter case while a second group was presented the items using a mixture of letter cases. There were 16 subjects in each treatment group, with four subjects representing each level of reading ability.

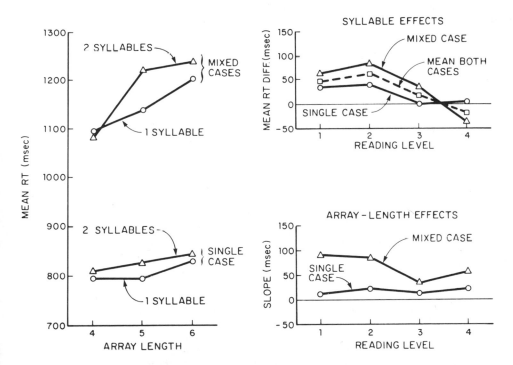

Figure 9.   Mean response latencies for single and mixed case stimulus presentation obtained in the lexical decision experiment. On the left, mean latencies are shown for words and pseudowords varying in length and number of syllables. On the right, the magnitude of syllable effects (difference between 2 and 1 syllable items) and of array-length effects (slopes) are shown for readers at each of 4 ability levels.

Reaction time changes obtained as a result of case mixing are shown in Figure 9. There was an increase in magnitude of array-length effects from an average of 17 msec in the single-case condition, to an average of 66 msec in the mixed-case condition. The interaction between visual familiarity (single- vs. mixed-case presentation) and array length was significant at the .005 level. At the same time, there was no significant interaction between syllabic length and visual familiarity, $F(1,24) = .46$, $p = .50$), although the main effect of syllabic length was significant ($p < .05$). Two-syllable items required an average of 27 msec longer to process than did one-syllable items. The magnitudes of array length and syllable effects under each mode of stimulus presentation are shown at the right of Figure 9 for subjects at each reading level. Several trends are apparent. First, the effect of case mixing on slopes of array-length functions is greater for low ability readers than for high ability readers. Second, syllable effects disappear in the case of high ability readers, but are present in the case of low ability readers.

The effects of case mixing on mean response latencies for words in each frequency class are shown in Figure 10. There are no significant differences among subjects at the four reading levels when the single case mode of presentation is employed. However, when visually unfamiliar stimuli are used, we find an increase in the height and slope of the reaction time functions. The overall mean response latencies for words and pseudowords presented in single- and mixed-case modes are shown in Figure 11 for subjects at each reading level. Mean reaction times for the poorest group of readers jumped from 866 msec in the single-case condition to 1281 msec in the mixed-case condition when words were judged, and from 831 msec to 1629 msec when pseudowords were judged. However, only small effects of visual familiarity on response latency were found for the two strong groups of readers. The magnitude of the frequency effect is plotted in Figure 12 as a function of reading level. For the two poorest groups of readers, there is an increase in size of frequency effects when visually unfamiliar stimuli are employed. No such increase is found for high ability readers. This suggests that the adequacy of a phonemic translation, as a cue for lexical retrieval, depends upon the reading level of the subjects. The types of errors made by good and poor readers lend additional support to this interpretation.

In Figure 13, we see that the major source of errors was a failure of subjects to identify low frequency words correctly. While the error rates in recognizing low frequency words are not affected by the mixing of letter cases to produce visually unfamiliar stimuli, error rates in decoding and categorizing pseudowords are influenced substantially by visual familiarity. There were more errors when the pseudowords were presented in a mixture of letter cases than when they were presented in a single-letter case. The overall error rates for poor readers were higher than those for good readers. This was due to two sources: Poor readers were less able to recognize low frequency words than were good readers (39% correct compared with 58% correct), and poor readers were

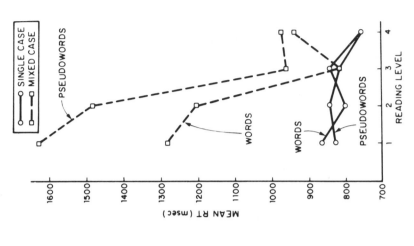

Figure 11. Overall mean lexical decision latencies for words and pseudowords presented under single and mixed case conditions, plotted as a function of the subjects' reading level.

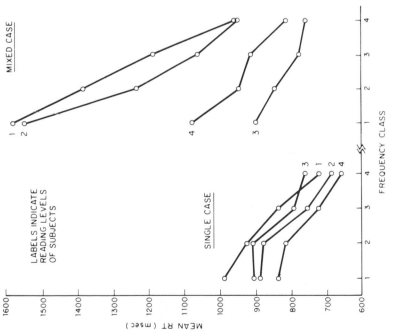

Figure 10. Mean lexical decision latencies are shown for words belonging to four frequency classes, presented under single case and mixed case conditions. Data are plotted separately for subjects at each reading level. The frequency classes represented the following intervals: 1 = 1/M (Million) or fewer, 2 = 2/M to 5/M, 3 = 6/M to 29/M, and 4 = 30/M or greater.

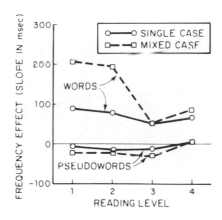

Figure 12. Magnitude of the word frequency effect obtained with words and
pseudowords, using single and mixed case modes of presentation. The
ordinate values are magnitudes of negative fitted slopes, and represent
decreases in reaction time for unit increases in frequency class.
Frequency effects are plotted as a function of subjects' reading ability.

less able to accurately decode linguistically regular pseudowords (82%
correct compared with 93% correct for good readers).

In summary, the strong effects of case mixing on reaction times and
errors in making lexical decisions demonstrate that the visual
familiarity and integrity of multiletter units is essential to the
process of word recognition. The interaction between array length and
visual familiarity supports the conclusion that decoding processes -
dependent as they are on the number of units to be decoded - proceed at
a slower pace when the units to be decoded are individual letters. On
the other hand, the minimal influence of case mixing on the magnitude of
syllable effects suggests that syllabication and stress assignment occur
after a phonemic representation has been built that is independent of
the visual familiarity of the stimulus. Poor readers were found to be
particularly susceptible to stimulus manipulations that increase demands
placed on the decoding system - in the present case, by reducing visual
familiarity. This deficiency in decoding ability may be due to an
imperfect mastery of rules for phonic analysis, to deficits in more
basic processing subsystems (e.g., immediate memory) that are utilized
in decoding, or to both of these sources. That subjects of varying
reading ability do not differ in times for retrieving low and high
frequency words that are visually familiar suggests that their skill
deficiencies may be localized at the perceptual and decoding levels;
however, the effect of case mixing on word frequency effects for poor
readers shows that times for lexical retrieval can be elevated if the
stimulus representation used in accessing the lexicon is of uncertain
accuracy and quality.

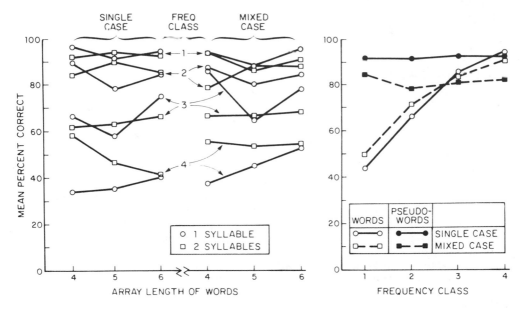

Figure 13. Percentage of correct lexical decisions for words varying in length, number of syllables, and frequency class (shown on the left), and for pseudowords and words varying in frequency class (shown on the right).

Conclusions

We have demonstrated that there are striking differences among readers in perceptual and decoding skills, and in their use of such skills in making lexical identifications. We have not, however, so far found any substantial differences among readers in times for lexical retrieval beyond those that are attributable to skill differences at the perceptual and decoding levels. Differences among readers at the lexical level are those dealing with variations in the extent of vocabulary.

The question can be asked, why do readers who differ in skills at the perceptual and decoding levels also differ in their ability to comprehend written discourse, as required in the Nelson-Denny Reading Test. Two possibilities come to mind:

1. Processing capacity and automaticity of decoding. Perfetti and Hogaboam (1975) have suggested that decoding and phrase-level processes compete for limited processing resources. Thus, a reader who must constantly shift his attention from phrase-level processing (e.g.,

building semantic representations, drawing inferences, solving problems of reference, etc.) to individual word decoding will have greater difficulty in comprehension of a text than will a reader who decodes swiftly and automatically, and who can concentrate processing resources on the problem of text understanding.

   2. Covariance of skill deficiencies across levels of processing. Another possibility is that, due to educational and cultural factors, readers who differ in perceptual and decoding skills are also likely to differ in higher-level skills involved in understanding text. These phrase-level skills, apart from the conditions under which they are learned, may he functionally independent of lower-level decoding skills. If this is the case, tests of reading comprehension that have been matched to a reader's level of proficiency in decoding should continue to show reliable differences in readers' responses to comprehension items. Whatever the resolution of this issue, I feel that on the basis of our results, it is feasible to measure differences among subjects in processing efficiency and accuracy within specified domains, through the use of experimental methods of analysis. Hopefully, the results of this effort will provide measures that can be used to evaluate the effects of instruction and to suggest alternative strategies for improving reading ability.

Footnotes

   This research was sponsored by the Personnel and Training Research Programs, Psychological Sciences Division, Office of Naval Research, under Contract No. N0014-76-0461, Contract Authority Identification Number, NR 154-386. I would like to thank Richard Pew and Marilyn Adams for fruitful discussions during many phases of the work, and Barbara Freeman and Jessica Kurzon, who implemented the experimental design.

   1. Bigrams were selected on the basis of frequencies of occurrence and positional likelihoods in four-letter words as recorded in the Mayzner and Tresselt (1965) tables. Twelve bigrams were selected for each combination of location (Positions 1 and 2, 2 and 3, and 3 and 4), bigram probability (low, middle, and high), and positional likelihood (low and high). There were no significant differences among these groups of bigrams in (a) the product of the probabilities of the individual letters, or (b) the product of the positional likelihoods of the individual letters.

   2. Note that other theorists (e.g., Spoehr & Smith, 1973) have favored a theory of syllabication prior to decoding.

   3. In this and subsequent analyses reported, distinctions between upper and lower single-case presentations are ignored. In a prior analysis of variance of single-case data, no significant effects of case were observed.

Reference Note

1. Landauer, T. K., Didner, R. S., & Fowlkes, E. B.   Processing stages in word naming: Reaction time effects of letter degradation and word frequency. Technical Memorandum, Bell Laboratories, Murray Hill, NJ, 1976.

References

Mayzner, M. S., & Tresselt, M. E. Tables of single-letter and bigram frequency counts for various word-length and letter position combinations.   Psychonomic Monograph Supplements, 1965,   1(2), 13-32.

Perfetti, C. A., & Hogaboam, T. The relationship between single word decoding and reading comprehension skill. Journal of Educational Psychology, 1975, 67, 461-469.

Spoehr, K. T., & Smith, E. E.   The role of syllables in perceptual processing. Cognitive Psychology, 1973, 5, 71-89.

Venezky, R. L.   The structure of English orthography.   The Hague: Mouton and Co., 1970.

A FUNCTIONAL ANALYSIS OF READING DISABILITY: THE UTILIZATION OF INTRAWORD REDUNDANCY BY GOOD AND POOR READERS

G. Scheerer-Neumann
Arbeitseinheit Kognitive Psychologie
Ruhr Universität
Bochum, Federal Republic of Germany

The Impact of Cognitive Psychology on the Study of Reading Disability

Research on reading disability has expanded considerably in the past twenty-five years. Even though scientists from different fields are working at the problem, the questions asked are surprisingly similar. Neurologists, psychologists, and educational researchers are trying to discover the basic causes of failure to learn how to read. The hypotheses set forth depend, of course, on the scientific background of the researchers. Thus, inheritance (Critchley, 1970), minimal brain dysfunction (Wender, 1971), perceptual deficits (Malmquist, 1958) and inadequate teaching methods (Schlee, 1976), to name but a few, have all been offered as hypotheses of the basic origin of reading disability.

While this approach may have some explanatory value, I feel that it does not offer all the information needed to develop a remedial program for the child who has already failed in learning to read. The assumption of "inheritance" does not offer any advice at all; the diagnosis "minimal brain dysfunction" could indicate a drug treatment that may improve a child's readiness to learn but does not teach him to read; remedial programs trying to compensate for a general perceptual deficit and thereby improve reading have not been successful at all (cf. Baker, 1973). By asking why these programs have failed, we might get some clue to the direction in which to proceed.

The expectation that perceptual training could improve reading is apparently based on the assumption that "perception" can be regarded as an entity that can be trained by any task as long as the stimulus material is visual. However, numerous studies that more or less subscribe to the information processing approach (cf. Neisser, 1967; Haber, 1969) have shown that most of the processes mediating recognition and retention of visual stimuli cannot be regarded as a set of invariant, structural features of the system (in the sense of Atkinson & Shiffrin, 1968); instead they have to be looked upon as control processes that depend, among other factors, on the task requirements, certain aspects of the stimulus material (e.g., verbal codability) and

171

the subject's experience.

It follows that like any other cognitive process, early reading should be understood as a set of <u>specific</u> component processes; whether some of these component processes could be "mimicked" and trained with figural stimulus material is a matter for further research. At our present state of knowledge, I question the relevance of most non-reading tasks both for the study and the treatment of reading disability. Instead, I feel that information that is truly relevant for the development of remedial reading programs could be obtained by applying an information processing approach to reading disability.   If we succeeded in identifying the elements or component processes of reading that cause problems for the retarded reader, but are mastered by his achieving age-mate, we could develop remedial programs specifically directed at those processes or system components.

A Model of Word Recognition

As a prerequisite for a functional analysis of reading disability, we need a model that specifies the operations and other system components involved in reading. At this point we may already feel inclined to give up. Geyer (1972) has counted no less than 48 different partial or comprehensive models of reading, and quite a few have been added since.   Still, the situation is not as chaotic as it may seem at first glance. The number of apparently competing models can already be reduced if we exclude those models that do not really offer alternatives but are concerned with different aspects of reading.   The models remaining for each aspect of reading are very often not mutually exclusive either, but should rather be looked upon as alternative process   configurations   that are utilized according to subjects' experience, the specific task demands, and the parameters of stimulus input. Still the picture is complicated enough. I therefore started my functional analysis of reading disability with a comparatively simple unit of reading, namely the reading of single words.

The most important (and by now quite venerable) question asked about the reading of single words refers to the size of the functional unit. Whole words, word shapes, spelling patterns, syllables, and letters all have been offered as the only, or at least the most important, unit in reading. The assumption of whole-word patterns or word shapes as the basic unit in reading can be refuted by a number of experiments showing that orthographically legal non-words or redundant letter strings are perceived almost as well as real words (Gibson, 1970; Baron, 1975). While this result has been obtained quite consistently, the mechanism of the utilization of redundancy or orthographic structure is still open to question.

Two of the explanations under discussion deserve closer inspection: the   "fast scan" hypothesis presented by Mewhort (1966) and the "unitization" hypothesis advocated by Gibson (1970), among others.   The fast scan hypothesis postulates a left-to-right encoding process (the "scan"), which operates on single letters; the higher transitional probability in redundant letter strings would allow the scan to operate faster, thereby increasing performance, given a constant processing time. The unitization hypothesis proposes a chunking process, which reduces the number of functional units in redundant as opposed to unrelated letter strings. The chunks thus formed could correspond to spelling patterns (Gibson, 1970) or to syllables (Spoehr & Smith, 1973).

I favor the unitization hypothesis for the following reason: Several experiments have shown that any alteration in the stimulus pattern that could counteract the chunking process, such as spacing (Mewhort, 1966) or alternate coloring of the letters (Wolff, Note 1), reduces performance considerably with highly redundant stimuli, while there is almost no effect with material of low redundancy.

My model of word recognition belongs to the unitization type. As a first stage of processing I propose a parallel visual process, which parses the letter string into chunks; for the German language I suppose that these chunks would mainly correspond to syllables. Once the chunks are established, the scanning process is initiated. It operates on the chunks as units in a left-to-right manner on the chunks. The relevance of the parsing process for reading is apparent. It determines the number of chunks that have to be scanned, thereby controlling the complexity of the task. Given the central function of the parsing process, I felt that poor readers might not have acquired the appropriate strategy and would therefore be forced to proceed on a letter-by-letter basis. While letter-by-letter scanning need not lead to reading errors by itself, it should increase the difficulty of the task to such an extent that letter omissions, inversions, and replacements could hardly be avoided. On the basis of these considerations, the first experiment was designed to test the hypothesis that reading disabled children do not use intraword redundancy to the same extent as good readers; the purpose of the second experiment was to deal with the mechanisms involved.

Experiment 1

Method

Subjects. The subjects were 16 normal and 16 poor readers from third grade, selected according to their performance in an oral reading test, the Zürcher Lesetest (Linder & Grissemann, 1967). The test consists of two subtests: reading of isolated words and paragraph reading. None of the poor readers reached a percentile of 15; all of the normal readers scored at 90 or above. None of the poor readers included in the experiment failed in naming single letters. The two groups were matched according to sex (eight boys in each group), age (mean age in both groups: 9.4 years) and non-verbal I.Q. (Raven Coloured Progressive Matrices); I.Q. scores were 111 and 109 for normal and poor readers, respectively.[1] All children were tested for their visual acuity.

Stimuli and apparatus. Stimuli were strings of eight lower case letters, either of first or of fourth order of approximation to German. Stimuli were presented by a three-channel projection tachistoscope. Each stimulus was preceded by a fixation cross adjusted between the fourth and fifth letter and followed by a crosshatched mask. The visual angle subtended about five degrees.

Design and procedure. Each child received 15 trials in each order of approximation, including three practice trials; conditions were run in a pure list design. The children responded by writing down the letters on a prepared answer sheet. Exposure time was adjusted individually so that accuracy was fixed on first order of approximation at about three letters out of eight.

Results and Discussion

Responses were scored only with respect to letter identity. Figure 1 shows the percentage of letters reported correctly. It can be seen that both groups improved their performance with fourth order as compared to first order of approximation; however, the difference was considerably larger for the good readers. The interaction between order of approximation and reading ability was highly significant, F (1,30)=17.5, p<.001).

The data are thus quite straightforward: reading-disabled children do not utilize intraword redundancy to the same extent as skilled readers, although there is an indication that they make some use of it.

The mean exposure times needed to reach the criterion of three letters on first order strings differed significantly between the groups, t (30)=2,71, p<.05; mean exposure times were 175 msec and 250 msec for normal and poor readers, respectively. While there is additional evidence that poor readers might take longer to identify single letters (Scholz, 1976), I cannot ignore that some of my first order stimuli contained transitional probabilities higher than chance. Given the present data, I cannot decide upon this issue.

The main result of the experiment - better utilization of intraword redundancy by normal as compared to poor readers - is not new. As early as 1927, Hoffman had shown that normal readers surpassed poor readers in the tachistoscopic recognition of common words, while there was a much smaller difference with respect to consonant strings. More recently, Wallach (1963) has found a considerable correlation between the utilization of intraword redundancy and reading ability. The inferiority of poor readers on structured stimuli is not specific to the tachistoscopic whole-report paradigm; it has also been demonstrated in an experiment using a visual search technique (Mason, 1975) and in a same/different comparison task (Scholz, 1976; Scheerer-Neumann, Note 2).

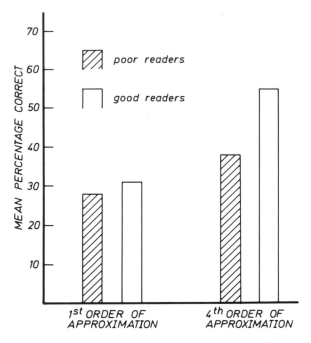

Figure 1.   Accuracy of report as a function of approximation to German and reading
             ability.

These studies confirm the proposed relationship between reading
ability and utilization of intraword redundancy. However, they do not
reveal the mechanisms involved, a knowledge of which is crucial for any
attempt to remediate the deficit of poor readers. My second experiment
was therefore designed to demonstrate that the inferiority of poor
readers on structured stimuli can indeed be attributed to a specific
deficit in parsing and chunking.

Experiment 2

The rationale of this experiment was the following: If poor
readers do not use a parsing strategy by themselves, they should improve
their performance when presented with stimulus material that is already
grouped into syllables. Good readers should not profit that much from a
syllable grouping manipulation, since it might only save them some
processing time without generally affecting their strategy. On the
other hand, grouping the letters across syllables should impede normal
readers, because it would counteract their strategy.

Method

     The subject sample and basic method (exposure times, number of
trials, etc.) were identical to Experiment 1. Only stimuli of fourth
order of approximation were used. The eight letters were grouped by
inserting spaces of the size of single letters. The screen was slightly
removed in order to keep the width of the grouped stimuli identical to
the ungrouped stimuli. There were two conditions. In the
within-syllable-grouping condition, there were three syllables of two or
three letters each. In the across-syllable-grouping condition, spaces
were inserted within syllable boundaries; unfortunately, I could not
tear apart all the syllables, since it seemed indispensable to keep
Number 3 and size of letter groups (two-three letters) comparable to the
within-syllable-grouping condition. Thus, at least one syllable
remained intact in each stimulus. The order of presentation of
conditions was counterbalanced in a Latin square design, including the
two conditions of Experiment 1.

Results and Discussion

     Figure 2 shows the percentage of letters reported correctly in
comparison to the data of Experiment 1. It can be seen that although
both groups profited from the syllable grouping and were impeded by the
across-syllable-grouping manipulation, the size of the effects is in the
predicted direction.

     According to Newman-Keuls comparison of means, there are
significant differences between the means of all three conditions
(within-syllable grouping, no grouping, and across-syllable grouping)
for the normal readers; for the poor readers, only the differences
between no-grouping and within-syllable-grouping as well as between
within-syllable-grouping and across-syllable-grouping, reach
significance ($p < .05$).

     The data address two issues: They demonstrate that parsing and
chunking are indeed important mechanisms in the utilization of intraword
redundancy, at least in third-grade children. They also show that poor
readers can be induced to take advantage of higher order structure when
an appropriate strategy is provided for them.

                              General Discussion

     Taken together, the results of Experiments 1 and 2 demonstrate that
one of the poor readers' problems is probably their inability to make
use of the higher order structure of words, but also suggest that the
unitization hypothesis is more adequate than the fast scanning
hypothesis in explaining how intraword redundancy is utilized.

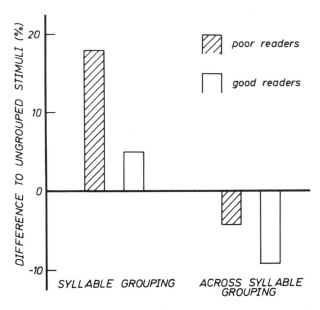

Figure 2.   Accuracy of report in the grouping conditions compared to the
ungrouped condition (fourth order of approximation only).

        Are these results relevant for instruction?   I have developed a
very preliminary version of a remedial reading program that tries to
teach children to analyze words into syllables as a first step of word
recognition.   Although   the   children participated in only 12 45-minute
sessions, particularly the very low-skilled readers showed a   remarkable
improvement compared to an untrained control group.   I will pursue this
project further.   The   crucial   point   would   be   to   go   back   to   the
laboratory after training.   I   would   only   be   satisfied if improved
reading   would   be   accompanied   by   better   utilization   of   intraword
redundancy   and   by a stronger impediment with across-syllable grouping.
This would be a prerequisite for the claim   that   in   this   very   narrow
field,   an   information processing   analysis and instruction can indeed
benefit from each other.

Footnotes

The experiments were run by H. Ahola, U. König, and U. Reckermann as part of their Diploma-theses.

I wish to thank Dr. Rudolf Müller for letting us use his yet unpublished norms for the Ravens test.

Reference Notes

1. Wolff, P. Verarbeitung der Identitäts- und Positionsinformation tachistoskopisch gebotener verbaler Reize. Dissertation, Bochum, in preparation.

2. Scheerer-Neumann, G. Formvergleich und Namensvergleich bei leseschwachen Kindern. Paper presented at the 19 Tagung experimentell arbeitender Psychologen, March 1977.

References

Atkinson, R. C., & Shiffrin, R. M. Human memory: A proposed system and its control processes. In K. W. Spence & J. T. Spence (Eds.), The psychology of learning and motivation, Vol. 2. New York: Academic Press, 1968.

Baker, G. P. Does perceptual training improve reading? Academic Therapy, 1973, 9, 41-45.

Baron, J. Successive stages in word recognition. In P. M. A. Rabbitt & S. Dornic (Eds.), Attention and performance V. London, New York: Academic Press, 1975.

Critchley, M. The dyslexic child. London: W. Heinemann Medical Books Limited, 1970.

Geyer, J. J. Comprehensive and partial models related to the reading process. Reading Research Quarterly, 1972, 7, 541-587.

Gibson, E. J. The ontogeny of reading. American Psychologist, 1970, 25, 136-143.

Haber, R. N. (Eds.). Information-processing approaches to visual perception. New York: Holt, Rinehart & Winston, 1969.

Hoffmann, J. Experimentell-psychologische Untersuchungen über Leseleistungen von Schulkindern. Archiv für die gesamte Psychologie, 1927, 58, 325-388.

Linder, M., & Grissemann, H. Zürcher Lesetest. Bern: Hans Huber, 1967.

Malmquist, E. Factors related to reading disability in the first grade of elementary school. Dissertation, University of Stockholm, Stockholm, 1958.

Mason, M. Reading ability and letter search time: Effects of orthographic structure defined by single-letter positional frequency. Journal of Experimental Psychology: General, 1975, 104, 146-166.

Mewhort, D. J. K. Sequential redundancy and letter spacing as determinants of tachistoscopic recognition. Canadian Journal of Psychology, 1966, 20, 435-444.

Neisser, U. Cognitive psychology. New York: Appleton-Century-Crofts, 1967.

Schlee, J. Legasthenieforschung am Ende? München: Urban & Schwarzenberg, 1976.

Scholz, R. Informationsverarbeitung bei Legasthenikern: Visuelle und phonetische Codierung. Unveröffentlichte Diplom-Arbeit, Bochum, 1976.

Spoehr, K. T., & Smith, E. E. The role of syllables in perceptual processing. Cognitive Psychology, 1973, 5, 71-89.

Wallach, M. A. Perceptual recognition of approximations to English in relation to spelling achievement. Journal of Educational Psychology, 1963, 54, 57-62.

Wender, P. H. Minimal brain dysfunction in children. New York: Wiley-Interscience, 1971.

LEARNING TO READ: VISUAL CUES TO WORD RECOGNITION

Keith Rayner and Carla Posnansky
University of Rochester
Center for Development, Learning, and Instruction
Rochester, New York, U.S.A.

The study of reading has a rich history in experimental psychology. Around the turn of the century,some of the most prominent experimental psychologists were conducting vigorous programs to study reading (cf. Huey, 1908/1968; Woodworth, 1938). While behaviorism depressed psychologists' interest in reading for almost a half a century, they have once again become interested in the basic processes involved in skilled reading and learning to read (Gibson & Levin, 1975). These processes are, of course, also of fundamental interest to educators who must deal with reading instruction.

Both early and recent researchers have been interested in studying the way that adults and children recognize words. Part of this interest is related to the fact that determining the basis of word recognition should have important implications for reading instruction and for understanding the processes involved in skilled reading. However, some researchers have questioned the relevance of word recognition studies to reading by pointing out that in everyday reading, words are seen in the context of sentences. Since it is true that skilled reading does involve contextual constraints, data from single word recognition tasks that are generalized to a skilled reading task have to be interpreted cautiously. However, children learning to read are often faced with the task of learning words in isolation, so we feel that the word recognition task seems particularly relevant to studying how children learn to read.

Still another caution is in order here. Researchers investigating adult word recognition should be extremely careful about generalizing their results to children. LaBerge and Samuels (1974) have pointed out that many processes that are automatic for adult readers are probably time-consuming, difficult processes for children learning to read. A classic case of inappropriate generalizations to children as a result of experiments with adults concerns the well-known experiments of Cattell in 1885-1886 (cf. Gibson & Levin, 1975). Cattell found that with a single 10 msec tachistoscopic flash, adult subjects could recognize three or four random letters, two unconnected words, and as many as four short words that made up a meaningful phrase. He concluded that the

words were read whole and not letter by letter. Upon hearing of
Cattell's results, the educational community concluded that since adults
read whole words, the most appropriate way of teaching children to read
would be a whole word approach. Of course, the basic flaw in this
generalization was the assumption that adults and children do the same
thing when they read. In the present paper, we will review a series of
experiments carried out with children in our laboratory. Our general
strategy has been to compare children who are learning to read with
literate older children and adults.

Marchbanks and Levin (1965) have reported that when children are
initially presented with a trigram stimulus and subsequently asked to
choose from four allternatives a word-like response that resembles the
stimulus, alternatives having the same first letter as a previously
presented stimulus are those most frequently chosen. Alternatives
having only the same overall word shape (no letters in common) with the
stimulus are those chosen least often. These findings hold for both
kindergarten and first-grade children. Unfortunately, the results of
this study and other similar studies have suggested to teachers that
word shape is not an important cue in word recognition for beginning
readers (Samuels, 1970). The additional finding that the use of word
shape for identification decreases with age (Fisher & Price, 1970)
conflicts with the finding that skilled readers use this cue from
parafoveal vision when reading (Rayner, 1975; McConkie & Rayner, 1976).
It should also be noted that a fair test of the extent to which word
shape is a viable cue has not been provided in the studies mentioned,
since word shape was manipulated independently of specific letters in
these studies. In actual texts, word shape never appears as a separate
entity from the letters that make up the word.

In order to assess more accurately the importance of word shape for
beginning readers, Rayner and Hagelberg (1975) carried out a series of
studies designed to deal with the criticisms of the delayed recognition
task mentioned above. Kindergarten children, first-grade children, and
adults were shown either a stimulus trigram or quingram and asked to
point to the response alternative most like the stimulus. However, half
of the response alternatives maintained the shape while the other half
altered the shape. Two alternatives also maintained each letter in its
correct serial position. Table 1 shows examples of the stimulus and
response alternatives. Rayner and Hagelberg found that kindergarten
children and first graders who were poor readers did not have a
consistent pattern of responses. First-grade children who were good
readers were clearly relying upon the first letter as the most important
cue. Adult, skilled readers chose alternatives with more distinctive
features in common with the stimulus (i.e., same-shape alternative)
about 90% of the time, while children beginning the reading process
chose such alternatives only 50-60% of the time.

Because of the large differences between the responses of the
beginning and skilled readers, another study (Rayner,1976) was carried
out with children from kindergarten through sixth grade and adults.

Table 1.   Examples of Stimulus Trigrams and Quingrams and the Response Alternatives

Stimulus	Response Alternatives	
	Same Shape	Different Shape
a. cug	cwq	cqn
	ouq	jun
	owg	jqg
b. bfa	bte	bsl
	dfe	efl
	dta	esa
c. mogad	mcqeb	mwnlr
	noqeb	tonlr
	ncgeb	twglr
	ncqab	twnar
	ncqed	twnld
d. fduhe	fbwka	frqpb
	tdwka	sdqpb
	tbuka	srupb
	tbwha	srqhb
	tbwke	srqpe

Quadrigrams were used in addition to trigrams and quingrams. Figure 1 shows the results of this experiment. Chance performance for choosing the first letter was 25% and for choosing the same shape alternatives was 50%. The results of Figure 1 make it clear that beginning readers rely very heavily on the first letter. Word shape becomes increasingly important with increasing reading skill, while the relative importance of the first letter decreases. Alternatives with the same first letter were still chosen above the chance level, but it is clear that older subjects did not rely on the first letter as their major cue.

In another recent study (Rayner & Press, Note 1) using good and poor readers from second, fourth, and sixth grade, we have found that good and poor readers within each of these grade levels did not differ from each other in terms of the visual cues they used. They did differ, however, when they were shown nonwords that differed in orthographic legitimacy. Poor readers in fourth and sixth grade were considerably poorer than good readers at choosing the alternative (among four) that was most like a real word. Likewise, there were clear developmental differences, such that the youngest readers performed at the chance level in terms of their responses.

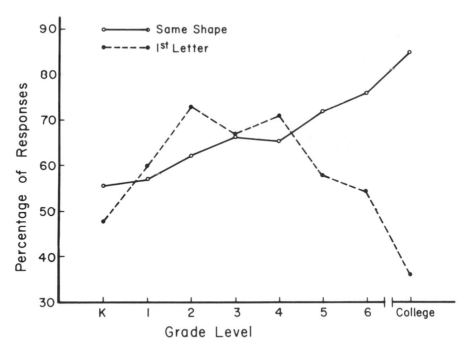

Figure 1.   Percentage of responses based on shape or initial letter similarity across grade level.

More recently, we have employed a modified Stroop paradigm in which print is superimposed on line drawings in order to examine the processing that occurs when children access the meaning of a printed word (cf. Chri, 1976; Golinkoff & Rosinski, 1976; Rosinski, Golinkoff, & Kukish, 1975). In the task, children named the picture presented regardless of the print on that picture. It had been reported by previous investigators that children do suffer from semantic interference in this paradigm. In our laboratory, we are currently using a more powerful, tachistoscopic version of this interference paradigm to study children's processing of the printed word in more detail (Posnansky & Rayner, 1977; Rayner & Posnansky, 1977).

In our first experiment, first-, third-, and sixth-grade children were asked to name pictures of line drawings that were presented tachistoscopically for 100 msec. Print was superimposed on each picture and the type of print printed on a particular picture came from one of six alternatives, which involved lexical, end-letter, and/or word shape changes. These alternatives are described completely in Figure 2. The mean reaction times for picture naming under each of these conditions were analyzed across grade levels; and hence reading ability levels of the subjects. Results indicated that for subjects in the third grade or older, conditions that preserved more of the visual features of the picture label resulted in faster naming times than those conditions that altered features (see Figure 2). When both word shape and end-letters of the picture label were preserved in the superimposed print, reaction times were the fastest of all nonword conditions. The picture label itself resulted in the fastest naming times and the alternative word (or Stroop) condition resulted in the slowest naming times.

The fact that all the nonword conditions were intermediate to these two word conditions allows us to conclude that there is some semantic interference generated in this paradigm, and the ordering of the nonword conditions allows us to conclude that the visual features studied were processed enroute to word meaning. First-grade readers performed more comparably under all the nonword conditions, suggesting that they were less able to take advantage of certain visual features. This finding is consistent with results found previously in the delayed recognition task (Rayner, 1976) and may be explained by the fact that beginning readers spend more time analyzing the features of each individual letter, while older, more skilled readers are able to analyze visual features from more than one letter at a time. Given the brief duration of the exposures in our tachistoscopic experiment, perhaps the beginning, first-grade readers processes the first letter, and upon encountering it or the next letter, they would know there was a problem since the printed stimulus did not match the picture. Thus, all of the nonwords were equally troublesome to the beginning reader. On the other hand, more skilled readers were able to abstract visual features from a number of letter positions simultaneously. In this case, the conditions violating the word shape and end-letters would be more interfering than the condition that did not.

The task we have just described can also be used to assess the extent to which phonemic recoding occurs when the meaning of a word is accessed. In another series of experiments, we have manipulated the degree to which the print superimposed on pictures is a phonemic match for the picture label. The presence or absence of a phonemic match has been varied factorially with the presence or absence of word shape and semantic content (i.e., homophones versus nonwords). We have found evidence of an equal degree of phonemic recoding for both beginning and more skilled (third-grade) readers. In addition, we are currently employing this versatile and powerful interference paradigm in order to determine the importance of word length as a cue to beginning and skilled readers, and to determine the extent to which semantic-conceptual interference is present in this task. Our current investigation of this latter hypothesis includes the factorial manipulation of both visual features (end-letters and word shape) and category membership.

The results of both the experiments we have completed and those currently underway have particular relevance for beginning reading instruction. Our results show that beginning readers (a) rely very heavily on the first letter in word identification, (b) are not sensitive to orthographic constraints in words, (c) do not take advantage of word shape information, and (d) do not process information

PICTURE

PRINTED IN PICTURE'S CENTER	CHARACTERISTICS	MEAN REACTION TIME (IN MSEC)		
		First Graders	Third Graders	Sixth Graders
heart	actual label	974.4	912.1	833.0
hcost	(1) preserves overall word shape of label (ascending and descending letters) / (2) preserves initial and final letters of label	1074.6	973.1	836.6
hskft	preserves initial and final letters of label	1052.0	1052.6	898.2
bcsof	preserves overall word shape of label	1058.8	1029.4	901.6
gkfsu	preserves neither word shape nor any letters	1088.0	1078.6	929.9
plant	labels another real word (same word frequency)	1140.6	1167.7	981.5

Figure 2.   Examples of stimulus manipulations with mean reaction time to stimulus types as a function of grade.

from a number of letter positions simultaneously. While it would seem feasible that reading development could be facilitated by specific instruction in which children are told, for example, to pay attention to word shape by presenting an outline around the word to make it distinctive

(e.g., dog),

our intuition is that such direct instructional strategies will not be effective. That is, all of the differences we have found between beginning readers and skilled readers relate to the idea that beginning readers must learn to process higher-order features of words. Thus, higher-order processing will result from experience with a lot of words. That word shape becomes important with increasing reading skill really reflects the fact that readers are processing the featural information from letters simultaneously. As we pointed out earlier in this paper, the shape of a word results from the features of the letters that comprise the word. The fact that beginning readers are not aware of orthographic regularities further points out that they do not process words in terms of higher-order features.

Given that trying to specifically point out differences in word shape between various words may not be a fruitful endeavor, what can teachers do to optimize children's ability to recognize words? Since beginning readers focus so heavily on beginning letters, we suggest that a great deal of discrimination training in which the first letter is held constant will prove beneficial for children. Thus, the teacher could show the child the word dog and dad simultaneously and show how they differ. In this case, to learn the word, the child has to direct the locus of attention away from the first letter. In summary, our research suggests that beginning readers do not process higher-order features from words and that teachers should develop techniques that force children to attend to salient features of the word other than the beginning letter.

Footnotes

This work was supported in part by grant number BNS76-05017 from the National Science Foundation to the first author. The authors wish to express gratitude to the Diocese of Rochester Catholic Schools (Sister Roberta Tierney, Superintendent) and their faculties and staff for their cooperation in the research described here.

Reference Note

1. Rayner, K., & Press, S. H. Visual and orthographic cues in children's word recognition (Center for Development, Learning, and Instruction working paper). Unpublished manuscript, University of Rochester, 1977.

References

Ehri, L. C. Do words readily interfere in naming pictures?   Child
    Development, 1976, 47, 502-505.

Fisher, V. L., & Price, J. H. Cues to word similarity used by children
    and adults: Supplementary report. Perceptual and Motor Skills,
    1970, 31, 849-850.

Gibson, E. J., & Levin, H. The psychology of reading.   Cambridge, MA:
    M.I.T. Press, 1975.

Golinkoff, R. M., & Rosinski, R. R. Decoding, semantic processing, and
    reading comprehension skill. Child Development, 1976, 47, 252-258.

Huey, E. B. The psychology and pedagogy of reading.   Cambridge, MA:
    M.I.T. Press, 1968. (Originally published, 1908.)

LaBerge, D., & Samuels, S. J. Toward a theory of automatic information
    processing in reading. Cognitive Psychology, 1974, 6, 293-323.

Marchbanks, G., & Levin, H. Cues by which children recognize words.
    Journal of Educational Psychology, 1965, 56, 57-61.

McConkie, G. W., & Rayner, K. The span of the effective stimulus during
    a fixation in reading.   Perception and Psychophysics, 1975, 17,
    578-586.

Posnansky, C. J., & Rayner, K. Visual-feature and response components
    in a picture-word interference task with beginning and skilled
    readers. Journal of Experimental Child Psychology, 1977.

Rayner, K. The perceptual span and peripheral cues in reading.
    Cognitive Psychology, 1975, 7, 65-81.

Rayner, K. Developmental changes in word recognition strategies.
    Journal of Educational Psychology, 1976, 68, 323-329.

Rayner, K., & Hagelberg, E. M. Word recognition cues for beginning and
    skilled readers.   Journal of Experimental Child Psychology, 1975,
    20, 444-455.

Rayner, K., & Posnansky, C. J. Stages of processing in word
    identification. Journal of Experimental Psychology: General, in
    press.

Rosinski, R. R., Golinkoff, R. M., & Kukish, K. Automatic semantic
    processing in a picture-word interference task. Child Development,
    1975, 46, 247-253.

Samuels, S. J. Modes of word recognition. In H. Singer & R. B. Ruddell (Eds.), Theoretical models and processes of reading. Newark, DE: International Reading Association, 1970.

Woodworth, R. S. Experimental psychology. New York: Holt, 1938.

STUDYING INDIVIDUAL DIFFERENCES IN READING

James L. McClelland and Mark D. Jackson
University of California, San Diego
LaJolla, California, U.S.A.

Perhaps as much as any other natural human activity, reading is a very complex process. Those of us who take an analytic attitude toward reading tend to think of it as a process that emerges from several simpler component information processing activities. We speak of the processes that control the movements of the eyes, guiding them to the the successive points of fixation in the text, and of the processes of letter and word identification. Some researchers stress the importance of phonological encoding processes, and syntactic processes are obviously important. Finally, we speak of the semantic processes that result in the comprehension of what is read, integrating the incoming information with information already stored in the reader's memory. An analytic approach may be necessary if we are to make progress toward an understanding of the reading process. At the same time, however, we should not lose sight of the fact that reading is not merely the concatenation of the components into which we divide it for the sake of analysis. In the fluent reader, it is clear that the components are all highly interdependent (Rumelhart, 1977).

These interdependencies are what make the study of individual differences in reading difficult. Because the components are interdependent, we cannot simply take at face value the individual differences we might observe in the more directly visible components of reading. A notorious case in point comes from early attempts to study individual differences (see Tinker, 1965, for a discussion). Early researchers (cf. Huey, 1908) discovered that faster readers made larger eye movements and fewer regressions than slower readers. Some inferred from this that the basis of individual differences lay in the control of eye movements, and many programs of reading improvement were developed that mainly stressed eye-movement training. Finally, of course, wiser heads prevailed, and we now believe that slow readers do not make shorter saccades because they have poor control over their eyes, but because limitations in other components of the reading process force them to spend more time processing a given amount of text (Tinker, 1961; Gilbert, 1959; Jackson & McClelland, 1975). More generally, this example illustrates the lesson that a difference between fast and slow readers on one particularly visible component of the complex reading

process is not sufficient to demonstrate that individual differences   in
reading actually arise from that component itself.

How are   we   to   go   about   isolating   the   sources   of   individual
differences   in   a complex process like reading, where it is likely that
every component of the process depends   on   every   other   one?   In   the
discussion   that   follows,   we   will consider various attempts.   We will
then turn to an application of an approach we have   adopted   from   Firth
(Note   1)   to   study   the role of individual differences in phonological
encoding in adult readers.

The obvious   way   to   get   around   the   problem   of   interdependent
component   processes   is   to   devise an information processing task that
retains some important aspects of the   reading   process   and   eliminates
others, and then determine whether individual differences in reading are
correlated with differences in the performance of the task.   If   so,   we
will be in a fairly good position to conclude that some processing skill
that contributes to the performance of our task is at   least   correlated
with   a   source   of   individual   differences in reading ability.   A nice
example of this research strategy comes from a study by Gilbert   (1959).
He   showed   phrases   and   sentences   up to five words long to readers of
varying ability under brief exposure conditions where multiple fixations
were   not   possible,   and   found that faster readers were able to report
more of the contents of the longer displays.   Gilbert's   results   nicely
suggest   that some processing skill underlying the ability to encode the
contents of a visual display is   at   least   related   to   one   source   of
individual differences in reading.

When we wish to go further than Gilbert's simple demonstration to a
more detailed analysis of the exact sources of individual differences in
reading ability, difficulties begin to arise.   One problem   we   face   is
that   the   set   of   possible   processing skills that might reasonably be
thought   to   underlie   the   ability   to   read   is   very   large   and   not
necessarily   mutually exclusive.   Even if we restrict ourselves to those
processing   abilities   that   might   underlie   efficient   performance   in
encoding   the   contents of a single fixation, there are many overlapping
possibilities.   What follows is a partial list.   It will be   clear   that
some   of   these   possible   sources   are   general   information processing
capacities, while   others   are   more   particular   potential   sources   of
individual   differences.   Further,   some of the possibilities, at least
within some theories, could underlie others on the list.

    1.   General   speed   and   efficiency   of   processing   visual
       information.

    2.   Capacity of short-term verbal memory.

    3.   Efficiency of the processes that translate   information
       from a visual to a verbal storage mode.

4. Ability to access stored representations of the letters, words, and/or phrases in the display.

5. Knowledge of orthographic constraints of English.

6. Knowledge of syntactic constraints of English.

Clearly, even if our goal is only to understand why faster readers are able to encode the contents of single fixations more efficiently than slower readers, we have a big job ahead of us.

We may wish to proceed by constructing single tasks that control for all but one of these possible sources of individual differences at a time, and see if any differences remain. The problem is that it is often impossible to construct a single task that adequately controls all of the possible sources of individual differences except the one of interest. Sometimes, however, it is possible to devise a pair of tasks (call them a and b), such that the only difference between the tasks appears to be that one (say, a) taps a specific processing ability of interest (call it x) and the other (b) does not. If it then turns out that individual differences in reading are related to differences in performing task a but not task b, we will be able to say that ability x is at least correlated with some source of individual differences in reading ability.

An example of the use of this strategy comes from Mason and Katz (1976). They wished to show that one important source of individual differences in reading lies in the use of knowledge of the positions that different letters are likely to occupy within words. For example, efficient readers might be more likely to use the fact that vowels tend to occur in medial positions while consonants tend to occur in initial and final positions. This hypothesis appears to be a special case of Item 5 in the list above. To test this hypothesis, Mason and Katz devised a task in which readers were required to search through a string of unfamiliar Greek letters to determine whether a predesignated target was present or absent. In one condition, the displays were constructed so that each target letter could only occur in a subset of the possible display locations, in an attempt to simulate the position constraints that operate in words. Mason and Katz predicted that good readers would be more likely to use the fact that each target could only occur in certain positions, and therefore, that they should be able to determine whether the target was present or absent faster than poor readers could. Since there are a large number of possible sources of individual differences that might result in better performance for faster readers in this task, Mason and Katz also included a condition in which all of the possible targets could occur in each of the possible display locations. Their hypothesis predicted an advantage for good readers in the condition where letter position was constrained, but not in the control condition. In fact, the prediction was supported by their results.

This experiment by Mason and Katz illustrates an important and valuable method that can be employed when a single task cannot adequately isolate a potential source of individual differences. In addition, however, the experiment illustrates a conceptual trap that is easy to fall into in individual differences research. Merely finding a task that differentiates good and poor readers does not permit us to conclude that the ability to perform this task itself is actually a source of individual differences in reading. Instead, some more general ability or skill may be responsible for the particular performance difference we are able to isolate in a specific experiment. Indeed, we may explain Mason and Katz's results simply by supposing that individual differences in the ability to read are due in part to individual differences in the ability to notice and use any regularities that will facilitate performance of the task at hand. This hypothesis is sufficient to account for the results, even if the set of regularities that readers use in reading (as opposed to visual search) does not include the letter-position regularities Mason and Katz manipulated in their experiment. It is, therefore, quite possible that differential use of letter position regularities per se is not a direct source of individual differences in reading ability.

This discussion of Mason and Katz's experiment illustrates a very general problem facing anyone who wishes to isolate a specific determinant of individual differences in reading ability. It is quite often possible to point to a more general potential determinant of individual differences that could account for differences between good and poor readers. One strategy that has often been used to overcome this problem is to equate groups of good and poor readers for some general factor such as I.Q., and then see if differences between the groups can still be obtained. This is the approach taken in a large number of studies by Perfetti, Lesgold, and their collaborators (Perfetti & Lesgold, in press). The approach is acceptable if the aim is only to point to the existence of a specific processing skill that is relatively uncorrelated with I.Q., and to identify this skill as a correlate of reading ability. However, this approach has several potential weaknesses: (a) By equating groups on I.Q., we might be eliminating exactly the source of differences that we wish to examine. An I.Q. score represents a collection of individual differences, and the specific ability that one wishes to isolate may well be a partial determinant of I.Q. In such a case, matching for I.Q. will have the effect of controlling the ability of interest. (b) By equating for I.Q., we can easily magnify a minor correlate of individual differences in reading ability beyond its true importance. If, indeed, I.Q. is strongly related to individual differences in reading ability, then groups that match in I.Q. and differ in reading ability will differ more strongly on factors that would have contributed only weakly to individual differences in reading ability, had we not force-equated the groups for I.Q. (c) Finally, because of statistical regression artifacts, the matching of groups on the basis of an I.Q. test will probably produce less than perfect matching of "true" I.Q. If whatever the I.Q. test measures is correlated with reading ability, and if there is any error of measurement in the test, then groups of good and poor readers who are matched for I.Q. test scores will differ systematically in true I.Q. A group of individuals who do well on a reading test but poorly on an I.Q. test will tend to include too many individuals who are actually more intelligent than their test scores indicate, and similarly, a group of individuals who do well on an I.Q. test but poorly on a reading test will tend to include too many individuals who are actually less intelligent than their scores indicate.

A recent study of individual differences in reading ability among eight-year-old readers by Firth (Note 1) illustrates these potential difficulties. Firth constructed four groups: good readers of high intelligence, good readers of average intelligence, poor readers of high intelligence, and poor readers of average intelligence. The groups were then tested on a large number of tasks. We will consider two of these tasks for purposes of illustration. One task tested the ability to sound out (produce the correct phonological code for) unfamiliar pronounceable nonwords (nonsense word test). The other task tested the ability to guess missing words from a sentence context. For example, given the context, "Before you put on your shoes you should put on your ...," the subject might be expected to guess "socks." Firth found that performance on the nonsense word test correlated highly with reading ability, but that the ability to guess words from context did not correlate with reading ability at all.

Firth's results suggest that individual differences in reading ability among eight-year-old readers are not due to individual differences in the ability to infer from context, but to differences in the phonological encoding skills underlying the ability to sound out novel letter strings. But, before we can accept this conclusion, we have to consider the possibility that the results are produced largely by the procedures Firth used to select subjects. If the ability to guess from context is a partial determinant of individual differences in reading ability, and if this ability is heavily correlated with intelligence, then controlling intelligence would be expected to diminish this factor's contribution to whatever differences in reading ability remained. And, if the ability to sound out nonwords were only a partial determinant of individual differences in reading ability, uncorrelated with intelligence, then we would expect it to assume greater importance when groups are matched for intelligence.

It is a simple matter to get around these matching artifacts. Instead of matching groups on I.Q., we need only give all subjects we plan to test an I.Q. test along with all the other more specific tests we wish to give, and then examine the pattern of correlations between reading ability and all of our other test scores, including intelligence. Indeed, Firth himself did just this in a second study of six-year-old readers. In this study (Firth, Note 1), he simply tested 100 children on a wide range of tests, including an I.Q. test and the nonsense word and guessing tests already described, and then looked to see which test scores actually correlated with reading ability. The result was that intelligence simply did not correlate very well with reading ability in this group of subjects. The ability to guess words in context also fared poorly, compared to the ability to sound out pronounceable nonwords. Thus, the data from this second study go a lot further than the results of the first in supporting the view that the major source of individual differences in beginning reading is the ability to carry out the phonological encoding operations required to sound out words.

This review has not done full justice to Firth's very impressive research. Because he tested readers on a large number of tasks and determined which scores correlated with reading ability and which did not, he was able to contrast a variety of specific and general hypotheses about the sources of individual differences in reading ability. This approach is particularly useful if we suspect that there is more than one source of individual differences in reading ability, as we almost certainly must when we consider adult readers. By using a multi-task approach, and by adding to it the techniques of partial correlation and regression analysis, we gain considerable power. We may contrast models in which several separate sources of individual differences come together to determine reading proficiency, against others in which one underlying source of individual differences accounts for differences in a range of processing tasks. In the remainder of this paper, we will illustrate the usefulness of this approach by applying it to an analysis of individual differences among readers at the university undergraduate level. In particular, we will show how these techniques can be used to address one important question about individual differences in reading ability: Is the ability to encode words phonologically a direct determinant of individual differences in the ability to read effectively for meaning?

Before we turn to our own research, it is worth considering other recent studies that bear on this issue. The results of several studies performed on high school and college students show that there is a correlation between phonological encoding skills and individual differences in reading ability (Chall, 1967; Calfea, Venezky, & Chapman, 1969; Frederiksen, in this volume). These results might be seen as support for the view that phonological encoding is required for accessing meaning, and therefore, that individual differences in phonological encoding skills are directly responsible for individual differences in the ability to read effectively for meaning. However, there are now several studies indicating that access to the meaning of a word does not depend on prior phonological encoding (Baron, 1973; Szumski, Note 2; Frederiksen & Kroll, 1976).

One possible way to resolve the apparent conflict between the individual differences studies on the one hand and the lexical access studies on the other would be to suggest that phonological encoding plays an important role in aspects of the reading process other than lexical access. Indeed, two recent experiments suggest that forming a phonological representation of a sentence may facilitate both memorization of the sentence and determination of its syntactic acceptability (Levy, 1975; Kleiman, 1975). However, neither of these tasks is precisely like the task of reading for meaning, and Levy's latest research (Levy, in this volume) suggests that formation of a phonological representation does not affect memory for semantic content.

Another possible way to resolve the apparent conflict is to suggest that individual differences in phonological encoding skills may reflect a more basic processing ability that differentiates good and poor readers. Specifically, both reading for meaning and phonological encoding depend on accessing memory from print. We suggest that individual differences in the speed and efficiency of this memory access process may lie at the source of the correlation between phonological encoding skills and the ability to read for meaning.

That both reading for meaning and phonological encoding depend on accessing memory hardly needs to be demonstrated. As Höffding (1891) pointed out a long time ago, we cannot associate the present sight of bread with butter without first associating the present sight of bread with traces of previous experiences with bread. Similarly, we cannot associate the present sight of a letter with the sound of that letter without first associating the present sight of the letter with traces of previous experiences with the letter itself. Thus, all we really need to show is that the correlation of reading ability with phonological encoding skill can be accounted for by the correlation of both abilities with a more general ability to access information in memory.

Our evidence comes from a study in which we compared fast and average college student readers on a large number of information processing tasks (Jackson & McClelland, Note 3, experiment 2). The fast reader group consisted of individuals who scored in the top 25% of a group of college undergraduates in mean performance on two tests of effective reading speed (speed times probability of correct response on a comprehension test). The average reader group consisted of individuals who scored in the bottom 25% of the larger group. For present purposes, we will only be concerned with three of the tasks. All three required subjects to compare two simultaneously presented stimuli and to determine whether they were the same or different according to a criterion specified in advance by the experimenter. One task was designed to pick up individual differences in the speed of accessing letter identity information from print. In this task (letter task; Posner, Boies, Eichelman, & Taylor, 1969; Hunt, Lunneborg, & Lewis, 1975), subjects were shown two letters, one of which was uppercase and one of which was lowercase. Sometimes, the two letters had the same identity (A a) and sometimes they did not (A b). The subjects simply had to determine whether the two letters were the same or different in identity and respond appropriately by pressing one button to indicate a same response and another to indicate a different response. A second task was designed to assess individual differences in speed of processing visual information, completing comparison processes and executing a response independently of accessing information in memory. In this task (dot pattern task), the stimuli were pairs of arrays of eight dots placed two to a row in a four-by-four grid. The arrays were constructed randomly, and we removed from the set of possible stimuli any array that was reminiscent of a familiar pattern or object. Sometimes, the two arrays were identical, and sometimes, they differed in that a single dot was displaced one cell to the left or right in one member of the pair. Thus, careful scrutiny was required to determine whether the two members of the pair were identical or not. As before, the subject had to determine whether the stimuli were the same or different and respond appropriately. Our third task (homophone task) was designed to tap individual differences in phonological encoding ability. The stimuli were pairs of pronounceable four-letter nonsense words. On some trials, both members of the pair would normally be pronounced the same (MERM-MURM); on others, the two members of the pair would normally be pronounced differently (MESP-MUSP). The subject's task was simply to determine whether or not the nonsense words would normally be pronounced the same or different and respond accordingly. In all three tasks, subjects were instructed to respond as rapidly as possible, consistent with accurate performance.

The results are shown in Table 1, averaged over same and different responses. The fast readers showed a 78 msec advantage over the average readers in the letter matching task (p<.025), and the correlation of reaction time in this task with one measure of effective reading speed was -.33; with the other it was -.34 (p = .07 and .06 respectively, one

Table 1. Mean Reaction Times and Error Rates for the Letter, Dot Pattern, and Homophone Tasks

	Reaction Times	
Task	Fast	Average
letter	586	664
dot pattern	1256	1230
homophone	1221	1365

	Error Rates	
letter	6.0	6.8
dot pattern	15.8	17.3
homophone	23.0	24.3

tailed; note that a negative correlation indicates that faster reaction
times are related to greater effective reading speed scores). The fast
readers showed an even larger mean advantage over the average readers in
the homophone task (144 msec), but the overall reaction times were
considerably longer, and the difference between groups was only
marginally reliable (p<.1, one- tailed). The correlation of reaction
time in this task with one measure of effective reading speed was -.27;
with the other it was -.22 (p=.1 in the first instance but p>.1 in the
second). The slight, nonsignificant (p>.5) difference between groups in
the dot-pattern task actually favored the slow readers, and the
correlations of reaction time in the dot- pattern task with the two
measures of effective reading speed were .10 and .08 (p>.5 in both
cases). In all three tasks, error rates were quite similar for the two
groups (p>.5 in all three cases).

What can we conclude from these results? Since we found no
difference between groups on the dot pattern task, our data do not
suggest that the differences we obtained in the letter and homophone
tasks were simply the result of any very general processing advantage
for faster readers independent of accessing information in memory. It
seems likely that the difference we found on the letter task is due to
the fact that it requires subjects to access and use information in
memory, while the dot-pattern task does not. It remains to be
determined whether the letter task reflects a memory access skill that
can be generalized to all types of familiar stimuli, or whether the
ability that is tapped by this task is restricted to accessing
representations of alphabetic stimuli from visual displays composed of
letters.

With regard to the homophone task, matters are somewhat more
ambiguous. To begin with, the relation between performance on this task
and effective reading speed is weak at best. But let us accept the
somewhat marginal statistical results for this task as reflecting a true
difference between fast and average reader groups in the ability to
perform the homophone task. The results we have presented thus far do
not permit us to determine whether the relation between performance on
the homophone task and effective reading can be accounted for completely
by a correlation of both homophone task performance and effective
reading speed with letter task performance. However, by using
correlational techniques, we are able to answer this question. The
correlation of letter reaction time with homophone reaction time was
.66, indicating that about half of the variance in the homophone
reaction time scores can be accounted for by the letter reaction time
scores. When we control for the letter reaction time score, the partial
correlation of the homophone reaction time score with one measure of
effective reading speed drops to -.07; with the other it becomes .01.
Thus, in spite of the fact that the size of the difference between the
fast and average readers was nearly twice as large in the homophone task
as it was in the letter task, our data provide absolutely no indication
that processes specific to phonological encoding of pronounceable letter
strings, as distinct from those involved in accessing representations of

letters from print, are correlated with individual differences in the ability to read effectively for meaning.

It should be clear that there could well be individual differences in skills specific to phonological encoding, and such differences could well be correlated with individual differences in the ability to read aloud, independent of any more general ability to access the relevant memory information from print. All our results suggest is that such differences may not be direct determinants of individual differences within our population of college students in the ability to read effectively for meaning. Firth's (Note 1) findings strongly suggest that the ability to sound out nonsense words is very important in early reading for meaning at a later stage. Finally, of course, it is possible that there is a slight role of phonological encoding skills per se in determining individual differences in the ability to read effectively for meaning, and our experiment simply failed to detect it. However, it is worth pointing out that our two measures of effective reading speed correlated .84 with each other, and that the split-half reliabilities of our letter and homophone reaction time scores were .94 and .90 respectively. Thus, there is not much room for error of measurement or attenuation of a true effect by random error in these results. It might be argued that a stronger partial correlation between phonological encoding and effective reading speed would have been obtained with a different sample of subjects from the same population. However, in the absence of such a partial, the results seem most compatible with the view that phonological encoding is at best an optional or secondary source of individual differences in the ability to read effectively for meaning in the mature reader.

The results we have reported here form only a part of a larger study of the determinants of individual differences in reading ability (Jackson & McClelland, Note 3). Several different analyses performed on the results of a large number of tasks, including a homophone task in which the stimuli were pairs of words rather than nonwords, support the conclusions reached here. In addition, it appears that the memory access component of individual differences in reading is relatively independent of a generalized language comprehension skill as measured by a test of comprehension of spoken language. Together, the generalized language comprehension skill and the memory access skill account for almost all of the nonerror variance in effective reading speed in our group of subjects.

The conclusion that individual differences in speed and efficiency of memory access is an important determinant of individual differences in reading agrees with the conclusions of Perfetti and Lesgold (in press). As they point out, accessing representations of the meanings of words in memory must play a crucial role in the comprehension of written text. It is also worth noting that accessing information in memory may well influence several other important components of the reading process as well. Within the context of models in which all components of the process are strongly interdependent (e.g., Rumelhart, 1977), it is clear that accessing syntactic, semantic, and lexical information in memory must be an important determinant not only of comprehension itself, but of the actual process of picking up information from the printed page. Faster access to the semantic and syntactic properties of words picked up in one reading fixation will leave the faster reader in a better position to use contextual information to infer letters and words he has not fully processed from the page, and to guide the movements of the eye to an advantageous position for picking up information on the next fixation. Indeed, if we adopt an interactive model of reading, there is hardly any aspect of the reading process that will not be facilitated by more efficient access to information in memory.

Footnotes

Preparation of this paper was supported by NSF Grant BNS76-24830 to the first author. We would like to thank our colleagues in the LNR and the M&N research groups for helpful discussions, and Robert Glushko for extensive comments on one draft of this paper.

Reference Notes

1. Firth, I. Components of reading disability. Unpublished doctoral dissertation, University of New South Wales, Kensington, N. S. W., Australia, 1972.

2. Szumski, J. The effects of specific visual experience on rapid visual word identification. Unpublished masters thesis, McMaster University, 1974.

3. Jackson, M, & McClelland, J. Processing determinants of reading speed. Manuscript submitted for publication, 1977.

References

Baron, J. Phonemic stage not necessary in reading. Quarterly Journal of Experimental Psychology, 1973, 25, 241-246.

Calfee, R., Venezky, R., & Chapman, R. Pronunciation of synthetic words with predictable and unpredictable letter-sound correspondences (Technical report 71). Madison: Wisconsin Research and Development Center for Cognitive Learning, 1969.

Chall, J. Learning to read: The great debate. New York: McGraw-Hill, 1967.

Frederiksen, J. R. Assessment of perceptual decoding and lexical skills
    and their relation to reading proficiency. In this volume.

Frederiksen, J. R., & Kroll, J. F. Spelling and sound: Approaches to
    the internal lexicon. Journal of Experimental Psychology: Human
    Perception and Performance, 1976, 2, 361-379.

Gilbert, L. Speed of processing visual stimuli and its relation to
    reading. Journal of Educational Psychology, 1959, 55 , 8-14.

Höffding, H. Outlines of psychology. New York: Macmillan, 1891.

Huey, E. B.   The psychology and pedagogy of reading.   New   York:
    Macmillan, 1908; Cambridge, MA: MIT Press, 1968.

Hunt, E., Lunneborg, C., & Lewis, J. What does it mean to be high
    verbal? Cognitive Psychology, 1975, 7, 194-227.

Jackson, M., & McClelland, J. Sensory and cognitive determinants of
    reading speed. Journal of Verbal Learning and Verbal Behavior,
    1975, 14, 565-574.

Kleiman, G. Speech recoding in reading. Journal of Verbal Learning and
    Verbal Behavior, 1975, 14, 323-340.

Levy, B. Vocalization and suppression effects in sentence memory.
    Journal of Verbal Learning and Verbal Behavior, 1975, 14, 304-316.

Levy, B. Speech processing during reading. In this volume.

Mason, M., & Katz, L.   Visual processing of nonlinguistic strings:
    Redundancy effects and reading ability. Journal of Experimental
    Psychology: General, 1976, 105, 338-348.

Perfetti, C., & Lesgold, A.   Discourse comprehension and sources of
    individual differences.   In M. Just & P. Carpenter (Eds.),
    Cognitive processes in comprehension. Hillsdale, NJ: Lawrence
    Erlbaum Assoc., in press.

Posner, M., Boies, S., Eichelman,, W., & Taylor, R. Retention of visual
    and name codes of single letters. Journal of Experimental
    Psychology Monographs, 1969, 79,(1), part 2.

Rumelhart, D. E. Toward an interactive model of reading. In S. Dornic
    (Ed.), Attention and performance VI. Hillsdale, NJ: Lawrence
    Erlbaum Assoc., 1977.

Tinker, M. A. Basis for effective reading. Minneapolis: University of
    Minnesota Press, 1965.

MEMORY FOR ON-GOING SPOKEN DISCOURSE

R. J. Jarvella, J. G. Snodgrass, and A. P. Adler
Project Group in Psycholinguistics
Max Planck Gesellschaft
Nijmegen, The Netherlands
and
New York and Rockefeller Universities
New York, U.S.A.

Much of the information that man acquires about the world is acquired using language. Speech and writing, in fact, are so pervasive as sources of material for human learning that our use of them is easy to take for granted. Yet, at present, remarkably little is known about how people process linguistic messages of even the most common variety.

This chapter reports a pair of experiments that were aimed at discovering how language of one typical form - namely, spoken connected discourse - may be understood. In this work, we try to combine reports by listeners of speech just heard in discourse with later checks on their understanding. The general approach rests partly on the assumption that, as a story unfolds, it is natural for a person hearing it both to keep up an analysis of the on-going text and to integrate what he learns from this with what has gone before.

The current studies extend a line of previous research in which a central concern has been the changing contents of immediate memory as discourse is heard. This has been studied using a variety of recall and recognition paradigms (see Jarvella, in press, for a review). Full sentences and clauses, which may be the smallest linguistic segments that are themselves interpretable in a story context, have been of special interest. Given the known short-term memory limitations of human listeners, it would not be too surprising if information was accumulated and processed from these segments largely as wholes. We have tried to look at people's verbatim memory representation for constituents on these levels, at the time they are heard, and shortly afterwards.

Our early work (Jarvella, 1971, 1972) did suggest that sentences themselves, and clauses within them, tend to function as units in "running" memory. Specifically, it was found that only the final sentence of discourse could be remembered well and that perfect verbatim recall was often limited to the last clause heard. Serial position

curves for probability of correct recall showed a sharp decrease, going
from the last sentence heard, into the one before it; these curves were
flat only within the final clause. The implications of these findings
for discourse processing, however, now seem less certain than they once
did.   What may be concluded most strongly from them is that just after
presentation of a full segment on either the clause or sentence level,
it is quite accurately represented in memory, and the one preceding it
is largely not. By this time, evidently, full-scale processing has
passed from one segment to the next.

Rather than pursuing the question of when the short-term memory
representation for a heard segment is degraded, or whether this is
brought about to some degree by any following clause or sentence,
subsequent research (e.g., Jarvella & Herman, 1972; Jarvella, 1973;
Marslen-Wilson & Tyler, 1976) has concentrated on the effects of other
linguistic factors. Therefore, how abruptly this change takes place and
what is responsible for it remain largely a matter of conjecture.   The
present paper tries to address both of these ignored issues.

As mentioned above, two studies will be reported. In both, small
groups of adult listeners heard a pair of discourse passages (taken from
Jarvella, 1971), which were interrupted at various points to test for
immediate recall. The first experiment was an attempt to replicate and
work backwards from earlier results. Recall of a clause or sentence was
tested after varying sized fractions of the following clause of the
discourse had also been heard. Here, it was the course of forgetting
that was investigated. The second experiment, on the other hand, was an
attempt to work forwards from the earlier findings. One- and two-clause
sentences, heard last in the discourses, were recalled when followed by
a clause or sentence instruction to write them down, or simply by an
extended pause.   Here, the question asked was whether grammatical but
fully uninformative segments would produce a similar effect of
forgetting as segments which, in the first study and previously, were
part of the story themselves.

Experiment I

Method

Two narrative passages, each about 1500 words long, served as the
materials.   One was about a case of political slander and the other
about a union election. Each passage contained 12 episodes, ranging
from about 50 to 250 words in length. Before being specially altered
for the experimental manipulation, eight episodes from each passage (the
others were distractors) had two alternative endings. Either a short
sentence preceded a long one, or a long sentence came before a short
one.   Together, the two sentences always consisted of three clauses,
seven, six, and seven words long; across endings, the final two clauses
were the same. The following is an example:

SHORT-LONG: "The confidence of Kofach was not unfounded. To stack the meeting for McDonald, the union had even brought in outsiders."

LONG-SHORT: "Kofach had been persuaded by the international to stack the meeting for McDonald.   The union had even brought in outsiders."

It had been shown previously that the final clause of either type of ending was remembered best by listeners, the middle clause was remembered better when it belonged to the final sentence, and the nonfinal sentences were remembered worst of all.

In the present experiment, the episodes were cut short, and presented without their final clause, or with part, most, or all of it present. For example, each of the endings shown above was shortened to end just after the middle clause (with "McDonald") and in the three forms underlined below:

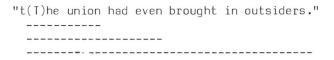

"t(T)he union had even brought in outsiders."

Thus, the first clause of the long final sentence in episodes was followed by zero, two, four, or all seven words of the second clause; or the long nonfinal sentence was similarly followed by zero, two, four, or all seven words of the short final one. Eight balanced versions of the passages were constructed and presented to listeners via a tape recorder.

Sixty-four students from New York universities served as subjects. During each passage, recall of the test sentences was prompted using tone signals; from the 16 specially designed episodes, only the long sentences were cued.   Subjects were instructed to write down the sentence being prompted as accurately as possible, word for word. Following each passage, they were asked to write a summary of what happened in it.

Results

All subjects' summaries indicated they had understood and remembered the meaning of the passages. Hence, we will be concerned here only with verbatim written recall of the test sentences.   For the sake of brevity, only a single measure will be reported: If a word recalled was from the sentence prompted, it was scored as correct regardless of the order in which it appeared in the response. This type of measure has previously been found to be highly positively correlated with ordered recall and recall of full segments. Significance levels reported were reached by both subjects and items using nonparametric statistics.

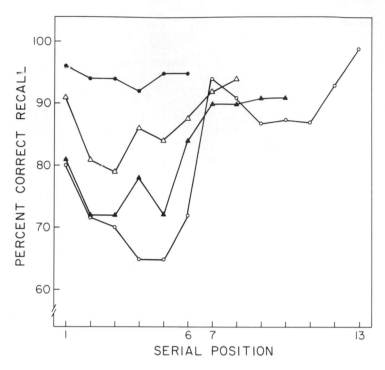

Figure 1.   Word recall by serial position in long final sentences: ● = first clause only; △ = plus two
words; ▲ = plus four words; ○ = plus all seven words of second clause.

     Figure 1 plots percent correct recall for the final   sentences   in
the SHORT-LONG condition, where the amount of the final clause heard was
varied.   The clause boundary lies between the sixth and   seventh   words
from   the   left.   Recall for these sentences' initial clause was highly
accurate (94.7% correct) and the serial position curve was   fairly   flat
only when no part of the later clause followed it. As the second clause
was heard, recall of the first one became   progressively   weaker.   With
the first two words of the later clause heard, recall in the earlier one
dropped to 85.4%, with four words to 76.4%, and with all seven words, to
70.7%.   Interestingly,   the   only significant decrease observed between
adjacent curves shown was between no further speech heard and the first
two words of the second clause ($\underline{p} < .01$ two-tailed).

     It is evident from Figure 1 that it was just at the clause boundary
that   these   sentences were segmented in memory. In all three instances
where additional material was heard, accuracy   of   recall   rose   sharply
from the end of the first clause into the beginning of the second, while
the average level of recall in the second   clause   was   about   the   same
whether   two,   four,   or   all   seven words were heard (92.9%, 90.7%, and
91.2%, respectively).

For the nonfinal sentences from the LONG-SHORT condition (not shown), results were quite comparable. Followed by zero, two, four, and all seven words from the following short sentence, word recall for these items averaged 76.9%, 57.9%, 51.7%, and 37.1%, respectively. Again, the only stepwise difference that was significant was between no further speech heard and the first two words of the next segment ($p<.01$ two-tailed). Secondly, accuracy of recall rose substantially at the beginning of these sentences' second clause, except where the full following sentence was heard. In each case, the first word of this clause was recalled better than those in the six other positions falling in the middle of the sentence.

Discussion

To recapitulate, for both clauses and sentences, hearing only two words of a new constituent was sufficient for recall of the previous one to fall off significantly. Therefore, memory for the exact form of a clause heard in discourse seems to persist until it is complete, but if a new clause follows, it often does not persist beyond this time. At the sentence level, there is a similar phenomenon. As one sentence begins, the integrity of the prior one's representation in memory may be promptly destroyed.

Still, exactly what kind of processing gives rise to this rapid forgetting is not fully evident. Are we to infer, for example, that listening to any following sentence or clause will produce the effect, and it is therefore based on syntax itself, or that meaning also must be processed from the new segment heard? Accordingly, it seems reasonable to test whether a noninformative clause or sentence will lead to much the same result as one relevant to the story. This test was attempted in the following study in a rather crude way, by using clause and sentence instructions to cue recall.

Experiment II

Method

The same materials were used as in Experiment I. This time, however, the test items were presented in their full original form. Thus, the final sentence heard for these episodes was 13 words long in the SHORT-LONG condition, and seven words long in the LONG-SHORT condition. The passages were recorded in three ways. In one form, the episodes were read aloud, separated only by extended pauses, as in Jarvella (1971). In a second, a clause was always appended to the final sentence saying:

"and now write down this sentence."

In the third form, a sentence of the same length was added instead, saying:

"Now write down the last sentence."

Sixty students from New York universities served as subjects. Where extended pauses were used, subjects were told simply to write down, word-for-word, the last sentence heard. In the other conditions, subjects were told to write down the last sentence going up to, but not including, the instructions. After each passage, subjects answered a series of true-false questions about it.

Results

Subjects' answers to the true-false questions were generally correct, indicating that they had a good idea of what had happened in the passages. Their recall responses were scored and analyzed as in the previous study. Figure 2 shows the corresponding serial position curves found. There were two obvious effects of clause recency in this second experiment. The first of these largely replicates Experiment I. The earlier clauses of the long sentences that were prompted were recalled more poorly (85.9% correct) than either their later clause (92.2%), or the identical (later) clause given as a separate sentence (96.6%) ($p<.001$ for each one-tailed). Secondly, recall of the cued sentences as a whole was also worse when they were followed by instructions than by silence ($p<.001$ for sentences, $p<.05$ for clauses, both one-tailed).

What is perhaps most striking about Figure 2 is that neither the sentence nor clause instructions that were added at the ends of episodes affected the shape of the recall functions very much. Compared with the clause recency effect shown in Figure 1, or that in Figure 2(a) between the first and second clauses of long sentences heard, the effect of processing an uninformative second clause in Figure 2(b) was a slight decrease in accuracy throughout the first clause. Secondly, the clause and sentence instructions had little effect on the recall function for the full 13-word sentences shown in Figure 2(a), compared with the nonfinal sentences prompted in the earlier experiment. The final clause in the sentences shown appears hardly affected at all.

Conclusion

Two parallel divergent results were obtained in these studies. On the one hand, the course of verbatim memory for the first clause of a sentence was quite different, depending on whether the second clause was also part of the discourse itself, or a recall instruction. On the other hand, recall of a two-clause sentence was substantially impaired when the sentence following it was itself part of the story, but not when it was an instruction to recall. The results of the second experiment weakly support the view that hearing any sentence or clause in discourse will lead to forgetting of the prior one; the "sentence" effect was also greater than that for clauses ($p=.06$ by subjects overall). However, other processing of immediately heard segments in discourse than perception of their clause- or sentence-hood per se

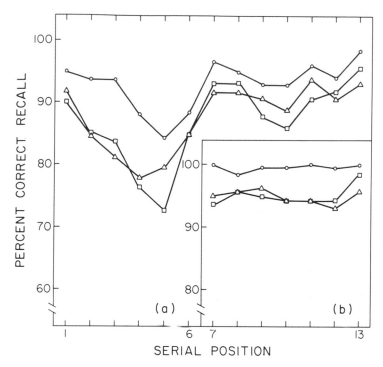

Figure 2.   Word recall by serial position in 13-word (a) and 7-word (b) final sentences: ○ = no further speech heard; △ = plus clause instruction; □ = plus sentence instruction.

appeared to lead to rapid forgetting of the ones preceding them.   This processing may indeed have been for units that were syntactically circumscribed, but processing of syntax itself seems to have had only a marginal effect.

      The generality of the present results is, of course, limited.   Not all linguistic messages we process are spoken or continuous, or require such close monitoring. What knowledge is acquired from them will also depend on other factors, some of which are considered elsewhere in this volume.   Still, the kind of basic linguistic processing suggested here is probably common to many contexts where learning from text is of interest. That other results are often dependent on it may be worth remembering.

210   R.J. Jarvella, J.G. Snodgrass, and A.P. Adler

This research was supported in part by a grant from the Volkswagen
Foundation to the Max Planck Gesellschaft, and by the United States
National Institute of Education (Grant G-76-0101) to the Rockefeller
University.   The authors wish to thank Lisa Rosen for technical
assistance, and W. J. M. Levelt and G. A. Miller for helpful comments.

References

Jarvella, R. J. Syntactic processing of connected speech.   Journal of
Verbal Learning and Verbal Behavior, 1971, <u>10</u>, 409-416.

Jarvella, R. J. Speech processing memory. In C. P. Smith (Ed.), 1972
conference on speech communication and processing.   New York:
Institute of Electrical and Electronics Engineers, 1972.

Jarvella, R. J.   Coreference and short-term memory for   discourse.
Journal of Experimental Psychology, 1973, <u>98</u>, 426-428.

Jarvella, R. J.   Immediate memory   in   discourse   processing.   In
G. H. Bower (Ed.), The psychology of learning and motivation:
Advances in research and theory (Vol. 12).   New York: Academic
Press, in press.

Jarvella, R. J., & Herman, S. J.   Clause structure of sentences and
speech   processing.   Perception and Psychophysics, 1972, <u>11</u>,
381-384.

Marslcn-Wilson, W., & Tyler, L. K. Memory and levels of processing in a
psycholinguistic context.   Journal of Experimental Psychology:
Human Learning and Memory, 1976, <u>2</u>, 112-119.

PRECURSORS OF READING: PATTERN DRAWING AND PICTURE COMPREHENSION

S. Farnham-Diggory
University of Delaware
Newark, Delaware, U.S.A.

I would like to acknowledge Dr. Siegler's elegant demonstration of the first point I would like to make - that readiness is not magic. There are always going to be mechanisms - some particular things that a child must do in order to succeed on a task. Dr. Siegler has shown how a task involving the balance beam can be analyzed, in order to pinpoint certain mechanisms. I am going to be analyzing two other tasks which - like the balance beam - are typically found in kindergartens: pattern drawing, and picture comprehension.

These two tasks are considered to help prepare children for reading. The general notion - the informal theory operating in the kindergarten - is that mastery on tasks of this sort is a signal that a child is ready for reading instruction. I am not testing that proposition. On the contrary, my point is that we will not be able to test such propositions until we have detailed models of both readiness tasks and reading tasks. Not until we have such models will we be in a position to investigate the questions of whether or not there are connections and relationships among readiness and reading; whether or not specific instruction can accelerate readiness performance; and whether or not improvement on a readiness task will transfer to a reading task.

I will have nothing more to say here about a model of reading, except to note that I am confident that Dr. Anderson's group at the University of Illinois is going to be able to produce the models we need. My concern in this paper is with the analysis of two readiness tasks. I can only give you samples of the analysis, which is very complex and detailed. But, I believe the samples will illustrate the promise of this approach to school tasks.

Pattern Drawing

Let me begin with pattern drawing. By pattern drawing, I mean specifically the ability to draw simple geometrical forms - squares, triangles, diamonds - from memory. This is different from pattern copying, where the pattern remains in front of the child. In our

211

experiments, the child was shown a particular pattern, such as a square, for five seconds, and then the pattern was removed, and the child drew it from memory. In that way, we made sure a child knew which pattern was meant, whether or not he knew exactly what it was called.

The idea in this case was to record the <u>process</u> of drawing a pattern, not merely the <u>product</u> - the completed drawing. Traditionally, only products are examined. But what is the child doing inside his head in order to produce a drawing? We begin with a very detailed description of a stream of behavior, and construct a hypothetical model of the internal processes that could be producing that behavior.

The first problem obviously is to record the process of drawing a pattern. But how should the recording be made? Where do you put the camera? Over the shoulder looking down at the hand? Then you miss the eye-movements. Do you put the camera out in front, looking at the face? Then you miss the hand-movements.

Our solution was to have a child draw on transparent plastic sheets, backed against a transparent plexiglass panel, rather like an artist drawing on an easel. The video cameras were in front and photographed the child <u>through</u> the plexiglass panel. One camera photographed the whole child, and a second camera photographed only the child's eyes. Both cameras recorded on the same tape, in a split-screen effect. The lower two-thirds of the recorded image showed the whole child, and the top one-third contained a close-up of the child's eyes. That made it possible to be sure exactly where the child's eyes and hands were, at the same moment in time. To make the scoring easier for us, the child drew on a matrix of nine black dots. We could later refer to those dots by number, and could say that the child's eyes were on Dot 3 while his hand was at Dot 5, and so on.

The next problem was to categorize the pattern drawing behavior. One interesting type of behavior we called <u>tracking</u> - where the eye looked ahead, and the drawing hand caught up to it. Another interesting type we called <u>monitoring</u> - where the hand and eye were in the same place, so that the eye was watching the hand. The amount of time spent alternating from tracking to monitoring could be determined exactly from the videotapes. We could also count alternation units - the number of times the child switched from tracking to monitoring in a continuous sequence. Table 1 shows the tracking times, hand monitoring times, and length of the alternation sequences, for eight 5-year-old children drawing eight patterns. The children's names arc down the side; you can see there werc four boys and four girls. The patterns they drew are across the top. The times are in milliseconds.

Some children and some patterns produced more alternation units than others did. The square U produced an average of ten alternation units; the Stair, only an average of six. Tammy alternated a lot; Helen, only half as much. The children generally spent more time watching their hands than tracking - at least twice as much time,

Table 1. Number of Alternation Units, Mean Tracking Time (msec), and Mean Hand Monitoring Time (msec) During Alteration Sequences

	+	⊔	⊓	□	△	▽	◇	⌐	Mean	Mean Tracking Time	Mean Hand Monitoring Time
Lewis	9	14	7	3	10	4	15	8	8.7	493	824
Randy	3	12	12	10	10	13	9	9	9.7	498	812
Terry	10	6	9	4	8	2	4	7	6.2	435	1765
Jimmy	5	13	3	9	11	8	6	10	8.1	574	1338
Tammy	9	14	13	6	8	9	17	5	10.1	604	1088
Helen	5	6	4	7	8	11	0	2	5.4	540	979
Tina	6	11	7	16	4	10	4	4	7.7	554	1125
Mary	5	7	8	14	10	11	16	9	10.0	440	1490
Mean	6.5	10.4	7.9	8.6	8.6	8.5	8.9	6.7	8.2		
Mean Tracking Time	454	460	513	512	592	517	552	535		517	
Mean Hand Monitoring Time	1254	1210	1377	961	1268	1065	1082	1129			1167

usually more. This suggests that children learn about trajectories, and become able to make predictions about where lines are going to end up, by observing their own hand movements during drawing. Hand- watching may be a mechanism of operational development in Piaget's terms (Piaget & Inhelder, 1967, 1971).

The most interesting numbers in the table are the mean tracking times, which average 500 msec. That means a child looked ahead, on the average, just far enough for his hand to need about 0.5 sec to catch up to where his eyes were. This is especially interesting because we have known since Woodworth's (1899) experiments that 0.5 sec is about how long you need to register visual information. If a hand moves faster than that, the head will not have time to register where that hand is going. Child after child, and pattern after pattern, the rate at which these children moved their eyes ahead indicates they had developed a tracking rhythm that coordinated hand and mind.

I believe the same type of coordination is necessary in reading. I would expect that children who could not rhythmically coordinate eye, hand, and mind in pattern drawing might also be unable to coordinate eye and mind in reading. That may be the basis of the fact that pattern drawing skills are moderately predictive of reading skills. We plan to test this hypothesis in the future.

There are many additional ways of analyzing the processes of pattern drawing. Figure 1 shows Tina drawing two patterns, a square and a diamond. The symbols at T1 mean that Tina has looked at the lower middle dot, and is drawing toward it (tracking). That goes on for 332 milliseconds. The symbols at T2 mean that she is monitoring her hand, for 1345 msec. At T3, she is tracking again, for 381 msec. The solid line is the part she has drawn. You can follow her drawing of the square all the way to T14, where the square is completed.

Now look at the next two columns, where she is supposed to be drawing a diamond. Like many 5-year-olds, Tina cannot draw diamonds, and ends up drawing another square. If we just looked at the two completed squares – at T14 and at T28 – we would not see anything different. Look especially at T22. The symbols there mean that Tina had paused after drawing two sides of the squares and was looking around "wildly." All those arrows signify eye movements.

Look back at T9, where Tina had completed those same two lines in the process of drawing an intentional square. No wild looks. Back at T22, it is clear Tina must have realized something was wrong.

According to Piaget, 5-year-olds cannot draw diamonds because they lack the reversibility operations necessary for producing mirror images. The events at T22 suggest that Tina realized something was wrong just at the point where she should have activated a mirror image concept. Either she could not activate the concept, or her attempts to activate it led her to discover she was not drawing a diamond. We are planning experiments to investigate that question.

What might this have to do with reading? Reading is very much a matter of unpacking concepts, in sequence, when you need them. A child's ability to unpack a mirror-image concept, at the point that it is needed in a serial drawing task, may well be related to the ability to unpack concepts during reading.

Picture Comprehension

We now turn to the second readiness task: picture comprehension. This task grew from the very common types of classification exercises that go on in kindergarten, where a teacher shows the child pictures of foods, clothing, or animals, and asks "which of these go together," or some variation of that. The child is supposed to recognize that all the foods "go together," all the clothing articles "go together," and so forth.

A process model of such a task would include the following notions. To decide that spinach and cereal "go together," you have to postulate a person or agent who is performing an action with reference to objects. For example, a hat and shoes "go together" because a person can wear a hat, and a person can also wear shoes.

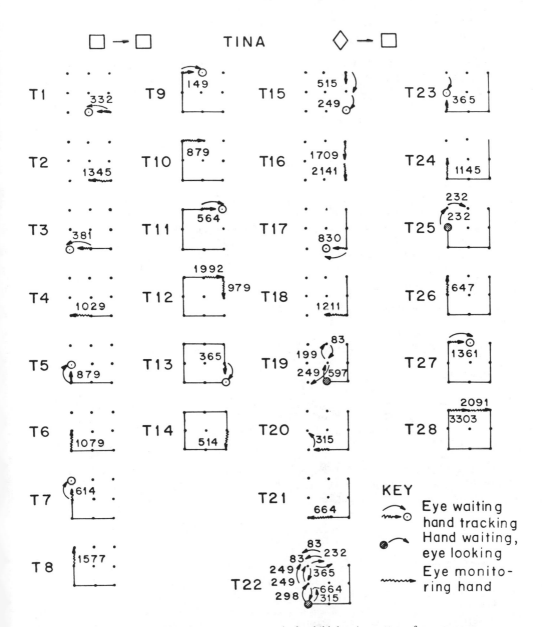

Figure 1.   Eye- and hand-movement protocol of a child drawing patterns from memory.

   That is how we came to design a picture comprehension task that
involved a person performing some kind of activity, and an object which
might or might not "go with" that scene. For example, think of a
postman delivering mail. Then think of a tricycle. Does the tricycle
"go with" the postman scene?

   We recorded the time it took subjects to decide whether the object
"went with" the scene or did not. The decision - yes or no - was up to
the subject. Having obtained a measure of the subject's decision time,
we stopped the clock and asked the subject why he made that particular
decision.

   If you analyze these explanations, you will discover that only a
small number of mental activities and tests are actually occurring.
Figure 2 shows a preliminary model of the decision process. First, an
explanation can reveal that the subject is testing the proposition that
a particular object is a customary part of a scene. For example, think
of a man carrying a garbage can. Now think of a vacuum cleaner. Do
they go together? Suppose a subject says something like, "No, a garbage
collector doesn't normally use a vacuum cleaner." Or, my favorite
response from several 5-year-olds, "No, because the garbage man only
delivers garbage."

   Those are Level 1 decisions. The subject has noticed, or
registered, the agent and the action - the man carrying out the garbage
- and has apparently asked himself the question: Is a vacuum cleaner a
customary part of that scene? He has decided it was not. His
consideration of the possibilities did not go any farther than that.

   But some explanations reveal that a subject has gone farther. He
has generated some explicit ideas about the actions associated with the
object - like vacuuming activities - and has mentally tested the
possibility that the person - the garbage man - might also do those
actions. This is what we call a Level 2 test. For example: Steven
says, "No, because a sweeper's to sweep dirt in, and a garbage man's to
carry garbage." Or Dirk says, "Yes, because a vacuum cleaner cleans up,
and the garbage man is cleaning up something too." In those cases, the
subject's explanation reveals that he thought explicitly about what you
do with the object in question.

   And still a third test is possible. You might be concerned over
whether or not the actions associated with the object - vacuuming
activities - are compatible with the action of the scene - carrying out
garbage. That is, can the two activities be performed at the same time,
or in the same place? If a subject's explanation reveals that he has
worried about compatibility, we call it a Level 3 explanation. Here is
an example: "Yes, because after he finished his garbage collection job
and went home he could clean his rug with the vacuum cleaner." The
subject has articulated his concern over the compatibility of the action
of vacuuming with the action of carrying out garbage.

DECISION CHART FOR "BELONGINGNESS" SCHEMATA

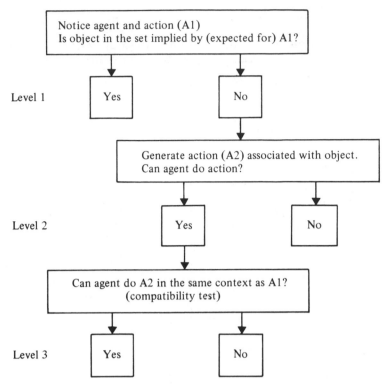

Figure 2. Model of the sequence of decision processes involved in answering such questions as "Here is a garbage man carrying out garbage (Al). Does a vacuum cleaner go with that scene ?"

The model in Figure 2 suggests that the tests are made in order from Level 1 to Level 3. That means Level 3 tests should be longest, and the Level 1 tests should be shortest, with the Level 2 tests in between. The model also specifies that the yes decisions are made before the no decisions, which means that the yes decisions should be faster.

Let us look now at the decision times of some 5-year-olds and adults who had each looked at a number of pictures like those described, and had given reasons why two pictures did or did not "go together." We grouped their Level 1 explanations, and averaged the decision times preceding those explanations. We grouped their Level 2 explanations, and similarly for the Level 3 set. So, we had an average decision time for Level 1, 2, and 3 decisions - regardless of which pictures were actually involved.

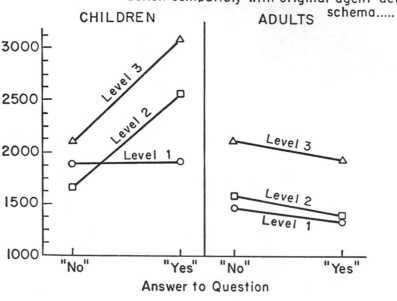

Figure 3. Decision times (msec) for children and adults whose explanations revealed they had made Level 1, Level 2, or Level 3 decisions (see Fig. 2).

The data for children and adults are shown in Figure 3. Adults take progressively longer to make Level 1, Level 2, and Level 3 decisons, as we expected. They also take a little longer to make no decisions than yes decisions at every level, as our model would also specify. Children take progressively longer to make Level 1, Level 2, and Level 3 yes decisions, but their yes decisions all have taken longer than their no decisions - contrary to our model.

Five-year-olds seem to make only one type of no decision - a relatively fast one, of the Level 1 variety. No, something is not a

usual part of an activity. As you can see in Figure 3, all the <u>no</u>
decisions are relatively fast, and they all seem to take about the same
amount of time. This is regardless of what the children say.   A child
may give a complicated Level 3 explanation of why something did <u>not</u> go
with something else. But, he actually decided <u>no</u> too fast for that
complicated explanation to have been part of the decision. Kindergarten
children seem to decide <u>no</u> first, and make up reasons afterwards.

But, this is not true of their <u>yes</u> responses.   As Figure 3
suggests, apparently a 5-year-old can delay a <u>yes</u> decision until after
he has checked out a rationale. Is the object in the set implied by the
original scene?   "Yes...but...," the child may say to himself, as he
checks out the Level 2 possibilities, and then the Level 3 ones.
Kindergarten children seem able to anchor a reasoning process in an
affirmative possibility, but not in a negative one. An adult may say to
himself, "Well, I <u>don't</u> think that's the case, but..." and then check
out additional possibilities before concluding a definite <u>no</u>.   Five-
year-olds do not seem to be able to do this. They cannot anchor a chain
of reasoning in a negative.

This sounds very much as if young children are not capable of using
negation operations, which is one of Piaget's most vigorous claims.
Along with reversibility, negation is not supposed to be present at the
age of five. The child may recognize a negative, and use complex forms
of negation in his language. But he is not - according to Piaget -
basing a train of reasoning processes on a negative. Negation is in the
language, but not yet in the reasoning process.

Analyzing the picture comprehension task in this way immediately
suggests some of the connections between that task and reading.
Certainly, reading comprehension is heavily dependent upon the child's
ability to test out a set of possible relations, to explore his semantic
net, and to find remote connections.

In conclusion, these two experiments have suggested some ways in
which we can construct a science of reading readiness, rather than a
readiness folklore, which is all we have at present. The growth of the
science depends, in my opinion, upon the development of methodologies
that permit fine-grained analyses.   It is not until we   analyze
kindergarten tasks in "slow motion," so to speak, that we can detect
their critical mental substrate.   If Piaget and other cognitive
theorists are right, theoretical principles should be visible in the
kindergarten as well as in the laboratory.

<u>References</u>

Farnham-Diggory, S.   <u>Cognitive</u> <u>processes</u> <u>in</u> <u>education</u>.   New   York:
      Harper & Row, 1972.

Piaget, J., & Inhelder, B. The child's conception of space. New York:
    Norton & Co., 1967.

Piaget, J., & Inhelder, B. Mental imagery in the child. New York:
    Basic Books, 1971.

Woodworth, R. S. The accuracy of voluntary movement. Psychological
    Review, 1899, Whole No. 13.

DEVELOPMENTAL CHANGES IN HEMISPHERIC PROCESSING FOR COGNITIVE SKILLS AND THE RELATIONSHIP TO READING ABILITY

Jules B. Davidoff
University of Edinburgh
Edinburgh, Scotland, U. K.

B. P. Cone and J. P. Scully
University of Wales at Swansea
Swansea, Wales, U. K.

Recent applications of the techniques and methodologies of cognitive psychology have had considerable implications for the study of brain function. Clinical observations concerning the fact that the disruption of specific cognitive tasks is critically dependent upon injury to particular areas of the brain have been backed up by evidence from information processing experiments with normal subjects. It is now clear that the time-honoured dichotomy between verbal and non-verbal skills has a real basis in terms of hemispheric specialization. In the majority of right-handed individuals, this latter-day phrenological analysis puts language-based skills in the left hemisphere and perceptually based skills in the right hemisphere. The verification of this dichotomy, which has been variously called digital versus analog or serial versus parallel processing or analytic versus wholistic analysis, is seen in the normal population by the application of two laboratory-based techniques.

The first of these is the method of dichotic stimulation, in which auditory material is simultaneously presented to the two ears. This methodology was successfully employed by Broadbent (1958) in the study of the role of a buffer store in memory. A reanalysis of these data by Kimura (1961) revealed considerable preference for the reception of input arriving at the right ear; this result has become known as a right ear advantage. This effect is still present when the necessary controls for order of ear report are carried out. Since contralateral brain pathways are presumably predominant over ipsilateral pathways, we may assume that the language-based hemisphere must be in control. The reverse seems to be the case for non-verbal sounds. Curry (1967) reported that environmental sounds can be shown to have a left ear advantage, presumably because in this case the right hemisphere is in control.

221

The second basic methodology employs visual presentations, and like the auditory methodology, has a physiological basis. The two retinae are divided anatomically into halves. The nasal half of the left eye and the temporal half of the right eye feed the right hemisphere occipital area, whereas the nasal half of the right eye and the temporal half of the left eye feed the left hemisphere occipital region. This method requires exact registration of the stimulus in the visual field, but once this has been established, it is possible to project stimuli, initially, to one hemisphere alone. This is done tachistoscopically with exposure times of less than 100 msec and with the subject looking straight ahead at a fixation point. A left visual field advantage is then found for non-verbal tasks (Kimura & Durnford, 1974), and a right visual field advantage for words (McKeever & Huling, 1970).

These effects are not without variation in adults. Indeed, Kinsbourne (1973) maintains that variations in individual attention and temporary hemispheric activation are at the very heart of these hemispheric biases. It is also known that these hemispheric specializations for information processing go through a period of plasticity in early life. Hemidecortication even of the left hemisphere does not seem to be as damaging in the child as it is in the adult, and the remaining hemisphere is able to take over both verbal and non-verbal functions. It becomes essential to study the relationship between hemispheric functions in a developmental manner to see if any change can be reliably associated with progressive educational attainment. Is it the case, for example, that one can estimate the verbal or spatial skill attainment of the individual child by investigating the hemispheric biases of that child?

Turning first to tasks that have been associated with the right hemisphere, does the left visual field advantage associated with visuo-spatial tasks or the left ear advantage associated with tone recognition remain constant during development? To this end, children were given tasks of dot detection and environmental sound identification. For the latter task, 194 right handed children (as assessed by the Harris Laterality Tests) were divided into groups, with girls and boys in each of five age groups (4, 6, 8, 10 and 12 years). They heard a dichotic tape that presented common environmental sounds for which verbal identification was required. Half of the children in each age group were of middle socio-economic status (SES) and half were of lower SES. These two groups attended different schools. The most pronounced left ear advantage was observed at age four for all groups, showing that the right hemisphere is predominant for this task at an early age. At age 12, left ear advantage was again present for all groups. However, between these ages an inverted U-shaped curve was seen for both SES groups and for both sexes. In all groups, the peak of the curve denoted a right ear advantage. The hemispheric advantage was computed by the proportion of left ear errors to total errors, expressed as a percentage, because this measure is relatively unbiased by the subject's overall accuracy (Papcun, Krashen, Terbeek, Remington, & Harshman, 1974). A three way analysis of variance (school x age x sex)

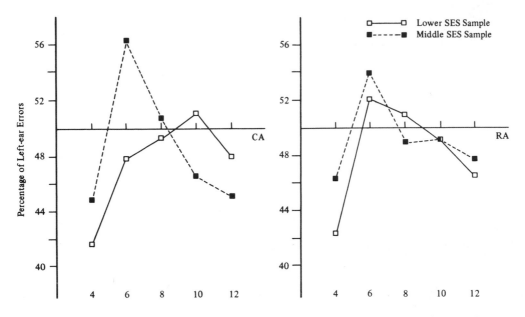

Figure 1.   Median percentage of left-ear errors plotted against Chronological Age (CA) (left panel) and plotted against Reading Age (RA) (right panel).

produced a significant age effect, $F(4,177)=4.99$, $p<.005$. This means that the hemisphere advantage differed at the five age groups. The school x age interaction (see Figure 1a) produced a trend ($p<.2$) for the middle SES children to peak into the left hemisphere earlier than the lower SES children. A non-parametric analysis (Mann-Whitney U-test) at age six reveals that for the middle SES children (n=20) there is a greater right ear advantage ($p<.05$) for the lower SES children (n=18). At age 10, exactly the reverse is the case with the lower SES children (n=22) having a greater right ear advantage ($p<.02$) than the middle SES children (n=18).

This finding of an age difference with respect to hemisphere advantage means a normally right hemisphere task is performed better by the left hemisphere at a given point in the schooling process before a return to right hemisphere processing superiority. It can also be seen that there is a considerable SES difference in the age of the language hemisphere take-over. Socio-economic status differences in hemispheric function have been noted before in children with the identification of dichotic digits. Geffner and Hochberg (1971) found no right ear advantage for a lower socio-economic status sample, but this was not repeated in a subsequent study by Dorman and Geffner (1974). This finding was, however, repeated by Borowy and Goebel (1976). Analysis in terms of SES must inevitably confound mental age with chronological age. Thus, as an index of verbal acquisition, each child was given the Burt

(re-arranged) Word Reading Test and the three-way analysis of variance
re-run, using reading age groups rather than chronological age groups.
This analysis produces just one significant effect, that of age,
$F(4,174)=2.78$, $p<.05$, showing once more that the hemisphere difference
is not the same at all ages. Indeed, this significant effect is made up
solely of a quadratic component, $F(1,192)=11.81$, $p<.001$, and a cubic
component, $F(1,193)=9.45$, $p<.005$, produced from the uptake into the left
hemisphere and the not-so-complete return to the right hemisphere (see
Figure 1b). It is important to notice the complete absence of any SES
effect at reading age six on the Mann-Whitney test. The middle SES
children (n=18) do not differ ($p>.3$) from the lower SES children (n=18).
Similarly, at reading age 10 the middle SES children (n=18) do not
differ ($p>.4$) from the lower SES (n=20).

This finding clearly emphasizes the need to use cognitive measures
of development when dealing with changing hemispheric functions. If
brain organization underlies such cognitive skills, chronological age
may well be a less informative variable to relate to the ontogeny of the
skill than mental age.

Witelson (1977) has suggested that developmental dyslexia in boys
is associated with an ambilaterlity for right hemisphere tasks. The
right hemisphere task reported above supports that view to some extent.
Girls did produce less lateralized performance, though not significantly
so, as Witelson (1976) reported. Poor reading skill is also associated
with an ambilaterality for the right hemisphere task. However, the
subjects used here were not dyslexic but normal. This ambilaterality
for children with developmental dyslexia (Orton, 1937) may therefore be
a result of the cognitive stage that the child has reached. It would
seem that beginning to read produces a change in hemispheric dominance
for non-linguistic material. Does it also produce a change for
linguistic material? To see if this was the case, 120 children at age
6, 8 and 10 listened to a dichotic stop consonant ($\underline{pa}$, $\underline{ga}$, etc.) tape.
This task has been associated with a steady right ear advantage for ages
five and upwards. However a percentage-of-errors analysis of the
results produced a significant age effect, $F(2,108)=7.60$, $p<.005$. This
occurred because the 6-year-old group showed much less right ear
advantage. Indeed, it was the lower SES 6-year-olds with an average
left ear advantage who were mainly responsible for this effect,
$F(2,108)=2.74$, $p<.075$. Once the right ear advantage had been
established at a reading age of six, then the effect was indeed constant
with increasing age. This diminished right ear advantage at age six was
not due to a "floor" effect from lowered accuracy, as these children
still performed well above chance level, and in any case an increase in
accuracy does not cause an increase of percentage of errors. This
diminished right ear advantage seen at an early reading age means that a
different recall strategy is being used. When a left hemisphere
strategy is displayed, however, it does not diminish with age when
dealing with stop consonants as it does when dealing with environmental
sounds. If more linguistic stimuli are used (Forgays, 1953; Ingram,
1975) there is perhaps no reason to doubt that the right ear advantage

may continue to increase until well after the age of six years.

It is clear that the relationship between cerebral dominance and a given task is not static. It has been observed, for example, that familiarity with music (Bever & Chiarello, 1974) causes a switch from left ear advantage to right ear advantage. A similar dynamic interaction must also occur for linguistic material since there is nothing intrinsic to a symbol to make it verbal. Papcun et al. (1974) have indeed shown that naive Morse code operators have a left ear advantage rather than right ear advantage if the set of alternatives in a Morse dichotic presentation becomes at all large. The environmental sounds experiment shows that this reversal of hemisphere advantage occurs as a normal pattern of events. This act of learning to read becomes such an important event that some strategy, maybe verbal labelling, is even applied to the processing of material that does not require linguistic operations. Indeed, the presence of this presumed verbal bias could be taken to indicate the stage to which reading was developed.

If learning to read is associated with such important changes in cognitive strategy in the identification of environmental sounds, then it is reasonable to ask whether other non-verbal (right hemisphere) tasks might not suffer the same fate. In the dot detection task (n=96) used for children of ages 6, 8, and 10, a similar curvilinear relationship between field advantage and age was found, $F(2,84)=2.44$, $p<.1$), but only for the boys. There was, in general, a much greater left visual field advantage for boys, $F(1,84)=7.34$, $p<.01$. This latter finding reproduces the findings of greater male lateralization reviewed by Fairweather (1976). The curvilinear relationship has been shown in a similar task by Schaller and Dziadosz (in press). The sex difference is confirmed by Rudel, Denckla, and Spalten (1974) and Witelson (1976). It is interesting to see the similarity between the present dot detection experiment and the last two experiments. Rudel et al. obtained a U-shaped curve only for their male subjects in a task of identifying Braille letters by touch in normally sighted children, with the smallest right hemisphere advantage at age nine. Witelson (1976) found that boys alone are specialized in the right hemisphere for a visual-tactile matching task. The smallest right hemisphere advantage is found at age eight, which is the same age as in the dot detection task here. Whereas girls seem to have a verbal strategy as indicated by the left hemisphere advantage seen fairly constantly for these tasks, boys seem to be more plastic when trying a verbal strategy at the onset of reading (or a little later) but then revert to a more perceptually based strategy. It is, perhaps, no accident that Coltheart, Hull, and Slater (1975) found that girls made different errors from boys when performing letter crossing-out tasks. Girls missed a letter more often if it was silent in English, suggesting a phonological coding. This was seen in another task where naming letters in the alphabet containing an ee sound produced fewer errors for girls than boys, whereas boys produced fewer errors when asked to name the curved letters of the alphabet.

In summary, one observes three effects. There is a difference in coding strategies between boys and girls, with girls using left-hemisphere-based skills. Secondly, there is an effect of learning to read that is associated with an increasing left hemisphere advantage for linguistic tasks, and even for a normally right hemisphere task. In this case there is a return, for boys to the right hemisphere for visual tasks, and for both sexes in auditory tasks. This dynamic view of cerebral dominance gives a far more accurate picture of the development of cognitive skills than previous neuropsychological approaches.

Footnote

The authors are grateful to Professor C. I. Berlin for providing the dichotic CV tape. We would also like to thank Mrs. Thomas and Mr. Ellis of the Hafod and Mayals schools for their help. This work was supported by S.S.R.C. Grant HR 3780/1.

References

Berlin, C. I., Hughes, L. F., Lowe-Bell, S. S., & Berlin, H. L. Dichotic right ear advantage in children 5 to 13. Cortex, 1973, 9, 394-402.

Bever, T. G., & Chiarello, R. J. Cerebral dominance in musicians and non-musicians. Science, 1974, 185, 537-539.

Borowy, T., & Goebel, R. Cerebral lateralization of speech: The effects of age, sex, race and socioeconomic class. Neuropsychologia, 1976, 14, 363-369.

Broadbent, D. E. Perception and communication. London: Pergamon, 1958.

Coltheart, M., Hull, E., & Slater, D. Sex differences in imagery and reading. Nature, 1975, 253, 438-40.

Curry, F. A comparison of left and right handed subjects on verbal and non-verbal dichotic listening tasks. Cortex, 1967, 3, 343-352.

Dorman, M. F., & Geffner, D. S. Hemispheric specialization for speech perception in six-year-old black and white children from low and middle socioeconomic classes. Cortex, 1974, 10, 171-176.

Fairweather, H. Sex differences in cognition. Cognition, 1976, 4, 231-280.

Forgays, D. G. The development of differential word recognition. Journal of Experimental Psychology, 1953, 45, 165-168.

Geffner, D., & Hochberg, I. Ear laterality performance of children from low and middle socioeconomic levels on a verbal dichotic listening task. Cortex, 1971, 2, 193-203.

Ingram, D. Cerebral speech lateralization in young children. Neuropsychologia, 1975, 13, 103-105.

Kimura, D. Cerebral dominance and the perception of verbal stimuli. Canadian Journal of Psychology, 1961, 15, 166-171.

Kimura, D., & Durnford, M. Normal studies of hemisphere function in the human brain. In S. Dimond & J. E. Beaumont (Eds.), Hemisphere function in the human brain. London: Elek, 1974.

Kinsbourne, M. The control of attention by interaction between the cerebral hemispheres. In S. Kornblum (Ed.), Attention and performance IV. New York: Academic Press, 1973.

McKeever, W. F., & Huling, M. D. Left cerebral hemisphere superiority in tachistoscopic word-recognition performances. Perceptual and Motor Skills, 1970, 30, 763-766.

Orton, S. T. Reading, writing and speech problems in children. London: Chapman and Hall, 1937.

Papcun, G., Krashen, S., Terbeek, D., Remington, R., & Harshman, R. Is the left hemisphere specialized for speech language and/or something else? Journal of the Acoustical Society of America, 1974, 55, 319-327.

Rudel, R. G., Denckla, M. B., & Spalten, E. The functional asymmetry of Braille letter learning in normal sighted childrren. Neurology, 1974, 24, 733-738.

Schaller, M. J., & Dziadosz, G. M. Development changes in foveal tachistoscopic recognition between pre-reading and reading children. Developmental Psychology, in press.

Thomson, M. E. A comparison of laterality effects in dyslexics and controls using verbal dichotic listening tasks. Neuropsychologia, 1976, 14, 263-265.

Witelson, S. F. Sex and the single hemisphere: Specialization of the right hemisphere for spatial processing. Science, 1976, 193, 425-427.

Witelson, S. F. Developmental dyslexia: Two right hemispheres and none left. Science, 1977, 195, 309-311.

Section IV

PROBLEM SOLVING AND COMPONENTS OF INTELLIGENCE

The papers included in this section represent two major and closely interrelated research topics and each is represented by a major invited address. The address by Doerner explicates three major theoretical and instructional concerns. The first of these concerns is the understanding and teaching of general problem solving and reasoning skills. In discussing this issue, Doerner specifies some elements of a taxonomy of the problem solving requirements that determine the strategies necessary and available for problem solution. The second major concern is which problem-solving skills should be taught, and here he contrasts the results of research on process training vs. strategy training. These two initial topics of discussion are extended in the papers by Neches and Hayes and by de Leeuw. Neches and Hayes discuss the importance of strategy transformations in the distinction between novice and expert performance. The authors present a preliminary taxonomy of strategy transformations that seems to have potential generality for a number of cognitive domains. The paper by de Leeuw describes the results of research comparing algorithmic and heuristic methods for training the problem solving skills involved in deductive and inductive reasoning tasks.

The third issue discussed by Doerner is the diagnosis of cognitive skills. Much of this discussion focuses on the use of intelligence tests for measuring cognitive skills and the lack of a theoretical basis for interpreting the results of such testing. This challenge is met quite squarely in the major address by Sternberg. He details a methodology for analyzing the component processes underlying performance and individual differences on standardized aptitude and intelligence tests. The application and results of such a methodology are illustrated for the analysis of deductive and inductive reasoning tasks. Sternberg further argues for the importance of such individual difference analyses and their practical utility and applicability. The paper by Snow complements that of Sternberg and reports the general results of eye movement and strategy analyses of solution behaviors of skilled and less-skilled individuals on a variety of tasks reflecting various aptitude factors. The types of reasoning tasks being studied by Sternberg and Snow and their methodologies receive further suppport in the work of Groner and Keller on the modeling and analysis of performance in a specific deductive reasoning task, the six-term problem.

The paper by Elshout further argues for the importance and relevance of studying the cognitive skills represented by tasks found in intelligence and aptitude tests. In his paper, he argues that the tasks and factors represented in psychometric studies reflect fundamental limitations of the human information processing system. Some of these limitations are highlighted in the paper by Hitch on the analysis of strategies and forgetting in mental arithmetic tasks. The final paper of this section by van der Veer, van Muylwijk and van de Wolde is an investigation of the relationships among associative learning styles, information processing, and aptitude measures.

THEORETICAL ADVANCES OF COGNITIVE PSYCHOLOGY
RELEVANT TO INSTRUCTION

Dietrich Dörner
Justus Liebig University
Giessen, West Germany

Before discussing which theoretical advances in cognitive psychology are relevant for instruction, it is important to discuss which type of instruction is relevant.

It is unclear whether the development of school curricula in West Germany is typical of the development of school curricula in other countries, but it seems apparent in Germany, during the last decades, that the knowledge that should be taught to pupils has been constantly increasing. The results have been the introduction of new courses and the restructuring of old courses to make them more "relevant" to daily life.

This pattern seems to occur as a reaction of the school to certain environmental demands. For example, the reports of the Club of Rome and other authors in dealing with the rapid depletion of raw materials and energy and various ecological problems, has led to a restructuring of biology curricula to include extensive discussion of ecological questions.

In viewing this development, the picture comes to mind of the traveler who arrives too late for his departing train and who must then run panting after it, only to miss it after all. The schoool system struggles zealously to do justice to the burning problems of the moment by introducing corresponding curricular reforms, but it can hardly complete these reforms before the burning problems change and new ones appear.

What is the source of this problem? In my opinion, the school should stop competing with actuality because, for obvious reasons, it cannot achieve perfect "relevance." What else could be done? In my opinion, there is only one reasonable alternative to the course caricatured above: After laying a groundwork of essential cultural knowledge and skills, the school should try to teach general problem solving ability. Why provide pupils with an extensive knowledge of nuclear power plants today simply because the topic is "in" at the moment, when totally different topics will be important tomorrow? It

231

would be more useful to supply pupils with techniques enabling them, ad
hoc, to obtain the necessary information about an important topic, and
to teach them techniques for adequately processing the available
information. If that were to succeed, there would be no need to worry
about actuality.   In that case, education would be always ahead of,
rather than chasing after, the actual situation.

        Until now, the school system has only been concerned with the
epistemic part of the cognitive structure; the heuristic part appeared
at best in pedagogical programs, where the demand that schools should
also teach creative thinking has been heard for a long time. In
practice, however, these programs have not caused much of a
breakthrough.   Presumably, that is because no one really knew how to
teach creative thinking. This paper will be confined mainly to those
theoretical developments of cognitive psychology that are essential for
the teaching of creative thinking.

Cognitive Structure

        The view of cognitive structure that is presently dominant in
cognitive psychology assumes the existence of two substructures: an
epistemic structure, containing a number of models for those spheres of
reality that are of importance to the individual (including schemes for
actions), and a heuristic or production structure, which operates on the
epistemic structure in those cases where the capability of the latter is
insufficient.

        The primary theoretical progress in cognitive psychology, with
respect to the epistemic structure, seems to be the concept of the
semantic network (see Kintsch, 1974; and the work of the LNR-group, see
Norman, 1973).   The concept of an active semantic network capable of
answering difficult questions about a sphere of reality has obvious
relevance for planning of lessons. The representation of knowledge as a
complex semantic network in standardized form allows a direct deduction
to be made about suitable types of teaching sequences. It makes
directly evident, for example, where the central concepts are located
and how they are interconnected to each other.

        The other part of the cognitive structure, the heuristic structure,
can be regarded as consisting of a more or less organized "library" of
heuristic strategies. The signal for the employment of the heuristic
structure is a dissonance arising within the epistemical structure
(e.g., a dissonance between actual information and stored knowledge).
Such dissonances signal the epistemic structure's lack of ability in
guiding behavior; it is the task of the heuristic structure to restore
the individual's capability for action.

        The components of the heuristic structure, the heuristic
strategies, consist of single mental operations arranged side by side in
defined organizational forms. Examples of mental operations that are

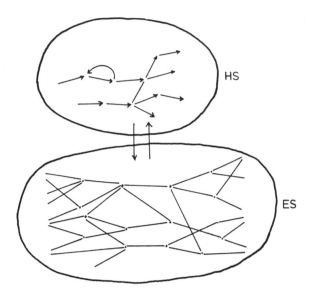

Figure 1. Schema of human cognitive structure as consisting of an epistemical (ES) and a heuristical (HS) structure.

elements of such heuristic strategies include comparing, abstracting, analyzing characteristics, ordering, etc. (see Lompscher, 1972). An example for the organization of such mental operations to heuristic strategies is the General Problem Solver (see Newell & Simon, 1972).

Until now, no apparent <u>systematic</u> discussion of the possibilities of improving the heuristic structure exists. In the following sections, the framework of such a systematic approach will be presented. Established theoretical developments will be discussed, as well as those that, until now, did not exist, but seem to be necessitated by the results of some empirical investigations.

A Taxonomy of Cognitive Requirements

When one aims at improving an individual's cognitive capability, then it pays to ask which requirements cognition should satisfy. When a general view of the specific requirements involved in human cognition is not at hand, then one runs the risk of taking action in irrelevant directions. Furthermore, it is not possible to equip a problem solver with a diagnostic system to control the specific employment of his or her heuristic strategies. No one who is considering influencing physical fitness would concentrate on increasing the muscle strength of the small toe. When one considers existing programs cooncerned with improving cognitive capability, however, one cannot resist the impression that a "training of the small toe" seems to be taking place.

To improve cognitive abilities, one should have precise conceptions as to which requirements demand preparation. Until now, only poor examples of a taxonomy for mental requirements exist. There is a differentiation between tasks and problems and between well- and ill-defined problems. Tasks involve reproductive thinking, calling upon already existing programs, so to speak; problems demand productive thinking: something new must be created. The distinction between well- and ill-defined problems concerns criteria for judging the products of the problem solving process. A well-defined problem is one for which an algorithm exists for making the decision that the goal state has been reached; such an algorithm does not exist for an ill-defined problem.

The distinctions depicted above are much too coarse to be applied as guidelines for designing cognitive curricula. A summary of the experimental work on problem solving in this paper proposes the following two ingredients for a taxonomy of the cognitive requirements of productive thinking:

1. A list of the requirements resulting from the nature of the problem.

2. A list of the requirements resulting from the nature of the sphere of reality in which the problem appears.

Requirements of a Problem

Consider one group of requirements. A problem is defined in the following way: An individual is in a situation that, for certain reasons, is not desirable. He seeks a different situation without knowing how the desired transformation should appear. The problem situation is marked by one or several barriers. The characteristic requirements of a problem lie in the peculiarity of the barriers present in it. In the case of solving a mathematical proof, for instance, the barriers lie in the fact that the specific combination of the operators leading from the start to the goal is unknown. This is a combination-barrier: One knows what the aspired goal situation looks like; one also knows (as a good mathematician) the operators, which perform the transformation as well; yet their combination is unknown.

If one wants to make gold from lead, the situation is different. Here it is also exactly known what is to be achieved. One must assume, however, that deciding operations are unknown, as well as the specific combination of operations. Not only must the known facts be cleverly combined, but a new operator must also be discovered. It is necessary to consider an enlargement of the class of possible transformations (see Klix, 1971, p. 679). This is an example of an invention-barrier, which demands cognitive processes different than those of a combination-barrier.

Now consider a chess-problem. This is clearly a well-defined problem, although the requirements of solving such a problem are different from the requirements of solving a mathematical proof. There is no invention-barrier in the chess-problem: New operators are not to be invented: the possible steps are given by the system of rules. An important barrier in a chess game is the correct goal projection, i.e., the construction of a concrete image of that which should be achieved. It should first be clear what is really desired, if aimless actions are to be avoided. The necessity of first having to make a very abstract conception concrete appears not only in chess but especially in the area of artistic creative processes. Often it is identical with the production of a work of art. Here there is the barrier of making a goal assume a concrete form, which requires other cognitive processes than those barriers already described.

A problem is characterized by the specific type of barriers that it contains. Different barriers can appear in one single problem. The concept of the barrier and the typology of barriers described above differentiates the old distinction between well- and ill-defined problems. Now theoretically, an infinite number of problem types can be discerned, each representing a specific combination of barriers. The specific types of barriers call for specific types of problem solving strategies.

To characterize the situation roughly, it is possible to say that a combination-barrier, above all, demands sharp analytical thinking. This type of thinking is perhaps most strikingly represented by the work of Newell and Simon (1972), although the General Problem Solver is not the only conceivable type of analytical thinking. In contrast, the invention-barrier demands a style of thinking that Bartlett (1958) has named "adventurous thinking." Trial and error and analogy transfer are important here.

The barrier of concretizing demands a type of thinking that could be called "dialectical thinking." A deciding factor here is what Reitman (1965) called "successive constraint proliferation." While a picture of the goal situation is developing, each hypothesis about the nature of the goal forces new constraints. This places a heavy price on bad hypotheses. For example, the choice of the first line in a poem is free; but the next one must already harmonize with the first in terms of rhythm, rhyme, and content. The process depends upon the discovery and disposal of contradictions in the emerging structure.

Requirements Imposed by a "Sphere of Reality"

The type of barriers in a problem determines or should determine the type of problem solving strategy, whereas the type of the sphere of reality to which the problem belongs determines the "tactics" of the problem solving process, i.e., the ways in which elementary operations are tailored to the specific details of the problem space.

Consider the group of requirements that arise from the type of reality sphere. One can formally describe a sphere of reality as a network of "circumstances," or "situations," and operations. The sphere of reality called "chess game" consists of all possible constellations of figures on the board, and the moves permitting the player to change one constellation to form another. Figure 2 symbolically shows the picture of a reality sphere. A sphere of reality has specific features for the problem solver based on which of certain demands are placed on the individual's cognitive capability. Without claim to completeness, here are some of these requirements.

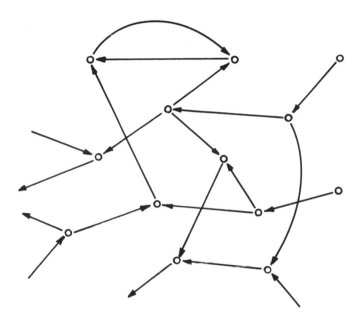

Figure 2. A sphere of reality as a network of situations (○) and transformations (→).

Consider the situation of a chess player and compare it with the situation of a minister of finance. Each is confronted with a problem. The problems are not only different with regard to the types of barriers, they differ in the requirements of the different types of spheres of reality, too. The nature of these differences indicates some of the characteristic features of spheres of reality. While one can perceive the given facts of a mathematical problem or a chess problem exactly, an economic situation is so complex that it is totally impossible to grasp all of its attributes. One can take as much time as needed to solve a chess problem, but one is under pressure in the economic situation because the situation has its own dynamics and develops on its own, even without anyone having to make any decisions.

When situations are very complex in a sphere of reality and decisions have to be made under time pressure, the limited human capacity of cognitive processing requires "condensing" of the situations in such a way that they become manageable. This "condensation" can take place by processes of abstraction or by combining single elements into configurations ("Gestaltbildung").

When the components of the situations in a sphere of reality are to a large extent interdependent, as, for example, in ecological systems, then specific demands arise. In such cases the operators are necessarily "wideband-operators" with a large spectrum of effects. This means that the effects of an operation "radiate" in the system's network. Side effects appear next to the aspired main effects. The construction of the Aswan Dam in Egypt, for example, had the desired main effect of enlarging the supply of energy. Side effcts appeared, however, that for the most part had not been considered when the dam was planned. Water devoid of mud under the dam intensified the erosion of the river bed, the water level sank, the ground water level sank (causing a need to change the irrigation canals and to sink them deeper), the Nile delta ceased growing, and the number of sardine fisheries on the delta coast sharply decreased. A sphere of reality with radiating effects, such as this, surely demands other requirements than a sphere of reality without these characteristics.

One can still list a number of other features of reality spheres that demand a certain type of information processing. The transformation of an equation in mathematics, for example, is an operation that can easily be reversed, but a decision concerning economic policy is quite a different case. The extent of reversibility of the operators is an important feature of a sphere of reality. The uncertainty of the effects and the breadth of the application field of the operators are other features of a sphere of reality that determine (or should determine) the "tactics" of a problem solving process. When the operators of a sphere of reality demand a great number of conditions for their application, i.e., have a narrow application field, then it is necessary to plan with many intermediary goals.

The present experimental results show the effects of the characteristics of situations and operations on the problem solving process. Bronner's (1975) results, for instance, indicate a characteristic change of problem solving behavior under time pressure that cannot be trivially attributed to the reduction of time. Dörner and Reither (Note 1) gave subjects a computer model of an African third-world nation to manipulate, and found that this country was ruined in less than 10 (simulated) years. The reasons for the failure did not lie in the good intentions of the subjects, but in the unsuitability of their habits of thinking when dealing with heavily meshed dynamic systems.

Figure 3 summarizes a suggestion for a taxonomy of the requirements once again: The specific type of barriers within a problem determine the general cognitive strategy, whereas the features of the sphere of reality determine the specific modification of the "tactics" of the problem solving processes, i.e., the modification of single mental operations (see Dörner, 1976).   Based on the categorization of a specific problem according to type of barriers and features of the sphere of reality, it is posible to give detailed specifications of the specific cognitive requirements of a problem.   Such a taxonomy is useful: (a) for the instructor as a guiding line for the design of instruction; (b) for the problem solver to help him in identifying his special difficulties and in overcoming them; and (c) for the researcher to plan investigations and to get an impression about the generalizability of his results.

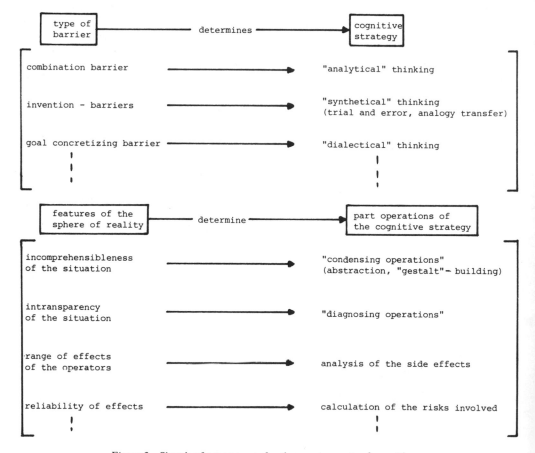

Figure 3. Sketch of a taxonomy for the requirements of a problem.

The Training of Productive Thinking

If one knows the requirements of problem situations, it becomes possible to design training methods to change the cognitive structure in the desired direction. This section will attempt to systematize the different forms of training methods and to examine their efficiency.

Practice Training

One can approach the training of thinking in different ways. The most primitive form of training in thinking involves simply confronting individuals with cognitive challenges, preferably all of a different nature, and hoping that problem solving ability develops as a result of confrontation with such problems, just as muscle develops as a result of constant exercise. The theoretical background of such an assumption can be reinforcement theory; one could assume that an individual's heuristic structure is not rigid, but possesses a certain chance instability, because of which the completion of heuristical programs is never quite identical, but takes slightly varied forms, similar to the way in which the genetic code constantly mutates. Similar to biological mutation it could happen now that particular heuristic mutations prove to be better suited than others for problem solving and will therefore be retained, according to the law of effect.

The hypothesis of a quasi-mutative change in the human cognitive structure was discussed by Selz (1924). According To Selz's assumption, the heuristic structure would change approximately in the way described by the "shaping of behavior" model postulated by reinforcement theory and by instrumental conditioning. This form of training will here be called "practice-training."

Tactical Training

If one considers thinking and problem solving as consisting of the ordering together of basic mental operations, then it can be meaningful to increase cognitive performance ability by training individual cognitive operations. It is possible to train such mental functions as comparing, analyzing, generalizing, classifying, ordering, etc., and hope that improving the constituents also brings an improvement in the whole process. This seems to be the most popular approach at the moment.

Preschool programs and training programs for older pupils and adults usually teach basic mental operations. Optical discrimination, memory capacity, mastery of the concept of number, reading ability, and imagination are all taught in the preschool programs. The training methods offered for adults contain such tasks as finding common factors, performing multiple classifications, completing incomplete texts, etc. The usual way of testing the effectiveness of such programs seemed to support the assumption that it is possible to generate a more or less substantial improvement of cognitive ability, because more or less significant increases in IQ scores are obtained with such programs (Klauer, 1975; Gray & Klaus, 1965). The results of such investigations must be treated with great caution. We have empirical results that support the hypothesis that tactical training may lead to an improvement of IQ, but not necessarily to an improvement of problem solving ability.

Hartung & Hartung (Note 2) investigated whether problem solving ability, in addition to IQ, can be improved by intelligence training methods. Their intelligence training consisted of training the following operations: (a) optical differentiation, (b) form perception, (c) memory, (d) logical thinking, and (e) concept formation. They chose those groups of operations based on the Sesame Street television program and the Baar program (Baar, 1952).

Optical differentiation dealt with selecting pictures from a series of pictures that deviated from the others. Form perception involved the identification of figures where only the contours were given. The memory exercises tested the retention of optically presented objects over a certain period of time. The exercises in logical thinking contained tasks that depended on the recognition of regularities within series. Concept formation consisted of exercises in which children choose from a series of presented objects those that did not belong to the same category as the others.

Hartung and Hartung (Note 2) trained children for four weeks in the performance of the operations, and tested their intelligence three times during the training procedure. After the conclusion of the training and a latency period of six weeks, they tested intelligence once again, in order to determine the persistence of the effects. Figure 4 shows the results of this training program.

Clearly, the test performances of both of the trained groups (E+ and E-) improved until the third test, whereas there was no reliable improvement in performance by the untrained groups (C+ and C-). Likewise, it is manifest that the training did not leave any lasting effects, for the posttest given after a latency period of six weeks did not show any remaining difference between groups E+ and C+, nor between E- and C-.

More interesting is the fact that the clear increase in intelligence test performance had no relationship to the child's performance in solving complex problems. Hartung and Hartung let the children solve problems from time to time; during the training these required construction of transformations consisting of many steps. Figure 5 shows such a problem. The children simultaneously received the problem situation and a choice of "magic wands." With the help of these "magic wands" certain features of the given object could be changed. Often the possibility of employing an operator ("magic wand") depended on certain conditions. In the example of Figure 5, an umbrella must be

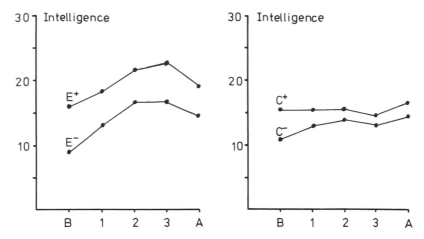

Figure 4. Effects of an intelligence-training program. E$^+$ and E$^-$ refer to the experimental groups, C$^+$ and C$^-$ to the control groups.

present before a flower pot can become a vase. Such conditions require detours and the formation of subgoals.

Figure 6 shows the percentage of problems solved by the experimental and the control groups. The impression that the problem solving ability of the subjects increased is deceptive. The difference is not statistically signficant. That means that the statistically significant increase in performance on the intelligence test by the experimental group did not result in a detectable increase in problem solving skills. If one correlates the extent of the increase in performance on the intelligence test with the subject problem solving ability, a slightly negative non-significant correlation results, r = -0.139.

These results may be explained in the following way: The trained operations are necessary but in no way sufficient conditions for complex cognitive abilities. The training of these operations may boost IQ; however, the improvement is uninteresting with regard to the improvement of general cognitive performance ability. The decisive factor seems to be strategic: the subjects do not lack the inventory of basic operations, but rather lack possibilities for integrating these basic operations into complex forms of thinking. This strategic ability, however, has not been trained.

The ability to perform individual cognitive operations such as comparing, ordering, classifying, etc., are necessary but in no way sufficient prerequisites for a complex problem solving process. To these individual abilities must be added the ability to combine individual operations into larger sequences of organizations, the

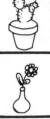

Here is a cactus in a flowerpot

It would like to be a flower in a vase

Help it with your magic wands

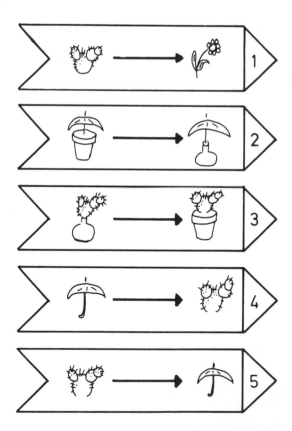

Figure 5. A magic problem and a choice of "magic wands."

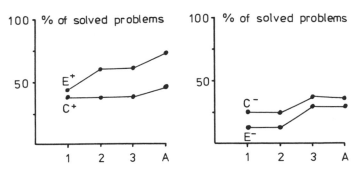

Figure 6. Percentage of solved problems for groups with (E$^+$,E$^-$) and without (C$^+$,C$^-$) an intelligence-training.

ability to break up these bonds in order to build new sequences, etc. To a great extent, intelligence tests do not measure the organizational form of cognitive operations, nor do they test the ability to change such forms of organization.

It is certainly conceivable that intelligence tests permit a good evaluation of the cognitive performance ability of an individual; on the other hand, an increase in the mastery of individual cognitive operations does not necessarily lead to an increase in cognitive performance ability. It is also conceivable that an individual's cognitive performance ability is not so limited by his or her ability to perform individual cognitive operations, but rather by the ability to meaningfully organize these operations. An electrical engineer does not necessarily become better qualified for that profession when he or she is taught to manufacture solder joints in half the time needed previously. The production of solder joints is in fact a necessary but in no way sufficient condition for such employment. It would be much more important to instruct him or her in strategies for searching for defects, strategies for construction and time usage, etc.

A good electrical engineer is usually able to solder well, but improving the ability to solder does not necessarily make a better electrical engineer. One has the clear impression that when preschool programs teach cognitive abilities, they improve the "solder ability" of individuals by teaching individual cognitive operations without doing much for the essential cognitive performance ability.

A limitation is conceivable in the mastery of individual cognitive operations, beyond which an additional improvement does not bring any increase in the cognitive performance ability. An electrical engineer must be able to solder, i.e., must be able to produce a stable joint with a limited consumption of material and within a limited amount of time; beyond a certain limit, however, an additional gain from economizing time and material does not bring any more gain in professional ability.

The Hartung and Hartung experiment (Note 2) does not devalue tactical training. One should ponder the following two questions, however, before administering such a form of cognitive training. First, are the single mental operations to be taught really <u>essential</u> parts of complex cognitive activity? (Or are they only essential for the solving of intelligence tests?) Second, is the current performance of these single mental operations really the limiting factor for cognitive capability? It may be that a further improvement of a certain mental operation is possible but not necessary. It is only of little relevance to improve the road-holding ability of a car so that it can take sharp turns with a speed of 200 km/h, when the tiny motor only allows a speed of 80 km/h. To improve something one must concentrate on the current limiting factor. This may sound trivial, but many preschool intelligence and creativity programs do not appear to consider this point.

Statistical Training and the Role of Self-Reflection

Thinking is not only a series of elementary cognitive operations but an organized sequence. For that reason, a third type of training consists of teaching the organization of single steps to form a total sequence. We call this type of teaching "strategical training." Strategical training can consist, for example, of teaching individuals a General Problem Solver - like organization form for single steps and hoping that this has a beneficial effect on the individual's ability to solve corresponding problems.

A good example for strategical training is Hayes' (1976) course for teaching problem solving skills. Hayes provided his subjects with a <u>diagnostic</u> <u>system</u> that had to serve the function of providing students with information about their current problem solving skills, and with procedures for examining their own problem solving procedures. In a theory-practice section, the students were confronted with a number of problem solving <u>strategies</u> (for instance, trial and error and heuristic search) and problem solving <u>tactics</u> (for instance, techniques for inducing rules, techniques for the management of short-term memory, techniques for decision making). Hayes' course is progressive for several reasons. First, the underlying philosophy is a <u>wholistic</u> view of human cognitive functioning. Cognitive processes are regarded not as <u>aggregations</u> of single mental operations, but as <u>organizations</u>. After a long period of factor-analytic intelligence research, it seems important to stress this point. Second, cognitive functioning is not regarded as comparable to a computer running through an algorithm, but as a process that actively can be interrupted and directed to other topics. <u>Self reflection</u> plays an important role; the student has to learn to examine his or her own problem solving processes and to use the information provided by such examinations to improve his or her cognitive structures. After a long period when psychologists refused to deal with processes such as self-reflection or with the phenomena of consciousness (closely related to self-reflection), this also seems an essential point (see Mandler, 1975).

It can be shown that strategic (i.e., wholistic) training and self-reflection have clear effects on the development of problem solving ability. One can show that the demand for self-reflection, even without any training, leads to an improvement of problem solving ability. Combined with some sort of strategic training, the effects seem to be still better. Figure 7 summarizes a series of experiments on the influence of strategic training and the demand for self-reflection on the development of problem solving skills.

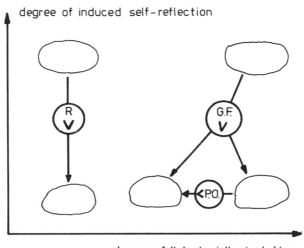

degree of "strategic" orientation
of the training

Figure 7. Results of some experiments with different forms of "strategic" training. The ordinate indicates the degree of induced self-reflection in the experimental and control groups, respectively. The abscissa indicates the degree of strategic orientation of the training. The "<" signs indicate the direction of the significant differences between the experimental and control groups.

Reither (1977, R in Figure 7) showed that subjects who were forced into self-reflection after every problem solving attempt learned to solve problems far better than subjects who were not stopped for self-reflection. Putz-Osterloh (1974, PO in Figure 7) was able to show that subjects who had been "strategically" trained proved better at problem solving than subjects who had only been "tactically" trained. Goetze and Frommling (Note 3, GF in Figure 7) showed that subjects with a good background of general problem solving theory and with strategic self-reflective training were far better in solving "ill-defined" problems than subjects who had been specially prepared with certain "creativity techniques" (brain-storming, synectics) for solving such problems. Their training procedure for the strategic self-reflective training was very similar to the Hayes course described above.

If one compares these results with those of the Hartung and Hartung (Note 2) experiment described above, the central point becomes clear. The limiting factor of cognitive ability seems to be the organizational one. Developing the efficiency of single mental operations does not seem to be very important; the crucial point is strategic flexibility.

Diagnosing Cognitive Skills

If one intends to improve human cognitive structures, one should be able to ascertain the specific cognitive weaknesses and strengths of an individual. This is necessary to plan and evaluate courses for teaching problem solving. The current means for the diagnosis of human cognitive abilites are intelligence tests. The history of intelligence testing will not be reviewed here, but it seems necessary to emphasize that intelligence tests have been developed largely independent of cognitive psychology and without the background of satisfactory theory (see McNeemar, 1964). Although one need not fully accept Putnam's remark (1973) that intelligence research in the past 75 years has nothing whatsoever to do with intelligence, it cannot be overlooked that the existing tests do not permit a satisfactory diagnosis of human cognitive abilities.

It is hardly disputable that intelligence tests have something to do with cognitive capability, that is, with intelligence. The specific relationship, though, is unclear. A series of experiments clearly suggest that the conventional validity assumptions must be treated with a great deal of caution. For example, in a series of investigations it was found that one of the subtests contained in a battery of tests based on Thurstone's theory, the test of the spatial factor continually correlated with problem solving skills in different areas. This subtest dealt with test problems that were, in the test-author's opinion, authoritative for measuring the ability to recode surface information into spatial information. Figure 8 depicts a simple item from this test. Of all the subjects of the battery, the performance on this test had the best correlations with the reaction time and number of errors in the solution of proof problems in propositional calculus, with the achievement in solving complicated puzzle problems (TANGRAMs), and with the solution time and number of errors in solving problems with a complicated circuit breaker apparatus. The correlation coefficients of this "space-test" with problem solving skills and a range from .63 to .80 and were statistically significant. It is notable that no other subtest of the battery, especially none of the reasoning tests, correlated substantially with the problem solving skills. One would have expected the opposite result from the usual validity assumptions.

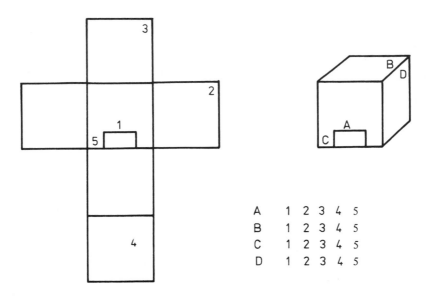

Figure 8. Items from a "space-factor test" which correlates highly with problem solving skills.

Putz-Osterloh and Luer (1975) investigated this phenomenon and found, based on exact examinations of the solution process in the spatial test problems, that these problems can be solved using two different strategies. Some of the tasks can be more reasonably attacked with one of these strategies, other tasks better with the second. Someone who has a command of both strategies and is in the position of applying the more suitable one according to the requirements of the problem is especially successful in this test. The quintessence of the examination by Putz-Osterloh and Luer was that the "test of space conception" is not essentially a test of this ability, but rather a test to determine the strategic flexibility of the subject. It is small wonder, therefore, that this test correlates with problem solving ability.

Other investigations support the assumption that one must be very cautious with the prominent interpretations of test validity. One should assume at once that the ability to learn and retain, as usually measured, relate to the further development of problem solving ability, for certainly operations and strategies must also be learned and retained.

Döring (Note 4) is currently examining whether one can predict the further development of problem solving abiity based on the usual ways of testing the capacity for learning and memory. He has measured the following traits in his subjects: (a) For short-term memory capacity (observation capability), subjects were shown a list of 26 simple nouns for a short time; immediately after the stimuli were shown they wrote down all the nouns they had retained. (b) For learning speed, the time required for the subjects to memorize a list of nonsense syllables was measured. (c) For memory capacity (ability to retain meaningful material), approximately 40 minutes after the original test subjects were tested to determine how many nouns they could reproduce. (d) For memory capacity (ability to retain nonsense material), approximately 40 minutes after the original showing subjects were tested to see how many nonsense syllables they could reproduce.

Döring attempted to measure subjects' problem solving behavior and its further development after practice. Subjects had to solve a total of 12 problems with a circuit breaker apparatus, shown in Figure 9. Problems consisted of generating certain light combinations with the help of the switches. The difficulty of such problems stem from the fact that the switches are dependent on one another in a complicated manner. For example, the third circuit breaker was only functional when the first switch was in the upper, and the fourth in the lower position. The subjects did not know the system of dependencies initially, but could learn it when manipulating the apparatus.

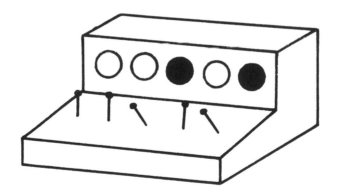

Figure 9. Circuit breaker problem apparatus.

The 12 problems the subjects had to solve were divided into two conditions, A and B. Conditions A and B differed from one another in terms of their types of interdependencies between the switch connections. Subjects had to solve six problems of each type. In this way, not only the solution time and number of errors in the individual problems could be measured, but also the progress of learning <u>within</u> a problem group and the transfer from one problem group to another.

The learning progress within a task group is mainly due to the fact that subjects remembered the system of interdependencies. The transfer from one group of tasks to another cannot be explained in this way, however, for the interdependencies changed. We assume that the transfer from one task group to another was determined mainly by the further development of the particular subject's heuristic capabilities.

One can conceive of the learning progress within a task group as an indicator for the progress in the creation of an epistemic strucuture, i.e., in the creation of an image of a certain sphere of reality. One can conceive of the transfer from one task group to another as an indicator for the development of the heuristic structure, i.e., as an indicator for the further development of general problem solving ability.[1]

The learning progress within a task group was measured by the average decrease in the perceptual number of false switches from problem to problem. The transfer from one condition to the other was measured by the reduction of the total number of trial switch movements from the one task group to the other.

Table 1 shows the correlations existing between the two measures of epistemic and heuristic development of problem solving ability and the memory measure for short-term memory (STM), learning speed (tempo) (LT), long-term memory for meaningful material (LTM+), and nonsense material (LTM-). One can see from the table that only one of the usual learning measures correlates significantly with either of the measures of problem solving development. Long-term memory for meaningful material correlates with heuristic development of problem solving ability. Even this correlation is too small to be of importance.

Does the development of cognitive capacity not have something to do with memory? That is surely not to be derived from this experiment. The results are interpreted in the following manner. The elementary human capability of absorbing and storing information is a necessary but in no way sufficient condition for cognitive development. The elementary skills of storing and retaining information are normally so well developed in indivduals with normal intelligence that they allow cognitive development. If the elementary memory skills lie above a certain threshold, the further development of cognitive abilities does not depend on them any more. It is supposed that strategic aspects of memory storing are of great importance beyond this threshold. These strategic aspects could consist of the way in which an individual can relate absorbed information to other information at hand. However, this ability is tested only to a small extent by learning lists of nonsense syllables.

Table 1.   Correlations Between Measures of Learning and Retaining Capacity and the Development of
            Epistemical and Heuristical Cognitive Skills.

	STM	LT	LTM$^+$	LTM$^-$	EL
LT	.42**				
LTM$^+$	.67**	.47**			
LTM$^-$	.33*	.31*	.46**		
EL	−.10	−.03	−.12	−.21	
HL	−.14	.02	−.33*	−.16	.15

Summary

      To improve the general cognitive abilities of an individual, it is
necessary to provide a system that allows the person to ascertain the
specific requirements of a problem.   This paper has attempted to give
the framework of such a system.   Furthermore, it is necessary to provide
a person with the strategies and tactics of problem solving.   Regarding
these results,   it does not seem very important to teach single mental
operations,   as   in   most preschool programs or in creativity and
intelligence programs.   More   essential is the teaching of strategic
flexibility in problem solving.   In this context, the   investigation of
the   possibilities of self-reflection seems to be of great importance.
Finally, it seems necessary to develop the diagnostic tools for
measuring   the efficiency of cognitive capabilities.   Conventional
intelligence testing, having developed without the background   of
cognitive theory, has unclear relationships to the parameters of complex
cognitive activities, and seems to fail in diagnosing important aspects
of cognitive capability.

Footnotes

      1. Of course, a certain sensorimotor adaptation to the
experimental   conditions (e.g., skill in manipulating the levers) could
be involved in this transfer as well as in the learing progress within a
task group.   We believe we have reasons for the assumption, however,
that the extent of such adaptation effects is so negligible that one can

ignore it. Such an adaptation must show up mainly in a decrease in the solution times. On the other hand, a reduction in the number of mistakes caused by switching could only be due to a change in the epistemic or heuristic structure. Because solution time and number of false switches have a rather high correlation with one another r = 0.75, the influence of sensorimotor adaptation can only be negligible.

Reference Notes

1. Dörner, D., & Reither, F. Über das Problemlösen in sehr komplexen Realitätsbereichen. Z. exp. angew. Psychol. (in print).

2. Hartung, C., & Hartung, P. Die Kurz- und langfristige Wirkung eines Intelligenztrainingsprogrammes auf die Testintelligenz und Problemlösefähigkeit bei Kindern unterschiedlichen Intelligenzniveaus. Unpublished thesis, University of Giessen, West Germany, 1977.

3. Goetze, U., & Frommling, J. Möglichkeiten des Problemlösetrainings an Problemen mit offenem Operatorinventar. Unpublished thesis. West Germany: University of Kiel, 1976.

4. Döring, J Gedächtnis, Lernen und Problemlösen. Unpublished thesis. West Germany: University of Giessen, 1977.

References

Baar, E. Schulreife-Entwicklungshilfe. West Germany: Wein, 1952.

Bartlett, F. Thinking. An experimental and social study. London: Unwin University Books, 1958.

Bronner, R. Zeitdruck in Entscheidungsprozessen. Management International Review, 1975, 15, 81-93.

Dörner, D. Problemlösen als Informationsverarbeitung. Stuttgart, West Germany: Kohlhammer, 1976.

Gray, S. W., & Klaus, R. A. An experimental program for culturally deprived children. Child Development, 1965, 36, 887-898.

Hayes, J. R. It's the thought that counts: New approaches to educational theory. In D. Klahr (Ed.), Cognition and instruction. Hillsdale, NJ: Lawrence Erlbaum, 1976.

Kintsche, W. The representation of meaning in memory. Hillsdale, NJ: Lawrence Erlbaum, 1974.

Klauer, K. J. Intelligenztraining im Kindesalter. West Germany:
    Beltz, Weinheim und Basel, 1975.

Klix, F. Information und Verhalten. Bern, Switzerland: Huber, 1971.

Lumpscher, J. (Ed.) Theoretische und experimentelle Untersuchungen zur
    Entwicklung geistiger Fähigkeiten. East Berlin: Volk und Wissen,
    1972.

Mandler, G. Consciousness: Respectable, useful, and probably
    necessary. In R. L. Solso (Ed.), Information processing and
    cognition. Hillsdale, NJ: Lawrence Erlbaum, 1975.

McNemar, Q. Lost: Our intelligence. Why? American Psychologist,
    1964, 19, 871-882.

Newell, A., & Simon, H. A. Human problem solving. Englewood Cliffs,
    NJ: Prentice Hall, 1972.

Norman, D. A. Memory, knowledge and the answering of questions. In R.
    L. Solso (Ed.), Contemporary issues in cognitive psychology. New
    York: Wiley, 1973.

Putnam, H. Reductionism and the nature of psychology. Cognition, 1973,
    2, 131-146.

Putz-Osterloh, W. Über die Effektivität von Problemlösungstraining.
    Z. f. Psychologie, 1974, 182, 253-276.

Putz-Osterloh, W., & Luer, G. Informationsverarbeitung bei einem Test
    zur Erfassung der Raumvorstellung. Diagnostica, 1975, XXI/4,
    166-181.

Reither, F. Der Einfluss der Selbstreflexion auf Strategie und
    Qualität des Problemlösens. In H. K. Garten (Ed.), Diagnose
    von Lernprozesen. Westermann, Braunschweig, 1977.

Reitman, W. R. Cognition and thought. Wiley: New York, 1965.

Selz, O. Die Gesetze der produktiven und reproduktiven
    Geistestätigkeit. Bonn, West Germany: Cohen, 1924.

Thurstone, L. L. Primary mental abilities. Psychometric Monographs 1,
    1938.

PROGRESS TOWARDS A TAXONOMY OF STRATEGY TRANSFORMATIONS

Robert Neches and J. R. Hayes
Department of Psychology
Carnegie-Mellon University
Pittsburgh, PA 15213

The difference between the performance of an expert and a novice seems not so much a matter of what the expert has been taught as of what he has learned by himself. That is, it often appears that the expert has taken the strategies taught him, and through practice has discovered ways to modify them into much more efficient and powerful procedures.

Expert strategies are often quite complex and therefore may be unsuitable for direct instruction. Our only instructional alternative may be to teach a simple initial strategy and work to promote its transformation into the expert strategy. A theory of strategy transformations would help us to do this, and thus has important implications for education. As Resnick (1976) suggests, such a theory would allow us to design easily learned novice strategies with the desirable property of being readily transformable into expert strategies. Further, it would enable us to promote the transformation process by explicitly teaching students techniques for improving their strategies.

The first step towards a theory of strategy transformations is to determine what sort of transformations are possible, i.e., to develop a taxonomy of strategy transformations. In this paper, we report progress in defining such a taxonomy.

We have observed transformations of strategies in a complex sequence generation task involving arithmetic and symbolic manipulations. The task and the particular initial strategy we have used have both been analyzed in detail by Greeno and Simon (1974). They have also been studied experimentally by Gerritsen, Gregg, and Simon (1975). We became interested in this particular task/strategy combination because of the large range of strategy transformations possible.

Eight different types of strategy transformations are described below. Although we first observed them in the environment of the sequence generation task, their application appears to be quite general, as we will attempt to demonstrate by presenting a number of examples from other tasks.

253

Types of Strategy Transformations

Reduction to Results

Reduction to results changes a procedure for finding results from a computational process to a memory retrieval process. That is, it places in long term memory a set of connections between potential inputs and their outcomes under the original procedure. This set of connections allows the information processing system to know what the procedure's result would be without actually performing the procedure itself. This can obviously be useful when the results of the procedure are needed frequently, particularly if the procedure has only a few possible results.

Groen and Parkman (1972), for example, found that for most digit pairs, young children compute the sum of two digits by a counting procedure. They interpreted their data for adults as indicating that, most of the time, adults add by retrieving sums from memory. Children did appear to have certain sums in memory, such as 1+1, 2+2, 3+3, and so on.

The critical step in making this transformation is the detection of regularities, i.e., noticing that some procedure P always has result r_1 when performed on some input i_1 result, r_2 on input i_2, and so on. Some basic constraints of the human information processing system affect this step. For example, the frequency with which a regularity occurs can play a critical role in its detection (Howes, 1957).

Note also that relating inputs and results requires that the inputs still be available to the information processing system when the results are found. It seems likely that circumstances favoring this availability will facilitate reduction to results. These circumstances might be predictable from our knowledge about short-term memory limitations (Miller, 1956; Waugh & Norman, 1965).

Reduction to a Rule

Reduction to a rule replaces a procedure with a rule or function describing its results. Like reduction to results, this allows the result of the procedure to be predicted without actually carrying it out. This is useful when the procedure is complicated, but its effects are simple.

For example, our sequence generation task requires decoding a "pattern description" of a form such as "4 CCXY." The letters stand for arithmetic operators (e.g., "Add 3"). Each digit in the sequence is obtained by applying some combination of the operators to the number given. Figure 1 describes the procedure subjects learn for determining what combination to use at each position in a sequence. Not surprisingly, subjects find this quite complicated. A much simpler rule is this: Use the leftmost operator not used on the previous turn, and any operators on its right that were used on the previous turn.

SELECT: To select the operators to be applied in generating the
nth digit in a sequence, let $i = n - l$, and then:

a) convert i to its four bit binary equivalent (e.g.,
1 becomes "0001", 2 becomes "0010", 3
becomes "0011", etc.).

b) "Flip" the binary pattern by reading it right to
left (e.g., "0001" becomes "1000", "0010"
becomes "0100", and "0011" becomes
"1100").

c) Choose the operators to be applied by lining up
the flipped bit-pattern beneath the operator
list; all operators with a "1" below are
selected (e.g., "1000" selects the first
operator, "0100" selects the second, "1100"
the first and second, and so on).

Figure 1. A procedure for selecting operators from a digit sequence "pattern description" in order to
compute the individual digits. Based on the "Binary Recompute" method of Greeno and Simon
(1974).

New rules such as this are perhaps constructed by searching for
constant relations either within ordered sets of results (e.g., that
some function f exists such that for any result

$$r_n, r_n = f(r_{n-1}),$$

or across the pairs of inputs and results (e.g., that for all inputs

$$i_n r_n = f(i_n)).$$

Replacement with Another Method

Replacement with another method consists of replacing one procedure
with a pre-existing one that achieves the same goals. For example,
people who must stack coins may at first laboriously count out the same
number of coins for each stack; they quickly learn to create one stack
by counting, and the remaining stacks by simply matching them to the
first stack. Replacing the numerical count with this perceptual test
greatly speeds the task.

Replacement transformations often involve retrieval from a
repertoire of already familiar methods. Retrieval might depend on
similarity detection processes. One process, result matching, might
notice when two methods produce identical results given the same inputs.
In our task, for example, adding 3 and subtracting 3 are equivalent

operations because arithmetic is restricted to the integers 1 through 6
- larger or smaller values (e.g., 6+3, 2-2) are normalized by
subtracting or adding 6, respectively. Subjects generally report
noticing this equivalence just after performing both operations on the
same number. (The coin-stacking example might also be accounted for by
this mechanism, assuming there exists a visual height-comparison
procedure announcing "same" or "different" that matches results with the
numerical count).

Another similarity detection process, description matching, might
notice when two procedures are identical with respect to a semantic
description of their goals or effects. This could give an alternative
accounting of the coin-stacking example, in which the switch is made on
the basis of prior knowledge about the relation of number and size for
collections of same-sized objects.

Unit Building

Unit building, or chunking applied to strategies, groups operations
into a set that is accessible as a single unit. In carrying out a
strategy, elements that at first are executed separately, later are
grouped to form a unit. In memory tasks, separate information elements
may be grouped to form "chunks" (Miller, 1956), which are accessible as
units. In perceptual-motor tasks, several simpler acts may be
integrated to form a single complex act.

A classic example of perceptual-motor unit building is in Bryan and
Harter's studies on the acquisition of skill at sending telegraph
messages (cited in Woodworth, 1938, p. 159): Subjects improve from
transmitting character-by-character to sending whole words smoothly, and
sometimes even phrases and complete sentences. Unit building can also
be seen in problem-solving tasks such as the problem shown in Figure 2a.
Figure 2b lists a sequence of moves that solve the problem, but consider
how hard it would be to remember this sequence. Figure 2c illustrates a
more memorable organization, "do four episodes of moving every piece
clockwise." The units formed here (the four rotations) seem best
described as memory units.

In the first example, building larger units improves efficiency.
There is no reason to expect this in the second example, but the new
organization does seem likely to increase ease of recalling or
reconstructing the strategy.

In spite of the differences, a single process might account for
both examples - that of searching for what Klahr and Wallace (1976) call
"consistent sequences" of actions. If sequences of actions are examined
by an information processor, then frequently recurring sub-sequences may
be discovered at some level of description. (For example, if P_1, P_2,
P_3, P_4, P_5, and P_9, P_2, P_3, P_4, P_7 are two sequences of processes, then
P_2, P_3, P_4 is a recurring sub-sequence). These sub-sequences, Klahr and
Wallace's consistent sequences, are potential new units.

Given a 3 x 3 chess board with
black knights in the two upper
corners and white knights in
the two lower corners, move
the white knights to the top
corners and the black knights
to the bottom corners. Only
chess moves legal for knights
may be used.

	1	2	3
A	BK1		BK2
B			
C	WK1		WK2

A

Problem statement and
initial configuration.

BK1 to B3
BK2 to C2
WK2 to B1
WK1 to A2

BK1 to C1
BK2 to A1
WK2 to A3
WK1 to C3

BK1 to A2
BK2 to B3
WK2 to C2
WK1 to B1

BK1 to C3
BK2 to C1
WK2 to A1
WK1 to A3

B

Units of individual moves

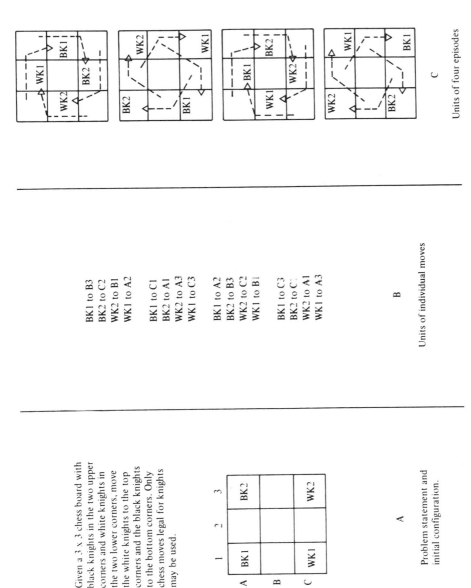

C

Units of four episodes

Figure 2. A simple puzzle (A), for which the solution strategy can be organized by units of individual moves (B), or by
more mnemonic units of clockwise rotations (C).

Deletion of Unnecessary Parts

Deletion of unnecessary parts eliminates inessential operations and otherwise simplifies the strategy's flow of control. For example, Neisser (1964) reports that experienced subjects locate a "Z" embedded in round letters ("GSQO" etc.) twice as fast as when it is among angular letters ("VMWX" etc.). The latter task requires searching for a particular configuration of angles; in the former, detecting any angle is sufficient. Neisser observes that subjects "construct" a recognition scheme during practice, and that, "with repeated scans, they discover the perceptual operations. . . minimally sufficient for the problem" (p. 96) (emphasis added).

Transformations, especially this one, cause problems if used inappropriately. Bhaskar and Simon (in press), for example, study a physics graduate student's difficulties with a simple problem caused by using his "favorite form" of an equation without noticing its irrelevance to the problem. He seemed to have eliminated a test for problem-type that was once part of his strategy for physics problems.

Deletion of unnecessary parts often might involve examining sequences of procedures, inputs, and results that are generated when a strategy is applied. Certain patterns, if invariant across sequences, can indicate unnecessary processing. That is, if one operation uses another's results and then duplicates that operation's input, the two cancel; they are unnecessary whenever appearing together. Here is another case: If a test succeeds if and only if some earlier test does, the later test is unnecessary. (Say that in Neisser's task, finding a "Z" meant looking for a diagonal, and then for two horizontals. In the round-letter condition, if the first test succeeds, the second always will also.)

People also use general knowledge in identifying unnecessary operations. Imagine a task calling for adding and then subtracting the same numbers, as our sequence generation task sometimes does. Prior knowledge that addition and subtraction are converse operations is likely to play a role in eliminating this redundancy; there is no need to wait for a pattern to appear.

Saving of Partial Results

Saving of partial results can reduce processing effort by retaining intermediate values that will be used again later in a procedure, thus avoiding the need for their recomputation. This differs from reduction to results by being useful when results recur within problems but not across them. To see this, one need only look at simple cases such as multiplication of numbers containing repeating digits. Clearly, one can save considerable effort in multiplying, say, 333 by 528 if one remembers that $3 \times 528 = 1584$ after first computing it. Then, rather than doing additional multiplications, one can find 30×528 and

300 X 528 simply by appending zeroes.

A simple set of processes might account for saving of partial results. The transformation is useful when an operation is repeated frequently with the same input, which is easily detected when examining sequences of procedures, inputs, and results. In such cases, procedures for remembering the operation's result can be inserted after its first occurrence, and resulting operations for retrieval can replace any succeeding occurrences.

Re-ordering

Re-ordering, changing the sequence in which operations are performed, can reduce the number of times a step is performed or the number of items that must be remembered at a given point in time. The latter is nicely illustrated by an example in Hunter's (1968) discussion of highly skilled arithmeticians. Try multiplying 234 by 567 entirely in your head using the method usually taught in grammar school:

$$
\begin{array}{r}
234 \\
\times\ 567 \\
\hline
1638 \\
1404 \\
1170 \\
\hline
132678
\end{array}
$$

The conventional method first computes three products: 7 X 234 = 1638, 6 X 234 = 1404, and 5 X 234 = 1170. These are adjusted for position, then added. Hunter observes that, " . . . without jotting down the intermediate steps, . . . there is too much to hold in temporary memory." One "must remember the four digits of the first product, . . . the second product, and the . . . third; then . . . recall these digits, in a different order, so as to add the three products; and all this must be done at the same time as . . . the component calculative steps" (p. 348).

Performing basically the same steps in a different order makes this problem easily manageable. If the computation is done in reverse, then a running total of the products can be kept in working memory:

Product Computed	Running Total
200 X 500 = 100,000	100,000
200 X 60 = 12,000	112,000
200 X 7 = 1,400	113,400
30 X 500 = 15,000	128,400

```
30 X  60 =   1,800              130,200

30 X   7 =    210               130,410

 4 X 500 =   2,000              132,410

 4 X  60 =    240               132,650

 4 X   7 =     28               132,678
```

Since only the running total needs to be remembered across computations, the task can easily be performed within the limits of short-term memory.

Re-ordering to reduce memory demands might involve noticing when operations usedpreviously obtained results. If many intervening operations delay using a result after obtaining it, then demands on short-term memory might be reduced by moving the related operations closer together.

Re-orderings also often appear to use general knowledge. For example, our task implicitly requires doing series of additions and subtractions in range-restricted arithmetic. Subjects are taught to do such series left-to-right e.g., [(((4+3)-2)+3)-3], but often report using different orders to reduce the nuisance of intermediate results going out of range e.g., [4+((3-2)+(3-3))]. This requires applying knowledge that basic arithmetic operations are associative and recognizing that certain operations will become unnecessary. Processes using knowledge in this way are likely very different from those described in the preceding paragraph.

Method Switching

Method switching, which might also be called "special case handling," depends on the existence of alternative procedures that are easier to use under certain circumstances than the regularly followed strategy. If such procedures exist, then it is possible to test for those circumstances and switch to the alternate procedure when appropriate.

For example, the data of Woods, Resnick, and Groen (1975) on second and fourth graders' subtraction strategies indicate that children perform identity subtractions (e.g., "9 - 9 = ?") significantly faster than most other problems; unlike all other problems, solution time is fairly insensitive to the operand values. It appears that children use the following rule in their subtraction strategy: If the minuend and subtrahend are equal, simply answer "zero." As mentioned earlier, Groen and Parkman (1972) found similar effects in children's addition strategies. Identity additions (e.g., 2+2) seemed to use memory retrieval; all others apparently required computation.

The ability to switch methods requires processes that both identify special cases and develop appropriate strategies for those cases. Our subjects' self-reports suggest that the identification process operates by first noticing unusual individual cases and then looking out for additional instances. Hayes and Clark (1970) suggest a similar process in a task of inducing word boundaries in an artificial language.

Once special-case circumstances are identified, the processes for developing an appropriate method might simply utilize the strategy transformations already described. For example, in the special case of equal operands, children in the studies just cited seemingly have reduced addition and subtraction to results. The multiplication example of partial result saving is another illustration; the transformation is useful only when there are repeated digits.

Some Taxonomies of Cognitive Development

Since there may be some parallels, it seems worthwhile to compare our typology of strategy transformations to some taxonomies of cognitive development. We will consider here Flavell's (1972) taxonomy, since it references all of the other explicit taxonomies of which we are aware (e.g., Werner, 1957; Flavell & Wohlwill, 1969; Van den Daele, 1969). We will also consider a taxonomy implicit in the work of Klahr and Wallace (1976).

Flavell's classification scheme provides five possible relationships between "items," his generic term for any cognitive unit (subsuming skills, concepts, beliefs, etc.). These relationships are summarized in Figure 3.

There is no contradiction between Flavell's categorization and ours, but there are some significant differences. The most important difference is in the kind of description being offered. Flavell focuses on general relationships, while we focus on particular changes. Thus, various groupings of transformation types may be needed to produce some of Flavell's relationships, and some transformations can produce different relationships when applied in different circumstances. As the comparison of taxonomies in Figure 4 shows, though, the match-up between transformation types and Flavell's categories is fairly straightforward.

Klahr and Wallace (1976) offer an implicit categorization based on the notion that cognitive development has its basis in the information processing system's capacity for self-modification, a view shared by such as Simon (1962) and Quillian, Wortman, and Baylor (1964). Klahr and Wallace suggest two general principles for self-modifying systems: consistency detection and redundancy elimination. In the first, described earlier, commonly recurring sequences of actions are detected and grouped. In the second, these sequences are examined for unnecessary operations or overly restrictive tests, which can then be eliminated. Klahr and Wallace describe how processes based on their two

Addition: A later item joins an earlier item
              without replacing it.

Substitution: An initial item largely supplants
                an initial item.

Modification: An initial item is extended in
                one of three ways.
      --Differentiation: An item's range of application
                          is divided among several more
                          specialized items.

      --Generalization: An item's range of application
                          is broadened.

      --Stabilization: The smoothness and efficiency
                          of utilizing an item is increased.

Inclusion: A later item uses an earlier item as
              a component.

Mediation: An initial item plays a role in the
              formation of a later item, but
              has no on-going role in that item.

Figure 3. Five possible relationships between cognitive-developmental "items" proposed by Flavell (1972).

principles might operate in several developmental tasks, such as quantification, class inclusion, quantity conservation, and transitivity of quantity.

Once more, there are no contradictions between Klahr and Wallace's organization and ours, but there are some significant differences. They focus on general principles, the construction of operations from smaller operations, and the deletion of sub-operations from larger operations, while we consider particular processes. Thus, some of the processes we have proposed are related to their first principle, while others are more closely related to the second. For example, unit building and replacement with another method are consistency detection processes. Deleting unnecessary parts, saving of partial results, and the reduction transformations are all redundancy elimination processes.

In summary, Flavell offers a change description, describing possible relationships between two states. Klahr and Wallace provide a process description, describing principles governing the processes that produce changes. Our categorization is a hybrid; we suggest both more

Relationships	Corresponding strategy transformation type
Addition:	Method-switching (with higher level goals determining choices between strategies).
Substitution:	Reduction to a rule Replacement with another method
Modification: --Differentiation:	Method-switching
--Generalization:	No corresponding type
-- Stabilization:	Reduction to results Unit building Deletion of unnecessary parts Saving of partial results Re-ordering
Inclusion:	Replacement with another method Unit building

Figure 4. Strategy transformations that can produce the cognitive-developmental relationships proposed by Flavell (1972).

specific types of changes and processes for realizing them. The advantages of such a hybrid categorization, we believe, lie in each description testing the other. A change description alone requires that proposed processes be sufficient to produce those changes, but provides little guidance as to what the actual processes might be. A pure process description suggests conditions for which information processors might test, but it cannot make detailed suggestions about actions taken when those conditions are met. A hybrid description can do both.

Towards a Taxonomy of Strategy Transformations

We have presented a list of eight different strategy transformation types, and attempted to demonstrate their generality by giving examples from a range of experimental and practical situations. There is a certain sense of commonality between some of these types, and of dissimilarity between others, which we would like to capture by proposing some dimensions along which these transformations might be categorized.

One distinction worth considering is that between formally based versus heuristically based transformations. This refers to the source of information suggesting a transformation, e.g., a description of the strategy as opposed to experience using the strategy in its task environment. While formally based transformations such as those used by optimizing compilers (Allen & Cocke, 1972) may have equivalents in humans, we have primarily been interested in heuristically based transformations.

The formal versus heuristic distinction suggests a dimension based on what must be known before the transformation can be made. This dimension might distinguish: (a) meta-knowledge about strategies; (b) general knowledge about the world, in particular about task domains and familiar methods for operating within them; and (c) feedback from performance of particular strategies. We have suggested several types of feedback: sequences of inputs from the task environment, and of procedure names and results within the information processor. Each of our strategy transformations appear to be at least partially dependent on some combination of these three types.

We would also like to look more closely at categorizing strategy transformations by benefits or tradeoffs. Strategies make varying demands on processing effort and memory load. These demands can arise either in accessing a strategy or in applying it. It would be worthwhile to see where different strategy transformations are beneficial, and to ask how an information processing system might determine, in advance, which transformation will be useful.

Another direction in refining the taxonomy is to explore transformations that alter problem representations, reconceptualizing a task in such a way that a new strategy suggests itself. There is ample reason to believe that such changes are important; in several tasks, new representations permit much more powerful strategies (Amarel, 1968; Simon, 1975). Experimentally induced changes in representation have produced important change in problem-solving behavior (Hayes & Simon, 1977).

The most interesting dimension of a taxonomy, we feel, would concern the processes underlying strategy transformations. We have implicitly suggested two categories in this paper: knowledge-based processes, and pattern detection processes. Our focus has been largely on the latter category. We have suggested a number of processes that realize our transformation types. Most have involved inducing a pattern in sequences of operations composing a strategy, along with their inputs and results. Recent progress on a system that discovers rules governing simple scientific domains that use a similar pattern-induction approach (Langley, Note 1) has encouraged us to consider computer models of these processes. While pattern induction processes cannot account for all strategy changes, we find it provocative that processes can be suggested for so many different transformation types within this framework.

Conclusions

The strategy transformation types and tentative taxonomy presented here represent very early steps towards a theory of how people modify their strategies through experience. We believe they are useful steps. The transformation types seem to have broad application, and the taxonomy provides a domain-independent vocabulary for discussing strategy modifications. The taxonomy also suggests both theoretical and empirical questions.

This leads us to consider the relative roles of world knowledge and of pattern induction processes. In addition, there are intriguing similarities between our strategy transformation taxonomy and some taxonomies of cognitive development. Although we consider changes in explicitly taught strategies over periods of only hours, rather than development in broad categories over periods of years, the descriptions offered contain a number of parallels.

Our efforts suggest several empirical questions. What other types of transformations are possible? What circumstances motivate making particular transformations? How does one strategy change influence the likelihoods for other possible changes? How can we predict the direction in which an initial strategy will change?

Answers to questions such as these will help us formulate a theory of strategy transformation processes. We believe that such a theory has a number of instructional applications. In particular, it can help us to design instructionally optimal novice strategies, and suggest ways to teach students how to modify their strategies more efficiently.

Footnote

The authors would like to thank Lee W. Gregg, David Klahr, Patrick W. Langley, and Herbert A. Simon for their comments and suggestions on earlier drafts of this paper. This research was supported in part by a research grant from the Alfred P. Sloan Foundation, and by NIMH Research Grant No. MH07722.

Reference Note

1. Langley, P. W. BACON: A production system that discovers empirical laws. Pittsburgh: Department of Psychology, Carnegie-Mellon University, Paper submitted for publication, 1977.

References

Allen, F. E., & Cocke, J. A catalogue of optimizing transformations.
    In R. Rustin (Ed.), Design and optimization of compilers.
    Englewood Cliffs, New Jersey: Prentice-Hall Inc., 1972.

Amarel, S. On representations of problems of reasoning about actions.
    In D. Michie (Ed.), Machine intelligence 3. New York: American
    Elsevier, 1968.

Bhaskar, R., & Simon, H. A.   Problem solving in semantically rich
    domains: An example from engineering thermodynamics. Cognitive
    Science, in press.

Flavell, J. H.   An analysis of cognitive-developmental sequences.
    Genetic Psychology Monographs, 1972, 86(2), 279-350.

Flavell, J. H., & Wohlwill, J. F.   Formal and functional aspects of
    cognitive development.   In D. Elkind & J. H. Flavell (Eds.),
    Studies in cognitive development: Essays in honor of Jean Piaget.
    New York: Oxford University Press, 1969.

Gerritsen, R., Gregg, L. W., & Simon, H. A. Task structure and subject
    strategies as determinants of latencies (CIP working paper 292).
    Pittsburgh: Carnegie-Mellon University, Department of Psychology,
    1975.

Greeno, J. G., & Simon, H. A.   Processes for sequence production.
    Psychological Review, 1974, 81, 187-198.

Groen, G. J., & Parkman, J. M.   A chronometric analysis of simple
    addition. Psychological Review, 1972, 79, 329-343.

Hayes, J. R., & Clark, H. H. Experiments in the segmentation of an
    artificial speech analogue.   In J. R. Hayes (Ed.), Cognition and
    the development of language. New York: John Wiley and Sons Inc.,
    1970.

Hayes, J. R., & Simon, H. A. Psychological differences among problem
    solving isomorphs.   In N. Castellon, Jr., D. Pisoni, & G. Potts
    (Eds.), Cognitive theory, Vol. II. Potomac, Maryland: Lawrence
    Erlbaum Associates, 1977.

Howes, D. H.   On the relationship between the intelligibility and
    frequency of occurrence of English words.   Journal of the
    Acoustical Society of America, 1957, 29, 296-305.

Hunter, I. M. L.   Mental   calculation.   In   P. C. Wason   & P. N. Johnson-Laird (Eds.), Thinking and reasoning. Baltimore: Penguin Books, 1968.

Klahr, D.,   &   Wallace, J. G.   Cognitive   development: An information-processing view. Hillsdale, New Jersey: Lawrence Erlbaum Associates, 1976.

Miller, G. A. The magical number seven, plus or minus two: Some limits on our capacity for processing information. Psychological Review, 1956, 63, 81-97.

Neisser, U. Visual search. Scientific American, 1964, 210(6), 94-102.

Resnick, L. B. Task analysis in instructional design: Some cases from mathematics. In D. Klahr (Ed.), Cognition and instruction. Hillsdale, New Jersey: Lawrence Erlbaum Associates, 1976.

Quillian, M. R., Wortman, P. M., & Baylor, G. W. The programmable Piaget: Behavior from the standpoint of a radical computerist (CIP working paper 78). Pittsburgh: Department of Psychology, Carnegie-Mellon University, 1964.

Simon, H. A. An information processing theory of intellectual development. Monographs of the Society for Research in Child Development, 1962, 27(2, Serial No. 82).

Simon, H. A. The functional equivalence of problem-solving skills. Cognitive Psychology, 1975, 7, 268-288.

Van den Daele, L. D. Qualitative models in developmental analysis. Developmental Psychology, 1969, 1, 303-310.

Waugh, N. C., & Norman, D. A. Primary memory. Psychological Review, 1965, 72, 89-104.

Werner, H. The concept of development from a comparative and organismic point of view. In D. B. Harris (Ed.), The concept of development. Minneapolis: University of Minnesota Press, 1957.

Woods, S. S., Resnick, L. B., & Groen, G. J. An experimental test of five process models for subtraction. Journal of Educational Psychology, 1975, 67, 17-21.

Woodworth, R. S. Experimental psychology. New York: Henry Holt and Company, 1938.

TEACHING PROBLEM SOLVING: THE EFFECT OF ALGORITHMIC AND HEURISTIC PROBLEM-SOLVING TRAINING IN RELATION TO TASK COMPLEXITY AND RELEVANT APTITUDES

L. de Leeuw
Free University
Amsterdam, Netherlands

The teaching of problem solving has been attempted for a long time. Selz (1935) reports remarkable success from systematic training programs given to elementary school pupils. Teaching thinking or problem solving can be done by training pupils in using adequate problem solving methods. What kind of problem solving methods are adequate? Some primary questions are connected with this point: First, what are the important dimensions of problem solving methods? Second, what are the important criteria for the effectiveness of problem solving training? Third, are there so-called aptitude treatment interactions between important treatment dimensions and certain personality variables? Finally, are the differential effects of the treatments the same for all criteria or not?

One important dimension of problem solving methods is the degree of prescribedness of the solutions process. One can prescribe the solution process in detail, leaving nothing to the invention of the pupil. This kind of solution process is described by the Russian psychologist Landa (1969) as an algorithmic one: a series of operations and decisions, which, if run through in the proper way, offers solution guarantee. This is what is called a TOTE-system by Miller, Galanter and Pribram (1960). Landa has taught algorithmic processes to pupils to help them master complex grammatical rules from the Russian language.

One could leave more thinking steps to the pupil's inventions, however, by letting him discover certain relations by himself. In this situation, help can be given if it is asked for or if the pupil makes too many mistakes. In this case, one is teaching problem solving in a heuristic way. In this situation there is no solution guarantee. Algorithmic and heuristic problem solving methods do not form a dichotomy. Landa (1971) makes a distinction between algorithmic, semi-algorithmic, semi-heuristic, and heuristic prescriptions. Kuljutkin (1970) has elucidated the distinction between algorithmic and heuristic problem solving methods by stating that in heuristic problem solving situations, in contrast with algorithmic ones, the crucial relations are not known; they have to be discovered to find the

269

solution. In the algorithmic situation, the problem solver scans, in a
systematic way, a small repertoire of possible relations from which he
chooses the crucial one; here there is no discovery of relations, but a
check on the presence of known relations.

The distinction between algorithmic and heuristic learning of
problem solving is somewhat related - but not synonymous - to the
distinction between rule learning and discovery learning.

The critical remarks that Wittrock (1966) made while talking about
research in the area of discovery learning are relevant here, too.
According to his critical remarks, one has in this type of research to
take care of: (a) exact operational definition of the treatments, (b)
the replicability of the treatments, (c) well-definedness of the
criteria, (d) the possibility that each pupil can work according to his
own rate and follow his own way through the problems, (e) random
assignment of pupils to the different treatments, (f) adequate
statistical analysis of the results, and (g) premature extrapolation of
results.   Some of these points regard the internal, some the external
validity of this kind of experiment. Cronbach (1966) adds to this list:
(h) the desirability of taking personality factors into account in
looking at the differential effects of the treatments.

We want to add three points to the list: (i) The differential
effects of various problem solving methods have to be investigated in
relation to the complexity of the class of problems trained; (j) There
have to be several criteria, that is, not only tests containing the
trained problem types, but also tests containing transfer problem types;
and (k) There have to be short and long-term effect criteria.

Research Issues

The above-mentioned viewpoints are realized in our research project
as follows. The differential effects of training in algorithmic versus
heuristic problem solving methods are investigated within two domains of
thinking, deductive and inductive reasoning. Within these domains the
following topics are chosen respectively: (a) judging the logical
validity of syllogisms, and (b) extrapolation of number series. Within
each topic two levels of complexity are distinguished in such a way that
the more complex category contains subtypes that are a superset of the
subtypes of the less complex category. Each of these two categories is
taught to different groups of pupils in an algorithmic or a heuristic
way. In this way a 2 x 2 design is created.   One of the important
research issues is the question of whether there is an interaction
between the algorithmic versus heuristic factor and the complexity of
the problem class.

By presenting the problems and feedback by means of
computer-assisted instruction, and using a very adaptive teaching logic,
each pupil goes through the problems in his own way and at his own rate.

Feedback and hints can be given in a multiconditional way, based on the recording by the computer of the response history of the pupil. As courseware and software are necessarily preconstructed, the treatments are exactly operationally defined and replicable. Pupils are assigned to the four different teaching programs by matching them on pretest scores. Important criteria are a test existing of problems of the trained type, and transfer tests, whose content is more or less related to the problems for which a solution method was presented. A distinction is made between horizontal, vertical, and non-specific transfer. All tests are taken three times: as pre-, post- and retention tests. The remainder of this paper reports only the number series extrapolation part of the research.

With respect to aptitude treatment interactions (ATI), the following potential aptitudes were chosen: IQ, numerical ability, achievement motivation, negative fear of failure, positive fear of failure, field dependency, interference-proneness. The two kinds of fear of failure are described in Hermans (1972). Other terms for these concepts are debilitating, and facilitating anxiety. Pupils with a high degree of negative fear of failure are handicapped by their fear in unstructured and/or stressful situations. In these situations they become underachievers. The reverse is true for pupils who score high on positive fear of failure. It was hypothesized that pupils high on negative fear of failure would do better with a problem solving method that offers a high degree of prescription for their behavior, i.e., with an algorithmic method in contrast to a heuristic method. This should not be the case, or even the reverse relation could exist for pupils low on negative fear of failure. No directed aptitude treatment interaction effects were predicted for the other aptitudes. With respect to ATI, these measures were used in an exploratory way. A positive correlation of IQ, numerical ability, and achievement motivation with the criterion variables was predicted. The factor field-dependency was chosen to determine the effect in situations where negative transfer effects were expected, based on fixedness to learned types of operations.

Method

Subjects

Sixty-four fifth and sixth grade elementary school pupils were trained in extrapolating number series; sixteen pupils were in each cell of the design.

Procedure

For brevity, a very short description will be given. Pupils took all tests three times: pre-, post- and retention tests. The posttests were taken within one to three days after the last training session; the retention tests were taken about two months after the posttest.

Each pupil took the programs individually during two or three sessions.
Learning time within each category was similar for each matched pair of
students.

     Apparatus.   The instructional programs were controlled by   a
DEC-PDP-8-computer.   Problems and feedback were presented and responses
given on different types of terminals: random access image projector,
scope (CRT) and teletype.

     Teaching logic. A thorough description of the teaching logics of
the training programs would be lengthy. Suffice it to say that a small
number of standard teaching logics were used in such a way that a very
responsive adaptive environment existed. The algorithm is built up of
identification and transformation subalgorithms.   In the algorithmic
version, learning to a criterion took place at the different levels of
the algorithm (mastery learning). This is described in more detail in
de Leeuw (1975a, 1975b).

     Instruction problem test. At the end of the last training session
a test containing the problems used in instruction was presented. This
test functioned for the algorithmic program pupils as a criterion of
mastery of the problem-category.   This test is called the Internal
Instruction Problems Test. The test containing the instruction problems
that was taken some days later is called the External Instruction
Problems Test.

     Horizontal transfer test. The test contains figure series that can
be reduced to number series of the types which were originally trained.

     Vertical transfer tests. These tests contain number series that go
to (few) step(s) further than the ones used in training and/or form a
combination of the subtypes used in training.

     Non-specific transfer tests. These tests contain: (a) problems
requiring interpolation of the trained number series; (b) fixedness
problems, that is, problems requiring a quite different approach than
the learned ones; and (c) subtests and factor score from the Numerical
Ability test.

                              Results

     Some of the most interesting results will be reported briefly.
Multiple regression analysis was applied as a method of data analysis.
This method offers possibilities to combine dichotomous and continuous
independent variables (predictors) in one analysis. The mean scores on
the Internal Instruction Problems Test (in percentages correct) for the
algorithmic and heuristic groups within complexity level 1 (Algorithmic
Category 1 and Heuristic Category 1, respectively), are 93.9 and 77.0,
$F(1,30)$ = 6.25, p = .018.   For complexity level 2, the means of
Algorithmic Category 2 and Heuristic Category 2 are 86.1 and 62.2,

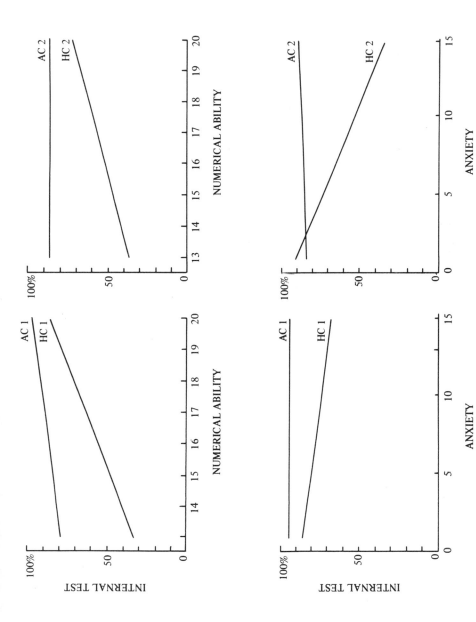

Figure 1. Aptitude-treatment interaction between algorithmic/heuristic treatments and numerical ability (top panels) and anxiety (bottom panels) for the internal instruction problems test.

$\underline{F}(1,30)$ = 8.83, $\underline{p}$ = .006. Within both complexity levels, the algorithmic group is performing at a significantly higher and nearly perfect level. Achievement for Category 1 (C1) is somewhat higher than for Category 2 (C2), but this difference is not significant.

Generally, it can be said that with the Internal Instruction Problems Test as a criterion, the algorithmic teaching program is more effective overall than the heuristic one. The influence of this treatment factor appears to depend upon the aptitudes of numerical ability or negative fear of failure (an anxiety dimension). The ATI between numerical ability and the algorithmic/heuristic treatment is significant for Category 1 only, $\underline{F}(2.29)$ = 10.92, $\underline{p}$ = .003. For Category 2 the trend is in the same direction but is not significant. The reverse relation holds for the interaction between negative fear of failure and the algorithmic heuristic treatment: for Category 2 this is significant, $\underline{F}(2,29)$ = 4.69, $\underline{p}$ = .039; for Category 1 the trend is similar but not significant. These ATI's are depicted in Figure 1.

In contrast, the differential effects of the algorithmic/heuristic treatments are reversed for the External Instruction Problems Test, taken some days after the last training session. Overall, the heuristic version now shows a significantly higher result than the algorithmic one, $\underline{F}(2,61)$ = 7.75, $\underline{p}$ = .007. This reversed effect is caused by a very sharp drop in the achievement from Internal to External Instruction Problems Test at the algorithmic level (from 90.0 to 52.0). The achievement of the heuristic group stays at about the same level (from 69.6 to 66.5).

The same type of ATI's that were found for the Internal Instruction Problems Test appear for the Vertical-Transfer posttest. Negative fear of failure is an important predictor of achievement in the heuristic group. The relation of this aptitude with achievement in the algorithmic group is not so strong. The ATI is significant for both Category 1 and Category 2, and strongest for Category 2, $\underline{F}(3,28)$ = 5.21, $\underline{p}$ = .030 and $\underline{F}(3,28)$ = 11.55, $\underline{p}$ = .002, respectively.

For the horizontal transfer measures, neither main effects or interactions were found. For the problem types for which fixedness to the trained approach could have a detrimental effect, neither main effects or interaction effects were present. Field dependency, measured by the Embedded Figures Test (EFT), however, appears to be a predictor of achievement, especially when the problem class is complex. For the posttest of the fixedness-problems, the partial correlations, after incorporating the pretest score and the algorithmic/heuristic treatment factor in the equation, are for Category 1 and Category 2, .17 and .42 ($\underline{p}$ = .372 and .002, respectively). This relation between field dependency and susceptibility to set is also found for the retention test of the fixedness problems. Partial correlations are .27 and .41 ($\underline{p}$ = .152 and .023, respectively).

References

Cronbach, L. J. The logic of experiments on discovery. In L. S. Schulman & E. R. Keislar (Eds.), Learning by discovery: A critical appraisal. Chicago: Rand McNally, 1966.

Hermans, H. J. M., ter Laak, J. J. F., & Maes, P. C. J. M. Achievement motivation and fear of failure in family and school. Developmental Psychology, 1972, 6, 520-528.

Kuljutkin, Ju.N. Heuristische methoden in het oplossingproces, 1970. Summary in C. F. van Parreren en W. A. van Loon-Vervoorn, Teksten en analyses Sowjetpsychologie 1: Denken. Groningen: Tjeenk Willink, 1975.

Landa, L. N. Algorithmierung im Unterricht. Berlin: Volk und Wissen, 1969.

Landa, L. N. Instructional grammar and types of thinking activity. In Proceedings of the XVII International Congress of Applied Psychology. Luik: 1971.

Leeuw, L. de Computer gestuurd denken; training in het hanteren van algorithmische en heuristische probleemoplossingsmethoden. Pedagogische Studjen, 1975, 52, 377-393. (a)

Leeuw, L. de Teaching of algorithmic and heuristic problem solving methods by computer-assisted instruction. In O. Lecarne & R. Lewis (Eds.), Computers in education: Informatique et enseignements. Amsterdam: North-Holland Publishing Company, 1975. (b)

Miller, G. A., Galanter, E. H., & Pribram, H. H. Plans and the structure of behavior. New York: Holt, 1960.

Plompt, Tj. Statistische technieken voor aptitude-treatment interaction (ATI) onderzoek. Technische Hogeschool Twente, no. 23, 1972.

Selz, O. Versuche zur Hebung des Intelligenzniveaus. Ein Beitrag zur Theorie der Intelligenz und ihrer erziehlichen Beeinflussung. Zeitschrift fur Psychologie, 1935, 134, 236-301.

Wittrock, M. C. The learning by discovery hypothesis. In L. S. Schulman & E. R. Keislar (Eds.), Learning by discovery: A critical appraisal. Chicago: Rand McNally, 1966.

COMPONENTIAL INVESTIGATIONS OF HUMAN INTELLIGENCE

Robert J. Sternberg
Department of Psychology
Yale University
New Haven, Connecticut, U.S.A.

For the past several years, I have been using a set of procedures that I call "componential analysis" to investigate performance in a variety of reasoning tasks: analogies, linear syllogisms, categorical syllogisms, classification problems, and series completion problems. The goal of componential analysis is to identify the component mental operations underlying a series of related information processing tasks, and to discover the organization of these component operations in terms of their relationships both to each other and to higher-order constellations of mental abilities. From a psychometric point of view, componential analysis may be viewed as a detailed algorithm for construct validation - the effort to elaborate the inferred traits (in our case, mental operations) determining test behavior (Campbell, 1960). From an information processing point of view, componential analysis may be viewed as a set of procedures for discovering the identity and organization of a set of elementary information processes (Newell & Simon, 1972).

The purpose of this paper is to describe briefly the procedures of componential analysis, and to illustrate its application in both laboratory and classroom settings. The paper is divided into four parts. In the first, I will summarize the procedures used in componential analysis. A detailed description of these procedures can be found in Sternberg (1977b), although the present paper includes material not previously published regarding componential procedures. In order to concretize the description of procedures, I will show how the procedures have been applied in the investigation of two reasoning tasks - linear syllogisms and analogies. In the second part of the paper, I will present some data from a series of experiments on linear syllogisms. These data, collected in a laboratory setting, show the usefulness of componential analysis as a tool in experimental investigations of human intelligence. Some of the assets of the methodology will be explicitly pointed out. In the third part of the paper, I will present data from an experiment on the development of analogical reasoning. These data, collected in a classroom setting, show that componential analysis can be practically as well as theoretically useful. Some of the practical assets of componential

277

analysis will be noted and discussed. In the fourth part of the paper, I will discuss some implications of the present work for the investigation of intelligence.

Procedures of Componential Analysis

A componential analysis consists of five steps: identification of component processes, identification of the combination rule for different component processes, identification of the combination rule for multiple executions of the same component process, discovery of component latencies and difficulties, and discovery of relations of components to each other and to higher-order mental abilities. We shall discuss each of these steps in turn.

Identification of Component Processes

The first step in a componential analysis is the identification of a set of elementary information processes, or components, that is believed to be sufficient to solve the problem type under investigation. Consider as examples first linear syllogisms and then analogies.

Components of linear syllogistic reasoning. A linear syllogism, or three-term series problem, consists of two premises and a question. The first premise describes a relation between two items in a linear array, for example, Jim is taller than Jon. The second premise describes a relation between one of the items previously described and a third item in the linear array, for example, Jon is taller than Jay. The question requires a transitive inference about the relation between the nonadjacent items in the array, for example, Who is tallest? In this case, solution of the problem requires the subject to infer the relation between the two nonadjacent items, Jim (the tallest person) and Jay (the shortest person).

According to the proposed model of linear syllogistic reasoning (Sternberg, Note 1), as many as 10 component processes may be required to solve linear syllogisms of various kinds. These processes will be illustrated with reference to the sample problem, C is not as tall as B; A is not as short as B; Who is shortest?

1. Premise reading (mandatory). The subject must read each of the two premises, "C is not as tall as B" and "A is not as short as B," in order to comprehend their surface structure.

2. Linguistic encoding of comparative relation (mandatory). The subject encodes the surface-structural form into a deep-structure proposition relating the two terms of a premise. Encoding of a premise with a marked adjective (such as short) is assumed to take longer than encoding of a premise with an unmarked adjective (such as tall). In the example, the first premise is encoded as (C is tall+; B is tall); the

second premise is encoded as (A is short+; B is short). Note that only the comparative and not the negative has, so far, been processed.

   3. Encoding of negation (optional). If a premise is a negative equative, that is, one with the relation "not as ___ as," it is necessary to reformulate the deep-structural encoding to take the negation into account. The roles of the terms in the proposition are reversed, so that the first proposition becomes (B is tall+; C is tall) and the second one becomes (B is short+; A is short). This reformulation, used only for negative equatives, is assumed to require additional processing time.

   4. Spatial seriation of comparative relation (mandatory). Having encoded the premises into deep-structural propositions, the subject is now able to seriate the terms of each premise spatially. A propositional encoding is assumed to be prerequisite for spatial seriation. The subject may seriate the two terms of each premise in either a preferred (usually top-down) or nonpreferred (usually bottom-up) direction. It is assumed that the subject's choice of direction depends upon whether or not the adjective in the original premise was marked or not. The preferred direction is used for unmarked adjectives, the nonpreferred direction for marked adjectives. In the example, B and C are seriated top-down into one spatial array,

B
C.

B and A are seriated bottom-up into a second spatial array,

A
B.

   5. Pivot search (optional). Once the subject has seriated the terms in each of the two premises into two spatial arrays, the subject must locate the middle (pivot) term that will enable him or her to combine the two arrays into a single array. The pivot is assumed to be immediately available if either (a) it appears in two affirmative premises, or (b) it was the last term to be seriated in a negative equative. (The principles behind this availability are described in Sternberg, Note 1.) In the example, the last term to be seriated was A (the tallest term). The subject inquires whether A is the pivot. Since it is not, the subject must use additional time locating the pivot, B, which of course is the only term that appears in both premises.

   6. Seriations of the two arrays into a single array (mandatory). Having found the pivot, the subject is prepared to combine the two separate arrays into a single, integrated spatial array. The subject combines the two single arrays according to the order of the original premises. In the example, the subject starts seriation in the bottom half of the array, and ends up in the top half. Thus, he or she links the second pair of terms, A and B, to the first pair, C and B, forming the spatial array,

A
B
C.

7. Question reading (mandatory). Next, the subject must read the
question that he or she will be required to answer. If the question
contains a marked adjective, as does the question in the example, it is
assumed to take longer to encode, and the subject is assumed to have to
search for the response to the question in the nonpreferred end of the
array.   A marked adjective in the question, therefore, increases
response latency. The example question "Who is shortest"?   contains
such an adjective.

8. Response search (optional).   After seriation was completed
(Step 6), the "mind's eye" of the subject ended up either in the top or
bottom half of the spatial array. If the question has as its answer the
term that is in the half of the array in which the subject has ended up,
then the response is immediately available. If the answer term is in
the other half of the array, however, then the response is not available
and must be sought. This search requires additional time.   In the
example, the subject ended up in the top half of the array, completing
seriation with the A and B terms. The question, however, asks who is
shortest. The subject must, therefore, search for the response, finding
it in the bottom half of the array.

9. Establishment of congruence (optional).   The processes
described above are sufficient to establish a correct answer, and under
some circumstances, a response is immediately forthcoming. If, however,
subjects were careless in their spatial representation of the problem,
they have available to them their propositional representation by which
they can check the accuracy of their response. If the linguistic
encoding of the proposed response is congruent with their linguistic
encoding of the corresponding premise . term, then the response
immediately passes the congruence check. If the two are incongruent,
however, congruence of the response term to the premise term is
established, taking additional time. In the example, C, the shortest
term, was encoded as tall (relative to B, which was tall+). The
question, however, asks who is shortest. Congruence must therefore be
established by formulating the question in terms of who is least tall.

10. Response (mandatory).   The final operation is response,
whereby the subject communicates his or her choice of an answer. In the
example, the subject responds with C.

Components of analogical reasoning. An analogy is a problem of the
form A : B :: C : D (A is to B as C is to D). In a standard analogy
task, there will be several alternative D options, and the subject's
goal will be to choose the best of available options. For simplicity,
we shall assume that two options are available, D_1 and D_2.   Can one
identify a set of component processes that is sufficient to solve all
problems of this kind?   I have proposed such a set of processes

(Sternberg, 1977a, 1977b), and will describe them with reference to the simple analogy, Washington : 1 :: Lincoln : (a. 10, b. 5).

1. Encoding (mandatory). In encoding an analogy term, the subject identifies the term, retrieves from long-term memory the attributes that may be relevant for analogy solution, retrieves from long-term memory a value corresponding to each attribute, and stores the results as an attribute-value list in working memory. In encoding Washington, the subject might store in working memory the facts that Washington was the first president, a portrait on a dollar bill, and a Revolutionary War hero. In attribute-value notation, these facts would be represented ((president (first)), (portrait on currency (dollar)), (war hero (Revolutionary))).

2. Inference (mandatory). In inference, the subject discovers the relation between A and B analogy terms. The relation is stored as a list of attributes with values in working memory. In inferring the relation between Washington and 1, the subject might store in working memory relations such as that Washington was the first president, and is the portrait on a one-dollar bill. In attribute-value notation, these facts are represented ((president (ordinal position (first))), (portrait on currency (amount (dollar)))). The first term (president, portrait on currency) in each relation comes from the encoding of A analogy term. The second term (ordinal position, amount) in each relation comes from the encoding of the B analogy term. The third and innermost term is newly inferred.

3. Mapping (optional).[1] In mapping, the subject discovers the higher-order relation between A and C analogy terms. The relation is higher-order in the sense that it is what constitutes the "analogy" connecting the domain (first half) to the range (second range) of the problem. In mapping the relation between Washington and Lincoln, the subject might store in working memory relations such as that both Washington and Lincoln were presidents, are portraits on currency, and were war heroes, ((presidents (first, sixteenth)), (portraits on currency (dollar, five dollars)), (war heroes) Revoluntionary, Civil))). Mapping is used for all analogies with integral terms (see Garner, 1974), that is, ones in which values of one attribute are not perceptually or conceptually separable from values of other attributes. Most types of analogy terms are indeed integral.

4. Application (mandatory). In application, the subject attempts to apply from C to each answer option the rule he or she has inferred from A to B as mapped to C. In applying from Lincoln to 10 and 5, the subject finds that only one relation is of use in completing the analogy. Whereas Washington is the portrait on a one-dollar bill, Lincoln is the portrait on a five-dollar bill. In attribute-value notation, the relation from Lincoln to 10 is null: ( ); the relation from Lincoln to 5 is not null, however: ((portrait on currency (amount (five dollars)))).

5. Justification (optional). Justification is used when none of
the presented answers meets the subject's criterion for an acceptable
analogy. In such a case, the subject must check his or her preceding
operations,   and justify one of the presented answer options as
preferred, although nonideal. The need for justification can arise
either because of an error in previous processing, or because none of
the answers forms a good analogy. If, in the example, the subject had
failed to infer that Washington appears on a dollar bill, then the
subject would later had needed justification in order to choose a
response.

6. Response (mandatory). The subject responds by circling an
answer, pushing a button, or whatever, thereby communicating his or her
solution to the investigator. In the example, the preferred solution is
5.

Combination Rule for Different Component Processes

The second step in a componential analysis is to determine the
combination rule for different component processes. The combination
rule can be serial or parallel, exhaustive or self-terminating, holistic
or analytic.

Serial versus parallel processing. If subjects combine a set of
component operations serially, then their total response latency will be
the sum of the individual component latencies. If combination occurs in
parallel, response latency will equal the duration of the most
time-consuming component operation.[2]   In the theories of linear
syllogistic and analogical reasoning, the various component operations
described above are assumed to be combined serially. For example,
solution of linear syllogisms requires reading of a premise, followed by
linguistic encoding of the comparative relation, followed by encoding of
negation (if one is used), and so on.

Exhaustive versus self-terminating processing. If components are
combined exhaustively, then all operations stipulated by the theory will
be used in the solution of every problem of the type encompassed by the
theory, that is, all operations are mandatory. If components are
combined in self-terminating fashion, then not every operation need be
used in the solution of every problem, that is, at least some operations
are optional. The theories of linear syllogistic and analogical
reasoning both contain optional components, and hence involve
self-terminating processing across components. For example,
justification need be executed in the solution of an analogy only if
application fails to yield a unique response.

Holistic versus analytic processing. If components are combined in
a holistic fashion, then the total latency for combined executions of a
given operation will not be separable from the total latency for
combined executions of every other component. If components are

executed in an analytic fashion,   separability can be attained.   The
theories of linear syllogistic and analogical reasoning assume analytic
processing. For example, one can separate inference (or any other
component) time for each other component.

Combination Rule for Multiple Executions of the Same Component Process

     The third step in a componential analysis is to determine the
combination   rule for multiple executions of the same component process.
These multiple executions may be serial or parallel, exhaustive or
self-terminating, holistic or analytic, just as above.

     Serial versus parallel processing. If multiple executions of a
given   component are serial,   then   total   processing time for a given
component equals the sum of the processing times for each repetition of
the   component.   If processing is parallel, then total time for a given
component equals the time for the most time-consuming single execution
of that component.   Serial processing is assumed in the theories of
linear syllogistic and analogical reasoning. For example, the time   to
infer   the   relation between Washington and 1 is equal to the sum of the
times to infer that Washington was the first president, the portrait   on
a dollar bill, and a Revolutionary War hero.

     Exhaustive versus self-terminating processing.   If processing is
exhaustive, then whenever a component is used in solution of an item, it
is executed the maximum possible number of times for that item type.   If
processing is self-terminating, the component need not be executed the
maximum possible number of times. In the theory of linear syllogistic
reasoning, exhaustive processing is assumed.   For example, if both
premises contain negatives, the subject is assumed always to process
both negatives.   Different models under the theory of analogical
reasoning make different assumptions about which components   are
exhaustive and which self-terminating (Sternberg, 1977a, 1977b).   In
what appears to be the preferred model, encoding and inference are found
to be exhaustive with respect to the attributes stored in working
memory; mapping, application, and justification are found to be
self-terminating.   In the sample analogy, for instance, a subject can
arrive at the correct solution without ever mapping the relation stating
that both Washington and Lincoln were war heroes.

     Holistic versus analytic processing. If multiple executions of
component processes are holistic, then it is not possible to separate
the amount of time spent on each execution of the process, even though
it may be possible to separate total time spent for that process from
total time spent for other processes.   If multiple executions are
analytic, then time for each single execution can be determined. The
theory of linear syllogistic reasoning assumes exclusively analytic
processing.   The time for processing a negation in the first premise,
for example, can be separated from the time for processing a negation in
the second premise. The theory of analogical reasoning stipulates that

holistic processing may be used when some analogies are of the
degenerate forms $\underline{A} : \underline{A} :: \underline{A} : \underline{A}$, $\underline{A} : \underline{B} :: \underline{A} : \underline{B}$, and $\underline{A} : \underline{A} :: \underline{B} : \underline{B}$.
In such analogies, a simple template match between the fourth term and
the stem term it repeats can determine whether a given fourth term is
satisfactory or not.

In completing this section, I would like to emphasize the
importance of distinguishing between combination rules for execution of
different components and for multiple executions of the same component.
They need not, and often will not, be the same. The two rules should be
specified separately.

Component Latencies and Difficulties

The fourth step in a componential analysis is to estimate the
latencies and difficulties of the individual components theorized to be
used in processing. In order to make these estimates, the investigator
must quantify the information processing model or models, predicting
subjects' latencies and error rates from a set of independent variables.
Corresponding to each independent variable is an estimated parameter
that represents the latency or difficulty of a single component process.

Latency and difficulty parameters, as estimated from modeling of
response times and error rates, respectively, do not necessarily
correspond to each other in magnitude. For example, I have found that
in analogical reasoning, encoding tends to be a time-consuming process,
and thus to have a large latency parameter estimate. In the solution of
nonverbal analogies, however, few of the errors subjects make are due to
errors in encoding, so that the difficulty estimate for encoding tends
to be small in value.

Individual differences in component latencies and difficulties are
almost inevitable. In componential analyses of a variety of reasoning
tasks, I have found that individual differences in global reasoning
performance are due almost entirely to differences in speed and
accuracy, not to differences in operations or strategies for combining
operations. Differences in parameter estimates are of key importance in
the next and last step of the analysis.

Relations of Components to Each Other and to Higher-order Abilities

In componential analysis, the component is the fundamental unit of
analysis, much as the factor is the fundamental unit in factor analysis,
and in the psychometric tradition in general. Reference abilities (as
measured by standard ability tests) are conceived of in terms of a
linear model combining component scores, rather than in terms of a
linear model combining factor scores. Specifically, reference abilities
are defined as constellations of components that, in combination, form
stable patterns of individual differences across tasks. In order to

understand the composition of abilities, we seek to model them in terms of the component processes that, in combination, constitute the abilities. An important step in the analysis, therefore, is to model ability test or factor scores in terms of individual component scores. The dependent variable is a score on an ability test or factor. The independent variables are component latencies or difficulties as estimated for each individual. If these component scores account for almost all of the reliable variance in the test or factor score, then one is assumed to have achieved understanding of the composition of the ability. Single correlations of component scores with ability scores are also helpful in elucidating the nature of the abilities. Finally, it is important to intercorrelate the component scores with each other in order to determine the extent to which duration or difficulty of each component process is related to duration or difficulty of each of the other processes.

Correlations of component latencies or difficulties with ability test scores can provide an important source of convergent and discriminant validation for a model of information processing. In the proposed model of linear syllogistic reasoning, for example, certain operations are hypothesized to be linguistic, and other operations to be spatial. Component process scores for the linguistic operations should be strongly related to scores on verbal reasoning tests, but only weakly related to scores on spatial operations. This logic assumes that verbal and spatial scores are not themselves highly correlated. In the samples I have used, they are not.

<u>Componential Analysis in a Laboratory Setting</u>

<u>A Componential Analysis of Linear Syllogistic Reasoning</u>

Four experiments were conducted to test the proposed theory of linear syllogistic reasoning. The experiments differed in certain aspects of the items and of the experimental paradigm used to test the theory. I shall present here a summary of the results from one of those experiments, Experiment 3, which used standard items and testing procedures. I will draw upon results of the other experiments only in analyses of individual differences. The results of the other experiments corroborated the findings reported below.

<u>Method</u>. Subjects were 18 Yale undergraduates who participated for course credit. All subjects received 32 types of linear syllogisms that varied in whether (a) the first premise adjective was marked or not, (b) the second premise adjective was marked or not, (c) the question adjective was marked or not, (d) the premises were affirmative or negative equative, and (e) the solution to the problem appeared in the first or second premise. Each subject received each of the 32 types of linear syllogisms three times, with each of three adjective pairs: <u>tall-short</u>, <u>good-bad</u>, <u>fast-slow</u>. Subjects also received eight types of two-term series problems. A two-term series problem takes a form such

Table 1.   Major Results of Linear Syllogisms Experiment

I. Means and Standard Errors

A. Overall

	$\overline{X}$	$S_{\overline{X}}$
1. 3-term series	7.00 ±	.17
2. 2-term series	3.18 ±	.13

B. By Adjective

1. tall-short	7.05 ±	.17
2. good-bad	7.02 ±	.18
3. fast-slow	6.94 ±	.19

C. By Session

1. Session 1	7.98 ±	.23
2. Session 2	7.02 ±	.17
3 Session 3	6.02 ±	.13

II. Group Model Fits

A. Overall

	$\underline{R}^2$	RMSD
1. 3-term series		
a. Mixed model	.84	.39
b. Linguistic model	.69	.54
c. Spatial model	.58	.63

B. By 2- & 3-term series combined

1. 3-term series		
a. Mixed model	.84	.39
b. Linguistic model	.69	.54
c. Spatial model	.58	.63
2. 2- & 3-term series combined		
a. Mixed model	.97	.35
b. Linguistic model	.96	.43
c. Spatial model	.94	.51

B. By Adjective

1. tall-short		
a. Mixed model	.75	.49
b. Linguistic model	.71	.52
c. Spatial model	.53	.66
2. good-bad		
a. Mixed model	.74	.53
b. Linguistic model	.63	.62
c. Spatial model	.60	.65
3. fast-slow		
a. Mixed model	.83	.44
b. Linguistic model	.56	.71
c. Spatial model	.46	.79

		R^2	RMSD
C. By Session			
1. Session 1			
	a. Mixed model	.71	.73
	b. Linguistic model	.63	.80
	c. Spatial model	.49	.94
2. Session 2			
	a. Mixed model	.81	.44
	b. Linguistic model	.67	.57
	c. Spatial model	.59	.63
3. Session 3			
	a. Mixed model	.81	.34
	b. Linguistic model	.54	.52
	c. Spatial model	.50	.54

III. Individual Model Fits
    A. 3-term series

	R^2	RMSD
1. Mixed model	.51	1.03
2. Linguistic model	.43	1.10
3. Spatial model	.36	1.15

    B. 2- & 3-term series combined

	R^2	RMSD
1. Mixed model	.87	.80
2. Linguistic model	.86	.85
3. Spatial model	.83	.89

IV. Distrubution of Component Latencies (see Figure 1)

V.   Statistically Significant Parameter Intercorrelations ($p < \leqslant r$ ($p < .05$)

(Encoding, Negation)	.58
(Encoding, Marking)	.56
(Encoding, Pivot Search)	.74
(Encoding, Response Search)	.43
(Marking, Pivot Search)	.45
(Marking, Response Search)	.66
(Response, Noncongruence)	.67

VI.   Correlations between Parameters and Composite Reference Ability Scores
    (Combined Samples of Four Experiments, N = 106)

	Verbal	Spatial
Encoding	−.25**	−.51***
Negation	−.14	−.34**
Marking	−.20	−.36***
Pivot Search	−.16	−.25**
Response Search	−.26**	−.35***
Noncongrence	−.31*	−.24
Response	−.30**	−.09

*$p < .05$
**$p < .01$
***$p < .001$

as $\underline{A}$ is taller than $\underline{B}$; Who is tallest? (The superlative form of the adjective is generally used for consistency with the three-term series problems, even though the comparative form of the adjective is grammatically correct.) The two-term series problems varied in whether (a) the premise adjective was marked, (b) the question adjective was marked, and (c) the premise was an affirmative or a negative equative. Each type of two-term series problem was presented four times with each of the three adjective pairs mentioned above. All items were presented over three sessions, using a Gerbrands two-field tachistoscope. Following testing in each session, subjects received a variety of verbal reasoning, spatial visualization, and abstract reasoning tests.

Results. Results of the experiment will be discussed in six parts, with each part corresponding to one of data sets I-VI in Table 1.

I. Means and Standard Errors. Three-term series problems took subjects an average of seven seconds to solve. There were no consistent trends in adjective difficulty. There was a consistent trend across sessions, however: Subjects became faster with practice.

II. Group Model Fits. Three basic models of linear syllogistic reasoning are compared in Sternberg (Note 1). These models are the mixed spatial-linguistic model described earlier, a linguistic model based upon (but not identical to) the model of Clark (1969), and a spatial model based upon (but not identical to) the models of DeSota and Huttenlocher (DeSoto, London, & Handel, 1965; Huttenlocher, 1968; Huttenlocher & Higgins, 1971). Space limitations preclude a detailed description of the latter two models, although these models are described in the original report (Sternberg, Note 1).

Table 1 reports comparative group model fits for the three-term series data, the combined two- and three-term series data, and for each adjective and each session. The results are unequivocal, supporting the mixed spatial-linguistic model over either of the other two models in every comparison. None of the models are identical to the true model, however. The mixed model can be rejected relative to the true model at the 5% level of significance, whereas the linguistic and spatial models can both be rejected at the .1% level.

III. Individual Model Fits. Each of the three models was fit to the data of individual subjects. As would be expected from the group results, the mixed model was superior to the other two models. The relative fits of the three models were compared for individual subjects, and it was found that the mixed model was best for 14 subjects, the linguistic model for 2 subjects, and the spatial model for 2 subjects. Thus, there appear to have been only minor differences in strategy.

IV. Distribution of Component Latencies. How did subjects spend their time in solving linear syllogisms? Figure 1 shows the distribution of component times for those parameters that could be estimated from the data in this experiment. The encoding parameter

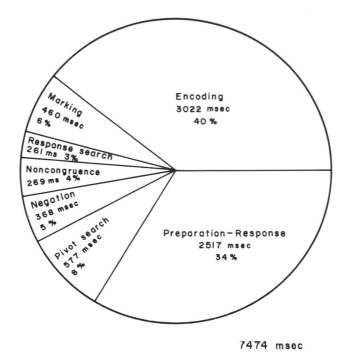

Figure 1.   Amounts of time spent in each operation for a typical negative equative
linear syllogism.

includes some seriation for unmarked comparatives, seriation of the   two
single arrays into a combined array integrating all of the relational
information, and some premise reading. The marking parameter   includes
both linguistic encoding of premises into deep-structure propositions,
and spatial seriation of the propositional information into a two-item
array. The response parameter includes response, question reading, some
premise reading, and some seriation of the   two   single   arrays   into   a
combined spatial array. The truly time-consuming part of the solution
processes is the combination of information from the two premises.

     V. Statistically Significant Parameter Intercorrelations.   As   can
be seen in the table, not all parameter estimates were statistically
independent across subjects; nor were they expected to be independent,
since   all   operations   were   hypothesized   to   be either spatial   or
linguistic. Two parameters - encoding and marking - are significantly
correlated with at least three other parameters. Since both of these
parameters were estimated as confoundings of spatial and linguistic
processes (as described in Part IV above), more statistically reliable
correlations with other parameters were to be expected.

VI. <u>Correlations</u> between <u>Parameters</u> and <u>Composite</u> <u>Reference</u> <u>Ability</u> <u>Scores</u>. In order to provide the statistical power necessary for an adequate test of the correlational hypotheses, correlations of parameter estimates with verbal and spatial tests were computed for the combined set of experiments. As described in Part IV above, the encoding parameter consisted primarily of spatial operations and secondarily of linguistic operations. The pattern of correlations shown in Table 1 is consistent with this mixture. Negation was predicted by the mixed model to be a linguistic operation. The data are inconsistent with this prediction: Negation is significantly correlated with spatial but not with linguistic scores. Subjects may negate premises, therefore, by interchanging the positions of the terms in spatial arrays representing premise information. For example, the terms in A-B are flipped in space so as to become represented as B-A. Marking was hypothesized to consist of one linguistic operation and one spatial operation. The correlations are consistent with this hypothesis. Pivot search and response search were both hypothesized to be spatial operations, and indeed, both parameters show significant correlations with the spatial scores. Response search, however, also shows a lower but significant correlation with the verbal scores. I am unable to explain this correlation. Noncongruence is hypothesized by the mixed model to be a linguistic operation, and the data bear out this hypothesis. Finally, response is estimated as a confounded parameter including primarily linguistic operations, and the data are consistent with this analysis.

Taken as a whole, the experimental data provide very good support for the mixed spatial-linguistic model of linear syllogistic reasoning. The data also show the power of componential analysis to provide stringent tests of well specified information processing hypotheses. Some of the assets of the method of analysis will now be explicitly noted.

<u>Assets</u> <u>of</u> <u>Componential</u> <u>Analysis</u> <u>in</u> <u>Testing</u> <u>Theory</u>

The major alternative to understanding individual differences in terms of component processes is that of understanding individual differences in terms of factors. What are the advantages of the componential framework?

<u>Inferential</u> <u>power</u>. Inferential statistics for mathematical modeling are well developed, and it is relatively easy to disconfirm one model relative to another. Inferential statistics for factor analysis are rather poorly developed, however, making it difficult to compare models, except in the case of maximum-likelihood methods (Lawley & Maxwell, 1963).

<u>Uniqueness</u> <u>of</u> <u>parameter</u> <u>estimates</u>. The parameter estimates for a given componential model are unique (unless the number of parameters exceeds the available number of degrees of freedom). The factor

loadings for a given factor analysis are nonunique, however, because the axes in a given factor space are subject to rotation. The nonuniqueness of the factor loadings leaves the investigator with the very difficult, mathematically arbitrary decision of how to rotate the axes. The exception to this difficulty is found in confirmatory maximum-likelihood factor analysis (Jöreskog, 1966, Jöreskog & Lawley, 1968).

Determinancy of parameter estimates. The parameter estimates, or component scores, are uniquely determined. Factor scores obtained under a common factor model, however, are indeterminate, and can only be estimated.

Interpretability of parameters estimates. The parameter estimates from a componential analysis are directly interpretable in terms of the contribution of each component process to either item latency or difficulty. The factor loadings of factor analysis are susceptible to no such direct interpretation, however. Indeed, there is considerable question as to how factors should even be interpreted (see Sternberg, 1977b).

Componential Analysis in a Classroom Setting

A Componential Analysis of the Development of Analogical Reasoning

Two experiments were conducted to test the proposed theory of analogical reasoning, and to trace the development of analogical reasoning processes over time. I shall present here a summary of the results from the first experiment (see Sternberg & Rifkin, Note 2, for further details). The results from the second experiment further elucidate the nature of analogical reasoning and its development, but these results cannot be presented here for lack of space.

Method. Our sample consisted of 19 second graders, 22 fourth graders, 18 sixth graders, and 17 adults. The children were students in a religious day school; the adults were students at Yale University.

All subjects received identical test materials. Of interest here are two of these materials, schematic-picture analogies and geometric analogies. The schematic-picture analogies depicted people varying in four binary attributes: hat color (white, black), suit pattern (striped, polka-dotted), hand gear (briefcase, umbrella), and footwear (shoes, boots). The geometric analogies constituted the complete nonverbal analogies subtest of the Cognitive Abilities Test, a multilevel test of mental ability for grades 3 to 12. The analogies differed from the ones presented in the actual Cognitive Abilities Test, however, in that we deleted three of the original five answer options. We retained only the correct option and a randomly selected option.

All subjects received 24 booklets of schematic-picture test analogies, plus 11 experimental booklets of no further interest to the

present discussion. Each booklet contained 16 analogies, and was timed
for 64 seconds. The analogies within a given booklet were homogeneous
in difficulty, as measured by the number of attribute values changed
from the A to B analogy term, the A to C analogy term, and the D_1 to D_2
analogy term. Since the identities of the particular attribute values
in each analogy varied, however, no two analogies were identical. For
example, if hat color and footwear varied from A to B in one analogy,
suit pattern and handgear might vary from A to B in another analogy.
Both were counted as two attribute-value changes.   Order of test
booklets and order of pages within test booklets were randomized across
subjects.

        Subjects had 30 minutes to complete the 60 geometric analogies.
Almost all subjects finished the test within the time.

        Results. It is convenient to divide the results into sections
representing the procedures of componential analysis described earlier.
These procedures are applied here to the understanding of cognitive
development.

        1. Acquisition of components. There was no evidence of component
acquisition for solution of schematic-picture analogies in the grade two
to adult range.   Subjects at each age level appear to have used
encoding, inference, application, and response in the solution of these
analogies. Mapping was not used at any age level, presumably because of
the nonintegral (separable) nature of the stimulus attributes.

        2. Acquisition of combination rule for different components.
According to the theory of analogical reasoning described earlier,
subjects use an additive rule for combining different   component
operations.   An additive combination rule for the four components
described above provided an excellent fit to the data at each age level.
The best additive model accounted for 91%, 95%, 90%, and 94% of the
variance at grades two, four, six, and adulthood respectively (with
respective RMSDs of .65 sec, .28 sec, .30 sec, and .32 sec).   There was
unexplained true variance at the grade six and adult levels.   Combined
over age levels, the fit of the best model was 96% (RMSD = .31 sec).
The best additive model accounted for 26%, 86%, 52% and 65% of the
variance in the error rates for each of the respective age levels (with
respective RMSDs of .03, .02, .02, and .01).   There were small amounts
of unexplained true variance again at the grade six and adult levels.
The fit for the combined levels was 86% (RMSD = .01).

        3. Acquisition of combination rule for multiple executions of
single components.   The same additive model provided the best fit to the
data at each age level. This model was one in which inference and
application were both self-terminating.   Encoding was also
self-terminating. Subjects encoded attribute-values only as they needed
them, rather than encoding all attribute-values in immediate succession.
A schematic flow chart for this model is shown in Figure 2.   Note that
subjects encode, infer, and apply the minimum number of attributes

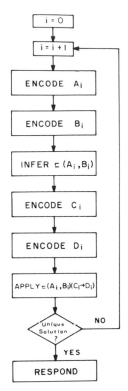

Figure 2.   Flow chart of processes used in solving schematic-picture analogies.

necessary to select   a unique response to a given analogy.   This
preferred model   is   used only for separable attributes; a different
preferred model   is found for stimuli   with   integral   attributes
(Sternberg, 1977a, 1977b).

    4. Changes in component latencies.   Although there   were   no
developmental trends in any of the analyses reported above, there were
clear developmental trends in the component latency data, as   shown in
Figure 3.

    As would be expected, there is a monotone decrease in overall
solution latency between grades two and four and between grades four and
six (as shown by the top line in the graph). At this point, solution
latency levels off.   Error rates, not shown in the graph, decreased
monotonically across age levels: .107, .080, .063, .015.

    Inference-application time (the two were confounded   in   the
preferred model) decreased between grades two and four and between
grades four and six. It increased trivially between grade six and
adulthood.

    Encoding time showed a sharp decrease in latency between grades two
and four, followed by a nontrivial increasing trend between grades four

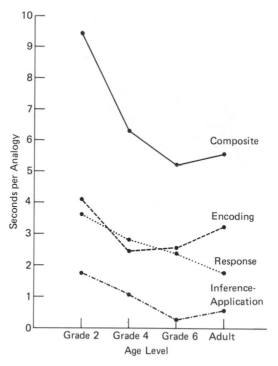

Figure 3.   Overall and component latencies in solution of schematic-picture
analogies.

and six and between grade six and adulthood.   The initial decrease
almost certainly reflects cognitive development. What factors, however,
might account for the subsequent increase in encoding time? It has been
found previously (Sternberg, 1977b) that among adults, better reasoners
spend proportionately longer amounts of time encoding than do poorer
reasoners.   The difference appears to be one of strategy, in that more
careful, thorough encoding of an analogy term may facilitate subsequent
processing of the stimulus (say, in inference or in application).   The
increase may, therefore, reflect a strategy of more thorough encoding by
older subjects.

        Response component time decreases monotonically across all age
levels.

        5. Relations of components to each other and to higher-order
abilities.   Two   pairs of parameters were significantly correlated ($p <$
.05),   encoding   and   inference-application   (r =   .49),   and
inference-application and response (r = .61).   Each of the component
scores was also correlated across subjects with scores on the geometric
analogies   test.   The   pattern of correlations was consistent with that

reported in Sternberg (1977a, 1977b) for "People Piece" analogies, which also consist of schematic figures. Response was the only component score showing a strong and significant correlation with higher-order reasoning, r = -.46, p < .001. Significant correlations between inference, mapping, application, and reasoning seem only to be obtained when discovery of stimulus attributes is a nontrivial task. In schematic-picture analogies, of course, the attributes are obvious, so that discovery of attributes is trivial.

In conclusion, the results reported above suggest that componential analysis can be used successfully in a classroom setting to isolate the loci of development in analogical (and possibly other) reasoning tasks. The method of analysis has several advantages over other methods, which will now be discussed.

Assets of Componential Analysis in a Practical Setting

Origins of individual differences. Componential analysis provides a useful way of explaining the origin of individual differences in global behavioral performance. Traditional psychometric tests can tell us that one student is superior to another in reasoning, but they provide little insight into the nature of this superiority. A componential analysis identifies a number of possible sources of significant variation among individuals.

Suppose an individual has difficulty relative to his or her peers in solving analogical reasoning problems. In many cases, teachers' expectations for the student's performance will be lowered, and the student may well be relegated to a lower track in school. But suppose an effort is made to provide remedial training. How might one begin? In order to provide remedial training, one must first know the source of the student's difficulty. Componential modeling of the individual's response data may enable the teacher to learn whether the student's difficulty is in unavailability of a critical component operation, use of a nonoptimal combination rule for either different components or multiple executions of the same component, prolonged component latency, or unusual component difficulty. The latter two problems are probably the most difficult to remedy. But if the student's problem is in the use of an incorrect or inefficient strategy, it may be possible through componential modeling to determine the nature of the strategy the student is using, and to see how it differs from the typical or optimal strategy.

Construct validation. Componential analysis provides a useful way of simultaneously validating a test, and a theory of how subjects perform on the test. The theory is validated by testing the extent to which mathematical models of information processing fit observed latency and error data. The test is validated by showing that performance on it can be understood in terms of nontrivial processing components, and by showing that these components are correlated with scores on standard

reference ability tests.   If no model seems to fit the data, then one
must question whether the test measures performance on any well-defined
set of information processing components. If some model fits the data,
but the components of this model are uncorrelated with any standard
reference ability tests, one must question whether the isolated
component processes are of any interest beyond the single test, that is,
whether they have any generality.   If procedures of both internal
validation (modeling) and external validations (correlations with
ability   tests) are successful, then one attains a comprehensive
understanding of the nature and value of the test investigated.

Criterion-referenced scores. Component scores or values can be
criterion-referenced.   For example, latency components are generally
expressed in terms of time per component execution, or in terms of total
time spent in a particular component operation on a given type of
problem. The scores are derived from each individual's response data
without reference to the data of other individuals, that is, the scores
are directly interpretable without any normative reference.

Individualized assessment of measurement error.   In   typical
psychometric analyses, indices of measurement error, such as the
standard error of measurement and the standard error of estimate, are
derived from group data and are, therefore, averages over subjects. But
we all know that accuracy of measurement differs widely for different
individuals.   In componential analysis, estimates of error are always
computed for each indivdual's data as well as for the group data.   Such
estimates may be for overall error, as measured by the standard error of
measurement or the standard error of estimate. Or, the estimates may be
for particular sources of error.   If linear regression or a closely
related technique is used for modeling, it is possible to derive the
standard error of each component score for each individual. The teacher
is thereby able to assess how much confidence can be placed in a
particular component score for a particular individual.

Intellectual development. The componential framework is useful for
charting a child's intellectual development as he or she proceeds
through school. It should be possible, at least in theory, to determine
which of the sources of individual differences described above are
responsible for improvements in global performance. Thus, in addition
to observing the almost inevitable increases in mental age that occur
over time during childhood, one can observe what aspects of performance
are responsible for this increase.

Implications for the Investigation of Intelligence

For almost 80 years, the primary model for the study of
intelligence was the factor model. But this long-lasting model was not
intended by the pioneers in the human abilities movement to be the
ultimate framework for the understanding of human abilities. According
to Thurston (1947), "the factorial methods were developed for the study

of individual differences among people but the individual differences may be regarded as an avenue of approach to the study of the processes which underlie these differences" (p. 55).

If the ultimate purpose of factor analysis is indeed the study of the processes that underlie individual differences, then it would seem desirable to attempt to model individual differences in these processes directly, rather than through intervening "factors" whose relation to processes is uncertain. Componential analysis provides one way of modeling individual differences in processes directly. By decomposing each individual's global score into a set of underlying process scores, the investigator is able to appreciate each individual's standing on each of the hypothesized sources of individual differences. At this level of elementary process analysis, the needs of experimental psychology and of counseling or educational psychology seem to converge, because it is only through understanding of the basic sources of individual differences that we will be able to design instructional treatments that either effectively take these individual differences into account, or seek to reduce them.

Footnotes

This research was supported by National Science Foundation Grant BNS-76-05311 to Robert J. Sternberg.

1. Mapping was formerly believed to be mandatory (Sternberg, 1977a, 1977b), but subsequent research has shown it to be optional.

2. The mathematical combination rules described for serial and parallel processing are for simple cases of each. More elaborate rules are required for more complex cases.

Reference Notes

1. Sternberg, R. J. Representation and process in transitive inference. Manuscript submitted for publication, 1977.

2. Sternberg, R. J., & Rifkin, B. The development of analogical reasoning. Manuscript submitted for publication, 1977.

References

Campbell, D. T. Recommendations for APA test standards regarding construct, trait, or discriminant validity. American Psychologist, 1960, 15, 546-553.

Clark, H. H.   Linguistic   processes   in   deductive   reasoning.
    Psychological Review, 1969, 76, 387-404.

DeSoto, C. B., London, M., & Handel, S. Social reasoning and spatial
    paralogic. Journal of Personality and Social Psychology, 1965, 2,
    513-521.

Garner, W. R. The processing of information and structure.   Hillsdale,
    NJ: Lawrence Erlbaum Associates, 1974.

Huttenlocher, J. Constructing spatial images: A strategy in reasoning.
    Psychological Review, 1968, 75, 550-560.

Huttenlocher, J., & Higgins, E. T.   Adjectives,   comparatives,   and
    syllogisms. Psychological Review, 1971, 78, 487-504.

Jöreskog, K. G.   Testing   a   simple   structure   hypothesis   in   factor
    analysis. Pyschometrika, 1966, 31, 165-178.

Jöreskog, K. G., & Lawley, D. N. New methods in maximum likelihood
    factor analysis. British Journal of Mathematical and Statistical
    Psychology, 1968, 21, 85-96.

Lawley, D. N., & Maxwell, A. E.   Factor analysis as a statistical
    method. London: Butterworth, 1963.

Newell, A., & Simon, H. Human problem solving. Englewood Cliffs, NJ:
    Prentice-Hall, 1972.

Spearman, C.   The nature of "intelligence" and the principles of
    cognition. London: Macmillan, 1923.

Sternberg, R. J.   Component   processes   in   analogical   reasoning.
    Psychological Review, 1977, 84, 353-378. (a)

Sternberg, R. J. Intelligence, information processing, and analogical
    reasoning: The   componential   analysis   of   human   abilities.
    Hillsdale, NJ: Lawrence Erlbaum Associates, 1977. (b)

Thurstone, L. L. Multiple factor analysis.   Chicago: University   of
    Chicago Press, 1947.

EYE FIXATION AND STRATEGY ANALYSES OF
INDIVIDUAL DIFFERENCES IN COGNITIVE APTITUDES

Richard E. Snow
Stanford University
Stanford, California, U.S.A.

A vast literature in educational psychology attests to the fact that individual differences in learner aptitudes predict learning outcomes. A substantial body of literature also now demonstrates that aptitude variables often interact with instructional treatment variables in these predictions (Cronbach & Snow, 1977). Aptitude main effects and aptitude-instructional treatment interactions (ATI), frequently account for a larger proportion of variation in learning outcome than do treatment main effects alone. ATI findings, in particular, have important implications for the development of instructional theory and research and for instructional improvement. They suggest how instruction can be made adaptive to student differences. But if practical and theoretical use is to be made of these ideas, then individual differences in aptitude for learning will need to be understood at a more analytic process level. Traditional research on aptitude sought mainly to improve the predictive power of measures, and to build a taxonomy of aptitude constructs based on correlational studies. With the growth of a cognitive experimental psychology of information processing, coupled with the development of ATI research on instruction, it now seems possible to pursue a process theory of aptitude. This paper notes some recent findings and reports one new study in a continuing program of research toward obtaining such a theory.

Background

Aptitudes are individual difference variables that predict learning in a particular situation. The defining characteristic of aptitude, then, is relation to learning. A recent review of research on aptitude (Snow, 1977) has suggested two constellations, called "aptitude complexes," into which many of the better substantiated ATI findings seem to fit. One of these centers on the construct of intelligence or general mental ability (abbreviated as G) and its division into verbal-crystallized ability, fluid-analytic ability, and spatial-visualization ability. G appears to interact when instructional treatments differ in the information processing burden they place on the

299

learner. The other is a complex of anxiety and motivation for achievement via independent work versus conformity of instructional prescriptions. These variables seem to enter interactions when treatments are more versus less structured by the teacher. There is reason to believe that the two complexes interrelate, since some investigations show cognitive ability and anxiety entering into higher-order ATI. As a start toward a process theory, however, the present research concentrates on G.

The cognitive ability tests used to measure G aptitudes are cognitive tasks, not different in kind from the tasks used in cognitive psychology laboratories to study human information processing. Several lines of recent work suggest that ability tests can be analyzed in information processing terms (e.g., Glaser, 1976; Resnick, 1976) and a number of task-specific process models now exist (e.g., Sternberg, 1977). Correlations also occur with some frequency between test scores and information processing measures (e.g., Hunt & Lansman, 1975). Hunt's work in particular yields the hypothesis that verbal-crystallized ability is associated with speed of coding and temporal order operations in short-term memory. However, other studies suggest that relationships of this sort are unlikely to be so simple. Chiang and Atkinson (1976) confirmed Hunt's result for males only, finding the opposite trend for females. Further analysis of Chiang-Anderson data (Snow, 1976; Snow, Marshalek & Lohman, 1976) suggested that rather than one-to-one correspondences between ability test scores and the parameters of particular information processing tasks, we should expect complex networks of interrelationships, including nonadditive combinations of variables. Further, process models are required that apply not only to specific tests or tasks but to all tasks purporting to reflect a particular aptitude construct. Thus, a method of analysis is needed by which information processing can be examined both within and between tasks, and the construct validity of process model components can be established.

Two exploratory devices that should be helpful in this connection are introspective reports and eye movement records. Computer simulation research has long relied on subject introspections about processing strategies, sequences, and styles. The advent of modern cognitive psychology, and some recent technological advances, has renewed interest in eye movement tracking during cognitive processing (e.g., Monty & Senders, 1976). Just and Carpenter (1976) have now applied this approach to the study of test-like cognitive tasks, including mental rotation, sentence-picture comparison, and quantitative comparison. Their data suggest that eye fixation sequences can be linked to processing models. Further, both introspection and eye tracking can be applied across tasks, and their use in combination may provide a form of construct validation.

Purpose

The present study was thus designed to explore information processing characteristics of performance on a range of tasks representing the aptitude constructs traditionally associated with G. It was hoped that a provisional process model of individual differences in G could be obtained.

Method

From each of eight mental ability tests, six items plus practice items were chosen and administered to 48 subjects under conditions allowing film recording of each subject's sequence of eye fixations during item solution. The tests from which items were selected represented a spectrum of ability factors, as identified in the factor analytic literature, ranging from verbal-crystallized ability, through fluid-analytic ability, to spatial visualization and visual-perceptual closure abilities. The tests were: Vocabulary, Verbal Analogies, Raven Matrices, Embedded Figures, Paper Folding, Paper Form Board, Street Gestalt Completion, and Harshman Gestalt Completion. Items were depicted on slides for rear-screen projection in a viewing box equipped with a super-8 film camera, with eye fixations recorded through a system of mirrors. The box was designed to be portable and to involve minimal discomfort or unusual posture demands on the subject. Reaction time and correctness of response were separately recorded. In a following session, subjects also introspected about their performance strategies on each type of test item, as well as their test-taking strategies in general. Paper versions of sample items were placed before the subjects. Special questionnaires were designed for each test and used by an interviewer as a checklist while the subject talked. The subject then reviewed and verified the completed questionnaire. Responses were recorded separately for test items originally answered correctly or incorrectly.

Subjects were selected from a pool of 241 California high school students for whom factor scores from a larger reference battery of ability tests were available. The subject samples represent extreme groups on fluid-analytic ability and verbal-crystallized ability. Subject selection also balanced on sex and a measure of cerebral laterality (eyedness) to yield a 2 x 2 x 2 x 2 design. Statistical analysis used multiple regression and correlation methods. Both significance tests and estimates of the strength of relationships were of interest. Exploration of the eye movement and introspection data also relied on informal graphical methods.

Results

Overall performance. The first stage of analysis examined correctness and reaction time for the eight tests. With total correct score as dependent variable, results were as expected for all types of items except Raven Matrices. In general, verbal items yielded main effects favoring high verbal-crystallized ability while spatial and visual-perceptual items yielded main effects favoring high fluid-analytic ability. Raven, and some Gestalt items, failed to show consistent differences, perhaps because these items had to be modified for slide presentation. On figural and spatial tests, males showed a slight advantage over females. No sex differences occurred on the verbal tests. The reaction time analysis also included items as a design factor, to detect systematic changes across practice within tests. Unlike the correctness analysis, results were mixed, without consistent main effects associated with reference ability factors. On some items and tests, high ability subjects showed shorter reaction times than did low ability subjects, but in general the reaction time data seemed to reflect more complex kinds of underlying individual differences in information processing than can be captured by simple generalizations associated with reference abilities. Item difficulty of course varied within tasks and this was a complicating factor in the reaction time data. There were, however, some sex and eyedness main effects and interactions here, mostly on the verbal tests. Males and left-eyed subjects, particularly if they were also low in verbal-crystallized ability, were slower in responding.

Introspective Strategies. Analysis then proceeded to the self-reported strategy data. Here, a scoring system had to be devised to capture the major strategy differences reflecting hypothesized process variables, while still allowing exploratory study of a range of other possibilities. The system adopted indexed 13 variables separately for items answered correctly and for items answered incorrectly. The list included reported use of subvocal verbalizing, general mental imagery, specific visualized spatial techniques, a form of template matching, guessing, double checking, apparent serial versus holistic processing, and exhaustive search of response alternatives. Results showed both general trends in strategies used across tests and some strategy differences specific to particular tests.

With respect to general statements, it was found, for example, that low-low ability (i.e., low G) subjects reported more use of sub-vocal verbalizing and general mental imagery, but less systematic attention to all parts of the stimulus and response alternatives in an item, than did high-high ability subjects. High G subjects were more likely to report skimming all the response alternatives in an item and attempting each item in turn without skipping around, when performing most kinds of tests. Low G subjects indicated that they often skipped around in tests, searching for easy items, and often did not examine all response alternatives in an item. On a number of tests, high G subjects also seemed to double check more often and more systematically than did low G subjects. The single strategy index yielding the most consistently high correlations (in the range .40 to .60 approximately) with a large variety of G measures (including Wechsler full scale IQ) reflected subjects' reported use of mental template-like construction of correct answers from stimulus analysis, followed by rapid skimming of response alternatives to find a match. Other strategy indices showed only spotty, inconsistent correlations with reference abilities, and with each other.

Findings for test-specific strategies were not necessarily consistent with those for the more general indices. For example, while low G subjects reported more use of visual imagery in general, high G subjects were more likely to report use of specific imagery strategies when visualizing rotations in spatial ability tests. Also, reported strategies sometimes differed on correct versus incorrect items. Some subjects appeared to adopt the same strategy across items despite the perception that the answer produced might sometimes be wrong. Other subjects seemed to change strategies between right and wrong items in such a way as to suggest the functioning of a kind of autocriticism or executive control; they shifted to a new strategy when a normally preferred one proved unproductive. One example of this occurred in contrasting high and low fluid-ability subjects on their use of specific spatial techniques on correct versus incorrect spatial test items. Some high fluid-ability subjects reported using this strategy on all items whether or not they were correct, while others shifted to a second strategy on difficult items. Some low fluid ability subjects reported use of this strategy only as a second choice when another strategy failed. Thus, subjects appear to differ in strategic flexibility. Some subjects appear to be relatively inflexible, or perhaps some strategies are simply unavailable to them. Among the more flexible individuals, strategies seem to be ordered differently for use by different subjects, and chosen as a function of internal executive evaluation.

Eye-Movement Analysis. Analysis of the eye fixation data also explored a variety of scoring procedures and indices. Some of these were designed to parallel basic differences in information-processing models, e.g., degree of systematic serial processing of stimulus features, exhaustive versus self-terminating study of response alternatives. Other indices were chosen to represent aspects of classical definitions of intelligence, e.g., flexibility and adaptation of performance within and between items, both within tasks and from task to task. Still others were based on more informal information processing hyptheses, e.g, early versus late examination of response alternatives, degree of switching between stimulus parts and response alternatives, rapid scanning versus concentrated study of stimulus and/or response features, and amount of double checking. A large number of more specific variables were scored for the purpose of building usable indices. Again, account was taken of eye fixation differences on correctly versus incorrectly answered items.

It was possible to decompose total reaction time for each item into parts presumed to be associated with different stages or steps of processing, using apparent major shifts in eye fixation patterns to demarcate steps. These stages were tentatively labelled "orientation," "analysis," and "decision," but it was evident that boundaries between stages were often unclear. Some subjects appeared to cycle through these steps several times, often in a rather disorderly fashion. Others seemed to spend almost all their time in analysis, some shifting between stimulus and response parts of the item, and some not; orienting and decision moves were hardly detectable at all for these subjects. Some eye movement indices were found to be positively associated with reference abilities (e.g., degree of systematic serial processing of stimulus features, early concentration on stimulus versus rapid switching between stimulus and response alternatives, rapidity of adaptation across items within tests). Some also changed relation to ability measures across items (e.g., memory span related to stimulus-response switching only on some early items). Many other indices showed marked individual differences but little apparent relation to reference abilities (e.g., exhaustive versus self-terminating use of response alternatives, component reaction times). Substantial differences were noted between tests, but the principle trends suggested that eye fixation indices related more to G than to special ability profiles.

It is not clear that a fine grain analysis of eye movement variables provides the most meaningful or useful level of measurement of individual differences in this domain. There were many puzzling correlations and shifts in correlations involving fine grain indices. While statistically significant, such correlations do not readily yield psychological interpretations. The statistical analyses completed on these data at the time of this writing have therefore not been entirely satisfying, and our interpretations and further analyses continue to rely also on molar categorizations of the eye movement records. Figure 1 suggests some of the kinds of results and the levels of analysis that are possible. Parts a and b show records of a high G and a low G subject, respectively, on one item from the Paper Folding Test, a spatial ability measure. Parts c and d of the figure show the same two subjects, respectively, on one Vocabulary test item. The two subjects differ more on fluid-analytic and spatial ability reference scores than on verbal-crystallized ability reference scores, and this seems to be reflected in a gross way in their eye tracks; their fixation patterns differ more on the spatial item than on the verbal item.

On Paper Folding, the subject's task is to examine the upper row of pictures, understand the series of folds made in the piece of paper, and note where the whole is punched in the folded paper in the final frame. He must then decide what the paper would look like when unfolded, and find it among the five alternatives in the lower row. The high G subject (Figure 1a) seems to perform a systematic analysis of the folding and unfolding steps in the stimulus row. He is particularly concerned with the first fold, which is also the last unfold. The

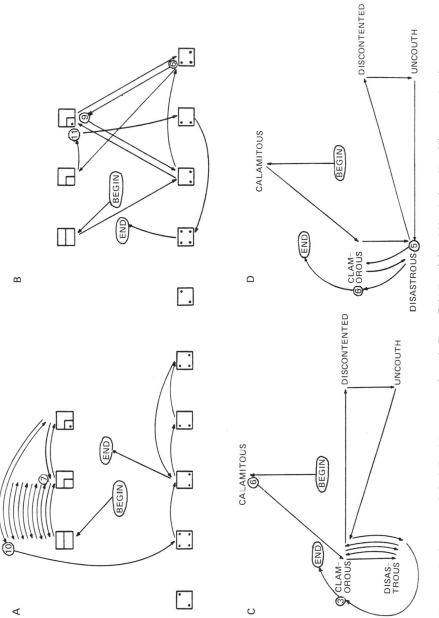

Figure 1. Performance of a high-G subject on items from the Paper Fold Test (A) and Vocabulary Test (C) compared with performance of a low-G subject (B and D).

circled numbers at several points indicate long gazes (measured in film frames; four frames = one second). Only after this systematic analysis of the stimulus does he look at the response row. He systematically scans across the response alternatives, orally responding that "b" is correct just after looking at it. He then completes his scan, checks back to be sure, and finishes. His later self-report was consistent with the pattern shown, indicating he folded and unfolded the paper mentally, constructed a template of the correct pattern, skimmed the alternatives to find a match, and checked back to be sure. The pattern for the low G subject on the same item is unsystematic. He continually jumps from stimulus row to response row, apparently without clear purpose. He never moves directly between the first two stimulus parts, the ones that the high G subject spent most of his time comparing. He responds incorrectly. He reported later that he was unable to visualize the folding process and ultimately guessed.

For the Vocabulary item (in Figures 1c and d), alternative "c" is correct. Here the high G subject starts by studying the stimulus word for six frames (about (1 1/2 seconds), then moves to a comparison of the two most likely alternatives. After this, he checks the other two alternatives, hesitates, then responds correctly. He reported knowing stimulus words as direct associates and eliminating alternatives that were obviously wrong. The low G subject spends only a quarter of a second on the stimulus word, then scans the alternatives, before comparing the two most likely alternatives. He spends more than a second studying each of these two response terms with few shifts.between them, and then responds correctly. He reported looking carefully at one alternative and analyzing word roots.

It should be clear that scoring could be based on gross classification, on identification of several intermediate critical features, and/or on quantification of time and direction of moves step by step. We have tried so far to work at all levels, and are not yet prepared to recommend which, if any, is best for process analysis. Incidentally, the most striking contrast in Figure 1, that between systematic and apparently unsystematic analysis of the Paper Folding sequence, for high and low G subjects, respectively, was also found for many other items and pairs of subjects, but not all. Several variations on this trend were evident, and there appear to be at least four categories of subjects between these two extremes.

Discussion

Our findings are tentative and we are now redoing the analyses in an attempt to develop an improved scheme for indexing the contrasts of particular interest. No conclusions are warranted; data analysis is still in progress, and interaction-produced scoring keys and results will still need to be cross-validated in a new sample.

It is possible to speculate from this initial experience, however, on the form of a process model of aptitude derived from such data. In addition to the three-stage conception noted earlier, it seems possible to distinguish four classes of variables important in analyzing individual differences in information processing within and across stages. These classes can be identified as: parameter variables, reflecting differences within a particular processing step, (e.g., time spent on each target); sequence variables, reflecting differences in the order in which processing steps are taken (e.g., stimulus looking before response looking versus rapid alternation); route variables, representing the inclusion of different steps by different subjects (e.g., double-checking vs. not, or systematic comparison of stimulus parts versus not); and summation variables, reflecting differences in gross adaptations across items or tasks. For the present, this fourth kind of individual difference might be thought of as "flexibility" or "adaptation" of approach as the series of items continues. It is not certain yet whether this summative kind of process difference will be clearly demonstrable. But, it is interesting to note that Binet's original definition of intelligence, at the beginning of this century, emphasized among other things "flexibility" and "adaptation" in problem solving.

Our analyses so far suggest that reference abilities may be less associated with specific parameter variables than with variables from the other three classes. Extended correlational research will be needed to link eye fixation and self-reported strategy indices to one another in distinguishing these classes of process variables, and thus to build a processing description of ability test factors. Eye movement records and introspections do seem to provide at least some important parts of the needed within-task and cross-task descriptions.

Aptitudes have been found useful in analyzing instructional effects, and cognitive processing conceptions now appear useful in analyzing aptitudes. ATI research as depicted in Cronbach and Snow (1977) is but a way-station along the road to more penetrating process analyses of individual differences in learning from instruction. Cognitive psychologists cannot analyze all possible tasks in detail and ATI results should help us decide where to focus process analyses. Also, exploratory correlational study of eye movement patterns and introspective reports should help guide and evaluate the construction of formal models of aptitude processes. In effect, the approach reported here may serve as an "advance organizer" for the kind of systematic componential analyses advocated by Sternberg (1977). Ultimately, improved and newly understood aptitude measures may provide an important avenue through which cognitive processing models can be brought to bear on the improvement of instruction in real school settings.

Footnotes

This report is based on preliminary findings from one study in a continuing series supported by Office of Naval Research Contract N00014-75-C-0882. The opinions expressed do not necessarily reflect those of ONR, and no official endorsement should be inferred.

Other individuals participating in this research will appear as co-authors of the final technical report. They are D. Coffing, D. Lohman, B. Marshalek, N. Webb, and E. Yalow.

References

Chiang, A., & Atkinson, R. C.   Individual   differences   and interrelationships among a select set of cognitive skills. Memory and Cognition, 1976, 4, 661-672.

Cronbach, L. J., & Snow, R. E. Aptitudes and instructional methods: A handbook of research on interactions. New York: Irvington, 1977.

Glaser, R. Components of a psychology of instruction: Toward a science of design. Review of Educational Research, 1976, 46, 1-24.

Hunt, E., & Lansman, M. Cognitive theory applied to individual differences. In W. K. Estes (Ed.), Handbook of learning and cognitive processes. Hillsdale, NJ: Erlbaum, 1975.

Just, M. A., & Carpenter, P. A. Eye fixations and cognitive processes. Cognitive Psychology, 1976, 8, 441-480.

Monty, R. A., & Senders, J. W. (Eds.) Eye movements and psychological processes. Hillsdale, NJ: Erlbaum, 1976.

Snow, R. E. Research on aptitudes: A progress report. In L. S. Shulman (Ed.), Review of Research in Education, Volume 4, 1977.

Snow, R. E. Theory and method for research on aptitude processes: A prospectus (Technical Report 2). Stanford, CA: Aptitude Research Project, School of Education, Stanford University, 1976.

Snow, R. E., Marshalek, B., & Lohman, D. F. Correlation of selected cognitive abilites and cognitive processing parameters: An exploratory study (Technical Report 3). Stanford, CA: Aptitude Research Project, School of Education, Stanford University, 1976.

Sternberg, R. Intelligence, information processing, and analogical reasoning: The componential analysis of human abilities. Hillsdale, NJ: Erlbaum, 1977.

HYPOTHESIS TESTING STRATEGIES AND INSTRUCTION

Rudolf Groner and Beat Keller
University of Bern
Bern, Switzerland

The research reported in this paper is based on the assumption that the process of thinking can be considered as an active internalized kind of experimentation, where the anticipation of the result precedes the collection of corroborating or disconfirming evidence. Some decades ago, the term hypothesis was used for this kind of mental activity and applied to a wide variety of thought problems (Dewey, 1933; Claparède, 1933; Piaget, 1949). Later, a number of formal theories (e.g., Bower & Trabasso, 1964; Falmagne, 1970; Millward & Wickens, 1974; Levine, 1975) have focussed on the concept identification paradigm. Despite the advantages of the formalized models in making strong parametric predictions, a number of objections might be raised. First, the models are restricted to a rather narrow domain of tasks in a rather artificial setting. There is little positive evidence to indicate how these findings generalize to other task domains. Second, the conventional dependent variables (e.g., statistics over the number of correct solutions, or distributions of solution latencies) represent the final product of a presumably long series of theoretical events. This is partly the reason why it is necessary to estimate, a posteriori, the values of parameters from the same set of data that is going to be used for testing the theory. If that part of the process that is reflected by the parameters (e.g., hypothesis sampling) could be directly observed, the methodological shortcomings of parameter-fitting could be avoided. In any event, it would be more desirable to collect data during the problem solving process. Finally, in order to arrive at strong quantitative predictions, the models have to be explicit in every detail. Therefore, a model might fail due to some ad hoc assumptions that are not at the center of the psychological interest, having been made for formal reasons. Some of these shortcomings might be avoided by the following changes in the conventional strategy.

The Task Domain

Extensive research has also been done with concept identification in the present paradigm (Groner, 1977, briefly summarized in Groner, 1976), but the area of applicability of a formalized hypothesis-testing model is going to be extended to a second task domain, multi-term series

Fred is taller than Jack	Sid is taller than Bill
Sam is taller than Bill	Sam is taller than Jack
John is taller than Jack	Sid is taller than Jack
John is taller than Sam	Fred is taller than John
Jack is taller than Bill	Sam is taller than Sid

Figure 1. An example of a six-term series problem (unit of eye movement analysis: one entire premise, as indicated by the 5 × 2 grid).

problems. A lot of theoretical effort has been spent by other authors in the past, with inconclusive results on a special case of this task, the so-called three term series problem (for a critical survey, see Johnson-Laird, 1972).   Figure 1 shows an example of a six-terms series problem requiring the successive ordering of a six named persons (called "terms") in accordance with ten statements about pairs of them (called "premises," or more generally "instances").

What is Measured?

The approach to be discussed below still allows for the prediction of the conventional dependent variables (Groner & Groner, 1974), but also has been generalized to apply to an additional class of data, eye movements (summarized in Groner, 1977), which are supposed to measure selective attention during a problem solving process. To make such a generalization possible, however, some assumptions have to be made explicit. These can be tested empirically.

The first assumption is that relatively complex visual processes, like the reading of premises in Figure 1 (or identification of attributes of the concept) require a foveal fixation, i.e., the axis of the eye has to be moved to the stimulus to be analyzed. This assumption is supported by numerous experimental results (cf. Lévy-Schoen, 1969), in which stimuli were more than a foveal diameter apart, and it was possible to identify the temporal pattern of attention from the foveal fixation pattern.   We also assume that in tasks that require large short-term memory (STM) capacity, the subject attempts to reduce his STM load.   The stimulus display has been tested empirically (Groner, 1975a, 1977) by removing the information after the subject had read it at least once, but had not yet solved the problem. Even with a very simple problem involving only three premises (which were designed to be recalled easily, if the subject would have attempted to store them), only 13% of the subjects were able to solve the problem.

Since the subject does not know in advance where to find the relevant information, he first has to search for it in the stimulus display. Two classes of eye movements can be distinguished, <u>scanning fixations</u>, which are associated with the stimulus search, and <u>processing fixations</u>, which are supposed to take place after the relevant information has been found and used for solving the problem. This distinction was empirically tested in an experiment (Groner, 1975b, 1977) where the subject's hypothesis was under the control of the experimenter. It was found that in certain tasks (e.g., concept identification) or arithmetic problems, the two classes of eye fixations can be distinguished by only considering the duration of the fixation. In the experiment reported here, no separation between scanning and processing will be attempted, but the distinction has to be made to avoid the difficulty that – if only processing were postulated – the subject would have to know in advance what he is looking at. Similar to Just and Carpenter (1976), we do not take as elementary units of the experimental analysis the saccadic eye movements as directly observed, but rather the fixation anywhere within an entire informational unit of the display (i.e., a whole premise or attribute). The method of registration has been described elsewhere (Groner, Kaufmann, Bischof & Hirsbrunner, 1974) in more detail.

The Generalized Hypothesis Model

To avoid the pitfall of inappropriate <u>ad</u> <u>hoc</u> assumptions, we attempted to start with a model formulation as general as possible, which in a first step leaves the essential features undetermined. In a second step, the assumptions are specified, but in a systematic and relatively exhaustive fashion, with each set of compatible assumptions creating a separate model variant. The model is not presented here in a complete and formal way (see Groner, 1975c, 1977). The most relevant assumptions follow.

The distinction between <u>verification</u> and <u>falsification</u> can be traced back to the old issue of incremental or all-or-none learning mechanisms. In the incremental processes the plausibility of different hypotheses changes only gradually with new instances. In the present context the result of a series of experiments (cf. Groner, 1977) suggests that "verificatory" or incremental effects might be present – if present at all with adult subjects – only during the initial stages of the problem solving process, where it could be interpreted as a hypothesis generating strategy. The conjecture of incremental change would be faulted if a single contradictory instance were sufficient for abandoning the hypothesis, in which case an all-or-none mechanism would have to be assumed.

A second assumption relates to the <u>number</u> of <u>hypotheses</u> <u>simultaneously</u> <u>processed</u>. The efficiency of the strategy might be drastically increased by the simultaneous evaluation of more than one hypothesis. While Bruner, Goodnow, and Austin (1956) speculated about some quite sophisticated strategies involving several current hypotheses (e.g., "simultaneous scanning"), Restle (1962) has shown that their additional efficiency will be zero when accompanied by an independent resampling scheme (see below). An additional argument against multiple hypothesis evaluation is that under these conditions, the STM processing load appears unrealistic for most humans.

Another way of increasing the efficiency might be realized by keeping track of all hypotheses previously falsified, and not resampling them. If the subject has the choice between instances, as provided by the selection paradigm of Bruner et al. (1956), instances could be chosen in a systematic, non-repetitive way. In probabilistic hypothesis models, these <u>memory</u> <u>asumptions</u> are equivalent to a sampling scheme without replacement, i.e., to conditional probabilities.

By stating the above assumptions in a more formal manner and creating all combinations between them, it is possible to arrive at a large number of model variants. By means of the theory of Markov processes, or through computer simulation, one can derive exact quantitative predictions on numerous statistics, e.g., the number of eye fixations required to arrive at the solution in a six-term series problem. Thus, an efficiency hierarchy of model variants can be established, where the actual human performance can be measured in terms of the model variant with comparable problem solving efficiency.

In the following section, two variants of the model, as applied to the six-term series problem, are introduced.

<u>Hypothesis</u> <u>Testing</u> <u>Model</u> <u>Variant</u> <u>I</u> <u>and</u> <u>II</u>

Variant I is the simplest and therefore least efficient strategy, but it is also minimal in its strain on the STM processing load. Since both Variants I and II assume only all-or-none mechanisms, they will be called hypothesis <u>testing</u> strategies.

To illustrate Variant I by an example, the term to the left side of the premise, which is activated by the first eye fixation (let us say in Figure 1, "John is taller than Sam"==>John) will be selected as a (single) hypothesis (here, "John is the tallest"). If the experimental conditions provide a randomization of the spatial arrangement of the ten premises, the relative frequency of a term showing up on the left can be taken as the probability of that term to be selected in the hypothesis (thus, the probability for John amounts to 0.2; for Sam 0.3; etc.). In a next step, more premises are scanned and processed according to an independent resampling scheme, and the hypothesis is maintained as long as it is compatible with the newly fixated premises. The condition of compatibility means that there exists (among the not yet ordered terms) no term that is still taller than the one contained in the hypothesis. Thus, in our example there is only one premise that is capable of falsifying the hypothesis (i.e., "Fred is taller than John"), and it will be scanned with probability 0.1, in which case the next premise will deliver a new hypothesis (with probability 0.2 again, "John is the tallest").

If the sampling of scanned premises is assumed to be independent, a problem arises as to when the process will ever finish. Therefore, another probability is introduced that stops the process and is supposed to indicate when a hypothesis will be accepted as a solution. The numerical value of 0.10 was found to be adequate. Such a probability also seems quite plausible since it generates an average of ten verifications until the hypothesis finally is accepted.

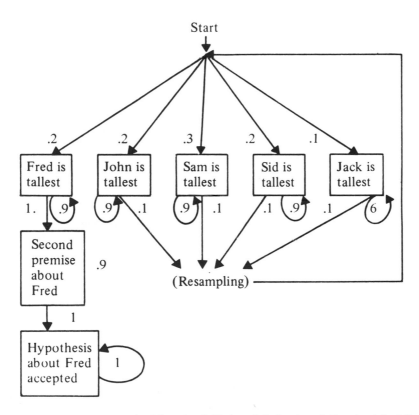

Figure 2. Hypothesis testing model, variant I; Markov chain for the solution about the tallest.

Figure 2 shows the states and transition probabilities of the Markov chain up to the point at which a solution about the tallest has been found. It is a straightforward matter to extend the model for the second tallest, third, and up to the sixth, requiring a total of 33 states. In its complete version, there are ten more states for ending up at an incorrect solution when the falsifying premise did not show up in an identical inspection series as with verification. In a natural way, this allows for strong predictions of particular errors.

Model Variant II is made more efficient by replacing the independence-of-resampling assumptions with a partial dependence. First, a perfect memory for instances is assumed, i.e., no premise will be scanned more than once during the same hypothesis. The memory for the previously falsified hypotheses goes back only to the last falsified hypothesis that will not be resampled. Figure 3 shows the corresponding Markov chain of this model variant. The left-most branch would be activated with the correct hypothesis and would consume exactly ten fixations (i.e., the number of premises in the display). The next branch to the right would be entered when the first premise involved term $\underline{b}$ (here: John). After that, eight of the nine remaining premises will be irrelevant (=branch down) and only will falsify the hypothesis (=branch to the left), and next the same happens with the remaining eight premises, and so on. At the bottom of this branch, the next scanned premise might contain a new hypothesis, but if $\underline{b}$ is sampled again, the resampling for a new hypothesis will continue until an eligible hypothesis is scanned. As it will have been noted, the stopping problem of Variant I does not occur in Variant II, since an exhaustive search will guarantee the correct solution. This property of Variant II might be considered as positive from the standpoint of problem solving efficiency, but negative with regard to predictive power, because no errors could be predicted.

For an exact description of the solution over all six order positions, one needs not less than 151 states, but under suitable experimental conditions there is not a single free parameter to be estimated. By powering the matrices of transition probabilities (e.g., Feller, 1957, chapter 15), the predicted probability distribution over the number of fixations can be computed, since every state transition corresponds to a new eye fixation. The empirical observations are the number of eye fixations (in the above defined sense) spent by the subjects before arriving at a final solution.

The lines of Figure 4 show the predicted probability distributions, and the circles represent the observations of 15 subjects (relatively unselected paid volunteers), each solving two six-term series problems without any special instructions. As will be noted, there is a remarkably similar tendency between Variant I and the data. Though being aware of the pitfall of accepting the null-hypothesis, the sad fact remains that normal subjects without special instructions behave on the efficiency level of the most inefficient hypothesis testing strategy.

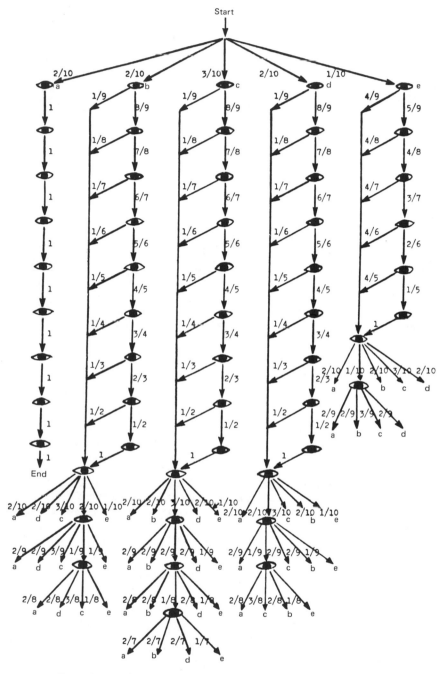

Figure 3. Model variant II; Markov chain for determining the "tallest."

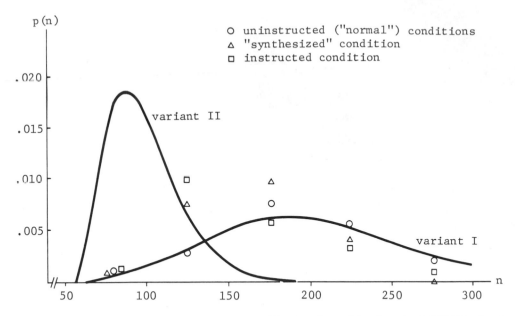

Figure 4. Six-term series problem. Predicted number of fixations for model variants I and II (full lines) and empirical results (relative frequencies in intervals of 50 fixations).

The Experimental Simulation of the Hypothesis Testing Model Variant I

In another small pilot study, we tried to simulate the processes of Variant I in a different experimental condition. Previous to the experiment, a series of hypotheses were randomly drawn in accordance with the sampling probabilities of Variant I. During this experiment, the subject was presented with the same display (Figure 1), but now had to decide on the truth of the hypothesis spoken by the experimenter (e.g., experimenter: "John is the tallest" - subject: "False"). The fixation paths of six subjects, each solving two problems under this condition, were assembled over all artificial hypotheses, and then inserted into Figure 4, represented as triangles. There is no statistically significant difference between the simulated and the "natural" (i.e., uninstructed) condition.

In this way, it is possible to "synthesize" postulated strategies from smaller, more rigorously controlled experimental units.

Where the Instruction Comes In

As a logical next step, the question arises about whether a more efficient strategy can be induced by proper instruction. While there seems little doubt that Variant II could be synthesized according to the methodology of the previous section, a more interesting question is whether the whole strategy of a higher variant can be communicated to the subjects by means of verbal instruction. In a third experiment, 12 subjects received a thorough instruction about the strategy underlying Variant II. They were taught to select immediately a hypothesis from the first premise encountered, and to search in a systematic, non-repetitive way. The squares in Figure 4 (based on 23 observations) do show a marked improvement under the instruction condition. Obviously, however, the instruction was not sufficient to bring the information gathering strategy of our subjects into a strict correspondence with the predictions of Variant II. The most striking difference is the fairly constant delay of about 20 fixations between the predictions and the subjects. There are at least two explanations that would account for this delay: The subjects read the whole set of premises before starting to look for the biggest one, despite the explicit instruction not to do so; or possibly, the subjects made a "double test," i.e., having found a solution, they looked a second time through the whole set of premises to make sure that they had not overlooked contradicting information the first time. A further fine grain analysis of the data might narrow down these possibilities. The important point now, however, is that we have demonstrated the effect of a goal directed instruction on molecular measures of cognitive behavior.

Footnotes

This study was supported by the Swiss National Science Foundation Grant 1.0810.74.

References

Bower, G. H., & Trabasso, T. R. Concept identification. In R. C. Atkinson (Ed.), Studies in mathematical psychology. Stanford: University of Stanford Press, 1964.

Bruner, J. S., Goodnow, J. J., & Austin, G. A. A study of thinking. New York: Wiley, 1956.

Claparède, E. La genèse de l'hypothèse. Archives de Psychologie, 1933, 24, 2-155.

Dewey, J. How we think. Boston: Heath, 1933.

Falmagne, R. Construction of a hypothesis testing model for concept
    identification. Journal of Mathematical Psychology, 1970, 7,
    60-96.

Feller, W. An introduction to probability and its applications, Volume
    I, second edition. New York: Wiley, 1957.

Groner, R. Cue utilization and memory structure in logical thinking.
    In J. R. Royce & W. W. Rozeboom (Eds.), The psychology of
    knowing. New York: Gordon & Breach, 1972.

Groner, R. Methodische und psychologische Probleme bei der Messung und
    Interpretation von Augenbewegungen. Psychologische Rundschau,
    1975, 26, 76-80. (a)

Groner, R. Die Präzisierung von Denktheorien mit Hilfe von
    Augenbewegungen. Schweizerische Zeitschrift für Psychologie,
    1975, 34, 260-262. (b)

Groner, R. Verallgemeinerte Hyppothesenmodelle für Ordnungsaufgaben
    und Konzepterwerb. In W. H. Tack (Ed.), Bericht über den
    28.Kongress der Deutschen Gesellschaft für Psychologie in Salzburg
    1974. Göttingen: Hogrefe, 1975. (c)

Groner, R. Eye movements and hypothesis testing behavior. Paper
    presented at the 21st International Congress of Psychology, July
    1976, in Paris, France.

Groner, R. Hypothesen im Denkvorgang. Bern, Verla Hans Huber, 1977.

Groner, R., Kaufmann, F., Bischof, W. F., & Hirsbrunner, H. Das Berner
    System zur Analyse von Blickrichtung und Pupillengrösse.
    Forschungsberichte aus dem Psychologischen Institut der
    Universität Bern, 1972.

Groner, R., & Groner, M. A hypothesis testing model for the three-term
    series problem. Research Reports from the Psychology Department,
    University of Bern, 1974.

Johnson Laird, P. M. The three-term series problem. Cognition, 1972,
    1, 57-82.

Just, M. A., & Carpenter, P, A. Fye fixations and cognitive processes.
    Cognitive Psychology, 1976, 8, 441-480.

Levine, A. A cognitive theory of learning: Research on hypothesis
    theory. New York: Erlbaum, 1975.

Lévy-Schoen, A. L. L'étude des mouvements oculaires. Paris: Presse
    Universitaire Franaise, 1969.

Millward, R. B., & Wickens, I. D. Concept identification models. In D. H. Krantz, R. C. Atkinson, R. D. Luce, & P. Suppes (Eds.), Learning, memory and thinking. Contemporary developments in mathematical psychology, Volume 1. San Francisco: Freeman, 1974.

Millward, T. D., & Spoehr, I. D. Direct measurement of hypothesis-sampling strategies. Cognitive Psychology, 1973, 4, 1-38.

Nahinsky, I. D. A hypothesis sampling model for conjunctive concept identification. Journal of Mathematical Psychology, 1970, 7, 293-316.

Newell, A., & Simon, H. A. Human problem solving. Englewood Cliffs: Prentice-Hall, 1972.

Piaget, J. La psychologie de l'intelligence. Paris: Collin, 1974.

Piaget, J. Introduction to J. H. Flavell. The developmental psychology of Jean Piaget. Princeton: Van Nostrand, 1963.

Restle, F. The selection of strategies in cue learning. Psychological Review, 1962, 69, 329-343.

THE CHARACTERISTIC DEMANDS OF INTELLECTUAL PROBLEMS

J. J. Elshout
Instituut voor Cognitie Onderzoek
Universiteit van Amsterdam
Amsterdam

Among theorists of intelligence there are divergent view on the intrinsic interest of the activities elicited by mental tests. On the one hand, there are those who hold that what a person does in trying to solve a test problem is of high interest, both from an ecological and a theoretical point of view. On the other hand, there is the opinion that the way people cope with tests of intelligence is only interesting insofar as the level of performance on the test is indicative of the underlying capacities. Only the capacities are of real interest, both ecologically and psychologically. Correlated with the distinction mentioned are differing views about how tests should be constructed, how test batteries should be assembled, and about the most informative way to factor-analyze the results. Those who see test items as interesting cognitive tasks tend to prefer item-homogeneous tests. They also favor methods of battery assembly and analysis that leave us with a fine-grained description, with factors of a level of specificity that hold the promise of homogeneity of cognitive process (like Guilford's system). Theorists in the other camp prefer an item and test sampling approach, and they like their factors to be few and broad, so as to ensure a better coverage of the underlying capacities that have their real interest (like the Cattell-Horn system).

Test Items as Cognitive Tasks

Two 1976 publications appeared from writers who aim to interpret and characterize the so-called primary level factors of intelligence according to a model of cognitive functioning suggested by recent work in cognitive psychology. This endeavor should be interesting to educational psychologists for at least two reasons. What Carroll (1976) and Elshout (1976) do for the relatively simple problems typically used in intelligence research, amounts to psychological task analysis. Psychological task analysis, one of the more complex tasks at which schooling aims, is also one of the major areas within educational psychology. It is not unrealistic to hope for a transfer of both theory and methodology to take place, in the direction from the simple to the complex. There should also be some direct profit from the analysis of

321

competent performance on intelligence test type problems. There seems
to be a great interest in the schools in furthering intelligence itself,
in teaching students to think. What this means, precisely, is certainly
debatable, but there seemo to be some agreement that it means teaching
studento the mental skills that are necessary for solving intelligence
test type problems.

Concordant Views

The conclusions independently reached by Carroll and Elshout and
others from their research are similar in many important respects. This
is not terribly surprising, because the approaches are very similar in
important ways. Both derive their theoretical base from the information
processing approach to cognitive processes. Also, both seem to agree on
the level of specificity of factors at which the contact between
psychometrically oriented research and cognitive psychology can be
expected to prove most fruitful. Carroll analyzes 48 tests representing
24 primary factors from the French, Ekstrom and Price (1967) kit of
reference tests, while Elshout takes the work of the Guilford and
Hoepfner (1971) (and his own work in the same vein) as the point of
departure.   Since all but three of the factors that are included in the
French et al. set also fit in Guilford's system, we may conclude that
there is agreement as to the optimal grain of analysis.

A very important point of agreement concerns the complexity of
cognitive tasks: All cognitive tasks, even the items of so-called
factor pure tests, involve many more capacities (factors) than will be
uncovered by factor analysis. The point is that a capacity will only
appear in factor analysis if the task in question is taxing enough with
respect to that capacity. Only then will individual differences in that
capacity be reflected in the test results. This point is crucial for
understanding the factor analytic strategy.   It is also of great
importance for the methodology of analyzing test problems as cognitive
tasks: One should look for the ways the task is made <u>taxing</u>. This is
what makes the test problems stand out in the factor space. Those task
features that contribute to its factor loadings can be labeled as the
<u>taxing features</u> of the task. They bring to the fore the limitations of
the problem solving system, and are also responsible for the
correlations between basic abilities, on the one hand, and performance
on the tests on the other.

What are the general points Carroll and Elshout agree upon? First,
starting with an information processing model of cogitive functioning
and stressing only those process components on which real demands are
put, <u>primary level factors do not seem to have anything in common</u>. They
involve different processes.

Secondly, tasks that best measure the same factor <u>are very similar
in their characteristic features</u>. Elshout states this second conclusion
most strongly. In his view, tests of intelligence correlate to the

degree   in   which they are <u>parallel</u>, in the sense that they call for the
same   problem   solving   activities.   The   alternative   explanation   of
correlation   in   the   sphere   of   intelligence,   i.e.,   different mental
activities that draw on correlated resources (capacities), is   rejected.
In order to appreciate this strong version of the second conclusion, one
must remember   that   according   to   accepted   methodology,   the   use   of
parallel tests should be avoided in factor analytic research.

A third conclusion that Carroll and Elshout both   draw   from   their
work is that intelligence indeed is interesting.   Stated more precisely,
looking at the type of problem solving behavior one typically encounters
at   the   item   level   from   the   point of view of information processing
theory, it seems obvious that the skills involved have direct   relevance
to   achievement   in   school and in life.   Tests of intelligence are more
than just indicators for underlying "brainpowers."

Discordant Views

Carroll's analyses lead him to conclude that even   relatively   pure
factor   tests always have several taxing features.   Elshout would agree.
But if I understand Carroll   correctly,   he   postulates   an   independent
ability   for   each   feature   of the task, and he seems to think of those
feature-coupled abilities (for instance, an ability to   scan   a   sensory
register)   as   the   <u>real</u>   basic abilities involved.   That means that the
primary abilities arrived at by factor analysis would   just   be   surface
phenomena.   They are <u>not</u> <u>unitary</u>, and what is more, they are <u>accidental</u>.
Tests do correlate to the   extent   that   they   have   important,   taxing,
features   in common.   The psychometric factors, in this view, do no more
than reflect the accidental clustering of   item   types   in   the   feature
space.   Add   a test, take a test, and the accidental pattern of feature
overlap will change;   and, the psychometric factor   will   swing   another
way.   Therefore,   there   will   never be a <u>non</u>-arbitrary way to classify
primary factors.   Also, the methods of test   psychology   are   unsuitable
for measuring the real basic abilities.   Elshout does not agree.

The main point of   my   criticism   is   that   it   is   psychologically
implausible   that   feature-bound   basic   abilities   can   have   developed
independently.   To give an example, it is possible that our analysis   of
a   certain   task   discovers a feature of search in long-term memory;   on
the basis of this,   a   searching-of-LTM   ability   may   be   hypothesized.
What,   in   this   particular   task,   are   sought are hypotheses about the
structure of number series.   In Carroll's view this would   be   a   second
feature,   with its own dimension of   individual   differences   associated to
it: Some people have more series patterns stored than others.   In   my
view,   however,   it is most probable that the form LTM-search takes, the
tactics used, is highly dependent on the type   of   LTM-content   searched
for,   on   the   way   it   is structured LTM, and so forth;   also, that the
amount of patterns stored   and   the   way   they   are   stored   are   highly
dependent   on   the   way the person has used and managed his knowledge of
number patterns in the part.   If this kind of developmental   interaction

is indeed what takes place, what we have to expect in this particular
task are not two dimensions of ability, but only one: being able to
produce suitable hypotheses about the structure of number series.

Primary Factors as Mental Skills

Like many others before me, I think that what primary factors
measure are mental skills. People do profit from their experience, that
is basic. And when they learn in situation A, they will profit from
that learning in situation B to the degree in which A and B are similar
in the ways that count for our system. There is a lot to say about
"being similar," and transfer is difficult to predict, but transfer does
occur. The environment helps by having a structure, such that similar
problems tend to co-occur in time and place. Our schools are based on
this principle (learning to add and to subtract go together). But
outside of the school, we also find clusterings of intellectual tasks
that are important to use ecologically and that have taxing features in
common. For instance, a person who has encountered the problem of
having to push a wagon uphill will most probably know about the problem
of preventing a wagon from going downhill.

The point is that the structured coherence of the world we live in
cooperates with the laws of transfer to make every individual develop a
great number of separate intellectual skills, one to a higher level,
another to a lower level, depending on experience and certain hardware
factors. We see such mental skills as coherent wholes of procedural and
propositional knowledge, both reflexive (verbalizable) and prereflexive
in kind. Such a whole is geared to a family of problems, bound together
by the environment and their psychological similarity. The question is
what the basis of this psychological similarity is. I propose that a
problem family (corresponding to a primary factor) is bound together by
the similiarities between the configurations of taxing features that
characterize each of the family members. The term "configuration" is
chosen here to stress that, in my view, the demands put upon our system
by the taxing feature do not stand side by side, but interact. By
interacting they form, so to speak, a knot of problematicity, different
for each problem type. These "knots" I have called the characteristic
demands of problem types (Elshout, 1976).

The Characteristic Demand of a Problem

How should we go about analyzing the characteristic demands in
terms of a model of cognitive functioning? Remember that a problem
feature only carries interest for us in this context if it is taxing,
and recall that it can only be taxing because the human information
processing system has certain limitations (without limitations there
would be no individual differences, and thus no correlation, no factors,
etc.) Our central proposition is that at the psychological core of each
characteristic demand is an interaction of three basic limitations of

the system. By basic I do not mean that they are necessarily to be
localized in the hardware of our system (they could also be limitations
in certain kinds of knowledge), but that at least they are ecologically
central.   I take my point of departure from Guilford's Structure of
Intellect Model, because it describes the correlational data quite well,
in my opinion, and also because its categories are compatible with the
categories of present day cognitive psychology. My suggestion is that
each of the five types of process, each of the four modalities of
representation, and each of the six ways in which problem information
may be organized, as represented in the SI-model, corresponds to one
basic limitation of the system, 15 in all. The <u>actual</u> limitations we
have to surmount when solving particular problems are the result of the
interaction of one limitation from each of the three main categories
(type of process, of modality, of form of organization).

Two <u>Problem</u> <u>Types</u>: <u>An</u> <u>Analysis</u> <u>of</u> <u>their</u>
<u>Characteristic</u> <u>Demands</u>

Let me try to give you an impression of how the interaction of
basic limitations works at the level of concrete problems.

One of the five important process types the Structure of Intellect
Model distinguishes is called cognition. This concept covers processes
like understanding, comprehending, becoming or being aware   that
something is the case.   The limitation of the problem solver most
obviously stressed by test items that call for cognition abilities
(SI-terminology) is the limited capacity of our working or active
memory. The taxing feature of this problem type is the complexity of
the problem information, calling for the application of strong
information reducing and structuring schemata. Following a difficult
figural transformation (the unfolding of a figure from 2-D to 3-D, for
example), and solving a verbal arithmetical reasoning item, are both
cases in point.   The form complexity takes in each of these two
modalities of representation, figural and semantic, differs, however.
This is what we mean by the interaction of limitations.

What makes <u>figural</u> information difficult in problem solving tasks
is typically that there are so many different but equally valid ways to
encode a concrete given, like a figure. Arbitrariness of encoding is
the general, characteristic difficulty of figural information. Trial
and error and shifts of representation will be necessary, tending to
overload working memory.

Problems presented in the <u>semantic</u> modality, on the other hand, are
typically difficult because of the looseness, ambiguity, and the
openness of natural language. A lot of context, both from the situation
and mobilized from semantic memory, is needed to arrive at a reasonably
"closed" interpretation of any problem text. Many of the mistakes we
observe when subjects try to solve arithmetical reasoning problems
(thinking aloud) can indeed be characterized as an inability to come to

a workable problem representation. There is too much detail and the presentation is too confusing to hold the information in short-term memory without the help of a good schema. Whereas in the visual unfolding problem, the subject complains that his mental image "crumbles," with verbal problems the subject has to read the problem again and again and again.

The form of the information involved interacts with the kind of process and modality in producing the actual characteristic demand of the problem situation. The situation described in the given of a verbal arithmetical problem is called a system in Structure of Intellect theory: Boats go up and down a river, in certain directions, with certain speeds and loads of fuel, etc. The information about systems is typically presented sequentially. Instead of reducing the complexity, this piecemeal presentation adds to it, because the representation of what is already given should depend on and be integrated with what is yet to come. This situation offers many chances of interference between the initial representation of early information and the representation called for in the end. An example: A ship goes from A to B, along a river. It arrives at C one hour before it arrives at B, etc. You thought that C would come after B? Well, not along this river!

The form of information involved in unfolding problems is called a transformation in SI terms. The subject is presented with pictures of a flat figure and of a solid folded from it. He has to understand how this transformation came about, which line became which edge, etc. The characteristic problems of transformations have been extensively studied by Gestalt psychologists. Let me try to sum up their findings this way: If you have to see or understand something as something else (other form, other function, etc.), two representations have to be formed, one of the "before," and one of the "after," and mutual interference will result. For instance: The grey stripe "on top" in the one figure may most easily be encoded as "on bottom" in the other figure. The resolution of conflicts like these will obviously lead to a greater working load of active memory, giving the complexity that characterizes cognition, and giving the arbitrariness that characterizes figural encoding, which has its own flavor, typical of the situation where the restructuring of information is what the problem is about.

I have illustrated what I mean by the interaction of limitations. This was done by describing two problem types, starting with the limitation typically stressed by the type of process involved, in this case memory limitation, adding detail and specificity to this by describing how overloading of working memory takes different forms, depending first on the modality of representations, and secondly on the organization of this information; systems make things difficult in different ways than those involved in transformations. This presentation suggests a hierarchy: process type being most important, type of information being least important. This is not intended, however. I could also have told my story the other way around, starting with an explanation of what typically makes systems, or transformations, or classes, etc., difficult; then showing how this difficulty is specified by the process involved: understanding, memorizing, etc.; and then by showing the modality of information involved: natural language, behavior, meaningless symbols, etc.

The Taxing Features of the 15 Categories of the SI-Model

It is, of course, out of the question to describe all the 120 interactions, all the 120 characteristic demands, that the theory is meant to account for. To be honest, I have not even started to work them all out. What I can do, to give at least an impression of the direction this would take, is list the main limitations of our intellectual system, corresponding to the main categories of Guilford's SI model. This model distinguishes five main types of cognitive processes. They are listed below, each followed by a characterization, in encapsuled form, of the main difficulty involved.

1. Cognition: The relatively small capacity of our active memory, leading to overload in complex situations.

2. Memory: The need to ensure that the cue information that is able to activate the information to be memorized will be at hand in the future, at the moment of recall.

3. Convergent production: Certain problems call for the execution of complex procedures, which have to be interpreted in sequence because they have not yet been assimilated; this entails problems of keeping track.

4. Divergent production: Because divergent production means recall of information that has only weak bonds with the cues in the problem, heuristic methods are needed that make good use of what is elicited by the problem cues.

5. Evaluation: When comparing information to a standard, the difficulty arises (given a time-press) of choosing the optimal depth of interpretation.

There are four modes of representation, the content categories in the SI model.

1. Figural: Concrete and meaningless material may be encoded in an endless variety of valid (but possibly for a particular problem, irrelevant) ways. Finding the relevant, arbitrarily "correct" representation forces the system to abstract, to discount, and to disregard.

2. Symbolic: Arbitrary symbols can by their nature only have an extrinsic, conventional relation to the way they are arranged. Symbolic information is not transparent.

3. Semantic: Our semantic representations of the world and ourselves, mediated by natural language, suffer from fuzziness, looseness, ambiguity, etc., which leads to great problems of matching semantic patterns.

4. Behavioral: Information about the "inner world" of others has to be inferred from overt behavior, which means "going beyond the information given" in a rather drastic way.

The theory distinguishes between six kinds of difficulties, associated with the six products of the SI model.

1. Units: Their problematicity centers around the difficulty of achieving and maintaining invariance despite the ever-changing appearance of the world.

2. Classes: The difficulty of problems about classes lies in the need to disregard the criticality of the characteristics of the individual items in favor of the commonality of the characteristics that define the class.

3. Relations: The relativity of relations forces the problem solver to "decanter," in the Piagetian sense, i.e., to see the object as being part of different relations (bigger than and smaller than) at the same time.

4. Systems: The involved nature of systems leads to interference between the representations of parts and between earlier and later representations.

5. Transformations: Restructuring information introduces the problem of maintaining and using two conflicting representations of the same information.

6. Implications: Tasks involving implications force us to treat as logically necessary (to schematize) what in effect is contingent.

Conclusion

We have stated that primary factors (e.g., 120 factors in the SI system) measure important mental skills. We have suggested, but not yet stated, that those mental skills may be viewed as (partial!) solutions to the problems of our limitations as processors of information, with an emphasis on those limitations that are most central to our ability to adapt in our ecology.

References

Carroll, J. B. Psychometric tests as cognitive tasks: A new "Structure
    of   intellect."   In   L.   B.   Resnick (Ed.), The nature of
    intelligence. Hillsdale, NJ: Lawrence Erlbaum Associates, 1976.

Elshout, J. J. Karakteristieke Moeilijkheden in het Denken. Academisch
    Proefschrift. Universiteit van Amsterdam, 1976.

French, J. W., Ekstrom, R. B., & Price, L. A.   Manual   for   kit   of
    reference tests for cognitive factors. Princeton, NJ: Educational
    Testing Service, 1967.

MENTAL ARITHMETIC: SHORT-TERM STORAGE
AND INFORMATION PROCESSING IN A COGNITIVE SKILL

G. J. Hitch
Medical Research Council, Applied Psychology Unit
Cambridge, England, U.K.

Although there have been rapid increases in both the number and sophistication of calculating aids in recent years, the simpler sorts of mental arithmetic will probably keep their place as common and useful skills. An understanding of the psychological processes that they entail should therefore be of some general value. There are at least two fairly good reasons for supposing that such an understanding might be possible. First, people are usually able to give clear verbal reports about their strategies for doing mental arithmetic. These reports give insights into some of the characteristics of performance. Second, it seems probable that mental calculation involves cognitive systems about which a good deal is already known from pure research. For example, it is known that people have a far greater capacity for written than for mental calculation. This is presumably because written information is relatively permanent, whereas information held temporarily in memory, as in mental calculation, is rapidly forgotten. The characteristics of short-term retention form a whole area of experimental psychology, and can hopefully be shown to apply to mental arithmetic.

This paper is concerned with the general nature of mental arithmetic and the hypothesis that errors of mental calculation are largely due to short-term forgetting. We shall consider two factors determining the amount of forgetting that occurs: the interval for which information is stored, and the total amount of information that has to be retained. Before exploring these factors, we must discuss the types of strategy that people typically employ.

Strategies in Mental Calculation

The studies that will be described are variations of a basic situation in which a person first hears two numbers and then adds or multiplies them, producing the answer in writing. The complexity of the problems is best described by citing examples, such as 325 + 431 and 327 x 5.

331

It has been suggested by Hunter (1964) and Lindsay and Norman
(1972), among others, that mental calculations involving multi-place
numbers are carried out in a series of elementary stages. Thus an
addition like 325 + 431 would involve the steps 1 + 5 = 6, 3 + 2 - 5,
and 4 + 3 = 7. In a study of mental multiplication, Danserau and Gregg
(1966) found there was indeed a high correlation between solution times
for different problems and the numbers of stages they would be expected
to involve. However, there appears to have been no investigation of the
order in which individual stages are executed, a factor that might be of
some importance in determining performance. An initial study was aimed
at exploring this question by taking note of people's subjective
reports.

Experiment 1

Thirty subjects, including housewives, laboratory staff members,
and naval personnel, carried out five additions in which a two-place
number was added to a three-place number (e.g., 357 + 32). There was an
initial practice question followed by examples of each of the four
carrying patterns that can occur. After doing the calculations,
subjects were asked about the methods they had used.

All 30 subjects reported using strategies in which the problems
were broken down into a set of elementary stages, with only occasional
exceptions. Table 1 shows that there was considerable variation in the
order in which individual stages were carried out.

Most people reported using a constant strategy for all the
additions regardless of the carrying requirements. The most common of
these strategies was the familiar "units, tens, hundreds" sequence, but
not everyone reported this particular order. There were also people who
reported varying their strategy according to the carrying pattern of the
addition, and here too there was diversity from person to person in the
actual orderings that were favored.

The variety of these subjective reports strongly suggests that a
complete description of the processes of mental arithmetic will
incorporate strategy as a flexible component. It is also clear that it
would be prudent to try to control for subjects' strategies in studies
of calculation performance.

Short-Term Storage in Mental Arithmetic

The superiority of written arithmetic suggests that mental
arithmetic is limited by the need to store temporary information in
memory. The analysis of step-by-step strategies allows the role of
temporary storage to be examined in some detail. For example,
information used for the first time during a later stage of calculation
must of necessity have been held in store during the execution of

Table 1.   Subjective Reports of Calculation Strategies in Additions Such As 352 + 43. (U = Units, T = Tens, H = Hundreds, N = Number of subjects reporting strategy.)

All subjects (N = 30)	
Constant strategies (N = 21)	Conditional strategies (N = 9)
UTH (N = 11)	UTH if carrying, HTU otherwise (N = 6)
HTU (N = 4)	UTH if carrying, HUT otherwise (N = 2)
HUT (N = 3)	HUT if carrying, HTU otherwise (N = 1)
TUH (N = 3)	

earlier intervening steps. A typical step can be regarded as involving first the retrieval of appropriate information and then its arithmetic combination. Thus the tens step in a problem like 235 + 214 would consist of retrieving the digits 3 and 1 from temporary storage and then combining them using the long-term knowledge that 3 + 1 = 4.

Memory over brief intervals is normally assumed to depend on short-term storage (STS) (see, e.g., Atkinson & Shiffrin, 1971), and one of the characteristics of this type of storage is the rapid loss of information during any activity interpolated between presentation and recall. We might, therefore, expect appreciable forgetting during the course of a calculation. A consequence of this would be that in a mental addition consisting of a number of similar steps, likc 343 + 215 (where there is no carrying to complicate matters), the later steps would show more errors. Experiment 2 tested this prediction.

Experiment 2

Subjects were given additions involving two three-place numbers, and added them using the "units, tens, hundreds" strategy. They were not specifically instructed to use this method, but they reported using it voluntarily.   The addends were presented auditorily and subjects wrote their answers on prepared sheets.   Assuming that each partial result was written as soon as it was calculated, we would expect rapid forgetting of the addends to give a distribution of least errors in the units, intermediate errors in the tens, and most errors in the hundreds.

The experiment also included conditions of normal written arithmetic and a "hybrid" type of arithmetic that was part-written and part-mental. In all conditions, the subject listened to the two numbers to be added. In the "written" condition, both numbers were also printed on the answer sheet. In the two "hybrid" conditions, either the first or second number was printed, and in the "mental" condition the answer sheet was blank. The purpose of these manipulations was to examine the relationship between written and mental arithmetic with regard to their differential dependence on short-term storage. On the simple assumption that numbers continuously present on the page do not have to be retrieved from the subject's memory, we would expect total errors to decrease as the amount of written information increases.

The subjects were 25 housewives. They did a series of problems that included examples of all the possible patterns of carrying, under each of the four conditions. Total errors were 22% in the mental condition, 8% when only the first addend was printed, 7% when only the second was printed, and 3% when both were printed. The two hybrid conditions did not differ from each other, but did differ from both the mental and written conditions (p < .01 by Sign Tests). As expected, increasing the number of digits to be retrieved from the subjects' own memories led to an increase in errors.

Data from problems that did not involve carrying were used to assess the distribution of errors across partial results. This restriction ensured that each partial result depended on a single addition of equivalent complexity, and avoided any imbalances due to carrying operations. There were too few errors in the hybrid and written conditions to assess the distributions, but in the mental condition the results were clear. Sign tests showed that there was a higher proportion of errors in the hundreds (.31) than in the tens (.18) and more in the tens than in the units (.09).

The overall comparison between mental, written, and hybrid conditions gives simple confirmation that each retrieval from short-term storage contributes to the total number of calculation errors. This comparison was clear when based on total errors in all problems, but less clear when only problems without carrying were considered, probably because of a "floor" effect. Data from the mental condition suggest that the forgetting of individual items is increased by interpolated activity during the interval prior to retrieval and combination.

Thus far, we have talked as though forgetting the initially presented information were the only source of calculation error. However, this is almost certainly an oversimplification. A further consideration of the nature of the task shows that each calculation stage produces its own information, such as interim carry figures or partial results. This information also must presumably be stored during any stages interpolated between initial generation and subsequent use.

Two experiments (Hitch, note 1) studied the forgetting of partial results by varying the interval between initially computing them and finally writing them down. In one study, subjects added pairs of numbers like 325 + 34 using the "units, tens, hundreds" strategy. In one condition, they were instructed to write each partial result as soon as it was calculated. In another, they were only allowed to write the partial results after all of them had been mentally calculated. The experiment showed that delaying output of a partial result reliably increased the chance of it being wrong. The second experiment confirmed this conclusion in a situation where subjects used a different calculation strategy. Rapid forgetting, therefore, seems to apply to the results of interim calculation stages as well as to the initially presented information.

Experiment 3

Although it is known that the short-term forgetting of individual items increases markedly with the amount of activity interpolated before retrieval (Peterson & Peterson, 1959), such activity may not be the only determinant of recall. The difficulty of recalling an item might also be increased by the presence of other items in store, as suggested by Melton (1963) and discussed by Lindsay and Norman (1972) in the context of mental arithmetic. Indeed a comparison between the conditions of Experiment 2 suggests that the forgetting of individual digits was less marked when only three as opposed to six digits had to be remembered. Performance in the hybrid conditions was much closer to the written condition than to the mental one.

Experiment 3 examined performance in mental multiplications designed to test for storage load effects. Subjects were given examples of three types of multiplication in which a two, three, or four-place number was to be multiplied by an integer, e.g., 38 x 4, 453 x 6, 6345 x 5. Presentation was auditory, and subjects were instructed to multiply in the usual way, beginning with the units figure of the first term and proceeding through the tens, etc., writing down each partial result as soon as it was computed. The first two digits of the product (i.e., the units and tens) were assumed to involve the same operations in all three types of problems. The units required only simple multiplication, whereas the tens required both multiplication and carrying from the previous column. For example, in the problem 453 x 6, the units are obtained by 6 x 3 = (1)8 and the tens are obtained by 6 x 5 = (3)0; 0 + 1 = 1. Because of both rapid forgetting and the different number of operations, we would expect there to be more errors in the tens than in the units. Such a result would merely confirm the conclusions that have already been drawn. The more interesting question was whether errors in these two stages would also depend on the number of digits held simultaneously in memory but not yet processed. If such extra digits did cause an increase in difficulty, we could argue for an effect of "storage load" on recall, over and above that of interpolated activity.

Table 2. Mental Multiplication. Units and Tens Errors as a Function of Problem Complexity. Figures
          Denote Mean Error Probabilities

	Type of problem		
	e.g. 38	e.g. 453	e.g. 6345
	x4	x6	x5
Units	.08	.04	.04
Tens	.13	.23	.31

The subjects taking part in the experiment were 32 housewives. Table 2 shows the observed error rates for units' and tens' partial results as a function of type of problem.

As expected, errors in the units were generally less frequent than errors in the tens. The differences were significant for problems involving three- and four-place numbers (p < .01 Sign Tests), but not for problems with two-place numbers.

Turning to the effects of type of problem, there were no reliable differences in units errors, but tens errors did increase with size of the first term of the multiplcation. However, the only significant difference was that between problems with two- and four-place numbers (p < .01, Sign Test).

The results, therefore, give tentative evidence for an effect of storage load. They seem to show that when information is utilized immediately after presentation, as in the case of multiplying the units, it is recalled well regardless of the number of items simultaneously in store. When there is an interval before using information, however, as in the case of multiplying the tens, storage load does seem to have some effect.

Conclusions

The experiments confirm what is generally believed, namely that most errors of mental arithmetic occur because of the rapid forgetting of temporary information. In more detail, it has been shown that calculations consist of a number of discrete stages, ordered according to a particular strategy. It seems that the strategy determines the intervals over which both initial and interim information has to be held in store. Information is progressively forgotten while in storage, primarily as a function of the number of interpolated stages before its recall, and partly as a function of the total amount of information simultaneously being held.[1]

From this general account, it can be seen that computational strategies are likely to be of great importance in determining both overall levels of mental arithmetic performance and detailed patterns of error. The most efficient strategies will be ones that minimize the effects of rapid forgetting, or at least localize such effects in less important components of the final answer. In this respect, the common "units, tens, hundreds" type of strategy is probably a relatively poor one since it gives highest errors on the most significant figure of the answer. This would be undesirable if, for instance, the numbers represented amounts of money, and a better strategy might be to tackle the most significant figures first, so that these have the highest chance of being correct. Such a strategy would be optimal provided it could successfully cope with carrying, which is necessarily directed from lower to higher figures. Nevertheless, it should be clear that there are grounds for expecting an effect of strategy on the amount and pattern of errors due to forgetting.

So far, we have assumed that the forgetting that has been observed in mental calculation reflects verbal short-term memory. The effects of interpolated activity and storage load are consistent with this view, but do not give direct evidence that the traces are verbal. However, Sokolov and his co-workers (Sokolov, 1972) have found electromyographic evidence for covert articulation during mental arithmetic, and have shown that suppressing covert articulation by having the subject pronounce irrelevant speech-sounds during mental calculation impairs performance. It is fairly clear, then, that the task does have a verbal component. Nevertheless, it would probably be incorrect to rule out the possibility of other components. Hayes (1973), for example, obtained clear subjective reports of the use of visual imagery during elementary calculation, and this is clearly a component that merits further investigation. So far, my own attempts at separating "imagers" from "verbalizers" have been unsuccessful, and I am inclined to believe, at least for the present, that the forgetting is of verbally coded information.

Beyond the domain of mental arithemtic, it is becoming clear that short-term storage is a common feature of many cognitive tasks, including reasoning, comprehension, and learning (Baddeley & Hitch, 1974). It may, therefore, be possible to generalize from arithmetic to other tasks, and suggest that one feature of "good" cognitive strategies is that they will minimize any deleterious effects of short-term forgetting on performance. It seems likely that this generalization will apply most clearly in tasks that are serial in nature, with a degree of option about the sequence of stages.

Footnotes

Parts of this research will be reported in more detail in a   paper
currently being prepared for publication (see reference note).

1. A mathematical model of performance (Hitch, note 1) achieves a
reasonable measure of success even though it assumes only an effect of
interpolated activity and no effect of storage load.

Reference Note

1. Hitch, G. J. The role of short-term working storage in mental
arithmetic. In preparation.

References

Atkinson, R. C., & Shiffrin, R. M. The control of short-term memory.
    Scientific American, 1971, 225, 82-90.

Baddeley, A. D. & Hitch, G. J.   Working memory.   In G. H.   Bower
    (Ed.), The psychology of learning and motivation: Advances in
    research and theory. Volume 8. New York: Academic Press, 1974.

Danserau, D. F., & Gregg, L. W. An information processing analysis of
    mental multiplication. Psychonomic Science, 1966, 6, 71-72.

Hayes, J. R.   On the function of visual   imagery   in   elementary
    mathematics. In W. G. Chase (Ed.), Visual informtion processing,
    New York: Academic Press, 1973.

Hunter, I. M. L. Memory. Harmondsworth: Penguin Books, 1964.

Lindsay, P. H., & Norman, ,D. A.   Human information processing: An
    introduction to psychology. New York: Academic Press, 1972.

Melton, A. W.   Implications of short-term memory for a general theory of
    memory.   Journal of Verbal Learning and Verbal Behavior, 1963, 2,
    1-21.

Peterson, L. R., & Peterson, M. J. Short-term retention of individual
    items. Journal of Experimental Psychology, 1959, 58, 193-198.

Sokolov, A. N. Inner speech and thought. New York: Plenum, 1972.

COGNITIVE STYLES AND DIFFERENTIAL LEARNING CAPACITIES
IN PAIRED-ASSOCIATE LEARNING

G. C. van der Veer, E. van Muylwijk and G. J. E. van de Wolde
Free University
Amsterdam, Netherlands

In the last few years we have carried out several learning experiments on paired associates (v. Bolhuis & v. d. Veer, 1973; v. d. Veer, 1970), with stimuli with which our subjects were unfamiliar, while the responses were well known: the letters of the alphabet (except Q). Each task concerned the acquisition of 25 pairs presented visually by the use of slides and according to the anticipation method. After presentation of the stimulus alone (the "stimulus slide"), the subject was shown both stimulus and response combined into a single picture (the "response slide"). The group of stimuli used within a single experiment was always homogeneous in nature, e.g., braille symbols, semaphore flags, or Holzman inkblots.

For our adult subjects, a 20 min learning period on these tasks usually resulted in correct recall of 20-25 pairs when tested immediately thereafter. In some experiments, the exposure times of both stimulus and response slides were fixed (at values specified by the particular experimental condition); in other cases, the subject directed the rate of presentation himself by pushing a single button, or the exposure times were matched with those a fellow subject had chosen for the same slides. Our subjects knew that they would be judged by their performance on a posttest, and they were not instructed to give overt responses during the learning period. By means of subsequent structured interviews, we were able to develop descriptions of the different learning mechanisms used by the subjects. These mechanisms could be detected for each individual pair that a student learned. The mechanisms in general were responsible for a stable process that started as soon as the stimulus was presented; and led to the response letter. The same process turned out to be at work in recall after three days. These mechanisms are referred to as "Operators" by Bower (1972) and, when the verbal apparatus is involved, as "Natural Language Mediators" by Prytulak (1971). We made a distinction among three ways in which learning took place, resulting in three qualitatively different mediations: verbal mediation (V), image mediation (I), and rote learning (R).

Learning Mechanisms

Verbal Mediation

In verbal mediations (a) the stimulus (a non-verbal, visual item) is named, described or interpreted in terms of a verbal code, e.g., "This picture represents a kidney." (b) The response (an alphabetic symbol) is coded to a word/name. Often but not always, the response is the first character of this code. In some cases there are deliberate "spelling mistakes" in the code, e.g., response C coded to "cidney" instead of "kidney." (c) The stimulus and response codes are connected with the help of a more or less reasonable verbal chain in such a way that the presentation of the stimulus, with the help of its code and this chain, results in the response, e.g., "The picture represents a mountain-landscape. My brother likes mountain-climbing. His name ends with the letter S." The chain may be rather elaborate, or short, with the shortest version existing in the code for the stimulus occurring in the same time code for the response, e.g., "The picture represents a Frog, so this is the F from Frog."

In many cases, the process of constructing these mediations is more specifically started either from a code for the stimulus, which is afterwards developed to a chain that ultimately leads to the response, or from a code connected to the response, from which a chain is generated back to a suitable code for the stimulus. There are a number of cases, however, in which one seems to develop separate codes for the single stimulus and the single response, which are coupled afterwards with a verbal mediation. In addition, there remain a number of cases for which we cannot find a clear picture of the development in time and direction, perhaps because of the high speed and spontaneity of the creation.

Image Mediations (I)

In image mediations, (a) a visual image of the response character is superimposed upon (a part of) the visual stimulus, resulting in a "Gestalt." To this end, the image of the response letter may be transformed or rotated. After learning has taken place, the next presentations of the stimulus evoke this Gestalt, from which the response is read off. In most cases it seems that the process starts from the response image, which is somehow fitted into the stimulus by means of a scanning process. There are cases, however, in which the stimulus seems to persuade the subject to recognize the response letter in it. And of course there are situations in which we get no clear picture of how and where the learning process starts. (b) In this type of learning mechanism, the connection is formed by creation of a visual mediator incorporating (parts of) the stimulus and response, without prior coding of either of those in another modality.

Rote-Learning (R)

With this category, we refer to a kind of direct coupling of the stimulus with the response letter, without a logical verbal connection or visual image mediation. Under the present conditions, the response is always taken in its verbal meaning, that is, the single character, or sometimes a simple word chosen more or less at random, starting with the character. The stimulus is, in some cases, labeled with a verbal code, describing the image (e.g., "this landscape is P"), but in other instances the stimulus is taken in its image value ("this is P"), and sometimes cannot even be named or described in any detail after the experiment. The memorization activity, with active perception of stimulus and response picture, seems to be sufficient to form a "trace" in memory, which helps to reproduce the response upon presentation of the stimulus.

We observed that our subjects were always learning very actively, and, except when using mechanism R, very creatively. We also discovered that the type of mediation in its elaborated form tended to be sustained during the total experiment, and was even present at a recall test after three days. In the great majority of cases, different judges agreed about the type of mediation construction, as detectable from the interview. We found three aspects responsible for the variation in mediation-category:

1. Kind of learning material, that is to say, in our case, primarily the nature of the class of stimuli: e.g., semaphore flags or inkblots. There is a close relation between kind of material and frequency of using a special type of mediation. For example, for 34 subjects learning both semaphore flags and inkblots, we tested the difference in number of mediations, of each category between these two learning materials. The number of I and R mediations did not differ significantly between the two types of material. The number of V mediations differed very significantly: The student T was 4.04, the inkblot material leading to more V mediations. ($T \leq 1.7$ is significant at 5% level.)

2. Individual pairs within the different learned alphabets, e.g., certain inkblot character combinations, are learned preferably by means of the one method, other more frequently with V. This turns out to be a function not of the individual characters, but of the stimulus letter combination within each type of stimulus material.

3. Differences between subjects. Every subject turns out to have his own preference for one special kind of learning mechanism (or in a minority of cases, for two mechanisms) that he uses whenever the material permits. This preference is constant over different kinds of materials, be it inkblots or semaphore flags. For the same 34 subjects, we correlated the number of V, I and R mediations for both learning experiments. The correlations turned out to be V = .84, I = .52, and R = .75 (a correlation coefficient $\leq$ .30 is significant at 5% level).

These individual differences do not lead to systematic differences in quantitative learning results, nor in systematically different preferences for rate of presentation, findings which contradict the results of studies reported by Marshall, Chatfield, & Janek (1975) and Owens, Werder, & Marshall (1974). The only trend we found in our data thus far (but not clear enough to be certain about) is that one looks slightly longer to those pairs that are eventually learned with a non-favorite mediation category.

Cognitive Styles

We expected a relation between these obvious differences in individual preference for certain mediation mechanisms and certain specific abilities and handicaps in the area of cognitive functioning:

1. In order to be successful in using the I mediation, one should not be too seriously handicapped by field dependency (e.g., Witkin, Moore, Goodenough, & Cox, 1975): In most cases, a certain amount of restructuring and abstraction of the concrete visual stimulus is needed before the response may be projected in the image at learning time, and read back at recall time.

2. The construction of V mediations demands a definite amount of verbal creativity. Herewith we refer to the ability to make new associations between known verbal notions or concepts within reasonably short time. A study by Sanders and Dudycha (1975) has shown that verbal fluency is a good predictor of performance on a long paired associate task. In the course of this creation process, one often has to check several association chains before coming to a successful one. That is to say, a certain amount of response competition (of the type in the Stroop Color-Word Test (Jensen & Rohwer, 1966; v. Dam, 1972) must be dealt with in order to be able to trace back the correct path to recall.

In R type learning, the above mentioned abilities seem to be of little importance. Facility to transport items from short-term memory (STM) to long-term memory (LTM) seems to be the most important condition. The object to be transported in this case is always a piece of new information: the contingency of a new stimulus and a well-known response. In recall, the stimulus should later evoke this unit of stored information.

We constructed a test battery, to establish a profile of abilities in the regions mentioned. This consisted of the following measures:

1. Field dependence. The score is constructed from the discrepancy between two versions of an abstract picture identification task, one of which is obscured by irrelevant disturbing elements in the pictures to be identified. Unlike most field dependency tests, this one is constructed to partial out elements like clerical speed and accuracy. Our score did not correlate with general intelligence as measured with

the Raven Advanced Progressive Matrices Test.

2. Channel capacity between STM and LTM. This device consists of two parts, both presented visually. We did a one trial learning-recognition test for unknown verbal material (Hungarian nouns and adjectives) and non-verbal material (line drawings of "three dimensional" objects). The score denotes the amount of new material that can be stored within a very short exposure and rehearsal time (5 sec). The two scores had a very low correlation (.21) in a group of over 100 subjects, so we had to treat them as different abilities.

3. Verbal creativity. Familiar nouns or adjectives in the native language of the subjects should be combined with others to form combinations that are themselves again correct nouns and adjectives, e.g., we gave the subject the two words BLACK and BOX. The subject had to find a word like MAIL, in order to form BLACKMAIL and MAILBOX. By the use of well-known words, we tried to separate the factor of verbal creativity from such intelligence aspects as "vocabulary."

4. Interference proneness, with respect to response competition. This ability we measured by means of both the classical Stroop Color-Word Test ("Stroop I") variant of the Stroop ("Stroop II") in which the first card has the names of the numbers ONE to NINE (excluding FUUR), with the instruction to read the card as quickly as possible. The second card shows boys' names, consisting of three to five characters, with the instruction to call the number of characters as quickly as possible. The third card is identical with the first, but with the instructions for the second card. Compared to the original Stroop, color blind or weak subjects in this test are no longer in a special position. In order to partial out practice effects, the best score turned out to be the time on third card divided by the time on second card. The two measures correlated .40 in a group of 100 subjects.

Out of a group of 108 subjects, we selected those who scored extremely high and low on one or more of these measures. We ended up with 34 subjects who were prepared to participate in two paired-associate learning experiments. From the results of these experiments we scored the amount of V, I, and R mediation they used. Because this group is very small, the results of a factor analysis are to be interpreted with caution. The variables in the analysis were: a) the Raven's Advanced Progressive Matrices Test, b) Stroop I and Stroop II, c) Embedded Figures Test (field-dependence), d) Channel Capacity for Figures and Words, e) V, I, and R scores (learning styles) (these measures are not totally dependent, about half of the subjects did not learn all pairs). The first two eigenvectors could be interpreted. From this analysis and the correlation-matrix, we draw the following tentative conclusions.

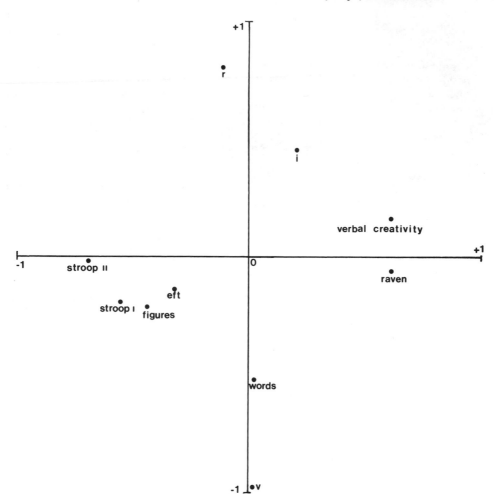

Figure 1. Factor analysis—space of first 2 eigenvectors.

1.   There seems to be no relation between learning style (number of
V, I and R mediations) and general intelligence. Combined with prior
results indicating that there is no relation between paired-associate
learning style and learning results, and with our findings that these
learning styles are consistent and reliably measurable, we conclude that
we have found an independent cognitive style variable, not merely an
aspect of intelligence.

2.   There is no relation between the V learning style and verbal
creativity (when measured in a group of 108, there was hardly any
relation between verbal creativity and the Raven, but in the

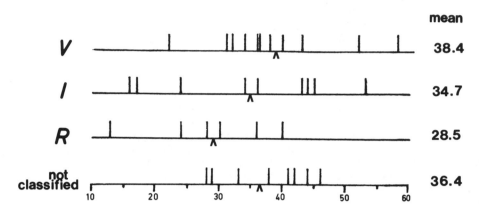

Figure 2. Memory for words.

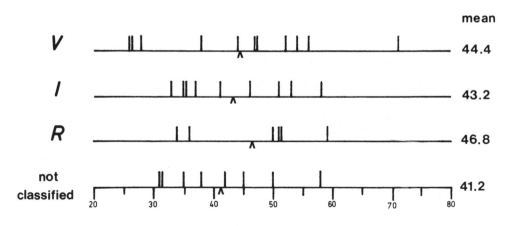

Figure 3. Verbal creativity.

experimental group of 34, there was a substantive positive relation between both tests). We will return to this finding in Conclusion 4.

3. Field dependence and interference proneness, with respect to response competition (Stroop), have no detectable relation with our learning styles.

4. Memory (channel) capacity for words predicts in the direction of V mediations (correlation = .38). In order to illustrate these relations, we categorized our subjects into three groups, each having evidently one favorite learning mechanism, and one group for which this was not evident. The scores for these groups on our memory capacity scale for words is shown in Figure 2. If we draw a comparable figure with the scores on "Verbal Creativity" (Figure 3), we see that both those subjects scoring very low and those scoring high on this test belong to the outspoken V group. The mediations used in the V category are, in the case of some of these subjects, perhaps very commonplace for them, but in order to work with those, they need the ability to store these verbal associations in long-term memory within a relatively short time.

For individuals who do not possess this ability in a sufficient amount, the use of I and R mediations is more suitable. But we have at this moment no idea whether and how we are able to indicate the best choice out of these two, based on some measure of special ability.

References

Bolhuis, J. v., & Veer, G. C. v. d.   Mathematical models for grouped paired-associate learning tasks. In Proceeding of the Second Prague Conference on Psychology of Human Learning and Problem Solving. Prague: 1973.

Bower, G. H. Stimulus sampling theory of encoding variability. In A. W. Melton & E. Martin (Eds.), Coding processes in human memory. New York: Wiley, 1972.

Dam, G. v.   Categories of interference and susceptibility to interference. Unpublished doctoral dissertation, State University of Utrecht, 1972.

Jensen, A. R., & Rohwer, W. D. Jr.   The Stroop color-word test: A review. Acta Psychologica, 1966, 25, 36-93.

Marshall, P. H., Chatfield, D. C., & Janek, E. J.   The effects of natural language mediation on response recognition following paired-associate learning. Bulletin of the Psychonomic Society, 1975, 5, 411-412.

Owens, J. M., Werder, P. R., & Marshall, P. H. A component analysis of natural language mediators obtained in paired-associate learning. Bulletin of the Psychonomic Society, 1974, 4, 512-514.

Prytulak, L. S. Natural language mediation. Cognitive Psychology, 1971, 2, 1-56.

Sanders, M. S., & Dudycha, A. L. Prediction of learning speed on long paired-associate tests. The Journal of General Psychology, 1975, 93, 297-298.

Veer, G. C. v. d. Mathematical learning models as tools for computer assisted instruction. In Proceedings of the International Federation for Information Processing world conference (Vol. 1). Amsterdam: 1970.

Witkin, H. A., Moore, C. A., Goodenough, D. R. & Cox, P. W. Field-dependent and field-independent cognitive styles and their educational implications. Research Bulletin 75-24. Princeton, New Jersey: Educational Testing Service, June 1975.

Section V

COGNITIVE DEVELOPMENT

        The papers in this section reflect the strong influence that Piaget
has had on theory and research in the area of cognitive development.
Many of the issues discussed in this section are in response to
Piagetian theory and its implications for instruction. Oléron begins
his invited address by providing an overview of what is meant by a
cognitive skill; he then points out that most psychological research on
cognitive skill development has focused on material objects and logical
systems while largely ignoring the larger social and psychological world
in which the child develops. In the context of his discussion of
intellectual development, Oléron discusses problems with Piagetian
theory and the need to consider functional aspects of development which
may not fit within formal logical systems. Oléron also presents a
discussion of the importance of psychological and social competence
within a theory of cognitive development.

        Certain of these same themes seem to be apparent in Oerter's
discussion of the isomorphism that develops between environmental
structure and internal cognitive structure, within his model of
cognitive socialization. He illustrates this course of development with
the concepts of work and time and reports results that illustrate
develomental changes in understanding and effective utilization of these
concepts in problem solving situations. Oerter also shows how identical
problem structures can produce quite different levels of performance
depending on the degree of isomorphism between the problem situation and
the individual's cognitive structure.

        The paper by Siegler is an elegant illustration of the analysis of
different levels of cognitive skill. The research he reports is
concerned with levels of rule complexity for responding to balance scale
problems and the different performance characteristics associated with
each specific rule system. Siegler also shows how instruction needs to
be matched to specific cognitive deficiencies before it can be
effective. The appropriate interpretation and analysis of different
levels of performance on cognitive tasks is further examined by the
papers by Gold and by Harris and Singleton. Gold's paper considers
possible sources of a child's failure to conserve quantity and problems
in interpreting failure as a deficiency in logical structures. In the
Harris and Singleton paper consideration is given to children's failures

on certain measurement problems and the inferences that can be drawn from such failures. These papers are followed by Murray's general discussion of the types of training strategies that have been developed in attempts to teach conservation. He argues that these training strategies may have broad applicability and serve as general teaching strategies for a variety of concepts. The final paper by Yuille and Catchpole is an analysis of some theoretical and empirical issues surrounding simple associative learning in children.

DEVELOPMENT OF COGNITIVE SKILLS

Pierre Oléron
Université Réné Descartes
Sorbonne
Paris, France

The use of the expression "cognitive skills" implies several presuppositions whose explanation can be useful for what follows.

1. The concept of a skill does not have it origin exclusively in behaviorism. The behaviorist proposition states, rather, that it is necessary only to consider those elements external to the student (stimulus, response, reinforcement). The idea of a skill, however, is closely related to that of efficiency (cf. Elliot & Connolly, 1974, p. 135: "to an extent skill is synonomous with efficiency"); in other words, what the subject is able to make, succeed in, and produce. A skill is defined by its actions and the effects of these actions.[1] The skill is thus the ability to produce certain actions. Its existence, as well as its development in the individual, is measured on the basis of what the person can do in a given situation. (This situation is representative, in general, of a class of situations, and can be standardized, as in the case of tests.)

The use of the words "cognition" and "cognitive" implies, however, the rejection of a behaviorist attitude and the refusal to consider only behavior. For example, Hayes (1976) mentioned the opposition between behavioral objectives and cognitive objectives in education, and reminded us that the term "cognitive" implies the consideration of those mechanisms of processes underlying behavior.

The negative aspects of this choice are clear. Its positive aspects are, however, not so clear. Each of us probably agrees upon the fact that the word "cognition" and the expressions in which it is used can be interpreted in various ways. For certain authors it means the consideration of information processing. For others, it suggests the description of sequences of operations that are expressed by diagrams or flow charts. For still others, it refers to logical or mathematical networks or structures. The latter usage is illustrated by Piaget, whom we will consider in some detail below, as a specialist on cognitive development.

In any case, cognitive skills necessarily deviate from their behaviorist definition ("correctly organized sequence of action") in order to take the form of interpretations, hypotheses, theoretical models, or the consequences of such models. (The same evolution can be observed in the notion of competence, narrowly related to the notion of skill.) It is impossible, under these conditions, to enumerate and describe skills with perfect precision; it is necessary, instead, to make room for analyses and discussions whose speculative character cannot be disguised.

2.   It is important to distinguish three types or levels of skills (however arbitrary they may be). The first level consists of skills that can be called natural or spontaneous. It is these that appear in the course of development, and are maintained in the framework of the organism's spontaneous activity. Second level skills are based on the natural dispositions of the organism, but their development and improvement depend, in part, on practice prescribed by the school, in particular, and later on by one's profession. The third level skills can be called instrumental skills. They are situated on "top" of the preceding skills to a certain extent, and intervene to increase the latter's efficiency by mobilizing and coordinating them, as well as adding some specific procedures.

These three levels can be illustrated by taking memory as an example. The first level skills relate to the mnemonic abilities that concern experienced events, and allow for their storage and recall. The middle skills correspond to the consolidated memories required in school (such as facts, dates, numbers, procedures, calculations, rules of grammar and spelling, etc.). The function of the third level skills is to call up the procedures that improve memory storage and retrieval, such as mnemonic devices, repetition, organization, summaries, note taking, etc.

Another example is given by perception, where we can also distinguish these three levels. The first level skills include identification and discrimination of objects and human faces, which appear in the child's first year. Acquisition of reading skills and the identification of non-verbal symbols (drawings, musical notes) are included in the second level, while the third contains systematic observation, cue detection, and similar skills.

3.   If one considers the objects to which cognitive activities are applied, two major domains appear: (a) the world of physical objects and materials and (b) the world of facts and psychological/sociological actions. There is an important point to be made here. There exists an extraordinary disproportion between the interest given to those cognitive activities focused on the first domain, and the attention given those with which the second is concerned. Almost all of the studies on cognition, and especially its development, address only the first domain. Researchers have acted as though cognitive skills were limited to physical objects, their properties, and the laws they obey.

One has only to look at the titles and contents of Piaget's works (see Piaget & Inhelder, 1969) to realize this. There, one discovers experiments on space, time, number, physical causality, physical quantities, etc. This is also apparent when one looks at the tasks presented to children, whether as practical tests or as part of experiments. Tasks utilizing language are either formal or they are related to the properties of physical objects more often than to social relations or psychological characteristics. As for tasks of a nonverbal nature, they refer in a privileged, semi-exclusive way to material objects or representations that express material characteristics such as form, number, spatial relations, etc.

The discordance is extremely surprising, since a large part of the life of the child (and of the adult) is made up of contacts with other people in the framework of social organizations, institutions, and habits. This life is determined by motivations, reactions, attitudes, emotions, enthusiasms, and rejections, all of which are linked to the origins of actions and reactions and are not easily understood via the theories of either physics or logic. An unbiased view of the world cannot help but bring out the surprising difference between the representation of cognitive activity viewed through the work of psychologists (even the greatest ones!), and the content and effective application of this activity. Consider the information diffused by mass media, whether it be news, political articles, or publicity, which well represents life and its daily preoccupations. What rapport can be established between this information and the psychologist asking his or her subjects to order a set of sticks, to deplace a quantity of liquid in order to test conservation, or to group red tokens with red ones and green tokens with green ones? This question cannot be avoided by claiming that the activities reflected by mass media have nothing to do with cognition; that would be to suppose that, in this field, man has no cognition concerning what he does! This unflattering picture is clearly inaccurate, even if the percentage of errors here is considerably higher than in the natural sciences. The question would also remain unanswered by claiming that those fields are of no importance and that what counts alone, or above all, comes from logic, mathematics, and the physical, spatial, and geometrical characteristics of the environment.

The only worthwhile answer is either to recognize the fact that psychology has locked itself into an area that corresponds only to a very limited sector of knowledge, or to admit that the cognitive processes whose analysis is based on experience with the physical world, mathematics, and logic, have universal merit and apply also to those psychological and sociological sectors from which they would erroneously have been separated. This point will be taken up later.

Perceptual Development

The examination of cognitive development necessarily implies a reference to perception: One part of cognitive activity takes place at the perceptual level, acting upon concrete objects that are present. One way to represent cognitive development consists of describing it as the transition from low-level perceptual activities to which the young child is limited, to abstract ones that progressively establish themselves. However, the division of cognitive activities into concrete and abstract categories, as well as the description of development as the transition from one to the other, however useful it may be (we will use it below), can only be taken as an approximation. In fact, abstract activities are not substituted for concrete ones. Cognitive activity is always in close contact with perceived objects, which are not replaced by "intellectual" objects (as Plato proposed in his theory of ideas). What is characteristic of cognitive development is the way in which perceived objects are dealt with, as well as the construction and utilization of symbolic representations that express and reconstruct their particular properties, but that always fall back upon perceived information for verification (this is observed in scientific procedure).

Perceptual skills develop in the child well in advance of school. Present work greatly emphasizes the earlier formation of perceptual organization. This does not signify that it is independent of exercise and learning. These are realized by physical contact with the environment. Adult contacts with the child are informal and do not offer any explicit form of teaching.

Preschool teaching and training of underprivileged children, in the framework of compensatory education, deal with concrete objects. The child's perception of the characteristics of concrete objects is one aspect of the training. Children are destined, however, to develop general capacities of attention, discrimination, and conceptualization (or even verbal expression), whose perception is only one opportunity.[2]

There are multiple forms of perceptual development; not all of them will be reviewed here. Certain works deal with them in a detailed manner and can be used as references for further information (e.g., Kidd & Rivoire, 1966; Pick & Pick, 1970; Vurpilot, 1972; Cohen & Salapatek, 1975; cf. also articles found in Stone, Smith & Murphy, 1973). Moreover, it is impossible to forget the role that visual images play in our civilization. This led to the idea of "visual literacy," i.e., a competence to identify information communicated by drawings, television, and the movies, and to extract new information and even cultural elements.

Elkind (1969) refers to "figurative perception" or perception of graphical representations. These figures or representations are important in the child's life, since they are found in books and magazines used for education or play. They are the ingredient of television programs as well as the movies. There is early identification of drawings and photographs in the child (by two years of age, Elkind notes). Certain precocious skills condition the structuring of complex representations, such as depth estimation from cues given by overlap or relative size (cf. Olson & Boswell, 1976).

Elkind (1969) noted that a transition takes place from figurative perception, in the true sense, to sign perception, which comes into play in reading (including the reading of numbers and musical notes). He refers to thematic perception, which is the understanding of the theme of those scenes represented, and, finally, to aesthetic perception. As he remarks, these activities are of a cognitive nature, even though their application takes place on perceptual material. They develop later than the identification of objects or people and even later with material that is more complex and whose interpretation implies more information transmitted in a cultural framework (the same for the understanding of humorous or comic elements).

The role of cognitive factors in perception and the dependence of perception on acquired knowledge and activities dealing with identification, categorization, and inference, is one of the classic themes of psychology (as it was in philosophy).[3] One can turn to Vernon (1966) on this point. The inverse relation should not be forgotten, however: The contribution of perception to intellectual functioning. The problem will not be presented in a general way (as in epistemology), and even the intermediary role of Piagetian schemas between perception and thought will be mentioned only in passing. But the aspects of figurative perception mentioned above are important in education because of the figures, schemas, and illustrations that occupy a great part of school books. These figural aids, in turn, depend for full effectiveness on the development and training of interpretative and integrative skills in the child. While many analyses on kinds of schemas and on their efficiency in learning have been performed on adults, they are less frequently done on children (cf., however, Vezin, 1974).

Intellectual Development

Piaget presented the most systematic and comprehensive theory of intellectual development. Moreover, his influence led psychologists to recognize the originality of cognitive processes and to use the words "Cognitive" and "Cognition" frequently. But the amplitude of this theory, in addition to the number of times it has been referred to, make it impossible and unnecessary to describe it at length. We will retain only what seems significant for the topic of this conference.

The guiding principle of Piagetian theory is that intellectual development is characterized by the formation of systems or structures of a logical or logico-mathematical kind. It has to be treated as a sequence or succession of such structures. The order in which these structures develop is a function of their increasing complexity; a given structure can appear only if preceded by a simpler structure that provides the conditions or prerequisites of its formation.

To prove a structure's existence, it must be shown that the child is simultaneously successful in those tasks requiring mastery of a certain structure after he or she has acquired that structure. As Piaget himself notes (e.g., 1971), this simultaneity is a consequence of the theory. Computation of correlations or factor analyses for scores obtained on such tasks are classical means for the testing of this simultaneity. Another way for this testing is given by learning experiments. Training whose purpose is to form or consolidate intellectual structures should have results different from that dealing with specific skills. The benefits of the latter are limited to the particular activities practiced. On the former, however, the progress should be more general and cover all the activities and skills related to the structure in question. The theory can be tested as follows. If the training relating to these structures ("operational") is shown to be possible and efficient, this would argue in favor of the theory. If, however, the training is inefficient or results only in partial effects, there would be reason to question the theory or at least to point out factors not fully taken into account.

The research carried out along these lines makes it difficult to draw a clear-cut conclusion. One thing, however, seems certain. The logico-structural theory of development described above does not appear to be sustained entirely.

Piaget himself admits that success in tasks relating to the same structure is sometimes not completely simultaneous. These "horizontal decalages" show up clearly in experiments dealing with the various aspects of conservation of quantity. Many studies employing diversified tasks have found similar results: A subject often performs at different levels depending on the nature of the task. Schirk and Laroche (1970) found, for example, that only 25% of a group of adults (mean age, 23-years-old) could be characterized as homogeneous with respect to performance level on the various experimental tasks.

Statistical correlations and factorial analyses point in the same direction. Several times, only weak correlations were found to exist between subject performances on tests supposedly related to the same stage of development. Factor analyses, such as those reported by Winkelman (1974) on conservation tasks, failed to single out any one factor that corresponded to "operativity."

Piaget interpreted these "horizontal decalages" by calling attention to characteristics of the objects of intellectual activity. Perceptual characteristics are particularly relevant. Operations are facilitated when they go in the same direction and are made more difficult when they go in the opposite direction. Generally, these decalages show, according to Inhelder, Sinclair and Bovet (1974, p. 29), "the resistances erected by reality" against "the structuring activity of the subject." These resistances, according to these authors, can be considered from two points of view: "properties of the objects . . . and processes of subject's activity at grip with them" (p. 298). This indicates that perceptual aspects are not the only factors, as it is also necessary to consider the way in which the subject approaches and deals with the proposed tasks.

The point of this observation is to reveal the <u>functional</u> aspects of cognitive development and to show that, even within the Genevan School, it is neither described nor interpeted solely in terms of structures. In fact, the functional aspects have been mentioned numerous times by Piaget, who includes them in his description of operational development, but does not present them systematically or give them the same weight as the structures.

A number of studies have shown that the effects of training can extend to tasks different from those used during the sessions. Inhelder, Sinclair, and Bovet (1974) reported progress in inclusion after training on conservation as well as the converse. Bideaud (1977) also found similar results concerning training on inclusion problems and performance on conservation. These results obtained in the laboratory can be compared with other observations; recent replications of some Piagetian tasks show subjects' performance levels frequently to be higher than that reported by Piaget or his immediate successors (e.g., Bideaud, 1977; Botson & Deliège, 1974). The differences between the subjects tested previously and now can be related to changes in teaching practices and school curricula, especially to the introduction of modern mathematics for young children.

These results can be interpreted as results of mobilization or formation of structures that are common to the tasks used in both training and testing sessions (whether they take place in the laboratory or in the school). Modern mathematics, for example, provides the opportunity to work with logical relations and to construct structures that seem to be related directly to operational thought as defined by Piaget.

There are, however, other possible interpretations of these results. Training in intellectual activities has complicated effects (as it involves components that are complex, too). It involves the way the subject approaches, deals with, and organizes thought-objects. This pertains to the subject's attitudes with respect to these objects and how they are directed and expressed by instrumental interventions. In a task of classification, for example, the possibility of picking out the common traits of several physically diverse elements (such as form, etc.) is related to their individuality and complexity. Practice in modern mathematics leads pupils to depict certain objects as circles, rectangles, etc. Confronted with the same figures, children in more traditional classes use such terms as "moons," "plates," "discs," "doors," "tables." This diversity and its strong relation to concrete examples can act so as to obstruct the formation of categorical classification (Bideaud, 1977).[4] Authors who have studied the development of mathematical thought have pointed out the limits of a purely structuralist approach. These studies bring to light the role of perceptual elements, formulas, or rules memorized, and symbolic means of expression such as numeration systems or graphs, without which mathematical thought and reasoning would be unable to take place (although these may also hinder its progression; see Pelnard-Considère, 1976).

The preeminence of logic is difficult to justify when extended to reasoning concerning the physical or psychological world, which is subject to the rule of causality. The formal model of Inhelder and Piaget (1955), proposed to account for inductive reasoning of the adolescent, proves to be inadequate as one analyzes more closely the correspondence that these authors try to establish between the devices on which the subject reasons and the logical formulations (see Oléron, 1977).

The fact that numerous adults also appear not to have attained the formal level that marks the completion of the logical structures constitutes an analogous objection, serious enought that Piaget (1972) recognized it as such and offered several interpretations. These interpretations suggest that factors such as the interest or training of subjects must be considered along with pure logical structures.

Thus, a theory that purports to describe intellectual development by calling attention to structures and their filiation cannot be realized without allowing room for the functional aspects. It is necessary to deal with them if a description of development is to be offered that takes into account all the data. Laboratory subjects' activity is able to fit into a model of logical structure, but only in part.

Unfortunately, the functional description of development cannot be established with the precision of the logical models (precision that explains the preference for them). However, all the research, including that using models made as elaborated as possible, have regularly mentioned a certain number of skills that must correspond to reality, even if attained in an empirical or approximate way.

Without proposing definitions or even accepting the same terms, they refer to the abilities to abstract, consider, or vary a single element among others; to take into account all the data; to complete them; to go beyond the information given (the title of a well-known book by Bruner); to draw conclusions; to seek causes; to change a point of view or a way of approaching a problem; to avoid perceptual or descriptive traps inherent in a situation; to retrieve and use acquired knowledge; and to resort to diverse tools such as verbal analyses of the situation, calculation, imagination, anticipation, invention, etc.

Two characteristics proposed elsewhere (Oléron, 1972) as a definition of intelligence can serve as the guideline for the presentation of its development. These two characteristics are: (a) the formation and utilization of long pathways, and (b) the formation and utilization of models.

The typical behavior of the young child is to respond immediately (when physically able to do so) to the properties of the perceived stimuli. Progress consists of going through long pathways characterized by a representation of the situation, utilization of acquired knowledge, inferences, etc.

The utilization of long pathways is marked by a negative aspect: It hinders the utilization of a shorter pathway when it is apparently - but only apparently - available. Thurstone (1924), in a rather unknown passage, mentioned this inhibition as a characteristic of intelligence. This observation was shown to be quite true, but little mention has been made of it since. However, observing a child's behavior reveals, or at least enables one to induce, the development of this ability.

The typically human long pathways include representations of reality (and in some cases representations of the subject himself). Typically, too, these representations are not copies of perceived reality, but rather a reconstruction, most frequently in an abstract form. In order to proceed along these pathways, the child must be able to master these representations and integrate them to the situation and to his action; it is in this way that he or she solves the tasks with which he or she is confronted. That this is the core of intellectual development results from the fact that any author, whatever be his or her system, mentions, as described above, this transition to representation or to the abstract rules of action as well as the related conflicts and facilitations. Along the same lines, one of the main problems of teaching is to assure and make easier the transition to the abstract forms proposed (or imposed) by society and culture.

When speaking abuut the relations between the concrete and the abstract there is a tendency to do so from the perspective of a succession, where one leads to the other. This perspective, coming from philosophy that focuses its attention on the objects of thought, inhibits one's realization of the pattern of the intellectual processes and their development. On the other hand, abstraction originates in perception and action. But more important is the fact that it is communicated by culture, language, and school. The progressive mastery that the child attains results from a kind of battle, in which the child is helped by the adult, but must resist the suggestions of his or her immediate perceptions and actions. The conflict inherent in cognitive development was deservedly mentioned by Piaget (e.g., in relation with his theory of cognitive equilibrium; see 1957), moving away from the temptation to interpret the interrelationship of structures as an automatic process, as well as the progress resulting from experience with conflict (for example, in the learning of operational concepts).

Intellectual development also implies the child's ability to experience conflicts between different aspects of reality and to get over them (preference being given to the most abstract representation).

The active nature of the psychological processes, recognized by most psychologists, is due to the fact that these processes can be linked to the subject's physical action on the environment (greatly emphasized by Piaget). It is due even more and more specifically to the subject taking command of his activity and directing it according to the appropriate strategies. The word "strategy" as used by psychologists is recent. Binet (1911), however, in one of his definitions of intelligence, mentioned "direction" as a character trait that is in part, at least, its forerunner. The taking charge of his or her own activity is an important aspect of the subject's development. It is one way of utilizing long pathways, as it corresponds to a desensitization (at least partially) toward the immediate environmental pressures and suggestions.

This taking command is not properly brought out in typical experimental situations; these situations give rise to a constraint from which it is difficult for the subject to escape, even if he or she wavers between various possible responses (e.g., for the conservation of quantity). A method much less employed but more adequate is one in which the subject is encouraged to ask questions in order to obtain the information necessary to solve a problem (the prototype is the game of 20 questions). Nguyen-Xuan, Lemaire, and Rousseau (1974), who refined this method, showed, among others, that the child's capacity to exploit all of the information given increases with age. More specifically, the child becomes able to infer from this information the implied consequences that are not, however, the object of an explicit question or answer. This is shown by the decrease in the question's redundancy and the appearance of an optimal strategy that enables the resolution of a problem by asking the minimum number of questions necessary.

One intellectual skill that is rarely mentioned is evaluation or judgment, even though the value of such age-old neighboring concepts as "common sense," "discrimination," and "the critical mind" have been commonly recognized. Binet (1911) had made room for censorship ("censure") in one of his definitions of intelligence, and had noted its deficiency in the young child. Censorship is the ability to criticize, evaluate, and appreciate. Guilford (in his research on adults) gave a large place to factors of evaluation (Guilford, 1967; Guilford & Hoepfner, 1971). He refers to it in a broad sense (as does Binet). The essence of judgment is to be found in the comparison between what is given or proposed (by the situation, other people, or by the subject himself) and the criteria of what is seemingly probable. It exerts a kind of regulatory function on the subject's activities and keeps them adapted to the situation by discriminating between the probable and improbable. It is this skill that dissuades the pupil from giving as the solution of a problem (e.g., in physics) a figure that is the result of an apparently correct calculation, but that has little rapport with the data's order of magnitude. Similarly, in a translation, this skill keeps one from sentences that do not agree with the whole text.

This skill can mislead the subject who is presented with situations too new to conform to his or her habitual modes of thinking, or who is faced with a formal type of reasoning (where it is essential to avoid the guidelines of reality or experience). In this case, however, it can be said that a judgment deficiency exists, since the subject had to understand that he or she is confronting a new situation or a kind of test that is unfamiliar.

This ability clearly marks the opposition between short and long pathways. It corresponds to giving up the short pathway, where the subject is governed by the action taken, for a pathway that integrates reflection on that action in addition to taking into account other available information than that immediately concerning the situation.

There is not room in this paper for the development of these analyses. However, two points are too important not to be mentioned.

1. Developmental studies reveal how slow and difficult the transition is from elementary intellectual activities to more elaborate forms (short pathways to long ones). It is not enough, in explaining development, to mention deficiencies that temporarily affect the child and that will disappear with maturation. One must also take into account the tendency of every organism to continue in its current behaviors. Pressures and demands are necessary to force a change to a more elaborate behavior. This is not clearly observed in the case of a "normal" child, who develops within the favorable conditions of experience, stimulation, and imitation. Children not subject to the same conditions allow a better view. This is the case for children who are socially and culturally deprived or physically handicapped, in particular, deaf children (born deaf or having become deaf at an early age). Deaf children show signs of retardation in certain domains of intellectual development. These deficits can be explained as the clinging to response modes determined by perceptual characteristics of objects and the difficulty of giving up these response modes in favor of others. For example, deaf children are inferior to hearing children in tests of conservation of quantity. but it is not enough to show them the reality of conservation and even less helpful to explain notions such as compensation, which logically conditions conservation, in order to make them acquire it immediately (Oléron, Corroyer, & Legros, 1977).

The pathway followed by the organism in reaction to the environment is not a simple geographic course that can be changed when a new path is available. It corresponds to strategies, attitudes, and response habits. Any teacher knows that it is necessary for the student to accept and practice new strategies, attitudes, and habits. A theory of cognitive development is seriously lacking if it does not take into account modes of functioning and strategies, and considers only an ideal subject reduced to an abstract succession of structures.

2. The teacher's dream is to give students the key to knowledge
and skill so that they attain the capability to solve problems of very
different types and acquire a competence that extends well beyond the
educational content. The structuralist conception of cognition and its
development is hopeful for the realization of this dream; whereas
structures are general and cover, in a coordinated manner, the entire
domain of activity corresponding to a certain level of development, it
is the teaching allowing for their formation or for their reinforcement
that can attain the hoped-for result. The limits that have been
mentioned concerning the validity of the structuralist theory make the
realization of this pedagogical dream relatively improbable. There
remains, however, the advantage stemming from any functional exercise,
and the reality of "transfer of training" that has always preoccupied
psychologists and teachers.

It is necessary, however, to take into account another source of
restriction, namely that concerning the content or objects of
intellectual activity. Intelligence can be characterized by the ability
to solve problems, and it has never been doubted that a problem is
hardly solved by the simple application of logical or mathematical
formulas. This is especially so with physical, psychological, or
political problems. General problem-solving ability is determined by
working skills, which can be trained using very different materials.
but information concerning the domain to which the problem relates and
the application and knowledge of specific procedural rules remain
essential. The doctor who delivers a diagnosis and the policeman who
discovers a guilty party both respect the rules of logic, but their
success is based on the use of acquired knowledge and habit that are
specific to their disciplines. It is this knowledge that permits them
to act and succeed. The efficiency of the action is related to
"regional competencies" with which teaching must deal. Collins offers a
judicious remark on problems that are poorly structured and the role of
the knowledge necessary to solve them. "It turns out that most of
life's problems are ill-structured and so acquiring factual knowledge is
crucial to understanding most problems" (Collins, 1976, p. 288).

Psychological Competence

The words that describe the skills dealt with in this section are
imprecise as well as poorly defined. What is distinguished by "social
competence" covers two distinct domains (see Hess, 1974). The most
common usage, which corresponds to social intelligence, refers to
knowledge and skills relative to other people. It concerns
interpersonal relations and the corresponding behaviors that, according
to the expression used by Hess, are "person relevant." In another sense,
social competence refers to the institutions, structures, and
organization of the society in which the subject lives
("system-relevant" according to Hess' terminology).

It seems that a more suitable terminology can be established by keeping the adjective "social" for the second usage and by adapting and generalizing the expression "psychological competence" to refer to relations concerning other individuals. However, psychological competence is not limited only to relations with others. It also includes reference to oneself (self-consciousness, behavior adapted to this consciousness, and self-management). The narrow relation between self-consciousness and the consciousness of others as well as their interactions justify regrouping those skills and abilities under the same terms. It is the psychological competence defined in such a manner that will be considered here.

It has been emphasized above that few studies have investigated the notion of psychological competence. This can be explained by philosophical and historical reasons (see Oléron, 1975). It may also be asked whether knowledge of cognitive development implies that psychological competence should be considered separately. Do not the studies on intellectual development bring to light universal traits or characteristics regardless of the objects on which the activity takes place? This is the question that will be examined.

It is difficult to question that the framework defined by logic and mathematics has a universal validity and that it can be applied to all sorts of objects, including psychological or social ones. The philosopher Bergson (1932) came out in favor of the opposite position, which carries little weight, however, compared to the development of psychology and sociology. In fact, the universality of logic and mathematics is a postulate that conditions their existence as sciences. But this condition of epistomological order does not imply that the child or adult concretely experiences psychological and social reality in the same way and according to the same regularities as physical objects.

The alternative of not dealing with psychological competence as a separate ability is supported by a certain number of arguments.

1. From the viewpoint of those procedures that lead to the acquisition of knowledge, the observed facts must always be integrated into the model's construction. This is true whether they are properties of the physical world or those that come into play in psychological life or society. The child attains knowledge of physical objects as a function of the ability to interpret perceptions and to accept that appearance and reality may differ (as in acquisition ' of quantity conservation: The displaced liquid and the deformed ball of clay appear different, but in reality, the amount of liquid and weight remain unchanged). In exactly the same way, it is necessary to go beyond the speech and actions of others in order to discern reality. The intentions, feelings, or dispositions of the speaker are not always explicitly indicated. In certain cases, they purposely resist interpretation; in others they are disguised as intentions or dispositions different from the real ones. Moreover, they are not

always consistent with the reality they supposedly describe. Psychological competence is attained only when one knows the existence of concealment, lies, machiavellianism, and, even less obvious, the speaker's lack of consciousness of his or her own desires and attitudes, not to mention the simple rules of politeness that dictate silence or discretion vis-a-vis thoughts and feelings.

2. Piaget's first studies (1923), which dealt with child communication, led to the notion of egocentricity, which has since been greatly expanded. According to his observations, egocentricity gives way to "socialized thought" or the ability (at about seven years) to take into account another person's point of view at the same time as the occurrence of operational thought. This coincidence suggests a strong relationship, indeed, and even an identity between psychological competence and the intelligence that acts on physical objects. Studies on the developmental aspects of spatial representation (Piaget & Inhelder, 1948) also situated at seven to eight years the time at which the child is regularly able to take on another's viewpoint in a task that brings perspective to play.

In favor of a contrasting theory, let it be noted that the arguments mentioned above can be contested. It has been shown that knowledge, in general, results from going beyond appearances in order to construct models of reality. This does not imply, however, that the models for different domains are in themselves identical. What was said above concerning the limitations of logic in its relation to physical events dominated by the laws of causality can be extended here. Several examples can be given as illustration.

1. The notion of ambivalence is of fundamental importance in understanding the behaviors and interactions of human beings. This is, however, a concept that goes against the logical principle of non-contradiction: The same object is at the same time desired and rejected.

2. The logical, mathematical, and physical laws are without exception. It is not the same for societal laws. The child learns by experience that one cannot escape gravity. Parents, however, show him or her examples of infractions that can be committed in a car with respect to parking regulations and speed limits. Television, comics, and even classical works given numerous examples of breaking the law (the "outlaw" is a kind of artistic and journalistic institution). The child learns that the rules imposed by his or her family can be broken, and that the transgression, even where the parents are aware of it, is not punished each time or is punished with different degrees of severity. A part of the child's competence consists of avoiding punishment or learning its degree by choosing the moment at which the parents feel the least severe or by acting in ways to "soften them up."

3. Intellectual development is complete, according to Piaget, (e.g., Piaget & Inhelder, 1969) when the child becomes able to take into account the totality of elements pertaining to a situation (and to form a structure out of them). Observation of people and society shows the reality of _partial_ viewpoints. Social classes, lobbies, political parties, and adherents to philosophical, moral or religious doctrines all have different points of view and act in ways to advance them to the detriment of their adversaries. The competent person is one who knows how to employ those measures necessary to have his or her cause and that of the group he or she requests triumph, rather than one who gives equal weight to his own interests as well as to those of opponents. (The efficient chief of a Union would never consider the interests of the employer as important as those of the worker.) The child can only acquire knowledge of these facts. Even if this knowledge is acquired relatively late, the child has at least experienced the differences in opinion between self and parents, brothers and sisters, friends, and teachers. This gives the child the chance to develop competence by using those measures that will assure some success.

4. With respect to the argument of the late appearance of the child's ability to take another's point of view, it can be noted that its substance is rather weak. In the first place, it establishes, for the most part, a coincidence between two aspects of development, which is far from proving the existence of identity or dependence. The usage of such expressions as "décentration," and "se décentrer" appears indifferently to designate behaviors relative to objects or people. This suggests that the same skill might be used in both cases. The uniqueness of a word, however, has never succeeded in establishing a uniqueness among the facts to which it refers. One meaning of "décentration" is to admit - without being necessarily conscious of the fact - that another person has an opinion or is found to be in a situation different from oneself. The other meaning concerns the fact of one's taking into consideration more than one characteristic aspect of an object or situation (e.g., both height and width in a conservation task). Isn't this a kind of awareness in the first case and a lack of rigidity in the second?

In any case, research going back to Piaget's first study (1923) has shown that the ability to take on another's point of view comes about much earlier than had been thought (Salama-Cazacu, 1966; Beaudichon, 1968, in communication; Flavell, e.g., Salatas & Flavell, 1976, in perspective). The findings by Piaget and those who followed his procedure that this ability appears relatively late in development can be explained by the complexity of his tasks. When working with concrete material of high motivation content, it appears that children adapt themselves quite early to their listener when they have a message to communicate, just as they also distinguish what they see from that seen by another person (Lempers, Flavell, & Flavell, 1977).

We have argued in favor of the specificity of psychological competence, but do not pretend that this specificity is absolute. It is clear, on the other hand, that when situations are complex, their complexity requires general intellectual skills that are also manifest in situations that are not psychological. The specificity of psychological competence is clear enough, however, to make mention of two of its consequences at the educational level.

1. The first is that it is impossible to develop psychological competence without exercises and programs directly related to its development. Intuitively, no one has illusions as to the universality of logic and mathematics. No one believes that the ability to understand and to solve problems relative to human relations results primarily from the application of these disciplines and the skills that ensue from their application. However, the importance of these disciplines and the identification of intelligence by these skills makes it difficult to accord the weight and prestige merited by psychological competence. The subjects taught in schools (literature, history) allow only the empirical and marginal practice of this ability. It is precisely this empiricism and marginality that should be dispensed with: Psychological competence can be trained early (see Oléron, 1969).

2. One aspect of psychological competence is self-knowledge; that is, self-knowledge acquired by the pupil not as a person (which must not be excluded) but as a subject who perceives, understands, learns, evaluates, decides, and organizes his or her actions. A large part of the pupil's activities consists of memorization. The knowledge of mnemonic processes, referred to by Flavell (1971, 76) as meta-memory, can increase the efficiency with which things are memorized. Glaser (1977) speaks of "self-management" (and "self-management skills") as necessary for success in academic tasks. Self-management, as described by Glaser, goes beyond psychological competence, to which he does not explicitly refer. It seems only logical, however, to include it here.

Language, Memory, Motivation

The notion of language development will not be discussed here. It is difficult, however, not to refer to language when dealing with cognitive development.[5]

The relation between language and cognition is known to have a double meaning: Language acquisition depends on cognitive development; language helps cognitive development along. The first relation will not be considered. It remains for those who study language acquisition to find out the factors on which it depends. It should be noted, however, that research on meaning acquisition enables one to reach certain aspects of cognitive development. The fact that the child does not understand certain words or interprets them differently than an adult is related to misunderstanding certain relations or, for example, the way in which the child conceives of the environment. Clark (1973) offers a good example of this in what she calls "non-linguistic strategies" in meaning acquisition. The child develops certain schemas relative to the objects in the environment and interprets the words he or she hears as a function of these schemas; the meaning evolves in conjunction with the evolution of the schemas. Along the same lines, the usage of certain verb forms depends on the attainment of a certain level of cognitive development (e.g., the passive forms and their relation with the acquisition of reversibility; Beilin, 1975). It is methodologically interesting to note the resurgence indirectly given to the study of cognitive development by way of language comprehension. But one must be careful with this method, as there exists no real parallel between observed progress in cognitive development and in verbal development (cf. Beilin, 1975).

With respect to the assistance given by language to cognitive development, it is necessary to avoid falling into a discussion between "language and thought" and "language and cognition." This line of thought often includes irrelevant arguments and poorly founded postulates. It is useful to show that certain verbal acquisitions depend on cognitive development (as we have just said). But, one may not conclude in general that language is of no help to cognitive development, as there is not a symmetrical relationship between the interrelations of "thought-language" and "language-thought." As stated elsewhere (Oléron, 1972), a certain level of muscular development is necessary for man to make use of a tool; once in his hand, however, his strength is greatly increased. The same analogy applies to language, at least in certain domains. That is clearer in a functional rather than a structural perspective, as one obvious aspect of the working of intelligence is the application of instrumental activities.

Language assists cognitive development by transmitting knowledge to the child. The acquisition of knowledge is closely related to intellectual activity. As mentioned earlier, abstract notions or concepts are constituted only in part by a direct elaboration of what is perceived or manipulated. They are constructed for the most part by appropriate symbols and by elaborations that take place in the framework of the historical evolution of society.

On the other hand, the usage of language is at least partially an intellectual exercise. The comprehension of a statement implies the comprehension of its relation to the situation in which it is produced, as well as to the preceding declarations, and to the presumed intention of the speaker. Production implies adapting the sentence to the knowledge of its receiver, so that it conveys its intended meaning, as well as the utilization of words and expressions that respect the rules of semantics and syntax.

From both points of view, language implies the utilization of long pathways. Thus, its practice is a form of training in the use of such pathways. It creates habits and attitudes that lead the child to take into account more than what is suggested by the present situation. This interpretation helps us to understand certain delays in cognitive development of children deprived of spontaneous language acquisition (cf. Oléron, 1972).

A very old tradition separates and even opposes memory and intelligence. The contemporary trend is to join them together. The way in which the role of acquired knowledge relates to the practice and development of intellectual activities, as explained beforehand, provides an argument in this direction. It draws attention to the fact that intelligence does not function in a vacuum, but on data that have been discovered, transmitted, and acquired.

In the opposite direction, Piaget and Inhelder (1968) showed that memory depends on the level of the child's intellectual development. Various authors assert that memorization does not operate in a raw and literal manner, but incorporates interpretations and inferences (Bransford, Barclay, & Franks, 1972; Paris, 1975), and even the retrieval of information is assimilable to the solution of a problem (Lindsay & Norman, 1972). Furthermore, research in models of human memory have led certain authors to refer to structures that are, in the end, intellectual ones (e.g., Lindsay & Norman, 1972).

The novelty of this approach does not lie in the facts themselves, but in the discoveries made in the psychological laboratory or, at the least, the importance attached to them. Everyone's experience, and the analysis of the communication of knowledge in school have always shown the existence of mnemonic activity concerned with meaning, implying comprehension and using diverse techniques or procedures in view of better storage or retrieval.

Should the limitation of an intellectual theory of memory be argued against? The storage of information, knowledge and know-how is built upon an original and irreducible base that instrumental interventions and logical relations can only help to reinforce. Without mentioning the part played by images (cf. Paivio, 1971), we note that inferences are sometimes set forth when, in fact, associations or groupings of perception come into play (cf. Oléron & Corroyer, 1977).

Let us consider motivation. It is the traditional norm to treat cognitive processes separately from affectivity. This is a convenient and indispensable abstraction for a theoretical analysis, but one must always keep in mind that this is only an abstraction. There exists perhaps an internal principle that causes cognitive structures to develop and become more complex through purely logical necessities. If this principle does exist, however, it can encounter obstacles strong enough to result in the loss of a great deal of its efficiency. In dealing earlier with the passage from concrete to abstract and from short pathways to long ones, mention was made of the tendency and temptation to remain at one level without ever going beyond it. In order that further progress be made, intellectual abilities are necessary, but so are motivational factors.

More generally, mention should also be made of what Connolly and Bruner (1974) have called "emotional skills." They offer the example of self-confidence. In fact, this is important in enabling one to tackle one's studies and school work with the feeling "that one can do things with a certain likelihood of success" (p. 5). These authors remind us how much the feelings of failure and powerlessness contribute to sidetrack certain children from learning the intellectual activities required in school, particularly in socially deprived groups.

This, in turn, leads to socio-economic factors. We cannot forget their role in determining cognitive development.

Footnotes

1. "A correctly organized sequence of actions constitutes what is generally considered as a skill. . ." (Elliott & Connolly, 1974, p. 136).

2. A complete study of the development of perceptual skills should mention the pedagogical interventions in the case of children with a sensorial handicap (development of exploration, discrimination and tactile identification of objects in the blind, training deaf children to distinguish as acutely as their residual hearing permits them, as well as the nature, pitch and intensity of sounds, the different positions and movement of the lips to allow them to be read, and the various tactile, proprioceptive and visual information which condition speech rehabilitation.

3. In the last century, Helmholtz referred to unconscious reasoning as the heart of perception. Boring (1950) has given a good summary of his theory.

4. The studies by Goldstein & Scherer (1941) on "concrete attitude" and by Wallon (Ascoli & Wallon, 1950) on "precategorical thought" report suggestions of the same kind.

5. It should be noted that the chapter by Ginsburg and Koslowski, 1976, includes a section on language acquisition.

References

Ascoli, G., & Wallon, H. Comment l'enfant sait claser les objets. Enfance, 1950, 3, 411-433.

Beaudichon, J. La communication entre enfants: Transmission des connaissances relatives à un matérial concret. Psychologie franaise, 1968, 3, 265-280.

Beilin, H. Studies in the cognitive basis of language development. New
    York: Academic Press, 1975.

Bergson, H. L'évolution créatrice. Paris: Alcan, forty-first edition,
    1932.

Bideaud, J. L'atteinte de la notion d'inclusion: Evolution comparée
    d'acquisitions provoquées par apprentissage et d'acquisitions
    spontanées. Enfance, 1977, (in press).

Binet, A. Les idées modernes sur les enfants. Paris: Flammarion,
    1911.

Boring, E. G.   A history of experimental psychology.   New   York:
    Appleton-Century-Croft, second edit., 1950.

Botson, C., & Deliège, M. Le dévelopment intellectuel de l'enfant.
    Bruxelles: Direction Générale de l'Organisation des Etudes, 1974.

Bransford, J. ., Barclay, J. R. & Franks, J. J. Sentence memory: A
    constructive versus interpretive approach. Cognitive Psychology,
    1972, 3, 193-209.

Clark, E. V. Non-linguistic strategies and the acquisition of word
    meanings. Cognition, 1973, 2, 161-182.

Cohen, L. B., & Salapatek, P. (Eds.) Infant perception: From sensation
    to cognition, Vol. 1. New York: Academic Press, 1975.

Collins, A. Education and understanding. In D. Klahr (Ed.), Cognition
    and instruction. Hillsdale, NJ: Erlbaum, 1976.

Connolly, K. & Bruner, J. Competence: Its nature and nurture.   In K.
    Connolly & J. Bruner (Eds.), The growth of competence. New York:
    Academic Press, 1974.

Elkind, D. Developmental studies of figurative perception. In L.   P.
    Lipsitt & H. W. Reese (Eds.), Advances in child development and
    behavior, Vol. 4. New York: Academic Press, 1969.

Elliott, J., & Connolly, K.   Hierarchical   structure   in   skill
    development. In K. Connolly & J. Bruner (Eds.), The growth of
    competence. New York: Academic Press, 1974.

Flavell, J. H. First discussant's comment: What is development of
    memory the development of? Human Development, 1971, 14, 272-278.

Flavell, J. H.   The development of meta communication.   Symposium
    language and cognition, Twenty-first International Congress of
    Psychology, Paris, July 1976.

Ginsburg, H. & Koslowski, B. Cognitive development. Annual Review of Psychology, 1976, 27, 29-61.

Guilford, J. P. The nature of human intelligence. New York: McGraw-Hill, 1967.

Guilford, J. P. & Hoepfner, R. The analysis of intelligence. New York: McGraw-Hill, 1971.

Glaser, R. Adaptative education: Individual diversity and learning. New York: Holt, Rinehart & Winston, 1977.

Goldstein, K. & Scherer, M. Abstract and concrete behavior. An experimental study with special tests. Psychological Monographs, 1941, 53(239).

Hayes, J. R. It's the thought that counts: New approaches to educational theory. In D. Klahr (Ed.), Cognition and instruction. Hillsdale, NJ: Lawrence Erlbaum, 1976.

Hess, R. D. Social competence and the educational process. In K. Connolly & J. Bruner (Eds.), The growth of competence. New York: Academic Press, 1974.

Inhelder, B., & Piaget, J. De la logique de l'enfant à la logique de l'adolescent. Paris: Presses Universitaires de France, 1955.

Inhelder, B., Sinclair, H. & Bovet, M. Apprentissage et structures de la connaissance. Paris: Presses Universitaires de France, 1974.

Kidd, A. H. & Rivoire, J. L. Perceptual development in children. New York: International Universities Press, 1966.

Lempers, J. D., Flavell, E. R. & Flavell, J. H. The development in very young children of tacit knowledge concerning visual perception. Genetic Psychology Monographs, 1977, 95, 3-53.

Lindsay, P. H. & Norman, D. A. Human information processing. New York: Academic Press, 1972.

Nguyen-Xuan, A., Lemaire, F. & Rosseau, J. La sélection des informations dans la résolution du problème de serie à trois termes. Journal de Psychologie, 1974, 297-317.

Oléron, P. Pour un enseignement des sciences humaines a l'école. L'Education, 1969, 32, 7-9.

Oléron, P. Language et developpement mental. Bruxelles: Dessart, 1972.

Oléron, P.   Pour   un   dépassement   du   concept   d'intelligence. International Review of Applied Psychology, 1975, 24, 107-116.

Oléron, P. Le raisonnement. Paris: Presses Universitaires de France, Coll. Que Sais-Je, 1977.

Oléron, P. & Corroyer, D.   Inférences dans la mémoire non verbale: Realité ou artefact?   In Psychologie expérimentale et comparée. Paris: Presses Universitaires de France, 1977.

Oléron, P., Corroyer, D., & Legros, S.   Effets   de   deux   types d'entrainement en vue de l'atteinte des conservations par des enfants sourds. Bulletin de Psychologie, 1977, 30, 312-324.

Olson, R. K., & Boswell, S. L.   Pictorial   depth   sensitivity   in two-year-old children. Child Development, 1976, 47, 1175-1178.

Paivio, A. Imagery and verbal processes. New York: Holt, Rinehart, and Winston, 1971.

Paris, S. G. Integration and inteference in children's comprehension and memory. In F. Restle, R. M. Shiffrin, N. J. Castellan, H. R. Lindman, & D. B. Pisoni (Eds.), Cognitive theory, Vol. 1. Hillsdale, NJ: Lawrence Erlbaum, 1975.

Pelnard-Considère, J.   Nature   et   développement   du   raisonnement mathématique. L'Orientation Scholaire et Professionnelle, 1976, 5, 349-364.

Piaget, J.   Le langage et la pensée chez l'enfant.   Neuchatel: Delachaux et Niestlé, 1923.

Piaget, J. Logique et équilibre dans les comportements du suject.   In Etudes d'épistemologie génétique, Vol. 2. Paris: Presses Universitaires de France, 1957.

Piaget, J. The theory of stages in cognitive development. In D. R. Green, M. P. Ford, & G. B. Flamer (Eds.), Measurement and Piaget. New York: McGraw-Hill, 1971.

Piaget, J. Intellectual evolution from adolescence to adulthood. Human Development, 1972, 15, 1-12.

Piaget, J., & Inhelder, B. La représentation de l'espace chez l'enfant. Paris: Presses Universitaires de France, 1948.

Piaget, J., & Inhelder, B. Mémoire et intelligence.   Paris: Presses Universitaires de France, 1968.

Piaget, J. & Inhelder, B. Les opérations intellectuelles et leur développement. In P. Fraisse & J. Piaget (Eds.), Traité de Psychologie Expérimentale, Vol. 7. Paris: Presses Universitaires de France, second edition, 1969.

Pick, H. L. Jr., & Pick, A. D. Sensory and perceptual development. In P. H. Mussen (Ed.), Carmichael's Manual of Child Psychology. New York: Wiley, 1970.

Salatas, H., & Flavell, J. H. Perspective taking: The development of two components of knowledge. Child Development, 1976, 47, 103-109.

Schirk, A., & Laroche, J. Etude des opérations intellectuelles chez des adultes de la promotion supérieure du travail. Travail Humain, 1970, 1-2, 99-112..

Slama-Cazacu, T. Le dialogue chez les petits enfants. Sa signification et quelques-unes de ses particularités. Bulletin de Psychologie, 1966, 19, 688-697.

Stone, L. J., Smith, H. T., & Murphy, L. B. The competent infant. Research and commentary. New York: Basic Books, 1973.

Thurstone, L. L. The nature of intelligence. New York: Harcourt Brace, 1924.

Vernon, M. D. Perception in relation to cognition. In A. H. Kidd & J. L. Rivoire (Eds.), Perceptual development in children. New York: International Universities Press, 1966.

Vezin, J. F. Etude comparée de schèmas plus ou moins concrets et d'énoncés verbaux: Mise en correspondance et rôle dans l'apprentissage en fonction de l'âge. Enfance, 1974, 1-2, 21-44.

Vurpillot, E. Le monde visuel du jeune enfant. Paris: Presses Universitaires de France, 1972.

Winkelmann, W. Factorial analysis of children's conservation task performance. Child Development, 1974, 45, 843-848.

THE INFLUENCE OF ENVIRONMENTAL STRUCTURE ON COGNITIVE DEVELOPMENT
DURING ADOLESCENCE: A THEORETICAL MODEL AND EMPIRICAL TESTING

Rolf Oerter
University of Augsburg
Augsburg, Federal Republic of Germany

Environment and Individual: The Linkage of
Two Frames of Reference

Research in cognitive psychology has focused on cognitive
structures and operations in information processing systems (man or
computer). Structures and processes are analyzed independently of the
environmental structure. They are understood as general features of the
individual's cognitive capacity, which - though developing in
interaction with the environment - are seen as qualitatively completely
different from environmental structure. Thus, the concepts of
intelligence and of cognitive skills are genuinely "psychological,"
trying to explain human nature as an entity "sui generis," separable
from its environment (Resnick, 1976; Guilford, 1967; Piaget, 1946).

One of the consequences of this procedure has been the division
into contents and processes, or formal structures, respectively. On the
other hand, theories have focused on general formal features of
information processing and have neglected relations between contents and
structures or processes. Ecological research and ethology on the other
hand have concentrated on the common relationships between environment
and individual, calling into question the independence of environment
and individual (Bronfenbrenner, Note 1; Kelly, 1955; Leontjew, 1964).
A model will be presented that assumes the common relationships between
environmental structure and individual cognitive structure. On the
basis of this model some conclusions for cognitive development during
adolescence will be drawn. Finally, empirical evidence relating to the
model and cognitive development will be presented.

A Model of Cognitive Socialization

The principal assumption of the model is that isomorphism exists
between environmental structure and individual cognitive structure.
Environmental structure is named "objective structure" (OS). It is
conceived as the total structure of society comprehending nature
transformed by mankind and culture with its system of knowledge, its

375

social order, economic system, and its concrete material expression in
the form of products and goods.   The objective structure is to   be   seen
in   relation   to the subjective structure.   The latter concept comprises
human cognitive abilities, acquired as the result of learning,   as   well
as   basic   cognitive   unit   (Mischel, 1973) and the concept of cognitive
structure (Piaget, 1946;   Ausubel, 1967;   Flammer, Note 2).

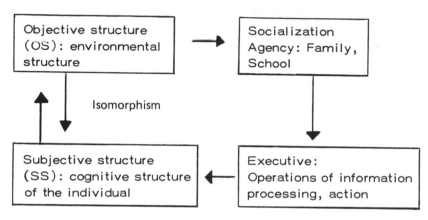

Figure 1. A simplified model of cognitive socialization (see Oerter et al., 1977).

        It is assumed that the   main   process   of   cognitive   socialization
consists   in   the   successive   transition   of   the   individual cognitive
structure (SS) from lower levels to higher levels of isomorphism between
subjective and objective structure.   Thus, the essential features of the
subjective structure cannot   be   found   in   general   formal   aspects   of
information   processing   but   rather   in   content aspects. Furthermore,
information processing seems to depend on contents and they are   assumed
to   be   isomorphic to processes or relations in the objective structure.
For example, logical thinking could not develop if logical relations did
not   exist   in   the   environment.   This statement is in accordance with
Piaget's position that the individual constructs the   physical   laws   by
assimilation   and   accommodation   of   the environment.   In Figure 1, two
subsystems   are   introduced   that   promote   the   process   of   producing
isomorphism   between OS and SS.   The first subsystem is the executive of
the   individual   (Neisser,   1967)   handling   the   actual   information
processing.   The executive also comprises actual external behavior that
produces results and effects in the environment.   Thus, the executive is
conceived   as   the   locus   of activity joining OS and SS.   This position
bears a close resemblance to the concept   of   activity (Tätigkeit)   in
Soviet   psychology   (Rubinstein,   1962;   Leontjew,   1964).   The second

subsystem is a part of the OS. Its functions are well known. However, let me make one important point: Family and school select a sample of elements from the OS and this sample need not to be representative for all regions of life, especially for professional life. Thus, one preliminary conclusion can be drawn: Effective instruction depends primarily on the selection of a representative sample of elements from the OS. Only under this condition will the individual be able to maintain transfer to regions outside of family and school.

Some Relevant Features of the OS

In order to understand cognitive development better and to describe cognitive capacity, it is necessary to look for relevant features of the OS that may determine the SS. Subsequently, we shall choose two categories as examples: (a) the category of work, and (b) the category of time. These categories together with the categories of object, life space, and organization are described in more detail in Oerter, Dreher, and Dreher (1977).

Work. This concepts seems to exist on at least five levels.

1. No separation between work (activity) and product. This level is realized in the OS as "nature" where animals are active without being aware of the results of their activities. In human structure this level is activated, for example, when the child is playing.

2. Separation of work and product, both remaining in relation to each other. In the OS this level can be observed when a concrete product is made; for example, when an artisan is making a special article. In the subjective structure this level is in operation, for example, when a child is building a tower or drawing a painting.

3. Separation between work and the contents of the result. This is the most common level in highly industrialized societies where everybody earns money for any kind of work. The general measure for work is the time spent working. In the SS we may infer the existence of this level when the individual is able to neglect a concrete valence of the task, as might be the case when a student achieves in order to get a good grade even though he is not interested in the subject at all.

4. Separation between work and effect. Using tools and machines corresponds to this level, but it is also reflected in the high status of the genius who produces extraordinary results apparently without appearing to make any effort. In the subjective structure this level is developed when the individual evaluates a result independently of the effort necessary for gaining the result.

5. Separation between the person and the work or the product, respectively. This level determines the economic processes where the products (goods) are not only separated from the process of work but

also from the persons who planned and organized their manufacture. The
SS on this level conceives the human being as an entity who is opposed
to the world and, simultaneously, is freed from activities directed
toward self-preservation.

     Time. As a second example the concept of time is analyzed and at
least four levels can be discerned.

     1. Time is not differentiated from the event as a whole.   There
exists a basic level in the OS where the speed of processes is
programmed by nature. Propagation is another example of programmed
sequence within an unchangeable time interval. On the corresponding
subjective level, the individual is active without being aware that time
passes.

     2. Time becomes an external factor. In the OS there are divisions
of daily periods and of the annual cycle as well as of the life cycle.
In the SS time is experienced within separate regions of the life space
(e.g., the daily round).

     3. Time becomes composed of duration (time   interval)   and
termination (time marks). In the OS work has to be done with a certain
time interval; in the SS time is experienced as an external condition
with the behavior being controlled by this condition.

     4. Time becomes an objective general entity. Now time is used as
a measure for work and time exists independently of individual human
beings. In the SS time is conceived as a general, uniform, universal
entity.

     The levels for the categories of "time" and "work" can be used in
predicting the development of cognitive structure during childhood and
adolescence. We may expect that the highest levels develop rather later
and will be built up only by the time adulthood is reached. Special
hypotheses can be formulated after some methods of measurement have been
described.

                Empirical Evidence: Three Developmental Studies

The Organization Problem

     The problem consists of ordering simultaneously presented tasks at
different places to be carried out within certain time limits. The
tasks are: Returning gloves to an acquaintance (locus: acquaintance;
3 min.   stay; time limit: 4:30 p.m.); fetching a book from a friend
(locus: school; time limit: 1:00 p.m.); sports for one and a half
hour (locus: playground;   time limits: from 2:30 p.m. until 4:00
p.m., plus 5 min. for changing clothes before and after sports);   and
buying stamps (locus: post office;   5 min stay; time limit: 6:00
p.m.). Distances between the different places are expressed as time

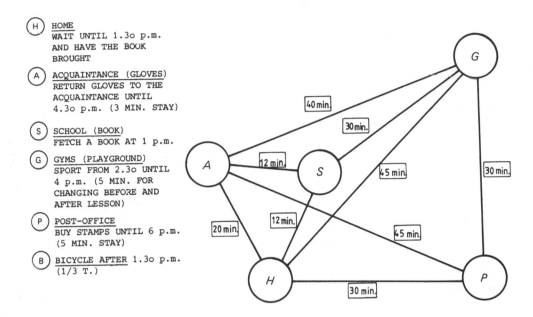

H HOME
WAIT UNTIL 1.3o p.m.
AND HAVE THE BOOK
BROUGHT

A ACQUAINTANCE (GLOVES)
RETURN GLOVES TO THE
ACQUAINTANCE UNTIL
4.3o p.m. (3 MIN. STAY)

S SCHOOL (BOOK)
FETCH A BOOK AT 1 p.m.

G GYMS (PLAYGROUND)
SPORT FROM 2.3o UNTIL
4 p.m. (5 MIN. FOR
CHANGING BEFORE AND
AFTER LESSON)

P POST-OFFICE
BUY STAMPS UNTIL 6 p.m.
(5 MIN. STAY)

B BICYCLE AFTER 1.3o p.m.
(1/3 T.)

Figure 2. Plan of the organization task.

distances, for example 20 min. from "home" to "acquaintance." Two
further conditions were introduced. First, one could stay at home until
a friend brings the book. In this case, he would arrive by 1:30 p.m.
The second condition is that one could use the bicycle, which is
available at 1:30 p.m., when the parents who have the key to the bicycle
return. By using the bicycle, only one-third of the time that is spent
for walking would be required.

Subjects and procedure. Six hundred and ninety subjects from grade
4 to 8 of the "Hauptschule" (elementary and secondary modern school) and
students in further education were tested under several conditions. The
information for the single tasks contained in the problem was printed on
cards that lay covered near the points on the plan marking each place,
and near the lines representing the routes. A special method of
recording was used that enabled the experimenter to record the
problem-solving behavior exactly.

Hypotheses and results. Only some hypotheses are selected because
the whole system of corresponding levels has not been described in
detail here (see Oerter et al., 1977).

Table 1.   Developmental Changes in Observing Time Limits

	subjects					
	4th grade	5th grade	6th grade	7th grade	8th grade	college students
solutions regarding time limits	25 (24)	32 (32)	39 (39)	54 (44)	39 (42)	138 (92)
solutions without regarding time limits	81 (76)	69 (68)	61 (61)	68 (56)	54 (58)	12 (8)
n	106 (100)	101 (100)	100 (100)	122 (100)	93 (100)	150 (100)

percent in brackets

$x^2 = 158.1$ s. $(p < .001)$ C = 0.44

1.   We expected that younger groups would take less notice of   time limits even though they had developed the time concept at a much earlier stage in their lives (Piaget, 1946).   This assumption   is   derived   from the   objectivation of time during development.   The results are shown in Table 1.   There is a gradual increase in observing time limits   followed by a marked ascent between 15-year-old students and adults.

2.   It was expected that older subjects would use the bicycle   more often   in   accordance with the level where tools and machines facilitate human work.   The results in Table 2 confirm this assumption: There is a gradual increase with age in using the bicycle.

3.   It was assumed that "having the book   brought"   is   more   often found   in   older groups according to the higher level of category "work" where persons become interchangeable and separated from the   process   of making   products.   The results are shown in Table 3.   It seems that the main developmental change occurs in late adolescence.   If this is   true, the   results   would   confirm   the   constructed sequence of level four to level five on the dimension of work.

Table 2.   Developmental Changes in Using the Bicycle as a Task Element

	4th grade	5th grade	subjects 6th grade	7th grade	8th grade	college students
solutions using the bicycle	28 (26)	22 (22)	38 (38)	56 (46)	43 (46)	120 (80)
solutions with walking all routes	78 (74)	79 (78)	62 (62)	66 (54)	50 (54)	30 (20)
n	106 (100)	101 (100)	100 (100)	122 (100)	93 (100)	150 (100)

percent in brackets

$x^2 = 110.65$ s. $(p < .001)$ $C = 0.37$

Table 3.   Developmental Changes in Using the Task Element "Having the Book Brought"

	4th - 6th grade	subjects 7th - 8th grade	college students
fetching the book	298 (97)	212 (95.5)	91 (61)
having the book brought	9 (3)	10 (4.5)	59 (39)
n	307 (100)	222 (100)	150 (100)

percent in brackets

comparison of grades 7/8 with adults $x^2 = 70.92$ s. $(p < .001)$

$$\phi = 0.43$$

The results presented in this section show that there is a remarkable gain in cognitive capacity during adolescence and youth. Until now there have not been many attempts to postulate new cognitive levels beyond the stages of Piaget. It seems that using real-life problems can help to diocover new dimensions of cognitive development that are more related to everyday life situations.

The Domino Game

In a next step of testing the model of isomorphism between OS and SS, we argued that the main condition for a successful solution of a problem must be a sufficient degree of isomorphism between SS and the problem situation. Thus, two problems with the same structure could offer different difficulties for the problem solver depending on whether isomorphism exists or not. In order to test this assumption a second problem was constructed that had a structure identical to that of the organization problem. The organization problem was transformed into a so-called Domino Game (Figure 3). The whole distance from 12:30 to 6:00 p.m. was represented as a long band on which the subject had to lay single stripes. The stripes represented all possible routes between the places. The stripes were ordered according to the places where the routes began. The bicycle condition was represented as stripes that were one-third as long. Different colored markers on the time band designated the time limits to be observed. For the subject, the task consisted of laying stripes on the long band whereby several rules had to be observed. The rules corresponded to the time limits given in the organization task. In effect, each type of stripe had to be ordered on the band without transgressing given demarcations. The condition of having the book brought could not be introduced. Thus, the structure of the Domino task was a little less complex than the structure of the organization task.

Fifteen subjects from each of three age groups from Hauptschule students (two secondary modern school groups, one of 11 years of age and the other 15 years of age, the final group being composed of students in further education) were run through the task individually. They solved, in varying sequence, the organization problem and the Domino Game. The material was presented as it is shown in Figure 3. The rules were printed on cards that lay covered above the band with the corresponding stripes lying below them. The subject could take as much time as he wanted. The amount of time needed for solution was recorded (for further detail see Oerter et al., 1977).

Hypotheses and results. It was expected that the Domino Game would be interpreted differently by different age groups. The rules of the game do not seem very meaningful for an adult. Thus, an adult might

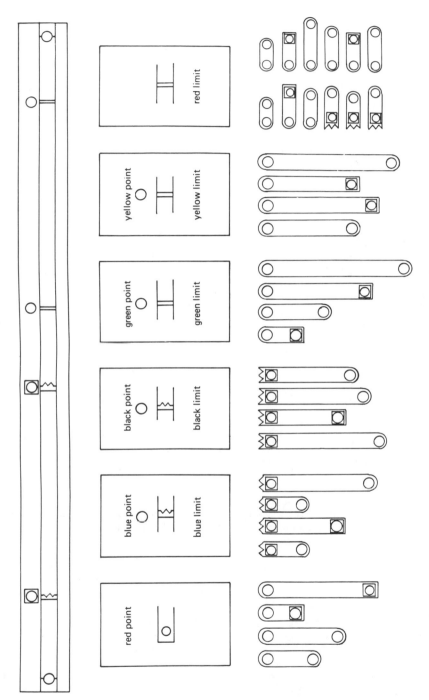

Figure 3. Domino task: materials.

spend more time solving the Domino Task than younger subjects. The
11-year old child, on the other hand, living in a world with many rules
that make no sense to him, would deal with the task without searching
for a deeper meaning. Comparing the organization task and the Domino
Task we should therefore expect an interaction of age and type of
problem: Adults would need less time for. the organization task and
spend more time in solving the Domino Task, whereas children would spend
more time on the organization problem than on the Domino Task.

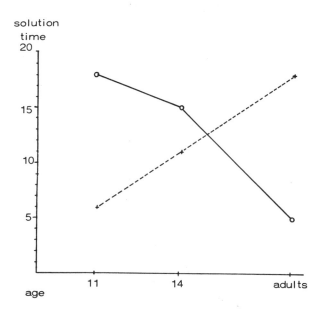

Figure 4. Interaction of task type and age in problem-solving behavior expressed in amount of time needed
for solution. (o ——— o, organization task; + – – – +, domino task).

The results as presented in Figure 4 show the predicted interaction
between age and task type. Notice that some adults spent more than 30
min solving the Domino problem! A second piece of evidence can be seen
in the number of correct solutions. The youngest group produced more
than twice the total of correct solutions to the Domino Problem than to
the organization problem. This result is in sharp contrast to the usual
assumption that a problem can be defined by structural features only.
It may stimulate further search for relevant features in the OS that
determine the SS via the principle of isomorphism.

Evaluation of Alternative Performance:
Developmental Change in the Concept of Work

In our discussion of different levels for the category of work, we
argued for an increasing separation of man and product.   One conclusion
was that an individual would reach a cognitive level where he would
evaluate performance more highly when it led to a product with a low
effort,   whereas   at   an   earlier   cognitive level of   socialization,
performance would be scored better when the person involved achieved a
product with great effort and diligence.   In order to examine the
expected change in evaluation of working processes, pairs of short
stories were presented in which a person performed a task either with
great industry but relatively low intelligence and creativity or with
more intelligence but low effort.   The subject was asked which of the
two persons performed better.   They were also asked how they would do
the job themselves and how their superior would judge their performance.
One hundred fifty subjects from age 11 to adulthood (student teachers)
were tested.   School type, grade, and sex were controlled.

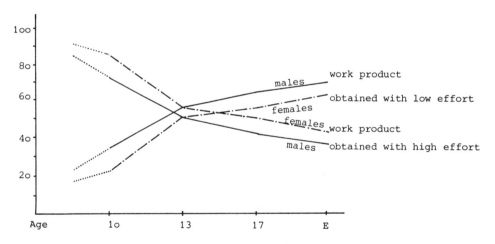

Figure 5. Developmental changes in evaluation of two different types of task performance. Notice that the
scores of 'low' vs. 'high' effort are dependent on each other marking the percentile number of
chosen alternatives.

As is discernible from Figure 5, there is a gradual change with age
in the expected direction.   However, there were substantial differences
between types of school and sexes.   For example, some groups attended
parochial schools and showed retardation in comparison with their
contemporaries who attended other schools.   Of course "retardation" in

this context means a level of isomorphism that is related to a segment
of the OS with typical traditional norms. Such norms are reflected in
some proverbs, for example "ohne Fleiss kein Preis" (a rolling stone
gathers no moss), "was du heute kannst hesorgen, das verschiebe nicht
auf morqen" (don't put off till tomorrow what you can do today).

Conclusions

The present results may provide encouragement for further studies
in our area. The following conclusions, though preliminary, may be
drawn:

1. Cognitive development continues during youth and adulthood.
There seem to be qualitatively new levels beyond the stage of formal
operations proposed by Piaget.

2. Cognitive development cannot be described with only formal
aspects of structure and operation, but may be more adequately conceived
by defining content features.

3. "Psychological absolutism" should be replaced by a form of
"psychological relativism" that takes account of aspects of a basic
environment-individual-interdependence.

The following are some interesting research directions suggested by
the present results:

1. Studying cognitive performance in complex everyday life
situations. This kind of research would prevent the construction of a
theory of cognitive processes that cannot be related to problem-solving
in real-life situations.

2. Studying cognitive development in youth and adulthood.
Variations in cognitive processes, dependent on individual and
developmental differences, may lead to a better understanding of
cognitive skills and structures.

3. A more systematic study of the objective structure, especially
of segments that are relevant for the individual during a specific
period of life. Analyzing the environmental structure may become the
key to understanding an individual's reasoning in a specific situation.

4. The comparison of OS segments within and outside of school and
derivation of corresponding differences in the subjective structure.
Similarities and dissimilarities between environmental structures may be
responsible for consistency and inconsistency in the subjective
structure.

Reference Notes

1. Bronfenbrenner, U.   The ecology of human development in retrospect and prospect.   Paper presented at the International Conference of Ecological Factors in Human Development, sponsored by the International Society for the Study of Behavioral Development, University of Surrey, Guilford, England, July, 1975.

2. Flammer, A.   Individuelle kognitive Strukturen und Lernoptimierung.   Referat auf dem Symposium Anwendungsorientierte Diagnostik, Bad Homburg, 1975.

References

Ausubel, D. P. A cognitive structure theory of school learning. In L. Siegel (Ed.), Instruction: Some contemporary viewpoints. San Francisco: Chandler, 1967.

Guilford, J. P. The nature of intelligence. New York: McGraw Hill, 1967.

Kelly, G. A. The psychology of personal constructs. New York: Norton, 1955.

Leontjew, A. N. Probleme der Entwicklung des Psychischen. Berlin: VEB, 1964.

Mischel, W. Toward a cognitive social learning reconceptualization of personality. Psychological Review, 1973, 80, 253-283.

Neisser, U. Cognitive psychology. New York: Appleton, 1967.

Oerter, R., Dreher, E., & Dreher, M.   Kognitive Sozialisation und subjektive Struktur. München: Oldenbourg, 1977.

Piaget, j. Psychologie der Intelligenz. Zurich: Rascher, 1946.

Resnick, L. B. (Ed.) The nature of intelligence. New York: Lawrence Erlbaum Associates, 1976.

Rubinstein, S. L. Sein und Bawusstsein. Berlin: VEB, 1962.

COGNITION, INSTRUCTION, DEVELOPMENT, AND INDIVIDUAL DIFFERENCES

Robert S. Siegler
Carnegie-Mellon University
Pittsburgh, Pennsylvania, U.S.A.

The purpose of this paper is to address four questions in the areas of cognition, instruction, development, and individual differences. The questions are the following:

1. What states of knowledge underlie different levels of task performance?

2. What are the alternative strategies that might result in any given level of task performance?

3. For a particular level of performance, what is the optimal level of difficulty for an instructional sequence?

4. When and why will two learners at the same initial performance level learn differently from the same instructional sequence?

All of these questions, and Question one in particular, demand rigorous methods for assessing what individual children know. Siegler (1976) described one such methodology based on two assumptions. One assumption is that children's problem solving strategies are rule-governed, with the rules progressing in sophistication with age. The second assumption is that a powerful means of validating hypothesized rule progressions is to create problem sets that yield sharply differing patterns of correct answers and errors, depending on what rule is being used. Within this framework, developmental decrements in performance are particularly revealing. That is, if younger children consistently adhere to Rule A and older children to Rule B, and neither rule is entirely correct, it should be possible to create types of problems on which the younger children will be correct more often than the older ones. To the extent that developmental decrements in performance are unusual, the validity of the hypothesized rule progression would receive relatively strong confirmation from such findings. In addition, to the extent that individual children's patterns of correct answers and errors corresponded to those predicted, the rules would be supported as characterizations of individual performance.

389

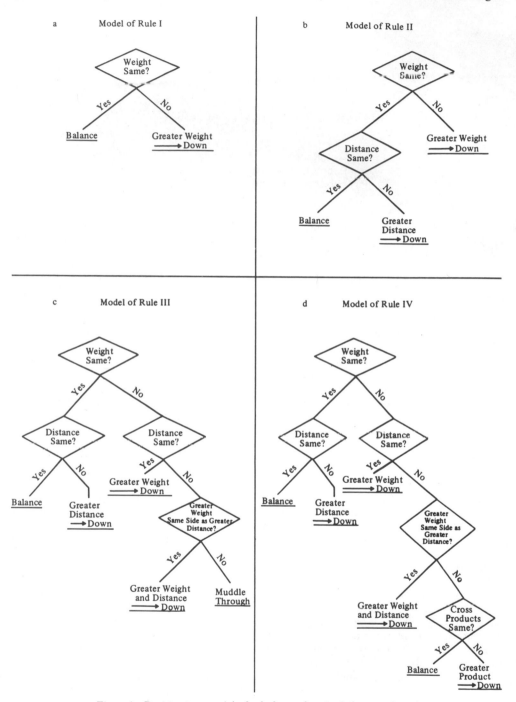

Figure 1. Decision tree model of rule for performing balance scale task.

The way in which this system works is best illustrated by an example. In an earlier paper (Siegler, 1976), I applied the methodology to a variant of Inhelder and Piaget's (1958) balance scale problem. The type of balance scale that was used consisted of a two arm balance, with several pegs located at equal intervals along each arm. Small circular disks, all of equal weight, were placed on the pegs in various configurations, while the balance was prevented from tipping by means of a lever. The subjects' basic task was to predict the direction in which the balance scale would move if it were allowed to do so.

A rational task analysis of the balance scale problem, Inhelder and Piaget's (1958) empirical description, and my own pilot work suggested that the different types of knowledge that children have about this task could be represented in the form of binary decision trees (Figure 1). A child using Rule I considers only the numbers of weights on each side: If they are the same, the child predicts balance, otherwise he predicts that the side with the greatest weight will go down. For a Rule II child, a difference in weight still is conclusive, but if weight is equal on the two sides, then the distance dimension is also considered. In this latter case, if the distances from the fulcrum are unequal, the child predicts that the side with the weight further away will go down; otherwise, the two sides will balance. A child using Rule III tests both weight and distance in all cases. If both dimensions are equal, the child predicts balance; if only one is equal, then the other one determines the outcome; if they are both unequal, but on the same side with respect to their inequality, then that side will go down. In a situation in which one side has the greater weight while the other has the weights farther from the fulcrum, however, a Rule III child does not have a consistent way to resolve the conflict. Therefore, he simply "muddles through" or guesses. Finally, Rule IV represents mature knowledge of the task; the child computes the torques on each side by multiplying the amounts of weight on each peg by the peg's ordinal distance from the fulcrum (the pegs are equidistant from each other, so that the third peg from the fulcrum is three times as far away as the first one), and then compares the sums of the products on the two sides. Thus, if there were five weights on the third peg to the left of the fulcrum, and four weights on the fourth peg to the right, $5 \times 3 = 15$; $4 \times 4 = 16$; $15 < 16$; so right side down.

But how can we determine whether children are actually using these rules? This is where the rule assessment methodology comes in. It is possible to establish which - if any - of these four rules accurately describe a child's knowledge by examining his pattern of predictions for the following six types of problems (see Table 1 for an example of each type):

1. Balance problems, with the same configuration of weights on pegs on each side of the balance.

Table 1.   Predictions for Percentage of Correct Answers and Error Patterns on Posttest for Children Using Different Rules

Problem type	Rules				Predicted developmental trend
	I	II	III	IV	
Balance	100	100	100	100	No change-all children at high level
Weight	100	100	100	100	No change-all children at high level
Distance	0 (Should say "balance")	100	100	100	Dramatic improvement with age
Conflict-weight	100	100	33 (Chance responding)	100	Decline with age Possible upturn in oldest group
Conflict-distance	0 (Should say "right down")	0 (Should say "right down")	33 (Chance responding)	100	Improvement with age
Conflict-balance	0 (Should say "right down")	0 (Should say "right down")	33 (Chance responding)	100	Improvement with age

2. Weight problems, with unequal amounts of weight equidistant from the fulcrum.

3. Distance problems, with equal amounts of weight different distances from the fulcrum.

4. Conflict-weight problems, with more weight on one side and more "distance" (i.e., occupied pegs further from the fulcrum) on the other, and the configuration arranged so that the side with more weight goes down.

5. Conflict-distance problems, similar to conflict-weight except that the side with greater distance goes down.

   6. Conflict-balance problems, like other conflict problems, except that the scale remains balanced.

   Children whose knowledge corresponded to the different rules would display dramatically different patterns of predictions on the six types of problems. Those using Rule I would consistently make correct predictions on balance, weight, and conflict-weight problems, and they would never be correct on the three other problem types. Children using Rule II would behave similarly, but they would also correctly solve distance problems. Those following Rule III would consistently make accurate predictions on weight, balance, and distance problems, and would perform at a chance level on all conflict items. Those using Rule IV would solve all problems of all types.

   To the extent that there is a correlation between children's ages and the rules that best represent their knowledge, there should be a clear developmental pattern on each problem types. Most interesting is the predicted developmental decrement in performance on conflict-weight problems. Younger children, using Rules I and II, should consistently get these problems right, while older children, using Rule III, will "muddle through" on them and be correct only one-third of the time. Another prediction of the rule models is that performance on distance problems should show the most dramatic improvement with age, from 0% correct for those who use Rule I, to 100% correct on all subsequent rules. Finally, there should be consistently correct responding among children using all rules on balance and on weight problems.

   These predictions have been primarily at the group level. The rule models also allow unambiguous prediction of individual performance. That is, the statement that a child is using Rule I or Rule II or Rule IV should tell us what response he will make on each posttest problem. On any item, a child can predict one of three outcomes: The left side will go down, the right side will go down, or the scale will balance. Given the usual 24 item posttest (four items from each of the six problem types) this means that there are 3^{24} distinct possible patterns of responses; of these, less than one-millionth fit the criterion for rule usage that has been adopted (20 of 24 responses conforming to a rule). Thus, the likelihood that a random responder would be misclassified as using a rule is almost nonexistent. In addition, to insure that children are in fact using the particular rule that we say they are, rather than some related formula, supplementary internal safeguards have been adopted. For example, in addition to the 20 of 24 total response criterion, children classified as using Rule I must also say "it will balance" on at least three of the four distance problems; those classified as using Rules II, III, or IV must choose the side with the weights farther from the fulcrum on at least three of the four problems. These supplementary criteria add to the discriminatory power of the rule classifications.

As mentioned earlier, this methodology has been applied to Inhelder and Piaget's balance scale problem; 5, 9, 13, and 17-year-olds who attended a girls' upper-middle class private school in Pittsburgh were presented the various problems. It was found that the rule models accurately characterized the predictions of 90% of the individual children. This ranged from 80% of the 5-year-olds to 100% of the 17-year-olds. The rule models were successful in characterizing both children's spontaneous performance and their performance following instruction. Children's explanations of how they made their choices closely followed their predictions; more than 90% of children were classified as using the same rule on the two measures by "blind" raters. The expectations at the group level were also confirmed. Performance on conflict-weight problems declined from 89% correct among the 5-year-olds to 51% correct among the 17-year-olds. Performance improved most dramatically on the distance problems, from 9% correct among 5-year-olds to 88% correct among 9-year-olds and 100% correct among 13 and 17 year-olds. Finally, performance was consistently high on weight and balance problems, ranging from 88% to 100% correct among the various age groups. Thus, there was considerable support for the rule models as characterizations of children's knowledge, both at the level of individuals and at the level of groups.

A number of other tasks have been studied using this rule assessment methodology, including Inhelder and Piaget's (1958) projection of shadows task, Bruner and Kenney's (1966) water jar task, and a probability concept task described by Chapman (1975). In each case, the proposed rules have been found to characterize the performance of more than 80% of children aged 5 to 17 years at a level of probability extremely unlikely to be the product of a random response process (cf. Siegler, in press). Thus the rule assessment methodology allows precise answers to Question One - it leads to explicit characterizations of the differences in knowledge that underlie different levels of task performance.

Klahr and Siegler (in press) focused on Question Two, the issue of alternative strategies resulting in a given level of performance. The emphasis here was on possible strategic variations among children using a particular rule (Rule III) on the balance scale task. The initial methodology was closely related to that used previously, but differed slightly in that impromptu questions, intended to reveal the child's underlying reasoning, were used to supplement the usual predictions test. Videotapes were made of the children's performance and their reactions to the experimenter's questions to allow detailed and repeated scrutiny of all that transpired; the videotapes were subsequently used as the raw data for production system analyses. These production systems allowed us to identify substantial variation in the way that children who were ostensibly using the same rule reached their predictions.

Consider the reactions of one 8-year-old girl, Jan, to experience with balance scale problems. The most striking feature of Jan's comments was the way in which she appeared to represent distance and weight on conflict problems. Both dimensions were treated as dichotomous; more than two weights were treated as "big"; otherwise weight was "little"; if the third or fourth peg was occupied, then distance was "big"; otherwise it was "little." If there was "big weight" on one side and "big distance" on the other, Jan would decide on the basis of an index that shifted from reliance on one dimension to reliance on the other each time a response was made. The production system correctly predicted 11 of Jan's 12 responses to the conflict problems, a considerable improvement over the previous Rule III prediction that children would "muddle through" on them.

This analysis raises some provocative questions concerning the relative advantages and disadvantages of the production system and decision tree representations. Production systems offer the advantage of providing considerably greater detail about what each child is doing, and also are closely linked to an emerging general theory of human cognition (cf. Klahr & Wallace, 1976). On the other hand, the decision trees are testable to a much greater extent and can go beyond the mass of details likely to be present in individual performance to bring out underlying age-related unities. Which language is preferable therefore appears to depend largely on the purpose of the investigation (cf. Klahr & Siegler, in press).

Question Three concerns the optimal level of difficulty for an instructional sequence. One common research approach to this problem has been to compare the efficacy of "near" training to that of "far" training. The issue has tended to be defined along the lines of the stage issue. Advocates of Piaget's (1970), Kohlberg's (1969), and Werner's (1948) stage systems have argued that children derive relatively little benefit from training that is far beyond their existing level, because they are unable to assimilate it; this argument has been made for conservation tasks (Strauss, 1972), class inclusion tasks (Kuhn, 1972), and moral development tasks (Turiel, 1966). Non-stage theorists, on the other hand, have argued that such findings are due to measurement artifacts, and that learning is independent of developmental stage (Bandura, 1969; Brainerd, 1977). The rule assessment methodology seemed to provide a useful metric for investigating the question, since it gave an unambiguous meaning to the phrases "near training" and "far training" (training on problems that are one rule versus two rules advanced from the learner's existing knowledge).

I have addressed the near versus far training issue within the context of studying developmental differences in learning. The research is aimed at a hypothetical question: If two children of different ages but with identical initial knowledge about a task are presented the same learning experience, will they emerge with the same final knowledge? The experiments have three phases: pretest, feedback, and posttest. In the pretest session, children of different ages, say 5 and 8-year-olds, are selected for spontaneously using a particular rule, say Rule I. Then, in the feedback session, they are given experience with control problems (problems at their existing level), near problems (problems that will be mastered in the rule immediately beyond their level), or far problems (problems two or more rules advanced). Finally, after their experience, they are given the usual posttest.

Table 2. Number of Children Using Different Rules—Experiment 2

		Rule			
Age and treatment		Rule I	Rule II	Rule III	Unclassifiable
5-year-olds	Control	8	0	0	2
	Distance problems	3	4	1	2
	Conflict problems	5	0	0	5
8-year-olds	Control	5	3	0	2
	Distance problems	0	8	1	1
	Conflict problems	0	2	5	3
	Total	21	17	7	15

The results of two experiments of this type, one involving the balance scale task and one involving the projection of shadows task, are shown in Table 2. The results indicate that the relative efficacy of near and far problems depends on the ages of the learners and on the particular problems involved. On the balance scale task, both 5 and 8-year-olds benefitted from the near training; substantial numbers of children of each age moved from Rule I to Rule II. Given the far training, by contrast, the reactions of the two age groups differed; 8-year-olds derived substantial benefits, often advancing to Rule III, while 5-year-olds derived no benefits whatsoever. On the shadows task, the 8-year-olds derived greater benefits from both the near and the far problems; neither type of experience proved of much help to the 5-year-olds. Thus, as any good, seasoned teacher could doubtlessly have told us, there is no absolute answer to the near versus far training issue, nor to the more general issue of the optimal level of instructional difficulty. It depends at minimum on the ages of the children, the particular task involved, and the particular instructional procedure.

The variable effects of far instruction on the balance scale problem led directly to Question Four: Why will two learners at the same initial level of knowledge learn differently from a particular instructional sequence? The above-mentioned protocol and production system analyses, together with past research reports such as those of Hagen (1972), Gelman (1969), and Pick, Christy, and Frankel (1972) led to the encoding hypothesis - "Five-year-olds are less able to acquire new information than 8-year-olds because their encoding of stimuli is less adequate." That is, it appeared from detailed observation that young children either encoded the balance scale configuration in terms of absolute values such as "big" and "little," or they did not encode the distance dimension at all, merely attending to the amounts of weight. The question was how to test this hypothesis. It seemed that several converging types of evidence would allow reasonable opportunity for disconfirmation. If the encoding hypothesis was correct, it would seem to have the following directing implications: (a) that if a measure of encoding independent of predictive knowledge could be devised, it would reveal that both 5 and 8-year-olds correctly encoded weight, but that only the 8-year-olds encoded distance; and (b) that if it were possible to teach 5-year-olds to encode both dimensions, then they would be able to benefit from the "far" instruction that previously had aided only the older children.

The first step was to find a means by which children's encoding could be assessed independent of their predictive performance. Chase and Simon's (1973) reconstruction paradigm suggested a means by which this could be accomplished. Their experiment involved briefly presenting chess masters and non-masters with either organized or disorganized arrangements of chess pieces, and then asking them to reproduce the exact configuration of pieces that they had observed. Chess masters were found to be greatly superior in reproducing the ordered arrangements, but not at all more accurate in reproducing the random ones. The explanation advanced was that the chess masters imposed a high level organization on the orderly arrangements that they could not impose on disorganized configurations, and that was never available to non-masters.

In the current experiments, older and younger children were briefly presented arrangements of weights on pegs of the balance scale. Then the scale was hidden from sight, and a second identical scale was presented; the task was to reproduce on the second balance scale the arrangement of disks on pegs that had been observed on the first apparatus. It should be noted that this paradigm allowed fully independent assessment of encoding on the weight and distance dimensions. A child could reproduce the correct amount of weight on each side of the fulcrum, could reproduce the correct distance of the weights from the fulcrum, could do both, or could do neither.

The prediction that followed from the encoding hypothesis was that older children, who had learned from the far training, would encode both weight and distance dimensions, while younger children, who had not, would encode only the weight dimension. This prediction was tested in Experiment 3a by presenting 5 and 8-year-olds with 26 encoding problems in which they were told that their job was to "look how the weights are set on the pegs on my balance scale and then make the same problem by putting the weights on the pegs on yours." Children were allowed to observe the initial configuration for 10 seconds; there was no time limit for reproduction, though both 5 and 8-year-olds usually finished quickly.

Table 3.   Percentage of Correct Encodings—Experiment 3

	5-year-olds		8-year-olds	
Experiment	Weight encodings	Distance encodings	Weight encodings	Distance encodings
3a	51	16	73	56
3b	54	9		
3c	54	19	64	73
3d	52	51	72	76

As shown in Table 3, the pattern of performance on the encoding task was as the encoding hypothesis predicted. Eight-year-olds performed well on both weight and distance dimensions; 5-year-olds did almost as well as the older children on the weight dimension, but far more poorly on the distance dimension. Thus, the first criterion appeared to be met.

Before continuing to the second criterion, there were several alternative interpretations of the initial finding that needed to be considered. One was that the younger children would have been able to encode in the same way as the older ones, but simply did not have sufficient time. To test this interpretation, in Experiment 3b a new group of 5-year-olds were provided the same problems, but with 15 rather than 10 sec exposure. The results, shown in Table 3, were similar to those previously found. It remained logically possible that still longer times would have produced different results, but the lack of any trend in this direction, and the observation that most of the children said they were ready to do the reproduction before the end of the 15 seconds, seemed to indicate against the possibility.

Another alternative interpretation was that the 5-year-olds simply did not understand the task, that is, did not understand that both weight and distance dimensions were important. Therefore, in Experiment 3c the instructions were adjusted to be extremely explicit:

> The idea for the first game is for you to look at how the weights are set on the pegs on the balance scale, and then to make the same problem by putting the weights on the pegs on yours. You want it to be the same problem in two ways. You want the same number of weights on each side of

your   scale   as I had on my scale, and you want the weights
on each side of your scale to be the same distance from the
center as they were on my scale.

Again, the alternative interpretation was not supported by the evidence.
The pattern of performance was similar on distance and weight dimensions
for the 8-year-olds, but the 5-year-olds were considerably   less
successful in encoding distance than weight (Table 3).

Now the second test could be attempted: Would it be possible to
teach 5-year-olds to encode both dimensions, and if so, would this lead
to their being able to benefit from the far training?   First, in
Experiment 3d an attempt was made to teach children of both ages how to
encode. The instructions were the same as those quoted above, until
children were told that they wanted "the same number of weights on each
side of your scale as I had on my scale and . . . the weights on each
side of your scale to be the same distance from the center as they were
on my scale." Then they were told:

> You do it like this. First you count the number of
> weights on this side - one, two, three, four. Then you
> count the number of pegs the weights are from the center -
> first, second, third.   So you say to yourself, "four
> weights on the third peg." Then you would do the same for
> the other side - one, two, three, four, five weights on the
> first, second, third peg. So it would be five weights on
> the third peg.   Then you would say, "four weights on the
> third peg and five weights on the third peg." Then you
> would put the right numer of weights on the right pegs on
> each side.

The child and experimenter did this procedure together for seven trials,
with the child taking increasing responsibility for its execution.   Then
the child was given the usual encoding and predictions tasks.

This encoding instruction changed the pattern of 5-year-olds'
encoding substantially and as predicted. As shown in Table 3, they now
correctly encoded 52% of problems on the weight dimension and 51% on the
distance dimension.   The corresponding figures for 8-year-olds were 72%
and 76%. Thus, while the absolute levels of performance differed
between the age groups, the patterns of encoding on weight and distance
dimensions were very similar.   The procedure had no effect on children's
predictive performance;   the large majority continued to use Rule I.
This was clear evidence that the instruction did not constitute a
general shotgun approach to teaching children about the balance scale,
but rather was focused on the proposed explanatory variable, encoding.

This set the stage for the second major test. If encoding was the
factor that prevented young children from learning, and now they knew
how to encode, they now should be able to learn.   Therefore, in
Experiment 3c, 5 and 8-year-olds who had been given encoding instruction

were brought back and given the far training sequence described previously. If the encoding hypothesis was correct, both groups would now be able to benefit.

Table 4.   Number of Children Using Rules—Experiment 3

		Rules used			
Experiment	Age	I	II	III	Unclassifiable
3a	5-years	9	0	0	1
	8-years	8	1	0	1
3b	5-years	7	0	0	3
3c	5-years	7	0	0	3
	8-years	6	2	1	1
3d	5-years	6	0	0	4
	8-years	6	1	0	3
3e	5-years	1	3	4	2
	8-years	0	3	7	0

As shown in Table 4, this was indeed the case. Where previously, none of the 10 5-year-olds benefitted from the instruction, now 7 of 10 did. At the very least, reducing the differential encoding substantially reduced the differential responsiveness to experience that had been present earlier.

A similar set of experiments has been undertaken to explain the differential reactions of 5 and 8-year-olds to experience with the projection of shadows task. In this task children had been asked to judge which of two T-shaped bars, differing in horizontal span and in distance from a light source, would cast a longer shadow or whether the shadows would be the same lengths (cf. Siegler, 1977). As on the balance scale task, 8-year-olds, initially using the same performance rule as 5-year-olds, had been much better able to learn new, more sophisticated strategies. First, it was established that the encodings of the shadows task differed; 8-year-olds encoded both the span of the bar and its distance from the light source, while the 5-year-olds encoded only the bar's span. Then it was demonstrated that 5-year-olds could be taught to encode both dimensions through an instructional procedure patterned directly after the balance scale instruction. Then the final test - some 5 and 8-year-olds were given the near training, and others the far training, neither of which had previously been helpful to the younger children.

As in the balance scale task, following encoding training, the reactions to experience of the two age groups were similar; both benefitted from near training, neither benefitted from far training. This is consistent with earlier findings that the shadows task is generally more difficult than the balance scale (cf. Lee, 1971); it also supports the view that the encoding hypothesis may explain a substantial part of the differential ability of older and younger children to learn on a variety of problems.

New Directions

This program of research is currently being extended in a number of directions. One involves its application to new psychological tasks, among them Bruner and Kenney's (1966) water jar problem, Chapman's (1975) probability concept problem, and some traditional conservation problems (cf. Siegler & Vage, in press). On all of these tasks, the proposed rule systems have proved to be accurate characterizations of children's predictive performance. Another new direction involves extending the work to younger children, 3 and 4-year-olds. This line of research suggests that, at least on the above-described tasks, rule usage is something that develops; 3-year-olds do not use any of the proposed rules on the balance scale, shadows, or probability tasks; approximately 50% of 4-year-olds perform in a rule-governed manner, and between 80% and 90% of 5-year-olds do (cf. Siegler, in press). This finding raises the issue of whether rule-governedness, as such, is a basic dimension of development. Finally, research is in progress to determine the consistency of rule usage both across tasks and across time. Preliminary results indicate that children tend to use rules of comparable complexity over a variety of different tasks, and that they tend to use the same rule on a given test over different occasions.

References

Bandura, A. Principles of behavior modification. New York: Holt, Rinehart, & Winston, 1969.

Brainerd, C. J. Cognitive development and concept learning: An interpretive review. Psychological Bulletin, 1977, in press.

Bruner, J. S., & Kenney, H. On relational concepts. In J. S. Bruner, R. R. Olver, & P. M. Greenfield (Eds.), Studies in cognitive growth. New York: Wiley, 1966.

Chapman, R. H.   The   development   of   children's   understanding   of
    proportions. Child Development, 1975, 46, 141-148.

Chase, W. G., & Simon, H. A.   The mind's eye in chess.   In W. G. Chase
    (Ed.), Visual information processing. New York: Academic Press,
    1973.

Gelman, R. Conservation acquisition: A problem of learning to attend
    to relevant attributes. Journal of Experimental Child Psychology,
    1969, 7, 167-187.

Hagen, J. W. Strategies for remembering. In S. Farnham-Diggory (Ed.),
    Information processing in children.   New York: Academic Press,
    1972.

Inhelder, B., & Piaget, J.   The growth of logical thinking from
    childhood to adolescence. New York: Basic Books, 1958.

Klahr, D., & Siegler, R. S. The representation of children's knowledge.
    In H.   Reese & L. Lipsitt (Eds.), Advances in child development
    and behavior, Volume 12, in press.

Klahr, D., & Wallace, J. G.   Cognitive   development: An
    information-processing view. Hillsdale, NJ: Erlbaum, 1976.

Kohlberg, L. Stage and sequence: The cognitive development approach to
    socialization.   In D. A. Goslin (Ed.), Handbook of socialization
    theory and research. Chicago: Rand-McNally, 1969.

Kuhn, D.   Mechanisms of change in the development of cognitive
    structures. Child Development, 1972, 43, 833-844.

Lee, L. C. The concommitant development of cognitive and moral modes of
    thought: A test of selected deductions from Piaget's theory.
    Genetic Psychology Monographs, 1971, 85, 93-146.

Piaget, J. Piaget's theory. In P. H. Mussen (Ed.), Carmichael's
    manual of child psychology, Volume 1. New York: Wiley, 1970.

Pick, A. D., Christy, M. D., & Frankel, G. W. A developmental study of
    visual   selective   attention.   Journal of Experimental Child
    Psychology, 1972, 14, 165-175.

Siegler, R. S.   Three aspects of cognitive development.   Cognitive
    Psychology, 1976, 8, 481-520.

Siegler, R. S. The origins of scientific reasoning. In R. S. Siegler
    (Ed.), Children's thinking: What develops?   Hillsdale, NJ:
    Erlbaum, in press.

Siegler, R. S., & Vage, S.   The   development   of   a   proportionality concept: Judging relative fullness.   Journal of Experimental Child Psychology, 1977, in press.

Strauss, S.   Inducing cognitive development and learning: A   review   of short-term   training experiments.   I.   The organismic-developmental approach.   Cognition, 1972, 1, 329-357.

Turiel, E.   An experimental test of the sequentiality   of   developmental stages   in   the child's moral judgment.   Journal of Personality and Social Psychology, 1966, 3, 611-618.

Werner, H.   Comparative psycholgoy of   mental   development.   New   York: International Universities Press, 1948.

ON THE MEANING OF NONCONSERVATION

Ron Gold
University of Oxford
Oxford, England, U.K.

In this brief paper, I would like to address myself to the question of whether young children's failure on Piaget's (1952) conservation task indicates a genuine belief in nonconservation. All of you will be familiar with the conservation task: The young child is given, for example, two rows of counters in one-one correspondence, and agrees that the rows have equal numbers of buttons. One row is then expanded or contracted and the child now says that one of the rows (usually the longer) has more than the other. Obviously, the child does not understand the question asked of him in the way an adult understands it. The issue is, however, why he doesn't understand it.

Piaget's position is clear. The child, he says, doesn't understand the question because he can't understand it, because he doesn't have the concept being asked about. The question refers to the number n of counters present. But what is this concept n other than that which is conserved? In the absence of conservation, n has no meaning. When Piaget says, therefore, that nonconservation is due to a conceptual deficit, this is merely to say that the child genuinely fails to realize that the number remains constant. Thus, Piaget (1952) says:

> It would be absurd to suggest that they imagine that the actual number of objects varies, since the basis of our whole interpretation is our belief that these children do not yet possess the notion of number. (p. 48)

Other workers in the field have, however, disagreed with this point of view. Gelman (1969) and Bryant (1972) have, for example, argued that the nonconservation response does not reflect a genuine belief in nonconservation, that it is a failure in performance rather than competence. They argue that the young child does have the concept n at his disposal, that he does conserve. He gets the question wrong, they argue, because his attention is drawn to features of the problem other than n, and this leads him to misinterpret the question asked. The salient difference in length between the rows of counters causes the child to be tricked into thinking that the question refers to this dimension rather than to n, and he answers accordingly. It isn't that

405

he can't understand the question, but that he misunderstands it.   The
fault is the E's: Were the question posed clearly, the S could   get   it
right.

     So this is the problem.   Does the response reflect a genuine belief
in   nonconservation   or   not?   Is   it   due to a conceptual deficit (and
therefore relatively profound in Piaget's terms), or   due   merely   to   a
linguistic deficit (relatively trivial according to Piaget)?

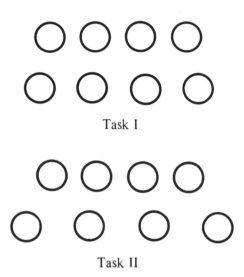

Task I

Task II

Figure 1. Post-transformation displays in two conservation-of-number tasks.

     What sort of evidence bears on this question?   It   is   tempting   to
cite   pairs   of similar tasks, in which one is easier than the other, as
relevant.   Consider,   for   example,   Figure   1,   in   which   the
post-transformation   presentations   of two number conservation tasks are
shown.   Task I is slightly easier than task II, and it   is   tempting   to
argue   that if the child doesn't misunderstand the question as referring
to length in I, he must also not misunderstand it in   II,   so   that   his
incorrect   response   in   the   latter   must   be due to the absence of the
necessary concept.

     Just such arguments are used by Piaget to   support   his   view   that
incorrect   responses   are   due   to   conceptual   failure.   On reflection,
however, the reasoning is seen to be specious.   The   disparity   between
the row lengths is much greater in the case of II than in the case of I,

so that the child's attention would be drawn to length much more in the former. According to Gelman and Bryant's theory, this greater attention to length would cause the child to misinterpret the question more often, so that, contrary to Piaget's assumption, misinterpretation of the question would be more likely to occur in II than in I.

Intuitively, indeed, Piaget's argument could equally well be turned on its head. It might be claimed that a child who exhibits the concept "four" in one situation (task I) must also have that concept in another (task II), so that his incorrect response in the latter must be due to misunderstanding of the question. Again, however, this reasoning is specious. Just as Piaget claims, a concept may be present in one context but absent in another; there is no reason why it should be acquired all of a piece, independently of the situation in which it is applied.

How, then, may one decide whether nonconservation is due to absence of a concept or to misinterpretation of the question? I suggest that the problem demands the use of a training study. It would be a somewhat unusual one, however, for its essential feature would be that no concept of conservation at all would be taught. Rather, the aim would simply be to teach the nonconserver what the conservation question is about in order to cause him to reinterpret it correctly.

How can one be sure that no concept has in fact been taught in a successful training study? The primary criterion would seem to involve the ease of acquisition. To the extent that a difficult concept is lacking in the nonconserver, it should take time and effort for it to be acquired; the acquisition curve should reflect this comparatively slow attainment. While such a curve, if it occurred in the training phase, could not definitely be said to show concept acquisition rather than reinterpretation of the question, the possibility of the former could not be ruled out. Only where an acquisition is virtually instantaneous can one legitimately infer that no substantive concept has been taught. That is, only where the subjects respond correctly right from the start of the training session, as well as in the posttest, can one say that no concept has been taught.

What sort of training is most likely to yield such a result? It would involve giving the child an extremely easy task, in which the number cue n is highly salient. The aim would simply be to develop in the subject a set to interpret the questions asked of him in terms of n. One would then see whether this set is spontaneously and fully generalized to the normal conservation task given in the posttest. If this occurs, it seems likely that the successful "training" was due simply to the reinterpretation by the subject of the experimenter's question, and not to the acquisition of a conservation concept as such.

I would now like to describe a study that seems to me to be of this type. In the normal number conservation task, the subject is asked a question of the form "Do the rows have the same number of buttons, or does one row have more buttons?" I wanted to compare this with a condition in which the subjects were asked instead how many buttons there were in the post-transformation rows, given no other information than the number that had been there before the transformation. In this condition, subjects are asked to reply in terms of a specific number of buttons, rather than in terms of global judgments, such as "more"; I will, therefore, refer to this task as the specific number task.

In the experiment, all subjects were given both the normal task and the specific number task. Half the subjects received the normal task first, and half the specific number task first. Two days separated the presentation of the different tasks.

Each task began in the same way, with two rows of counters being presented in one-one correspondence. Subjects counted each row and were asked three questions: "Do the rows have the same number of buttons? Does this row have more buttons? Does that row have more buttons?" (These three standard questions will be referred to collectively as the "SMM question.") Subjects who failed to assert the pre-transformation equality were eliminated. For the subjects who did agree that the sets were equal, the transformation (expansion or contraction) was then performed. The procedure following this differed for the two types of task: (a) In the normal task, subjects were asked the SMM question again. (b) In the specific number task, subjects were asked how many counters there would be now if they counted each of the rows. (The question about the untransformed row was included in order to check that the subjects remembered how many counters there had been before the transformation.) On the first two trials, if they hesitated before replying, the question was repeated, thus: "How many are there really?"

Six trials of each task were given with equal numbers of counters (four, five, or six) in each row. A seventh trial, in which one counter was added to one of the lines, was used to detect subjects who had given correct responses mindlessly on the equality trials. The subjects ranged in age from four years ten months to six years five months.

Within each task, subjects tended to get all trials right or none at all. The results are summarized in Table 1, the criterion for correct response being five out of six equality trials plus the seventh, addition trial, correct. Two features of the results are immediately obvious. One is that the subjects found the specific number task very easy indeed. The second is the very strong order effect, such that the normal, SMM task was greatly facilitated by prior presentation of the specific number task. Without my intending it, the experiment had become, essentially, a training study of just the type described earlier, i.e., in which no concept acquisition could have occurred.

The next step was, obviously, to carry out a full, proper training study. The pretest consisted of normal (i.e., SMM) conservation trials, two using counters and one using beads in glasses. Subjects had to fail all three of these trials to be retained in the experiment. Training,

Table 1.   Comparison of Performance (measured by number of subjects attaining criterion) in SMM and
Specific Number Tasks (N = 42 for each order)

Order of Presentation	Specific Number	SMM
SMM First	38	17
Specific Number First	39	36

which was given five days later, consisted of eight specific number
trials, with equal numbers of counters in each row, plus one specific
number trial with unequal numbers of counters.   A control group was
given corresponding trials, but using the SMM question.   The first
posttest, given a day after the training, consisted of counters and
beads trials, with the SMM question.   The results are shown in Table 2,
the criterion being, for the counters, five out of six trials correct
(plus the inequality trial) and, for the beads, two out of three trials
correct (plus the inequality trial).   It is seen that there is good
acquisition of number conservation, and considerable generalization to
the beads task.

Table 2.   Number of Subjects Reaching Criterion in Study Presenting the Specific Number Task as
"Training"

	Training	Post (1) 1 day		Post (2) 6 wks.			Post (3) 14½ wks.		
		counters	beads	counters	beads	liquid	counters	beads	liquid
Experimental Group (N = 29)	25	23	20	22	20	19	24	23	21
Control Group (N = 29)	0	0	0	0	0	0	0	0	0

At this point, a problem occurred to me.   The purpose of the
training had been to give the subjects a set to respond to number n, so
that they would go on to interpret the SMM question in the posttest in

the same way. But could it have been that the training in fact merely
drew the subjects' attention to number name, rather than to number
itself? Piaget has drawn the distinction between conservation of
"quotité" (or number name) and conservation of "quantité" (real
quantity). A child may possess the former without the latter, so that,
for him, the number label "5," for example, represents a whole band on
the number scale rather than a single point, with one "5" being more or
less than another. Could it be that the subjects had learned to
reinterpret the SMM question in terms of quotité, rather than number?
That is, was it merely a sort of pseudo-conservation that they had
acquired?

The obvious way of testing the question was to add some continuous
quantity trials to the posttest. The particles in a liquid, for
example, are not identifiable in terms of number names, and a child who
conserves only quotité, but not quantity, should not be able to respond
correctly on such trials. Accordingly, I added two equality and one
inequality liquid trials to posttests (2) and (3) (6 weeks and 14.5
weeks after training). The criterion for correct response was one of
the equality trials plus the inequality trial correct. The results are
shown in Table 2. It is seen that good generalization to the liquid
task occurred.

One question remained. The posttest tasks had always been given in
the same order: counters, then beads, then liquid. Would the same
results for the liquid task be obtained if it were not preceded by two
easier tasks, themselves given in order of increasing difficulty? To
answer this question, I repeated the training study, eliminating all
subjects who failed training, and giving the posttest tasks in three
different orders. The results are shown in Table 3. It is seen that
while performance on the counters and beads tasks was only slightly
affected by order, the effect on the liquid task was much greater. Only
in the case of order I was considerable acquisition of liquid
conservation recorded.

This last result naturally casts some doubt on the study as a
whole. Of course, a negative result in a training study does not give
much information. The training, which only lasted 10-15 minutes, might
not have been extensive enough. And, in any case, to require of such
training that it push a nonconserver of number all the way on to
conservation of liquid (which is normally acquired about two years after
that of number) is perhaps to require a little much. Nevertheless, the
possibility must remain open that the subjects in the study did not
acquire the true conservation of quantity, but merely that of quotité.
I am fairly convinced that many conserving children do fail the
conservation task because they are systematically tricked into
misinterpreting the question. But demonstrating it conclusively - well,
that is another matter.

One point on which I must insist, however, is that the question is
a valid and important one. In the past, cognitive developmental

Table 3.   Effect of Posttest Order on Results: Number of Subjects Reaching Criterion (N = 25 for each order)

Post-test Order	Counters	Beads	Liquid
Counters ⟶ Beads ⟶ Liquid	22	20	14
Counters ⟶ Liquid ⟶ Beads	23	16	5
Liquid ⟶ Counters ⟶ Beads	20	16	3

psychologists have been too ready to assert that if a task requiring
logic is answered incorrectly by a child, it must be because he lacks
the logic required.   Cross-cultural psychologists have at last achieved
enlightenment on this point;   Cole, Gay, Glick, and Sharp (1971) write,
for example:

> If there is a general principle to be gleaned from the method
> upon which our work is based, it derives from our belief that
> the people we are working with always behave reasonably.   When
> their behavior appears unreasonable, it is to ourselves, our
> procedures, and our experimental tasks that we turn for an
> explanation.   (p. xv)

This approach is surely a wise one for the psychologist testing in a
strange culture.   But it is equally applicable to testing in our own.

References

Bryant, P. The understanding of invariance by very young children.
    Canadian Journal of Psychology, 1972, 26, 78-96.

Cole, M., Gay, J., Glick, J., & Sharp, D.   The cultural context of
    learning and thinking. London: Methuen, 1971.

Gelman, R. Conservation acquisition: A problem of learning to attend
    to relevant attributes. Journal of Experimental Child Psychology,
    1969, 7, 167-187.

Piaget, J.   The child's conception of number.   London: Routledge and
    Kegan Paul, 1952.

CHILDREN'S UNDERSTANDING OF MEASUREMENT

P. L. Harris
Free University, Amsterdam, The Netherlands

W. M. Singleton
Lancaster University, Lancaster, U.K.

In the teaching of logical and mathematical skills, psychology has often preached the value of patience. Piaget, especially, has suggested that certain types of training will be useless until the child has reached a particular stage. A key example of this argument concerns the young child's understanding of measurement. Piaget claims that young children do not understand transitivity. Knowing, for example, that A=B and that B=C, they fail to conclude that A=C. Measurement involves transitivity, since it requires the comparison of two items by means of a third item or scale, such as a ruler. A child who does not understand transitivity cannot use a measuring instrument to make an indirect comparison of two items.

To illustrate the young child's deficiencies, Piaget and his colleagues (Piaget, Inhelder, & Szeminska, 1960) asked children of four years and upwards to build a tower equal in height to one already built by the experimenter and located at some distance from the child. Strips of paper were available for use as a primitive ruler. Only at about seven or eight years did children pick up a strip of paper, place it alongside the experimenter's tower, and then place it alongside their own to check their equality. The four-year-olds did not use the strips of paper as a middle term, indicating their ignorance of transitivity according to Piaget.

Our results suggest that this conclusion is mistaken. We find that young children can use a measuring device intelligently. If they do show a deficiency, it is not a logical deficiency. Rather, they appear to be overconfident of their ability to make a direct comparison of two items without the use of a middle term. I shall describe some experiments to support these claims.

The first experiment showed that young children spontaneously use a measuring device. The child was first shown a tower that stood between two towers, one the same size and one different in size. The child was allowed to inspect these three towers so that he could see that the middle tower was equal in height to one of the two side towers. The middle tower was then moved to a table about 2 m from the child, and he was asked to build a tower of bricks to equal it in height.

Here the child had three options. First, he could look at the distant tower and attempt to copy it directly. Second, he could use the side tower, equal in height, as a guide or primitive ruler. Third, he could recall how the tower looked before it was moved, and base his copy on this memory.

A child copying the distant tower directly should be less accurate if it is hidden by a screen. A child using a side tower as a guide should be less accurate if this guide is removed. Finally, a child relying on memory should not be bothered if the tower to be copied is hidden or the guide tower removed.

To find out which strategy was used, children of four to six years made a copy with and without a nearby guide tower, and with and without a screen in front of the tower to be copied. Errors in copying for these four conditions are shown in Table 1.

Table 1.   Mean Number of Errors (bricks mis-estimated) in Relation to Age, Presence of Guide Tower, and Presence of Screen

	Guide tower present				Guide tower absent			
	Screen present		Screen absent		Screen present		Screen absent	
	Mean	SD	Mean	SD	Mean	SD	Mean	SD
Younger	0.38	1.10	0.46	0.83	2.29	1.76	1.88	1.57
Older	0.00	0.00	0.13	0.61	2.17	1.72	1.88	1.23

The screen had little effect, showing that children were not relying on direct visual inspection of the tower to be copied. The clear effect of the presence or absence of the guide tower, on the other hand, ruled out a memory-based strategy. We can conclude that the children used a measurement strategy at both ages. They spontaneously copied the nearby tower as an indirect way of copying the distant tower.

These results show that even very young children can use a guide tower as a middle term or ruler in order to check the equality of two items. True, the child's use of a middle term was somewhat less active than Piaget required. Subjects at no point needed to move the guide tower, but from a strictly logical point of view, they were not deficient. Bryant and Kopytynska (1976) also found that young children spontaneously adopt a measurement strategy. However, they report that only a minority of subjects measured if direct comparison was possible instead. Our results indicate that when direct comparison would lead to inaccuracy, even four-year-old children prefer a measurement strategy.

The four-year-old turned out to exhibit an intriguing deficiency, but it was not a logical deficiency. This is illustrated in our second experiment. We placed a black tower in front of the child. Three white towers were placed at different distances from this black tower: 90 cm, 45 cm, and immediately alongside. Four- and six-year-old children were then asked to say which of the white towers was bigger than the black tower. (Unknown to the child, all three towers were actually 0.75 cm taller than the black tower.)

Both age groups were confident that the white tower alongside the black tower was indeed bigger. When it came to the more distant white towers, however, an age difference emerged. The six-year-olds hesitated. They either said nothing, or said that they were unable to tell because the black and white towers were too far apart, and so forth. The younger children of four years were much more cavalier. The majority of them said that the two white towers were bigger than the black tower. This age change is illustrated in Table 2.

Table 2.   Number of "taller", "shorter" and "no comment" Responses by Younger and Older Children for Three Tower Loci in Experiment Two

	Middle tower		45 cm tower		90 cm tower	
	Younger	Older	Younger	Older	Younger	Older
"Taller"	24	24	15	7	15	9
"Shorter"	0	0	4	3	4	1
"No comment"	0	0	5	14	5	14

The older child appears to know that his eyes can sometimes mislead him, and so he reserves his judgment. The younger child, on the other hand, is more confident of his ability to compare two items at a distance from each other. To check this interpretation, we carried out a slightly different experiment. We asked children of four and six years to make a copy of a tower with three different sets of bricks: white, brown, and red. The three sets of bricks were all placed about 1 m from the tower to be copied. We reasoned that the younger children should be happy to build their tower further away from the tower to be copied, if they are more confident of the accuracy of their perceptual comparisons. Table 3 confirms this expectation. Although most of the older children built their copies alongside the tower to be copied, few of the younger children did this.

   Thus, we have two conclusions. Even very young children can use a middle term to establish the equality of two items; also, the younger child is more confident than the older child of his ability to make perceptual comparisons of length at a distance.

Table 3.   Mean Distance (in cms) of Child's Construction from Reference Tower

		Bricks			
	White	Brown	Red	mean	SD
Younger	52.6	49.1	53.2	51.6	44.9
Older	15.5	15.3	12.7	15.0	27.1

   In the final experiment, we attempted to put these two conclusions together. Does the young child realize that side-by-side comparisons, which a middle term permits, are more accurate than direct perceptual comparisons at a distance? Some support for this possibility could be obtained from Experiment 1. In that experiment, the younger children rejected a direct perceptual comparison strategy. Instead, they used the nearby tower as a guide in copying the distant tower. The younger children, however, might have done this out of sheer convenience, not because they knew that the nearby tower permitted greater accuracy. After all, the four-year-old children in Experiments 2 and 3 had been quite confident of their comparisons at a distance.

   In Experiment 4, subjects were presented with two strips of paper, placed far enough apart so that their 0.5 cm difference in length was imperceptible. We then asked 24 children of four years which strip was bigger. As expected, they chose randomly; 10 subjects were correct, and 14 were incorrect. We then moved the strips side-by-side so that the 0.5 cm difference was clearly visible. The strips of paper were then returned to their original position and the children were again asked to decide which of the two was longer.

   If children think that judgments for distant items are just as valid as judgments for side-by-side items, they should repeat the original random performance. If, on the other hand, they realize the superior accuracy of side-by-side judgments, they should be influenced by the difference visible when the two strips were placed alongside one another. They should revise their judgment and achieve greater accuracy on their second judgments.

This was exactly what happened. All 24 subjects now pointed to the objectively longer strip on their second judgment. In a control condition, subjects who were asked to make a second judgment, without the benefit of having seen a side-by-side display in the meantime, continued to choose randomly. Clearly, the improved accuracy for the experimental group was attributable to the opportunity to see the two items adjacent to one another.

In summary, the young child is logically capable. He is capable of using a middle term as a means of comparing two other items. On the other hand, he is also overconfident; he will make perceptual comparisons at a distance when an older child will refrain. Nonetheless, the younger child can benefit by being taught how to measure, because he accepts that side-by-side comparisons are more accurate than comparisons at a distance. Far from falling on deaf ears, then, the teaching of measurement would encourage the child to mistrust his eyes.

References

Bryant, P. E., & Kopytynska, H. Spontaneous measurement by young children. Nature, 1976, 260, 773.

Piaget, J., Inhelder, B., & Szeminska, A. The child's conception of geometry. New York: Basic Books, 1960.

TEACHING STRATEGIES AND CONSERVATION TRAINING

Frank B. Murray
Department of Educational Foundations
College of Education
University of Delaware

Between 1961 and 1976, about 140 research studies were published that were designed specifically, in one way or another, to train young children between four and seven years old to conserve. Seventy percent of these studies appeared between 1970 and 1975, and with only two percent of them appearing in 1976, it would appear that the conservation training preoccupation of developmental psychologists may have ended. Quite apart from the theoretical reasons that may have motivated and legitimized the attention scientific journals gave to this issue, the thesis of this paper is that in these studies, a number of precise teaching techniques were created and, more importantly, were evaluated. Moreover, the extensive experimental literature on conservation, of which the training literature is a small part, serendipitously provides a model for programmatic research in educational psychology. From its inception at the turn of the century, educational psychology was planned as the discipline of the psychology of the various subject matters in which variables that predicted and controlled the acquisition of subject matter would be charted and explained. The claim that teaching could be a science was to be based upon this new discipline. For various reasons, the discipline wandered in the following decades from this central purpose; but the developmental psychologists have, perhaps unwittingly, followed the program faithfully in their evaluation of the conservation phenomenon.

While conservation researchers have limited themselves generally to the concepts Piaget originally researched (e.g., number, amount, length, area, weight, time, volume, etc.), this limitation has been self-imposed, because the conservation paradigm can be applied without exception to any concept. When it is, it provides a diagnostic technique for measuring a person's understanding of a concept that is as old as Platonic dialectic, wherein various concepts like justice, virtue, goodness, etc., were each subjected to a series of relevant and irrelevant transformations by which their essences were finally apprehended. The point is that there is nothing in principle to distinguish the traditionally researched conservation concept from any other that might be of interest to the curriculum developer. It has been claimed by Piaget (1968) that conservation is reserved for

419

quantitative and not qualitative concepts, but this claim must give way
to the child's, not the researcher's, notion of a quantitative concept.
The concept of substance or mass may be quantitative for the physicist,
but it is probably not for children (and many adults), and yet it is
conserved by children about seven years of age. Moreover, Saltz and
Hamilton (1968) have shown that conservation of qualitative concepts
follows the same patterns that Piaget and others have claimed for
quantitative concepts. Quite simply, every concept comprises a set of
relevant attributes that define it. Sets of irrelevant attributes that
the concept excludes are often correlated and associated with the
relevant attributes. When they are, they make concept acquisition more
difficult (Bourne, 1966). When they vary, subjects may assume the
relevant attributes have varied also, in which case the concept will not
be conserved, since a change in an irrelevant attribute has been taken
by the subject to be a change in a relevant one. Under these
conditions, even adults may fail to conserve rather simple concepts of
numerical equivalence that prove less difficult for children (Odom,
Astor, & Cunningham, 1975).

Also, researchers have restricted themselves generally to the types
of transformations used by Piaget and his colleagues (viz., shape and
position). When this limitation, too, has been discarded, it becomes
possible to chart other important and unsuspected--yet arresting--errors
in children's thinking (e.g., fathers that are drunks are no longer
fathers, Saltz & Hamilton, 1968; or that making a clay ball colder
makes it heavier, and warmer makes it lighter, Murray & Johnson, 1975).
In this regard, incidentally, it seems that the connotations of the
concept to be conserved are excellent candidates as the labels for
seductive transformations. For example, "heavy" connotes large, rough,
strong, hard, etc. on the semantic differential, and changes in an
object's size, texture, hardness are judged by second graders to change
its weight also (Nummedal & Murray, 1969; Murray & Johnson, 1975).

Similarly, limitations in the type of material used as an exemplar
of a concept can be extended beyond the usual clay balls and poker chips
used by the Genevans, with the result that an even finer map of the
child's concept may be had as the basis for curriculum and instructional
planning (e.g., the weight of objects and the weight of oneself under
analogous transformations are not uniformly appreciated by young
children; Murray, 1969).

Since the conservation research has proceeded vigorously for 16
years, a number of otherwise troublesome assessment questions that
ordinarily plagued educational testing have been resolved for the
paradigm, at least in the sense that sources of error are known. A set
of inherently theoretical criterion questions remain, however. Various
question formats, verbal and nonverbal procedures, and unobtrusive
techniques exist (Murray, 1968, 1970), and some have been standardized
(e.g., Goldschmidt & Bentler, 1968); and this has led to more precise
evaluation of concept attainment. Moreover, the influence of variables
like SES, IQ (MA), sex, cognitive style, cultural milieu, degree of

prior schooling, etc., have been researched with the overwhelming result that the primary variable in explaining and predicting conservation variation is the child's mental age.

A number of reviews of the conservation training literature exist (e.g., Beilin, 1971, in press; Brainerd, 1973; Brainerd & Allen, 1971; Glaser & Resnick, 1972; Goldschmidt, 1971; Peill, 1975; Strauss, 1972, 1974/75). Because Piagetian theory had claimed that conceptual development was under the sufficient control of unique and largely unmodifiable structural mechanisms, the intent of the early studies was to demonstrate that conservation could be trained and was amenable to conventional learning procedures. The failure of the first dozen training attempts (Flavell, 1963) undoubtedly motivated the subsequent attempts, with the result that there is no longer doubt that conservation can be taught (e.g., Beilin, in press). Still, there is an overwhelming and somewhat pessimistic result that training--even highly individualized training--is only successful (by whatever criteria) with about half the children in the sample, or more precisely, that the children make about half the gains in conservation performance that could be made, although the gains are stable for as long as a month and are significantly different from pretest or control group subjects' performance. This result seems to be as true for procedures that take as little as five minutes as it is for those that have taken an hour. The use of fixed-trials or trials-to-criterion procedures is somewhat determined by the researcher's assumptions about the trainability of conservation. Moreover, with the exception of the social interaction techniques, no one type of training strategy, regardless of its theoretical inspiration, has been shown to be superior to any other.

It also seems to be a well supported, but not surprising, principle in this literature that the training effort needed to bring a behavior to criterion is most successful with behaviors that were initially closest to the criterion. Using each researcher's criterion of success, 50 percent of 62 attempts to train 4-5 year olds succeeded, while 70 percent of 60 attempts with 6-8 year olds succeeded. The evidence for aptitude treatment interactions in this literature, like all others, is scant, but there remains the theoretical issue of whether training is constrained by the child's developmental level. The Genevans (Inhelder, Sinclair, & Bovet, 1974) claim training is only successful with transitional children who give prior evidence of some conservation--either with a simpler concept, content, or transformation. Murray (1972) and Murray, Ames and Botvin (in press), however, have reported no significant differences in the training gains between nonconservers who had exhibited no pretest conservation and those who had exhibited some. Brainerd (in press) concluded that, to date, there is no compelling evidence that training is constrained by preoperational or transitional cognitive levels in that each receives equal benefit from training.

It should be noted that many of these training strategies have face validity as classroom techniques, and in many instances would seem to be a teacher's first response to a child who thought, for example, that the number of objects in a patterned array changed when the pattern changed.

What follows is a formal description of the general training paradigm (Steps 1-6 below) and descriptions of eight primary varieties of training that have been researched and have direct classroom applicability.

Conservation Training Paradigm

It is established by virtue of some measurement procedure, however primitive (e.g., counting, weighing, hefting,eyeballing, etc.) that

1. $\underline{Axy} = \underline{Bxy}$ Where $\underline{A}$ and $\underline{B}$ are identical objects with respect to at least two attributes, $\underline{x}$ and $\underline{y}$; where $\underline{x}$ is the property in question, say weight, and $\underline{y}$ is some other property, say shape.

2. $\underline{Bxy} \overset{ty}{\rightarrow} \underline{B^1 xy}^1$ Object $\underline{B}$ is transformed with respect to $\underline{y}$ into $\underline{B^1}$ by a transformation ($\underline{t}$) that is irrelevant with respect to $\underline{x}$, because it does not change $\underline{x}$; it only changes $\underline{y}$ ($\underline{ty}$). Relevant transformations ($\underline{tx}$) change $\underline{x}$ as it is measured or indicated by the measurement procedure in (1) above. Some guarantee that the child was aware of the transformation should be provided in the procedure.

3. Conservation Questions (Q1): Is $\underline{B^1 xy}^1 = $ or $\neq \underline{Axy}$?

    (Q2): Why?

4. Training procedure (4.1-4.8 below).

5. Q1.

6. Any of the additional criteria (6.1-6.7), depending on the theoretical viewpoint of the experimenter, may be employed:

    6.1 Q2 may be asked.

    6.2 Q1 and Q2 may be asked at a later time (day, week, month).

    6.3 It may be suggested that $\underline{B^1 xy}^1 \gtrless \underline{Axy}$ for various reasons (counter-suggestion).

6.4 Q1 and Q2 may be asked about different $\underline{A}$'s and $\underline{B}$'s with respect to $\underline{x}$ and with respect to some or different $\underline{y}$'s and $\underline{ty}$'s (specific transfer, i.e., the same conservations on different objects and by different transformations).

6.5 Q1 and Q2 may be asked about different $\underline{x}$'s and same or different $\underline{y}$'s and $\underline{ty}$'s (nonspecific transfer, i.e., different conservations).

6.6 Differently structured tasks may be assessed (seriation, transitivity, identity, classification, etc.).

6.7 Training procedure may be reinstated until Q1 answered correctly (trials to criterion).

It should be noted that Step 3 of the paradigm should not be answerable simply from an inspection or measurement of $\underline{B}^1$ and $\underline{A}$; if it is, discrimination and not conservation is assessed. The conservation judgment, $\underline{B}^1\underline{xy}^1 = \underline{Axy}$, is not a judgment as much as it is a deduction based on four premises. Two of these are given explicitly in the experimental procedure, $\underline{Axy} = \underline{Bxy}$ and $\underline{Bxy} \overset{ty}{\to} \underline{B}^1\underline{xy}^1$, and two must be supplied implicitly by the subject, viz., $\underline{B}^1\underline{xy}^1 = \underline{Bxy}$, and knowledge of transitivity (if $\underline{A} = \underline{B}$ and $\underline{B} = \underline{B}^1$, then $\underline{A} = \underline{B}^1$). This analysis of the paradigm reveals appropriate items for training, namely the underlying logical structure and the knowledge that $\underline{B}^1\underline{xy}^1 = \underline{Bxy}$, although some procedures have focused upon the conclusion.

Incidentally, nonconservation can be a deduction, and in that sense, nonconservation represents a logical competence equal to that presumed for conservation. Nonconservation follows from the implicit premises, $\underline{B}^1\underline{xy}^1 \gtrless \underline{Bxy}$ and "if $\underline{A} = \underline{B}$ and $\underline{B} \gtrless \underline{B}^1$, then $\underline{A} \gtrless \underline{B}^1$." Murray and Armstrong (1976) have shown some nonconservers do, in fact, feel their judgments are necessary.

The analysis also reveals that the usual acceptable answers to Q2 are inadequate (e.g., Murray & Johnson, 1969) because they do not provide or represent any information that features in the conservation deduction. They do not provide transitivity or the knowledge that $\underline{B}^1\underline{xy}^1 = \underline{Bxy}$.

Each training procedure may be viewed as implicitly focusing upon one or another aspect of the paradigm--its explicit and implicit premises and conclusion--although not every trainer has appreciated that the judgment itself is not the object of instruction, but rather deduction of the judgment from the premises.

The Training Procedure

Each procedure has a well-established pedagogical counterpart in the education literature, and is based upon different assumptions about the nature of the child's competence and the causes of the nonconservation response at Step 3. To some extent they center upon whether the source of the error is presumed to be rooted in competence factors or performance factors, and whether the error stems from insufficient information about one or another of each step of the paradigm. Operationally, the procedures are as follows:

4.1 Feedback (law of effect strategies to provide the conclusion $\overline{Axy} = \overline{B^1xy^1}$ to some extent obviate the deduction, although $\overline{Bxy} = \overline{B^1xy^1}$ may be provided).

    4.11 Some measurement procedure applied to $\underline{B^1xy^1}$ and $\underline{Axy}$ to demonstrate equality with $\underline{Axy}$, or

    4.12 $\underline{Axy} = \underline{B^1xy^1}$ validated by authority and reinforcement and "$\underline{Axy} \neq \underline{B^1xy^1}$" response simply punished or extinguished.

4.2 Cognitive conflict (an instance of reductio ad absurdum to provide $\underline{B^1xy^1} = \underline{Bxy}$). $\underline{Bxy}$ simultaneously transformed (sometimes successively) by $\underline{ty}$ and $\underline{tx}$ to $B^1x^1y^1$, such that the outcome with respect to $\underline{x}$ hopefully conflicts and is untenable. For example, a clay ball may be fattened with clay subtracted so that the transformed ball appears both heavier and lighter. If $\underline{B^1xy^1}$ is taken as greater than $\underline{Bxy}$, and B^1xy^1 can be seen also as less than $\underline{Bxy}$, this inconsistency requires resolution by the hypothesis that $\underline{B^1xy^1} = \underline{Bxy}$. The likely outcomes are:

    4.21 The conflict is ignored and $\underline{ty}$ and $\underline{tx}$ are taken as separate and independent events (i.e., ball was heavier, then lighter).

    4.22 The conflict is maintained as a paradox or mystery.

    4.23 The conflict is avoided by forced response (Q1) to authority of the experimenter.

    4.24 $\underline{ty}$ is accepted as changing $\underline{x}$, and $\underline{tx}$ is rejected (nonconservation).

    4.25 $\underline{tx}$ is accepted as changing $\underline{x}$, and $\underline{ty}$ is rejected (conservation).

4.3 Training by analogy or apperception (apparent-real discrimination to provide $Axy = B^1xy^1$, or break down correlation between x and y as an illusion). The particular procedure presupposes that a prior distinction has been acquired to which the effects of tx and ty may be linked. In this case it is supposed that a distinction between appearance and reality has been acquired, and made an instance of this. It creates two questions for Q1: "Does Axy look heavier, etc. than B^1xy^1?" (Q_L) and "Is Axy really heavier, than B^1xy^1?" (Q_I) and follows each with feedback (4.1) so that Q_L elicits $Axy \neq B^1xy^1$ and Q_I elicits $Axy = B^1xy^1$. Other appropriate analogies, metaphors, etc., could be used but the procedure is hazardous because there are no necessary links between an event and its metaphor or analogy.

4.4 Cue reduction or shaping (screening to minimize or eliminate effects of ty). Child is prevented from concluding $B^1xy^1 \gtrless Axy$ by masking or screening the effects of ty of or by performing ty slowly so that the $Axy = Bxy$ is preserved as long as possible; a slow motion strategy to preserve the initial equality. To some extent this procedure violates Step 2 of the paradigm.

4.5 Discrimination training (to demonstrate that x and y are independent; assign Q1 to only). The independence of x and y is demonstrated by the measurement procedure for x used in Step 1 after tx and ty are performed on B as follows:

4.51 tx and no ty with the result that x changes
$(Bxy \underset{\rightarrow}{tx} B^1xy^1$; B and B^1 measured).

4.52 no tx and ty with the result that x does not change
$(Bxy \underset{\neq}{ty} B^1xy^1$; B and B^1 measured).

4.53 tx and ty with the result that x changes Bxy $tx ty$ $B^1x^1y^1$; B and B^1 measured).

4.54 no tx and no ty with the result that x does not change
$(Bxy \underset{0}{\rightarrow} Bxy$; B and B^1 measured).

4.6 Verbal rule instruction (algorithmic learning at any step in paradigm). Child is given a rule, such as, if no tx then no change in x (if nothing is added or subtracted, then nothing changes). Provides a verbal mediator for any strategy as well. This is teaching by telling.

4.7 Theoretical prerequisites training. The prerequisites vary with the theory, from an empirical hierarchy analysis of every step of the paradigm, to the abstract Genevan structures that provide the intellectual competence to make the deduction. For example,

4.71 Training on multiplication of classes and relations (the appropriate logical groupings).

4.72 Training on operativity features (e.g., reversibility by inversion $\underline{B^1xy^1ty} \rightleftarrows \underline{Bxy}$ reversibility by reciprocity or compensation, i.e., $\underline{ty}$ analyzed as having component effects, $\underline{y_1}$ and $\underline{y_2}$ where $\underline{y_1}$ and $\underline{y_2} = \underline{y}$. Change in shape in $\underline{y}$ is composed of change in height, $\underline{y_1}$, and width, $\underline{y_2}$, Effects of $\underline{y_1}$ and $\underline{y_2}$ conflict (4.2) and can be coordinated with $\underline{tx}$ effects by (4.5) to provide an integrated understanding of covariation and independence of $\underline{x}$ and $\underline{y}$.

4.73 Training on simpler conservation tasks, viz., identity forms, discontinuous materials, more primitive concepts, etc.

4.8 <u>Social interaction, imitation, cognitive dissonance, role playing</u> (provides $\underline{Axy} = \underline{B^1xy^1}$ to guarantee conflict with $\underline{Axy} \neq \underline{B^1xy^1}$). Nonconservers must come to a group agreement with conservers, and/or must role play as a conserver. A distinction is presumed between information derived personally from actions on the world and information in acquiesence to other minds.

While some of these strategies in some theories have superiority over others, and some have pedagogical superiority in certain educational philosophies (e.g., discovery versus telling), there is no compelling empirical superiority of any except class (4.8), which leads to very high response levels in all subjects. This only suggests that confirmation of one's beliefs by another mind may be a critical feature of intellectual development, since (4.8) may include all the features of the other procedures.

These instructional strategies are presented in this abstract notation to demonstrate their applicability to any concept as well as to set forth the structure of variations that do exist in the various conservation training attempts.

The recommendations for instructional design are that every curricular concept be analyzed as a conservation concept into its relevant and irrelevant attributes. The source of the relevant attributes is the academic discipline in which the concept resides. The source of the interesting irrelevant attributes, namely those that are confused with relevant attributes, is developmental cognitive psychology. The conservation paradigm provides a diagnostic device for assessing understanding by probing the pupil's discrimination of the relevant from irrelevant attributes, and of his appreciation of the necessity of the relationships. The training strategies are evaluated procedures for providing information and/or competence for segregating and integrating the relevant and irrelevant attributes. At present, each appears to be a sufficient but not necessary device for instruction and conceptual development.

References

Beilin, H. The training and acquisition of logical operations. In M. Rosskopf, L. Steffe, & S. Taback, Piagetian cognitive-development research and mathematical education. Washington, DC: National Council of Teachers of Mathematics, Inc., 1971.

Beilin, H. Inducing conservation through training. In G. Steiner (Ed.), Psychology of 20th century, Piaget and beyond, Vol. 7. Bern: Kinder, in press.

Bourne, L. Human conceptual behavior. Boston: Allyn & Bacon, 1966.

Brainerd, C. J. Cognitive development and concept learning: An interpretive review. Psychological Bulletin, in press.

Brainerd, C. J. Neo-Piagetian training experiments revisited: Is there any support for the cognitive-developmental stage hypothesis? Cognition, 1973, 2, 349-370.

Brainerd, C. J., & Allen, T. Experimental inducements of the conservation of first order quantitative invariants. Psychological Bulletin, 1971, 75, 128-44.

Flavell, J. The developmental psychology of Jean Piaget. New York: Van Nostrand, 1963.

Glaser, R., & Resnick, L. B. Instructional psychology. In P. H. Mussen & M. Rosenweig (Eds.), Annual review of psychology. Palo Alto, CA: Annual Reviews, 1972.

Goldschmidt, M. The role of experience in the rate and sequence of cognitive development. In D. R. Green, M. Ford, & G. Flammer (Eds.). Measurement and Piaget. New York: McGraw-Hill, 1971.

Goldschmidt, M., & Bentler, P. Concept assessment kit--Conservation manual. San Diego: Educational and Industrial Testing Service, 1968.

Inhelder, B., Sinclair, H., & Bovet, M. Learning and the development of cognition. Cambridge, MA: Harvard University Press, 1974.

Murray, F. B. Operational conservation of illusion-distorted length.
    British Journal of Educational Psychology, 1968, 38(2), 189-193.

Murray, F. B. Conservation of mass, weight, and volume in self and
    object. Psychological Reports, 1969, 25, 941-942.

Murray, F. B.   Verbal and nonverbal measures of conservation   of
    illusion-distorted length. Journal for Research in Mathematics
    Education, 1970, 9-15.

Murray, F. B.   The acquisition of conservation through social
    interaction. Developmental Psychology, 1972, 6,(1), 1-6.

Murray, F. B., Ames, G., & Botvin, G. The acquisition of conservation
    through cognitive dissonance. Journal of Educational Psychology,
    in press.

Murray, F. B., & Armstrong, S.   Necessity in conservation and
    nonconservation. Developmental Psychology, 1976, 12, 483-484.

Murray, F. B., & Johnson, P. E. Reversibility in the non-conservation
    of weight. Psychonomic Science, 1969, 16(6), 285-286.

Murray, F. B., & Johnson, P. E. Relevant and irrelevant factors in the
    child's concept of weight. Journal of Educational Psychology,
    1975, 67, 705-711.

Nummedal, S., & Murray, F. B.   Semantic aspects of conservation.
    Psychonomic Science, 1969, 16, 323-324.

Odom, R., Astor, E., & Cunningham, J. Adults thinking the way we think
    children think but children don't think that way: A study of
    perceptual salience and problem solving. Bulletin of the
    Psychonomic Society, 1975, 6, 545-548.

Peill, E. J. Invention and discovery of reality: The acquisition of
    conservation of amount. New York: Wiley & Sons, 1975.

Piaget, J. On the concept of memory and identity. Barre, Mass.: Clark
    University Press, 1968.

Saltz, E., & Hamilton, H. Concept conservation under positively and
    negatively evaluated transformations. Journal of Experimental
    Child Psychology, 1968, 6, 44-51.

Strauss, S. Inducing cognitive development and learning: A review of
    short-term training experiments I, The organismic-developmental
    approach. Cognition, 1972, 1, 329-357.

Strauss, S. A reply to Brainerd. Cognition, 1974/75, 3, 155-185.

IMAGERY AND CHILDREN'S ASSOCIATIVE LEARNING

John C. Yuille and Michael J. Catchpole
University of British Columbia
Vancouver, B. C., Canada

During the past five years, we have collaborated in a series of research studies concerned with children's associative memory, or what Piaget and Inhelder (1973) have called "memory in the strict sense." This paper is a review of that work. In addition, we have included some thoughts about the role of this type of research within the general context of theories of cognition (see also Yuille & Catchpole, in press). [1]

The principal goal of our research has been to determine the type of processing and storage that mediates associative memory in children. To this end, we have manipulated the learning instructions provided to children in associative tasks. That is, we have tried to affect the kind of learning strategy employed by the child through the use of instructional and training procedures. The selection of instructional techniques was determined by major theories of children's associative learning: those of Paivio (1970) and Rohwer (1973). Paivio's views are representative of the widely held opinion that imagery plays a major role in children's learning (see also Reese, 1970; Yuille, 1974). The benefits of visual imagery codes were inferred from studies that show that picture pairs are more easily learned than word pairs (e.g., Rohwer & Levin, 1971), and that instructions to use images facilitate performance (e.g., Davidson & Adams, 1970). According to Paivio (1970), an image will serve as an effective associative code to the extent that it represents an interaction between the pair of to-be-associated items. For example, if a child wishes to remember the pair DOG-BALL, an interacting image of a dog chewing a ball will aid memory because of the interactive nature of the image. Later presentation of the cue DOG will permit retrieval of the entire image, and hence recall of BALL. Because of the central importance of this hypothesis, much of our research has concentrated on the role of imagery in children's learning.

The second major hypothesis related to the learning of associations in children was presented by Rohwer (1973), who argued that memory for associations is mediated by an abstract, amodal code. Specifically, he proposed that, at the time of presentation of a pair of items, the child forms a semantic code comprised of the meaning features of the two items. To the extent that the two items share common semantic components, they will be remembered easily. Rohwer called the process of finding shared components semantic elaboration, and he suggested that elaboration can be encouraged by instructions, as well as by embedding noun pairs in a sentence context. The second purpose of our research has been to examine Rohwer's ideas, and to contrast the semantic elaboration and imagery hypotheses.

We began by developing a training procedure designed to encourage children to form interactive images. The technique is simple: We display a number of pairs of objects, one at a time, and ask the child to picture the two objects playing together. After five minutes or so of this type of training, the child is given the principal learning task. Typical findings using this technique are illustrated in Table 1. The first-grade children tested in this study were presented with a set of 20 pairs of objects. Half of the children were provided with imagery training before the learning task, while the remaining children were told that the training pairs were examples of the type of learning material to follow (i.e., they received no special training). Note the very strong effect of the training found in the means on the left of Table 1, and note that training affected both recall and recognition measures of retention. It is important to emphasize that these effects are not transitory.

We returned and retested the same group of children a week after the original session. In this case a new set of objects constituted the learning task, and no additional training was provided. The means on the right in Table 1 indicate that the training continued to facilitate learning a week after it was provided. It appears that a long lasting improvement in associative learning ability can result from just five minutes of training.

Having established the value of the technique of imagery training, we turned our attention to determining the ages at which the procedure is effective. A comment made by Rohwer (1973) that children below about seven years of age will not benefit from mnemonic training, as well as the proposition of Piaget and Inhelder (1973) that preoperational children cannot form anticipatory images, encouraged us to work with children in the three- to six-year-old range. The results presented in Table 2 are from an illustrative experiment (Catchpole, Yuille, & Major, Note 1). Each of a number of preschool children was assigned to one of three groups, and given two sets of pairs of objects to learn. The learning of each set was separated by one week and in each case memory was tested by a recognition task. No training was provided for the learning of the first set of pairs, so that we could determine the effects of training as a within-subject variable. On this first test, the children in two groups were shown the two objects in each pair, side-by-side (Groups 1 and 3), while Group 2 saw the objects in each pair in some interaction. A week later, the second learning task was given, but this time the Group 3 children were given imagery training before the learning task. Groups 1 and 2 were treated the same as they were for the first learning test. An inspection of the means in Table 2

Table 1. Mean Correct Scores for Grade One Children Immediately after Training, and One Week after Training

	Immediate Test		Delayed Test	
	Recall	Recognition	Recall	Recognition
Imagery Training	7.46	8.26	6.95	9.82
No Training	3.18	4.59	2.50	3.64

From Yuille and Catchpole (1974)
Maximum Score = 20

reveals that the interactive presentation strongly facilitated learning, and this is noticeable in both testing sessions. This result is consistent with Paivio's notion that an interactive representation enhances memory. More important to the present discussion, the training effect was strong, even when each child served as his/her own control (i.e., Group 3). In addition, a comparison of Groups 2 and 3 indicates that the training is as effective as presenting the objects in an interaction.

The effectiveness of the training with preschool children casts some doubt on the limitations in imagery abilities that Piaget and Inhelder (1973) proposed for children in this age range. To examine this possibility more directly, we gave the trained children (Group 3) in this study two standard Piagetian tasks to assess their developmental level. There was no relationship between the cognitive level of the child (vis-a-vis concrete operations) and the extent to which he or she benefited from the training. To the extent that the training technique encourages the child to use anticipatory images to mediate learning, these results indicate that preoperational children do possess anticipatory imagery. This would indicate more rapid development of imagery abilities than Piaget and his co-workers have suggested. In fact, we believe that these results indicate a greater degree of figurative autonomy than proposed in Piaget's theory. That is, we believe that a child can attain flexible mnemonic abilities on the figurative plane in the absence of corresponding operative schemes. Further comments on this issue are made later in this paper.

The fact that the effect of the imagery training procedure is not simply motivational is illustrated by the results of two further experiments. In one study (Yuille & Catchpole, Note 2), we found that

Table 2.   Mean Recognition Scores for Two Separate Learning Tasks

	Test 1 (No Training)	Test 2
Group 1 (Objects side by-side)	3.07	3.27
Group 2 (Objects interacting)	6.86	6.79
Group 3 (Objects side by-side)	3.05 (Imagery Training) 6.26	

From Catchpole, Yuille, and Major (Note 1)
Maximum Score 10; Average age = 4 years, 4 months

imagery training was slightly more effective with object pairs than with word pairs (although the training was effective with both), while a verbal training procedure had the reverse effect. This differential effect of instructions was more dramatically illustrated in a study involving manipulation of the familiarity of the learning materials (Yuille, Note 3). In this case, preschool children (mean age of 4.5 years) were given eight pairs of two-dimensional cutouts to learn. For one group, the cutouts represented familiar objects, while for the other group the cutouts were of random (nonlabelable) forms. Half of each group received imagery training prior to learning, while the other half did not. The means for imagery training were 4.63 for familiar cutouts, and 2.13 for unfamiliar cutouts, while the respective means for no training were 1.90 and 1.21. This shows that although the training facilitated the learning of both types of material, its effect was considerably smaller with the unfamiliar materials.

Our next concern was with the locus of the training effect. Does imagery improve learning, or memory, or both? In a recently completed experiment (Yuille, Note 4), we had groups of first-grade children learn a set of 10 pairs of familiar cutouts, and both the trained and the untrained children were required to learn the pairs to a criterion of one perfect recall trial. A week later, recall was tested and the children were then required to relearn the list to the original criterion. The results are found in Table 3. Consistent with previous findings, the trained children showed more rapid learning than their untrained peers. However, a week later, with the two groups equated for the degree of original learning, the recall scores did not differ. In addition, the two groups showed equivalent relearning rates, another index of equal retention. It appears that the principal affect of imagery training is on the rate of associative learning in children. That is, imagery training encourages the rapid formation of associative links.

Table 3.   Performance Measures for Ten Pair List

	Original Learning (Trials to Criterion)	Delayed Recall	Relearning (Trials to Criterion)
Imagery Training	2.70	6.56	1.44
No Training	3.60	7.44	1.33

From Yuille (Note 4)

The final study presented in this review was concerned with the role of verb links in the learning of noun pairs. Rohwer (1973) has attributed the improvement in learning that results from the presence of verb links to semantic elaboration, while Paivio (1970; see also Yuille, 1974) believes that links improve the probability of generating an interactive imagery code. Thus the investigation of linked noun pair learning offers an opportunity to compare the two major theories of children's associative learning. To evaluate the role of verb links, we generated a pool of linked pairs, and had groups of children rate each sentence in terms of: (a) the appropriateness of the link to the noun pair (the characteristic that Rohwer considered central), and (b) the degree of interaction implied by the verb link (Paivio's central characteristic). Using the resulting ratings, we independently manipulated these two aspects of verb links in an associative learning study (see Table 4 for examples). Sixteen sentences (four of each of the four sentence types) were presented to Grade 5 and Grade 6 children to learn (the first nouns served as recall cues for the second nouns in the memory test). One-third of the children received no special instructions, one-third were given the imagery training procedure, and the remaining third were asked to "picture" the scene described by each sentence. The latter condition, which we have called imagery prompting, was intended to amplify the effects of the type of link (as far as the imagery hypothesis is concerned). The results, presented in Table 4, show that both link characteristics and instructions affected recall. Imagery training proved more effective than imagery prompting, but the latter instruction still helped recall relative to the uninstructed control. Appropriate verb links led to much better recall than inappropriate links (supporting Rohwer's hypothesis). However, Paivio's theory was not as well supported, in that the degree of interaction implied by the verb links only affected recall when the links were inappropriate. Paivio's views were further questioned by the fact that the instructional effects did not interact with the effects of the type of link. These results place some doubt on the notion that an interaction is a critical characteristic in a code mediating associative memory.

Table 4.   Verb Link Types and Examples of Sentence Types

Type of Verb Link

	Appropriate-Interacting	Appropriate-Non-interacting	Inappropriate-Interacting	Inappropriate-Non-interacting
Imagery Training	2.25	2.70	2.30	1.65
Imagery Prompting	2.35	2.20	1.65	1.40
No Train-ing	1.75	1.55	1.40	.80
Means	2.12	2.15	1.78	1.28

Maximum Score per Condition = 4

Type of Sentence	Example
Appropriate/Interacting	The BOAT hits the ROCK.
Appropriate/Non-interacting	The CAPTAIN smells the PIE.
Inappropriate/Interacting	The POSTMAN climbs the BUN.
Inappropriate/Non-interacting	The BUCKET hunts the VASE.

(Yuille and Catchpole, Note 6.)

The above review has indicated that imagery is a highly effective mnemonic in children's associative learning. This conclusion is supportive of some aspects of Paivio's model of learning and memory processes, although we would qualify the role that images play in memory. It appears that picturing an interaction is not as central as Paivio has suggested. Rather, the essential factor is the elaboration involved in representation. If a child is attempting to represent an association with a visual image, the effectiveness of that image is a direct function of the elaborative processing the child applies to the image. An interaction may be one form of elaboration, but it is by no means the only form, and certainly not the only effective form.

Our assertion that children's associative memory involves a degree of figurative independence contrasts with the conclusion of Wolff and Levin (for a summary of their work, see Levin, 1976). They have failed to obtain a positive effect of imagery training among preschool children unless, in addition to the training, the children were allowed to hold the two objects of each pair and interact them behind a screen (while attempting to image the interaction). As a consequence, Wolff and Levin have concluded that motor involvement is prerequisite to successful imagery training among preoperational children, and that this is consistent with Piaget's (1962) remarks concerning the sensori-motor roots of the image. Not only do our results contradict those of Wolff and Levin (see also Danner & Taylor, 1973) but their idea is weak on purely theoretical grounds. Piaget and Inhelder (1973) believe the image to arise from an act of pure accommodation, or imitation. The imitations of the preoperational child do not require or benefit from an external sensori-motor action; rather, the preoperational imitations are an internal abstract cognitive process in which the act of applying relevant schemes to a particular object leads to the generation of a particular schema or image. Sensori-motor imitations are related to image formation only in the direct sense that the accommodations of the interiorized schemes of the preoperational child are supposed to be analogous to the external accommodations of the sensori-motor schemes. Since sensori-motor accommodations do not lead to images, the interpretation of Piaget's theory offered by Wolff and Levin is inappropriate. It is more parsimonious to explain the facilitating effect of contact on image formation reported by Wolff and Levin as reflecting an instructional effect. That is, permitting their children to interact the objects clarified the imagery training procedure Wolff and Levin employed.

Our conclusion, then, is that associations are mediated by representations of relationships between items, and that the imagery mode is a viable one to represent such relations. This view is a blend of Rohwer's stress on elaborative processes and Paivio's concern with the imagery modality. Elaborative images appear to speed up the learning process, but it is not clear that they improve memory in comparison with other types of representations. Furthermore, the effects of delay on recall that were reported earlier, as well as the results of other studies not included in this review (e.g., Catchpole & Yuille, Note 5; Yuille & Catchpole, Note 2) indicate that the value of these elaborative codes may be quite transient. That is, while they facilitate recall for short periods after learning, this effect is short-lived. Perhaps Piaget and Inhelder (1973) are correct, and long-term retention of these figurative codes requires operative support.

Whether or not long-term retention of associations requires operative assistance, the research presented in this review indicates that children may possess figurative abilities that are partially independent of their operative abilities. Thus, a preoperative child can be taught to use a figurative mnemonic (interactive imagery) in spite of the absence of the operative schemes that are supposed to permit anticipatory imagery. We believe that certain figurative skills can be independently acquired, and we would speculate that such skills may assist developments on the operative plane. That is, the acquisition of flexible representational capacities may contribute to the achievement of logical structures.

Our results have some implications for research in the general area of "memory in the strict sense." First, there is a clear need to incorporate longer delays between learning and testing than has been the practice in most research. Variables that have strong effects on immediate memory tests may have little or no effect on performance a week later. Related to this, we must learn why some figurative memories become permanent (e.g., poems, songs, names, etc.) and others are so rapidly lost. Finally, researchers of figurative memory should attempt to relate their findings to the broader field of cognition. "Memory in the strict sense" must be interpreted within the context of the individual's general knowledge (i.e., "memory in the broad sense").

There are several implications of these findings for classroom instruction. First, it is apparent that pictorial materials facilitate learning (see also, Levin, 1976). Second, we have learned that a few minutes of training in simple organizational techniques (particularly those that are imagery based) can improve children's learning ability. A basic fault in current primary school curricula is that they do not include instruction in how to learn. While educators and psychologists have devoted a great deal of attention to the appropriate organization of content in order to improve learning, little attention has been paid to the direct development of the learning skills of the child. In effect, we expect the child to discover appropriate coding methods to aid learning. Our data, together with the findings of Levin, Paivio, Rohwer, and others, indicates that young children will benefit from training designed to improve their memory. The memory improvements reported in this research are testimony to the need for such training. Clearly, the children are not developing these techniques spontaneously. A variety of learning and memory devices, including both verbal and visual techniques, could be taught to children. Various coding techniques should be scaled in difficulty and introduced at appropriate grade levels.

The final point vis-a-vis instruction relates to the effect of an immediate recall opportunity on a child's subsequent ability (after days or weeks) to remember material. We have found that children's long-term memory for associative information is greatly improved if they are provided with a recall trial shortly after learning. This immediate recall trial has a stronger effect than an additional learning trial, and it appears to improve the organization of the material. Apparently, the child is able to examine the effectiveness of his/her coding and improve weak or inappropriate codes that resulted in recall difficulties. Poorly coded associations are quickly lost, so an immediate recall trial is most effective in allowing recoding. Teachers should be encouraged to provide their students with frequent opportunities for recall, or the children might be taught to practice recall on their own. One method to achieve the latter goal would involve each child maintaining a diary of school experiences. Adding to the diary two or three times each day would be an effective method of encouraging active recall.

Footnotes

1. Due to space limitations, the review of experimental results will omit details concerning the research procedures and the techniques employed to analyze the data. The reader is directed to the specific publications and preprints for these details.

Reference Notes

1. Catchpole, M. J., Yuille, J. C., & Major, C.   Preoperational imagery and object pair memory. Unpublished paper, 1977.

2. Yuille, J. C., & Catchpole, M. J. A comparison of verbal and imaginal mnemonics in children's associative learning. Unpublished paper, 1976.

3. Yuille, J. C. Familiarity and imagery training as factors in the learning of preschool children. Unpublished paper, 1977.

4. Yuille, J. C. Acquisition and retention components of imagery effects. Unpublished paper, 1977.

5. Catchpole, M. J., & Yuille, J. C. The effects of prepositional links and immediate recall on children's delayed memory for associations. Unpublished paper, 1977.

6. Yuille, J. C., & Catchpole, M. J. Semantic elaboration and interactive imagery as factors in the sentence context effect. Unpublished paper, 1977.

References

Danner, F. W. & Taylor, A. M.   Integrated   pictures   and   relational
    imagery   training   in children's learning.   Journal of Experimental
    Child Psychology, 1973, 16, 47-54.

Davidson, R. E., & Adams, J. F.   Verbal   and   imagery   processes   in
    children's   paired-associate   learning.   Journal   of   Experimental
    Child Psychology, 1970, 9, 429-435.

Levin, J. R.   What have we learned about maximizing what children learn.
    in   J.   R.   Levin & V. L.   Allen (Eds.), Cognitive learning in
    children.   New York: Academic Press, 1976.

Paivio, A. On the functional significance of imagery.   Psychological
    Bulletin, 1970, 73, 385-392.

Piaget, J.   Play, dreams, and imitation in childhood.   New   York:
    Norton, 1962.

Piaget, J., & Inhelder, B. Memory and intelligence. New York: Basic
    Books, 1973.

Reese, H. W. Imagery and contextual meaning.   Psychological Bulletin,
    1970, 73, 404-413.

Rohwer, W. D., Jr.   Elaboration   and   learning   in   children   and
    adolescence. In H. W. Reese (Ed.), Advances in child development
    and behavior, Vol. 8. New York: Academic Press, 1973.

Rohwer, W. D., Jr., & Levin, J. R.   Elaboration   preferences   and
    differences in learning proficiency.   In J.   Hellmuth (Ed.),
    Cognitive studies, Vol. 2. New York: Brunner/Megel, 1971.

Yuille, J. C.   Syntactic   facilitation   of   children's   associative
    learning: An instructional effect. Journal of Experimental Child
    Psychology, 1974, 18, 41-50.

Yuille, J. C. & Catchpole, M. J.   The   effects of delay and imagery
    training in recall and recognition of object pairs. Journal of
    Experimental Child Psychology, 1974, 17, 474-481.

Yuille, J. C., & Catchpole, M. J. The role of imagery in models of
    cognition. Journal of Mental Imagery, in press.

Section VI

APPROACHES TO INSTRUCTION

The papers in the section on instruction differ in tactic in comparison with other papers in this symposium. In most of the other papers, a discussion of some psychological experiment or theory is presented and then the author presents implications for instruction. In the three papers in this section, instructional problems are directly attacked and provide the basis for investigation.

Case integrates theoretical work from developmental psychology, specifically the work of Piaget and Pascual-Leone, into a set of explicit principles and techniques of instruction aimed at reducing the learning difficulties of young children. His detailed analyses and examples center around five general principles of instruction that have been applied explicitly or implicitly in successful training studies in the developmental psychology literature. These principles involve: (a) comparing the sequence of operations to be taught with the sequence of spontaneous operations and potentially misleading strategies that students might bring to the task; (b) designing training paradigms in which the goal of instruction is clear to children, and in which they can receive feedback that enables them to evaluate the adequacy of their current strategy; (c) presenting experience to students that insures that they will understand the limitations of their spontaneous approach to the task; (d) insuring that the number of items of information or operations to which students must attend at any one time does not exceed their memory capability; and (e) insuring that all information and operations of relevance to the strategy to be taught are already in the student's repertoire and are thoroughly learned prior to instruction. Case points out that although the above principles have been applied in successful training studies reported in the literature, their applicability to the more conventional tasks of instruction in education has not been demonstrated, and the gap that separates laboratory tasks from classroom tasks needs to be investigated.

Rothkopf's paper asks the following question: Since covert learning processes are complex and incompletely understood, what general and readily observable factors appear to be relevant to the success of instruction? The question is answered at an operational instructional level without reduction to underlying processes. He concentrates on techniques that can be manipulated in the design of instructional

439

settings: the physical presence of instructive events, the perception and representation of these events in instructionally appropriate ways, and the relationship between instructive events and assessments of performance and forgetting. Rothkopf emphasizes that the most significant problem for instruction centers on the conditions that determine whether an instructive event, once it is encountered, results in adequate learning. These conditions include: instructional materials that reflect relevant student experience, the disparity between instructional presentation and the competence to be learned, the cognitive burden of the information to be learned, and the processing and capacity limitations of the student.

Sticht describes global strategies of instruction required for dealing with personnel who enter instructional programs with low literacy skills. In one training approach, low cognitive skills are considered as a fixed characteristic of the person and the instruction is modified to adapt to the person's capabilities. A second strategy does not consider the person's low cognitive skills as fixed and attempts to provide basic literacy training to a level where the person can perform the learning tasks involved in a job skills training program. Sticht's discussion emphasizes the importance of the latter strategy and discusses (a) problems and procedures involved, such as the distinction between oral language knowledge and skill in recognizing the same language in print; (b) tailoring the relationship between the literacy to be learned and the literacy required for a job; and (c) the difference between reading to obtain information to do a job and reading to learn. A general question is raised about the extent to which fundamental changes in the cognitive competence of adults can be achieved. Sticht challenges a cognitive psychology of instruction with issues that arise in the context of real-life, large-scale educational efforts.

IMPLICATIONS OF DEVELOPMENTAL PSYCHOLOGY FOR THE DESIGN OF EFFECTIVE INSTRUCTION

Robbie Case
The Ontario Institute for Studies in Education
Toronto, Ontario, Canada

As anyone who has been a classroom teacher can attest, not all concepts or skills that children are asked to learn are of equal cognitive complexity. In any given curriculum, there are normally one or two tasks that stand out as being harder than the rest. Even when students are highly motivated, they master such tasks with great difficulty. In certain cases (for example, the addition of fractions), they may not master the tasks at all unless they are academically talented or unless they are given massive practice. The present paper addresses the question of how the teaching of such cognitively complex classroom tasks can be improved. It contends that a significant improvement can be achieved by basing the design of instruction on principles that derive from the study of cognitive development.

Empirical Characteristics of Cognitive-Developmental Tasks

From an empirical point of view, the sort of cognitive tasks that have been studied by developmental psychologists have two characteristics that make them relevant to the teaching of complex classroom tasks. First, although their content is normally quite familiar to the child, the understanding that they demand is not. In fact, it is sufficiently complex that it often takes years to acquire. Piaget's conservation task, for example, involves materials with which children are thoroughly familiar by age of three. However, the task itself is not normally mastered until age of seven or eight. Binet's figure copying task involves motor skills that are mastered by the age of four or five. In addition, it utilizes patterns that children can recognize and label by age of five or six. However, the task itself is not normally mastered until age of eight or nine.

The second empirical characteristic of cognitive-developmental tasks is that they are extremely difficult to teach by conventional methods. If one simply explains the conservation principle to a 5-year-old, or simply demonstrates the drawing of a diamond, the improvement in performance that is obtained is minimal. If the instruction is sufficiently extensive that some improvement in

441

performance is obtained, retention and transfer may nevertheless remain quite poor. Thus, although cognitive-developmental tasks are unlike classroom tasks in that they are eventually acquired spontaneously, they are similar in that they are cognitively complex and difficult to teach. Given this empirical similarity, it seems probable that there may be an underlying theoretical similarity as well.

Theoretical Characteristics of Cognitive-Developmental Tasks

From a theoretical point of view, most cognitive-developmental tasks again possess two closely related characteristics. The first is that they elicit strategies from young children that are reasonable, but incorrect. Table 1 presents a description of the strategies that young children use to solve three different Piagetian tasks. Consider first the task where the child is presented with two beakers of water, and asked to judge which contains the greater amount to drink. The 5-year-old's strategy on this task may be characterized as follows: "Estimate the height of the first beaker. Estimate the height of the second beaker. Choose the beaker with the taller column of liquid" (Piaget, 1957). This is, of course, a very reasonable strategy, and one that would probably work 90% of the time at home or at school, where drinking water would be offered in glasses of equal diameter.

Consider next a task called the Orange Juice Problem (Noelting, Note 1). On this task, children are presented with two small sets of cups, some of which are filled with water, some of which are filled with orange concentrate. They are asked which set will form a mixture that tastes more strongly of orange juice. The 5-year-old's strategy on the task may be characterized as follows: "Count the number of orange-concentrate cups in the first set. Count the number of orange-concentrate cups in the second set. Choose the set that has the greater number of such cups" (Noelting, Note 1). Again, this is an eminently reasonable strategy, and one that would guarantee success in any situation where the number of cups of water in the two sets was equal.

Finally, consider the Balance Task (Inhelder & Piaget, 1964). On this task, children are shown two sets of weights, each of which is on one arm of a balance beam. They are asked which side of the balance beam will go down when its supports are removed. The 5-year-old's strategy on this task may be characterized as follows: "Count the number of weights on the left-hand side. Count the number of weights on the right-hand side. Choose the side with the greater number of weights" (Siegler, 1976). Once again, this is a very reasonable strategy, and one that would probably work 90% of the time on playgrounds, where the seats of teetertotters are equal distances from the fulcrum. In all three of these examples, and in fact in almost any developmental task for which children's strategies can be described with precision, it is the case that the strategies that young children employ are not so much incorrect as they are incomplete.

Table 1. Strategies Observed at Two Age Levels on Three Piagetian Tasks

Visual Array			
Task Question	Which beaker has more water to drink?	Which mixture will taste more strongly of orange juice (indicated by shading)?	Which side will go down?
Response — 5-6 years	A has more, because it's taller.	A will taste more. It's got two juice. B's only got one.	A will go down. It's got more weights.
Response — 7-8	B has more. A is a bit taller, but B is much fatter.	B will taste more. A's got more water than juice. B doesn't.	B will go down. It's only got 2 weights, but they're so far out. A has 3 but they're right in close.

The second theoretical characteristic of cognitive developmental
tasks is that the strategy that they elicit from young children places a
lighter load on working memory than would the correct strategy.[1] This
property is most easily seen by looking down the columns of Table 1
rather than across them. The strategy used by 5-year-olds on Piaget's
liquid quantity task is to compare the two liquid columns with respect
to their height. The strategy used by 8-year-olds is to compare the
liquid heights and the liquid widths, and to try to effect some sort of
compensation. Table 2 traces the series of mental acts that each of
these two strategies entail. As may be seen, only two items must be
held in working memory in order to execute the most complex step of the
5-year-old's strategy: the height of beaker 1 and the height of beaker
2. By contrast, at least three items must be held in working memory in
order to execute the most complex step of the 8-year-old's strategy:
the width of beaker 1, the width of beaker 2, and the already computed
difference in height. A similar analysis may be made for both the
Orange Juice Problem and the Balance Problem.

Developmental psychologists are not yet agreed on how to compute
the quantitative load that a strategy places on a child's working
memory.[2] Nor are they agreed as to whether the measured growth in
children's working memory has a functional or structural basis (cf.
Case, 1978a; Chi, Note 2; Dempster, Note 3; Pascual-Leone, 1970;
Simon, 1972). There does appear to be a good agreement, however, with
regard to the following two points: (a) The strategies that lead young
children into error are reasonable but oversimplified, and (b) correct
strategies often place a greater burden on young children's working
memory than incorrect strategies.

Relationship Between Theoretical and Empirical Characteristics of Cognitive-Developmental Tasks

Once it is acknowledged that many developmental tasks share the
above two theoretical characteristics, it is a very short leap to assert
that it is these same two characteristics that are responsible for
producing the observed empirical phenomena, namely the long period of
failure under conditions of spontaneous acquisition, and the continued
failure in the face of conventional instruction. From the earliest days
in psychology, it has been known that it is difficult for subjects who
have a habitual way of viewing or responding to a particular task to
break that set and respond in a new way (cf. Dunker, 1945). Clinical
analyses reveal that this tendency may persist even in the face of
direct instruction (cf. Case, 1975). A subject will appear to have
grasped a particular point, but then ignore it and give his old response
a few minutes later. A similar point can be made with regard to the
load on working memory. From the earliest days in psychology it has
been known that the human working memory is limited (cf. Jacobs, 1887),
and that this may affect a subject's ability to grasp complex issues or

Table 2. Working Memory Demands for Executing Two Typical Strategies on Piaget's Quantity Assessment Task

Strategy	Steps Involved	Items In Working Memory		Memory Demand
Unidimensional Scanning (5 years)	Step 1: Note height A (H_A)	(i)	(H_A)	1
	Step 2: Compare to height B (H_B)	(i) (ii)	(H_A) (H_B)	2
	Step 3: Pick side for which height is greater	(i)	($H_A > H_B$)	1
Bidimensional Scanning (8 years)	Step 1: Note height A (H_A)	(i)	H_A	1
	Step 2: Compare to height B (H_B)	(i) (ii)	H_A H_B	2
	Step 3: Store difference	(i)	$H_A - H_B$	1
	Step 4: Note width B (W_B)	(i) (ii)	$H_A - H_2$ W_B	2
	Step 5: Compare to width A (W_A)	(i) (ii) (iii)	$H_A - H_B$ W_B W_A	3
	Step 6: Pick greater difference	(i) (ii)	$H_A - H_B$ $W_B - W_A$	2

problems. Clinical studies reveal that this problem may continue even in the face of instruction (Case, 1975). A child will appear to grasp one point perfectly, yet as the child's attention swings to the point with which he or she must integrate it, the child will appear to lose hold of the original understanding. Experimental evidence supports both of these clinical findings. It has been shown that children's ability to resist misleading and habitual sets correlates with their performance on developmental tasks (cf. Pascual-Leone, Note 4; Dale, Note 5). It has also been shown that the size of their working memory correlates both with their original performance and with their ability to profit from instruction (Case, Note 6). The following section will outline a method of instruction that is designed to take account of these two sources of task difficulty.

Theoretical Characteristics of Successful Instruction

For any task where the above two problems persist in the face of conventional instruction, it is clear that successful instruction must somehow accomplish the following two objectives: (a) It must demonstrate to the student that his or her current strategy can be improved upon; and, (b) it must minimize the load on the student's working memory.

Dealing with Incorrect Solution Strategies

Consider first the objective of demonstrating to the student that his or her current strategy can be improved upon. If this objective is to be accomplished, it seems necessary for the instruction to have the following characteristics:

1. It must provide the student with some meaningful procedure for determining whether or not his or her approach has been successful.

2. It must present the student with problems for which his or her current strategy will not work.

3. It must provide an explanation for why the current strategy will not work, if this is not apparent to the student already.

4. It must provide a demonstration of (or invite the student to discover) the correct strategy.

5. It must explain why the correct strategy works better, if this is not apparent to the student already.

6. It must provide a period of practice with coaching, together with the opportunity to transfer the new strategy to new situations.

Minimizing the Load on Working Memory

Consider next the objective of minimizing the load on the student's working memory. If this objective is to be accomplished, the instruction must have the following three characteristics:

1. It must reduce to a bare minimum the number of items of information that require the student's attention. By definition, the fewer the number of items of information with which the student must deal at any one time, the smaller the load on working memory.

2. It must insure that all cues to which the student must attend and all responses he or she must exhibit are familiar ones. The more familiar a cue, the less working memory need be devoted to the task of extracting it from its context. Similarly, the more familiar a response, the less working memory need be devoted to its execution (cf. Case, 1978a,b).

3. It must insure that all stimuli to which the subject must attend are salient, either because their physical characteristics make them stand out from their context, or because they are pointed out verbally by the instructor. Once again, the more salient a stimulus, the less working memory need be devoted to the task of extracting it.

The next section will examine several instructional programs that were designed to teach developmental competencies, and that were successful at doing so. It will attempt to demonstrate that these successful programs did, in fact, possess the two sets of theoretical characteristics that were mentioned earlier.

Examples of Successful Instruction

A Cognitive-Developmental Task: The Control of Variables

Consider first a task that was designed by Inhelder, and is often referred to as Bending Rods (Inhelder & Piaget, 1964). Children are presented with a set of rods as indicated in Figure 1, and are invited to explore the apparatus with a view to determining what makes some of the rods bend more than others. After they have conducted a preliminary investigation, they are asked (a) to list the variables that they think might determine rod flexibility, and (b) to design a careful experiment to determine whether or not each possible variable really does have the effect they believe it does. Although the task would appear to be an easy one to someone with formal training in science, it is, in fact, quite difficult. Even by the age of 15 or 16, it is failed by at least 50% of the children in an average population. As with most developmental tasks, the problem is not so much that the children's strategy is incorrect, as that it is incomplete. What children do is to isolate the variable that is of interest (say length), and vary it by choosing a long rod and a short rod. They then hang a weight on each rod, and check to see if the long rod bends more than the short rod. If it does, they take the result as proof of their original hypothesis. What children do not do is to check the pair of rods for any other difference that might possibly have made the long rod bend more than the short rod.

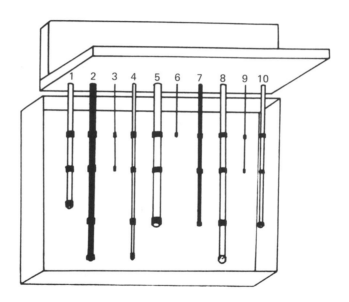

Figure 1. Apparatus for *Bending Rods*. Rod 1: wood, 13 × 0.125 in. Rod 2: brass, 20 × 0.1875 in. Rod 3: brass, 10 × 0.0625 in. Rod 4: wood, 20 × 0.125 in. Rod 5: wood, 16 × 0.3125 in. Rod 6: brass, 6 × 0.0625 in. Rod 7: brass, 16 × 0.125 in. Rod 8: wood, 20 × 0.1875 in. Rod 9: brass, 10 × 0.0625 in. Rod 10: wood, 16 × 0.125 in.

The majority of programs aimed at teaching students how to succeed on tasks such as Bending Rods have not been particularly successful (cf. Tomlinson-Keasey, 1972; Black, Note 7). However, there is one clear exception to this rule (Case, 1974a,b), and it is this program that will be analyzed.

According to the line of reasoning developed above, the first theoretical characteristic of effective instruction is that it should provide some means by which a student can assess the adequacy of his or her current strategy. For the Bending Rods task, this is a particular problem. A child who believes that length affects flexibility, and who sees that the long rod bends more than the short rod, has neither the cognitive motivation nor the means to see that his or her current strategy is inadequate. In the instructional program under consideration, however, this problem was solved by beginning with a different task.[3] Children were presented with an array of objects such as those illustrated in Figure 2a. They were asked to determine which weighed more, the dark-colored rods or the light-colored rods. Since the rods were securely embedded in blocks that could vary in weight themselves, the result was that the relative weight of the rods could only be established with certainty by controlling the type of block in which the rods were embedded. In this respect, the task was parallel to the Bending Rods test. As will no doubt be apparent, however, the task was also different from the Bending Rods test in several important respects. First, the subject had no basis for assuming that he or she knew the effect of the independent variable ahead of time; all the child knew was that one rod weighed more, not which one it was. Second, once the child had conducted an experiment to determine which of the two rods weighed more, it was possible for the experimenter to detach the rods from the blocks, and let the child do a more direct test to see if his or her conclusion had been correct. In fact, this was done after every trial. The instructor removed the rods from the blocks, and let the student test the validity of the conclusion he or she had drawn directly.

In addition to providing the motivation and means for a direct test, the Rod and Block paradigm satisfied the three criteria that were mentioned for minimizing the load on working memory. First, the paradigm is maximally simple. There is only one possibly confounding variable (the type of block), and the presence of this variable is highly salient. Second, the test of strategic adequacy (weighing) is itself a simple one. Again, only one cue need be attended to (the tilt of the balance), and this cue is a highly salient one. Finally, for both the original experiment and the more direct test, the situation is familiar, since pretraining is provided in how to work a balance.

The second theoretical characteristic that successful instruction should possess is that it should provide the student with a problem situation where the inadequacy of his or her current strategy can be plainly seen. In order to insure that this would be the case, children were presented with the array of objects illustrated in Figure 2b. Since their strategy was simply to select the first dark-colored and the first light-colored rod on which their gaze fell, they all chose the pair of blocks that was closest to them. Although the light-colored rod was made of aluminum and the dark-colored rod was made of brass, the dark-colored block had been weighted with lead inserts, whereas the light-colored block had not. Thus, the result was that the side of the

A

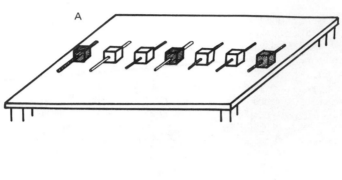

B

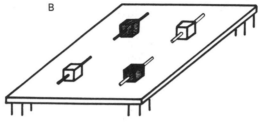

Figure 2. Materials for testing and training in the control-of-variables test.

balance with the light-colored rod on it tilted down. As soon as the children drew the conclusion that this rod was heavier (which they all did), the rods were removed and they were allowed to weigh them separately. Their error was thus immediately apparent.

The third theoretical characteristic that an effective instructional program should possess is the provision of a simple explanation for why the children's current strategy is inadequate. In the program under consideration, the instructor asked the children if they could figure out how they had been fooled. For those who could not figure out the answer on their own, the following explanation was provided:

"Feel these blocks. I fooled you because this block was so heavy that it pulled the balance down (gesture). It made the silver rod look heavier, even though it was not."

Note that the above explanation uses words that are familiar, sentences that are short, and grammatical constructions that are simple (e.g., the active voice). Note, too, that the explanation places a minimum load on working memory from the point of view of content. No reference is made to a "variable" as such, or even to relative weight.

The result is that the subject has to focus on only one item of information: the effect of the heavy block. The effect that a heavy weight can have is already familiar to children, but its salience is heightened by the instructor's verbal reference to it, by his or her gesture, and by the request that the child feel the block.

The fourth theoretical characteristic that an effective instructional sequence should possess is a clear demonstration of the correct strategy. In the program under consideration, the intructor achieved this by inviting the child to think of a way the child could have done the experiment so that he or she would have gotten the right answer. If the child could not figure this out independently, the instructor demonstrated the correct strategy as follows: He or she picked up a light block with a silver rod, and placed it on one side of the balance. He or she then picked up another light block with a brass rod, and placed it on the other side of the balance. Then the instructor said:

> "You should pick up two rods where the blocks are the same.
> See (releasing the balance). It doesn't fool you. The
> silver one doesn't look heavier this time."

Note once again that this demonstration places only a minimal load on the student's working memory. The words are familiar, the sentences short, and the constructions simple. In addition, the content is highly simplified, and the perceptual configuration extremely clear.

The fifth theoretical characteristic that an effective instructional program should possess is a clear explanation of why the correct strategy works the way it does. Such an explanation may not always be necessary. Students may grasp the principle on which the correct strategy is based spontaneously, at last at an intuitive level. However, in the program under consideration, the following elaboration was provided:

> "Now pay attention carefully and I'll explain why the
> blocks have to be the same (putting two differently-colored
> rods on the balance). Which is heavier? Right, the brass
> (putting light block on each pan, but not connecting them
> to rods). See, when the blocks are the same, the brass one
> still looks heavier. The blocks don't fool you because
> they're the same (demonstrating the equality). See, they
> balance. Even if I use these two (putting on two heavy
> blocks) it doesn't fool you because they're the same. They
> can't make the silver one look heavier. But look what
> happens when I put two different ones on. The silver one
> looks heavier, even though it isn't (demonstrating). It
> always works that way. If you make two blocks the same,
> they can't fool you. You can tell which rod is heavier.
> But if you don't, it (the heavy block) can fool you."

In retrospect, it seems possible that the above explanation could be further simplified. Nevertheless, even in the above form, it shows the child why the correct strategy works in terms that are relatively simple, and that refer back to the original explanation of how the child was fooled. The child was fooled originally by putting on a block that was so heavy that it obscured the effect of the rods. He or she avoids being fooled by making sure that one block is not heavier than the other.

The final characteristic that an effective instructional program should possess is that it should present a period of practice, coaching, and generalization. In the present program, such a period was provided for about 80 minutes spread across four sessions.

After the above demonstration had been provided, children were given several more examples in which the relative weights of two (new) rods had to be determined. During this period, they were allowed to proceed on their own, and the instructor only intervened if they made some error. After each trial, the rods were taken out and the accuracy of the inference was checked. If the child made an error, the above explanation and demonstration were repeated. On the second day, the same task was reviewed, and the child was presented with a situation in which the two variables in question could not be disassociated from each other physically. If an error was made, the instructor drew an analogy to the block situation and asked "How do you know it (e.g., bounced higher?) Because. . . (e.g., it's made of harder rubber?) Maybe it's just because (e.g., it was dropped from higher)." On the third day, the block demonstration was again reviewed, and a three variable problem was introduced. At the end of this session, the experimenter introduced a counter-suggestion: "Would this be another fair way to prove it?," thus sensitizing the child to the possibility that another test that yields the same results is not necessarily an adequate one. Finally, on the fourth day, again after a review, a task was introduced for which the number of variables was the same as in Bending Rods. Once again, the child was left to his or her own devices, and coaching was provided only if the child slipped back into the original inadequate strategy.

The practice and generalization inherent in the above sequence will no doubt be obvious. What may be less obvious, however, is that the three requirements for minimizing the load on working memory are once again met. First of all, new components are introduced to the task only one at a time. Second, they are introduced only after extensive practice on the basic strategy. Third, when they are introduced, the new component is always rendered salient by the instructor.

In summary, the above instructional sequence possesses all six of the theoretical characteristics that appear to be necessary if the children's original strategy on a task is to be treated. In addition, the sequence possesses all three of the characteristics necessary to minimize the load on working memory. The results of the program are also quite dramatic. After completing the program, the majority of 7-

and 8-year-olds perform virtually perfectly on the Bending Rods task on
their first exposure to it. The mean scores they obtain are thus higher
than those of untrained 15- and 16-year-olds.

    Although space does not permit a detailed description here,
programs with similar characteristics have been developed for teaching
other cognitive-developmental tasks. The results have been similar. To
date, the tasks for which this has been done include the Binet Maze Task
(Case, Note 8), Classification (Case, 1972), a Mnemonic Ordering Task
(Case, 1974a), the Wine and Water Task (Case, 1975), Conservation (Case,
Note 6), and Wason's Four Card Task (Weiss, Note 9).

A Difficult Classroom Task: The Missing Addend Problem

    Consider a difficult cognitive task of the sort encountered in the
classroom.   Children are presented with the following equation, and
asked to fill in the missing number.

$$4 + \fbox{\underline{}} = 7$$

    Although the task appears to be quite elementary, and although it
forms a part of most standard first grade curricula, like many cognitive
developmental tasks it is, in fact, quite difficult.   When they first
encounter the task, children almost universally fail it. In addition,
as with most cognitive developmental tasks, the strategy that they
exhibit is reasonable but inappropriate. Beginning with the number 4,
they increment it 7 times, thus arriving at 11 as the answer.   (This
would, of course, be the correct answer if the + and the = signs were
reversed.)   Finally,   as   is   again   the   case   with   most
cognitive-developmental tasks, most programs designed to teach the
missing addend problem have not been particularly successful, at least
in first grade (cf. O'Hara, 1975).   Once again, there is one notable
exception to this rule (Case, Note 10; Gold, Note 11), and it is this
exception that will be analyzed here.

    The first theoretical characteristic of effective instruction, it
will be remembered, is that it should introduce children to some simple
and meaningful paradigm, by means of which they can evaluate the
effectiveness of their current strategy.   In the program under
consideration, the first exercise in which these children participated
is shown in Figure 3.

    Note that this paradigm permits children to check the results of
their addition to a fashion that meets all the criteria for minimizing
the load on short-term memory. Few perceptual cues need to considered.
In addition, the cues in question are both highly familiar and highly
salient. Finally, the overall purpose of the task (to check to see if
two objects are identical) is set in a context that is also both
meaningful and familiar.

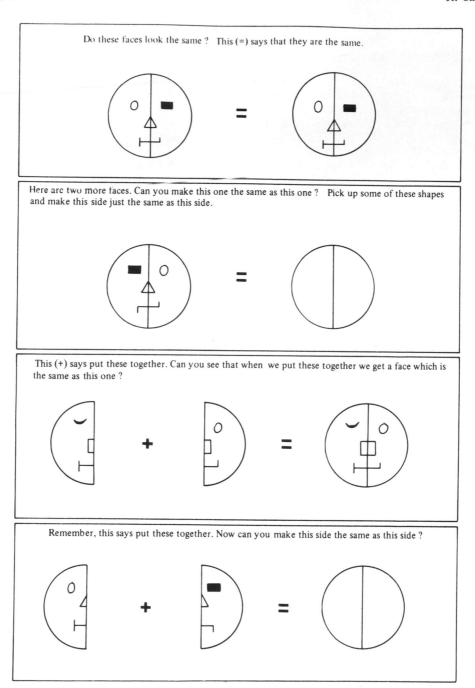

Figure 3. Example materials for an initial addition exercise.

The second theoretical characteristic of an effective instructional program is that it should present the children with example problems where the inadequacy of their spontaneous strategy will become apparent. In the program under consideration, this objective was attained almost immediately. The second set of exercises to which the child was exposed is shown in Figure 4.

The third characteristic of successful instruction is that it should provide children with a simple and clear explanation of why their current strategy is inappropriate. In the program under consideration, such an explanation was rarely necessary during the initial phases, since the inappropriateness of the incorrect strategy was clear from the nature of the paradigm itself. However, as the more formal components of the task were reintroduced (i.e., dot counting and numerical reading), the incorrect strategy was again observed quite frequently. Whenever it appeared, the following explanation was provided:

> "Remember, this (pointing at the plus) says put these together so that you get the same as this one. Put these together, and see if you get the same as this one."

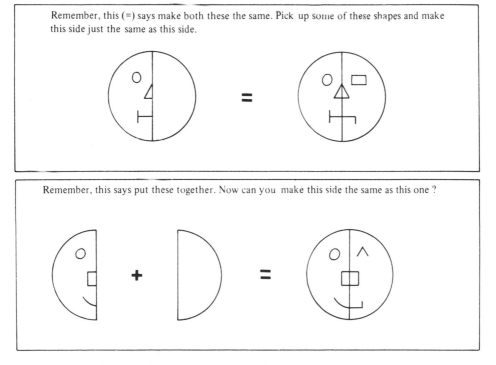

Figure 4. Example materials for subsequent addition exercises.

Note that, as with the Rod and Block example, the words used are all familiar, the sentences short, and the grammatical constructions similar. What the instructor does is to point out the cue that the subject ignored (in this case, the position of the plus), and remind the subject of the importance of this cue for the task at hand. The number of items to which the subject must attend is kept to bare minimum (one), the salience of this item is heightened by word and gesture, and the subject's own previous knowledge is drawn upon to make the explanation as simple and meaningful as possible.

The fourth characteristic of successful instruction is that it should provide children with a clear demonstration of the correct strategy. In the "faces" paradigm, this is not really necessary, since children spontaneously look for the parts that are missing, and put them in the appropriate place. Once a shift is made to numbers, however, this becomes a potential problem. One strategy that adults often use is to subtract the addend that is given from the total. The strategy used by 8-year-olds, however, which is equally correct, involves only addition (cf. Groen & Poll, 1973). In fact, the strategy is very much like that used by shopkeepers in making change. Beginning with the lower number, children count upward until they reach the higher number (often using their fingers). The number of times the lower number has been incremented is then the number that they place in the box.

In the program under consideration, considerable strategic flexibility was permitted, at least in the pilot phase. Some children seemed to find that the correct number "popped into their heads once they realized that they were looking for a missing addend," not a missing total. These children were given free rein to follow their intuitions, so long as they checked their answers by addition. Other children did not find that the number could be obtained so easily, and so they were provided with tokens to execute the above mentioned "storekeeper" strategy. Note that in both the choice of the strategy to be modeled, and in the provision of concrete props, the intent was again to minimize the load on working memory.

The fifth characteristic of successful instruction is that it should provide whatever verbal explanation is necessary to make the rationale for the correct strategy apparent. The explanation that was provided in the present program was the same as that provided for explaining the error of the incorrect strategy. Children were reminded of the meaning of the addition sign, and asked to check their answer after each trial to see that when the two addends were put together as the sign indicated, they did, in fact, yield the answer given on the other side of the equal sign.

The sixth characteristic of successful instruction is that it should provide the subject with a period of practice, coaching, and generalization. In the present program, as with the Rod and Blocks program, the components that were stripped from the task originally were gradually reintroduced at this point. Thus, the exercise and explanations already presented for the faces were repeated, first using dots and counting, and then using numerals. Once again, the pacing of the new exercises was such as to minimize the load on working memory, by maximizing the familiarity of the basic strategy and the goal toward which it was directed. Any time the subject made an error, the instructor referred back to the original paradigm, and reviewed the meaning of the basic signs involved.

In summary, like the successful programs that were designed to teach cognitive-developmental competencies, the above program would appear to possess all six of the theoretical characteristics that were hypothesized as necessary for dealing with children's original strategy on a task. In addition, the program appears to possess all three of the characteristics that were hypothesized as necessary for minimizing the load on working memory. The exact fashion in which these characteristics were realized in the classroom program were different from the way they were realized in the laboratory program. The general thrust was to head off the incorrect strategy rather than to trap children into it, and then explain their error. In addition, the explanations had to do with the meaning of culturally defined symbols, rather than observable effects in the physical world. These differences aside, however, it seems clear that the overall aims and structure of the two programs were remarkably similar. The same is true of the results.

The "faces" program was administered on an individual basis to 10 children in a standard California kindergarten. The standard curriculum was adapted so that it drew on the same specific examples, and could be presented in the same length of time (20 minutes). It was then administered to a matched set of 10 control children from the same classroom. As is shown in Table 3, the results were again quite dramatic. Only one subject out of 10 who received the standard curriculum scored as high as three out of five on a posttest given two days later. By contrast, only three subjects out of 10 in the group receiving the developmentally based program received scores that were lower than four out of five.

Although space does not permit their presentation here, a number of other instructional programs have recently been devised by my students, and tried out on small groups of children. To date, the evidence is clinical rather than experimental. Nevertheless, the approach appears to be quite successful. One student applied the approach to the teaching of perimeter, where the incorrect strategy is to count the squares on the graph paper around the perimeter of whatever shape appears, rather than to count the marks on the perimeter itself (Hunt, Note 12). Another student applied the approach to teaching children how to tell time, where the strategy is to use the available numerals to assign values to both the minutes and the hours (Steinback, Note 13). Another student applied the approach to the teaching of addition of fractions, where one of the incorrect strategies is to add both the denominators and the numerators (Stevens, Note 14). Finally,

Table 3. Score on Five Standard-Format Missing Addend Problems

Teacher-Assessed Ability	Developmental Boys	Method Girls	Conventional Boys	Method Girls
Very High	5	5	1	0
High	4	4	3	0
Medium	4	4	0	0
Low	5	2	0	0
Very Low	3	1	0	0

one student used the approach as an aid in teaching remedial phonics, where one incorrect strategy is to sound out the names of letters rather than their corresponding sounds (Frazer, Note 15).

Practical Applications of the Developmental Approach

On the basis of the above analysis, it seems reasonable to conclude that instruction that possesses the nine characteristics that were itemized can produce positive results, whether the task in question is drawn from the literature on cognitive development or from conventional classroom curricula. This being the case, it seems important to specify the type of task for which it is possible to design such a curriculum,[4] and the type of student for whom the benefits of doing so would be expected to be maximal.

Domain of Appropriate Tasks

The domain of tasks for which a developmentally based curriculum can be designed may be defined by the following three characteristics:

1. The task should be a difficult one for students to master, given current methods of instruction.

2. The task should have a specifiable objective and method of solution.

3. The task should be one that elicits consistent responses from those who fail it.

Domain of Appropriate Subjects

Given that a task possesses the above three properties, any student should profit from a curriculum that is designed according to the principles that have been itemized. On the other hand, however, it must be remembered that many tasks that possess these characteristics do so only because they have been placed at an appropriate grade level. If placed at a somewhat higher level, they will present little difficulty. This being the case, the students who would be expected to receive maximum benefit would be those from whom the strategy of simply delaying instruction would, for some reason, be inappropriate. These include the following groups:

1. Children who are mentally retarded. By definition, a retardate is one whose development lags behind that of his peer group and who reaches a lower terminal level. For such a child, the strategy of simply waiting for development to take its course is clearly not an advisable one.

2. Adults. For tasks that exhibit the above three properties (e.g., statistics), adults are in essentially the same position as retardates: Their intellectual development is complete, and no further understanding can be expected simply as a result of delaying instruction.

3. Children who are handicapped, or who come from cultural backgrounds that are different from the majority. While the strategy of delaying instruction may be quite effective with such children, it will do nothing to close the gap between them and their peers. Thus, any approach that permits a given task to be mastered at a lower level of initial understanding is clearly highly desirable.

4. Children who need remedial work in a particular subject area. The object of remedial work is, of course, to enable children to catch up with their peers. Clearly, this is another example in which the strategy of simply delaying instruction will not be effective.

Summary

The argument that has been advanced here may be summarized by means of the following four propositions:

1. Difficult classroom tasks and the tasks that have been studied by developmental psychologists exhibit a number of very similar empirical characteristics.

2. Two of the major sources of difficulty underlying cognitive-developmental tasks are the following: (a) Children come to the tasks with strategies that are reasonable but inappropriate, and (b) the acquisition of a more appropriate strategy by conventional methods

of instruction places a severe burden on children's working memory.   It
is likely that these difficulties underlie difficult classroom tasks as
well.

3.   Instruction that is designed to demonstrate to children that
their current strategy is inadequate, and to minimize the memorial
demands of acquiring a new strategy, can have dramatic effects. This is
true whether the task in question is drawn from the literature on
cognitive development, or from a conventional classroom curriculum.

4.   The practical situations in which curricula with these
characteristics would be expected to be most beneficial would be those
in which the instructional task possesses the above-mentioned
theoretical characteristics, and in which the alternative strategy of
simply delaying instruction is not a viable one.

Footnotes

1.   Working memory is defined as the maximum number of items that a
subject can hold in mind while working on a problem (cf. Pascual-Leone,
1970). This may be contrasted with short-term memory, which is the
maximum number of items a subject can store and retrieve when this is
the only task in which he or she is engaged. For young children, the
difference between working memory and short-term memory is often as high
as three or four units.

2.   The system employed in Table 2 is that presented in Case
(1978a).

3.   The task in question was designed by Robert Kenzie (Note 16).

4.   In the present article, I have concentrated exclusively on
describing the characteristics that effective instruction should
possess. For a description of how to design a program that has these
characteristics, see Case (1978b).

Reference Notes

1.   Noelting, G. Stages and mechanisms in the development of the
concept of proportion in the child and adolescent. Paper given at the
Fifth Interdisciplinary Seminar on Piagetian Theory and its Implications
for the Helping Professions. University of Southern California, Los
Angeles, 1975.

2.   Chi, M.   The development of short-term memory capacity.
Unpublished doctoral dissertation. Carnegie-Mellon University, 1975.

3. Dempster, F. A developmental investigation of memory span:
Storage capacity or organizational strategies? Unpublished doctoral
dissertation, University of California, Berkeley, 1976.

4. Pascual-Leone, J. Cognitive development and cognitive style.
Unpublished doctoral dissertation, University of Geneva, 1969.

5. Dale, L. A neo-Piagetian investigation of some factors
affecting performance on Piaget's flexibillity of rods problem.
Unpublished doctoral dissertation, La Trobe University, Australia, 1976.

6. Case, R. Maturation, experience, and intellectual development.
Final report, The Spencer Foundation, 1976.

7. Black, A. The coordination of logical and moral reasoning in
adolescence. Unpublished doctoral dissertation, University of
California, 1977.

8. Case, R. Difficulties encountered by disadvantaged children in
solving a visually represented problem. Unpublished Master's thesis,
University of Toronto, 1968.

9. Weiss, N. Predicting and eliminating errors in adult
problem-solving behavior: A task analytic approach. Unpublished course
assignment, University of California, Berkeley, 1975.

10. Case, R. The process of stage transition in cognitive
development. Final report, Project £ROIHDO91Y8-01, NIMHCD, 1977.

11. Gold, A. Effects of four training procedures on learning the
missing addend problem. Unpublished manuscript. University of
California, Berkeley, 1974.

12. Hunt, J. Teaching perimeter. Unpublished course assignment,
The Ontario Institute for Studies in Education, 1977.

13. Steinbach, R. Teaching Eric how to tell time. Unpublished
course assignment, The Ontario Institute for Studies in Education, 1977.

14. Stevens, R. Teaching the addition of fractions. Unpublished
course assignment, The Ontario Institute for Studies in Education, 1977.

15. Frazer, A. Teaching Michael to sound out words. Unpublished
course assignment, The Ontario Institute for Studies in Education, 1977.

16. Kenzie, R. Personal communication, July 1970.

References

Case, R. Learning and development: A neo-Piagetian interpretation.
     Human Development, 1972, 15, 339-358.

Case, R.   Mental strategies, mental capacity, and instruction: A
     neo-Piagetian   investigation.   Journal   of Experimental Child
     Psychology, 1974, 18, 382-397. (a)

Case, R. Structures and strictures, some functional limitations on the
     course   of cognitive growth.   Cognitive Psychology, 1974, 6,
     544-573. (b)

Case, R.   Gearing the demands of instruction to the   development
     capacities of the learner. Review of Educational Research, 1975,
     45, 59-87.

Case, R. Piaget and beyond: Toward a developmentally based theory and
     technology of instruction.   In R.   Glaser (Ed.), Advances in
     instructional psychology, Volume 1.   Hillsdale, NJ: Lawrence
     Erlbaum, 1978. (a)

Case, R.   Intellectual development from birth to adulthood: A
     neo-Piagetian interpretation.   In R.   Siegler (Ed.), Children's
     thinking: What develops? Hillsdale NJ: Lawrence Erlbaum, 1978.
     (b)

Dunker, K. On problem solving.   Psychological Monographs, 1945, 58,
     Whole No. 270.

Groen, G. J., & Poll, M. Subtraction and the solution of open sentence
     problems.   Journal of Experimental Child Psychology, 1973, 16,
     292-302.

Inhelder, B., & Piaget, J. The early growth of logic in the child:
     Classification and seriation. London: Routledge and Kegan Paul,
     1964.

Jacobs, J. Experiments on prehension. Mind, 1887, 12, 75-79.

O'Hara, E.   Piaget, the six-year-old, and   modern   math.   Todays
     Education, 1975, 64, 33-36.

Pascual-Leone, J. A mathematical model for the transition rule in
     Piaget's developmental stages.   Acta Psychologica, 1970, 63,
     301-345.

Piaget, J. Logique et équilibre dans les comportements du sujet. In L.
     Apostel,   B.   Mandelbrot,   &   J.   Piaget (Eds.),   Etudes
     D'épistemologie génétique, II: Logique et équilbre.   Paris:

Presses Universitaires de France, 1957.

Siegler, R. S.   Three aspects of cognitive development.   <u>Cognitive</u> <u>Psychology</u>, 1976, <u>8</u>, 481-520.

Simon, H. A.   On the development of the processor.   In S. Farnham-Diggory (Ed.), <u>Information</u> <u>processing</u> <u>in children</u>.   New York: Academic Press, 1972.

Tomlinson-Keasey, C.   Formal operations in females from eleven to fifty-four years of age.   <u>Developmental</u> <u>Psychology</u>, 1972, <u>6</u>(2), 364.

ON THE RECIPROCAL RELATIONSHIP BETWEEN PREVIOUS EXPERIENCE AND PROCESSING IN DETERMINING LEARNING OUTCOMES

Ernst Z. Rothkopf
Bell Laboratories
Murray Hill, New Jersey, U.S.A.

The learning process is complex and incompletely understood. Despite this, the general factors that appear relevant to the measured success of instruction are small in number. At least at the first level of approximation, they can be simply described. First there are those factors that determine that students will come in physical proximity of instructive events. In the case of written material, these factors include the incidence of instructive events in the text, and compliance by students with reading assignments and/or suggestions. The second class of factors are those that determine whether an instructive event, once it has been encountered, will be perceived and internally represented in instructionally appropriate ways. The third factor primarily determines test performance. This factor is related to (a) the semantic and structural disparity between instructive events and the test, as well as (b) forgetting. Whether the required skills are learned is determined by the opportunities for encounters with suitable instructive events, as well as by the likelihood of sufficient internal representation. The disparity and forgetting factor determines whether acquired competence is translated into appropriate test performance.

The conditions that determine whether an instructive event, once it is encountered, results in suitable learning, are the chief concerns of this paper. Research during the past decade has been strongly concerned with the important role of student processing activities used in translating the nominal instructive stimuli into effective instructive events (e.g., Bobrow & Bower, 1969; Craik & Lockhart, 1972; Hyde & Jenkins, 1973; Rothkopf, 1965, 1971, 1972a). I have concluded that translation of nominal stimulus into effective instructive stimulus has at least two components. These are (a) the likelihood of processing activities of sufficient quality, and (b) the nature of instruction-relevant knowledge that has been acquired by the student prior to instruction. My main thesis is that these two factors, processing and instruction-relevant experience, stand in reciprocal relationship to each other. This point of view implies that different qualities of processing are required with different degrees of instruction-relevant experience in order to achieve instructional success.

465

Previous Experience and Processing

The reasoning that led to this formulation will be illustrated in two ways: one, by examining two instructive events relevant to the reproduction of grasshoppers, and, two, by the analysis of correlational data from a previous experiment.

Consider two ways in which readers might learn that grasshoppers lay eggs in holes in the ground. Both of the following text elements (instructive events) would be sufficient for at least some of the readers in some situations: (a) Grasshoppers reproduce by laying eggs; these are laid in holes in the ground. (b) We attempted to capture a specimen during this important moment in the reproductive cycle. Unfortunately, I grabbed the grasshopper too hard and its ovipositor broke off in the small hole in the ground.

Instructive event (a) is simple and resembles the verbal description of the performance goal. It contains an infrequently used technical word, and requires an inference. Instructive event (b) will require processing levels that can be expected to be less common in the population of potential readers than those minimally required for instructive event (a). Moreover, readers who are not familiar with the word ovipositor (but who understand the Latin roots and in this way can extract the target information from the text), must engage in a less common level of processing than that required for success in readers who know the term well. If the reader knew neither ovipositor nor Latin, success is still possible if another information source such as a dictionary or knowledgeable parent is consulted. Broadly speaking, consulting other information sources is also a processing activity. It is a relatively unlikely event in general reading. This illustration may provide some intuitive grasp of why the reciprocal relationship between instruction-relevant knowledge and the likelihood of sufficient processing activities is a plausible and attractive conjecture.

Another line of reasoning that led us to the hypothesis that at least two related factors determine successful instruction can be illustrated from a recent study of goal-guided learning from written discourse (Rothkopf & Billington, 1975a). We looked at the correlation in average performance on 12 test items between groups of subjects operating in each of three treatments. Each test item measured the recall of a different information element in the text. Two of the groups, T_1 and T_2, involved goal-defining directions. This treatment was thought to affect mathemagenic activities (learning-relevant processing activities; see Rothkopf, 1972) relevant to the recall of information measured on the 12 test items. The third group, C, was not treated in any special way that would dispose them to attend selectively to the test-relevant information.

The idea that successful recall depends on at least two major factors (the experience factor E and the processing factor m) becomes interesting if it can be demonstrated that consistency in performance on the 12 test items was related to two separate factors. We reasoned from our data in the following way.

The proportion of correct responses for each of the 12 goal-relevant test items was determined for each treatment. Product-moment correlations were calculated in order to compare performance on the various test items between any two conditions.

1. If the two treatments T_1 and T_2 did not share a common factor, then the correlation between them, r_{TT}, would be zero. The actual r_{TT} correlation was .93 (p < .05). It was therefore concluded that the two experimental treatments shared a common factor.

2. If an experimental treatment and the control condition did not share a common factor, then the correlation between them, r_{TC}, would be zero. The best estimate of the correlation, r_{TC}, was found to be .60 (p < .05). From these data it was concluded that the experimental and control condition shared at least one common factor.

3. If the factor shared by the two experimental treatments was the same as the factor shared by treatment and control condition, the correlation between the two treatments, with the correlation to the control condition partialed out, would be zero (i.e., $r_{T_1 \cdot T_2} \cdot C = 0$). The partial correlation between T_1 and T_2, with the effect of the correlation to the control condition removed, was calculated to be .86 (p < .05). It was therefore concluded that at least one factor shared by the two experimental treatments was <u>not</u> also shared by the control condition.

The interpretation of the correlational results described above was consistent with the two factor theory. Performance on any test item depends on a priori experience ($\underline{E}$) with information relevant to the item. This "item ease" factor is shared by treatment and control conditions. The second component ($\underline{m}$, the mathemagenic operator) describes the nature of the learning-relevant processing and tends to have a different and larger value in the two experimental treatments than in the control.

In summary, these results indicated that in a suitable theoretical model (a) goal-descriptive direction and control treatment share at least one common factor; and, (b) that the two treatment conditions and the control condition each have at least one factor that is unique to them. We were also able to determine by other analysis (for details see Rothkopf & Billington, 1975a) that, (c) the shared factor probably interacts in a multiplicative way with the unique factor; and, (d) the unique factor for the control condition is a variable, while the unique factor for the goal-descriptive direction treatment is constant across test items.

For the data described above, we proposed a simple quasi-quantitative model. Performance on any specific test item is given for the control and the treatment groups respectively by the following equations:

$$\text{Control:} \quad P_C = E + (1 - E)m_C$$
$$\text{Treatment:} \quad P_T = E + (1 - E)m_T$$

where $\underline{E}$ is the pre-experiment experience factor shared by treatment and control. The variable mathemagenic operator m_C, is uniquely associated with the control condition. The variations in m_C probably reflected pre-experimentally established expectations of what was important in the text. The factor m_T, on the other hand, is a constant across items and is uniquely associated with the directions treatment. It reflects the impact of the goal-descriptive directions on learning and/or recall of goal-relevant information.

Experience and Mathemagenic Activity

Some processing is needed for learning regardless of the student's experience with the stimuli, concept structure, and metaphors of the instructional event. Beyond this minimal level it takes different and generally less likely processing, if the component elements of an instructional event are unfamiliar to the student, than if they are.

In general the experience factor (E) can be thought of as the main source of a hypothetical correlation in success produced by two presentations of the same instructional event widely spaced in time. It (E) would also contribute to correlations between effects of repetitions that are close together in time. The processing factors (m), on the other hand, would contribute only to hypothetical agreements in outcome between two presentations of the same instructional events that followed each other relatively closely in time, or that appeared in very similar situational contexts. The experience (E) relevant to an instructional event is under the control of relatively long-term factors. Processing factors, on the other hand, tend to be under the control of the more immediate and recent instructional environment.

Let us consider a possible theoretical mechanism for the interaction between $\underline{E}$ and $\underline{m}$. For this purpose it is assumed that a suitable instructive event is in the text (or any other instructional presentation) and that all students have at least nominally complied with the relevant reading assignments.

It is also assumed that experience level ε_i is found in the student population with probability E_i. If experience level is ε_i, the processing level sufficient for instructional success is assumed to be μ_i. A student at experience level ε_i, with respect to a given instructive event, will always learn if the processing level of the student is at least μ_i. The probability of processing levels of at least μ_i in the population is m_i. This relationship is illustrated in Figure 1, for a student population divided into three groups according to experience relevant to a given instructive event. Processing level μ_i is sufficient for experience ε_i, μ_j for ε_j, and μ_n for ε_n. The height of the curve in the upper panel of the figure is the probability of encountering at least processing level μ in the population of students. The areas of the flags are approximately proportional to the likelihood of successes, e.g., $E_i \times m_i$ is the proportion of students in the population at experience level ε_i who are also operating at processing level μ, which is the processing level sufficient for success in these students.

Expectations of success of a given instructive event for the entire student population, P_T, can be written:

(1) $$P_T = E_i m_i + E_j m_j + E_n m_n + E_e m_e$$

where E_i is the proportion of students in any given experience level i, and m_i, m_j, m_n, and m_e is the proportion of students who are operating at the minimum mathemagenic activity level or better required at their experience level for the successful outcome of the instructive event.

Experience level relevant to a particular instructive event can be ascertained by direct tests of knowledge, or by other approximate indicators such as the student's major field of concentration. If no special attempt is made to manipulate processing in a selective manner, the predictions that can be derived from formula (1) above for students classified according to experience may be like the instructional effectiveness profile in Figure 2. It shows hypothetical performance on questions about an analysis of variance problem following an instructive event, which described analysis of variance techniques using agricultural examples.

Estimates of processing activities can be obtained through experimental manipulations such as adjunct questions (e.g., Rothkopf, 1972b) or goal-descriptive directions (e.g., Rothkopf & Billington, 1975a, 1975b). Another method that offers some promise is to use inspection time data or eye movement measurements (see Rothkopf & Billington, Note 1) as indices of underlying processing activities.

Some Concluding Comments

The hypothesis about the reciprocal relationship between instruction-relevant experience and processing captures some aspects of aptitude-treatment interaction. It has also produced testable predictions about the effects of redundancy, density, and variety of instructive events on learning from text.

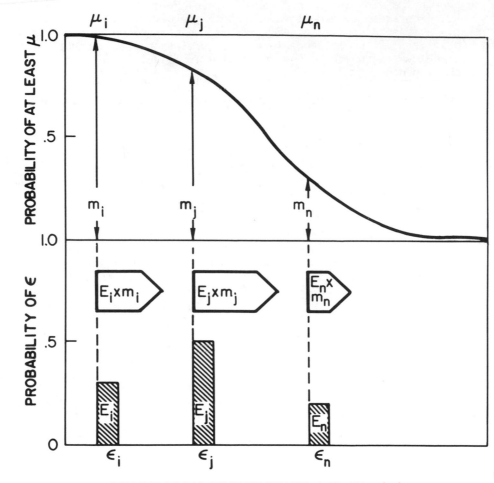

MATHEMAGENIC ACTIVITY LEVEL (μ)

Figure 1. Instructional success for subjects at successively lower experience levels $\in_i$, $\in_j$, and $\in_n$. Processing
levels μ_i, μ_j, and μ_n are sufficient for the correspondingly-labeled experience level. The curve
in the top panel is the probability (m) of encountering processing levels of at least μ in a given
reader population. The area of the flags indicates successful use of the instructive event and is
approximately proportional to the product of m and E (E = probability of experience level
$\in$ in population).

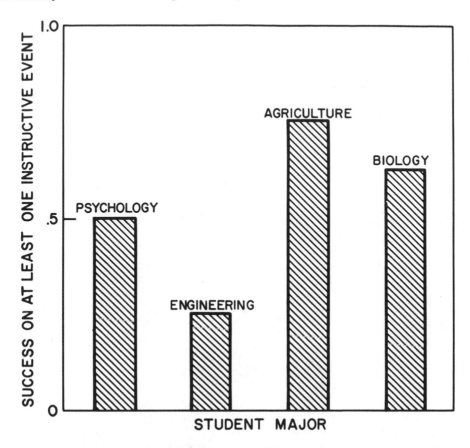

Figure 2. Instructional effectiveness profile showing successful performance on an analysis of variance
lesson that involved an agricultural illustration. The fictional data are shown for students in four
different fields of academic concentration.

The experiential factor, E, reflects instruction-relevant experience, disparity between instructional presentation and target competence, as well as the general cognitive burden in learning. The processing factor, m, reflects mathemagenic processing and the capacity limitations of the student. The theoretical approach described in this paper focuses on the likelihood that sufficient conditions for successful learning have been met, rather than on the exact nature of the underlying cognitive processes. A theory that spells out underlying processes would be intellectually more satisfying, but available observational techniques are not adequate for such a formulation. Theoretical emphasis on the likelihood that conditions prerequisite for successful instructional outcomes have been met represents a compromise between our overly rich intuitions and that which is practicable.

Footnotes

It should be noted that any characterization of the instruction-relevant experience of the student is in certain respects equivalent to descriptions of the difficulty of instructional material. A measure of the student's vocabulary leads to similar predictions as measures of the incidence of rare words in text. In this sense, E can also be viewed as reflecting the nature of the nominal stimulus.

Reference Note

1. Rothkopf, E. Z., & Billington,M. J. Goal-guided learning from written discourse: Inspection time and eye movement measures as indicators of underlying learning processes. Manuscript submitted for publication, 1977.

References

Bobrow, S. A., & Bower, G. H. Comprehension and recall of sentences. Journal of Experimental Psychology, 1969, 80, 55-61.

Craik, F. I. M., & Lockhart, R. S. Level of processing: A framework for memory research. Journal of Verbal Learning and Verbal Behavior, 1972, 11, 671-684.

Hyde, T. S., & Jenkins, J. J. Recall for words as a function of semantic, graphic, and syntactic orienting tasks. Journal of Verbal Learning and Verbal Behavior, 1973, 12, 471-480.

Rothkopf, E. Z. Some theoretical and experimental approaches to problems in written instruction. In J. D. Krumboltz (Ed.), Learning and the educational process. Chicago: Rand McNally, 1965.

Rothkopf, E. Z. Experiments on mathemagenic behavior and the technology of written instruction. In E. Z. Rothkopf & P. E. Johnson (Eds.), Verbal learning research and the technology of written instruction. New York: Columbia University Teachers College Press, 1971.

Rothkopf, E. Z. Structural text features and the control of processes in learning from written material. In R. O. Freedle & J. B. Carroll (Eds.), Language comprehension and the acquisition of knowledge. Washington, D.C.: V. H. Winston & Sons, 1972. (a)

Rothkopf, E. Z. Variable adjunct question schedules, interpersonal interaction, and incidental learning from written material. Journal of Educational Psychology, 1972, 63, 87-92. (b)

Rothkopf, E. Z., & Billington, M. J.   A two-factor model of   the   effect
     of   goal-descriptive   directions on learning from text.   Journal of
     Educational Psychology, 1975, 67, 692-704.   (a)

Rothkopf, E. Z., & Billington, M. J.   Relevance and similarity   of   text
     elements to descriptions of learning goals.   Journal of Educational
     Psychology, 1975, 67, 645-750.   (b)

COGNITIVE RESEARCH APPLIED TO LITERACY TRAINING

Thomas G. Sticht
National Institute of Education

The military services provide job skills training for millions of adults annually. This task is complicated by the wide range of cognitive capabilities that characterize the enlisted populations of the military services of most nations. For instance, it has been found in the United States that some people who enter the Army may require four times the amount of learning time as others to learn some job skill or knowledge (Fox, Taylor, & Caylor, 1969).

Though I am not certain of the situation in other countries, in the United States the task of providing job skills training is made more difficult because, in addition to having a wide spectrum of cognitive capabilities in the training population, there is overrepresentation of persons characterized by their slowness to learn, low performance on various aptitude tests, and poor performance on tests of academic skills (reading, arithmetic).

To cope with personnel having lower cognitive and literacy skills, the armed services of the United States have followed four strategies: non-acceptance of the less capable, assignment of less capable personnel to a limited number of jobs that do not demand high levels of cognitive capability, redesign of job skills training and job materials to accommodate the less literate personnel, and the provision of remedial literacy training to improve the cognitive capabilities of personnel.

The first two strategies, nonacceptance and limited assignments, depend for their success upon adequate assessment instruments for predicting who will be successful or unsuccessful on the job. The remaining two strategies involve the development of training programs for lower aptitude, less literate personnel. In one approach, the person's low cognitive skills are considered as a fixed characteristic of the person, and modification of job technical training programs to adapt to the person's lower-than-normal capabilities is attempted. In the fourth strategy, an attempt is made to produce a more adaptive person through the provision of basic literacy training to a level at which it is expected that the person can perform the literacy tasks of a job skills training program. In this case, then, the literacy demands of a job skills training program are considered as fixed, while the literacy skills of personnel are considered as changeable. Rather than

475

adapting the job skills training to the person, the person is adapted to meet the requirements of the job skills training.

Relationships among the Four Strategies

It is apparent that the four strategies are not independent. The first strategy, that of nonacceptance, determines what happens with the remaining strategies. If the level of cognitive ability required for acceptance is set high enough, then there is little need to worry about assigning people to jobs and job training programs that they cannot perform. Also, there is no need for remedial literacy training.

A major problem with the existing training systems of the armed services of the United States is that while they have accepted the selection strategy in concept, they cannot successfully implement it. There are at least two reasons for this. First, without the universal draft, there are simply not enough higher aptitude people applying for work in the military services to permit the setting of a very high cut-off level of cognitive ability. Second, the social goals of the United States increasingly stress the need for opportunities for upward mobility of ethnic and minority groups who have traditionally scored low on cognitive screening tests. The impact of this concern is clearly indicated by a recent government report, which calls for the development of "a policy to effectively address the illiteracy problem" (General Accounting Office, 1977).

Failure to come to grips with the fact that they are continuously going to have to train personnel having relatively low levels of cognitive abilities, has led the military services to implement a piecemeal training system in which the selection, classification, literacy training, and job skills training components are unrelated. For instance, selection and classification are based upon "aptitude" tests that have no clear relationship to the content and skills involved in either literacy or job training programs. Furthermore, until recently (cf. Sticht, 1975b), there has been little or no relationship between the content of literacy training and the content of job skills training programs. Rather, literacy has been construed as something one "gets" and then "applies." Thus, six to eight weeks of "general" literacy training has been provided in various Army, Navy, and Air Force locations in order to develop the required levels of literacy skills needed to complete basic military training or job skills training successfully. However, Army, Navy, and Air Force research (Sticht & Zapf, 1976) has failed to demonstrate that brief remedial reading programs are an effective approach to developing more competent, effective readers capable of contending with the reading demands of technical training programs and many other reading tasks demanded by military jobs. Usually, only one or two "years" of gain in "general" reading proficiency are produced, which may typically shrink to less than one "year" after a few weeks following the reading training.

Problems With Brief Literacy Programs for Adults

Failure to implement effective literacy training successfully appears to reflect, at least in part, an inadequate understanding of the concept of literacy. A major (though not the only) problem is the tendency to confuse the information processing skills of reading and writing with the knowledge expressed or received by those skills. For example, in a reading vocabulary test, it is possible to miss an item because one lacks knowledge of the word meaning. A person might be perfectly capable of saying the word out loud, however, thereby indicating skill in converting the printed word into a spoken word.

It is clear that if a person does not know the meaning of a word, then instructional practice must differ from what would be done if the person knew the meaning of a word when that word was spoken, but could not recognize the word when seeing it in printed form. If a person does not know the meaning of a word when it is presented in the printed form, and also does not know the meaning of a word when it is heard, then we may conclude that the person will have difficulty understanding reading material containing that word, but the problem is only secondarily a reading problem. Primarily, it is a language problem that no amount of instruction in sight/sound correspondences or sight/word recognition will remedy.

This distinction between the oral language knowledge that a person has, and his or her skill in recognizing the same language form in print, is a crucial one for understanding why brief reading programs are likely to produce only slight improvements in the ability to perform various tasks involving reading. The unspoken assumption in reading training programs for adults is that many illiterate or marginally literate people have a fairly well-developed oral language capability. Hence, a relatively brief period of training in decoding skills, i.e., providing knowledge of sight/sound correspondences and opportunities for practicing this knowledge to develop skill, is considered sufficient for unlocking the person's oral language skill via the printed word. At the extreme, we might imagine a person whose oral language skills and knowledge are equivalent to those of a typical 18-year-old with 12 years of education, but who had simply neglected to learn to read. In this case, a relatively brief period spent learning the heuristics of decoding would permit this person to bring this fully developed language skill to bear on the printed word. In such a case, the person might gain as much as 12 years of reading skill with only a few weeks of decoding training!

Unfortunately, a problem for adult literacy programs is that clients are likely to be poorly developed in both oral and written language skills. In Air Force-sponsored research (Sticht & Beck, 1976), men in a military literacy training program were administered a test of auding[1] and reading comprehension. The results showed that both oral and written language skills were at the fifth grade level. These findings were confirmed in research reported by Duffy (1976) with Navy personnel.

The fact that most marginally literate personnel score several years below the norm for their age group in auding indicates that their "literacy" problem is not restricted to the printed page. Rather, it reflects in large measure a language processing/comprehension problem. Low oral vocabulary scores indicate a lack of language knowledge, not just low skill in processing the connected discourse used in assessing paragraph comprehension. Because language knowledge is low, reading comprehension will tend to be low. Hence, even if a marginally literate person could decode printed language as well as he could spoken language, his low oral language skill would retard comprehension. An implication of this is that major improvements in reading skills of marginally literate personnel will require major improvements in language competence (e.g., vocabulary knowledge).

Carroll (1971) discusses problems involved in measuring growth in vocabulary (by auding or reading). He cites work by Edgar Dale in which Dale estimates that childen may finish first grade with a vocabulary of 3,000 words. Then he estimates that they will add about 1,000 words per year from then on through high school, with high school seniors knowing about 15,000 words.

Accepting this rate of growth, if marginally literate personnel typically have vocabularies like beginning fifth graders, then they know about 6,000 words. To achieve a sixth grade vocabulary, about 1,000 words will have to be learned. In a six week program in which six hours of active learning occurs each day (an unlikely situation), new words would have to be learned and retained at a rate of six per hour. To reach a seventh grade vocabulary level, 12 words per hour would have to be learned and retained. The problem enlarges when it is recognized that this rate of learning is based upon typical learning rates of typical children. Marginally literate personnel, however, usually require anywhere from two to four times as much time to learn verbal concepts as typical recruits do (Fox, Taylor, & Caylor, 1969). For these people, it seems unlikely that they could learn and retain six to 12 words per hour for six hours a day, or even half this number. As Carroll has pointed out "basic linguistic competence (at least with respect to grammar and vocabulary) is probably relatively unsusceptible to improvement except over long periods of time and with tremendous efforts . . . "(p. 130).

The foregoing considerations strongly suggest that the brief literacy programs that the Services have operated in the past, and are currently operating, take only the first few steps of a long journey. Furthermore, it does not seem unreasonable to expect that even the progress gained in the current programs will be lost, because no systematic efforts are made to continue to stimulate the less literate person to continue reading development after completion of literacy training; no developmental reading materials are provided, and no

officially scheduled time for continued literacy development is
provided.

A Comprehensive Literacy Training System for the Armed Services

The piecemeal nature of the existing selection, classification, and
job training system, supplemented from time to time with the inadequate,
brief literacy program discussed above, is clearly in need of an
overhaul.   Research is needed that would study methods to characterize
literacy and other cognitive (and noncognitive) demands of military jobs
validly, and to design and develop literacy training programs that
systematically teach job-related vocabulary and reading tasks, and that
are extensive enough to permit a long-term period for the development of
literacy skills.

Recently completed research for the Navy (Sticht, Fox, Hauke, &
Zapf, 1976) suggests the possibility that basic military training, job
technical school training, and correspondence course materials may be
modifiable such that literacy skills and job skills training can be
offered in an integrated manner. The concept is based on findings that
suggest that much (perhaps 25% to 50%) of what is currently taught in
these training programs is not considered relevant to their work by Navy
personnel.   That is, much of the current training programs may consist
of "nice-to-know" but not "need-to-know" information.   Thus, some
instruction time might be saved if the training programs were
systematically redesigned to effect a better match between training and
job requirements.

Additional time might be saved by converting training programs from
lock-step, lecture-oriented classrooms, to individualized, self-paced
programs with flexible entry and exit.   Where this has been done
elsewhere in military training programs, considerable overall savings in
person-hours (and hence cost) of training have been effected.

Because of the time, materials, and cost savings that may result
from the careful systems engineering of training, and the move to
self-pacing of instruction, it should be possible to incorporate
literacy training into the programs for those who need it. While they
would necessarily require more time to complete training programs under
this system, the exception is that overall training costs will drop, as
those capable of accelerated progress are permitted to move rapidly
through the streamlined programs.

Figure 1 presents a general plan for research and development to
produce a comprehensive, integrated job skills and literacy skills
career development system. The first phase of the plan calls for a
thorough analysis of reading within the Services, including the
determination of job-related reading tasks, so that reading training
objectives may be targeted to job requirements.

An additional aspect of the Phase 1.0 activities given in Figure 1 is the study of job skills training and the general education system within the Services to determine the feasibility of improving linkages in these systems, and potential for revising these systems to produce a more integrated job skills and literacy skills training system. The report by Sticht et al. (1976) illustrates the type of approach envisaged under the Phase 1.2 activities, and provides information concerning the Navy's current career development system, including information regarding job skills training, career counseling, and general educational systems. A general finding is that the linkages among these subsystems is very loose, if not totally absent. Initial efforts toward a comprehensive career development system that includes integrated job skills and reading skills training should include the formation of tighter administration and content linkages among those subsystems.

The Phase 2.0 activities of Figure 1 call for the evolutionary development of integrated job skills and literacy skills training programs for the three major stages of military career development: entry into the Service with basic military training, job technical school training, and assignment to on-the-job training at an active duty station.

Figure 2 illustrates the type of literacy/job skills training system that could be developed to integrate the three major stages of military career development. The example is for the U. S. Navy, and was developed under project SEAREAD (Sticht, Fox, Hauke, & Zapf, 1976). In the project, Navy personnel were interviewed to identify two kinds of reading tasks: reading-to-do and reading-to-learn tasks.

Reading-to-do tasks involve reading in which information is looked up and applied and can then be forgotten. This forms the bulk of the reading of job performers who are working daily (as contrasted with job trainees or instructors).

Reading-to-learn tasks require that what is read be learned in some more or less complete manner so that it can be used later on. This type of task is used mostly in training situations, where people must learn information so they can pass an examination.

Analysis of reading-to-do tasks revealed that they consisted of either fact finding tasks, in which the person already knew how to do a particular job, but needed some additional specific information/data to get the job done, or following directions tasks, involving the use of a manual or other document to find out how to do a job task.

Additional analysis revealed that the reading-to-do materials included texts, figures, tables, and combinations of texts and figures and texts and tables. Very few uses were found of figures and tables in combination, so this combination is excluded from Figure 2.

PHASE 1.0

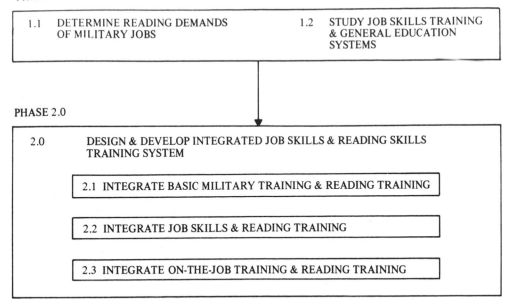

Figure 1. General plan for developing an integrated job skills and reading skills training system.

The reading-to-learn component of the literacy curriculum focuses on four major strategies for learning. The four strategies are based on an analysis of over 140 specific learning activities that Navy personnel reported using to learn. The most frequently used type of learning strategy, accounting for 25% of the responses, consisted of reading materials. The problem solve/question learning strategy consisted mostly of solving problems or answering questions given in the instructional materials. The relate/associate strategy included many activities that have the effect of adding elaborative encodings to what was read. This included talking with fellow students about the material, watching a related movie, using mnemonics, and other activities. The focus attention strategy included underlining, outlining, and other such activities that reduce the amount of materials to be attended.

The column headings of Figure 2 show the three major military training components: recruit training, technical school training (called A school training in the Navy), and training at the active duty station. Associated with each of these training components are job content areas. In recruit training, basic military subjects are taught

READING TASK	RECRUIT TRAINING	A SCHOOL TRAINING			DUTY STATION TRAINING/JOB PERFORMANCE		
	BASIC MILITARY	SERVICE MAINTENANCE	TECHNICAL MAINTENANCE	DATA GROUP	SERVICE MAINTENANCE	TECHNICAL MAINTENANCE	DATA GROUP

READING TO DO
 Fact-Finding
   Text
   Figures
   Tables
   Text & Figures
   Text & Tables							

Following Directions
   Text
   Figures
   Tables
   Text & Figures
   Text & Tables							

READING TO LEARN Re-read/Rehearse Problem Solve/Question Relate/Associate Focus Attention							

Figure 2. Research toward the Navy's integrated job skills and reading training system: job reading programs for three stages of job skills training.

to all new personnel. In technical school training, a great number of job training programs are available. Here we have made three major clusters of jobs: service maintenance; technical maintenance; and data oriented jobs, such as administrative, clerical, personnel, and so forth. Generally, the service maintenance jobs have the least demands for literacy skills.

The concept in Figure 2 is that literacy training involving reading-to-do and reading-to-learn tasks would be taught at each stage of training, using appropriate reading materials for each of the job cluster areas.

In a fully integrated job skills/literacy skills system, a very close coupling between the job skills tasks and associated reading tasks would be desirable. Preferably, students would get "hands-on" experience with materials, equipment, procedures, etc., prior to reading about these things. This would provide an opportunity for the experience-based learning of implicit knowledge needed to achieve a deeper comprehension of what is read.

Example of a Front-Loaded Job-Related Literacy Program

It is not practically feasible to attempt to convert from the current type of training to an integrated system such as outlined above, all at once. Rather, an evolutionary approach is needed. One such approach is to operate first in the current mode, in which literacy training is offered prior to job skills training. In military jargon, this is called a "front-loaded" training system. Following the development of a job-related, front-loaded literacy program, the next step would be to integrate that program with the job skills program for which it was prepared.

In the Navy project SEAREAD, an example of a front-loaded, fixed duration job skills program for A school training was designed to incorporate the reading-to-do and reading-to-learn components from Figure 2. The instruction curriculum of the A School Preparatory Training (ASPT) program consists of three Strands: Reading-to-Do, Reading-to-Learn, and Decoding, a strand not evidenced in Figure 2, but anticipated to be useful.

Strand I: Reading-to-Do

This strand is illustrated in the flow chart of Figure 3. Essentially, it takes the information of Figure 2 and places it into an instructional curriculum format, with learning modules based on the types of information sought (fact finding and following directions) and the types of information sources or displays (texts, figures, etc.). Each module is accompanied by pre- and post-proficiency tests (PT), which determine eligibility for the module training, and mastery of the

module.   Data obtained with these PTs provide <u>formative</u> data for module
development, and <u>criterion-referenced</u> achievement data for students. As
indicated in Figure 3, a pre- and post-summative reading test is
included. This test would be a Navy Reading Task Test assessing reading
skills needed in job skills training.

    The construction of module materials reflects the fact that Strand
I is primarily intended to provide extensive drill and practice in
performing Navy reading tasks. Thus, each module consists of source
materials and numerous worksheets, which require that the person perform
the tasks indicated by the module name.   The worksheets should be
designed to emphasize three dimensions: structure, content, and
difficulty.

    A structural worksheet causes the person to notice how   an
information source/display is put together, e.g., a table may have rows,
columns, headings, etc.   Specific questions should be developed to
require the processing of information about structural features.

    A content worksheet causes the person to attend to the content of
an information display, e.g., a fact-finding worksheet might ask a
person to locate a specific fact in a given display.

    The difficulty dimension is incorporated into both structural and
content worksheets.   Essentially, the idea is to start with easy
questions and gradually make them more difficult, in terms of the amount
of information to be presented, or in the amount of paraphrasing of the
questions, which places a stress on the student's vocabulary.

Strand II: Reading-For-Learning

    This strand contrasts with the Strand I activities in being
oriented toward the processing of information for future use, and hence
emphasizes the development of skill in manipulating written information
to increase its storage in and retrieval from memory. To process
information for learning, the person must be prepared in at least two
ways: He or she must have the knowledge base that can be brought
to bear in comprehending the material to be learned, and he must possess
knowledge of the skill in performing the types of intentional learning
strategies identified in Figure 2 (i.e., reread/rehearse, problem
solve/question, relate/associate, and focus attention).

    To promote the acquisition of a relevant knowledge base that will
help students learn better from their job training school materials,
much of which will be written at high levels of difficulty, e.g.,
readability levels of eleventh to twelfth grade (Duffy, 1976), Strand II
includes specially developed materials written at a lower difficulty
level that incorporates the basic concepts/topics within a career
cluster.

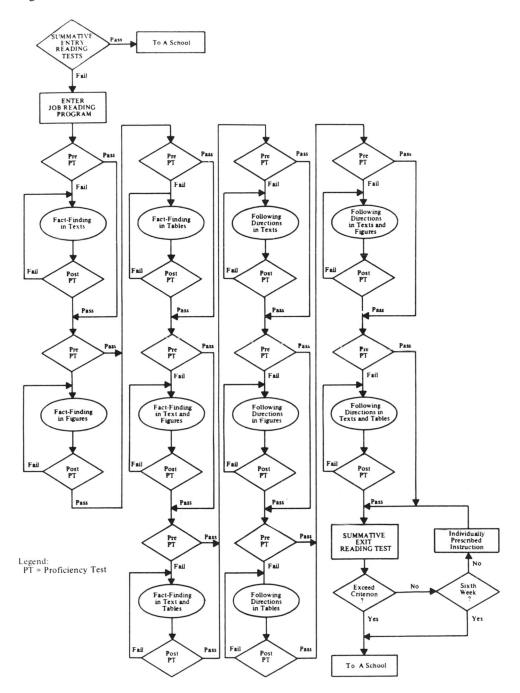

Figure 3. Strand I of A School Preparatory Training (ASPT).

The content materials can be developed in the form of 300 - 1,000 word passages, one for each major topic. Each passage can contain a high density of concepts, without the redundancy and elaboration usually needed to explicate concepts in written materials because in the Strand II activities each student will perform repeated readings of the materials, and will construct various elaborations in the course of performing the information processing activities for storing and retrieving information.

Figure 4 presents a fictitious set of content topics that might be developed for the Data Group career cluster. (The content areas are actually taken from the content area matrices developed for the Air Force's job-oriented reading program for duty station personnel; see Huff, Sticht, Joyner, Groff, & Burkett, 1977.) The figure also shows the information processing activities from Figure 2 as column headings. Cell entries suggest different types of specific activities that might be used for each content area and with each information processing activity.

The Strand II activities are to be taught in a classroom setting, with students working in teams or small groups, and with teacher demonstration and feedback. This approach permits students to take a break from the solo drill and practice of Strand I, and engage in a little more social activity. This is necessary under a front-loaded, full-day-of-study type of program in order to prevent boredom and fatigue.

Evaluation of Strand II activities is less systematic in the formative area than Strand I. In Strand II, student classroom products are evaluated by the teacher and other students in group discussion. In addition to providing the teacher with opportunities for evaluation, these discussions present the information in the written passages in a spoken form, and can be used for defining unfamiliar words and elaborating on unfamiliar concepts in words within the oral language of the students. The latter types of discussions should also be used to introduce a new content area for the first time. This oracy to literacy sequence is useful for bringing students' prior knowledge to bear on the learning of the new knowledge in the job content areas (cf. Sticht, Beck, Hauke, Kleiman, & James, 1974, for a discussion of relationships of oracy and literacy skills).

The informal evaluations can be supplemented by pre- and post-summative tests developed for each of the four categories of information processing. A paper by Sticht (Note 1) presents examples of two tests of Relate/Associate activities: skill in making classification tables and flow charts using content area passages. Additional tests can be developed for the remaining information processing activities. Additionally, pre- and posttest summative measures of the acquisition of the knowledge objectives included in the

CONTENT AREAS	REREAD/ REHEARSE	PROBLEM SOLVE/ QUESTION	RELATE/ ASSOCIATE	FOCUS ATTENTION
1 Career Field Progression (Skills upgrading process, skill levels, career field general structure)	Efficiency of Reading	Answering questions about who, what, where, when, why.	Classification matrix construction.	Underlining
2 Communications Security (Security classifications, methods of transmission, accountability of classified information)	Preview/ Review Techniques	Writing questions.	Drawing illustrations.	Outlining
i Supply Requisitions (Supplies and equipment custodial accounts, submission procedures, controlling documents & forms)	Skimming	Solving vocabulary test problems.	Constructing flow charts.	Summarizing
n Publications Management (System, updating procedures, files)	Scanning	Test taking practice.	Paraphrasing.	Notetaking

Figure 4.   Illustration of a partial matrix for Strand II: Reading-to-Learn content passages and information processing activities to be performed on the content passages for the Navy's Data Group career cluster.

content area passages should be constructed to measure the person's development of a knowledge base for learning by reading in A Schools.

Strand III: Decoding

The decoding component of the ASPT program is meant to provide students with knowledge useful for (a) transforming printed words into spoken words, and (b) transforming sentences into semantic representations. Additionally, the decoding strand provides practice to develop skill in efficiently transforming connected prose into meaning.

The knowledge useful for transforming printed words into spoken words is that generally known as phonics, or sight-sound correspondences. While people who develop reading skills in a "normal" manner over the school years may not possess conscious awareness of these correspondences (or at least not completely), and may not require explicit instruction in such knowledge, poorer readers may find this information of great value. Even though the number of sight-sound correspondence rules is so great that teaching all of these rules is out of the question, explicit instruction in a few that have broad generality can be of heuristic value for the poorer reader.

At a more complex level of analysis, knowledge for decoding sentences can also be a useful tool for poorer readers. The Army's functional literacy program contains a simplified approach to the decoding of sentences that divides all sentences into two basic parts: the main idea, and more about the main idea (cf. Sticht, 1975a). In turn, the main idea is broken into subject and action, while the "more about" component is discussed in terms of telling more about who, what, when, where, etc. This type of knowledge may be of most value for study purposes where complex texts must be analyzed.

The third part of the decoding strand simply provides practice in reading, with the intent to develop the capacity for reading and storing information presented in the printed form with the same efficiency and accuracy as one can use to process language in the spoken form.

Recently (Sticht & Beck, 1976), an experimental test for assessing discrepancies in oral and written language capacities has been developed for the Air Force test. This test might be examined for ideas on how to go about assessing the development of automaticity in reading, which, in the case of the Air Force test, is considered to be achieved when one uses printed language as accurately and efficiently as one uses the spoken language.

To briefly summarize, I have outlined an instructional curriculum for an A School Preparatory Training (ASPT) program that is conceived as occurring prior to A School, that offers training in the type of reading found in a career cluster relevant to the A School the person will be attending, and is of brief duration. The curriculum consists of three strands. Strand I emphasizes practice in performing reading for doing tasks. Strand II concentrates on reading-for-learning, presents a relevant career cluster knowledge base, and provides practice in performing the information processing strategies of reread/rehearse, problem solve/question, relate/associate, and focus attention, using the content knowledge base. Finally, Strand III offers knowledge of and provides practice for the development of skill in decoding printed words into spoken words, decoding sentences into semantic representations, and developing parity in automaticity of decoding printed and spoken languages.

An Integrated Job Skills/Reading Skills Training Program

The development of the front-loaded ASPT program permits a total concentration on the development of an effective job-oriented reading training program. Once considerable experience with such a program has been achieved, however, the next step is to develop an integrated job skills and reading skills program in which the daily training day contains both of these types of training.

To accomplish the integration of job skills and reading skills training, it is first necessary to develop a job skills training program that reduces the amount of total person-days of training, so that any extra time spent in reading training produces little or no increase in the total person-days spent in the resident training program. The object is to overcome the costs of a front-loaded program, which adds on to the time spent in the resident training pipelines.

There is precedence for the teaching of reading skills in the course of the training day. The Department of the Army book entitled Marginal Man and Military Service (1965) describes research projects by the Army and Air Force to teach "academic skills" during basic military training (i.e., recruit training). The reading was not job-related, however, nor was the basic military developed to be self-paced and performance-oriented. Rather, the traditional classroom/lecture lock-step procedures were in effect.

Only one case has been found in which the job skills training was first transformed from the traditional classroom to a self-paced, performance (rather than paper-and-pencil test)-oriented program, and then job-oriented reading training was introduced. Hungerland and Taylor (1975) describe the effects of introducing self-paced instruction in the Army's Supplyman course. They found that in the lock-step course, students were held in the program for 35 training days (seven weeks), while the average time in the self-paced course was 25 days (five weeks), with a range from 13 to 44 days. Only seven percent of the self-paced trainees required additional time (beyond seven weeks) to complete the course requirements. All graduates of the self-paced course met the same end-of-course test criterion as used in the regular lock-step course.

To incorporate reading training into the Supplyman course, the Clerical career cluster from the Army's job-related reading program (Sticht, 1975a) was modified to focus exclusively on the Supplyman's materials. Reading training was provided for two hours per day for students entering the Supplyman course who read below the eight grade level on a standardized reading test, and the special job-related reading tests used for summative evaluation of the job reading program. Integration of the job reading training with the ongoing self-paced, modular job skills training system was accomplished by directing students from their self-paced study in a Supplyman's module to the daily block of two hours of job reading instruction. They then returned to their job skills training--all within the normal training day.

Results showed that performance on the Army job reading task test (JRTT) increased from an average reading grade level of 5.5 before training to 7.2 after training, and the percentage of students meeting the minimal job reading requirement of seventh grade level on the JRTT increased from 16% before training to 53% at the end of the integrated training program. Additional details are given in Sticht (1975a).

This study suggests that it is feasible to introduce job training and job reading training within the same training day without adding to the overall training time of traditional classroom, lock-step technical school training programs. Though such reading training is not likely to be sufficient for the poorest readers who enter the armed services, the inclusion of reading training during basic military (recruit) training (before the person gets to technical school training), and the provision for reading training at the duty station (following technical school training), makes possible the long period of training needed by the poorest readers to utilize the printed language more adaptively for learning and task performance.

Opportunities for Cognitive Research

In this paper I have attempted to show, by example, how cognitive research can influence instruction. My example, military literacy training, was selected because it reflects one area of my research interests for the last decade. It is my hope that this rather detailed discussion of military literacy training will make it easier for potential users of this information to see the relevance of cognitive research to their training needs. Hopefully, others concerned with literacy development for children and adults will find some information of value to them, too.

For researchers inclined to the utilization of cognitive constructs in their work, the development of an integrated job skills training system, as outlined in Figure 1, offers many opportunities for intellectually and socially relevant and rewarding research. For instance, how should and can the reading and other cognitive demands of jobs be represented? What is "general literacy" and what is its relationship to the job-oriented literacy talked about in this paper? Can fundamental changes in adult cognitive competency be achieved in relatively brief periods? What competencies? How long a time period? What would represent a "fundamental" change? Rate of learning in new settings? Propensity to engage in new learning?

These are just a few of the important questions entailed by the problem of setting out to develop an integrated job/literacy training system. To me, it is important that such questions be posed within the context of a real life, large-scale effort. This reveals the enormity of the task of understanding that cognitive researchers face. It is not enough to understand how a given person performs a given task. Additionally, the cognitive researcher must understand the assemblage of a multitude of specific tasks over an extended period of time, during which both in and out of school activities may affect cognitive development (cf. Cole, Sharp, & Lave, 1976, for further discussion of the problem of assemblage of task skills).

Another reason for being concerned with cognitive research on real life problems is that, if we do our jobs correctly, we can reap a double reward: We can solve important problems, and at the same time develop more accurate theories of how cognition arises from and contributes to success in coping with the tasks of life.

Footnotes

The opinions expressed herein are those of the author and do not represent the opinions and/or policies of the National Institute of Education or the Department of Health, Education and Welfare. The research described in this paper was completed while the author was Senior Staff Scientist with the Human Resources Research Organization, Monterey, California. Thanks to Lynn Fox, Bob Hauke, Diana Welty Zapf, and John Caylor for their tireless efforts on Project SEAREAD, which forms the basis for most of this paper. Doctors Tom Duffy and Ed Aiken of the Navy Personnel Research and Development Center, San Diego, were technical monitors of Project SEAREAD and provided the support necessary to accomplish the work.

1. Auding refers to listening to speech in order to comprehend, and is a parallel term to reading, which refers to looking at printed language in order to comprehend.

Reference Note

1. Sticht, T. G. Comprehending reading at work. Paper presented
at the 12th Annual Carnegie Symposium on Cognition, Carnegie-Mellon
University, May 1976.

References

Carroll, J. B. Development of native language language skills beyond
     the early years. In C. E. Reed (Ed.), The learning of languages.
     New York: Appleton-Century-Crofts, 1971.

Cole, M., Sharp, D., & Lave, C. The cognitive consequences of
     education: Some empirical evidence and theoretical misgivings.
     The Urban Review, 1976, 9, 218-233.

Duffy, T. M. Literacy research in the Navy. In T. G. Sticht & D. Welty
     Zapf (Eds.), Reading and readability research in the armed
     services, Alexandria, Virginia: Human Resources Research
     Organization, September, 1976. HumRRO FR-WD-CA-76-4.

Fox, W., Taylor, J., & Caylor, J. Aptitude level and the acquisition of
     skills and knowledges in a variety of military training tasks.
     Alexandria, Virginia: Human Resources Research Organization, May
     1969. HumRRO Technical Report 69-6.

General Accounting Office. A need to address illiteracy problems in the
     military services. March 1977. Report Number FPCD-77-13.

Huff, K., Sticht, T., Joyner, J., Groff, S., & Burkett, J. A
     job-oriented reading program for the Air Force: Development and
     field evaluation. Alexandria, Virginia: Human Resources Research
     Organization, February 1977. HumRRO FR-WD-CA-77-3.

Hungerland, J., & Taylor, J. Self-paced instruction in a cognitively
     oriented skills course: Supplyman, MOS 76Y10. Alexandria,
     Virginia: Human Resources Research Organization, June 1975.
     HumRRO-TR-75-20.

Marginal man and military service: A review. Department of Army,
     January 1965.

Sticht, T. G. A program of Army functional job reading training:
     Development, implementation, and delivery system. Alexandria,
     Virginia: Human Resources Research Organization, June 1975. (a)
     HumRRO-FR-WD-CA-75-7.

Sticht, T. G. (Ed.).   Reading   for   working: A   functional   literacy
    anthology.   Alexandria,   Virginia: Human   Resources   Research
    Organization, 1975. (b)

Sticht, T. G., & Beck, L. J. Development of an experimental literacy
    assessment   battery.   Alexandria,   Virginia: Human   Resources
    Research Organization, June 1976. HumRRO-FR-WD-CA-76-5.

Sticht, T., Beck, L., Hauke, R., Kleiman, G., & James, J.   Auding and
    reading: A developmental model.   Alexandria, Virginia: Human
    Resources Research Organization, 1974.

Sticht, T. G., & Zapf, D. W.   Reading and readability in the armed
    services.   Alexandria,   Virginia: Human   Resources   Research
    Organization, September 1976. HumRRO FR-WD-CA-76-4.

Sticht, T., Fox, L., Hauke, R., & Zapf, D.   Reading in the   Navy.
    Alexandria,   Virginia: Human   Resources   Research   Organization,
    September 1976. HumRRO-FR-WD-CA-76-14.

SOME DIRECTIONS FOR A COGNITIVE PSYCHOLOGY OF INSTRUCTION

Robert Glaser, James W. Pellegrino, and Alan M. Lesgold
Learning Research and Development Center
University of Pittsburgh
Pittsburgh, Pennsylvania, U.S.A.

Modern cognitive psychology is today's dominant theoretical force in behavioral science. More than ever before, complex mental behaviors are being investigated in rigorous scientific ways. However, while cognitive psychology is becoming increasingly mature in its attempts to model the complexity of human performance, it is a fledgling in the domain of applications to education and instruction. At the present time, cognitive psychology's findings and techniques have not significantly influenced teaching practices, instructional processes, nor the design of conditions for learning.

This state of affairs is rather incongruous, since one of the major influences in the development of new cognitive theory was a body of research that was directly stimulated by applied problems. World War II led to a vast increase of research in human skills and performance, work referred to as "human engineering" or "human factors" research. Much of this work was concerned with the kind of human performance involved when individuals controlled complex man-machine systems. Of particular concern was the detection and transmission of the information required for human and machine decision making. Human behavior was studied in terms of its interactions with these systems, and comparisons and analogies were made between human processes and the mechanisms and operations of mechanical and electronic systems like servomechanisms and computers. As a result, a link was forged between research in human cognitive capacities and models of performance capabilities in terms of the hardware with which individuals interacted.

The general developments that came into prominence after World War II, including cybernetics, information theory, and control theory, provided explanatory principles for understanding cognitive processes in perception, concept formation, and language. Developments in probability theory, including statistical decision theory and operations research, led to a conception of cognitive processes in terms of state descriptions of human memory and the transformations that connected one state to the next. Computer science and computer-based information processing systems provided rigorous means for theory development through the simulation of human information processing activity in

495

learning and problem solving. In the 1950's, linguists began to realize that grammars could be thought of as formal, generative systems. This meant that mathematical tools were available to decide whether a given syntax was adequate to the language it meant to describe. And, in the new focus on the acquisition and structuring of knowledge, the work of Piaget on the developmental changes in modes of cognitive functioning now could be related to concepts of structure and process in cognitive theory. The force of this "succession of intellectual invasions" (Estes, 1975), coupled with the study of realistic performances (as compared with simplified laboratory paradigms) and the practical problems of skilled and complex human performance, became a shaping force in current psychological theory building and experimentation.

Cognitive psychology is now investigating problem solving, language development, thinking, understanding, attention, memory, imagery, the nature of intelligence, and the problems of comprehending written and oral discourse. These areas of human endeavor, which have only been peripheral aspects of behavioristic psychology, are the starting points for cognitive psychologists. In addition, there is the growing realization, as a result of experience in attempts to apply psychological knowledge and as a result of lessons learned in other fields of science, that application can be a significant test of a theory's adequacy as well as a useful social contribution.

In this frame of mind, cognitive psychologists are beginning to study instructional processes and the acquisition and utilization of the skills and knowledge of everyday life. They are attempting to contribute to the solution of problems arising outside of the laboratory by specifically focusing on how the acquisition of cognitive skills and knowledge is facilitated through the arrangement or design of conditions for learning. What seems to be emerging is a psychology of instruction - a prescriptive science of educational design. At the moment, however, cognitive psychology is striving for theoretical organization, and instructional psychology is looking for a systematic framework. Each endeavor contributes to the other. New findings and theory in cognitive psychology provide a basis for the development of frameworks for optimizing human performance through instruction. And, developing the frameworks required for instructional design and theories of teaching provides a strong way of testing the limitations of our knowledge of human cognition (Glaser, 1976).

The work described in this book is typical of much of the research in cognitive psychology now going on in a number of countries in the world. The focus is on theory construction, related experimental work, and on the development of techniques for investigating fundamental phenomena of human cognition, and it is apparent that the theories and techniques described are not yet highly developed for the purposes of instructional application. Nevertheless, the work reported does permit certain inferences to be made about next steps and immediate directions for the field of cognitive psychology, at least with respect to its interactions with an emerging instructional psychology. The sections below, which parallel the organization of this book, explore some of these directions.

Learning

The attempt to integrate theoretical and applied concerns about learning and instruction has brought one important goal into focus - the development of a rigorous theory of learning. Most cognitive research has been concerned with understanding how complex cognitive tasks are performed and to much less an extent with how these activities are learned - the latter problem being the central problem addressed by older behavioristic theories. The new psychological approaches have concentrated primarily on the analysis of performance and on what is learned. However, for significant influence upon educational practice, the problem of learning and the acquisition of performance - the how of learning and teaching - must also be considered. Cognitive psychologists have concentrated on the analysis of the information processes of human performance, especially perception, memory, and problem solving. However, the problem of how performance capability is acquired cannot be ignored by new theories of cognitive processes and their development. A significant number of the papers in this volume have addressed this latter issue, and we regard this as a portent of continued successful evolution of a cognitive psychology of learning and performance that will have strong implications for a psychology of instruction.

The papers in this book that directly address learning do so in different ways. Some consider old problems of learning with new theories and methodologies. Others insist upon the necessity for major reformulation of the problems to be attacked. Some, like van Parreren's paper are eclectic combinations of older and newer theoretical approaches. Van Parreren proposes a "building-block" theory of cognitive learning. The basic notion is that simpler cognitive skills can be coordinated and combined into higher-order skills and that the same lower-level skill can be a component of many higher-order skills. Further, when several lower-level skills are combined into a single skill of greater complexity, it is "abbreviated" in the sense that unnecessary mental operations or movements are eliminated. Thus, the whole, higher-order skill is something different than the sum of its parts. It can be thought of and executed as a unit. Among other properties, for example, such units can be referenced by a single name and are less demanding of attention than the totality of the components that compose them.

Other researchers have studied the evolution of complex skills from simple ones. As van Parreren points out, related ideas, such as those of Gagné (1965), arose in a behaviorist context. There is, however, an important difference between Gagné's early work and the research on "abbreviation" summarized by van Parreren. Gagné, in proposing the idea of a learning hierarchy, essentially was presenting a formalization and

ramification of the basic principles of S-R learning: analyze behavior
into   its   appropriate response units and then teach complex behaviors a
little bit at a time. Gagné differentiated levels   of   complexity   that
were   interconnected   by   learning   processes that were more or less the
same   as   those   postulated   in   fundamental   behavioristic   learning
paradigms.

     In contrast, Hebb (1949) emphasized that the critical   problem   was
one   of   understanding   the   mechanisms   whereby   richer,   more   complex
activities evolve out of simpler ones. Van Parreren's paper is one of
several   indicators   (see   also   Hayes-Roth,   1977)   of this concern for
identifying the   integrative   cognitive   processes   that   occur   when   a
complex performance is learned and mastered. The Russian research from
which van Parreren extracts the principles   of   abbreviation   emphasizes
the   detailed   understanding   of   the   transformations that occur when a
cluster of simple cognitive skills evolves into a   more   complex   skill.
Both   the   Russian   and recent related American work (e.g., Gagné, 1974;
Resnick, 1976b) of this type have taken place in the context   of   school
tasks   and are particularly good examples of mutual facilitation between
cognitive psychology and instructional science.

     Van Parreren's paper also contains within it hints of an   important
point   which   is   further amplified by Voss. Most cognitive learning is
really what is called transfer in the associationistic, verbal   learning
literature.   That is, what is acquired is heavily dependent upon what is
already known. However, Voss points out   that   the   classical   transfer
paradigms   are   inadequate   for characterizing cognitive learning. They
are both too restrictive and too general. They are too   restrictive   in
the   sense   that they have dealt with minimal knowledge bases. They are
too general because they have assumed   broad   applicability   to   a   wide
variety   of   tasks   without   taking   into   account   the   detailed
characteristics   of   specific   task   domains.   In   contrast,   Voss
reinterprets   the transfer problem in terms of knowledge structures that
exist for individuals in specific subject-matter areas and examines   how
individuals   with different degrees of subject-related knowledge use the
relationships and concepts they know in various   memory   and   processing
tasks.

     The mechanisms of transfer he suggests   involve   knowledge-specific
conceptual   relationships rather than the vague "common-elements" notion
of older   associationistic   theories.   The   dynamics   of   transfer   are
specific   to   the   knowledge   relations   of   a particular subject-matter
domain. A person with great knowledge in a particular domain identifies
material   from   that   domain   more   precisely   and   quickly   than   a
low-knowledge individual and this results in more facile   retrieval   for
the   high-knowledge   individual   when   that   information   is   needed   to
understand and learn additional information. The "common   elements"   in
Voss'   formulation   are   neither   single   words nor concepts, but rather
relationships between concepts and patterns of events. What is   learned
through   transfer   is   a   function   of   the   nature   of   a   particular
individual's knowledge relative to the nature of the knowledge structure

of the material being learned. An expert in a knowledge domain can quickly and flexibly encode new facts from that domain. The problem of instruction then becomes one of characterizing the knowledge structures of the expert as compared with the knowledge conceptualization of the novice and bringing the novice closer to the expert by some instructional form of means-end analysis.

An old and well-studied question in learning, the problem of concept learning (see, e.g., Bruner, Goodnow, & Austin, 1956; Hunt, 1962), is addressed in the paper by Frederick Hayes-Roth. The work described by F. Hayes-Roth is a good example of the depth of detail in which specific processing mechanisms can be analyzed through modern techniques and theoretical concepts as compared with older forms of theorizing in this area. He analyzes classic tasks in concept learning, using production system models and techniques of pattern recognition derived from artificial intelligence research, and develops a formal methodology in which relational descriptions of exemplars of a concept are represented in standard format so that a general structure can be abstracted as an hypothesis about the criterial properties of a concept. The same methodology permits abstraction of the conditions under which an operation should be performed and the rules for its execution. Thus, the methodology provides a theory of both conceptual and operational learning. It has been tested initially by generating successful computer learning algorithms for a variety of tasks. In subsequent work, the theory has been used to predict the performance of human subjects (e.g., Hayes-Roth & Hayes-Roth, 1977).

While the work of F. Hayes-Roth is exemplary cognitive psychology, the significant question to be asked is what advances are apparent as a result of the new theoretical frameworks and heuristics now available for investigating concept learning. It is, of course, too early to judge, but the knowledge provided by F. Hayes-Roth sounds a good deal like what has already been learned about concept acquisition. The research directions that he suggests sound very much like questions we have heard before, and his suggestions for instructional applications are what could be deduced from existing knowledge in the context of behavior theory. What is new is the rigorous assimilation of concept and procedure learning into a formal theory that is richly detailed. To be useful, this more complete understanding must lead to new experimental questions and practical tests of the forms of theorizing involved.

In contrast to the above work on elementary learning processes, Norman argues that modern cognitive psychology should address itself to the domains of human knowledge, skill, and expertise that take years of a life span to learn. The basic unit of analysis is some form of organized knowledge representation in human memory; these structural organizations are the significant aspects to be studied in understanding the acquisition of knowledge and skill. In making these assertions, Norman attempts to bring cognitive psychology closer to the problems of instruction. Norman describes three modes of learning that he and

Rumelhart have proposed: accretion, the addition of new information; restucturing, the understanding and the gaining of insight into the information obtained; and tuning, the refinement and efficiency of performance that comes about as a result of continued use. Of particular interest is the notion that these modes of learning are active at different times in the course of learning. Since the characteristics of learning change at different stages of knowledge acquisition, Norman suggests that instruction should proceed in different ways as a function of the degree of knowledge and skill acquired. This notion is reminiscent of the literature on the learning of psychomotor skills. Changes in the organization of motor routines occur at successive stages of learning, and different kinds of performance at various levels of learning need to be matched with appropriate instructional conditions in order for expert skill to be acquired. It should be noted that Piaget's proposed mechanisms for cognitive development are very similar to Norman's modes of learning. At present, the details of Piaget's assimilation and accommodation processes and Norman's modes of learning are not well enough developed to determine whether .the stage structure of cognitive development mirrors the more microscopic structure of cognitive learning, but the similarity is compelling.

     The necessity for research and theory development on the mechanisms of learning and on the nature of instructional conditions that foster transformations between learning stages becomes apparent in Norman's comments on instruction and on teaching strategies. He provides some very general suggestions about teaching, such as teaching students to be better learning theorists so that they can teach themselves, teaching students to debug their own performance, and confronting students with critical confusions. These are highly intuitive and bear little relationship to an existing theory of learning. A future goal for cognitive psychology must be to relate theories of learning more strongly to technologies of instruction.

Discourse Structure, Knowledge Structure, and the Nature of Understanding

     Until recently, the role of organization of information in the understanding of discourse was not readily studied in the laboratory. However, it has been a topic of discussion at a broader, rational level for as long as the enterprises of psychology and philosophy have been pursued. The early philosophical discussions concerned themselves with whether knowledge was innate and, therefore, needed only to be unlocked by experience, or whether it was impressed on the mind by the invariant patterns in the flow of experience. Modern psychology has instead been concerned with the environmental conditions and internal cognitive processes that structure what is learned rather than with the ultimate sources of the ability to know.

There are several sources that influence research within modern psychology on the problem of understanding new facts. In perception, the Gestalt school and the Gibsonian tradition are the major influences, the first emphasizing the biasing role of what is already known on the understanding of what is currently sensed, and the second emphasizing the patterning of energy in the world as the source for the structuring of knowledge in the mind. In the study of learning and the study of memory, there have been parallel viewpoints. Bartlett demonstrated the role of thought and its organization in determining what is remembered from a picture or story. On the other hand, the Skinnerian approach, while de-emphasizing the importance of structured knowledge, clearly places all structure effects in the input to the human information processing system rather than in the structure of that system. In the study of cognitive development, Piaget has added a new dimension to the subjective viewpoints of the Gestalt and Bartlett approaches - not only is structure located in the existing knowledge base a person brings to the system, but the properties of that structure evolve as knowledge is acquired and as the organism matures. The subjective and environmental perspectives are best thought of as complements, not alternatives.

These different viewpoints are represented in the work reported in this volume. Anderson and Voss point out the role played by what is known in the process of understanding a discourse, while Barbara Hayes-Roth and Thorndyke emphasize the role played by the discourse's own structure. What is striking, though, is not the range of viewpoints presented, but rather the convergence of all these papers toward the definition of the critical task for instructional psychology in the domain of discourse comprehension. This task is to analyze learning from and understanding of discourse as a process in which structured knowledge interacts with structured input within the constraints set down by the overall properties of the human cognitive system.

Cognitive psychologists have only begun to pursue this work. The work Anderson reports from his laboratory and elsewhere shows that knowledge structure interacts with message structure to determine comprehension. Further, the work he reports shows that a dynamic cognitive theory of comprehension is needed. That is, not all of what is known, but rather only the schemata that are currently active, interact with discourse structure during comprehension. Thus, both experiential and the contextual effects on comprehension are manifestations of the general principle that a sentence is understood relative to the information that the context in which it appears activates in a given learner.

A detailed quantitative or qualitative description of the role that knowledge structures play in guiding comprehension is not yet available. The Voss paper, with its discussion of the "flowing" chunk, offers a hint of a mechanism, but more is needed. Outside this volume, Rumelhart (1976) has discussed a model of reading in which knowledge plays a role at the perceptual level. He suggests a multilevel system in which the reader's knowledge includes probabilistic information that influences

what is recognized from a complex, noisy situation. Comprehension
consists of an interactive, Bayesian process that matches what has been
sensed to an evolving model of what is being understood in a manner that
is as consistent as possible with existing knowledge, i.e., the prior
conditional probabilities that relate hypotheses to categories of
perceptual and cognitive evidence.

We mention Rumelhart's work not because we are sure it is the best
approach, but rather to contrast it to the schema theorists (e.g.,
Anderson, this volume; Minsky, 1975; Schank & Abelson, 1977;
Winograd, 1975). Schemata have been represented, in almost all recent
works, as information structures, i.e., as declarative knowledge.
Rumelhart, in representing knowledge as a set of biases on processing,
makes a leap to a level of analysis and theorizing that is essential if
we are to make use of schema theory in an instructional psychology;
that is, he ties knowledge to processing. Effectively, this moves
knowledge representation from being completely declarative to being
partially procedural. We find it puzzling that schema theorists tend
not to think of schemata as procedures for comprehension, but rather as
organized bodies of declarative information. If schemata were thought
of procedurally, we would be more able to devise analyses of what needs
to be taught and more able to specify tests for mastery of given
subschemata. We might come to think of schemata as cognitive objectives
of instruction (e.g., Greeno, 1976a).

The work of B. Hayes-Roth and Thorndyke adds another dimension to
the perspective instructional psychologists can bring to structured
knowledge. In addition to studying how subjective knowledge structures
can guide comprehension, we can also study information relationships in
discourse that can exert influences on how sentences are understood. B.
Hayes-Roth (Hayes-Roth & Hayes-Roth, 1977; see also Swinney & Hakes,
1976) shows us that exact choice of wording will have an important
influence on which facts are learned from a text and how they are
integrated. Thorndyke further shows the influence of different forms of
discourse organization. These findings are not contradicted by
Jarvella's work showing that memory for what is read does not, for very
long, contain a record of the exact wording and syntax. Exact word
choices can be crucial in determining what is learned and when it can be
used. However, understanding is more than word storage; it is a
constructive process, which wording and discourse structure influence.
It is to be noted that the discourse variables that Hayes-Roth and
Thorndyke have shown to be influential are not directly measured by
formulas educators and publishers use to assess text difficulty.

Some of the hints for effective text writing that these authors
provide seem to conflict with aesthetic principles that have evolved in
the art of creative writing. The writer's aesthetic goal is based upon
the assumption that what is written is a piece of art, to be studied at
length and with slowly evolving understanding. The world of the school
child does not always admit this leisurely study process as an option.
Consequently, the nonredundant simplicity of the creative writer may not

always be optimal for textbooks. Perhaps the kind of research typified by B. Hayes-Roth and Thorndyke will cause textbook writers to go beyond the aesthetic of creative writing toward something more like the aesthetic of rhetoric. In textbook writing, as in architecture, beauty may lie in effective function.

Another issue raised in this book is whether the verbal medium is appropriate for conveying certain information. The issue is not addressed at length, however. Stenning's data suggest that people who receive verbal directions on how to find a specific location encode those directions in a spatially more specific manner than the directions specify (see Anderson & Ortony, 1975, for other evidence of the specificity and concreteness of mental representations). Considerable earlier work (see Bower, 1972) suggests that overspecified, mental-picture encodings are particularly well remembered. The interesting finding of Stenning's work is that this overspecificity is quite automatic, at least for adults in the task he studied.

Yuille and Catchpole, in their chapter, found that very young children show improved learning in artificial laboratory tasks after training in imagery procedures. The training emphasized the generation of highly specific, sensory-like representations. Earlier work (e.g., Lesgold, Golinkoff, & McCormick, 1975; Wolff & Levin, 1972) supports a relatively general assertion that elaborative procedures, which may need to be taught to children, facilitate rote learning. This effect may occur either because highly specific and detailed encodings are better remembered (cf. Lesgold & Goldman, 1973; Lockhart, Craik, & Jacoby, 1976), or alternatively, because a separate, powerful, nonverbal encoding system is brought into play. A strong explanation is yet to be developed.

Our ignorance extends to another instructional domain that is guided by only a small amount of existing research. This is the area of text illustration. We do not know if, or when, illustrations and diagrams facilitate learning from text, nor do we know which types are best, nor which populations most benefit from them. One reason for our ignorance has been the lack of an appropriate theoretical foundation for research in this area. Thus, there are a number of discrete experimental results about illustration and diagrams (Wright, 1977, is especially helpful), but these findings cannot be safely applied to new situations, since they are not related by generalizable theory. As discourse processing theories develop, it should become possible to extend hypotheses about the role of context in understanding to situations where the context is a picture or a diagram. However, there will also be a need for research on how diagrams are themselves understood, i.e., how they become part of the internal context for subsequent discourse.

Perceptual and Memory Processes in Reading

The papers on reading in this volume present evidence of significant progress toward an understanding of the reading difficulties that some children and adults face. Three different approaches that are converging toward that understanding can be seen in the papers by Levy, McClelland and Jackson, Rayner and Posnansky, and Frederiksen. Levy has developed a technique in which phonological processing mechanisms are suppressed by having the subject count aloud while reading. This suppression procedure lowers the level at which sentences can be processed (cf. Lockhart, Craik, & Jacoby, 1976). Instead of encodings that include specific order and item information, the encodings made under phonological suppression contain only vague gist.

The papers by Frederiksen and by McClelland and Jackson present evidence that is complementary to that of Levy; that is, poorer readers seem to be slower at accessing phonological codes. This evidence tempts us to suggest that educators build phonological skill curricula, and, indeed, some programs that emphasize phonological processing have been rather successful (e.g., DISTAR). The problem is that we do not know exactly what skill the poor readers lack, nor do we know much about how good readers acquire this skill. We discuss these two problems in turn.

While the results of Frederiksen and of McClelland and Jackson are empirically very parallel, the two chapters offer different explanations of the results. Frederiksen argues that speed of access to phonological codes is slower in less-skilled readers, while Jackson and McClelland produce correlational analyses that suggest a more general difference in memory access speed. Specifically, they show that of all the phonological processing tasks that correlate with reading speed, none account for additional variance beyond that accounted for by a letter-matching task that requires little phonological coding. Of course, the letter-matching task, when done quickly, might depend on phonological processing even if it can also be done without such activity. While further research is needed, the bulk of existing evidence seems to favor a specific phonological deficit in less-skilled readers, and it would seem useful to investigate the origins of phonological processing speed differences and the components of the curriculum that produce faster processing.

The need to build a more complete instructional model for reading is illustrated by the contrast between the papers by Rayner and Posnansky and by Frederiksen. Frederiksen, looking at high school students, finds reading ability differences to be reflected especially in tasks where fast processing of the pieces of a word is required. When Rayner and Posnansky look at young children, though, they find that learning to read involves a shift from piece-by-piece to wholistic processing of words. That is, as children learn to read, they shift away from the very piece-by-piece processing that Frederiksen says good readers do best. These two findings are not incompatible since processing of subword codes may still be necessary at some point in the process even if it is basically wholistic. However, a theory that explains both sets of phenomena in an efficient way is yet to be produced. This leaves instructional psychology in the position of having experimental support for more than one competing approach to reading instruction; e.g., both whole-word and phonics methods have data to which they can appeal.

Thus far, the work reported suggests an approach that emphasizes a scientific analysis of beginning, expert, and deficient readers and of the course of their instruction in reading. However, Farnham-Diggory's chapter suggests an alternative approach. She has selected tasks that teachers judge to be important predictors of reading achievement and analyzed the nature of those tasks with great precision. The next step would presumably be to compare these analyses with a task analysis of the reading process. Common elements of the predictor task and the reading task might then be discovered. These could perhaps be the basis of improved instruction. One problem with Farnham-Diggory's approach is that the analysis of performances that correlate with reading performance requires as much effort as the direct analysis of reading itself. And, there is less certainty that an analysis of any given reading correlate will be fruitful, especially if it is done before analysis of the reading process provides hints as to what components of the task are probably involved.

In general, a final matter that needs to be discussed is the task of more closely tying reading research to instructional practice. The intuitions of reading teachers will surely help us avoid perseveration on theoretical issues that are tangential to the task of building instructionally relevant cognitive theories. At least as important, though, is a need to report our results in a manner that permits the development of a psychology of instruction. In many cases, our results will confirm practitioners' beliefs and not influence instructional practice unless we can point out which beliefs have been disfirmed and how the precision of our theories improves on their intuitions as a source for curriculum design.

Reasoning, Problem Solving, and Intelligence

Schools typically espouse two complementary goals for students: learning basic skills such as reading, writing, and mathematics; and learning to reason and solve problems. The ability to reason and solve problems is certainly a function of one's basic factual or declarative knowledge, but it clearly extends beyond such knowledge into the domain of procedural knowledge and the "executive functions" of cognition. One of the major themes of this volume is the importance of problem-solving and reasoning skills as a domain of inquiry that might lead to new curriculum goals. For example, Doerner proposes that one of the primary objectives of instruction beyond the level of basic skills learning should be the teaching of creative thinking, i.e., reasoning and general problem-solving skills. Similarly, Oléron and Frijda (see also Resnick

& Glaser, 1976) view problem-solving skill as an important aspect of general intelligence.

Since there is consensus that understanding and teaching the skills underlying reasoning, problem solving, and general intelligence is a worthy goal, we need to determine whether our current knowledge about these skills is adequate for achieving that goal. While the study of thinking and problem solving has a long tradition within the associationistic and Gestalt schools, this field of research has not been systematic and has not generally fostered the development of a theory of problem-solving skill (Neimark & Santa, 1975). A recent exception to this negative evaluation has been the work done in the context of an information processing and computer simulation approach (e.g., Newell & Simon, 1972). One of the major contributions of this type of approach has been the level of detail with respect to enumerating the processes and assumptions embodied in a theory or model of problem solution. Unfortunately, the theories developed thus far have been largely task specific and, as Doerner points out, no particularly helpful taxonomy of problem-solving skills has evolved. What Doerner proposes is a preliminary taxonomy based upon different problem characteristics or "barriers," which necessitate different solution modes or strategies. The second major component of Doerner's taxonomy seems to reflect the complexity of the problem to be solved.

Although a taxonomy of problem-solving requirements does not constitute a theory of problem solving, it may contribute toward the development of such a theory (see Greeno, in press). It may also provide a partial basis for curriculum development. In principle, an individual could be instructed in the elements of the taxonomy and use this knowledge to select an appropriate problem-solving strategy. However, there is little or no direct evidence that this would be helpful. One might even expect that such an approach would lead to negative consequences since knowing such a taxonomy might present the problem solver with yet another problem, that of identifying the appropriate taxonomic category of the problem to be solved. Even if an individual could easily use the taxonomy, it is clear that we have yet to reach the point where we can specify the algorithms, heuristics, or basic components that make for effective and efficient problem solving in various problem domains. In order to train problem-solving skills, we must understand their nature and variety in two contexts: in terms of cognitive theory such as information processing theory and in terms of a theory and methodology of instruction concerned with optimizing human performance.

The lack of an adequate theoretical and empirical base for understanding what problem-solving skills to train, how to train them, and how to interpret the results of training studies is brought forth in the papers by Doerner, Frijda, and de Leeuw. Doerner distinguishes between training in the basic processes used in problem solving and training in strategies for assembling effective attacks on problems, and he discusses their respective effects on problem-solving proficiency.

This is a potentially useful distinction, but more specificity is required to predict success or failure for the particular instances of each type of training. We do not seem to understand why one type of training succeeded while another type failed. As an example, self-reflection is offered as a potentially important type of strategy training, but why, when, and how it helps remain to be determined.

Frijda discusses the general failure of attempts to improve problem-solving skills, but again we are uncertain about the theoretical analyses underlying the training efforts. It also seems unfortunate and premature to conclude, as Frijda seems to, that all efforts at teaching such skills are doomed to failure. This does not mean that we question Frijda's argument that there may be a substantial gap between what we teach and how the learner internalizes and then utilizes the information conveyed. Our basic concern is that the current problem for cognitive psychology is to sufficiently specify the declarative knowledge, the elementary information processing skills, and the higher-level executive functions that interact to produce problem-solving proficiency. Once we have detailed models of problem-solving competence and its acquisition, then we can begin to test the limits of instructional intervention. Without such information, we can do little but speculate about the utility and practicality of general and/or specific instruction in problem solving or reasoning.

One activity that may facilitate progress in this area is the investigation of problem-solving skills within subject-matter content areas. Much of the work on problem solving has concentrated on games, puzzles, and the like, although there are some studies of academically relevant areas (e.g., Bobrow, 1968; Greeno, 1976b; Landa, 1974; Paige & Simon, 1966). Studies of the latter type may at least define the skills necessary within certain instructional domains and thus be capable of immediate, albeit circumscribed, instructional application. Investigations of this kind can eventually accumulate into the basis for a "general" theory of problem-solving skill. Studies of the type described by Neches and Hayes on the strategy transformations that characterize the difference between novice and expert performance also may contribute toward a general understanding of problem-solving competence and its acquisition.

As mentioned earlier, there is some agreement that problem solving and intelligence are related concepts. Some might argue that the linking of these two concepts represents a step backwards, since we seem to know even less about intelligence than about problem solving. There are various ways of defining and studying intelligence (see Resnick, 1976a), and one of these is to consider performance on intelligence and aptitude tests as one facet of intelligent behavior and directly analyze the components of performance that give rise to individual differences in performance on such tests (Estes, 1974; Pellegrino & Glaser, 1977).

The mental test tradition has been oriented uniquely toward the selection of individuals and the prediction of intellectual (academic) achievement. An individual's general abilities are presumably assessed by standardized tests of aptitude and intelligence, and on the basis of these test scores, educational decisions are made. Social and scientific advances, however, now make it necessary and possible for us to understand intelligence and aptitude in different ways than we have in the past. Part of the necessity is reflected by a growing discontinuity between past and current thinking about the way in which individual differences should be viewed and assessed for the purposes of education. Present viewpoints emphasize the malleability and active functional development of cognitive skills and strongly recommend that the most significant use of measures of intelligence and aptitude should not be primarily for the purposes of prediction, but for indicating how intellectual performance can be improved.

If the goal of improving intellectual performance is to be achieved, we must develop the knowledge required to interpret intelligence and aptitude in terms of processes that enhance or retard cognitive performance. Instruction might then be implemented that adapts to these individual characteristics or directly or indirectly teaches prerequisite cognitive skills that facilitate learning and development. Such practical benefits seem to be the distant goals toward which some of the studies in this volume seem to be aimed.

The papers by Sternberg and Snow represent a direct attack on the problem of developing models of performance on aptitude test tasks that tap various types of reasoning abilities. The approach taken by Sternberg is a more microscopic analysis. Various possible models for task performance are explicitly detailed, and individual differences are specified in terms of the parameters of these models. This particular approach has certain strengths and corresponding weaknesses. One of the strengths is the specificity of the theoretical and empirical analysis, which seems to reflect a combination of psychometric rigor and general information processing constructs. A second strength is the ability to provide a characterization of the general processing stages and their sequencing for task solution. These strengths have certain negative consequences. In the attempt to model "typical" task performance, there is relatively little room for assessing changes in the organization of solution processes that occur within individuals as a function of experience and that may differentiate among levels of task competence. Snow's approach of looking at eye fixations and subject protocols allows for such flexibility, but it correspondingly lacks some of the theoretical rigor of Sternberg's approach. Thus, it would seem that the two approaches are complementary and may provide valuable insights into the elementary processes and executive functions or strategies that are assessed by reasoning tasks found on aptitude and intelligence tests.

A second potential problem with Sternberg's appproach relates directly to the diagnostic utility of the individual difference data arising from estimates of the various process parameters. The difficulty can best be pointed out by considering the following situation. Assume that one has followed all the necessary steps to do a componential analysis of individual differences in analogical reasoning tasks and has found that individuals systematically differ in encoding speed. What is the next step? The answer is unclear because we do not know precisely what encoding refers to and whether differences in the speed of executing the encoding process are related to the accuracy or successful execution of this process. Latency estimates typically tell us something about process speed when the process has been "successful," and error estimates tell us only about gross differences in process success. Even if we know that individuals differ by a value X in the parameter for successful process performance, we still do not know the source or meaning of the difference. Rather than having a score on a test, we now have several scores representing parameters of a model of task performance. Sternberg's approach gives some validation of the analysis of a task into components, but leaves the specifics of the various components largely undocumented. It would appear that the modeling efforts of Sternberg and the associated quantitative parameter estimations are only one first step toward a useful analysis of task performance. Again, the qualitative protocol data of the type collected by Snow could be invaluable in helping to understand the meaning of the processes and parameters and thereby move us closer toward the desired goal of being able to use tests as diagnostic instruments for assessing cognitive strengths and weaknesses.

In considering problem-solving skill, cognitive psychologists have clearly defined a goal that is instructionally significant. They have also begun to identify some of the important elements in problem solving (i.e., they are constructing the problem space for studying problem solving). Many of the issues raised by the papers in this volume and our own preceding comments reflect an initial attempt to specify the variety of questions that need to be addressed in any serious long-range attempt to study and improve cognitive functioning.

Cognitive Development

Attempts to develop a theory of instruction must be intimately related to extant theories of learning and cognitive development (Bruner, 1966). There is, however, a critical difference between developmental theory and research and instructional theory and practice. Bruner (1966) has emphasized that "theories of learning and development are descriptive rather than prescriptive. They tell us what happened after the fact: for example, that most children of six do not yet possess the notion of reversibility. A theory of instruction, on the other hand, might attempt to set forth the best means of leading the child toward the notion of reversibility" (p. 40). The papers in this book dealing with the topic of cognitive development raise important questions about the descriptive adequacy of current theory and the prescriptive implications of such theory.

In Oléron's discussion of cognitive skill development, he points out some of the inadequacies of Piagetian stage theory while simultaneously arguing for a consideration of the functional aspects of cognitive development. His discussion of psychological competence elaborates on the argument that a child develops in an environment that cannot be adequately represented by assumptions only about the growth of logical structures and systems. Oerter further elaborates on the role of the environment in shaping internal cognitive structures. While Oerter's data do not constitute proof of his model of cognitive socialization, they nonetheless reveal some interesting aspects in the development of problem-solving skill in a domain different from that studied by Piaget.

The general arguments put forth by Oléron and Oerter have strong implications for future research and theory in developmental psychology. However, the implications of this work for instruction are less clear. It would certainly seem reasonable to expect that theoretical and empirical research on cognitive development should influence instructional theory and practice, particularly since the latter require an analysis and understanding of the initial state of competence of the learner (Glaser, 1976). The division of cognitive development into rather gross stages of logical thought is descriptive rather than prescriptive theory. As a descriptive theory of stages of competence, it can be criticized, as Oléron has done, for the failure to adequately deal with performance heterogeneity (horizontal decalage) within a stage of development and for the failure to specify the processes that bring about major shifts between stages of development (competence). A note of caution must therefore be expressed about relying heavily on theories of cognitive development for an understanding of the process(es) of cognitive restructuring or accommodation. The explanation of transitions between different stages of cognitive development, i.e., between different levels of cognitive organization and structure, has been a particularly thorny problem in development theory, and it will not be easy to solve within any theory of learning that similarly postulates stages and levels of restructuring. This is not to say that such restructuring does not occur, but simply to note the past difficulty in detailing the processes involved.

Setting aside questions about the adequacy of stage theory as a descriptive theory, one can examine the prescriptive implications of such a theory. In one sense, the implications are negative, since the theory implies that instruction is inappropriate unless the learner has reached a proper level of cognitive structuring. If the child is not at the appropriate stage of logical thought, then there is the further problem of specifying how and whether conditions might be arranged to bring about the development of the appropriate structures. As a reaction to the static emphasis of stage theory, a considerable number of training studies have attempted to illustrate that cognitive development can be accelerated or affected by direct instruction. Murray has reviewed this body of research, and from it he gleans a set of assessment and concept training techniques that may have broad

applicability.   The interesting point about the training studies is not
whether they prove or disprove Piagetian stage theory, but instead   what
they can illustrate about the procedures for analyzing performance and
for teaching the prerequisite skills for successful performance.   It
remains to be seen whether the general training strategies outlined by
Murray can be broadly applied and in what circumstances they serve to
optimize the understanding and performance of new tasks.

     While macrotheories of stages of cognitive development do not seem
particularly   useful   when   attempting to formulate principles of
instructional   design,   some   empirical   results and methods   in
developmental research may have relevance for instructional situations.
The clearest illustration of such applicability is Case's discussion of
memory   limitations   in   children and the correlated tendency to employ
overly simplistic solution strategies in tasks that are sufficiently
complex so that they begin to tax working memory. The assessment of
performance deficiencies and concomitant attempts at remediation require
a careful task and performance analysis in which one attempts to specify
the elements of the task and their incorporation in the various possible
strategies that lead to different types of successful and unsuccessful
performance. In the paper by Case, this is illustrated by the analysis
of performance on the missing addend problem in arithmetic instruction.
A parallel type of analysis is presented by Siegler for the balance
scale problem. The basic theme in the work of both Case and Siegler is
that the child is following a systematic solution strategy, and the task
of the researcher (and teacher) is to determine the particular strategy
being used.

     In his research on cognitive development, Siegler has demonstrated
the importance of having explicit models for representing, contrasting,
and evaluating performance on different problem types. With such
information, it then becomes possible to specify the conditions that are
necessary to affect performance changes. In the case of the balance
scale problem, the critical factor in affecting strategy changes is the
encoding of all relevant dimensions. Modification of the encoding
process produces major changes in the level of solution strategy and is
a prerequisite for the acquisition of higher-level strategies. The type
of performance analysis carried out by Case and Siegler is also
represented in the work of Harris and Singleton on the appropriate
interpretation of a child's failure to make accurate measurement
decisions. What Harris and Singleton demonstrate is that deficient
performance need not imply inadequate cognitive structures. The same
type of inferential problem is discussed by Gold with respect to
conservation problems.

     The above work on Piagetian-type tasks shows that an information
processing analysis can be effectively utilized to explain, predict, and
influence cognitive performance arising from the systematic application
of an inappropriate strategy. The major problem that remains
unresolved, however, is how to go about making use of developmental
principles and theory in curriculum development and instructional design

such that the representational and performance deficiencies are minimized as a result of educational practices. This may necessitate detailed analyses of the instructional tasks and concepts that pose major problems for children. Analyses of this kind can lead to the development of new instructional methods that foster the acquisition of appropriate encoding, interpretive, and strategic processes. One of the goals of a prescriptive instructional theory is the optimization of performance, and it seems particularly crucial to incorporate developmental principles and analytic techniques that serve to optimize the development of intellect rather than simply remediate deficient performance.

Instruction

Attempts to develop instructional theory and a technology of instruction proceed in two ways in this volume. One tactic, which most of the papers in this volume have adopted, is to present implications that appear to arise from the results of a psychological experiment. A second tactic takes on an instructional problem more directly either by attempting to develop an instructional model or by building a specific instructional program. Case, Rothkopf, and Sticht use this second tactic. Case reflects on the experimental techniques reported in studies of child development and organizes them into a set of principles and techniques for optimizing children's acquisition of performance strategies in intellectual tasks by minimizing their learning difficulties. The relationship between the developmental literature and the principles and techniques he proposes is made by referencing studies from which principles can be derived or in which they are implied. In doing this, he refers to the work of Gagné on learning hierarchies, to the task-analysis, subject-protocol techniques of Newell and Simon, and to the training techniques for Piagetian tasks used by Gelman, Lefebre and Pinard, Siegler, and Case himself. Much of the experimentation reported by van Parreren in this volume is also highly relevant.

The two general psychological principles that form a basis for Case's instructional principles are: (a) that children tend to generalize a strategy learned in one situation to a similar novel situation, and (b) that children have a limited memory capacity for attending to various amounts of information. Since these characteristics for generalization (often overgeneralization) and limited memory capacity account for many learning difficulties that children experience in school settings, the optimization of instruction must take account of these characteristics of children's behavior. A theory of instruction should take account of such capacities and limitations of the learner and then concentrate on developing procedures for optimizing learning. It is this task of "designing conditions for optimization" that becomes the central focus of instruction. In this sense, the major emphasis of instructional theory or technology is different from psychological theory and experimentation; instructional work does not involve describing phenomena and developing descriptive theories about them, but is concerned with designing conditions to optimize performance. We shall return to this issue shortly.

Rothkopf's instructional theory is also based on two general psychological principles: (a) the relationship of level of processing to comprehension, and (b) the relationship between the semantic representation that an individual brings to learning and the knowledge structure to be acquired (a notion similar to that expressed by Voss and Anderson in their papers). These two aspects, the appropriate processing of text and the influence of prior knowledge, are reciprocally related to one another. The greater the experience level, the less the requirements for deep processing, and the less the experience, the greater the processing level required. It is the interplay between these two aspects that provide a basis for optimizing learning from textual materials and other such instructional events. Again, the task of instruction is to arrange conditions to optimize the acquisition of information. Unlike Case, Rothkopf does not give an example of actual instructional routines, but does refer to possible directions. Prior knowledge level can be assessed by direct or indirect tests of a student's knowledge in a particular subject-matter field, and estimates of processing activities can be obtained through appropriate text manipulations.

Both Case and Rothkopf reflect an important issue concerning the level of analysis at which instructional theory must be expressed. While the theory and experimentation from which they derive their instructional models is formulated in terms of basic cognitive processes, instructional technology requires specification in terms of conditions that can be manipulated at a practical level under educational conditions. This suggests that a theory of instruction needs to be a macrotheory of instructional operations and not a microtheory of learning processes, just as practical theories of engineering or medicine are organized around levels of description that correspond to the levels of their goals. Building theories and models of instruction at this macrolevel is a task for which cognitive psychologists are not particularly trained. Theory at such a level, however, would be a strong test of underlying scientific theories of human learning and development.

In contrast to Case and Rothkopf, Sticht takes on the development of a major instructional program. His work suggests the nature of such macroinstructional models and also raises questions for learning theory. He adopts two procedures as basic components of instructional technology - human engineering and skills training. Sticht's program is designed to establish an optimal combination of these two components. In human engineering, peoples' cognitive skills are considered fixed, and the attempt is made to design tasks so that they match the existing skills. In this procedure, the requirements for the tasks are well defined, so that groups can then be selected for training on these specific tasks. A task that requires reading, for example, can be divided into two levels of difficulty: (a) reading to follow directions and to find information to do a job; and (b) reading for new learning, where information must be learned to solve problems and acquire new skills. Certain individuals are selected for the first but not the second of these two levels. In the skills training approach, the skills of individuals are considered as variable, and instruction is designed to improve their level of skill and knowledge so that they can meet the requirements of a particular training program.

These macroinstructional manipulations suggest that some new research and new tools are needed for a cognitive psychology of instruction. Techniques must be developed to determine the knowledge structure and cognitive demands of various levels of knowledge and skill in different domains. The extent to which entering levels of aptitude and cognitive skills can be influenced by training must also be determined so that individuals can profit from available instructional programs. Other papers in this conference, particularly Sternberg's, are concerned with this second question and are investigating the nature of the cognitive skills that underlie measured aptitude and intelligence. Eventually, these individual differences that have been measured by psychometric tests might be understood in terms of cognitive processes that can be influenced by instruction.

Returning to the question of optimization, all three of the papers directly concerned with instruction imply the necessity for a change in tactic when one moves from a theory of learning to a theory of instruction. As indicated earlier, a theory of learning, like other scientific theories, is concerned with describing how things are and how things work; such theories are decriptive and explanatory. A theory of instruction, in contrast, is concerned with the design of conditions to bring about certain events. It is a normative theory that sets up criteria of performance and then specifies optimal conditions for meeting them. Cognitive psychologists interested in learning and instruction have been trained in techniques and approaches to psychological knowledge that emphasize the theoretical and empirical description of learning. They have not been trained and are less proficient in attacking the problems of prescriptive normative science concerned with designing conditions for optimizing performance outcomes.

A significant task, then, is for instructional theory to develop optimizing methods and models for the acquisition of complex domains of knowledge and skill. The procedures and models of instructional design will be based upon progress in the psychology of learning, but the work that also needs to be undertaken is the development of a theory of instructional design which, in its own right, becomes a test of its underlying theories of learning and cognition. There is no doubt that the adequacy of cognitive psychology can be assessed through attempts at building and testing models of instructional design. Such models should provide alternative instructional practices that can be tested against practical requirements, constraints, and values.

Finally, if the participants in this conference were asked what the general requirements are for building a theory of instruction, they would probably agree on the following kinds of work: (a) analysis of the structures of knowledge and skill that comprise objectives of instruction and that characterize high-knowledge, well-skilled individuals; (b) analysis of the intermediate knowledge states that characterize the transition from lack of knowledge to competence; (c) specification, in terms of a cognitive process theory, of the aptitudes for learning that individuals bring to an instructional situation; and (d) specification of the transformations that take place between various stages of acquisition and of the conditions that can be implemented to bring about change from one stage of knowledge to more advanced stages.

These requirements are more than sufficient to provide challenging work for instructional psychology. Those who take on this work, as we have suggested above, will need training in the design of optimization procedures based upon the developing cognitive psychology with which their work must interact. The task is substantial, as several authors in this volume have suggested. However, our mood is optimistic. The evolution of cognitive psychology has resulted in, at least, the ability to specify somewhat more clearly the knowledge that individuals acquire through instruction. Perhaps this conference is one sign that we are starting to acquire the knowledge required to systematically address the problems of instruction.

References

Anderson, R. C., & Ortony, A. On putting apples into bottles - A problem of polysemy. Cognitive Psychology, 1975, 7, 167-180.

Bobrow, D. G. Natural language input for a computer problem-solving system. In M. Minsky (Ed.), Semantic information processing. Cambridge, MA: M.I.T. Press, 1968.

Bower, G. H. Mental imagery and associative learning. In L. W. Gregg (Ed.), Cognition in learning and memory. New York: Wiley, 1972.

Bruner, J. S. Toward a theory of instruction. New York; W. W. Norton and Company, 1966.

Bruner, J. J., Goodnow, J. J., & Austin, G. A. A study of thinking. New York: Wiley, 1956.

DISTAR Reading Program (2nd ed.). Chicago: Science Research Associates, 1974.

Estes, W. K. Learning theory and intelligence. American Psychologist, 1974, 29, 740-749.

Estes, W. K. (Ed.) Handbook of learning and cognitive processes (Vol. 1). Hillsdale, NJ: Lawrence Erlbaum Associates, 1975.

Gagné, R. M. The conditions of learning. New York: Holt, Rinehart & Winston, 1965.

Gagné, R. M. Essentials of learning for instruction. Hinsdale, IL: Dryden Press, 1974.

Glaser, R. Components of a psychology of instruction: Toward a science of design. Review of Educational Research, 1976, 46, 1-24.

Greeno, J. G. Nature of problem-solving abilities. In W. K. Estes (Ed.), Handbook of learning and cognitive processes (Vol. 5). Hillsdale, NJ: Lawrence Erlbaum Associates, in press.

Greeno, J. G. Cognitive objectives of instruction: Knowledge for solving problems and answering questions. In D. Klahr (Ed.), Cognition and instruction. Hillsdale, NJ: Lawrence Erlbaum Associates, 1976. (a)

Greeno, J. G. Indefinite goals in well-structured problems. Psychological Review, 1976, 83, 479-491. (b)

Hayes-Roth, B. Evolution of cognitive structures and processses. Psychological Review, 1977, 84, 260-278.

Hayes-Roth, B., & Hayes-Roth, F. The prominence of lexical information in memory representations of meaning. Journal of Verbal Learning and Verbal Behavior, 1977, 16, 119-136.

Hebb, D. O. The organization of behavior: A neuropsychological theory. New York: Wiley, 1949.

Hunt, E. B. Concept learning: An information processing problem. New York: Wiley, 1962.

Landa, L. N. Algorithmization in learning and instruction. Englewood Cliffs, NJ: Educational Technology Publications, 1974.

Lesgold, A. M., & Goldman, S. R. Encoding uniqueness and the imagery mnemonic in associative learning. Journal of Verbal Learning and Verbal Behavior, 1973, 12, 193-202.

Lesgold, A. M., McCormick, C., & Golinkoff, R. M. Imagery training and children's prose learning. Journal of Educational Psychology, 1975, 67, 663-667.

Lockhart, R. S., Craik, F. I., & Jacoby, L. Depth of processing, recognition and recall. In J. Brown (Ed.), Recall and recognition. New York: Wiley, 1976.

Minsky, M. A framework for representing knowledge. In P. Winston (Ed.), The psychology of computer vision. New York: McGraw-Hill, 1975.

Neimark, E. D., & Santa, J. L. Thinking and concept attainment. Annual Review of Psychology, 1975, 26, 173-205.

Newell, A., & Simon, H. A. Human problem solving. Englewood Cliffs, NJ: Prentice-Hall, 1972.

Paige, J. M., & Simon, H. A. Cognitive processes in solving algebra word problems. In B. Kleinmuntz (Ed.), Problem solving: Research, method and theory. New York: Wiley, 1966.

Pellegrino, J., & Glaser, R. Cognitive components of individual differences. Paper presented at the meeting of the American Educational Research Association, New York, April 1977.

Resnick, L. B. (Ed.) The nature of intelligence. Hillsdale, NJ: Lawrence Erlbaum Associates, 1976. (a)

Resnick, L. B. Task analysis in instructional design: Some cases from mathematics. In D. Klahr (Ed.), Cognition and instruction. Hillsdale, NJ: Lawrence Erlbaum Associates, 1976. (b)

Resnick, L. B., & Glaser, R. Problem solving and intelligence. In L. B. Resnick (Ed.), The nature of intelligence. Hillsdale, NJ: Lawrence Erlbaum Associates, 1976.

Rumelhart, D. C. Toward an interactive model of reading (Technical Report No. 56). San Diego: University of California, Center for Human Information Processing, 1976.

Schank, R., & Abelson, R. Scripts, plans, goals and understanding: An inquiry into human knowledge structures. Hillsdale, NJ: Lawrence Erlbaum Associates, 1977.

Swinney, D. A., & Hakes, D. T. Effects of prior context upon lexical access during sentence comprehension. Journal of Verbal Learning and Verbal Behavior, 1976, 15, 681-689.

Winograd, T. Frame representations and the declarative-procedural controversy. In D. C. Bobrow & A. Collins (Eds.), Representations and understanding: Studies in cognitive psychology. New York: Academic Press, 1975.

Wolff, P., & Levin, J. R. The role of overt activity in children's imagery production. Child Development, 1972, 43, 537-547.

Wright, P. Presenting technical information: A survey of research findings. Instructional Science, 1977, 6, 93-134.

Intelligence tests
  problem solving and, 240-244
  246-247
  task analysis of, 321-328
Interference
  discourse processing and, 207-209
  knowledge structure and, 15-17,
  42-45, 85-89, 93-97
  learning strategies and, 342-346
Knowledge structure
  assessment of, 469
  cognitive development and, 18,
  359-362
  conceptual differentiation and,
  15-19
  context and, 15-18
  degree of knowledge and, 15-18
  discrepancy with instruction,
  54-55, 471
  environmental structure and,
  375-386
  individual differences in, 14-20
  instructional implications of,
  20-22, 45-47, 232-233, 465-471,
  498-503
  intelligence and, 323-324
  interference and, 15-17, 42-45,
  85-89, 93-97
  macrostructures and, 59-60
  mathemagenic activities and,
  468-471
  problem solving and, 54-55,
  232-233
  representation of, 29-36, 39-40,
  389-395
  transfer and, 14-22, 42-45,
  498-499
  transformation and, 51-58
Language
  cognitive development and, 366-368
  hemispheric specialization and,
  221-226
  schemata and, 366-367
  specificity and, 101-102
  (see also comprehension)
Learning
  by rules, 30-36
  discrepancy between instruction
  and knowledge, 55
  sequence of, 42-45, 500
  strategy differences in, 339-346
  transfer and, 13-22, 42-45
  types of, 40-42, 499-500

Learning theory
  instructional implications of,
  42-46, 497-500
Lexical access
  speech recoding and, 124-126,
  158-166
Literacy
  components of, 480-483
  instruction in, 475-490
Macrostructures
  formation of, 57-60
  transformations in, 52-53, 56-58
Mathemagenic activities
  assessment of, 469
  discourse processing and, 466-468
  instructional implications of, 47
  465-471
  knowledge structure and, 468-471
Mathematics
  abbreviation process in, 9
  measurement in, 413-417
  Piagetian theory and, 357-358,
  413-417
  transformations in, 54
Measurement
  cognitive development and,
  413-417
  instruction in, 417
Memory
  development of, 366-368
  requirements in problem solving,
  248-249
  (see also working memory)
Memory access
  reading ability and, 196-201
  speech recoding and, 199-200
Memory representation
  imagery and, 101-108, 111-117
  propositional theory of, 101-108
  specificity and, 101-108
Memory structure
  inference making and, 85-89
  knowledge modules in, 40-45
  text structure and, 19-20, 52-53,
  56-58, 86-89, 91-97
  types of, 83-85
  (see also knowledge structure)
Moral development, 362-366
Motivation
  cognitive development and,
  366-369